THE PROBLEM OF CRIME IN AMERICA

The President's Crime Commission Report carefully studied the threats to American citizens posed by lawlessness. Professor Isidore Silver's Introduction and Afterword considers the document as a whole and the crucial task force reports on which it was based. The subjects considered:

THE POLICE • THE COURTS • CORRECTIONS • SCIENCE AND TECHNOLOGY • ORGANIZED CRIME NARCOTICS AND DRUG ABUSE • JUVENILE DELINQUENCY AND YOUTH CRIME • DRUNKENNESS

"The Commission has made a substantial contribution, if we choose to listen, to the problem of understanding crime."
PROFESSOR ISIDORE SILVER, from the Introduction

"A comprehensive, sophisticated and highly detailed study."
The New York Times

Professor Silver's new work shows that the attempted solutions of the "Law and Order" problem suggested by the Presidential candidates, if followed, will cause this country to explode. He presents his own analysis and alternative solutions in his comments on the President's Crime Commission report. Professor Silver suggests the manner in which security can be restored in his exploration of the several causes of criminality. I hope that his words are heard by the men in the new administration who are responsible for helping this country meet the challenge of crime. We cannot, as all but the politicians know, reduce lawlessness by exacting more punitive sentences. I recommend the book.

MARTIN GARBUS, Director-Counsel of the Roger Baldwin Foundation, American Civil Liberties Union

THE CHALLENGE
OF CRIME
IN A FREE SOCIETY

A REPORT BY THE PRESIDENT'S
COMMISSION ON LAW
ENFORCEMENT AND
ADMINISTRATION OF JUSTICE

Introduction and Afterword by
Isidore Silver

 AVON PUBLISHERS OF BARD, CAMELOT, DISCUS AND EQUINOX BOOKS

AVON BOOKS
A division of
The Hearst Corporation
959 Eighth Avenue
New York, New York 10019

First Avon Printing, November, 1968
Third Printing, January, 1972

Cover photo courtesy of Francis Laping-D.P.I.

AVON TRADEMARK REG. U.S. PAT. OFF. AND
FOREIGN COUNTRIES, REGISTERED TRADEMARK—
MARCA REGISTRADA, HECHO EN CHICAGO, U.S.A.

Printed in the U.S.A.

Foreword

On July 23, 1965, recognizing the urgency of the Nation's crime problem and the depth of ignorance about it, President Johnson established this Commission on Law Enforcement and Administration of Justice, through Executive Order 11236.

This general report—"The Challenge of Crime in a Free Society"—embodies all the major findings we have drawn from our examination of every facet of crime and law enforcement in America. These are summarized in an opening section, and our recommendations are cataloged in a table following chapter 13. In addition, we are finishing the work on a series of volumes reflecting the detailed and extensive research and analysis underlying this report. These volumes, each dealing with a different major segment of the field of crime and law enforcement, will be issued shortly, as they are completed.

We have described, in appendix A, how the Commission went about its work. But one aspect deserves particular note. Our work was, as indeed it should and had to be, in the fullest sense, a joint undertaking.

We received the unstinting assistance of the Federal Bureau of Investigation, the U.S. Bureau of Prisons, the Department of Health, Education, and Welfare, and every other Federal agency we called on.

We had the invaluable assistance of many State, local, and private agencies and groups in this field.

We had at our service the special talent and knowledge of hundreds of expert consultants and advisers who contributed to our work.

And, most important, the foundation to our work came from a staff whose energy and endurance was exceeded only by its brilliance and imagination. Every member of this Commission joins me in expressing the warmest gratitude and admiration for James Vorenberg, professor at the Harvard Law School, the Executive Director of the Commission, who directed this extraordinary staff effort, and for each of his colleagues.

Nicholas deB. Katzenbach
Chairman

THE COMMISSION

Nicholas deB. Katzenbach, *Chairman*

THE STAFF

Executive Director:

James Vorenberg

Deputy Director:

Henry S. Ruth, Jr.

Associate Directors:

Gene S. Muehleisen
Elmer K. Nelson, Jr.
Lloyd E. Ohlin
Arthur Rosett

Assistant Directors:

David B. Burnham
Bruce J. Terris
Samuel G. Chapman (*Police*)
Howard Ohmart (*Corrections*)
Vincent O'Leary (*Corrections*)
Charles H. Rogovin (*Organized Crime*)

Director of Science and Technology:

Alfred Blumstein

William Caldwell	John L. McCausland
Weston R. Campbell, Jr.	Sheila Anne Mulvihill
Gerald M. Caplan	Albert W. Overby, Jr.
Roland Chilton	Nick Pappas
Joseph G. J. Connolly	John F. Quinn
Virginia N. Crawford	Robert Rice
Elizabeth Bartholet DuBois	Gordon D. Rowe
Paul B. Duruz	Susan Freeman Schapiro
Robert L. Emrich	Gerald Stern
Floyd Feeney	Keith Stubblefield
Victor Gioscia	Thelma C. Stevens
Sheldon Krantz	Martin Timin
Anthony Lapham	G. Joseph Vining

Richardson White, Jr.

Contents

Introduction

"Crime in the Streets"—to some a euphemism for racism, to others a fearful everyday possibility—promises to be America's Number One domestic political issue for many years to come. Under its currently fashionable rubric, "Law and Order," it will be the subject of uninformed "gut" speculation, political exploitation, and sociological generalization for at least the remainder of the decade and probably well beyond. Unfortunately Americans have a capacity for dramatizing unsubstantiated fears and eschewing hard analytical study of their social problems. The best evidence of this (admittedly subjective) conclusion is the almost complete lack of public discussion of the findings of the President's Commission on Law Enforcement and the Administration of Justice. In fact this edition constitutes the first popular reprint of the Commission report, almost two years after it was rendered. To those who seek facile solutions to the "crime problem" the Report will offer little succor, and perhaps that is why it has been studiously ignored despite the increasingly abrasive debate about its vital subject.

If the Report disappoints the impatient believer in miraculous nostrums by offering little more than complex and confused data about the "causes" of crime, it offers not much more to the skeptic. I am skeptical of any attempt to deal with law enforcement and the administration of justice without an accompanying inquiry into the nature of American Justice—and of the Laws which ostensibly embody and exemplify such Justice. A great criminologist once said, "Crime is not an entity in fact; it is an entity in Law." As we shall see, the Commission sedulously avoided discovering whether this entity is a meaningful one for our time.

To understand the Commission's difficulties, we need to comprehend its background and the reasons which animated

17

President Johnson to convoke such a body. The Commission was established through an Executive Order signed by President Johnson on July 23, 1965. No particular event, such as an assassination, triggered the directive: in fact the first public mention of any crime study occurred in a presidential message about general conditions in the District of Columbia, and the increasing crime rate was one of them. We must look to the general background of events, and determine just why such a body was established at that particular time.

The previous fall, Barry Goldwater had campaigned on the "lawlessness" theme. Although he had lost the election (for other reasons), the fears upon which this theme played were substantial, and, more importantly, Lyndon Johnson recognized their explosive potential. Johnson is not the sort of politician who overlooks actual or potential political issues, and it was quite clear that Goldwater had touched a sensitive nerve. Undoubtedly he believed that he could preempt the issue by proposing a bundle of anticrime legislation and, simultaneously, a grandiose study of the problem.

Also, the President was interested in enacting a far-ranging poverty program. He probably saw a true tie-in between the themes of poverty and lawlessness. Probably the Commission idea served the function of killing two rather large birds with a single hefty stone.

Other considerations may have been important. In June of 1964 the Supreme Court had decided the landmark, controversial Escobedo case, and held that the right to counsel arose at a certain point during police questioning of suspects. Although the decision was unclear, its backlash was profound. Public controversy—stimulated by police charges that law enforcement was being handcuffed—was still continuing in early 1965.

Barely two weeks before Johnson first publicly broached the idea of a National Commission, Lewis F. Powell, Jr., then president of the American Bar Association attacked the Supreme Court in a widely publicized speech.[1] Also, on March 3, 1965, the same day that Johnson met with Attorney-General Ramsey Clark and J. Edgar Hoover to discuss the forthcoming crime message to Congress, the Senate Subcommittee on Permanent Investigations issued a report on organized crime and narcotics which reiterated the by then two-year-old shocking revelations of Joseph Valachi.

On March 8, 1965, the President announced that a Com-

[1] Mr. Powell was appointed a Commissioner. He and six others wrote an additional view to the report wherein they repeated the arguments in Mr. Powell's speech.

mission, composed of "men and women of distinction," would be appointed to investigate the causes of crime. With typical Johnsonian caution, he elected to appease both sides of the controversy. Thus his message noted that crime could be reduced by programs to combat poverty, but added that:

All these (programs) are vital, but they are not enough. . . . We must arrest and reverse the trend toward lawlessness.

His "consensus" approach also encompassed the police-court dispute:

There is misunderstanding at times between law enforcement officers and some courts. We need to think less, however, about taking sides in such controversies and more about the common objective: law enforcement which is both fair and effective.

Although the crime message was replete with optimism, a *New York Times* editorial dated March 9, 1965, noted that the record of previous attempts to vigorously fight crime "gives little basis for optimism."

There is no reason to suppose that the citizen's commission the President proposes to appoint will have any more success in framing definitive answers (than had predecessor groups).

There is a certain syndrome about Presidential Commissions, and it operated here. The people are often "prominent" and "distinguished," but they are also rather ignorant of the problem they are supposed to analyze. Thus Kingman Brewster, Jr., president of Yale University and a former law professor (but, unfortunately, not a criminal law specialist), Otis Chandler, a publisher, and Robert F. Wagner, mayor of New York City were appointed to the Commission in the American spirit of enlightened amateurism.

Other Commissioners are involved in the activity being investigated, but have a vested interest in the analysis of such activity. Thus the Crime Commission also had Garrett H. Byrne, district attorney of Suffolk County, Massachusetts, Thomas J. Cahill, San Francisco chief of police, and Thomas C. Lynch, attorney general of California; they represented what might be called the "law enforcement establishment." Several distinguished lawyers and judges with varying backgrounds in the criminal law also were appointed; an eminent law professor was mixed into the brew; a prominent civil rights leader added some social spice; and the cake was topped off by the presence of two women (perhaps one over the normal quota for such bodies) with no discernible background for this work.

Attorney General Katzenbach was appointed chairman, and James Vorenberg, a Harvard law professor and head of the Office of Criminal Justice, a six-man section of the Justice Department, became Executive Director. Vorenberg was noted mostly for a mildly critical attack on the Escobedo decision.

The group covered the spectrum of opinion about crime. It was noncontroversial; in fact most of its members were unknown. It was also an aggregation of busy people. Although President Johnson asked the body to "build a broad base of public support for constructive action," without an eminent panel (or at least a chairman), and with the apparent internal cleavages, this would be difficult to accomplish.

Since, as with all Commissions, the group was busy, the bulk of the work, of necessity, had to fall upon the staff—a group of lawyers (with a sprinkling of sociologists). Because (a) the lawyers themselves knew little about the subject, and (b) the Commission was asked to report by the summer of 1966, the fundamental function of the staff was to find outside expert consultants and to audit their analyses to suit the Commissioners' concerns. The staff cast about for the known rather than nonestablishment experts, and was rewarded by the preparation of numerous studies which recapitulated and reinforced what these particular experts had been saying all along for years. Thus the staff functioned as middlemen between the experts and the Commissioners.

This approach virtually ruled out the possibility of innovation. The Commissioners had their concerns; the "experts" had their vested interests; and the staff was concerned with its own political survival. Consequently the Commission did little to study what *The New York Times* hoped would be "The roots of crime [which] go deep into the maladjustment of our society."

Thus the Commission's main function, at least insofar as it is reflected in the Report, was to distill and set forth extant knowledge about our system of criminal procedure. Means, not Ends, were studied, albeit very intensively and, in many instances, very well. However, we cannot discover very much about ourselves if we merely study the internal configurations of social events; we also must know something about their external boundaries. The substantive criminal law constitutes the external boundaries of the "system" of criminal justice. The substantive law—what law is—inevitably colors our thinking about how it operates and what it does.

Perhaps it could be argued that we don't know enough to analyze our laws as to whether the existence of some laws leads to substantial social problems, and whether those problems in turn affect the internal operations of the system. Yet I would argue that we cannot meaningfully discuss questions such as the function of the police and the courts without knowing that almost one-half of all arrests in America are made for "crimes" which don't harm anyone. One-third are for the crime of drunkenness, and the Report wisely argues that this crime should be eliminated from our statute books. Another 10 percent or so are made for crimes such as vagrancy, disturbing the peace, disorderly conduct, and the like. Quite obviously, these arrests mean that substantial police power and time are involved. Other "vice" crimes such as gambling and prostitution also consume substantive police activity. There is considerable evidence that police corruption is bred by the existence of these and similar laws. Could police activity be better directed to combat crimes of violence rather than load the criminal courts down with what many lawyers call "junk cases"?

The Commission used several rationalizations to avoid answering the complex questions posed by our junk laws (generally quaintly titled as "offenses against public order" and "offenses against decency"). Laws (often selectively enforced ones, it is true) against adultery, abortion, gambling, certain forms of homosexual conduct, and possession and use of narcotics are included in this category. Although the difficulties of labeling some of these activities as "criminal" were discussed in the Report, time after time we were told that "we don't know enough" to make firm recommendations, or that "more research is needed," or that "those concerned with penal administration should make further investigations" into the propriety of using the criminal process.

Evidently the Commission felt that it had quite enough to do to clear up other sorts of misconceptions about the criminal process without becoming involved in these thorny and controversial questions. The composition of the Commission also insured that certain issues would not be raised. The 19 Commissioners were "establishment" figures; they comprised a gamut of recognized (one hesitates to say "vested") interests running from police officials to moderate civil rights leaders. Since some member of some group might have been offended, a certain muting of tone can be detected. One Commission consultant who wrote a portion of the first draft of the Report later observed that:

21

*It may be said that the controversial character of these issues,
and the need to achieve consensus among 19 Commissioners
. . . quite understandably required some reduction in tone
and conclusions of my original draft.*

That rather mild characterization is intriguing; just how
much "reduction" occurred?

The muting took several different forms: the Police section
of the Report recognizes the presence of a certain degree of
community-police tension, but argues that mutual mispercep-
tion is at the heart of the controversy. Not much of substance
need be changed: the police should investigate their own misconduct, which, in any event, is not very serious. Increased
"professionalization," higher standards, better pay, development of sincere community relations programs are all regarded as panaceas. Yet the evidence obtained from police
sociologists, including cops on the firing line, indicates that
"professionalization" will: (a) be difficult (a "Horatio Alger
story" said one recent analysis); and (b) create new problems of overenforcement of some of the reprehensible laws
under which we now live.

Perhaps the most dismal section in the entire Report is the
chapter on Narcotics. We are offered little relief from the
misconceptions and banalities that plague common discussion
of this issue. Despite some excellent Task Force papers on
the subject, the only substantive recommendation made in
this chapter is for an end to mandatory minimum sentences
for certain narcotics law violations. The frustrating problems
of labeling college students as criminals for possession of marihuana (a relatively harmless substance) and penalizing heroin addicts for the "crime" of narcotics possession, which is
nothing more than penalizing them for being addicts, are virtually ignored. Instead the Report pays implied homage to
Harry Anslinger, former head of the Narcotics Bureau, and
the chief opponent of liberalization of penalties for the dubious crimes involved. Again, what one author has called
"The Crisis of Over Criminalization" is overlooked here.

The inability to recommend necessary sweeping changes
also was demonstrated by the Corrections section. The data
in that chapter clearly reveals that prisons serve no meaningful rehabilitative function, and that most money spent on
prisoners goes for the salaries of their custodians. America
also has the highest rates of sentencing in the world—and
there is no proof that longer sentences effectively rehabilitate.
Quite the opposite appears to be true. Paradoxically, the
longest sentences are imposed on violators of certain types of

laws, such as homicide, which we deem serious; yet, most of those so sentenced are in fact excellent prospects for rehabilitation outside of jail. Murderers, as is well known in penological circles, have the lowest rate of recidivism (commission of new crimes) and commit almost no new homicides—but they continue to receive the longest sentences. These sentences are totally unrelated to the two alleged goals of imprisonment, rehabilitation and isolation of dangerous people.

Other instances of "muting" are not very serious. The Report was obviously written with the President's Poverty Program in mind. In large part, it is a rationale for such a program. At times it oversimplifies the relationship between poverty and crime and poverty and delinquency. There are different forms of poverty, different types of communities in which poverty occurs, and varying forms of family reaction to that poverty, and they all play roles in determining whether delinquency and later criminality will arise. Sociologists are responsible for the Corrections section of the main Report, and they profoundly disagree with each other (as well as with other professionals, such as psychiatrists) on the "causes" of crime. Poverty should be eliminated for its own sake, because it dehumanizes the impoverished and is ethically intolerable in an affluent society. It may have a causal relationship to some crime, although the pace of social change within a particular area probably has more; and, given the disagreements in the scientific community, it probably is the best place to start if we want to eliminate adverse environmental conditions. Yet the Report should not claim more than it can prove; and were the slums razed tomorrow, crime would still exist.

Despite these not inconsiderable reservations, the Commission can still be commended for its ability (within its chosen range) to clear up some of the numerous misconceptions about the daily facts of life concerning crime.

Clearly, the American people are uninformed, or rather misinformed about the subject. The sensational stuff of which tabloid headlines are made is merely one aspect—and not the most important one—of the entire problem. For instance, Americans murder fewer people (per 100,000) than they did in 1933 (about one third less). The Commission's boldest attack focuses on the misconception that "Crime in the Streets" is rampant. The Commission found that the extent of crime and its increase may be partially or even wholly attributable to small changes in crime reporting or classification by the police. These, the Commission observes, "could have significant effects on the trend of reported crime."

23

Perhaps this factor even accounts for some of the strange discrepancies in crime rates in the same city. Los Angeles, for instance, is first in rape but only twentieth in murder in the statistics; New York ranks fifth in larceny of goods worth more than $50 but fifty-fourth for thefts of under $50. If the average, fairly middle-class white fears being mugged, murdered, or robbed by a vicious member (or gang) of some threatening minority group he has less to worry about than he thinks. Most crimes of violence against the person are neighborhood (often family) affairs of intra- (rather than inter-) racial hue. As the Report notes, "the most striking fact in the data is the extent of correlation in rate between victim and offender."

Burglary and larceny from premises—crimes rarely affecting the individual save as property owner—are much more pervasive. But the Report puts the matter into perspective:

The price fixing by 29 electrical equipment companies alone probably cost utilities and therefore the public, more money than is reported as stolen by burglars in a year.

Although the Report says little—and this is inexcusable—about riots and other urban disorders, its conclusion that rioters "were a more or less representative cross section of the Negro community, particularly of its young men, many of whom had lived in the neighborhood for many years and were steadily employed" belies the prevalent belief that "lawless elements" predominated. In this and in similar passages the Report foreshadowed the findings of the President's Riot Commission.

The Commission is appalled by the huge percentage of funds spent for salaries (85 to 90 percent of the 4 billion dollars per year spent on fighting crime) rather than for research and continued testing of well thought out correctional programs, some of which have proved successful.

In other areas our subjective impressions have greater validity. Our belief that most crimes are not solved or even reported (because we realize that they cannot be solved) is true. As the Report notes, "if a suspect is neither known to the victim nor arrested at the scene of the crime, the chance of ever arresting him is slim." We can only sympathize with the Report's bitter conclusion that "In the present state of police knowledge and organization many crimes are, in fact, not solvable." The Commission estimates that there may be 50 percent more robberies and, perhaps, four times as many rapes as reported and observes that in 1965, 78 percent of reported serious crimes against property were never solved.

Although serious crimes against the person such as murder and rape *are* frequently solved, others, such as burglary, often are not. The extent of unreported crime varies according to the nature of the crime (penny-ante thefts) or the social feelings of the victim (ghetto residents are pessimistic about law enforcement as they are about everything else).

Although the Report generally lacks much historical perspective, it does take the long view on the persistency of crime and delinquency in certain inner-city areas. These neighborhoods have always been characterized by substantial crime; as classes move into these areas of rapid change, as hopes for advancement rise, the struggle for social recognition frequently becomes criminal in nature. The same areas which today see crimes by Negroes and Puerto Ricans once were victimized by Irish, Italian, and Jewish high crime rates. What the Commission calls a "self-healing" process occurs as these groups become integrated into the larger society. To this extent, "crime" is natural and its "cure" is also natural. Insofar as new economic opportunities open up more slowly for present city inhabitants than for their predecessors, inner-city crime rates will remain high.

The Commission recognizes that crime is often a juvenile phenomenon—almost a stage through which adolescents must painfully pass. As the juvenile proportion of the population increases more rapidly than the population as a whole, crime also will inevitably increase. Most of us perceive that certain crimes, such as auto theft, are largely committed by juveniles; we do not realize that a large percentage of other crimes are also attributable to this highly confused age group. In 1965, 50 percent of known burglaries and larcenies were committed by those under eighteen years of age.

The Commission has little good to say—and, in truth, there is little good to be said—about our correctional system which, daily, must deal with a million people. Most state systems do not have separate juvenile detention facilities; nor are there separate facilities for offenders with differing problems. Most criminals graduate from misdemeanors (lesser crimes, though often ones characterized by violence) to serious felonies. Our judicial system is most inadequate at this early stage, just where much crime might be nipped in the bud by adequate correctional facilities for misdemeanants. Few of the lower courts (Magistrate's Courts, District Courts, Justices of the Peace, or whatever) provide for presentence reports for such minor crimes or for detention facilities separate from those provided for hardened criminals. There are virtually no rehabilitation programs in local jails.

In short, we abjectly fail just at the most crucial point—the onset of a criminal career.

"The Commission has been shocked by what it has seen in some lower courts." The question is whether the Commission has been shocked by the right things. True, as the Report observes, we must revamp the entire structure of the administration of justice to insure that: (a) defendants are accorded fair and expeditious hearings in decent (not dilapidated) court rooms; (b) hasty decisions by district attorneys to drop prosecutions do not set dangerous people free; (c) sentencing of those found guilty be made by judges who are knowledgeable rather than ignorant of the defendant's personality and life history; and (d) correctional institutions adopt programs such as work-study and halfway houses (such as community treatment centers) leading to useful rather than wasted lives after incarceration.

And still more must be done. The lower judiciary in America is (or should be) a source of shame. Judges are chosen or elected generally on the basis of political affiliation. They act punitively, especially toward children. They often ignore or illiberally define Supreme Court decisions. Clearly, "professionalization" is truly needed here. The American system of criminal justice has reached the point where it is assembly-line. More (and better) judges are part of the answer. They must receive formal judicial training. In fact, given present circumstances, it would not be too radical to suggest that we adopt (with appropriate modifications) the European system of professionally trained judges. Here, where most people meet the system, it is most inadequate; and the Commission gives us little to chew on.

The role of the police is at best only hesitantly and inadequately dealt with in the Report. Although this may be inevitable, given the Report's orientation, it is lamentable. The Commission recognizes that law enforcement is something more than the ritualistic invocation of and adherence to "pure" textbook maxims. The policeman does "not enact the laws that (he is) required to enforce, nor (does he) dispose of the criminals (he arrests)." This would imply that he has no choice about the laws he is required to enforce; yet we are also told, "How an individual policeman moves around that territory (of the criminal code) depends largely on his personal discretion." In fact he makes the most crucial decision of all—whether to invoke the criminal process, and that decision is not reviewable unless an arrest occurs. As he patrols his beat he comes into contact with numerous situations calling for instantaneous value judgments about his function. Since he is called upon to suppress crime as well as catch criminals he does things he considers necessary to pacify his "beat." He checks stores, and inquires about the presence of "suspicious" individuals.

The Commission clearly recognizes this vital aspect of the patrolman's daily routine and duly notes the kind of community antagonisms such conduct creates. How far should a policeman go in enforcing the laws of the community? If he goes too far, he can make many arrests for crimes such as disturbing the peace, disorderly conduct, petty assault, and (when he has nothing else) vagrancy. Not all laws are meant to be enforced all the time. Which ones should be, when, and against whom? The Commission certainly does not want effective law enforcement only against minority ethnic and racial groups, but it does not go much beyond this homily.

When a crime might have been committed, when can a policeman stop someone to inquire about his identity, his activities in the neighborhood, or other suspicious conduct? The Commission wants to meaningfully balance the interests of law enforcement against the liberty of the individual. Unfortunately it fails to clearly note the most obvious problem of "stop" and "frisk"—the distinction between "rousting" of ghetto youth as a harassment tactic and stopping suspicious people in a specific criminal situation.

This distinction was made in the recent Supreme Court cases of Terry against Ohio, and Sibron and Peters against New York. The Court clearly indicated that a hostile stop of a person for questioning can be justified only by a "reasonable suspicion" that he has committed, is committing, or is about to commit a crime, and that any search resulting from such temporary detention can be justified only by, again, a "reasonable suspicion" that the suspect has a weapon capable of causing harm to the policeman or to others. In addition the search must be "reasonable" in area—at least, initially, a "patting down" of the suspect's outer garments. Thus the Supreme Court has given Constitutional permission for nonarrest stops under carefully defined circumstances. The Commission's faint endeavor to allay community antagonism against indiscriminate stops and frisks has thus been partially aided by the Court, although numerous perplexing questions remain.

The problem of police misconduct is extensively discussed in the Police Section; but the Commission meanders around, probably in some embarrassment. It argues that misconduct is not as frequent as police critics maintain and is best controlled by interdepartmental review procedures. "When this kind of machinery is fully and fairly used it succeeds both in disciplining misbehaving officers and deterring others from misbehaving."

Although it may be unfair to cite recent events, such as the Chicago riot during the Democratic Convention, the New York City incident in which approximately 150 off-duty policemen allegedly assaulted some Negro militants in a courtroom hallway, and other altercations in Oakland and Berkeley, in criticism of the Commission's sanguine position about misconduct, these incidents were clearly foreshadowed by numerous similar ones in the early and middle '60's. The evidence—some of it analyzed in the Police Task Force Report itself—clearly indicates that such generalized misconduct usually will not be internally punished. For one thing, public fears about crime encourage police excesses: for another, such excesses are often obviously or tacitly approved by the political power structure. It is true that the police are often front-line victims of the resentment felt by minority groups toward the "Establishment," but this does not justify clearly illegal conduct. Neither does it justify self-imposed police immunity to complaints. It certainly cannot be the rationale for the Commission's belief that internal police sanctions can be effective. The evidence clearly supports the opposite thesis. Police notions of the need to preserve their own "integrity," their insular mentality, and fear of a threatening (and always hostile) outside world virtually insure that malefactors in their ranks will go unpunished.

Since the question is controversial, the Commission, as an alternative, recommends the establishment of an Ombudsman system of review for all governmental agencies, including the police. Yet, as one of the Task Force Reports indicates, civilian review boards have been effective, do not lower police morale, and do satisfy complainants.

Since the Report's orientation is toward reform and not revolution, as we have seen (though the latter might well be necessary in certain respects), it contributed little to the debate about what "crime" is or should be. The question of whether the criminal law is the appropriate sanction against offensive but not necessarily harmful conduct is a complex one. What is the state's role in protecting the individual against himself (narcotics, homosexual offenses, abortion), in suppressing potential disorder (breach of the peace), and in regulating offensive displays in public (drunkenness)? Apart from its recommendation that Drunkenness be removed from the criminal statute books (for many scientific as well as practical reasons), the Report merely notes that enforcement of the other laws tends to put a great strain on police resources, drives certain furtive practices underground but does not alleviate them, and often involves discriminatory and corrupt law enforcement. The arguments as to whether harmless conduct should be punished by criminal sanctions, and whether the cost to law enforcement integrity is worth the often intangible (and, perhaps, insubstantial) benefits to society should have received more attention.

If "crime in the streets" is the big problem to most Americans, the question of organized crime is a close second. Public interest in Joe Valachi and James Marcus is indicative of our great concern about the Mafia's influence on American life. The Commission is worried about organized crime and, more importantly, about America's casual attitude toward it. "The extraordinary thing about organized crime is that America has tolerated it for so long." We regularly deplore the Mafia (though we can't quite define it) but regularly tolerate its activities. In fact, "toleration" is too genteel a term; "affection" would be more accurate. Nowhere is American ambivalence —moral indignation accompanied by practical unconcern— about crime more pronounced than here. Gambling (which primarily consists of bookmaking and policy) does not appear to be very criminal to many of the same people who have tactile reactions to street crime. Yet the Report estimates that the annual gambling gross of the Mafia is somewhere around 9 billion dollars (later reliable estimates go as high as 20 billion dollars). Gambling provides the "juice" to corrupt public officials, to invest in and ultimately take over legitimate businesses, and to diminish respect for law and order.

The Report's study of the Mafia recapitulates what has been public information ever since the Kefauver hearings in 1952. Organized crime exists; it is not a figment of ever-suspicious law enforcers' imaginations, but rather a loose confederation of highly organized "families" governed by a commission of from nine to twelve men. It controls such activities as gambling, loan-sharking and wholesale importation of narcotics. It is "big business." "Organized crime takes about twice as much income from gambling and other illegal groups and services as criminals derive from all other kinds of criminal activity combined."

Although more of the Mafia's activities have become respectable, its business methods remain tainted by criminal practices. Mafia companies dilute the quality of goods sold and use unfair methods of competition ("the ordinary businessman is hard pressed to compete with a syndicate enterprise").

29

Large amounts of funds are siphoned off from otherwise "respectable" companies and banks subject to Mafia control, and these funds are "invested" in lucrative enterprises such as loan-sharking. Numerous bankruptcy fraud cases involve such financial finagling. Certain labor unions have also contributed to Mafia coffers, often through the manipulation of their pension funds. The Mafia has become involved in the sinews of the American economy (selling goods with "known and respected brand names," as the Report notes), and its economic influence grows geometrically.

The Commission recognizes that Mafia success is directly dependent upon its ability to corrupt law enforcement, for many semipublic profitable activities such as bookmaking cannot, by their nature, occur without protection. Fully one-half of the gross profits from gambling are plowed back into "juice." Thus Mafia presence in many large as well as smaller cities is directly related to corruption. "Today, no large city is completely controlled by organized crime, but in many there is a considerable degree of corruption."

Also, the Mafia provides services people want. Its crimes have few victims and few complainants. As the Report bluntly notes:

Organized criminal groups participate in any illegal activity that offers maximum profit at a minimum risk of law enforcement interference. They offer goods and services that millions of Americans desire even though declared illegal by their legislatures.

Although one of the Task Force papers (to be discussed in the Afterword) raises the issue of whether restrictive American laws act to *perpetuate* Mafia monopoly, the Commission itself does not discuss whether it would be easier to eliminate the Mafia or to render it impotent by allowing competitors to provide presently illegal services. Again, here as in other places, the Commission's interest (and a maddening one it is) is in description rather than prescription.

If the Report graphically demonstrates that many of our assumptions about "crime" are wrong, and that there are no magic solutions to a complex problem, what does it tell us about ourselves as a people? It informs us (unfortunately, by implication) that we worry about the tangible symptoms of our social problems without undertaking the uncomfortable task of analyzing the disease. Our perception of crime is often class oriented, and we conveniently forget that most crime (at least in terms of dollar amounts) is middle class and not lower class. Although forms of crime differ generally because criminal opportunities differ, most Americans occasionally violate the law. As one Commission survey of 10,000 households indicates, 91 percent of all Americans have violated laws that could have subjected them to a term of imprisonment at one time in their lives.

Most Americans tend to identify "crime" with the slum, the ghetto, the broken family, mental disorder, poor education, and other characteristics of poverty, and we feel some sort of obligation (often a minimal one) to "cure" these conditions. Yet the Report's chapter on Juvenile Delinquency and Youth Crime alludes to the strong prejudices against ghetto youth felt by middle-class society. Americans are conformists and quickly label deviant activity as criminal, especially when such activity is undertaken by the lower classes. We also place youth in a special category. Strangely enough, much conduct that would not subject an adult to any criminal charge whatever becomes the touchstone by which an adolescent is adjudged a "juvenile delinquent." Activities which at one time were labeled "youthful pranks" are now deemed, at least in the large urban centers, serious enough to come before the juvenile courts. In the suburbs, where parents have more influence over the law enforcement system, such activities are often handled more informally and without the stigmatizing label of "delinquency."

The Commission emphasizes that Americans tend to turn their social problems over to experts and trust them to come up with adequate (or, hopefully, magic) solutions. This process is simply inadequate where crime is concerned, because experts cannot change our style of life, and it is precisely this which causes much crime. To eliminate most crime we would have to curb the national appetite for "progress," "success," and for constant change.

Among the experts charged with controlling crime are judges, and they are frequently criticized for contributing to the "crime wave" by decisions which sharply restrict police practices. Although there is no proof that judicial decisions, especially those of the Supreme Court, have anything to do with the amount of crime in the country, we instinctively tend to seek and find convenient targets.

The average American's persistent and continuing distrust of "big" government plays its role in the crime picture. We prize "localism" and have no national police force; nor, I would suggest, should we have one. In a computerized society many of the benefits of integration can be achieved by regular cooperation; yet local police forces do tend to duplicate activities and to be wary of cooperation with each other and

31

with federal agencies for various competitive reasons. The Commission wants more pooling of intelligence systems and sharing of facilities by both police and prosecutors. Localism also makes the job of law enforcement infinitely more difficult, especially in the case of organized crime.

How was the Report received by the American people? What influence has it had? If the influence has not been significant, why?

Prior to the publication of the Report certain political problems arose; these difficulties damped President Johnson's enthusiasm for it, and thus initially impaired any prospects for widespread publicity. The dispute was over wiretapping and bugging. A majority of the Commission wanted to recommend new legislation to permit authorization of these surveillance techniques on the ground that they were effective weapons against organized crime. At that time, the President was emphatically opposed to all tapping and bugging except in national security cases. Leon Jaworski, a Texas attorney and the President's "man" on the panel, fought the proposal and threatened to write a strong dissent. Attorney General Katzenbach papered over the dispute by suggesting compromise language.

Despite the compromise (the Commission "believes" instead of "recommends"), President Johnson jumped the gun by delivering a message on crime to Congress on February 6, 1967, two weeks before the Report was issued. This maneuver was characterized by *The New York Times* as an attempt to focus "primary attention on his own program" rather than the Commission's. That message called for enactment of a "Safe Streets and Crime Control Act" designed to federally fund innovative state and local improvements in court and correction procedures. The message also contained suggestions for some modest antiorganized-crime laws and for federal funding of innovations in state juvenile delinquency treatment; most significantly, President Johnson wanted a strong antielectronic surveillance law (dubbed the "Right of Privacy Act of 1967").

When the Report was issued, it received substantial publicity. *The New York Times* called it a "comprehensive, sophisticated and highly detailed study." But that may have been its main drawback as well as its virtue. Its more than 200 recommendations were diffuse and generalized; more important, there was no listing of priorities. The Report was written in rather stultified prose and was dangerously unfocused. Its tone was measured and qualified, and it appeared to have been written for the professionals in the field rather than for a lay audience. When the *Times* noted that "The Commission Report is an intelligent guide to [the] investment [of funds in anticrime activities]," it clearly did not regard the document as inspirational.

The difficulties were emphasized by later events. A month after the Report came out, Johnson convened a meeting of more than 600 law enforcement personnel, judges, law professors, and legislators to ostensibly discuss its recommendations. The President's tendency to use these conclaves as sounding boards for his own legislative proposals was evident in his call for enactment of the "safe streets" bill. The amorphousness of the Report and its tendency to mute controversy were reflected in one description of the meeting:

After the first discussion session there was much grumbling among the delegates that the conference leaders were trying so hard to avoid controversy that little of importance was being discussed.

* * *

Several participants remarked that the range of subjects was so broad that nothing concrete was being decided. After the initial meetings some said they still did not know exactly what purpose the conference was supposed to serve.

As the Task Force Reports emerged, they received diminishing attention. The Reports on the Police and the Courts were front-page items in the *Times*, but, by May 15, 1967, the Organized Crime Report was shunted onto Page 46. Since the Report merely recapitulated the relevant chapter material of the main Report, this might not have been surprising. Perhaps more boldness could have reaped more publicity, for it was noted that:

There had been predictions that the official Report would contain explosive disclosures, but it did not live up to its advance billing.

Even the important Corrections and Juvenile Delinquency Reports received scanty coverage. In a short article about the last Task Force Report on "Crime and its Impact—An Assessment," *The New York Times* noted that the Commission had published more than 2 million words. Perhaps they were just too many.

Congressional opinion was not substantially influenced by the Report's breadth and humanity. Four months after publication, the House of Representatives passed a repressive District of Columbia Crime Bill by a vote of 355 to 14. "In passing the bill, the House displayed its impatience with what the Committee on the District of Columbia called 'the creed that most crime is the outgrowth of poverty and slums and ghettoes . . . and in general social and economic deprivation' " reported the *Times*.[2]

Eventually the Crime Bill passed the Senate (in modified though still noxious form), and the President signed the final act on December 27, 1967. Ironically, he expressed reservations about the bill's provisions for minimum sentences for those people convicted of violent crimes—at that time, a sterile reflection of the Commission's point of view.

Congress also emphasized its disenchantment with the Commission by passing the "safe streets" bill in radically revised form as the Omnibus Crime Control Act of 1968. Johnson got his federal funding program at the expense of other repressive provisions. The Commission's trimming of the sails about the problem of narcotics and drugs may have contributed somewhat to the current congressional drive to penalize simple possession of LSD.

Events rather than the Commission's recommendations, of course, account for the passage of the modest federal, and some state and local firearms control legislation. Other legislation inspired by the Report's recommendations, is still, as of this writing, meandering slowly through the congressional labyrinth. The Juvenile Delinquency Prevention and Control Act, embodying some Commission recommendations, (in the area of federal funding of state innovative programs for prevention and rehabilitation) was recently passed. Appropriations to implement its laudable purpose have not yet been passed by Congress.

Some "citizens' efforts," attributable to activities of the National Council on Crime and Delinquency (as well as to Commission publicity for such activities) have been undertaken; but, in perspective, the Report has so far been less influential than the recent riots, assassinations, and other acts of violence which characterize our turbulent era.

Despite the problems, the Commission has made a substantial contribution, if we choose to listen, to the problem of understanding crime. Crime is not an alien phenomenon, a cancer on the otherwise healthy skin of the body politic. Crime is often the direct result of the vagaries of what might be

2 The District of Columbia Crime Commission Report, issued on New Year's Day, 1967, resembled the National Commission's document's emphasis upon antipoverty recommendations.

called "the American character." What we believe as a people, what we tolerate, how we go about acquiring wealth, the standards we practice rather than preach determine the nature and extent of crime we get as a nation. We are dedicated to progress, to rapid change, to a belief that anything (or anybody) which is old is somehow useless and should be replaced. We encourage competition, emulation of those who have achieved wealth, and often wink at some of the unethical or illegal means by which such wealth has been acquired.

Our hypermodern society, with its urban anonymity and social alienation, has also contributed to crime. As the Report notes, "The fear of crimes of violence is not a simple fear of injury or death, or even of all crimes of violence, but, at bottom, a fear of strangers." These fears, as well as the crime rate, will doubtless increase as migration from country to city continues.

Despite our tolerance we are vaguely troubled by what we perceive to be our loose ethical standards, so we endorse all sorts of punitive laws covering most areas of human activity to control our impulses and to appease our sense of guilt.

This schizophrenic reaction to the American experience results in both the economic phenomenon of poverty, of economic backwaters in an otherwise affluent nation, and an overly punitive attitude toward deviance. Thus, paradoxically, our very attitudes operate to perpetuate both the conditions of crime and our frustration about these conditions.

Perhaps this schizophrenia is responsible for our traditional unconcern with the warnings of those who have investigated crime. One major effort to analyze crime and law enforcement was the so-called Wickersham Commission Reports of 1931. These studies, dramatic and bluntly worded, constituted the first systematic inquiry into the crime problem ever undertaken in America. The findings, especially about organized crime, the lack of police professionalization, and in other critical areas are haunting precursers of the present Report. We made some changes, as a result of the Wickersham Reports: Police brutality (apparently) diminished; some district attorney's offices became less political in nature; and better crime statistics were compiled. Those changes fell far short of those the Reports argued were necessary, and that deleterious experience threatens to be repeated now. Reluctantly we must conclude that the reason for inaction in both instances can be found only in our lack of a fundamental commitment to the requirements of fundamental change.

The Commission clearly believes that our entire Society is ready to seriously reexamine itself. I cannot be so sanguine;

35

for if the Commission was not ready to do so, why should we assume a more serious commitment by Society itself?

America, in 1968, is beset by self-doubt rather than dignified by self-understanding. Cynical politicians appease the worst appetites of our national character by declaiming against crime. Crime is always equated with the political failures of the last administration. Because overt racist appeals are not fashionable, covert eulogies to "law and order" are substituted. Both political parties have been hypnotized by the vote-getting potential of the crime theme. "Crime" as a political weapon is particularly potent, since there can be no conscientious objectors to this particular war. Thus the level of public debate descends on a downward spiral of clichés and mindlessness. The incessant reiteration of the theme has resulted in a war against our young, our disaffected, and our minorities. Our police, smarting from alleged court attacks, see themselves as the last bulwark to social anarchy and frighteningly, they and their political allies are convincing many of us that this is true.[3]

We must understand that crime is going to be with us forever, and that its appalling frequency can be somewhat mitigated if we understand its roots in our culture; and that self-understanding, and meaningful action based upon it, is necessary if we are to overcome the national schizophrenia that is the cause of so much social and personal malaise. The Report constitutes an essential prelude to the necessary commencement of that process of reexamination. The sad thing (about us, not only the Commission) is that there is precious little evidence that this is being done. Rather, if the 1968 Crime Control Act is a viable example, we become harsher, more punitive, and the malaise continues.

[3] Last summer, a confrontation of serious dimension between the police and the political leadership of New York City occurred. The president of the Patrolman's Benevolent Association, a police union, offered "guidelines" to the police in cases of demonstrations and riots on the theory that the mayor was preventing full enforcement of the laws and going easy on demonstrators. Although that particular brouhaha was settled by a strategic withdrawal by the P.B.A., the issues posed promise to be renewed by the recent activities of a newly-formed "splinter" organization called The Law Enforcement Society of New York. Among the Society's initial demands (some of which were later dropped) was a call for the dismissal of a judge who allegedly permitted courtroom discipline to break down. These incidents raise the issue of police autonomy from political control, albeit in the guise of a call for "total law enforcement." Of course, beneath the argument lies the phenomenon of police antipathy toward minorities, political as well as racial, and a desire for unreviewable use of law enforcement power. Perhaps it all relates back to the police victory on the New York City Civilian Review Board issue a few years ago.

Summary

THIS REPORT IS ABOUT CRIME in America—about those who commit it, about those who are its victims, and about what can be done to reduce it.

The report is the work of 19 commissioners, 63 staff members, 175 consultants, and hundreds of advisers. The commissioners, staff, consultants, and advisers come from every part of America and represent a broad range of opinion and profession.

In the process of developing the findings and recommendations of the report the Commission called three national conferences, conducted five national surveys, held hundreds of meetings, and interviewed tens of thousands of persons.

The report makes more than 200 specific recommendations —concrete steps the Commission believes can lead to a safer and more just society. These recommendations call for a greatly increased effort on the part of the Federal Government, the States, the counties, the cities, civic organizations, religious institutions, business groups, and individual citizens. They call for basic changes in the operations of police, schools, prosecutors, employment agencies, defenders, social workers, prisons, housing authorities, and probation and parole officers.

But the recommendations are more than just a list of new procedures, new tactics, and new techniques. They are a call for a revolution in the way America thinks about crime.

Many Americans take comfort in the view that crime is the vice of a handful of people. This view is inaccurate. In the United States today, one boy in six is referred to the juvenile court. A Commission survey shows that in 1965 more than two million Americans were received in prisons or juvenile training schools, or placed on probation. Another Commission study suggests that about 40 percent of all male children now living in the United States will be arrested for a nontraffic offense during their lives. An independent survey of 1,700 persons found that 91 percent of the sample admitted they had committed acts for which they might have received jail or prison sentences.

Many Americans also think of crime as a very narrow range of behavior. It is not. An enormous variety of acts make up the "crime problem." Crime is not just a tough teenager snatching a lady's purse. It is a professional thief stealing cars "on order." It is a well-heeled loan shark taking over a previously legitimate business for organized crime. It is a polite young man who suddenly and inexplicably murders his family. It is a corporation executive conspiring with competitors to keep prices high. No single formula, no single theory, no single generalization can explain the vast range of behavior called crime.

Many Americans think controlling crime is solely the task of the police, the courts, and correction agencies. In fact, as the Commission's report makes clear, crime cannot be controlled without the interest and participation of schools, businesses, social agencies, private groups, and individual citizens.

What, then, is America's experience with crime and how has this experience shaped the Nation's way of living? A new insight into these two questions is furnished by the Commission's National Survey of Criminal Victims. In this survey, the first of its kind conducted on such a scope 10,000 representative American households were asked about their experiences with crime, whether they reported those experiences to the police, and how those experiences affected their lives.

An important finding of the survey is that for the Nation as a whole there is far more crime than ever is reported. Burglaries occur about three times more often than they are reported to police. Aggravated assaults and larcenies over $50 occur twice as often as they are reported. There are 50 percent more robberies than are reported. In some areas, only one-tenth of the total number of certain kinds of crimes are reported to the police. Seventy-four percent of the neighborhood commercial establishments surveyed do not report to police the thefts committed by their employees.

The existence of crime, the talk about crime, the reports of crime, and the fear of crime have eroded the basic quality of life of many Americans. A Commission study conducted in high crime areas of two large cities found that:

☐ 43 percent of the respondents say they stay off the streets at night because of their fear of crime.

- ☐ 35 percent say they do not speak to strangers any more because of their fear of crime.
- ☐ 21 percent say they use cars and cabs at night because of their fear of crime.
- ☐ 20 percent say they would like to move to another neighborhood because of their fear of crime.

The findings of the Commission's national survey generally support those of the local surveys. One-third of a representative sample of all Americans say it is unsafe to walk alone at night in their neighborhoods. Slightly more than one-third say they keep firearms in the house for protection against criminals. Twenty-eight percent say they keep watchdogs for the same reason.

Under any circumstance, developing an effective response to the problem of crime in America is exceedingly difficult. And because of the changes expected in the population in the next decade, in years to come it will be more difficult. Young people commit a disproportionate share of crime and the number of young people in our society is growing at a much faster rate than the total population. Although the 15- to 17-year-old age group represents only 5.4 percent of the population, it accounts for 12.8 percent of all arrests. Fifteen and sixteen year olds have the highest arrest rate in the United States. The problem in the years ahead is dramatically foretold by the fact that 23 percent of the population is 10 or under.

Despite the seriousness of the problem today and the increasing challenge in the years ahead, the central conclusion of the Commission is that a significant reduction in crime is possible if the following objectives are vigorously pursued:

First, society must seek to prevent crime before it happens by assuring all Americans a stake in the benefits and responsibilities of American life, by strengthening law enforcement, and by reducing criminal opportunities.

Second, society's aim of reducing crime would be better served if the system of criminal justice developed a far broader range of techniques with which to deal with individual offenders.

Third, the system of criminal justice must eliminate existing injustices if it is to achieve its ideals and win the respect and cooperation of all citizens.

Fourth, the system of criminal justice must attract more people and better people—police, prosecutors, judges, defense attorneys, probation and parole officers, and corrections officials with more knowledge, expertise, initiative, and integrity.

Fifth, there must be much more operational and basic research into the problems of crime and criminal administration, by those both within and without the system of criminal justice.

Sixth, the police, courts, and correctional agencies must be given substantially greater amounts of money if they are to improve their ability to control crime.

Seventh, individual citizens, civic and business organizations, religious institutions, and all levels of government must take responsibility for planning and implementing the changes that must be made in the criminal justice system if crime is to be reduced.

In terms of specific recommendations, what do these seven objectives mean?

---

1. PREVENTING CRIME

◇ The prevention of crime covers a wide range of activities: Eliminating social conditions closely associated with crime; improving the ability of the criminal justice system to detect, apprehend, judge, and reintegrate into their communities those who commit crimes; and reducing the situations in which crimes are most likely to be committed.

Every effort must be made to strengthen the family, now often shattered by the grinding pressures of urban slums.

Slum schools must be given enough resources to make them as good as schools elsewhere and to enable them to compensate for the various handicaps suffered by the slum child—to rescue him from his environment.

Present efforts to combat school segregation, and the housing segregation that underlies it, must be continued and expanded.

Employment opportunities must be enlarged and young people provided with more effective vocational training and individual job counseling. Programs to create new kinds of jobs—such as probation aides, medical assistants, and teacher helpers—seem particularly promising and should be expanded.

The problem of increasing the ability of the police to detect and apprehend criminals is complicated. In one effort to find out how this objective could be achieved, the Commission conducted an analysis of 1,905 crimes reported to the Los Angeles Police Department during a recent month. The study showed the importance of identifying the perpetrator at the scene of the crime. Eighty-six percent of the crimes with named suspects were solved, but only 12 percent of the unnamed suspect crimes were solved. Another finding of the study was that there is a relationship between the speed of response and certainty of apprehension. On the average, response to emergency calls resulting in arrests was 50 percent faster than response to emergency calls not resulting in arrest. On the basis of this finding, and a cost effectiveness study to discover the best means to reduce response time, the Commission recommends an experimental program to develop computer-aided command-and-control systems for large police departments.

To insure the maximum use of such a system, headquarters must have a direct link with every onduty police officer. Because large scale production would result in a substantial reduction of the cost of miniature two-way radios, the Commission recommends that the Federal Government assume leadership in initiating a development program for such equipment and that it consider guaranteeing the sale of the first production lot of perhaps 20,000 units.

Two other steps to reduce police response time are recommended:

☐ Police callboxes, which are locked and inconspicuous in most cities, should be left open, brightly marked, and designated "public emergency callboxes."

☐ The telephone company should develop a single police number for each metropolitan area, and eventually for the entire United States.

Improving the effectiveness of law enforcement, however, is much more than just improving police response time. For example a study in Washington, D.C., found that courtroom time for a felony defendant who pleads guilty probably totals less than 1 hour, while the median time from his initial appearance to his disposition is 4 months.

In an effort to discover how courts can best speed the process of criminal justice, the known facts about felony cases in Washington were placed in a computer and the operation of the system was simulated. After a number of possible solutions to the problem of delay were tested, it appeared that the addition of a second grand jury—which, with supporting per-

41

sonnel, would cost less than $50,000 a year—would result in a 25-percent reduction in the time required for the typical felony case to move from initial appearance to trial.

The application of such analysis—when combined with the Commission's recommended timetable laying out timespans for each step in the criminal process—should help court systems to ascertain their procedural bottlenecks and develop ways to eliminate them.

Another way to prevent crime is to reduce the opportunity to commit it. Many crimes would not be committed, indeed many criminal careers would not begin, if there were fewer opportunities for crime.

Auto theft is a good example. According to FBI statistics, the key had been left in the ignition or the ignition had been left unlocked in 42 percent of all stolen cars. Even in those cars taken when the ignition was locked, at least 20 percent were stolen simply by shorting the ignition with such simple devices as paper clips or tinfoil. In one city, the elimination of the unlocked "off" position on the 1965 Chevrolet resulted in 50 percent fewer of those models being stolen in 1965 than were stolen in 1964.

On the basis of these findings, it appears that an important reduction in auto theft could be achieved simply by installing an ignition system that automatically ejects the key when the engine is turned off.

A major reason that it is important to reduce auto theft is that stealing a car is very often the criminal act that starts a boy on a course of lawbreaking.

Stricter gun controls also would reduce some kinds of crime. Here, the Commission recommends a strengthening of the Federal law governing the interstate shipment of firearms and enactment of State laws requiring the registration of all handguns, rifles, and shotguns, and prohibiting the sale or ownership of firearms by certain categories of persons—dangerous criminals, habitual drunkards, and drug addicts. After 5 years, the Commission recommends that Congress pass a Federal registration law applying to those States that have not passed their own registration laws.

---

2. NEW WAYS OF DEALING WITH OFFENDERS

☐ The Commission's second objective—the development of a far broader range of alternatives for dealing with offenders—is based on the belief that, while there are some who must be completely segregated from society, there are many instances in which segregation does more harm than good. Furthermore, by concentrating the resources of the police, the courts, and correctional agencies on the smaller number of offenders who really need them, it should be possible to give all offenders more effective treatment.

A specific and important example of this principle is the Commission's recommendation that every community consider establishing a Youth Services Bureau, a community-based center to which juveniles could be referred by the police, the courts, parents, schools, and social agencies for counseling, education, work, or recreation programs and job placement.

The Youth Services Bureau—an agency to handle many troubled and troublesome young people outside the criminal system—is needed in part because society has failed to give the juvenile court the resources that would allow it to function as its founders hoped it would. In a recent survey of juvenile court judges, for example, 83 percent said no psychologist or psychiatrist was available to their courts on a regular basis and one-third said they did not have probation officers or social workers. Even where there are probation officers, the Commission found, the average officer supervises 76 probationers, more than double the recommended caseload.

The California Youth Authority for the last 5 years has been conducting a controlled experiment to determine the effectiveness of another kind of alternative treatment program for juveniles. There, after initial screening, convicted juvenile delinquents are assigned on a random basis to either an experimental group or a control group. Those in the experimental group are returned to the community and receive intensive individual counseling, group counseling, group therapy, and family counseling. Those in the control group are assigned to California's regular institutional treatment program. The findings so far: 28 percent of the experimental group have had their paroles revoked, compared with 52 percent in the control group. Furthermore, the community treatment program is less expensive than institutional treatment.

To make community-based treatment possible for both adults and juveniles, the Commission recommends the development of an entirely new kind of correctional institution: located close to population centers; maintaining close relations with schools, employers, and universities; housing as few as 50 inmates; serving as a classification center, as the center for various kinds of community programs and as a port of reen-

43

try to the community for those difficult and dangerous offenders who have required treatment in facilities with tighter custody.

Such institutions would be useful in the operation of programs—strongly recommended by the Commission—that permit selected inmates to work or study in the community during the day and return to control at night, and programs that permit long-term inmates to become adjusted to society gradually rather than being discharged directly from maximum security institutions to the streets.

Another aspect of the Commission's conviction that different offenders with different problems should be treated in different ways, is its recommendation about the handling of public drunkenness, which, in 1965, accounted for one out of every three arrests in America. The great number of these arrests—some 2 million—burdens the police, clogs the lower courts and crowds the penal institutions. The Commission therefore recommends that communities develop civil detoxification units and comprehensive aftercare programs, and that with the development of such programs, drunkenness, not accompanied by other unlawful conduct, should not be a criminal offense.

Similarly, the Commission recommends the expanded use of civil commitment for drug addicts.

---

3. ELIMINATING UNFAIRNESS

◇ The third objective is to eliminate injustices so that the system of criminal justice can win the respect and cooperation of all citizens. Our society must give the police, the courts, and correctional agencies the resources and the mandate to provide fair and dignified treatment for all.

The Commission found overwhelming evidence of institutional shortcomings in almost every part of the United States.

A survey of the lower court operations in a number of large American cities found cramped and noisy courtrooms, undignified and perfunctory procedures, badly trained personnel overwhelmed by enormous caseloads. In short, the Commission found assembly line justice.

The Commission found that in at least three States, justices of the peace are paid only if they convict and collect a fee from the defendant, a practice held unconstitutional by the Supreme Court 40 years ago.

The Commission found that approximately one-fourth of the 400,000 children detained in 1965—for a variety of causes but including truancy, smoking, and running away from home—were held in adult jails and lockups, often with hardened criminals.

In addition to the creation of new kinds of institutions—such as the Youth Services Bureau and the small, community-based correctional centers—the Commission recommends several important procedural changes. It recommends counsel at various points in the criminal process.

For juveniles, the Commission recommends providing counsel whenever coercive action is a possibility.

For adults, the Commission recommends providing counsel to any criminal defendant who faces a significant penalty—excluding traffic and similar petty charges—if he cannot afford to provide counsel for himself.

In connection with this recommendation, the Commission asks each State to finance regular, statewide assigned counsel and defender systems for the indigent.

Counsel also should be provided in parole and probation revocation hearings.

Another kind of broad procedural change that the Commission recommends is that every State, county, and local jurisdiction provide judicial officers with sufficient information about individual defendants to permit the release without money bail of those who can be safely released.

In addition to eliminating the injustice of holding persons charged with a crime merely because they cannot afford bail, this recommendation also would save a good deal of money. New York City alone, for example, spends approximately $10 million a year holding persons who have not yet been found guilty of any crime.

Besides institutional injustices, the Commission found that while the great majority of criminal justice and law enforcement personnel perform their duties with fairness and understanding, even under the most trying circumstances, some take advantage of their official positions and act in a callous, corrupt, or brutal manner.

Injustice will not yield to simple solutions. Overcoming it requires a wide variety of remedies including improved methods of selecting personnel, the massive infusion of additional funds, the revamping of existing procedures and the adoption of more effective internal and external controls.

The relations between the police and urban poor deserve special mention. Here the Commission recommends that every large department—especially in communities with substantial minority populations—should have community-relations machinery consisting of a headquarters planning and supervising unit and precinct units to carry out recommended programs. Effective citizen advisory committees should be established in minority group neighborhoods. All departments with substantial minority populations should make special efforts to recruit minority group officers and to deploy and promote them fairly. They should have rigorous internal investigation units to examine complaints of misconduct. The Commission believes it is of the utmost importance to insure that complaints of unfair treatment are fairly dealt with.

Fair treatment of every individual—fair in fact and also perceived to be fair by those affected—is an essential element of justice and a principal objective of the American criminal justice system.

---

4. PERSONNEL

◇ The fourth objective is that higher levels of knowledge, expertise, initiative, and integrity be achieved by police, judges, prosecutors, defense attorneys, and correctional authorities so that the system of criminal justice can improve its ability to control crime.

The commission found one obstacle to recruiting better police officers was the standard requirement that all candidates —regardless of qualifications—begin their careers at the lowest level and normally remain at this level from 2 to 5 years before being eligible for promotion. Thus, a college graduate must enter a department at the same rank and pay and perform the same tasks as a person who enters with only a high school diploma or less.

The Commission recommends that police departments give up single entry and establish three levels at which candidates may begin their police careers. The Commission calls these three levels the "community service officer," the "police officer," and the "police agent."

This division, in addition to providing an entry place for the better educated, also would permit police departments to tap the special knowledge, skills, and understanding of those brought up in the slums.

The community service officer would be a uniformed but unarmed member of the police department. Two of his major responsibilities would be to maintain close relations with

46

juveniles in the area where he works and to be especially alert to crime-breeding conditions that other city agencies had not dealt with. Typically, the CSO might be under 21, might not be required to meet conventional education requirements, and might work out of a store-front office. Serving as an apprentice policeman—a substitute for the police cadet—the CSO would work as a member of a team with the police officer and police agent.

The police officer would respond to calls for service, perform routine patrol, render emergency services, make preliminary investigations, and enforce traffic regulations. In order to qualify as a police officer at the present time, a candidate should possess a high school diploma and should demonstrate a capacity for college work.

The police agent would do what ever police jobs were most complicated, most sensitive, and most demanding. He might be a specialist in police community-relations or juvenile delinquency. He might be in uniform patrolling a high-crime neighborhood. He might have staff duties. To become a police agent would require at least 2 years of college work and preferably a baccalaureate degree in the liberal arts or social sciences.

As an ultimate goal, the Commission recommends that all police personnel with general enforcement powers have baccalaureate degrees.

While candidates could enter the police service at any one of the three levels, they also could work their way up through the different categories as they met the basic education and other requirements.

In many jurisdictions there is a critical need for additional police personnel. Studies by the Commission indicate a recruiting need of 50,000 policemen in 1967 just to fill positions already authorized. In order to increase police effectiveness, additional staff specialists will be required, and when the community service officers are added manpower needs will be even greater.

The Commission also recommends that every State establish a commission on police standards to set minimum recruiting and training standards and to provide financial and technical assistance for local police departments.

In order to improve the quality of judges, prosecutors, and defense attorneys, the Commission recommends a variety of steps: Taking the selection of judges out of partisan politics; the more regular use of seminars, conferences, and institutes to train sitting judges; the establishment of judicial commissions to excuse physically or mentally incapacitated judges

47

from their duties without public humiliation; the general abolition of part-time district attorneys and assistant district attorneys; and a broad range of measures to develop a greatly enlarged and better trained pool of defense attorneys.

In the correctional system there is a critical shortage of probation and parole officers, teachers, caseworkers, vocational instructors, and group workers. The need for major manpower increases in this area was made clear by the findings from the Commissions national corrections survey:

☐ Less than 3 percent of all personnel working in local jails and institutions devote their time to treatment and training.

☐ Eleven States do not offer any kind of probation services for adult misdemeanants, six offer only the barest fragments of such services, and most States offer them on a spotty basis.

☐ Two-thirds of all State adult felony probationers are in caseloads of over 100 persons.

To meet the requirements of both the correctional agencies and the courts, the Commission has found an immediate need to double the Nation's pool of juvenile probation officers, triple the number of probation officers working with adult felons, and increase sevenfold the number of officers working with misdemeanants.

Another area with a critical need for large numbers of expert criminal justice officers is the complex one of controlling organized crime. Here, the Commission recommends that prosecutors and police in every State and city where organized crime is known to, or may, exist develop special organized crime units.

---

5. RESEARCH

◇ The fifth objective is that every segment of the system of criminal justice devote a significant part of its resources for research to insure the development of new and effective methods of controlling crime.

The Commission found that little research is being conducted into such matters as the economic impact of crime; the effects on crime of increasing or decreasing criminal sanctions; possible methods for improving the effectiveness of various procedures of the police, courts, and correctional agencies.

Organized crime is another area in which almost no research has been conducted. The commission found that the only group with any significant knowledge about this problem was law enforcement officials. Those in other disciplines—social scientists, economists and lawyers, for example—have not until recently considered the possibility of research projects on organized crime.

A small fraction of 1 percent of the criminal justice system's total budget is spent on research. This figure could be multiplied many times without approaching the 3 percent industry spends on research, much less the 15 percent the Defense Department spends. The Commission believes it should be multiplied many times.

That research is a powerful force for change in the field of criminal justice perhaps can best be documented by the history of the Vera Institute in New York City. Here the research of a small, nongovernment agency has in a very short time led to major changes in the bail procedures of approximately 100 cities, several States, and the Federal Government.

Because of the importance of research, the Commission recommends that major criminal justice agencies—such as State court and correctional systems and big-city police departments—organize operational research units as integral parts of their structures.

In addition, the criminal justice agencies should welcome the efforts of scholars and other independent experts to understand their problems and operations. These agencies cannot undertake needed research on their own; they urgently need the help of outsiders.

The Commission also recommends the establishment of several regional research institutes designed to concentrate a number of different disciplines on the problem of crime. It further recommends the establishment of an independent National Criminal Research Foundation to stimulate and coordinate research and disseminate its results.

One essential requirement for research is more complete information about the operation of the criminal process. To meet this requirement, the Commission recommends the creation of a National Criminal Justice Statistics Center. The Center's first responsibility would be to work with the FBI, the Children's Bureau, the Federal Bureau of Prisons, and other agencies to develop an integrated picture of the number of crimes reported to police, the number of persons arrested,

49

the number of accused persons prosecuted, the number of offenders placed on probation, in prison, and subsequently on parole.

Another major responsibility of the Center would be to continue the Commission's initial effort to develop a new yardstick to measure the extent of crime in our society as a supplement to the FBI's Uniform Crime Reports. The Commission believes that the Government should be able to plot the levels of different kinds of crime in a city or a State as precisely as the Labor Department and the Census Bureau now plot the rate of unemployment. Just as unemployment information is essential to sound economic planning, so some day may criminal information help official planning in the system of criminal justice.

---

6. MONEY

◊ Sixth, the police, the courts, and correctional agencies will require substantially more money if they are to control crime better.

Almost all of the specific recommendations made by the Commission will involve increased budgets. Substantially higher salaries must be offered to attract topflight candidates to the system of criminal justice. For example, the median annual salary for a patrolman in a large city today is $5,300. Typically, the maximum salary is something less than $1,000 above the starting salary. The Commission believes the most important change that can be made in police salary scales is to increase maximums sharply. An FBI agent, for example, starts at $8,421 a year and if he serves long and well enough can reach $16,905 a year without being promoted to a supervisory position. The Commission is aware that reaching such figures immediately is not possible in many cities, but it believes that there should be a large range from minimum to maximum everywhere.

The Commission also recommends new kinds of programs that will require additional funds: Youth Services Bureaus, greatly enlarged misdemeanant probation services and increased levels of research, for example.

The Commission believes some of the additional resources —especially those devoted to innovative programs and to training, education, and research—should be contributed by the Federal Government.

The Federal Government already is conducting a broad range of programs—aid to elementary and secondary schools, the Neighborhood Youth Corps, Project Head Start, and others—designed to attack directly the social problems often associated with crime.

Through such agencies as the Federal Bureau of Investigation, the Office of Law Enforcement Assistance, the Bureau of Prisons, and the Office of Manpower Development and Training, the Federal Government also offers comparatively limited financial and technical assistance to the police, the courts, and corrections authorities.

While the Commission is convinced State and local governments must continue to carry the major burden of criminal administration, it recommends a vastly enlarged program of Federal assistance to strengthen law enforcement, crime prevention, and the administration of justice.

The program of Federal support recommended by the Commission would be directed to eight major needs:

(1) State and local planning.

(2) Education and training of criminal justice personnel.

(3) Surveys and advisory services concerning the organization and operation of police departments, courts, prosecuting offices, and corrections agencies.

(4) Development of a coordinated national information system for operational and research purposes.

(5) Funding of limited numbers of demonstration programs in agencies of justice.

(6) Scientific and technological research and development.

(7) Development of national and regional research centers.

(8) Grants-in-aid for operational innovations.

The Commission is not in a position to recommend the exact amount of money that will be needed to carry out its proposed program. It believes, however, that a Federal program totaling hundreds of millions of dollars a year during the next decade could be effectively utilized. The Commission also believes the major responsibility for administering this program should lie within the Department of Justice.

The States, the cities, and the counties also will have to make substantial increases in their contributions to the system of criminal justice.

7. RESPONSIBILITY FOR CHANGE

◊ Seventh, individual citizens, social-service agencies, universities, religious institutions, civic and business groups, and all kinds of governmental agencies at all levels must become involved in planning and executing changes in the criminal justice system.

The Commission is convinced that the financial and technical assistance program it proposes can and should be only a small part of the national effort to develop a more effective and fair response to crime.

In March of 1966, President Johnson asked the Attorney General to invite each Governor to form a State committee on criminal administration. The response to this request has been encouraging: more than two-thirds of the States already have such committees or have indicated they intend to form them.

The Commission recommends that in every State and city there should be an agency, or one or more officials, with specific responsibility for planning improvements in criminal administration and encouraging their implementation.

Planning agencies, among other functions, play a key role in helping State legislatures and city councils decide where additional funds and manpower are most needed, what new programs should be adopted, and where and how existing agencies might pool their resources on either a metropolitan or regional basis.

The planning agencies should include both officials from the system of criminal justice and citizens from other professions. Plans to improve criminal administration will be impossible to put into effect unless those responsible for criminal administration help make them. On the other hand, crime prevention must be the task of the community as a whole.

While this report had concentrated on recommendations for action by governments, the Commission is convinced that governmental actions will not be enough. Crime is a social problem that is interwoven with almost every aspect of American life. Controlling it involves improving the quality of family life, the way schools are run, the way cities are planned, the way workers are hired. Controlling crime is the business of every American institution. Controlling crime is the business of every American.

Universities should increase their research on the problems of crime; private social welfare organizations and religious institutions should continue to experiment with advanced techniques of helping slum children overcome their environment; labor unions and businesses can enlarge their programs to provide prisoners with vocational training; professional and community organizations can help probation and parole workers with their work.

The responsibility of the individual citizen runs far deeper than cooperating with the police or accepting jury duty or insuring the safety of his family by installing adequate locks—important as they are. He must respect the law, refuse to cut corners, reject the cynical argument that "anything goes as long as you don't get caught."

Most important of all, he must, on his own and through the organizations he belongs to, interest himself in the problems of crime and criminal justice, seek information, express his views, use his vote wisely, get involved.

In sum, the Commission is sure that the Nation can control crime if it will.

"The problems of crime bring us together.

Even as we join in common action, we know

there can be no instant victory. Ancient evils

do not yield to easy conquest. We cannot

limit our efforts to enemies we can see. We

must, with equal resolve, seek out new

knowledge, new techniques, and new under-

standing."

—Message from President Johnson
to the Congress, March 9, 1966.

Chapter 1

The Challenge of Crime in a Free Society: Introduction

THERE IS MUCH CRIME in America, more than ever is reported, far more than ever is solved, far too much for the health of the Nation. Every American knows that. Every American is, in a sense, a victim of crime. Violence and theft have not only injured, often irreparably, hundreds of thousands of citizens, but have directly affected everyone. Some people have been impelled to uproot themselves and find new homes. Some have been made afraid to use public streets and parks. Some have come to doubt the worth of a society in which so many people behave so badly. Some have become distrustful of the Government's ability, or even desire, to protect them. Some have lapsed into the attitude that criminal behavior is normal human behavior and consequently have become indifferent to it, or have adopted it as a good way to get ahead in life. Some have become suspicious of those they conceive to be responsible for crime: adolescents or Negroes or drug addicts or college students or demonstrators; policemen who fail to solve crimes; judges who pass lenient sentences or write decisions restricting the activities of the police; parole boards that release prisoners who resume their criminal activities.

The most understandable mood into which many Americans have been plunged by crime is one of frustration and bewilderment. For "crime" is not a single simple phenomenon that can be examined, analyzed and described in one piece. It occurs in every part of the country and in every stratum of society. Its practitioners and its victims are people of all ages, incomes and backgrounds. Its trends are difficult

55

to ascertain. Its causes are legion. Its cures are speculative and controversial. An examination of any single kind of crime, let alone of "crime in America," raises a myriad of issues of the utmost complexity.

Consider the crime of robbery, which, since it involves both stealing and violence or the threat of it, is an especially hurtful and frightening one. In 1965 in America there were 118,916 robberies known to the police: 326 robberies a day; a robbery for every 1,630 Americans. Robbery takes dozens of forms, but suppose it took only four: forcible or violent purse-snatching by boys, muggings by drug addicts, store stickups by people with a sudden desperate need for money, and bank robberies by skillful professional criminals. The technical, organizational, legal, behavioral, economic and social problems that must be addressed if America is to deal with any degree of success with just those four kinds of events and those four kinds of persons are innumerable and refractory.

The underlying problems are ones that the criminal justice system can do little about. The unruliness of young people, widespread drug addiction, the existence of much poverty in a wealthy society, the pursuit of the dollar by any available means are phenomena the police, the courts, and the correctional apparatus, which must deal with crimes and criminals one by one, cannot confront directly. They are strands that can be disentangled from the fabric of American life only by the concerted action of all of society. They concern the Commission deeply, for unless society does take concerted action to change the general conditions and attitudes that are associated with crime, no improvement in law enforcement and administration of justice, the subjects this Commission was specifically asked to study, will be of much avail.

Of the everyday problems of the criminal justice system itself, certainly the most delicate and probably the most difficult concern the proper ways of dealing individually with individuals. Arrest and prosecution are likely to have quite different effects on delinquent boys and on hardened professional criminals. Sentencing occasional robbers and habitual robbers by the same standards is clearly inappropriate. Rehabilitating a drug addict is a procedure that has little in common with rehabilitating a holdup man. In short, there are no general prescriptions for dealing with "robbers." There are no general prescriptions for dealing with "robbery" either. Keeping streets and parks safe is not the same problem as keeping banks secure. Investigating a mugging and tracking down a band of prudent and well-organized bank robbers are two en-

56

tirely distinct police procedures. The kind of police patrol that will deter boys from street robberies is not likely to deter men with guns from holding up storekeepers.

Robbery is only one of 28 crimes on which the Federal Bureau of Investigation reports in its annual Uniform Crime Reports. In terms of frequency of occurrence, it ranks fifth among the UCR's "Index Crimes," the seven serious crimes that the FBI considers to be indicative of the general crime trends in the Nation. (The others are willful homicide, forcible rape, aggravated assault, burglary, theft of $50 or over, and motor vehicle theft.) The Index Crimes accounted for fewer than 1 million of the almost 5 million arrests that the UCR reports for 1965. Almost half of those arrests were for crimes that have no real victims (prostitution, gambling, narcotics use, vagrancy, juvenile curfew violations and the like) or for breaches of the public peace (drunkenness, disorderly conduct). Other crimes for which more than 50,000 people were arrested were such widely different kinds of behavior as vandalism, fraud, sex offenses other than rape or prostitution, driving while intoxicated, carrying weapons, and offenses against family or children. Each of the 28 categories of crime confronts the community and the criminal justice system, to a greater or a lesser degree, with unique social, legal, correctional, and law enforcement problems. Taken together they raise a multitude of questions about how the police, the courts, and corrections should be organized; how their personnel should be selected, trained and paid; what modern technology can do to help their work; what kinds of knowledge they need; what procedures they should use; what resources they should be given; what the relations between the community and the various parts of the criminal justice system should be.

And so, when the President asked the Commission to "deepen our understanding of the causes of crime and of how society should respond to the challenge of the present levels of crime," he gave it a formidable assignment.

Crime and society's response to it resemble a gigantic disassembled jigsaw puzzle whose pieces the Commission was asked to assemble into as complete and accurate a picture as it could. It was charged with discovering whether the popular picture of crime in America is how it really looks and, if not, what the differences are; with determining how poverty, discrimination and other social ills relate to crime; with ascertaining whether America's system of criminal justice really works the way the public thinks it does and the books say it

The pattern of a crime like robbery is, of course, irregular. A rash of robberies at a single time may give people the feeling that they are engulfed by danger and lawlessness. In Washington, D.C., for example, between 8 a.m., Friday, December 9, and 8 a.m., Saturday, December 10, 1966, an extraordinary total of 35 robberies that netted the robbers almost $16,000 was reported to the Metropolitan Police Department.

Friday, December 9:

9:15 a.m.	Strongarm robbery, street, $2.
10:00 a.m.	Armed robbery, liquor store, $1,500.
11:30 a.m.	Pocketbook snatched with force and violence, street, $3.
12:30 p.m.	Holdup with revolver, roofing company, $2,100.
2:40 p.m.	Holdup with gun, shoe store, $139.
3:20 p.m.	Holdup with gun, apartment, $92.
4:55 p.m.	Holdup with gun, bank, $8,716.
6:25 p.m.	Mugging, street, $5.
6:50 p.m.	Holdup with revolver, tourist home, $30.

7:00 p.m.	Strongarm robbery, street, $25.
7:05 p.m.	Holdup with gun, auto in parking lot, $61.
7:10 p.m.	Strongarm robbery, apartment house, $3.
7:15 p.m.	Holdup with revolver (employee shot twice), truck rental company, $200.
7:25 p.m.	Mugging, street, $5.
7:50 p.m.	Holdup with gun, transfer company, $1,400.

8:55 p.m.	Holdup with shotgun, newspaper substation, $100.

10:10 p.m.	Holdup with gun, hotel, $289.50.
10:15 p.m.	Strongarm robbery, street, $120.
10:30 p.m.	Holdup with gun, street, $59.50.
10:53 p.m.	Strongarm robbery, street, $175.

11:05 p.m.	Holdup, tavern, $40.
11:30 p.m.	Strongarm robbery, street, $3.
11:55 p.m.	Strongarm robbery, street, $51.

Saturday, December 10:

12:20 a.m.	Strongarm robbery, street, $19.

1:10 a.m.	Strongarm robbery, apartment house, $3.

3:25 a.m.	Strongarm robbery, street, $25.
3:50 a.m.	Holdup with knife, street, $23.
3:55 a.m.	Holdup with gun, street, $25.

4:20 a.m.	Robbery with intent to rape, street, 75 cents.
4:20 a.m.	Holdup with gun, carryout shop, $80.

6:25 a.m.	Holdup-rape, street, $20.
6:25 a.m.	Holdup with gun, tourist home, no amount listed.
6:45 a.m.	Holdup, street, $5.

7:30 a.m.	Holdup with knife, cleaners, $300.
7:40 a.m.	Strongarm robbery, street, $80.

should and, if it does not, where, when, how, and why it does not.

Commission observers rode in police cars, sat in courtrooms, visited prisons, walked the streets of city slums. Commission interviewers questioned victims of crime about their experiences; professional criminals about their methods of operation; citizens about their attitudes toward the police; convicts about their daily lives; policemen, prosecutors, judges and correctional officials about the jobs they perform and the problems they meet every working day. The Commission convened a conference at which State representatives, assigned by the Governors to work with the Commission, shared knowledge and exchanged opinions; it sponsored a symposium at which scientists and technological experts analyzed ways science and technology could be used to control crime; it co-sponsored a national conference on legal manpower needs.

The Commission brought to its offices in Washington, often for weeks or months, several hundred crime specialists —police, court and correctional officials, professors of criminal law, criminologists, sociologists, social workers, statisticians, psychiatrists, technological experts—so that they could tell in detail what they knew and what they thought. Members of the Commission's full-time staff, drawn from diverse professions and backgrounds, visited and corresponded with other hundreds of such experts. The staff collected its own statistics and other data, along with data from other agencies, for comparison and analysis. It read hundreds of books and papers dealing with subjects from police administration to juvenile-gang subcultures, from criminal sentencing codes to correctional theory.

The Commission did not—it could not—find out "everything" about crime and the criminal justice system. It became increasingly aware during its work that far from seeking to say the last word on crime, its task was rather a step in a long process of systematic inquiry that must be continued and expanded by others. But the work the Commission was able to do did deepen its understanding; and, the Commission hopes and believes, it does provide a basis for a vigorous and effective program for meeting crime's challenge to the Nation.

TOWARD UNDERSTANDING AND
PREVENTING CRIME

A skid-row drunk lying in a gutter is crime. So is the killing of an unfaithful wife. A Cosa Nostra conspiracy to bribe public officials is crime. So is a strong-arm robbery by a 15-year-old boy. The embezzlement of a corporation's funds by an executive is crime. So is the possession of marihuana cigarettes by a student. These crimes can no more be lumped together for purposes of analysis than can measles and schizophrenia, or lung cancer and a broken ankle. As with disease, so with crime: if causes are to be understood, if risks are to be evaluated, and if preventive or remedial actions are to be taken, each kind must be looked at separately. Thinking of "crime" as a whole is futile.

In any case it is impossible to answer with precision questions about the volume or trends of crime as a whole, or even of any particular kind of crime. Techniques for measuring crime are, and probably always will be imperfect. Successful crime, after all, is secret crime. The best, in fact almost the only, source of statistical information about crime volumes is the Uniform Crime Reports of the FBI. The UCR is the product of a nationwide system of crime reporting that the FBI has painstakingly developed over the years. Under this system local police agencies report the offenses they know of to the FBI; the UCR is a compilation of these reports. This compilation can be no better than the underlying information that local agencies supply to the FBI. And because the FBI has induced local agencies to improve their reporting methods year by year, it is important to distinguish better reporting from more crime.

What the UCR shows is a rise in the number of individual crimes over the years at a rate faster than the rise in America's population. It shows an especially rapid rise in crimes against property. Furthermore, Commission surveys of the experience of the public as victims of crime show that there is several times as much crime against both property and persons as is reported to the police. Even in the areas having the highest rates of crime in our large cities, the surveys suggested that citizens are victimized several times as often as official records indicate. As might be expected, crimes the public regards as most serious, particularly those involving violence, are generally better reported than less serious crimes.

While it is impossible to offer absolute statistical proof that every year there are more crimes per American than there were the year before, both available statistics and the facts of social change in America suggest that there are.

61

Obviously the most serious crimes are the ones that consist of or employ physical aggression: willful homicide, rape, robbery, and serious assault. The injuries such crimes inflict are grievous and irreparable. There is no way to undo the damage done to a child whose father is murdered or to a woman who has been forcibly violated. And though medicine may heal the wounds of a victim of a mugging, and law enforcement may recover his stolen property, they cannot restore to him the feeling of personal security that has been violently wrested from him.

To be sure, the amount of pain that crime causes is a minute fraction of the amount Americans suffer accidentally every year. There were approximately 10,000 willful homicides in 1965 and more than 40,000 motor-accident fatalities. There were slightly more than 100 serious assaults for every 100,000 Americans, and more than 12,000 injuries due to accidents in the home for every 100,000 Americans. The risk of being attacked by a stranger on a street is far less than the total of violent crimes might lead one to believe. The UCR estimates that in fully two-thirds of the cases of willful homicide and aggravated assault, the criminals and the victims are known to each other; very often they are members of the same family. Studies of rape indicate that in perhaps half the cases the criminal and victim are acquainted. Robbery is the principal source of violence from strangers.

The most damaging of the effects of violent crime is fear, and that fear must not be belittled. Suddenly becoming the object of a stranger's violent hostility is as frightening as any class of experience. A citizen who hears rapid footsteps behind him as he walks down a dark and otherwise deserted street cannot be expected to calculate that the chance of those footsteps having a sinister meaning is only one in a hundred or in a thousand or, if he does make such a calculation, to be calmed by its results. Any chance at all is frightening. And, in fact, when Commission interviewers asked a sample of citizens what they would do in just such a situation, the majority replied, "Run as fast as I could or call for help." Commission studies in several cities indicate that just this kind of fear has impelled hundreds of thousands of Americans to move their homes or change their habits.

Controlling violent crime presents a number of distinct problems. To the extent that these crimes occur on private premises, as most murders and rapes and many assaults do, they are little susceptible to deterrence by police patrol. To the extent that they are the passionate culmination of quarrels between acquaintances or relatives—as again many murders and assaults are—there is little that can be done to increase the deterrent effect of the threat of punishment. More than nine-tenths of all murders are cleared by arrest, and a high proportion of those arrested are convicted. Yet people continue to commit murders at about the same rate year after year. Almost a third of all robberies are committed by juveniles and are, therefore, one aspect of the enormously complicated phenomenon of juvenile delinquency. Some robberies are committed by drug addicts, and a certain number of rapes are committed by sexually pathological men (or boys). Effective treatment for these diseases, in the community or in the criminal justice system, has not yet been found. Finally, more than one-half of all willful homicides and armed robberies, and almost one-fifth of all aggravated assaults, involve the use of firearms. As long as there is no effective gun-control legislation, violent crimes and the injuries they inflict will be harder to reduce than they might otherwise be.

Only 13 percent of the total number of Index Crimes in the UCR for 1965 were crimes of violence. The remaining 87 percent were thefts: thefts of $50 or over in money or goods, automobile thefts, and burglaries (thefts that involve breaking into or otherwise unlawfully entering private premises). Of these three kinds of stealing, burglary was the most frequent; 1,173,201 burglaries were reported to the FBI in 1965, approximately one-half of them involving homes and one-half commercial establishments. Burglary is expensive; the FBI calculates that the worth of the property stolen by burglars in 1965 was some $284 million. Burglary is frightening; having one's home broken into and ransacked is an experience that unnerves almost anyone. Finally, burglars are seldom caught; only 25 percent of the burglaries known to the police in 1965 were solved, and many burglaries were not reported to the police.

Because burglary is so frequent, so costly, so upsetting and so difficult to control, it makes great demands on the criminal justice system. Preventing burglary demands imaginative methods of police patrol, and solving burglaries calls for great investigative patience and resourcefulness. Dealing with individual burglars appropriately is a difficult problem for prosecutors and judges; for while burglary is a serious crime that carries heavy penalties and many of its practitioners are habitual or professional criminals, many more are youthful or marginal offenders to whom criminal sanctions in their most

63

drastic form might do more harm than good. Burglars are probably the most numerous class of serious offenders in the correctional system. It is a plausible assumption that the prevalence of the two crimes of burglary and robbery is a significant, if not a major, reason for America's alarm about crime, and that finding effective ways of protecting the community from those two crimes would do much to make "crime" as a whole less frightening and to bring it within manageable bounds.

Larceny—stealing that does not involve either force or illegal entry—is by far the most frequent kind of stealing in America. It is less frightening than burglary because to a large, perhaps even to a preponderant extent, it is a crime of opportunity, a matter of making off with whatever happens to be lying around loose: Christmas presents in an unlocked car, merchandise on a store counter, a bicycle in a front yard, and so forth. Insofar as this is so, it is a crime that might be sharply reduced by the adoption of precautionary measures by citizens themselves. The reverse side of this is that it is an extremely difficult crime for the police to deal with; there are seldom physical clues to go on, as there are more likely to be in cases of breaking and entering, and the likelihood of the victim identifying the criminal is far less than in the case of a face-to-face crime like robbery. Only 20 percent of reported major larcenies are solved, and the solution rate for minor ones is considerably lower.

A unique feature of the crime of automobile theft is that, although only a quarter of all automobile thefts—and there were 486,568 reported to the FBI in 1965—are solved, some 87 percent of all stolen automobiles are recovered and returned to their owners. The overwhelming majority of automobile thefts are for the purpose of securing temporary transportation, often for "joyriding."

More than 60 percent of those arrested for this crime in 1965 were under 18 years of age, and 88 percent were under 25. However, automobile theft for the purpose of stripping automobiles of their parts or for reselling automobiles in remote parts of the country is a lucrative and growing part of professional crime, a Commission study of professional criminals indicates. What is especially suggestive about these facts is that, while much automobile theft is committed by young joyriders, some of it is calculating, professional crime that poses a major law enforcement problem. The estimated value of the unrecovered stolen automobiles in 1965 is $60 million. In other words, coping with automobile theft, like coping with every kind of serious crime, is a matter of dealing with many

64

kinds of people with many kinds of motives. No single response, by either the community or the criminal justice system, can be effective.

These three major crimes against property do not tell the whole story about stealing. In fact, the whole story cannot be told. There is no knowing how much embezzlement, fraud, loan sharking, and other forms of thievery from individuals or commercial institutions there is, or how much price-rigging, tax evasion, bribery, graft, and other forms of thievery from the public at large there is. The Commission's studies indicate that the economic losses those crimes cause are far greater than those caused by the three index crimes against property. Many crimes in this category are never discovered; they get lost in the complications and convolutions of business procedures. Many others are never reported to law enforcement agencies. Most people pay little heed to crimes of this sort when they worry about "crime in America," because those crimes do not, as a rule, offer an immediate, recognizable threat to personal safety.

However, it is possible to argue that, in one sense, those crimes are the most threatening of all—not just because they are so expensive, but because of their corrosive effect on the moral standards by which American business is conducted. Businessmen who defraud consumers promote cynicism towards society and disrespect for law. The Mafia or Cosa Nostra or the Syndicate, as it has variously been called, is deeply involved in business crime, and protects its position there by bribery and graft and, all too often, assault and murder. White-collar crime and organized crime are subjects about which the criminal justice system, and the community as a whole, have little knowledge. Acquiring such knowledge in a systematic way is an extremely high-priority obligation of those entrusted with protecting society from crime.

"Crimes without victims," crimes whose essence is providing people with goods or services that, though illegal, are in demand, are peculiarly vexatious to the criminal justice system. Gambling, narcotics, and prostitution offenses, and their like, are not only numerous, but they present policemen, prosecutors, judges, and correctional officials with problems they are ill-equipped to solve. Since such crimes have no direct victims, or at any rate no victims with complaints, investigating them obliges policemen to employ practices like relying on informants who may turn out to be accomplices, or walking the streets hoping to be solicited by prostitutes. These practices may be legal, but they are surely distasteful and they can lead, in addition, to discriminatory enforcement or out-and-out corruption.

When offenders of this sort are arrested, corrections or punishment seldom has much effect on them; they resume their activities as soon as they return to the street. Yet offenses of this sort cannot be ignored. Gambling is an activity that is controlled by organized criminals and is a major source of their wealth and power. The growing use of drugs, especially by young people, is a matter of profound concern to almost every parent in America and, of course, the distribution of narcotics is also an important part of the activities of organized crime. Often the statutes that deal with these offenses are obsolete or ambiguous. Treatment programs are still in an experimental stage. The connection between these offenses and social conditions is little understood. Finding ways of dealing with crimes without victims is not only a task for the criminal justice system but for legislators, doctors, sociologists, and social workers.

Finally, there are "petty offenses" and "breaches of the peace" like public drunkenness and public quarreling, which are the most numerous of all crimes. Most Americans have never actually seen a serious crime committed, but every American has seen a petty offense. Such offenses are undoubted public nuisances against which the public has every right to protect itself. Yet a curious thing about them is that usually the only person who suffers real damage from one of these crimes is the offender himself. Breaches of the peace are the most exasperating everyday problem of the criminal justice system. Petty offenders, many of whom, like chronic alcoholics, are repeated and incurable lawbreakers, occupy much of the time of policemen, clog the lower courts and crowd city and county jails.

CRIME AND SOCIAL CONDITIONS

Two striking facts that the UCR and every other examination of American crime disclose are that most crimes, wherever they are committed, are committed by boys and young men, and that most crimes, by whomever they are committed, are committed in cities. Three-quarters of the 1965 arrests for Index crimes, plus petty larceny and negligent manslaughter, were of people less than 25 years old. More 15-year-olds were arrested for those crimes than people of any other age, and 16-year-olds were a close second. Of 2,780,015 "offenses known to the police" in 1965—these were Index crimes—some 2 million occurred in cities, more

66

than half a million occurred in the suburbs, and about 170,000 occurred in rural areas. The number of city crimes per hundred thousand residents was over 1,800, the suburban rate was almost 1,200, and the rural rate was 616.9. In short, crime is evidently associated with two powerful social trends: the increasing urbanization of America and the increasing numerousness, restlessness, and restiveness of American youth. The two trends are not separate and distinct, of course. They are entangled with each other in many ways, and both are entangled with another trend, increasing affluence, that also appears to be intimately associated with crime. An abundance of material goods provides an abundance of motives and opportunities for stealing, and stealing is the fastest growing kind of crime.

For as long as crime statistics of any kind have been compiled, they have shown that males between the ages of 15 and 24 are the most crime-prone group in the population. For the last 5 years, as the result of the "baby boom" that took place after the Second World War, the 15–24 age group has been the fastest growing group in the population.

The fact that young people make up a larger part of the population than they did 10 years ago accounts for some of the recent increase in crime. This group will continue to grow disproportionately for at least 15 years more. And so it is probable that crime will continue to increase during this period, unless there are drastic changes in general social and economic conditions and in the effectiveness of the criminal justice system. However, population changes cannot be shown to account for all of the increase that is reported in juvenile and youth crime, nor can the probability that police reporting is more complete every year account for the increase. Moreover, there have been marked improvements in police efficiency and correctional resourcefulness in many localities in recent years, which, all other things being equal, might have reduced crime. It may be that young people are not only more numerous than ever, but more crime prone; it is impossible to be sure.

What appears to be happening throughout the country, in the cities and in the suburbs, among the poor and among the well-to-do, is that parental, and especially paternal, authority over young people is becoming weaker. The community is accustomed to rely upon this force as one guarantee that children will learn to fit themselves into society in an orderly and peaceable manner, that the natural and valuable rebelliousness of young people will not express itself in the form of warring violently on society or any of its members. The programs and activities of almost every kind of social institution with which children come in contact—schools, churches, social-service agencies, youth organizations—are predicated on the assumption that children acquire their fundamental attitudes toward life, their moral standards, in their homes. The social institutions provide children with many opportunities: to learn, to worship, to play, to socialize, to secure expert help in solving a variety of problems. However, offering opportunities is not the same thing as providing moral standards. The community's social institutions have so far not found ways to give young people the motivation to live moral lives; some of them have not even recognized their duty to seek for such ways. Young people who have not received strong and loving parental guidance, or whose experience leads them to believe that all of society is callous at best, or a racket at worst, tend to be unmotivated people, and therefore people with whom the community is most unprepared to cope. Much more to the point, they are people who are unprepared to cope with the many ambiguities and lacks that they find in the community. Boredom corrodes ambition and cynicism corrupts those with ethical sensitivity.

That there are all too many ambiguities and lacks in the community scarcely needs prolonged demonstration. Poverty and racial discrimination, bad housing and commercial exploitation, the enormous gap between American ideals and American achievements, and the many distressing consequences and implications of these conditions are national failings that are widely recognized. Their effects on young people have been greatly aggravated by the technological revolution of the last two decades, which has greatly reduced the market for unskilled labor. A job, earning one's own living, is probably the most important factor in making a person independent and making him responsible. Today education is a prerequisite for all but the most menial jobs; a great deal of education is a prerequisite for really promising ones.

And so there are two continually growing groups of discontented young people: those whose capacity or desire for becoming educated has not been developed by their homes or schools (or both), and who therefore are unemployed or even unemployable; and those whose entry into the adult working world has been delayed by the necessity of continuing their studies long past the point at which they have become physically and psychologically adult. Young people today are sorely discontented in the suburbs and on the campuses as well as in the slums.

However, there is no doubt that they more often express

this discontent criminally in the slums. So do older people. It is not hard to understand why. The conditions of life there, economic and social, conspire to make crime not only easy to engage in but easy to invent justifications for. A man who lives in the country or in a small town is likely to be conspicuous, under surveillance by his community so to speak, and therefore under its control. A city man is often almost invisible, socially isolated from his neighborhood and therefore incapable of being controlled by it. He has more opportunities for crime. At the same time in a city, much more than in a small community, he rubs constantly, abrasively, and impersonally against other people; he is likely to live his life unnoticed and unrespected, his hopes unfulfilled. He can fall easily into resentment against his neighbors and against society, into a feeling that he is in a jungle where force and cunning are the only means of survival. There have always been slums in the cities, and they have always been places where there was the most crime. What has made this condition even more menacing in recent years is that the slums, with all their squalor and turbulence, have more and more become ghettos, neighborhoods in which racial minorities are sequestered with little chance of escape. People who, though declared by the law to be equal, are prevented by society from improving their circumstances, even when they have the ability and the desire to do so, are people with extraordinary strains on their respect for the law and society.

It is with the young people and the slum dwellers who have been embittered by these painful social and economic pressures that the criminal justice system preponderantly deals. Society insists that individuals are responsible for their actions, and the criminal process operates on that assumption. However, society has not devised ways for ensuring that all its members have the ability to assume responsibility. It has let too many of them grow up untaught, unmotivated, unwanted. The criminal justice system has a great potential for dealing with individual instances of crime, but it was not designed to eliminate the conditions in which most crime breeds. It needs help. Warring on poverty, inadequate housing and unemployment, is warring on crime. A civil rights law is a law against crime. Money for schools is money against crime. Medical, psychiatric, and family-counseling services are services against crime. More broadly and most importantly every effort to improve life in America's "inner cities" is an effort against crime. A community's most enduring protection against crime is to right the wrongs and cure the illnesses that tempt men to harm their neighbors.

Finally, no system, however well staffed or organized, no level of material well-being for all, will rid a society of crime if there is not a widespread ethical motivation, and a widespread belief that by and large the government and the social order deserve credence, respect and loyalty.

AMERICA'S SYSTEM OF CRIMINAL JUSTICE

The system of criminal justice America uses to deal with those crimes it cannot prevent and those criminals it cannot deter is not a monolithic, or even a consistent, system. It was not designed or built in one piece at one time. Its philosophic core is that a person may be punished by the Government if, and only if, it has been proved by an impartial and deliberate process that he has violated a specific law. Around that core layer upon layer of institutions and procedures, some carefully constructed and some improvised, some inspired by principle and some by expediency, have accumulated. Parts of the system—magistrates' courts, trial by jury, bail—are of great antiquity. Other parts—juvenile courts, probation and parole, professional policemen—are relatively new. The entire system represents an adaptation of the English common law to America's peculiar structure of government, which allows each local community to construct institutions that fill its special needs. Every village, town, county, city, and State has its own criminal justice system, and there is a Federal one as well. All of them operate somewhat alike. No two of them operate precisely alike.

Any criminal justice system is an apparatus society uses to enforce the standards of conduct necessary to protect individuals and the community. It operates by apprehending, prosecuting, convicting, and sentencing those members of the community who violate the basic rules of group existence. The action taken against lawbreakers is designed to serve three purposes beyond the immediately punitive one. It removes dangerous people from the community; it deters others from criminal behavior; and it gives society an opportunity to attempt to transform lawbreakers into law-abiding citizens. What most significantly distinguishes the system of one country from that of another is the extent and the form of the protections it offers individuals in the process of determining guilt and imposing punishment. Our system of justice deliberately sacrifices much in efficiency and even in effectiveness in order to preserve local autonomy and to protect the individual. Sometimes it may seem to sacrifice too much. For example, the American system was not designed with Cosa Nostra-type criminal organizations in mind, and it has been notably unsuccessful to date in preventing such organizations from preying on society.

The criminal justice system has three separately organized parts—the police, the courts, and corrections—and each has distinct tasks. However, these parts are by no means independent of each other. What each one does and how it does it has a direct effect on the work of the others. The courts must deal, and can only deal, with those whom the police arrest; the business of corrections is with those delivered to it by the courts. How successfully corrections reforms convicts determines whether they will once again become police business and influences the sentences the judges pass; police activities are subject to court scrutiny and are often determined by court decisions. And so reforming or reorganizing any part or procedure of the system changes other parts or procedures. Furthermore, the criminal process, the method by which the system deals with individual cases, is not a hodgepodge of random actions. It is rather a continuum—an orderly progression of events—some of which, like arrest and trial, are highly visible and some of which, though of great importance, occur out of public view. A study of the system must begin by examining it as a whole.

The chart on the following page sets forth in simplified form the process of criminal administration and shows the many decision points along its course. Since felonies, misdemeanors, petty offenses, and juvenile cases generally follow quite different paths, they are shown separately.

The popular, or even the lawbook, theory of everyday criminal process oversimplifies in some respects and overcomplicates in others what usually happens. That theory is that when an infraction of the law occurs, a policeman finds, if he can, the probable offender, arrests him and brings him promptly before a magistrate. If the offense is minor, the magistrate disposes of it forthwith; if it is serious, he holds the defendant for further action and admits him to bail. The case then is turned over to a prosecuting attorney who charges the defendant with a specific statutory crime. This charge is subject to review by a judge at a preliminary hearing of the evidence and in many places if the offense charged is a felony, by a grand jury that can dismiss the charge, or affirm it by delivering it to a judge in the form of an indictment. If the defendant pleads "not guilty" to the charge he comes to trial; the facts of his case are marshaled by prosecuting and defense attorneys and presented, under the super-

A general view of The Criminal Justice System

This chart seeks to present a simple yet comprehensive view
of the movement of cases through the criminal justice system.
Procedures in individual jurisdictions may vary from the
pattern shown here. The differing weights of line indicate
the relative volumes of cases disposed of at various points
in the system, but this is only suggestive since no nationwide
data of this sort exists.

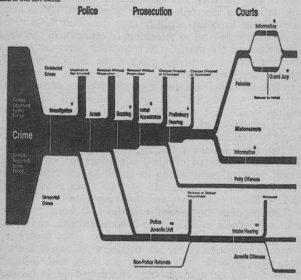

Police   **Prosecution**   **Courts**

1 May continue until trial.

2 Administrative record of arrest. First step at
which temporary release on bail may be
available.

3 Before magistrate, commissioner, or justice of
peace. Formal notice of charge, advice of
rights. Bail set. Summary trials for petty
offenses usually conducted here without
further processing.

4 Preliminary testing of evidence against
defendant. Charge may be reduced. No
separate preliminary hearing for misdemeanors
in some systems.

5 Charge filed by prosecutor on basis of
information submitted by police or citizens.
Alternative to grand jury indictment; often
used in felonies, almost always in
misdemeanors.

6 Reviews whether Government evidence
sufficient to justify trial. Some States have no
grand jury system; others seldom use it.

Corrections

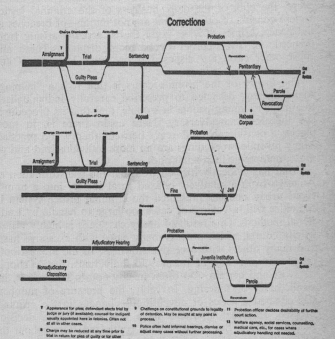

7 Appearance for plea; defendant elects trial by judge or jury (if available); counsel for indigent usually appointed here in felonies. Often not at all in other cases.

8 Charge may be reduced at any time prior to trial in return for plea of guilty or for other reasons.

9 Challenge on constitutional grounds to legality of detention. May be sought at any point in process.

10 Police often hold informal hearings, dismiss or adjust many cases without further processing.

11 Probation officer decides desirability of further court action.

12 Welfare agency, social services, counselling, medical care, etc., for cases where adjudicatory handling not needed.

vision of a judge, through witnesses, to a jury. If the jury finds the defendant guilty, he is sentenced by the judge to a term in prison, where a systematic attempt to convert him into a law-abiding citizen is made, or to a term of probation, under which he is permitted to live in the community as long as he behaves himself.

Some cases do proceed much like that, especially those involving offenses that are generally considered "major": serious acts of violence or thefts of large amounts of property. However, not all major cases follow this course, and, in any event, the bulk of the daily business of the criminal justice system consists of offenses that are not major—of breaches of the peace, crimes of vice, petty thefts, assaults arising from domestic or street-corner or barroom disputes. These and most other cases are disposed of in much less formal and much less deliberate ways.

The theory of the juvenile court is that it is a "helping" social agency, designed to prescribe carefully individualized treatment to young people in trouble, and that its procedures are therefore nonadversary. Here again there is, in most places, a considerable difference between theory and practice. Many juvenile proceedings are no more individualized and no more therapeutic than adult ones.

What has evidently happened is that the transformation of America from a relatively relaxed rural society into a tumultuous urban one has presented the criminal justice system in the cities with a volume of cases too large to handle by traditional methods. One result of heavy caseloads is highly visible in city courts, which process many cases with excessive haste and many others with excessive slowness. In the interest both of effectiveness and of fairness to individuals, justice should be swift and certain; too often in city courts today it is, instead, hasty or faltering. Invisibly, the pressure of numbers has effected a series of adventitious changes in the criminal process. Informal shortcuts have been used. The decision making process has often become routinized. Throughout the system the importance of individual judgment and discretion, as distinguished from stated rules and procedures, has increased. In effect, much decision making is being done on an administrative rather than on a judicial basis. Thus, an examination of how the criminal justice system works and a consideration of the changes needed to make it more effective and fair must focus on the extent to which invisible, administrative procedures depart from visible, traditional ones, and on the desirability of that departure.

At the very beginning of the process—or, more properly, before the process begins at all—something happens that is scarcely discussed in lawbooks and is seldom recognized by the public: law enforcement policy is made by the policeman. For policemen cannot and do not arrest all the offenders they encounter. It is doubtful that they arrest most of them. A criminal code, in practice, is not a set of specific instructions to policemen but a more or less rough map of the territory in which policemen work. How an individual policeman moves around that territory depends largely on his personal discretion.

That a policeman's duties compel him to exercise personal discretion many times every day is evident. Crime does not look the same on the street as it does in a legislative chamber. How much noise or profanity makes conduct "disorderly" within the meaning of the law? When must a quarrel be treated as a criminal assault: at the first threat or at the first shove or at the first blow, or after blood is drawn, or when a serious injury is inflicted? How suspicious must conduct be before there is "probable cause," the constitutional basis for an arrest? Every policeman, however complete or sketchy his education, is an interpreter of the law.

Every policeman, too, is an arbiter of social values, for he meets situation after situation in which invoking criminal sanctions is a questionable line of action. It is obvious that a boy throwing rocks at a school's windows is committing the statutory offense of vandalism, but it is often not at all obvious whether a policeman will better serve the interests of the community and of the boy by taking the boy home to his parents or by arresting him. Who are the boy's parents? Can they control him? Is he a frequent offender who has responded badly to leniency? Is vandalism so epidemic in the neighborhood that he should be made a cautionary example? With juveniles especially, the police exercise great discretion.

Finally, the manner in which a policeman works is influenced by practical matters: the legal strength of the available evidence, the willingness of victims to press charges and of witnesses to testify, the temper of the community, the time and information at the policeman's disposal. Much is at stake in how the policeman exercises this discretion. If he judges conduct not suspicious enough to justify intervention, the chance to prevent a robbery, rape, or murder may be lost. If he overestimates the seriousness of a situation or his actions are controlled by panic or prejudice, he may hurt or kill someone unnecessarily. His actions may even touch off a riot.

THE MAGISTRATE

In direct contrast to the policeman, the magistrate before whom a suspect is first brought usually exercises less discretion than the law allows him. He is entitled to inquire into the facts of the case, into whether there are grounds for holding the accused. He seldom does. He seldom can. The more promptly an arrested suspect is brought into magistrate's court, the less likelihood there is that much information about the arrest other than the arresting officer's statement will be available to the magistrate. Moreover many magistrates, especially in big cities, have such congested calendars that it is almost impossible for them to subject any case but an extraordinary one to prolonged scrutiny.

In practice the most important things, by far, that a magistrate does are to set the amount of a defendant's bail and in some jurisdictions to appoint counsel. Too seldom does either action get the careful attention it deserves. In many cases the magistrate accepts a waiver of counsel without insuring that the suspect knows the significance of legal representation.

Bail is a device to free an untried defendant and at the same time make sure he appears for trial. That is the sole stated legal purpose in America. The Eighth Amendment to the Constitution declares that it must not be "excessive." Appellate courts have declared that not just the seriousness of the charge against the defendant, but the suspect's personal, family, and employment situation, as they bear on the likelihood of his appearance, must be weighed before the amount of his bail is fixed. Yet more magistrates than not set bail according to standard rates: so and so many dollars for such and such an offense.

The persistence of money bail can best be explained not by its stated purpose but by the belief of police, prosecutors, and courts that the best way to keep a defendant from committing more crimes before trial is to set bail so high that he cannot obtain his release.

THE PROSECUTOR

The key administrative officer in the processing of cases is the prosecutor. Theoretically the examination of the evidence against a defendant by a judge at a preliminary hearing, and

76

its reexamination by a grand jury, are important parts of the process. Practically they seldom are because a prosecutor seldom has any difficulty in making a prima facie case against a defendant. In fact most defendants waive their rights to preliminary hearings and much more often than not grand juries indict precisely as prosecutors ask them to. The prosecutor wields almost undisputed sway over the pretrial progress of most cases. He decides whether to press a case or drop it. He determines the specific charge against a defendant. When the charge is reduced, as it is in as many as two-thirds of all cases in some cities, the prosecutor is usually the official who reduces it.

In the informal, noncriminal, nonadversary juvenile justice system there are no "magistrates" or "prosecutors" or "charges," or, in most instances, defense counsel. An arrested youth is brought before an intake officer who is likely to be a social worker or, in smaller communities, before a judge. On the basis of an informal inquiry into the facts and circumstances that led to the arrest, and of an interview with the youth himself, the intake officer or the judge decides whether or not a case should be the subject of formal court proceedings. If he decides it should be, he draws up a petition, describing the case. In very few places is bail a part of the juvenile system; a youth whose case is referred to court is either sent home with orders to reappear on a certain date, or remanded to custody. This decision, too, is made by the screening official. Thus, though these officials work in a quite different environment and according to quite different procedures from magistrates and prosecutors, they in fact exercise the same kind of discretionary control over what happens before the facts of a case are adjudicated.

THE PLEA AND THE SENTENCE

When a prosecutor reduces a charge it is ordinarily because there has been "plea bargaining" between him and a defense attorney. The issue at stake is how much the prosecutor will reduce his original charge or how lenient a sentence he will recommend, in return for a plea of guilty. There is no way of judging how many bargains reflect the prosecutor's belief that a lesser charge or sentence is justified and how many result from the fact that there may be in the system at any one time ten times as many cases as there are prosecutors or judges or courtrooms to handle them, should every one come to trial. In form, a plea bargain can be anything from a series of careful conferences to a hurried consultation in a courthouse corridor. In content it can be anything from a conscientious exploration of the facts and dispositional alternatives available and appropriate to a defendant, to a perfunctory deal. If the interests of a defendant are to be properly protected while his fate is being thus invisibly determined, he obviously needs just as good legal representation as the kind he needs at a public trial. Whether or not plea bargaining is a fair and effective method of disposing of criminal cases depends heavily on whether or not defendants are provided early with competent and conscientious counsel.

Plea bargaining is not only an invisible procedure but, in some jurisdictions, a theoretically unsanctioned one. In order to satisfy the court record, a defendant, his attorney, and the prosecutor will at the time of sentencing often ritually state to a judge that no bargain has been made. Plea bargaining may be a useful procedure, especially in congested urban jurisdictions, but neither the dignity of the law, nor the quality of justice, nor the protection of society from dangerous criminals is enhanced by its being conducted covertly.

In the juvenile system there is, of course, no plea bargaining in the sense described above. However, the entire juvenile process can involve extra-judicial negotiations about disposition. Furthermore, the entire juvenile process is by design invisible. Though intended to be helpful, the authority exercised often is coercive; juveniles, no less than adults, may need representation by counsel.

An enormously consequential kind of decision is the sentencing decision of a judge. The law recognizes the importance of fitting sentences to individual defendants by giving judges, in most instances, considerable latitude. For example the recently adopted New York Penal Code, which will go into effect in autumn of 1967, empowers a judge to impose upon a man convicted of armed robbery any sentence between a 5-year term of probation and a 25-year term in prison. Even when a judge has presided over a trial during which the facts of a case have been carefully set forth and has been given a probation report that carefully discusses a defendant's character, background, and problems, he cannot find it easy to choose a sentence. In perhaps nine-tenths of all cases there is no trial; the defendants are self-confessedly guilty.

In the lower or misdemeanor courts, the courts that process most criminal cases, probation reports are a rarity. Under such circumstances judges have little to go on and many sentences are bound to be based on conjecture or intuition. When a sentence is part of a plea bargain, which an overworked judge ratifies perfunctorily, it may not even be his conjecture or intuition on which the sentence is based, but a prosecutor's or a defense counsel's. But perhaps the greatest lack judges suffer from when they pass sentences is not time or information, but correctional alternatives. Some lower courts do not have any probation officers, and in almost every court the caseloads of probation officers are so heavy that a sentence of probation means, in fact, releasing an offender into the community with almost no supervision. Few States have a sufficient variety of correctional institutions or treatment programs to inspire judges with the confidence that sentences will lead to rehabilitation.

CORRECTIONS

The correctional apparatus to which guilty defendants are delivered is in every respect the most isolated part of the criminal justice system. Much of it is physically isolated; its institutions usually have thick walls and locked doors, and often they are situated in rural areas, remote from the courts where the institutions' inmates were tried and from the communities where they lived. The correctional apparatus is isolated in the sense that its officials do not have everyday working relationships with officials from the system's other branches, like those that commonly exist between policemen and prosecutors, or prosecutors and judges. It is isolated in the sense that what it does with, to, or for the people under its supervision is seldom governed by any but the most broadly written statutes, and is almost never scrutinized by appellate courts. Finally, it is isolated from the public partly by its invisibility and physical remoteness; partly by the inherent lack of drama in most of its activities, but perhaps most importantly by the fact that the correctional apparatus is often used—or misused—by both the criminal justice system and the public as a rug under which disturbing problems and people can be swept.

The most striking fact about the correctional apparatus today is that, although the rehabilitation of criminals is presumably its major purpose, the custody of criminals is actually its major task. On any given day there are well over a million people being "corrected" in America, two-thirds of them on probation or parole and one-third of them in prisons or jails. However, prisons and jails are where four-fifths of correctional money is spent and where nine-tenths of correctional employees work. Furthermore, fewer than one-fifth of the people who work in State prisons and local jails have jobs that are not essentially either custodial or administrative in character. Many jails have nothing but custodial and administrative personnel. Of course many jails are crowded with defendants who have not been able to furnish bail and who are not considered by the law to be appropriate objects of rehabilitation because it has not yet been determined that they are criminals who need it.

What this emphasis on custody means in practice is that the enormous potential of the correctional apparatus for making creative decisions about its treatment of convicts is largely unfulfilled. This is true not only of offenders in custody but of offenders on probation and parole. Most authorities agree that while probationers and parolees need varying degrees and kinds of supervision, an average of no more than 35 cases per officer is necessary for effective attention; 97 percent of all officers handling adults have larger caseloads than that. In the juvenile correctional system the situation is somewhat better. Juvenile institutions, which typically are training schools, have a higher proportion of treatment personnel and juvenile probation and parole officers generally have lighter caseloads. However, these comparatively rich resources are very far from being sufficiently rich.

Except for sentencing, no decision in the criminal process has more impact on the convicted offender than the parole decision, which determines how much of his maximum sentence a prisoner must serve. This again is an invisible administrative decision that is seldom open to attack or subject to review. It is made by parole board members who are often political appointees. Many are skilled and conscientious, but they generally are able to spend no more than a few minutes on a case. Parole decisions that are made in haste and on the basis of insufficient information, in the absence of parole machinery that can provide good supervision, are necessarily imperfect decisions. And since there is virtually no appeal from them, they can be made arbitrarily or discriminatorily. Just as carefully formulated and clearly stated law enforcement policies would help policemen, charge policies would help prosecutors and sentencing policies would help judges, so parole policies would help parole boards perform their delicate and important duties.

In sum, America's system of criminal justice is overcrowded and overworked, undermanned, underfinanced, and very often misunderstood. It needs more information and more knowledge. It needs more technical resources. It needs more coordination among its many parts. It needs more public support. It needs the help of community programs and institutions in dealing with offenders and potential offenders. It needs, above all, the willingness to reexamine old ways of doing things, to reform itself, to experiment, to run risks, to dare. It needs vision.

THE FOUNDATIONS OF A CRIME CONTROL PROGRAM

In the ensuing chapters of this report, the Commission's specific recommendations for improvements in the criminal justice system are set forth in detail. Here a brief identification of the general needs of the system is sufficient.

RESOURCES

The many specific needs of the criminal justice system—for manpower, for equipment, for facilities, for programs, for research, for money—are interlocking. Each one must be filled with the others in mind. Equipment cannot be operated, facilities manned, programs initiated or research conducted without personnel of many different kinds. It would be useless to seek to recruit more and better personnel if there were not more and better jobs for them to do. Programs cannot be conducted without equipment and facilities, and cannot be conducted effectively without research. Money is needed for everything. This discussion of the system's needs assumes that every need is dependent on the others.

The problem of personnel is at the root of most of the criminal justice system's problems. The system cannot operate fairly unless its personnel are fair. The system cannot operate swiftly and certainly unless its personnel are efficient and well-informed. The system cannot make wise decisions unless its personnel are thoughtful. In many places—many police departments, congested urban lower courts, the understaffed county jails, the entire prison, probation and parole apparatus —more manpower is needed. Probably the greatest manpower need of all, in view of the increasing—and overdue— involvement of defense counsel in all kinds of cases, is for lawyers who can handle criminal cases. Everywhere more skilled, better trained, more imaginative manpower is needed. Some positions are hard to fill. Often the pay is bad and the working conditions are difficult. In addition, an odd and injurious notion is widespread that there is something disreputable about being a policeman or a criminal lawyer or a prison guard. The fact is that there are few fields in which people have more opportunities to do important and responsible work than the criminal justice system. Recruiting such people in large numbers, training them fully and giving them the pay, the opportunities for advancement and the responsibility they deserve is a matter of great urgency.

Too much of the system is physically inadequate, antiquated or dilapidated. This condition goes beyond the obvious obsolescence of many correctional institutions and the squalor and congestion of many urban lower courts, which make it difficult to treat defendants or convicts humanely. The system's personnel often must work with poor facilities: recordkeeping systems that are clumsy and inefficient, communications equipment that makes speedy action difficult, an absence of all kinds of scientific and technological aids. Furthermore, in few States is there the variety of correctional facilities that could make a variety of correctional programs possible. Most institutions are always entirely custodial in a physical sense—with high walls, locked gates, and barred windows. New kinds of institutions, less forbidding in character and situated within reach of the community, are an immediate and pressing need.

Probably the single greatest technical limitation on the system's ability to make its decisions wisely and fairly is that the people in the system often are required to decide issues without enough information. A policeman who has just set out in pursuit of a speeding and suspicious looking car should be able to get immediate information as to whether or not the car is wanted; a judge about to sentence a criminal should know everything about him that the police know; and the correctional authorities to whom that criminal is delivered should know everything about him that the judge knows. When they make dispositional decisions, judges and corrections officials should be able to draw on the experience of the system in dealing with different offenders in different ways. Existing procedures must be made more efficient; and new procedures must be devised, so that information can flow more fully and swiftly among the system's many parts.

Finally, the nature of crime and the means of controlling it are subjects about which a surprisingly small amount of research has been done. What "deterrence" really means and involves, how different kinds of criminals are likely to respond to different kinds of treatment, what the objective effects of making various kinds of marginal behavior criminal have been, how much of the juvenile justice system's informality can be preserved without sacrificing fairness—and a multitude of other abstruse questions of this kind—are almost totally unanswerable today. There is almost as great a lack of operational knowledge. It is impossible to state accurately, for example, what proportions of police time are spent on the different sorts of police work, or how large a proportion of the drunks that come before lower courts are chronic offenders, or what personal characteristics best qualify a man to be an effective correctional official.

This lack of firm data of almost every kind has been the greatest obstacle to the Commission's work, in many instances requiring it to base its recommendations on fragmentary information, combined with the experienced judgment of those who have worked in this field. The process of change cannot await all the answers the Commission would like to have had. The criminal justice system is faced with too urgent a need for action to stand back for a generation and engage in research. At the same time self-education is one of the system's crucial responsibilities. Only by combining research with action can future programs be founded on knowledge rather than on informed or perceptive guesswork. Moreover, once knowledge is acquired, it is wasted if it is not shared. An east coast city must be able to draw on a west coast city's experience, a judge on a policeman's. Scattered about the country today are many individuals and groups with special knowledge about one aspect or another of law enforcement and the administration of justice. Often no one else in the system knows that these individuals and groups know anything. Sometimes these individuals and groups are themselves not aware, through lack of contact with the rest of the system, that they know something no one else knows. The system must devote itself to acquiring and diffusing knowledge, with special emphasis on exploring ways in which the criminal justice system and the universities can work together.

PUBLIC INVOLVEMENT AND SUPPORT

Each time a citizen fails to report an offense, declines to take the commonsense precautions against crime his police department tells him to, is disrespectful to an officer of the law, shirks his duty as a juror or performs it with a biased mind or a hate-filled heart, or refuses to hire a qualified man because he is an exconvict, he contributes his mite to crime. That much is obvious. A further duty of every citizen is to familiarize himself with the problems of crime and the criminal justice system so that when legislatures are considering criminal laws or appropriations for the system he can express informed views, and when politicians make crime an election issue he will not be panicked or deceived. The money that is needed to control crime will come, ultimately, from the public. That too, is obvious.

Beyond this, controlling crime depends to a great degree on interaction between the community and the criminal justice system. The need for the system and the universities to work together on research into crime and the ways to prevent or control it has been mentioned. Similarly, effective policing of slums and ghettos requires programs designed to improve relations between the police and the residents of such neighborhoods and enable them to work together. Community-based correctional programs require that organizations of many kinds, and individuals as well, involve themselves actively in the job of reintegrating offenders into the life of the community. Programs designed to reduce juvenile delinquency require the same kind of public involvement.

Above all, the Commission inquiries have convinced it that it is undesirable that offenders travel any further along the full course from arrest to charge to sentence to detention than is absolutely necessary for society's protection and the offenders' own welfare. Much of the congestion throughout the system, from police stations to prisons, is the result of the presence in the system of offenders who are there only because there is no other way of dealing with them. One of the system's greatest needs is for the community to establish institutions and agencies to which policemen, prosecutors, and judges can refer various kinds of offenders, without being compelled to bring the full force of criminal sanctions to bear on them. Doubtless, devising and instituting alternative ways of treating offenders is a long and complicated process. It must begin with an understanding by the community of the limited capacity of the criminal justice system for handling the whole problem of "crime." Until the public becomes fully aware of what the system can do and what it cannot do, it cannot give the system the help it needs.

A WILLINGNESS TO CHANGE

The inertia of the criminal justice system is great. More than 30 years ago the Wickersham Commission described the scandalous way in which justice was being administered in many of the country's "lower" courts, and urged that they be abolished; few of them have been abolished and many of the remaining ones are still a scandal. For centuries the imposition of money bail has discriminated against poor defendants, but only in the last few years has the movement to eliminate money bail for most defendants gained any momentum, and even so money bail is still used for almost everyone in the overwhelming majority of courts. State prisons that were built before 1850 and became obsolete before 1900 are still in operation. Police departments continue to insist that all policemen start their careers at the bottom and rise through the ranks slowly, despite the clearly damaging effect this has on the recruitment and effective use of able personnel. A third of the arrests and convictions in America every year are for drunkenness, though for many years almost everyone in the criminal justice system and out of it has recognized that the criminal process is an irrational means of dealing with drunks. The list of examples could extend for pages.

Many of the criminal justice system's difficulties stem from its reluctance to change old ways or, to put the same proposition in reverse, its reluctance to try new ones. The increasing volume of crime in America establishes conclusively that many of the old ways are not good enough. Innovation and experimentation in all parts of the criminal justice system are clearly imperative. They are imperative with respect both to entire agencies and to specific procedures. Court systems need reorganization and case-docketing methods need improvement; police-community relations programs are needed and so are ways of relieving detectives from the duty of typing their own reports; community-based correctional programs must be organized and the pay of prison guards must be raised. Recruitment and training, organization and management, research and development all require reexamination and reform.

The Commission believes that the first step toward improvement is for officials in all parts of the system to face their problems. The lower courts never will be reformed if their officials do not grapple with the hard fact that the quality of justice that is dispensed in them is disgracefully low. Any program to rehabilitate prisoners must begin with the acknowledgment of the fact that most prisons today do not even try to do this job. Until the police recognize that they exercise great discretion about whom they arrest and how they investigate, no effort to ensure that the discretion is exercised wisely can be made. It is futile to consider ways of making plea negotiation an open, regular procedure as long as prosecutors and defense attorneys state ritually to judges that pleas are not negotiated.

The Commission finds, first, that America must translate its well-founded alarm about crime into social action that will prevent crime. It has no doubt whatever that the most significant action that can be taken against crime is action designed to eliminate slums and ghettos, to improve education, to provide jobs, to make sure that every American is given the opportunities and the freedoms that will enable him to assume his responsibilities. We will not have dealt effectively with crime until we have alleviated the conditions that stimulate it. To speak of controlling crime only in terms of the work of the police, the courts and the correctional apparatus, is to refuse to face the fact that widespread crime implies a widespread failure by society as a whole.

The Commission finds, second, that America must translate its alarm about crime into action that will give the criminal justice system the wherewithal to do the job it is charged with doing. Every part of the system is undernourished. There is too little manpower and what there is is not well enough trained or well enough paid. Facilities and equipment are inadequate. Research programs that could lead to greater knowledge about crime and justice, and therefore to more effective operations, are almost nonexistent. To lament the increase in crime and at the same time to starve the agencies of law enforcement and justice is to whistle in the wind.

The Commission finds, third, that the officials of the criminal justice system itself must stop operating, as all too many do, by tradition or by rote. They must reexamine what they do. They must be honest about the system's shortcomings with the public and with themselves. They must be willing to take risks in order to make advances. They must be bold.

Those three things are what this report is about.

Chapter 2

Crime in America

THE MOST NATURAL AND FREQUENT question people ask about crime is "Why?" They ask it about individual crimes and about crime as a whole. In either case it is an almost impossible question to answer. Each single crime is a response to a specific situation by a person with an infinitely complicated psychological and emotional makeup who is subject to infinitely complicated external pressures. Crime as a whole is millions of such responses. To seek the "causes" of crime in human motivations alone is to risk losing one's way in the impenetrable thickets of the human psyche. Compulsive gambling was the cause of an embezzlement, one may say, or drug addiction the cause of a burglary or madness the cause of a homicide; but what caused the compulsion, the addiction, the madness? Why did they manifest themselves in those ways at those times?

There are some crimes so irrational, so unpredictable, so explosive, so resistant to analysis or explanation that they can no more be prevented or guarded against than earthquakes or tidal waves.

At the opposite end of the spectrum of crime are the carefully planned acts of professional criminals. The elaborately organized robbery of an armored car, the skillfully executed jewel theft, the murder of an informant by a Cosa Nostra "enforcer" are so deliberate, so calculated, so rational that understanding the motivations of those who commit such crimes does not show us how to prevent them. How to keep competent and intelligent men from taking up crime as a life work is as baffling a problem as how to predict and discourage sudden criminal outbursts.

To say this is not, of course, to belittle the efforts of psychiatrists and other behaviorial scientists to identify and to treat the personality traits that are associated with crime. Such efforts are an indispensable part of understanding and controlling crime. Many criminals can be rehabilitated. The point is that looking at the personal characteristics of offenders is only one of many ways, and not always the most helpful way, of looking at crime.

It is possible to say, for example, that many crimes are "caused" by their victims. Often the victim of an assault is the person who started the fight, or the victim of an automobile theft is a person who left his keys in his car, or the victim of a loan shark is a person who lost his rent money at the race track, or the victim of a confidence man is a person who thought he could get rich quick. The relationship of victims to crimes is a subject that so far has received little attention. Many crimes, no matter what kind of people their perpetrators were, would not have been committed if their victims had understood the risks they were running.

From another viewpoint, crime is "caused" by public tolerance of it, or reluctance or inability to take action against it. Corporate and business—"white-collar"—crime is closely associated with a widespread notion that, when making money is involved, anything goes. Shoplifting and employee theft may be made more safe by their victims' reluctance to report to the police—often due to a recognition that the likelihood of detection and successful prosecution are negligible. Very often slum residents feel they live in territory that it is useless for them even to try to defend. Many slum residents feel overwhelmed and helpless in the face of the flourishing vice and crime around them; many have received indifferent treatment from the criminal justice system when they have attempted to do their duty as complainants and witnesses; many fear reprisals, especially victims of rackets. When citizens do not get involved, criminals can act with relative impunity.

In a sense, social and economic conditions "cause" crime. Crime flourishes, and always has flourished, in city slums, those neighborhoods where overcrowding, economic deprivation, social disruption and racial discrimination are endemic. Crime flourishes in conditions of affluence, when there is much desire for material goods and many opportunities to acquire them illegally. Crime flourishes when there are many restless, relatively footloose young people in the population.

Crime flourishes when standards of morality are changing rapidly.

Finally, to the extent that the agencies of law enforcement and justice, and such community institutions as schools, churches and social service agencies, do not do their jobs effectively, they fail to prevent crime. If the police are inefficient or starved for manpower, otherwise preventable crimes will occur; if they are overzealous, people better left alone will be drawn into criminal careers. If the courts fail to separate the innocent from the guilty, the guilty may be turned loose to continue their depredations and the innocent may be criminalized. If the system fails to convict the guilty with reasonable certainty and promptness, deterrence of crime may be blunted. If correctional programs do not correct, a core of hardened and habitual criminals will continue to plague the community. If the community institutions that can shape the characters of young people do not take advantage of their opportunities, youth rebelliousness will turn into crime.

The causes of crime, then, are numerous and mysterious and intertwined. Even to begin to understand them, one must gather statistics about the amounts and trends of crime, estimate the costs of crime, study the conditions of life where crime thrives, identify criminals and the victims of crime, survey the public's attitudes toward crime. No one way of describing crime describes it well enough.

THE AMOUNT OF CRIME

There are more than 2800 Federal crimes and a much larger number of State and local ones. Some involve serious bodily harm, some stealing, some public morals or public order, some governmental revenues, some the creation of hazardous conditions, some the regulation of the economy. Some are perpetrated ruthlessly and systematically; others are spontaneous derelictions. Gambling and prostitution are willingly undertaken by both buyer and seller; murder and rape are violently imposed upon their victims. Vandalism is predominantly a crime of the young; driving while intoxicated, a crime of the adult. Many crime rates vary significantly from place to place.

The crimes that concern Americans the most are those that affect their personal safety—at home, at work, or in the streets. The most frequent and serious of these crimes of violence against the person are willful homicide, forcible rape, aggravated assault, and robbery. National statistics regarding the number of these offenses known to the police either from

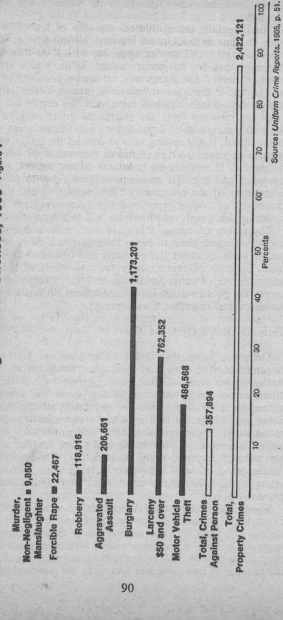

Estimated Number and Percentage of Index Offenses, 1965 Figure 1

Murder, Non-Negligent = 9,850
Manslaughter

Forcible Rape 22,467

Robbery 118,916

Aggravated Assault 206,661

Burglary 1,173,201

Larceny $50 and over 762,352

Motor Vehicle Theft 486,568

Total, Crimes Against Person 357,894

Total, Property Crimes 2,422,121

10 20 30 40 50 60 70 80 90 100

Percents

Source: *Uniform Crime Reports*, 1965, p. 51.

citizen complaints or through independent police discovery are collected from local police officials by the Federal Bureau of Investigation and published annually as a part of its report, "Crime in the United States, Uniform Crime Reports." The FBI also collects "offenses known" statistics for three property crimes: Burglary, larceny of $50 and over and motor vehicle theft. These seven crimes are grouped together in the UCR to form an Index of serious crimes. Figure 1 shows the totals for these offenses for 1965.

THE RISK OF HARM

Including robbery, the crimes of violence make up approximately 13 percent of the Index. The Index reports the number of incidents known to the police, not the number of criminals who committed them or the number of injuries they caused.

The risk of sudden attack by a stranger is perhaps best measured by the frequency of robberies since, according to UCR and other studies, about 70 percent of all willful killings, nearly two-thirds of all aggravated assaults and a high percentage of forcible rapes are committed by family members, friends, or other persons previously known to their victims. Robbery usually does not involve this prior victim-offender relationship.

Robbery, for UCR purposes, is the taking of property from a person by use or threat of force with or without a weapon. Nationally, about one-half of all robberies are street robberies, and slightly more than one-half involve weapons. Attempted robberies are an unknown percentage of the robberies reported to the UCR. The likelihood of injury is also unknown, but a survey by the District of Columbia Crime Commission of 297 robberies in Washington showed that some injury was inflicted in 25 percent of them. The likelihood of injury was found higher for "yokings" or "muggings" (unarmed robberies from the rear) than for armed robberies. Injuries occurred in 10 of 91 armed robberies as compared with 30 of 67 yokings.

Aggravated assault is assault with intent to kill or for the purpose of inflicting severe bodily injury, whether or not a dangerous weapon is used. It includes all cases of attempted homicide, but cases in which bodily injury is inflicted in the course of a robbery or a rape are included with those crimes rather than with aggravated assault. There are no national figures showing the percentage of aggravated assaults that involve injury, but a survey of 131 cases by the District of Columbia Crime Commission found injury in 84 percent of the

91

cases; 35 percent of the victims required hospitalization. A 1960 UCR study showed that juvenile gangs committed less than 4 percent of all aggravated assaults.

Forcible rape includes only those rapes or attempted rapes in which force or threat of force is used. About one-third of the UCR total is attempted rape. In a District of Columbia Crime Commission survey of 151 cases, about 25 percent of all rape victims were attacked with dangerous weapons; the survey did not show what percentage received bodily harm in addition to the rape.

About 15 percent of all criminal homicides, both nationally and in the District of Columbia Crime Commission surveys, occurred in the course of committing other offenses. These offenses appear in the homicide total rather than in the total for the other offense. In the District of Columbia Crime Commission surveys, less than one-half of 1 percent of the robberies and about 1 percent of the forcible rapes ended in homicide.

Some personal danger is also involved in the property crimes. Burglary is the unlawful entering of a building to commit a felony or a theft, whether force is used or not. About half of all burglaries involve residences, but the statistics do not distinguish inhabited parts of houses from garages and similar outlying parts. About half of all residential burglaries are committed in daylight and about half at night. A UCR survey indicates that 32 percent of the entries into residences are made through unlocked doors or windows. When an unlawful entry results in a violent confrontation with the occupant, the offense is counted as a robbery rather than a burglary. Of course, even when no confrontation takes place there is often a risk of confrontation. Nationally such confrontations occur in only one-fortieth of all residential burglaries. They account for nearly one-tenth of all robberies.

In summary, these figures suggest that, on the average, the likelihood of a serious personal attack on any American in a given year is about 1 in 550; together with the studies available they also suggest that the risk of serious attack from spouses, family members, friends, or acquaintances is almost twice as great as it is from strangers on the street. Commission and other studies, moreover, indicate that the risks of personal harm are spread very unevenly. The actual risk for slum dwellers is considerably more; for most Americans it is considerably less.

Except in the case of willful homicide, where the figures describe the extent of injury as well as the number of incidents, there is no national data on the likelihood of injury from attack. More limited studies indicate that while some injury may occur in two-thirds of all attacks, the risk in a given year of injury serious enough to require any degree of hospitalization of any individual is about 1 in 3,000 on the average, and much less for most Americans. These studies also suggest that the injury inflicted by family members or acquaintances is likely to be more severe than that from strangers. As shown by table 1, the risk of death from willful homicide is about 1 in 20,000.

Table 1.—Deaths From Other Than Natural Causes in 1965

[Per 100,000 inhabitants]

Motor vehicle accidents	25
Other accidents	12
Suicide	12
Falls	10
Willful homicide	5
Drowning	4
Fires	4

SOURCE: National Safety Council, "Accident Facts," 1965; Population Reference Bureau.

Criminal behavior accounts for a high percentage of motor vehicle deaths and injuries. In 1965 there were an estimated 49,000 motor vehicle deaths. Negligent manslaughter, which is largely a motor vehicle offense, accounted for more than 7,000 of these. Studies in several States indicate that an even higher percentage involve criminal behavior. They show that driving while intoxicated is probably involved in more than one-half of all motor vehicle deaths. These same studies show that driving while intoxicated is involved in more than 13 percent of the 1,800,000 nonfatal motor vehicle injuries each year.

For various statistical and other reasons, a number of serious crimes against or involving risk to the person, such as arson, kidnapping, child molestation, and simple assault, are not included in the UCR Index. In a study of 1,300 cases of delinquency in Philadelphia, offenses other than the seven Index crimes constituted 62 percent of all cases in which there was physical injury. Simple assault accounted for the largest percentage of these injuries. But its victims required medical attention in only one-fifth of the cases as opposed to three-fourths of the aggravated assaults, and hospitalization in 7 percent as opposed to 23 percent. Injury was more prevalent in conflicts between persons of the same age than in those in which the victim was older or younger than the attacker.

The three property crimes of burglary, automobile theft, and larceny of $50 and over make up 87 percent of Index crimes. The Index is a reasonably reliable indicator of the total number of property crimes reported to the police, but not a particularly good indicator of the seriousness of monetary loss from all property crimes. Commission studies tend to indicate that such non-Index crimes as fraud and embezzlement are more significant in terms of dollar volume. Fraud can be a particularly pernicious offense. It is not only expensive in total but all too often preys on the weak.

Many larcenies included in the Index total are misdemeanors rather than felonies under the laws of their own States. Auto thefts that involve only unauthorized use also are misdemeanors in many States. Many stolen automobiles are abandoned after a few hours, and more than 85 percent are ultimately recovered according to UCR studies. Studies in California indicate that about 20 percent of recovered cars are significantly damaged.

OTHER CRIMINAL OFFENSES

The seven crimes for which all offenses known are reported were selected in 1927 and modified in 1958 by a special advisory committee of the International Association of Chiefs of Police on the basis of their serious nature, their frequency, and the reliability of reporting from citizens to police. In 1965 reporting for these offenses included information supplied voluntarily by some 8,000 police agencies covering nearly 92 percent of the total population. The FBI tries vigorously to increase the number of jurisdictions that report each year and to promote uniform reporting and classification of the reported offenses.

The UCR Index does not and is not intended to assist in assessing all serious national crime problems. For example, offense statistics are not sufficient to assess the incidence of crime connected with corporate activity, commonly known as white-collar crime, or the total criminal acts committed by organized crime groups. Likewise, offense and arrest figures alone do not aid very much in analyzing the scope of professional crime—that is, the number and types of offenses committed by those whose principal employment and source of income are based upon the commission of criminal acts.

Except for larceny under $50 and negligent manslaughter,

for which there are some national offenses-known-to-the-police data, knowledge of the volume and trends of non-Index crimes depends upon arrest statistics. Since the police are not able to make arrests in many cases, these are necessarily less complete than the "offenses known" statistics. Moreover, the ratio between arrests and the number of offenses differs significantly from offense to offense—as is shown, for example, by the high percentage of reported cases in which arrests are made for murder (91 percent) and the relatively low percentage for larceny (20 percent). Reporting to the FBI for arrests covers less than 70 percent of the population. However, because arrest statistics are collected for a broader range of offenses—28 categories including the Index crimes —they show more of the diversity and magnitude of the many different crime problems. Property crimes do not loom so large in this picture.

Nearly 45 percent of all arrests are for such crimes without victims or against the public order as drunkenness, gambling, liquor law violations, vagrancy, and prostitution. As table 2 shows, drunkenness alone accounts for almost one-

Table 2.—Number and Rate of Arrests for the 10 Most Frequent Offenses, 1965

[4,062 agencies reporting; total population 134,095,000]

Rank	Offense	Number	Rate (per 100,000 population)	Percent of total arrests
1	Drunkenness	1,535,040	1,144.7	31.0
2	Disorderly conduct	570,122	425.2	11.5
3	Larceny (over and under $50)	385,726	286.2	7.7
4	Driving under the influence	241,511	180.1	4.9
5	Simple assault	207,615	154.8	4.2
6	Burglary	197,627	147.4	4.0
7	Liquor laws	179,219	133.7	3.6
8	Vagrancy	120,416	89.8	2.4
9	Gambling	114,294	85.2	2.3
10	Motor vehicle theft	101,763	75.9	2.1
	Total, 10 most frequent offenses	3,651,333	2,722.9	73.7
	Arrests for all offenses [1]	4,955,047	3,695.2	100.0

[1] Does not include arrests for traffic offenses.

SOURCE: "Uniform Crime Reports," 1965, pp. 108–109.

third of all arrests. This is not necessarily a good indication of the number of persons arrested for drunkenness, however, as some individuals may be arrested many times during the year. Arrest statistics measure the number of arrests, not the number of criminals.

More than 50 percent of all Federal criminal offenses relate to general law enforcement in territorial or maritime jurisdictions directly subject to Federal control, or are also State offenses (bank robberies, for example). Police statistics for these offenses are normally reported in the UCR, particularly when local law enforcement is involved. Such other Federal crimes as antitrust violations, food and drug violations and tax evasion are not included in the UCR. Although Federal crimes constitute only a small percentage of all offenses, crimes such as those shown in table 3 are an important part

Table 3.—Selected Federal Crimes
[Cases filed in court—1966]

Antitrust	7
Food and drug	350
Income tax evasion	863
Liquor revenue violations	2,729
Narcotics	2,293
Immigration	3,188

SOURCE: Department of Justice.

of the national crime picture.

THE EXTENT OF UNREPORTED CRIME

Although the police statistics indicate a lot of crime today, they do not begin to indicate the full amount. Crimes reported directly to prosecutors usually do not show up in the police statistics. Citizens often do not report crimes to the police. Some crimes reported to the police never get into the statistical system. Since better crime prevention and control programs depend upon a full and accurate knowledge about the amount and kinds of crime, the Commission initiated the first national survey ever made of crime victimization. The National Opinion Research Center of the University of Chicago surveyed 10,000 households, asking whether the person questioned, or any member of his or her household, had been a victim of crime during the past year, whether the crime had been reported and, if not, the reasons for not reporting.

More detailed surveys were undertaken in a number of high and medium crime rate precincts of Washington, Chicago, and Boston by the Bureau of Social Science Research of Washington, D.C., and the Survey Research Center of the University of Michigan. All of the surveys dealt primarily with households or individuals, although some data were obtained for certain kinds of businesses and other organizations.

These surveys show that the actual amount of crime in the United States today is several times that reported in the UCR. As table 4 shows, the amount of personal injury crime

Table 4.—Comparison of Survey and UCR Rates

[Per 100,000 population]

Index Crimes	NORC survey 1965–66	UCR rate for individuals 1965 [1]	UCR rate for individuals and organizations 1965 [1]
Willful homicide	3.0	5.1	5.1
Forcible rape	42.5	11.6	11.6
Robbery	94.0	61.4	61.4
Aggravated assault	218.3	106.6	106.6
Burglary	949.1	299.6	605.3
Larceny ($50 and over)	606.5	267.4	393.3
Motor vehicle theft	206.2	226.0	251.0
Total violence	357.8	184.7	184.7
Total property	1,761.8	793.0	1,249.6

[1] "Uniform Crime Reports," 1965, p. 51. The UCR national totals do not distinguish crimes committed against individuals or households from those committed against businesses or other organizations. The UCR rate for individuals is the published national rate adjusted to eliminate burglaries, larcenies, and vehicle thefts not committed against individuals or households. No adjustment was made for robbery.

reported to NORC is almost twice the UCR rate and the amount of property crime more than twice as much as the UCR rate for individuals. Forcible rapes were more than 3½ times the reported rate, burglaries three times, aggravated assaults and larcenies of $50 and over more than double, and robbery 50 percent greater than the reported rate. Only vehicle theft was lower and then by a small amount. (The single homicide reported is too small a number to be statistically useful.)

Even these rates probably understate the actual amounts of crime. The national survey was a survey of the victim experience of every member of a household based on interviews of one member. If the results are tabulated only for the family member who was interviewed, the amount of unreported victimization for some offenses is considerably higher. Apparently, the person interviewed remembered more of his own victimization than that of other members of his family.

The Washington, Boston, and Chicago surveys, based solely on victimization of the person interviewed, show even more clearly the disparity between reported and unreported amounts of crime. The clearest case is that of the survey in

Estimated Rates of Offense[1]

Comparison of Police[2] and BSSR Survey Data   Figure 2

3 WASHINGTON, D.C. PRECINCTS   Rates per 1000 Residents 18 Years or Over

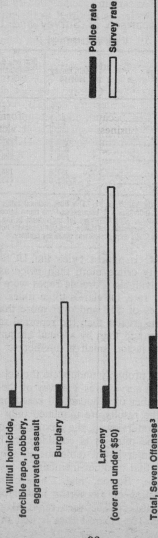

- ■ Police rate
- □ Survey rate

Wilful homicide, forcible rape, robbery, aggravated assault

Burglary

Larceny (over and under $50)

Total, Seven Offenses[3]

[1] Incidents involving more than one victim adjusted to count as only one offense. A victimization rate would count the incidence for each individual.

[2] Police statistics adjusted to eliminate nonresident and commercial victims and victims under 18 years of age.

[3] Wilful homicide, forcible rape, robbery, aggravated assault, burglary, larceny (over and under $50), and motor vehicle theft.

three Washington precincts, where, for the purpose of comparing survey results with crimes reported to the police, previous special studies made it possible to eliminate from police statistics crimes involving business and transient victims. As figure 2 indicates, for certain specific offenses against individuals the number of offenses reported to the survey per thousand residents 18 years or over ranged, depending on the offense, from 3 to 10 times more than the number contained in police statistics.

The survey in Boston and in one of the Chicago precincts indicated about three times as many Index crimes as the police statistics, in the other Chicago precinct about 1½ times as many. These survey rates are not fully comparable with the Washington results because adequate information did not exist for eliminating business and transient victims from the police statistics. If this computation would have been made,

Table 5.—Victims' Most Important Reason for Not Notifying Police [1]

[In percentages]

Crimes	Percent of cases in which police not notified	Reasons for not notifying police				
		Felt it was private matter or did not want to harm offender	Police could not be effective or would not want to be bothered	Did not want to take time	Too confused or did not know how to report	Fear of reprisal
Robbery	35	27	45	9	18	0
Aggravated assault	35	50	25	4	8	13
Simple assault	54	50	35	4	4	7
Burglary	42	30	63	4	2	2
Larceny ($50 and over)	40	23	62	7	7	0
Larceny (under $50)	63	31	58	7	3	(*)
Auto theft	11	20[2]	60[2]	0[2]	0[2]	20[2]
Malicious mischief	62	23	68	5	2	2
Consumer fraud	90	50	40	0	10	0
Other fraud (bad checks, swindling, etc.)	74	41	35	16	8	0
Sex offenses (other than forcible rape)	49	40	50	0	5	5
Family crimes (desertion, non-support, etc.)	50	65	17	10	0	7

SOURCE: NORC survey.

*Less than 0.5%.
[1] Willful homicide, forcible rape, and a few other crimes had too few cases to be statistically useful, and they are therefore excluded.
[2] There were only 5 instances in which auto theft was not reported.

the Boston and Chicago figures would undoubtedly have shown a closer similarity to the Washington findings.

In the national survey of households those victims saying that they had not notified the police of their victimization were asked why. The reason most frequently given for all offenses was that the police could not do anything. As table 5 shows, this reason was given by 68 percent of those not reporting malicious mischief, and by 60 or more percent of those not reporting burglaries, larcenies of $50 and over, and auto thefts. It is not clear whether these responses are accurate assessments of the victims' inability to help the police or merely rationalizations of their failure to report. The next most frequent reason was that the offense was a private matter or that the victim did not want to harm the offender. It was given by 50 percent or more of those who did not notify the police for aggravated and simple assaults, family crimes, and consumer frauds. Fear of reprisal, though least often cited, was strongest in the case of assaults and family crimes. The extent of failure to report to the police was highest for consumer fraud (90 percent) and lowest for auto theft (11 percent).

Table 6.—Offenses Known to the Police, 1960–65

[Rates per 100,000 population]

Offense	1960	1961	1962	1963	1964	1965
Willful homicide	5.0	4.7	4.5	4.5	4.8	5.1
Forcible rape	9.2	9.0	9.1	9.0	10.7	11.6
Robbery	51.6	50.0	51.1	53.0	58.4	61.4
Aggravated assault	82.5	82.2	84.9	88.6	101.8	106.6
Burglary	465.5	474.9	489.7	527.4	580.4	605.3
Larceny $50 and over	271.4	277.9	296.6	330.9	368.2	393.3
Motor vehicle theft	179.2	179.9	193.4	212.1	242.0	251.0
Total crimes against person	148.3	145.9	149.6	155.1	175.7	184.7
Total property crimes	916.1	932.7	979.7	1,070.4	1,190.6	1,249.6

SOURCE: FBI, Uniform Crime Reports Section, unpublished data.

The survey technique, as applied to criminal victimization, is still new and beset with a number of methodological problems. However, the Commission has found the information provided by the surveys of considerable value, and believes that the survey technique has a great untapped potential as a method for providing additional information about the nature and extent of our crime problem and the relative effectiveness of different programs to control crime.

There has always been too much crime. Virtually every generation since the founding of the Nation and before has felt itself threatened by the spectre of rising crime and violence.

A hundred years ago contemporary accounts of San Francisco told of extensive areas where "no decent man was in safety to walk the street after dark; while at all hours, both night and day, his property was jeopardized by incendiarism and burglary." Teenage gangs gave rise to the word "hoodlum"; while in one central New York City area, near Broadway, the police entered "only in pairs, and never unarmed." A noted chronicler of the period declared that "municipal law is a failure * * * we must soon fall back on the law of self preservation." "Alarming" increases in robbery and violent crimes were reported throughout the country prior to the Revolution. And in 1910 one author declared that "crime, especially its more violent forms, and among the young is increasing steadily and is threatening to bankrupt the Nation."

Crime and violence in the past took many forms. During the great railway strike of 1877 hundreds were killed across the country and almost 2 miles of railroad cars and buildings were burned in Pittsburgh in clashes between strikers and company police and the militia. It was nearly a half century later, after pitched battles in the steel industry in the late thirties, that the Nation's long history of labor violence subsided. The looting and takeover of New York for 3 days by mobs in the 1863 draft riots rivaled the violence of Watts, while racial disturbances in Atlanta in 1907, in Chicago, Washington, and East St. Louis in 1919, Detroit in 1943 and New York in 1900, 1935, and 1943 marred big city life in the first half of the 20th century. Lynchings took the lives of more than 4,500 persons throughout the country between 1882 and 1930. And the violence of Al Capone and Jesse James was so striking that they have left their marks permanently on our understanding of the eras in which they lived.

However, the fact that there has always been a lot of crime does not mean that the amount of crime never changes. It changes constantly, day and night, month to month, place to place. It is essential that society be able to tell when changes occur and what they are, that it be able to distinguish normal ups and downs from long-term trends. Whether the amount of crime is increasing or decreasing, and by how much, is an important question—for law enforcement, for the individual citizen who must run the risk of crime, and for the official

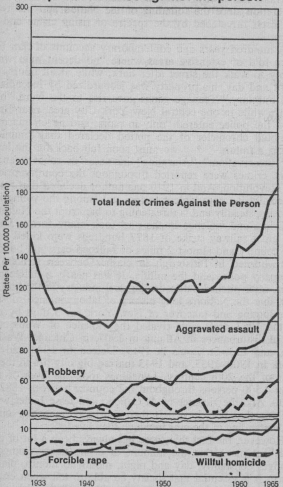

Index Crime Trends, 1933-1965 Figure 3
Reported Crimes against the person

(Rates Per 100,000 Population)

Total Index Crimes Against the Person

Aggravated assault

Robbery

Forcible rape

Willful homicide

NOTE: Scale for willful homicide and forcible rape enlarged,
to show trend.
Source: FBI, Uniform Crime Reports Section; unpublished data.

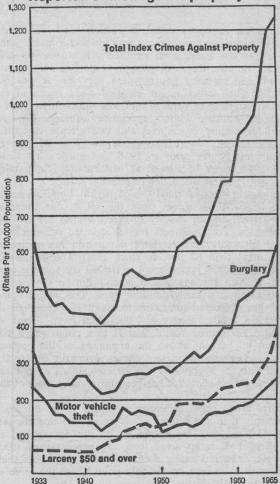

Index Crime Trends, 1933-1965 Figure 4
Reported Crimes against property

Total Index Crimes Against Property

Burglary

Motor vehicle theft

Larceny $50 and over

(Rates Per 100,000 Population)

1933 1940 1950 1960 1965

NOTE: The scale for this figure is not comparable with that used in Figure 3.

Source: FBI, Uniform Crime Reports Section; unpublished data.

who must plan and establish prevention and control programs. If it is true, as the Commission surveys tend to indicate, that society has not yet found fully reliable methods for measuring the volume of crime, it is even more true that it has failed to find such methods for measuring the trend of crime.

Unlike some European countries, which have maintained national statistics for more than a century and a quarter, the United States has maintained national crime statistics only since 1930. Because the rural areas were slow in coming into the system and reported poorly when they did, it was not until 1958, when other major changes were made in the UCR, that reporting of rural crimes was sufficient to allow a total national estimate without special adjustments. Changes in overall estimating procedures and two offense categories —rape and larceny—were also made in 1958. Because of these problems figures prior to 1958 and particularly those prior to 1940, must be viewed as neither fully comparable with nor nearly so reliable as later figures.

For crimes of violence the 1933–65 period, based on newly adjusted unpublished figures from the UCR, has been, as figure 3 shows, one of sharply divergent trends for the different offenses. Total numbers for all reported offenses have increased markedly; the Nation's population has increased also—by more than 47 percent since 1940. The number of offenses per 100,000 population has tripled for forcible rape and has doubled for aggravated assault during the period, both increasing at a fairly constant pace. The willful homicide rate has decreased somewhat to about 70 percent of its high in 1933, while robbery has fluctuated from a high in 1933 and a low during World War II to a point where it is now about 20 percent above the beginning of the postwar era. The overall rate for violent crimes, primarily due to the increased rate for aggravated assault, now stands at its highest point, well above what it has been throughout most of the period.

Property crime rates, as shown in figure 4, are up much more sharply than the crimes of violence. The rate for larceny of $50 and over has shown the greatest increase of all Index offenses. It is up more than 550 percent over 1933. The burglary rate has nearly doubled. The rate for auto theft has followed an uneven course to a point about the same as the rate of the early thirties.

The upward trend for 1960–65 as shown in table 6 has been faster than the long-term trend, up 25 percent for the violent crimes and 36 percent for the property crimes. The greatest increases in the period came in 1964, in forcible rape among crimes of violence and in vehicle theft among property crimes. Preliminary reports indicate that all Index offenses rose in 1966.

Arrest rates are in general much less complete and are available for many fewer years than are rates for offenses known to the police. However, they do provide another measure of the trend of crime. For crimes of violence, arrest rates rose 16 percent during 1960–65, considerably less than the 25 percent increase indicated by offenses known to the police. For property crimes, arrest rates have increased about 25 percent, as opposed to a 36 percent increase in offenses known to the police during 1960–65. Figure 5 compares the 1960–65 trend for arrests and offenses known for both crimes of violence and property crimes.

Prior to the year 1933, shown in figures 3 and 4, there is no estimated national rate for any offenses. UCR figures for a sizable number of individual cities, however, indicate that the 1930–32 rates, at least for those cities, were higher than the 1933 rates. Studies of such individual cities as Boston, Chicago, New York, and others indicate that in the twenties and the World War I years reported rates for many offenses were even higher. A recent study of crime in Buffalo, N.Y., from 1854 to 1946 showed arrest rates in that city for willful homicide, rape, and assault reaching their highest peak in the early 1870's, declining, rising again until 1918, and declining into the forties.

Trends for crimes against trust, vice crimes, and crimes against public order, based on arrest rates for 1960–65, follow a much more checkered pattern than do trends for Index offenses. For some offenses this is in part due to the fact that arrest patterns change significantly from time to time, as when New York recently decided not to make further arrests for public drunkenness. Based on comparable places covering about half the total population, arrest rates during 1960–65 rose 13 percent for simple assault, 13 percent for embezzlement and fraud, and 36 percent for narcotics violations, while for the same period, the rates declined 24 percent for gambling and 11 percent for drunkenness.

The picture portrayed by the official statistics in recent years, both in the total number of crimes and in the number of crimes per 100,000 Americans, is one of increasing crime. Crime always seems to be increasing, never going down. Up 5 percent this year, 10 the next, and the Commission's surveys have shown there is a great deal more crime than the official statistics show. The public can fairly wonder whether there is ever to be an end.

This official picture is also alarming because it seems so

pervasive. Crimes of violence are up in both the biggest and smallest cities, in the suburbs as well as in the rural areas. The same is true for property crimes. Young people are being arrested in ever increasing numbers. Offense rates for most crimes are rising every year and in every section of the country. That there are some bright spots does not change this dismal outlook. Rates for some offenses are still below those of the early thirties and perhaps of earlier periods. Willful homicide rates have been below the 1960 level through most of the last few years. Robbery rates continue to decline in the

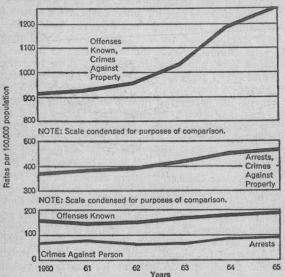

Reported Crimes Against Persons and Property, 1960-1965 Trends Arrests and Offenses Known to the Police

Figure 5

NOTE: Scale condensed for purposes of comparison.

NOTE: Scale condensed for purposes of comparison.

NOTE: Arrest rates include larceny over and under $50 but rates for offenses known to the police include only larcenies of $50 and over. All rates are based on estimates for the total population.

Source: FBI, Uniform Crime Reports Section; unpublished data.

rural areas and small towns, and arrest rates for many non-Index offenses have remained relatively stable.

Because the general picture is so disturbing and the questions it raises go to the very heart of concern about crime in the United States today, the Commission has made a special effort to evaluate as fully as possible the information available.

It has tried to determine just how far this picture is accurate, to see whether our cities and our countryside are more dangerous than they were before, to find out whether our youth and our citizens are becoming more crime prone than those who were in their same circumstances in earlier years, to see what lies behind any increases that may have occurred, and to determine what if anything this information tells us can be done to bring the crime rate down.

What is known about the trend of crime—in the total number of offenses; in the ratio of offenses to population, which measures roughly the risk of victimization; and in the relationship of crime trends to changes in the composition of the population, which measures roughly the crime proneness of various kinds of people—is almost wholly a product of statistics. Therefore the Commission has taken a particularly hard look at the current sources of statistical knowledge.

FACTORS AFFECTING THE REPORTING OF CRIME

From the time that police statistics first began to be maintained in France in the 1820's, it has been recognized that the validity of calculations of changes in crime rates was dependent upon a constant relationship between reported and unreported crime. Until the Commission surveys of unreported crime, however, no systematic effort of wide scale had ever been made to determine what the relationship between reported and unreported crime was. As shown earlier, these surveys have now indicated that the actual amount of crime is several times that reported to the police, even in some of the precincts with the highest reported crime rates. This margin of unreported crime raises the possibility that even small changes in the way that crime is reported by the public to the police, or classified and recorded by the police, could have significant effects on the trend of reported crime. There is strong reason to believe that a number of such changes have taken place within recent years.

Changing Expectations. One change of importance in the amount of crime that is reported in our society is the change in the expectations of the poor and members of minority groups about civil rights and social protection. Not long ago there was a tendency to dismiss reports of all but the most serious offenses in slum areas and segregated minority group districts. The poor and the segregated minority groups were left to take care of their own problems. Commission studies indicate that whatever the past pattern was, these areas now have a strong feeling of need for adequate police protection.

Crimes that were once unknown to the police, or ignored when complaints were received, are now much more likely to be reported and recorded as part of the regular statistical procedure.

The situation seems similar to that found in England. The University of Cambridge's Institute of Criminology, which in 1963 conducted an exhaustive study of the sharp rise in crimes of violence, concluded in its report that: *One of the main causes for an increase in the* recording *of violent crime appears to be a decrease in the toleration of aggressive and violent behaviour, even in those slum and poor tenement areas where violence has always been regarded as a normal and accepted way of settling quarrels, jealousies or even quite trivial arguments.*

Police Practice. Perhaps the most important change for reporting purposes that has taken place in the last 25 years is the change in the police. Notable progress has been made during this period in the professionalization of police forces. With this change, Commission studies indicate, there is a strong trend toward more formal actions, more formal records and less informal disposition of individual cases. This trend is particularly apparent in the way the police handle juveniles, where the greatest increases are reported, but seems to apply to other cases as well. It seems likely that professionalization also results in greater police efficiency in looking for crime. Increases in the number of clerks and statistical personnel, better methods for recording information, and the use of more intensive patrolling practices also tend to increase the amount of recorded crime. Because this process of professionalization has taken place over a period of time and because it is most often a gradual rather than an abrupt change, it is difficult to estimate what its cumulative effect has been.

Wholly different kinds of changes have occurred in a number of cities. In 1953 Philadelphia reported 28,560 Index crimes plus negligent manslaughter and larceny under $50, an increase of more than 70 percent over 1951. This sudden jump in crime, however, was not due to an invasion by criminals but to the discovery by a new administration that crime records had for years minimized the amount of crime in the city. One district had actually handled 5,000 complaints more than it had recorded.

The Commission could not attempt an exhaustive study of such changes in reporting procedures. It has noted in table 7 a number of instances in which the UCR indicated changes in reporting procedures for major cities during 1959–65. All of these changes have resulted in an increase in the level of

Table 7.—Reporting System Changes—UCR Index Figures Not Comparable With Prior Years

| Name of city | Years of increase | Amount of increase (Index offenses): | | |
		From	To	Percent increase
Baltimore	1964–65	18,637	26,193	40.5
Buffalo	1961–63	4,779	9,305	94.7
Chicago	1959–60	56,570	97,253	71.9
Cleveland	1963–64	10,584	17,254	63.0
Indianapolis	1961–62	7,416	10,926	47.3
Kansas City, Mo	1959–61 [1]	4,344	13,121	202.0
Memphis	1963–64	8,781	11,533	31.3
Miami	1963–64	10,750	13,610	26.6
Nashville	1962–63	6,595	9,343	41.7
Shreveport	1962–63	1,898	2,784	46.7
Syracuse	1963–64	3,365	4,527	34.5

[1] No report was published for Kansas City, Mo., for 1960.

SOURCE: "Uniform Crime Reports," 1959–1965.

reporting for all subsequent years. It has also noted that changes of this sort are still taking place, being indicated in 1966 for Detroit, Chattanooga, Worcester, Mass., and New York City among others.

Perhaps the clearest illustration of the impact that changes in reporting systems can have is that shown by the history of such changes in New York City and Chicago. These cities are two of the Nation's largest police jurisdictions, accounting in 1965 for 20 percent of all reported robberies and 7 percent of all reported burglaries. Changes in their reporting systems have several times produced large paper increases in crime. Figure 6 illustrates the pattern dramatically.

Although Chicago, with about 3 million people, has remained a little less than half the size of New York City with 7½ million throughout the period covered in figure 6, it was reporting in 1935 about 8 times as many robberies as New York City until 1949, when the FBI discontinued publication of New York reports because it no longer believed them. In 1950 New York discontinued its prior practice of allowing precincts to handle complaints directly and installed a central reporting system, through which citizens had to route all calls.

In the first year, robberies rose 400 percent and burglaries 1,300 percent, passing Chicago in volume for both offenses. In 1959 Chicago installed a central complaint bureau of its own, reporting thereafter several times more robberies than

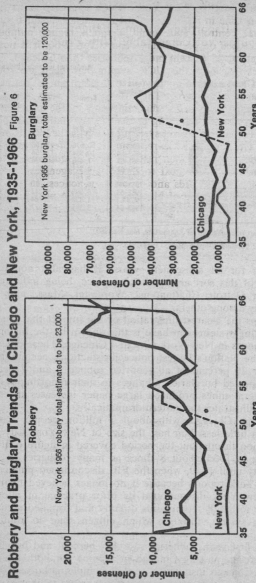

Robbery and Burglary Trends for Chicago and New York, 1935-1966   Figure 6

Robbery

New York 1966 robbery total estimated to be 23,000.

Number of Offenses: 20,000 / 15,000 / 10,000 / 5,000

Chicago

New York

Years: 35 40 45 50 55 60 66

*UCR did not report any data for New York, 1949-1951.
Source: Uniform Crime Reports, 1936-1966. 1966 figures estimated from 11 months' report.

Burglary

New York 1966 burglary total estimated to be 120,000.

Number of Offenses: 90,000 / 80,000 / 70,000 / 60,000 / 50,000 / 40,000 / 30,000 / 20,000 / 10,000

Chicago

New York

Years: 35 40 45 50 55 60 66

New York. In 1966 New York, which appeared to have had a sharp decline in robberies in the late fifties, again tightened its central controls and found a much higher number of offenses. Based on preliminary reports for 1966, it is now reporting about 25 percent more robberies than Chicago.

The existence of the UCR system has been one of the strongest forces pushing toward the adoption of better and more complete reporting. The FBI has been alert both to the need to encourage better reporting and to the problem that sizable changes in reporting present to the national statistical system. Through a careful system of checks the FBI is able to identify the units that are reporting on a different basis than the previous year. It then restricts its computations of trends from one year to the next to those police agencies that have had comparable records and reporting practices. In 1965, for example, computation of changes from 1964 were limited to agencies representing 82 percent of the U.S. population; 147 reporting agencies representing about 10 percent of the population were eliminated because of changes in reporting practices.

In order to make comparisons for periods greater than 1 year the UCR assumes that the city that underwent the change in reporting practices has had the same experience as other cities of its size and State throughout the period and reestimates the amount of crime for all prior years back to its base period of the 1937–40 average. In the 1960–65 period, use of this system reduces the 36 percent increase in Index crimes against the person based on published rates to a 25 percent increase, and the 39 percent increase in crimes against property to 36 percent. Cities are returned to the trend computation after they have had 2 years of comparable experience under the new system.

This system is perhaps as good as can be devised. It is obviously very hard, however, to estimate how much crime would have been reported in a major city in the year prior to that in which the system of reporting was changed, and even harder to say what the crime rate was 5 years earlier. It seems unlikely that the level of robbery in New York today is 13 times what it was in 1940 or triple what it was in 1960, but how does one decide for the purpose of long-term comparisons? The cities that have significantly changed their reporting systems since 1959 account for nearly 25 percent of all reported Index crimes against the person and about 16 percent of all reported Index property crimes. The real question is not the method of estimation, but whether the yardstick at the present time is too changeable to allow significant trend comparisons to be made at the national level.

A further problem is raised by the fact that a number of other large cities have not yet adopted the central complaint bureaus and strong staff controls necessary for an effective reporting program. In one of these cities Commission staff members were informed of a precinct file 13, where citizen complaints not forwarded to the central statistical office were filed for the purpose of answering insurance inquiries. The President's Commission on Crime in the District of Columbia recently criticized Washington's failure to record all offenses reported to the police. It is not clear how large this group of cities is, but disparities between cities of the same size for each of the Index offenses are so great that they seem most unlikely in the absence of some variation in reporting practice.

The reporting problem arises at least in part from the tendency of some cities, noted in 1931 by the Wickersham Commission, to "use these reports in order to advertise their freedom from crime as compared with other muncipalities." This tendency has apparently not yet been fully overcome. It sometimes arises from political pressure outside the police department and sometimes from the desire of the police to appear to be doing a good job of keeping the crime rate down. Defective or inefficient recording practices may also prevent crimes reported by citizens from becoming a part of the record.

The Commission believes that each city administration and each agency of justice has a duty to insure that its citizens are being informed of the full rate of reported crime in the community. Not to do so means that the community is being misled and that it has no benchmark to measure the effectiveness of its prevention and control program. It may also mean that the community is unaware of an increasing problem. In the case of large cities, not to report crime accurately also penalizes those administrations and police departments that are honest with their citizens by causing them to suffer unjust comparisons with other cities.

The Commission recommends:

Those cities that have not already done so should adopt centralized procedures for handling the receipt of reports of crime from citizens and institute the staff controls necessary to make those procedures effective.

Insurance. Another factor that probably increases the amount of reporting for some crimes is the sizable increase in insurance coverage against theft. It is difficult to evaluate this factor. However, because many persons believe that they must report a criminal event to the police in order to collect insurance, more reporting seems likely. Although not the only factor involved, one indication that this may be the case is the high rate of reporting for auto theft noted by the NORC survey. Insurance is usually involved in auto theft.

FACTORS INDICATING AN INCREASE IN CRIME

Many factors affect crime trends but they are not always easy to isolate. Murder is a seasonal offense. Rates are generally higher in the summer, except for December, which is often the highest month and almost always 5 to 20 percent above the yearly average. In December 1963, following the assassination of President Kennedy, murders were below the yearly average by 4 percent, one of the few years in the history of the UCR that this occurred. Since 1950 the pace of auto thefts has increased faster than but in the same direction as car registrations. During World War II, however, when there was rationing and a shortage of cars, rates for auto theft rose sharply. And in 1946 when cars came back in production and most other crimes were increasing, auto thefts fell off rapidly.

The introduction to the UCR provides a checklist of some of the many factors that must be taken into account in interpreting changes in crime rates and in the amount and type of crime that occurs from place to place:

Density and size of the community population and the metropolitan area of which it is a part.
Composition of the population with reference particularly to age, sex, and race.
Economic status and mores of the population.
Relative stability of population, including commuters, seasonal, and other transient types.
Climate, including seasonal weather conditions.
Educational, recreational, and religious characteristics.
Effective strength of the police force.
Standards governing appointments to the police force.
Policies of the prosecuting officials and the courts.
Attitude of the public toward law enforcement problems.
The administrative and investigative efficiency of the local law enforcement agency.

A number of these factors have been changing in ways that would lead one to expect increases in the amounts of certain kinds of crime.

Changing Age Composition. One of the most significant factors affecting crime rates is the age composition of the population. In 1965 more than 44 percent of all persons arrested for forcible rape, more than 39 percent for robbery, and more than 26 percent for willful homicide and aggravated assault were in the 18- to 24-year-old age group. For property crimes the highest percentages are found in the under 18 group—nearly 50 percent of all those arrested for burglary and larceny and more than 60 percent for auto theft.

For most of these offenses the rate of offense per individual in these age groups is many times that in older groups. Of course the differences are based on arrest figures, and the national figures on offenses cleared by arrest show that 75 to 80 percent of burglaries, larcenies, and auto thefts are unsolved. It is possible that older persons committing offenses against property are more successful at evading arrest, so that the age figures for arrests give a somewhat biased picture.

Because of the unusual birth rate in the postwar years, the youthful high-risk group—those in their teens and early twenties—has been increasing much faster than other groups in the population. Beginning in 1961 nearly 1 million more youths have reached the ages of maximum risk each year than did so in the prior year. Thus the volume of crime and the overall crime rate could be expected to grow whether the rate for any given age increased or not.

Commission studies based on 1960 arrest rates indicate that between 1960 and 1965 about 40 to 50 percent of the total increase in the arrests reported by UCR could have been expected as the result of increases in population and changes in the age composition of the population.

Urbanization. Rates for most crimes are highest in the big cities. Twenty-six core cities of more than 500,000 people, with less than 18 percent of the total population, account for more than half of all reported Index crimes against the person and more than 30 percent of all reported Index property crimes. One of every three robberies and nearly one of every five rapes occurs in cities of more than 1 million. The average rate for every Index crime except burglary, as table 8 shows, is at least twice as great—and often more—in these cities as in the suburbs or rural areas. With a few exceptions, average rates increase progressively as the size of the city becomes larger.

Suburban rates are closest to those of the smaller cities except for forcible rape where suburban rates are higher. Suburban rates appear to be going up as business and industry

114

Table 8.—Offenses Known by City Size, 1965

[Rates per 100,000 population]

Group	Willful homicide	Forcible rape	Robbery	Aggravated assault	Burglary	Larceny $50 and over	Motor vehicle theft
Cities over 1 million	10	26	221	246	930	734	586
500,000 to 1 million	10	20	165	182	1,009	555	640
250,000 to 500,000	7	15	122	142	1,045	550	468
100,000 to 250,000	6	11	73	151	871	556	353
50,000 to 100,000	4	8	49	85	675	492	297
25,000 to 50,000	3	6	33	71	562	443	212
10,000 to 25,000	2	6	19	67	462	309	141
Under 10,000	2	5	12	62	369	236	99
Rural	4	9	10	58	308	176	51
Suburban area	3	10	28	66	545	359	160
All places	5	12	61	107	605	420	251

SOURCE: "Uniform Crime Reports," 1965, table 1, p. 51 and table 6, p. 94.

increase—shopping centers are most frequently blamed by local police officials for rises in suburban crime.

Although rural rates are lower generally than those for cities, the differences have always been much greater for property crimes than for crimes against the person. Until the last few years rural rates for murder were close to those of the big cities, and rural rates for murder and rape still exceed those for small towns.

The country has for many years seen a steady increase in its urban population and a decline in the proportion of the population living in rural areas and smaller towns. Since 1930 the rural population has increased by less than 2 percent while the city population has increased by more than 50 percent. The increase in the cities and their suburbs since 1960 alone has been about 10 percent. Because of the higher crime rates in and around the larger cities, this trend toward urbanization has a considerable effect on the national rate for most Index crimes. Commission studies show that if metropolitan, small city, and rural crime rates for 1960 had remained constant through 1965, the increase that could have been expected due to urbanization would have been about 7 to 8 percent of the increase reported by the UCR.

It would obviously tell us a great deal about the trend of crime if we could analyze all together the changes that have been taking place in urbanization, age composition of the population, number of slum dwellers, and other factors such as sex, race, and level of income. The Commission has spent a considerable amount of time trying to make this kind of analysis. However, it was unable to analyze satisfactorily more than one or two factors in conjunction with each other on the basis of present information. As more factors were brought into the analysis the results differed in some instances substantially from those obtained when only one factor was analyzed. It also seemed clear that as the number of factors was increased, a more accurate picture of the effect of changing conditions on the rate of crime emerged.

On the basis of its study, the Commission estimates that the total expected increase in crime from 1960 to 1965 from these kinds of changes would be at least half, and possibly a great deal more, of the total increase in crime rates actually observed. The Commission's study clearly indicates the need for fuller reporting of arrest information and for the development of more compatibility between police statistics and information collected by other statistical agencies. The FBI has already made substantial progress in this direction in recent years but further steps are still needed.

Some Unexplained Variations. Some crimes are not so heavily concentrated in the urban areas as the Index offenses. Vandalism, liquor law violations, driving while intoxicated, forgery and counterfeiting, and embezzlement and fraud are much more evenly spread over cities of all sizes and rural areas. Narcotics violations, gambling, drunkenness, vagrancy, and disorderly conduct generally follow the same pattern as Index offenses.

The explanations that have been offered for urban areas having higher rates of crime than rural areas have usually centered around the larger number of criminal opportunities available, a greater likelihood of association with those who are already criminals, a more impersonal life that offers greater freedom and, in many cases, the harsher conditions of slum life—often in sharp and visible contrast to the affluence of nearby areas. That these factors operate differently with regard to crimes of violence and crimes against property, and with regard to more serious offenses, suggests that the relationship between the rate of crime and the degree of urbanization is a very complicated one.

This seems to be borne out by the disparities in rates between cities of the same size. While average rates of individual cities seem much more helter-skelter. Of the 56 cities in the country with more than 250,000 in population, only one, Los Angeles, of the 10 cities with the highest rates for all Index offenses is a city of over 1 million. Newark, the city with the highest rate for all Index offenses, is in the 250,000–500,000 category, as are 4 others. Philadelphia ranks 51st and New York, before its change in reporting, ranked 28th.

The patterns vary markedly from offense to offense even within the broad categories of crimes against the person and crimes against property. Los Angeles is 1st for rape and 4th for aggravated assault but 20th for murder, with a murder rate less than half that of St. Louis. Chicago has the highest rate for robbery but a relatively low rate for burglary. New York is 5th in larcenies $50 and over, but 54th for larcenies under $50. The risk of auto theft is about 50 percent greater in Boston than anywhere else in the country, but in Boston the likelihood of other kinds of theft is about the average for cities over 250,000. Table 9 shows the robbery rates for the country's 14 largest cities.

Table 9.—Robbery Rates in 1965—14 Largest Cities in Order of Size

[Per 100,000 population]

New York	114	Cleveland	213
Chicago	421	Washington	359
Los Angeles	293	St. Louis	327
Philadelphia	140	Milwaukee	28
Detroit	335	San Francisco	278
Baltimore	229	Boston	168
Houston	135	Dallas	79

SOURCE: FBI, Uniform Crime Reports Section, unpublished data.

Not very much study has been devoted to this kind of difference and the Commission was able to do little more than survey the literature already in existence. Some of the difference, perhaps a great deal, seems clearly attributable to differences in reporting. Disparities as great as 17 to 1 between Newark and Jersey City, or 10 to 1 between St. Louis and Milwaukee for certain offenses seem most unlikely in the absence of some reporting variation. There are significant differences, however, among cities in such factors as age, sex, race, and other population characteristics, economic status, character of industry, climate, and the like and it seems clear that there are real and substantial differences in the true amounts of crime.

The few studies that have been done in this area have failed altogether to account for the differences in offense rates in terms of characteristics such as these. These studies suggest that whatever factors are operating affect personal and property crimes differently, and substantially refute the idea that crime rate variations can be accounted for by any single factor such as urbanization, industrialization, or standard of living. These studies take us very little farther, however, than the differences in the rates themselves. Even when they offer some explanation of the differences between cities, the explanations they offer are not able to account for the variations within the cities themselves.

Given the large, often gigantic, differences in rates between cities, the Commission has been struck that so little has been done to learn the causes of these variations. If only a little were known as to why the robbery rate was 12 times as high in Chicago as in San Jose, it would be much easier to figure out what to do about robbery in Chicago. While no simple answers can be expected, the Commission strongly believes that further exploration of these differences could make an important contribution to the prevention and control of crime.

Increased Affluence. Another change that may result in more crime is increasing affluence. There are more goods around to be stolen. National wealth and all categories of merchandise have increased in terms of constant dollars more than fourfold since 1940—significantly more than the population or the rate of reported theft.

Increased affluence may also have meant that property is now protected less well than formerly. More than 40 percent of all auto thefts involve cars with the keys inside or the switch left open. A substantial percentage of residential burglaries occur in unlocked houses. Bicycles, whose theft constitutes 15 percent of all reported larcenies, are frequently left lying around. Larceny of goods and accessories from cars accounts for another 40 percent of all reported larceny.

Some increased business theft seems directly due to less protection. The recent rise in bank robbery seems due in large part to the development of small, poorly protected branch banks in the suburbs.

In retail establishments, managers choose to tolerate a high percentage of shoplifting rather than pay for additional clerks. Discount stores, for example, experience an inventory loss rate almost double that of the conventional department store. Studies indicate that there is in general more public tolerance for theft of property and goods from large organizations than from small ones, from big corporations or utilities than from small neighborhood establishments. Restraints on conduct that were effective in a more personal rural society do not seem as effective in an impersonal society of large organizations.

Inflation has also had an impact on some property crimes. Larceny, for example, is any stealing that does not involve force or fraud. The test of the seriousness of larceny is the value of the property stolen. The dividing line between "grand" and "petty" larceny for national reporting purposes is $50. Larceny of $50 and over is the Index offense that has increased the most over the history of the UCR, more than 550 percent since 1933. Because the purchasing power of the dollar today is only 40 percent of what it was in 1933, many thefts that would have been under $50 then are over $50 now. UCR figures on the value of property stolen, for example, indicate that the average value of a larceny has risen from $26 in 1940 to $84 in 1965.

Table 10.—Homicide Rates for Selected Countries
[Per 100,000 population]

Country	Rate	Year reported
Colombia	36.5	1962
Mexico	31.9	1960
South Africa	21.8	1960
United States	4.8	1962
Japan	1.5	1962
France	1.5	1962
Canada	1.4	1962
Federal Republic of Germany	1.2	1961
England/Wales	.7	1962
Ireland	.4	1962

SOURCE: "Demographic Yearbook," 15th issue, United Nations Publication, 1963, pp. 594–611.

OTHER COUNTRIES

Crime is a worldwide problem. For most offenses it is difficult to compare directly the rates between countries because of great differences in the definitions of crime and in reporting practices. It is clear, however, that there are great differences in the rates of crime among the various countries, and in the crime problems that they face. These differences are illustrated to some extent by the homicide rates for a number of countries shown in table 10. The comparisons show only the general range of difference, as definitions and reporting even of homicide vary to some extent. In the years covered by the table, Colombia had the highest rate for all countries and Ireland the lowest.

A comparison between crime rates in 1964 in West Germany and the north central United States, prepared by the FBI, indicates that the Federal Republic, including West Berlin, had a crime rate of 0.8 murders per 100,000 inhabitants,

10.6 rapes, 12.4 robberies, 1,628.2 larcenies, and 78.2 auto thefts, as opposed to 3.5 murders per 100,000 inhabitants for north central United States, 10.5 rapes, 76.2 robberies, 1,337.3 larcenies, and 234.7 auto thefts.

Commission and other studies of crime trends indicate that in most other countries officially reported rates for property offenses are rising rapidly, as they are in the United States, but that there is no definite pattern in the trend of crimes of violence in other countries. Since 1955 property crime rates have increased more than 200 percent in West Germany, the Netherlands, Sweden, and Finland, and over 100 percent in France, England and Wales, Italy, and Norway. Of the countries studied, property crime rates in Denmark, Belgium, and Switzerland remained relatively stable.

Crimes of violence could be studied in only a few countries. Rates declined in Belgium, Denmark, Norway, and Switzerland, but rose more than 150 percent in England and Wales between 1955 and 1964. Sexual offenses, which are usually kept as a separate statistic in Europe, also showed a mixed trend.

ASSESSING THE AMOUNT AND TREND OF CRIME

Because of the grave public concern about the crime problem in America today, the Commission has made a special effort to understand the amount and trend of crime and has reached the following conclusions:

1. The number of offenses—crimes of violence, crimes against property and most others as well—has been increasing. Naturally, population growth is one of the significant contributing factors in the total amount of crime.

2. Most forms of crime—especially crimes against property—are increasing faster than population growth. This means that the risk of victimization to the individual citizen for these crimes is increasing, although it is not possible to ascertain precisely the extent of the increase. All economic and social factors discussed above support, and indeed lead to, this conclusion.

The Commission found it very difficult to make accurate measurements of crime trends by relying solely on official figures, since it is likely that each year police agencies are to some degree dipping deeper into the vast reservoir of unreported crime. People are probably reporting more to the police as a reflection of higher expectations and greater confidence, and the police in turn are reflecting this in their statistics. In this sense more efficient policing may be leading to higher rates of reported crime. The diligence of the FBI in promoting more complete and accurate reporting through the development of professional police reporting procedures has clearly had an important effect on the completeness of reporting, but while this task of upgrading local reporting is under way, the FBI is faced with the problem, in computing national trends, of omitting for a time the places undergoing changes in reporting methods and estimating the amount of crime that occurred in those places in prior years.

3. Although the Commission concluded that there has been an increase in the volume and rate of crime in America, it has been unable to decide whether individual Americans today are more criminal than their counterparts 5, 10, or 25 years ago. To answer this question it would be necessary to make comparisons between persons of the same age, sex, race, place of residence, economic status and other factors at the different times: in other words, to decide whether the 15-year-old slum dweller or the 50-year-old businessman is inherently more criminal now than the 15-year-old slum dweller or the 50-year-old businessman in the past. Because of the many rapid and turbulent changes over these years in society as a whole and in the myriad conditions of life which affect crime, it was not possible for the Commission to make such a comparison. Nor do the data exist to make even simple comparisons of the incidence of crime among persons of the same age, sex, race, and place of residence at these different years.

4. There is a great deal of crime in America, some of it very serious, that is not reported to the police, or in some instances by the police. The national survey revealed that people are generally more likely to report serious crimes to the police, but the percent who indicated they did report to the police ranged from 10 percent for consumer fraud to 89 percent for auto theft. Estimates of the rate of victimization for Index offenses ranged from 2 per 100 persons in the national survey to 10 to 20 per 100 persons in the individual districts surveyed in 3 cities. The surveys produced rates of victimization that were from 2 to 10 times greater than the official rates for certain crimes.

5. What is needed to answer questions about the volume and trend of crime satisfactorily are a number of different crime indicators showing trends over a period of time to supplement the improved reporting by police agencies. The Commission experimented with development of public surveys of victims of crime and feels this can become a useful supplementary yardstick. Further development of the procedure is needed to improve the reliability and accuracy of the

findings. However, the Commission found these initial experiments produced useful results that justify more intensive efforts to gather such information on a regular basis. They should also be supplemented by new types of surveys and censuses which would provide better information about crime in areas where good information is lacking such as crimes by or against business and other organizations. The Commission also believes that an improved and greatly expanded procedure for the collection of arrest statistics would be of immense benefit in the assessment of the problem of juvenile delinquency.

6. Throughout its work the Commission has noted repeatedly the sharp differences in the amount and trends of reported crimes against property as compared with crimes against persons. It has noted that while property crimes are far more numerous than crimes against the person, and so dominate any reported trends, there is much public concern about crimes against persons. The more recent reports of the UCR have moved far toward separating the reporting of these two classes of crime altogether.

The Commission recommends:

The present Index of reported crime should be broken into two wholly separate parts, one for crimes of violence and the other for crimes against property.

The Commission also recommends, in principle, the development of additional indices to indicate the volume and trend of such other important crime problems as embezzlement, fraud, and other crimes against trust, crimes of vice that are associated with organized crime, and perhaps others. The Commission urges that consideration be given to practical methods for developing such indices.

The Commission also urges that the public media and others concerned with crime be careful to keep separate the various crime problems and not to deal with them as a unitary phenomenon. Whenever possible, crime should be reported relative to population as well as by the number of offenses, so as to provide a more accurate picture of risks of victimization in any particular locality.

7. The Commission believes that age, urbanization, and other shifts in the population already under way will likely operate over the next 5 to 10 years to increase the volume of offenses faster than population growth. Further dipping into the reservoirs of unreported crime will likely combine with this real increase in crime to produce even greater increases

in reported crime rates. Many of the basic social forces that tend to increase the amount of real crime are already taking effect and are for the most part irreversible. If society is to be successful in its desire to reduce the amount of real crime, it must find new ways to create the kinds of conditions and inducements—social, environmental, and psychological—that will bring about a greater commitment to law-abiding conduct and respect for the law on the part of all Americans and a better understanding of the great stake that all men have in being able to trust in the honesty and integrity of their fellow citizens.

THE ECONOMIC IMPACT OF CRIME

One way in which crime affects the lives of all Americans is that it costs all Americans money. Economic costs alone cannot determine attitudes about crime or policies toward crime, of course. The costs of lost or damaged lives, of fear and of suffering, and of the failure to control critical events cannot be measured solely in dollars and cents. Nor can the requirements of justice and law enforcement be established solely by use of economic measures. A high percentage of a police department's manpower may have to be committed to catch a single murderer or bombthrower. The poor, unemployed defendant in a minor criminal case is entitled to all the protections our constitutional system provides—without regard to monetary costs.

However, economic factors relating to crime are important in the formation of attitudes and policies. Crime in the United States today imposes a very heavy economic burden upon both the community as a whole and individual members of it. Risks and responses cannot be judged with maximum effectiveness until the full extent of economic loss has been ascertained. Researchers, policymakers, and operating agencies should know which crimes cause the greatest economic loss, which the least; on whom the costs of crime fall, and what the costs are to prevent or protect against it; whether a particular or general crime situation warrants further expenditures for control or prevention and, if so, what expenditures are likely to have the greatest impact.

The number of policemen, the size of a plant security staff, or the amount of insurance any individual or business carries are controlled to some degree by economics—the balance of the value to be gained against the burden of additional expenditures. If the protection of property is the objective, the economic loss from crime must be weighed directly against the cost of better prevention or control. In view of the importance and the frequency of such decisions, it is surprising that the cost information on which they are based is as fragmentary as it is. The lack of knowledge about which the Wickersham Commission complained 30 years ago is almost as great today.

Some cost data are now reported through the UCR and additional data are available from individual police forces, insurance companies, industrial security firms, trade associations, and others. However, the total amount of information is not nearly enough in quantity, quality, or detail to give an accurate overall picture.

The information available about the economic cost of crime is most usefully presented not as an overall figure, but as a series of separate private and public costs. Knowing the economic impact of each separate crime aids in identifying important areas for public concern and guides officials in making judgments about priorities for expenditure. Breakdowns of money now being spent on different parts of the criminal justice system, and within each separate part, may afford insights into past errors. For example, even excluding value judgments about rehabilitative methods, the fact that an adult probationer costs 38 cents a day and an adult offender in prison costs $5.24 a day suggests the need for reexamining current budget allocations in correctional practice.

Figure 7 represents six different categories of economic impacts both private and public. Numerous crimes were omitted because of the lack of figures. Estimates of doubtful reliability were used in other cases so that a fuller picture might be presented. Estimates do not include any amounts for pain and suffering. Except for alcohol, which is based on the amount of tax revenue lost, estimates for illegal goods and services are based on the gross amount of income to the seller. (Gambling includes only the percentage retained by organized crime, not the total amount gambled.) The totals should be taken to indicate rough orders of magnitude rather than precise details.

ECONOMIC IMPACT OF INDIVIDUAL CRIME

The picture of crime as seen through cost information is considerably different from that shown by statistics portraying the number of offenses known to the police or the number of arrests:

☐ Organized crime takes about twice as much income from gambling and other illegal goods and services as criminals derive from all other kinds of criminal activity combined.

Economic Impact of Crimes and Related Expenditures Figure 7
(Estimated in Millions of Dollars)

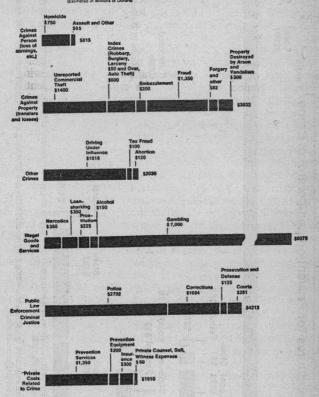

Crimes Against Person (loss of earnings, etc.)
- Homicide $750
- Assault and Other $65
- $815

Crimes Against Property (transfers and losses)
- Unreported Commercial Theft $1400
- Index Crimes (Robbery, Burglary, Larceny $50 and Over, Auto Theft) $600
- Embezzlement $200
- Fraud $1,350
- Forgery and other $82
- Property Destroyed by Arson and Vandalism $300
- $3932

Other Crimes
- Driving Under Influence $1818
- Tax Fraud $100
- Abortion $120
- $2038

Illegal Goods and Services
- Narcotics $350
- Loan-sharking $350
- Prostitution $225
- Alcohol $150
- Gambling $7,000
- $8075

Public Law Enforcement Criminal Justice
- Police $2792
- Corrections $1034
- Prosecution and Defense $125
- Courts $261
- $4212

Private Costs Related to Crime
- Prevention Services $1,350
- Prevention Equipment $200
- Insurance $300
- Private Counsel, Bail, Witness Expenses $60
- $1910

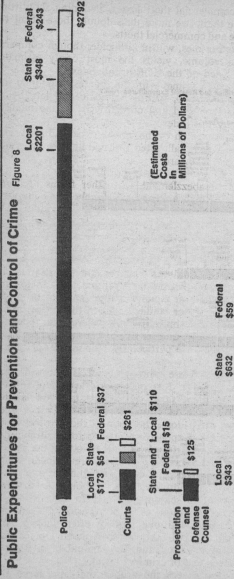

Public Expenditures for Prevention and Control of Crime Figure 8

(Estimated Costs In Millions of Dollars)

Police
Local $2201
State $348
Federal $243
$2792

Courts¹
Local $173 State $51 Federal $37
$261

Prosecution and Defense Counsel
State and Local $110
Federal $15
$125

Corrections
Local $343
State $632
Federal $59
$1034

Source: Bureau of the Census, Division of Governments (corrections and police); Bureau of the Budget (courts); Commission studies. All figures are for fiscal year ending June 30, 1965.

¹ Total court costs are estimated at $782 million—$109 Federal, $155 State and $518 local; criminal court costs were estimated at one-third of the total based on studies in several jurisdictions.

126

- ☐ Unreported commercial theft losses, including shoplifting and employee theft, are more than double those of all reported private and commercial thefts.
- ☐ Of the reported crimes, willful homicide, though comparatively low in volume, yields the most costly estimates among those listed on the UCR crime index.
- ☐ A list of the seven crimes with the greatest economic impact includes only two, willful homicide and larceny of $50 and over (reported and unreported), of the offenses included in the crime Index.
- ☐ Only a small proportion of the money expended for criminal justice agencies is allocated to rehabilitative programs for criminals or for research.

Employee theft, embezzlement, and other forms of crime involving business, which appear in relatively small numbers in the police statistics, loom very large in dollar volume. Direct stealing of cash and merchandise, manipulation of accounts and stock records, and other forms of these crimes, along with shoplifting, appear to constitute a tax of one to two percent on the total sales of retail enterprises, and significant amounts in other parts of business and industry. In the grocery trade, for example, the theft estimates for shoplifting and employee theft almost equal the total amount of profit. Yet Commission and other studies indicate that these crimes are largely dealt with by business itself. Merchants report to the police fewer than one-quarter of the known offenses. Estimates for these crimes are particularly incomplete for nonretail industries.

Fraud is another offense whose impact is not well conveyed by police statistics. Just one conspiracy involving the collapse of a fraudulent salad oil empire in 1964 created losses of $125–$175 million. Fraud is especially vicious when it attacks, as it so often does, the poor or those who live on the margin of poverty. Expensive nostrums for incurable diseases, home-improvement frauds, frauds involving the sale or repair of cars, and other criminal schemes create losses which are not only sizable in gross but are also significant and possibly devastating for individual victims. Although a very frequent offense, fraud is seldom reported to the police. In consumer and business fraud, as in tax evasion, the line between criminal conduct and civil fraud is often unclear. And just as the amount of civil tax evasion is much greater than the amount of criminal tax fraud, the amount of civil fraud probably far exceeds that of criminal fraud.

Cost analysis also places the crimes that appear so frequently in police statistics—robbery, burglary, larceny, and auto theft—in somewhat different perspective. The number of reported offenses for these crimes accounts for less than one-sixth the estimated total dollar loss for all property crimes and would constitute an even lower percentage if there were any accurate way of estimating the very large sums involved in extortion, blackmail, and other property crimes.

This is not to say, however, that the large amounts of police time and effort spent in dealing with these crimes are not important. Robbery and burglary, particularly residential burglary, have importance beyond the number of dollars involved. The effectiveness of the police in securing the return of better than 85 percent of the $500 million worth of cars stolen annually appears to be high, and without the efforts of the police the costs of these crimes would doubtless be higher. As with all categories of crime, the total cost of property crimes cannot be measured because of the large volume of unreported crimes; however, Commission surveys suggest that the crimes that are unreported involve less money per offense than those that are reported.

The economic impact of crimes causing death is surprisingly high. For 1965 there were an estimated 9,850 homicide victims. Of the estimated 49,000 people who lost their lives in highway accidents, more than half were killed in accidents involving either negligent manslaughter or driving under the influence of alcohol. An estimated 290 women died from complications resulting from illegal abortions (nearly one-fourth of all maternal deaths). Measured by the loss of future earnings at the time of death, these losses totaled more than $1½ billion.

The economic impact of other crimes is particularly difficult to assess. Antitrust violations reduce competition and unduly raise prices; building code violations, pure food and drug law violations, and other crimes affecting the consumer have important economic consequences, but they cannot be easily described without further information. Losses due to fear of crime, such as reduced sales in high crime locations, are real but beyond measure.

Economic impact must also be measured in terms of ultimate costs to society. Criminal acts causing property destruction or injury to persons not only result in serious losses to the victims or their families but also the withdrawal of wealth or productive capacity from the economy as a whole. Theft on the other hand does not destroy wealth but merely transfers it involuntarily from the victim, or perhaps his insurance company, to the thief. The bettor purchasing illegal betting services from organized crime may easily absorb the loss of a

10-cent, or even 10-dollar, bet. But from the point of view of society, gambling leaves much less wealth available for legitimate business. Perhaps more important, it is the proceeds of this crime tariff that organized crime collects from those who purchase its illegal wares that form the major source of income that organized crime requires to achieve and exercise economic and political power.

EXPENDITURES FOR CRIME PREVENTION AND CONTROL

Public expenditures, shown on figure 8, for the police, courts, and corrections—currently estimated at more than $4 billion a year—are borne primarily by taxpayers at the State and local level.

Both corrections costs and police costs have been growing, with corrections costs expanding at a more rapid rate. About 85–90 percent of all police costs are for salaries and wages, leaving only a small proportion for equipment or research. Ten to 15 percent of local police time and greater amounts for some State police units is spent on traffic control. Because it is difficult to distinguish the civil from the criminal allocations of police time, no adjustment has been made in figure 8. A small percentage of all correctional costs is spent for the treatment—as opposed to custody—of institutionalized offenders.

Many other public expenditures play a direct and important role in the prevention of crime. These include antipoverty, recreational, educational, and vocational programs. They have not been included in this tabulation, however, because most have social purposes that go far beyond preventing crime.

Private costs related to crime are also difficult to determine, particularly those for crime prevention and protection. While the $200 million spent annually for burglar alarms and other protective equipment clearly relates only to crime, the night watchman's additional duties indicate that only an undetermined percentage of his salary should be attributed to crime costs. Insurance awards neither increase nor decrease the total loss from crime, but merely spread it among all premium payers. The substantial overhead cost of insuring—the cost shown in figure 7—is, however, an additional burden that must be borne by those who seek protection from crime.

THE NEED FOR MORE DATA

The Commission recommends that the lack of information about the economic costs of crime in America be remedied

—not only to furnish a better basis for assessing the nature and amounts of the various kinds of losses but also as a means for developing new and improved measures of control. Much of the study needed to do this can be accomplished in Federal, State, and local criminal justice agencies. Business associations must also contribute to the effort and university research should be greatly expanded. The Federal statistics center proposed in chapter 13 could collect annual cost data, be the central repository for it, and disseminate it widely to relevant agencies. In addition, periodic censuses and surveys could provide more detailed information that would be useful in indicating crime problems of national scope and in evaluating the relative effectiveness of the various crime prevention and control measures adopted by individuals, businesses, and governments.

CRIME AND THE INNER CITY

One of the most fully documented facts about crime is that the common serious crimes that worry people most—murder, forcible rape, robbery, aggravated assault, and burglary—happen most often in the slums of large cities. Study after study in city after city in all regions of the country have traced the variations in the rates for these crimes. The results, with monotonous regularity, show that the offenses, the victims, and the offenders are found most frequently in the poorest, and most deteriorated and socially disorganized areas of cities.

Studies of the distribution of crime rates in cities and of the conditions of life most commonly associated with high crime rates have been conducted for well over a century in Europe and for many years in the United States. The findings have been remarkably consistent. Burglary, robbery, and serious assaults occur in areas characterized by low income, physical deterioration, dependency, racial and ethnic concentrations, broken homes, working mothers, low levels of education and vocational skill, high unemployment, high proportions of single males, overcrowded and substandard housing, high rates of tuberculosis and infant mortality, low rates of home ownership or single family dwellings, mixed land use, and high population density. Studies that have mapped the relationship of these factors and crime have found them following the same pattern from one area of the city to another.

Crime rates in American cities tend to be highest in the city center and decrease in relationship to distance from the

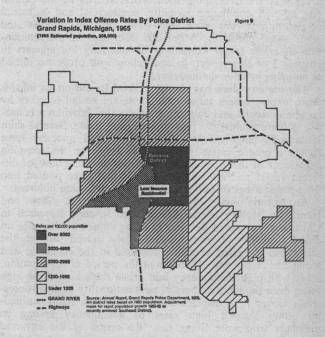

**Variation in Index Offense Rates By Police District
Grand Rapids, Michigan, 1965**
(1965 Estimated population, 208,000)

Figure 9

Business
District

Low Income
Residential

Rates per 100,000 population

- ■ Over 5000
- ▨ 3000-4999
- ▧ 2000-2999
- ▨ 1200-1999
- □ Under 1200
- ⚬⚬⚬ GRAND RIVER
- ⚬—⚬ Highways

Source: Annual Report, Grand Rapids Police Department, 1965.
All district rates based on 1960 population. Adjustment
made for rapid population growth 1960-65 in
recently annexed Southeast District.

center. This typical distribution of crime rates is found even in medium sized cities, such as the city of Grand Rapids, Mich., shown in figure 9. This pattern has been found to hold fairly well for both offenses and offenders, although it is sometimes broken by unusual features of geography, enclaves of socially well integrated ethnic groups, irregularities in the distribution of opportunities to commit crime, and unusual concentrations of commercial and industrial establishments in outlying areas. The major irregularity found is the clustering of offenses and offenders beyond city boundaries in satellite areas that are developing such characteristics of the central city as high population mobility, commercial and industrial concentrations, low economic status, broken families and other social problems. A detailed discussion of the relationship of crime to the conditions of inner-city life appears in chapter 3 of this report, in connection with programs aimed at reducing juvenile delinquency.

The big city slum has always exacted its toll on its inhabitants, except where those inhabitants are bound together by an intense social and cultural solidarity that provides a collective defense against the pressures of slum living. Several slum settlements inhabited by people of oriental ancestry have shown a unique capacity to do this. However, the common experience of the great successive waves of immigrants of different racial and ethnic backgrounds that have poured into the poorest areas of our large cities has been quite different.

An historic series of studies by Clifford R. Shaw and Henry D. McKay of the Institute of Juvenile Research in Chicago documented the disorganizing impact of slum life on different groups of immigrants as they moved through the slums and struggled to gain a foothold in the economic and social life of the city. Throughout the period of immigration, areas with high delinquency and crime rates kept these high rates, even though members of new nationality groups successively moved in to displace the older residents. Each nationality group showed high rates of delinquency among its members who were living near the center of the city and lower rates for those living in the better outlying residential areas. Also for each nationality group, those living in the poorer areas had more of all the other social problems commonly associated with life in the slums.

This same pattern of high rates in the slum neighborhoods and low rates in the better districts is true among the Negroes and members of other minority groups who have made up the most recent waves of migration to the big cities. As other groups before them, they have had to crowd into the areas where they can afford to live while they search for ways to live better. The disorganizing personal and social experiences with life in the slums are producing the same problems for the new minority group residents, including high rates of crime and delinquency. As they acquire a stake in urban society and move to better areas of the city, the crime rates and the incidence of other social problems drop to lower levels.

However, there are a number of reasons to expect more crime and related problems among the new migrants to the city than among the older immigrants. There have been major changes in the job market, greatly reducing the demand for unskilled labor, which is all most new migrants have to offer. At the same time the educational requirements for jobs have been rising. Discrimination in employment, education, and housing, based on such a visible criterion as color, is harder to break than discrimination based on language or ethnic background.

What these changes add up to is that slums are becoming ghettos from which escape is increasingly difficult. It could be predicted that this frustration of the aspirations that originally led Negroes and other minority groups to seek out the city would ultimately lead to more crime. Such evidence as exists suggests this is true.

RIOTS

One hypothesis about everyday crime in the slums is that much of it is a blind reaction to the conditions of slum living. The ghetto riots of 1964, 1965, and 1966 were crime in its most aggravated form. In the 1965 riot in the Watts section of Los Angeles alone, 34 persons were killed, 1,032 injured, and 3,952 arrested. Some 600 buildings were damaged. Some $40 million in property was destroyed.

The size of the threat to the community that riots offer cannot be reckoned as merely the sum of the individual acts of murder, assault, arson, theft, and vandalism that occur during them, of course. Riots are a mass repudiation of the standards of conduct citizens must adhere to if society is to remain not only safe, but civilized and free. They give a sort of moral license to the compulsively or habitually criminal members of the ghetto community to engage in their criminal activities, and to ordinarily law-abiding citizens to gratify such submerged tendencies toward violence and theft as they may have.

However, riots are every bit as complicated as any other form of crime, and another way of looking at them is as direct and deliberate attacks on ghetto conditions. This is what all the studies, particularly those of the Watts riots by the

McCone Commission, an independent nonpolitical body; by the attorney general of California; and by members of the faculty of the University of California at Los Angeles, show. Although once underway some riots were exploited by agitators, they were not deliberate in the sense that they were planned at the outset; the best evidence is that they were spontaneous outbursts, set off more often than not by some quite ordinary and proper action by a policeman. They were deliberate in the sense that they were directed, to an extent that varied from city to city, against specific targets.

The principal objects of attack were most often just those people or institutions, insofar as they were within reach, that the rioters thought of as being their principal oppressors: Policemen and white passers-by, or white-owned commercial establishments, especially those that charged high prices, dealt in inferior merchandise or employed harsh credit policies. Loan offices were a favorite target. Homes, schools, churches, and libraries were, by and large, left alone.

The studies also show that the rioters were not preponderantly wild adolescents, hoodlums, racial extremists, and radical agitators, as is sometimes asserted, although such people undoubtedly did take part. They were a more or less representative cross section of the Negro community, particularly of its younger men, many of whom had lived in the neighborhood for many years and were steadily employed. The studies show further that many of those who participated in the riots, when questioned subsequently about their motives, stated quite explicitly they had been protesting against, indeed trying to call the attention of the white community to, police misconduct, commercial exploitation and economic deprivation, and racial discrimination.

Along with all responsible citizens, the Commission believes strongly, of course, that riots must be suppressed promptly when they occur. No society can afford to tolerate violent and dangerous mass crime.

But a far more determined effort must be made to eradicate conditions that invite riots. Citizen reactions reported in the UCLA study of Watts provide useful clues to riot prevention. A majority (55 percent) of the Negroes interviewed felt that one result of the riot would be to diminish racial problems. The main stated reason for this belief was that help would now be forthcoming. It would be forthcoming because whites would now be more sympathetic to Negro problems (of the 62 percent of the Negroes who had opinions, over half believed that white sympathy would increase). The dilemma of Negroes emerges from the survey data as a constant theme: anger at discrimination, yet basic trust in America.

A full and adequate investigation of the causes of riots and the means for preventing them is a complex and difficult undertaking beyond the scope of the resources and mandate of this Commission. However, examination of the crimes that are committed during riots and of the conditions of life in the places where riots break out leads to the conclusion that the only enduring guarantee that riots will not occur is to answer the cry of "Help!" that Negroes have been uttering for many years, and that can be clearly heard even amid the destruction and bloodshed of a riot.

America must move more rapidly than it has so far done toward fundamental reorganization of the institutions of the slum community, and toward the abolition of the discriminatory practices that maintain the ghetto in existence. Measures to prevent delinquency, especially in the slums, that are proposed in the next chapter should also help prevent the ghetto riots that in recent years have killed and injured so many people, have destroyed so much property, have inspired so much fear, have so badly shaken the confidence of Americans in the capacity of their society to achieve long-needed reform in a peaceful manner.

Table 11.—Victimization by Income

[Rates per 100,000 population]

Offenses	Income			
	$0 to $2,999	$3,000 to $5,999	$6,000 to $9,999	Above $10,000
Total	2,369	2,331	1,820	2,237
Forcible rape	76	49	10	17
Robbery	172	121	48	34
Aggravated assault	229	316	144	252
Burglary	1,319	1,020	867	790
Larceny ($50 and over)	420	619	549	925
Motor vehicle theft	153	206	202	219
Number of respondents	(5,232)	(8,238)	(10,382)	(5,946)

SOURCE: NORC survey.

THE VICTIMS OF CRIME

One of the most neglected subjects in the study of crime is its victims: the persons, households, and businesses that bear the brunt of crime in the United States. Both the part the victim can play in the criminal act and the part he could have played in preventing it are often overlooked. If it could be determined with sufficient specificity that people or businesses with certain characteristics are more likely than others to be crime victims, and that crime is more likely to occur in some places than in others, efforts to control and prevent crime would be more productive. Then the public could be told where and when the risks of crime are greatest. Measures such as preventive police patrol and installation of burglar alarms and special locks could then be pursued more efficiently and effectively. Individuals could then substitute objective estimation of risk for the general apprehensiveness that today restricts—perhaps unnecessarily and at best haphazardly—their enjoyment of parks and their freedom of movement on the streets after dark.

Although information about victims and their relationships to offenders is recorded in the case files of the police and other criminal justice agencies, it is rarely used for systematic study of those relationships or the risks of victimization. To discover variations in victimization rates among different age, sex, race, and income groupings in the population, the Commission analyzed information on these items obtained in the national survey by NORC.

Rather striking variations in the risk of victimization for different types of crime appear among different income levels in the population. The results shown in table 11 indicate that the highest rates of victimization occur in the lower income

Table 12.—Victimization by Race

[Rates per 100,000 population]

Offenses	White	Nonwhite
Total	1,860	2,592
Forcible rape	22	82
Robbery	58	204
Aggravated assault	186	347
Burglary	822	1,306
Larceny ($50 and over)	608	367
Motor vehicle theft	164	286
Number of respondents	(27,484)	(4,902)

* SOURCE: NORC survey.

groups when all Index offenses except homicide are considered together. The risks of victimization from forcible rape, robbery, and burglary, are clearly concentrated in the lowest income group and decrease steadily at higher income levels.

136

The picture is somewhat more erratic for the offenses of aggravated assault, larceny of $50 and over, and vehicle theft. Victimization for larceny increases sharply in the highest income group.

National figures on rates of victimization also show sharp differences between whites and nonwhites (table 12). Nonwhites are victimized disproportionately by all Index crimes except larceny $50 and over.

The rates of victimization shown for Index offenses against men (table 13) are almost three times as great as those for women, but the higher rates of burglary, larceny and auto theft against men are in large measure an artifact of the survey procedure of assigning offenses against the household to the head of the household.

Table 13.—Victimization by Age and Sex

[Rates per 100,000 population]

Offense	Male						
	10–19	20–29	30–39	40–49	50–59	60 plus	All ages
Total	951	5,924	6,231	5,150	4,231	3,465	3,091
Robbery	61	257	112	210	181	98	112
Aggravated assault	399	824	337	263	181	146	287
Burglary	123	2,782	3,649	2,365	2,297	2,343	1,583
Larceny ($50 and over)	337	1,546	1,628	1,839	967	683	841
Motor vehicle theft	31	515	505	473	605	195	268
	Female						
	10–19	20–29	30–39	40–49	50–59	60 plus	All ages
Total	334	2,424	1,514	1,908	1,132	1,052	1,059
Forcible rape	91	238	104	48	0	0	83
Robbery	0	238	157	96	60	81	77
Aggravated assault	91	333	52	286	119	40	118
Burglary	30	665	574	524	298	445	314
Larceny ($50 and over)	122	570	470	620	536	405	337
Motor vehicle theft	0	380	157	334	119	81	130

SOURCE: NORC survey.

The victimization rate for women is highest in the 20 to 29 age group. In fact the victimization rates for women for all the Index offenses reported, with the exception of larceny, are greatest in this age group. The concentration of offenses against women in this age group is particularly noticeable for forcible rape and robbery and much less apparent in aggravated assault and the property crimes.

For men the highest Index total rate falls in the 30–39 age category, a result heavily influenced by the burglaries assigned to men as heads of households. Actually, all the Index

137

property offenses against men show peak rates in the older age categories. This is probably due not only to their role as household heads but also to the fact that at older ages they are likely to possess more property to be stolen. Crimes against the person, such as aggravated assault and robbery, are committed relatively more often against men who are from 20 to 29 years of age.

Thus, the findings from the national survey show that the risk of victimization is highest among the lower income groups for all Index offenses except homicide, larceny, and vehicle theft; it weighs most heavily on the nonwhites for all Index offenses except larceny; it is borne by men more often than women, except, of course, for forcible rape; and the risk is greatest for the age category 20 to 29, except for larceny against women, and burglary, larceny, and vehicle theft against men.

VICTIM-OFFENDER RELATIONSHIPS IN CRIMES OF VIOLENCE

The relations and interactions of victims and offenders prior to and during the criminal act are important facts to know for understanding and controlling crime and assessing personal risks more accurately. The relationships most often studied have been those involving crimes of violence against the person, especially homicide and forcible rape. Typical of the findings of these inquiries are the results of an analysis of criminal homicides in Philadelphia between 1948 and 1952. This study clearly demonstrated that it is not the marauding stranger who poses the greatest threat as a murderer. Only 12.2 percent of the murders were committed by strangers. In 28.2 percent of the cases studied, the murderer was a relative or a close friend. In 24.7 percent he was a member of the family. The murderer was an acquaintance of the victim in 13.5 percent of the cases.

These findings are very similar to those reported nationally in the UCR:

In 1965 killings within the family made up 31 percent of all murders. Over one-half of these involved spouse killing spouse and 16 percent parents killing children. Murder outside the family unit, usually the result of altercations among acquaintances, made up 48 percent of the willful killings. In the latter category romantic triangles or lovers' quarrels comprised 21 percent and killings resulting from drinking situations 17 percent. Felony murder, which is defined in this Program as those killings resulting from robberies, sex motives, gangland slayings, and other felonious activities, made up 16 percent of

138

these offenses. In another 5 percent of the total police were unable to identify the reasons for the killings; however, the circumstances were such as to suspect felony murder.

Unfortunately, no national statistics are available on relationships between victims and offenders in crimes other than criminal homicide. However, the District of Columbia Crime Commission surveyed a number of other crimes. Its findings on victim-offender relationships in rape and aggravated assault closely resemble those for murder:

Almost two-thirds of the 151 [rape] victims surveyed were attacked by persons with whom they were at least casually acquainted. Only 36 percent of the 224 assailants about whom some identifying information was obtained were complete strangers to their victims: 16 (7 percent) of the attackers were known to the victim by sight, although there had been no previous contact. Thirty-one (14 percent) of the 224 assailants were relatives, family friends or boy friends of the victims, and 88 (39 percent) were either acquaintances or neighbors.

And among 131 aggravated assault victims, only 25 (19 percent) were not acquainted with their assailants:

Fourteen (11 percent) of the victims were attacked by their spouses, 13 (10 percent) were attacked by other relatives, and 79 (60 percent) were assaulted by persons with whom they were at least casually acquainted.

Again, as in murder, a substantial number (20 percent) of the aggravated assaults surveyed by the District of Columbia Crime Commission involved a victim and offender who had had trouble with each other before.

Another source of the concern about crime, in addition to its violence and its frequency, is the extent to which it is assumed to involve interracial attacks. Therefore a key question in any assessment of the crime problem is to what extent men or women of one racial group victimize those of another. For evidence on the way in which the race and sex of victims and offenders might affect the probability of criminal assault, the Commission, with the cooperation of the Chicago Police Department, studied 13,713 cases of assaultive crimes against the person, other than homicide.

As shown in table 14, it is Negro males and females who are most likely to be victimized in crimes against the person. A Negro man in Chicago runs the risk of being a victim nearly six times as often as a white man, a Negro woman nearly eight times as often as a white woman.

The most striking fact in the data is the extent of the correlation in race between victim and offender. Table 14 shows that Negroes are most likely to assault Negroes, white most likely to assault whites. Thus, while Negro males account for two-thirds of all assaults, the offender who victimizes a white person is most likely also to be white.

The President's Commission on Crime in the District of Columbia discovered similar racial relationships in its 1966 survey of a number of serious crimes. Only 12 of 172 murders were interracial. Eighty-eight percent of rapes involved persons of the same race. Among 121 aggravated assaults for which identification of race was available, only 9 percent were interracial. Auto theft offenders in the District are three-fourths Negroes, their victims two-thirds Negroes. Robbery, the only crime of violence in which whites were victimized more often than Negroes, is also the only one that is predominantly interracial: in 56 percent of the robberies committed by Negroes in the District of Columbia, the victims are white.

Table 14.—Victim-Offender Relationships by Race and Sex in Assaultive Crimes Against the Person (Except Homicide)

	Offenses attributable to—				
	White offenders		Negro offenders		All types of offenders
	Male	Female	Male	Female	
Victim rate for each 100,000: [1]					
White males	201	9	129	4	342
White females	108	14	46	6	175
Negro males	58	3	1,636	256	1,953
Negro females	21	3	1,202	157	1,382
Total population [1]	130	10	350	45	535

[1] The rates are based only on persons 14 years of age or older in each race-sex category. The "total population" category in addition excludes persons from racial groups other than Negro or white.

SOURCE: Special tabulation from Chicago Police Department, Data Systems Division, for period September 1965 to March 1966.

The high proportions of both acquaintance between victim and offender and the intraracial character of offenses are further borne out by the findings of another study developed for the Commission. Analyzing data obtained from the Seattle Police Department, this study compared the census tract where the crime occurred with the tract (or other place) in which the offender lived. It found that a relatively large percentage of crimes against persons, as contrasted with crimes against property, had been committed in the offender's home tract—an area likely to be racially homogeneous and in which he is most likely to be known at least by sight.

This analysis shows that a failure to collect adequate data on victim-offender relationships may lead to a miscalculation of the source and nature of the risk of victimization. At present the Nation's view of the crime problem is shaped largely by official statistics which in turn are based on offenses known to the police and statistics concerning arrested offenders; they include very little about victims.

PLACE WHERE VICTIMIZATION OCCURS

Crime is more likely to occur in some places than in others, just as some persons are more likely than others to be the victims of criminal offenders. The police often distribute their preventive patrols according to spot maps that locate the time and place of occurrence of different types of crimes. Such information, however, has not been developed well enough to inform the public of the places it should avoid.

A well-designed information system should also provide crime rate figures for different types of business premises in

Table 15.—Victimization by Sex and Place of Occurrence for Major Crimes (Except Homicide) Against the Person

[In percent]

Place of occurrence	Victims of major crimes against person	
	Male	Female
School property	3.2	2.4
Residence	20.5	46.1
Transport property	1.4	.4
Taxis and delivery trucks	2.6	
Businesses	3.2	1.1
Taverns and liquor stores	5.7	2.8
Street	46.8	30.7
Parks	.8	.5
All other premises	16.0	16.0
Total percent	100.0	100.0
Total number	(8,047)	(5,666)

SOURCE: Special tabulation from Chicago Police Department, Data Systems Division, for period September 1965 to March 1966.

different areas of the city. Victimization rates based upon the number of drugstores, cleaning establishments, gas stations, taxicabs, banks, supermarkets, taverns, and other businesses in a neighborhood would furnish better indicators of the likelihood of crime in that neighborhood than exist at present. Determining such rates would require enumerating premises of different types and locating them by area. This information would help to test the effectiveness of control measures and to identify the nature of increases in crime by making it possible to detect changes in the pattern of risk for various businesses. It would also permit more refined calculations of risk for insurance purposes and guide the placement of alarm systems and other crime prevention devices.

The study of victimization of individuals carried out in cooperation with the Chicago Police Department recorded the types of premises for all major crimes against the person except homicide. Table 15 classifies victims by sex in relation to the place where the offense occurred. For assaultive crimes against the person, the street and the home are by far the most common places of occurrence. Men are more likely to be victimized on the street, and women are more likely to be victimized in residences.

The findings in general are closely related to the characteristic patterns of interaction among men and women in our society. Men are more likely to meet one another outside the home. A substantial portion of assaults arises from drinking —the tavern is the third most common setting for men to be victims of assault and battery—and some of the conflicts among drunks later erupt into street fights. Men and women more frequently engage in conflicts with each other in domestic settings.

COMPENSATION TO VICTIMS OF CRIME

Programs granting public compensation to victims for physical injuries from violent crimes have aroused increased interest in recent years. The community has evidenced concern for the plight of victims of muggings, stabbings, and other violence. In the absence of such programs victims generally suffer losses that are not compensated in any way. Their civil remedies are most likely to be unsuccessful because of the poor financial condition and prospects of most offenders. And the criminal law generally makes no effort to use its sanctions to insure restitution to the victim. Indeed it often aggravates the victim's problem by incarcerating the offender, thus preventing him from earning money to make restitution.

Two philosophies underlie the recent movements for victim compensation. The first argues that the government is responsible for preventing crime and therefore should be made responsible for compensating the victims of the crimes it fails to prevent. The second approach, an extension of welfare doctrines, rests on the belief that people in need, especially those in need because they have been victimized by events they could not avoid, are entitled to public aid.

The first modern victim-compensation programs were established in New Zealand and Great Britain in 1964. California's programs, which became effective in the beginning of 1966, was the first in the United States. Only victims with limited financial resources qualify for compensation under this program. New York's victim-compensation bill, enacted in 1966, also provides compensation only for those who would suffer "serious financial hardship" as a result of the crime. Various Federal victim-compensation bills, now before the Congress, have yet to receive public hearings. The Commission believes that such hearings would provide a national forum for a much needed debate over the philosophy, assumptions, and potential advantages and disadvantages of such programs generally, and the relative merits and design of a program on the Federal level in particular.

The Commission has been impressed by the consensus among legislators and law enforcement officials that some kind of State compensation for victims of violent crime is desirable. Recent public opinion polls indicate that a considerable majority of the public is in favor of victim compensation. The Commission believes that the general principle of victim compensation, especially to persons who suffer injury in violent crime, is sound and that the experiments now being conducted with different types of compensation programs are valuable.

COMMERCIAL ESTABLISHMENTS AND ORGANIZATIONS AS VICTIMS OF CRIME

It is very difficult to discover the exact extent to which businesses and organizations are the victims of crime. Few attempts are made to keep systematic records or report such crimes to any central place. Police agencies do not ordinarily separate the crimes against individuals from those against organizations. It was not possible in the short time available to the Commission to undertake a systematic census of victimization of different types of industrial, business, professional, religious, or civic organizations throughout the Nation. This task ought to be undertaken, and some assessment procedure developed, using reports, special sample surveys or similar devices.

The Commission was able to make a pilot survey, however, of a sample of neighborhood businesses and organizations in eight police precincts in Chicago, Washington, and Boston. The objective was to discover through interviews what types of victimization businesses and organizations had experienced from crimes such as burglary, robbery, shoplifting, passing of fraudulent checks, and employee theft.

Burglary and Robbery. Reports to the UCR indicate that nationally about half of all burglaries in 1965 were nonresidential, and that the average worth of the property stolen in such burglaries was about $225. In the Commission survey almost one of every five businesses and organizations in the eight neighborhood police precincts surveyed was burglarized at least once during the one-year period covered by the survey. Considering only those that were burglarized, 62 percent had from two to seven burglaries.

In both Chicago and Washington, but for some reason not in Boston, the burglary victimization rates were highest in the districts where the overall crime rates were highest. Precinct 13 in the District of Columbia, for example, had a victimization rate of 51.8 per 100 organizations—twice that of the precinct with the fewest burglaries—and a third of all the businesses and organizations sampled in that area had been victimized.

Nationally, reports to the UCR indicate that in 1965 9 percent of all robberies were of service stations or chainstores, almost 1 percent were of banks, and more than 20 percent were of other types of commercial establishments. The average value of the property reported stolen varies from $109 for service station robberies to $3,789 for bank robberies.

In the Commission survey the picture that emerges for victimization by robbery is similar to that for burglary, which occurs more frequently. Among the organizations that were robbed, 80 percent reported only one robbery but 2 percent had as many as five. While any business in a high crime rate area is obviously in danger, it appears that some businesses, like some people, are more likely than others to be victimized by crime. Clearly, the reasons for the differences need investigation as guides in prevention. The findings of the President's Commission on Crime in the District of Columbia with respect to the circumstances of housebreaking are suggestive of the way risks vary:

In 21 (7 percent) of the 313 commercial burglaries surveyed

144

housebreakers entered through unlocked doors and in 70 instances (22 percent) through unlocked windows. In 111 instances the housebreakers broke windows to gain entry, and locks were forced in 95. A total of 105 of the commercial establishments victimized were reported to have had burglar-resistant locks; 65 of these establishments, however, were entered other than by tampering with the lock. Sixty-four percent of the burglarized commercial establishments were located on the first floor.

Shoplifting. Shoplifting usually involves the theft of relatively small and inexpensive articles, although the professional shoplifter may steal expensive furs, clothes, and jewelry. It is heaviest in the chainstores and other larger stores which do the most retail business. However, it is the smaller establishments, particularly those that operate on a low margin of profit, to which shoplifting may make the difference between success and failure.

In the Commission survey, 35 percent of the neighborhood wholesale and retail establishments surprisingly reported no problem with shoplifting, while sizable percentages of other types of businesses, such as construction companies (30 percent), manufacturers of nondurables (33 percent), finance, insurance, and real estate firms (25 percent), which might not be expected to have any problem, reported some shoplifting difficulties. The average amount of shoplifting experienced by the nontrade establishments was considerably less than that for retail establishments.

As one might expect, the highest rates of shoplifting were reported in the high crime rate districts. The most common items carried off by shoplifters were food, liquor or beer, clothing and footwear, and miscellaneous small items worth less than $10. However, it is the total volume, rather than individual acts, that makes shoplifting a serious problem for most commercial enterprises.

Nationally most large retail businesses estimate their overall inventory shrinkage due to shoplifting, employee theft, and accounting errors at between 1 and 2 percent of total inventory. Experts in industrial and commercial security estimate that 75 to 80 percent of the inventory shrinkage is probably attributable to some type of dishonesty. Among the neighborhood businesses found by the Commission survey to have high rates of shoplifting, 60 percent placed their losses at less than 2 percent of total inventory; another 28 percent estimated they had lost between 2 and 6 percent. Surprisingly, 23 percent were unable to give any estimate at all of the amount of their losses due to shoplifting.

Employee Theft. According to security experts for retail and other commercial establishments, theft by employees accounts for a considerably larger volume of theft than shoplifting. Theft of merchandise or equipment by employees is particularly hard to control because detection is so difficult. Employees have opportunities for theft every working day, whereas the shoplifting customer cannot steal merchandise regularly from the same establishment without arousing suspicion.

Employee theft is also a problem in many industrial concerns. A recent survey by the National Industrial Conference Board of 473 companies indicated that 20 percent of all companies and nearly 30 percent of those with more than 1,000 employees had a serious problem with employee theft of tools, equipment, materials or company products. More than half of the companies with a problem of employee theft indicated trouble with both white and blue collar workers.

In neighborhood establishments surveyed by the Commission only 14 percent reported the discovery of any employee dishonesty. Among those, 40 percent estimated losses at no more than $50 a year. Most managers or owners surveyed attempted to establish the honesty of employees before hiring them. Nearly one-third made an effort to check references or to clear the employee with the local police department but 74 percent did not report to the police the discovery of theft by their own employees, preferring to discharge the employee or handle the matter in some other way by themselves.

CRIME AGAINST PUBLIC ORGANIZATIONS AND UTILITIES

Public organizations and utilities are repeatedly victimized by crime. While some of the crime committed against these organizations is reported to the police, it is not clear just how much goes unreported and how widespread it is.

To obtain some estimation, the Commission surveyed 48 such organizations in Boston, Chicago, and Washington with special attention to the police districts in which other surveys were being conducted.

The most prevalent and persistent problem reported was vandalism of buildings and equipment. Telephone companies, electric companies, schools, libraries, traffic and highway departments, parks, public transportation, and housing all are victims. Estimates of damage ranging up to $200,000 a year were quoted for such facilities as public housing, transportation, public parks, and recreation facilities in schools. The public school system in Washington, D.C., for example, provided data for 1965 showing a total of 26,500 window panes broken and replaced at a cost of $118,000. A similar report was received in Boston.

Larceny was also a frequently mentioned problem, involving such thefts as stealing loose equipment and personal possessions, theft from coin meters, and breaking and entering. Some organizations make a distinction between amateur and professional theft. For example, the telephone companies distinguish between the organized coinbox larceny using forged keys and the amateur forcible entry involving damage to the equipment. Employee theft was not reported as a serious problem except in hospitals where it represents the most common reason for the apprehension and discharge of employees.

Many public facilities reported problems with various forms of violence within their boundaries. Assaults and child molestation occur in parks, libraries, and schools. Emergency rooms of hospitals cited disturbances by drunken and disorderly persons. The threat of violent behavior or the presence of disorderly persons was reported to affect markedly the patronage of parks, libraries and after-school activities, especially in areas with high crime rates.

CHARACTERISTICS OF OFFENDERS

There is a common belief that the general population consists of a large group of law-abiding people and a small body of criminals. However, studies have shown that most people, when they are asked, remember having committed offenses for which they might have been sentenced if they had been apprehended. These studies of "self-reported" crime have generally been of juveniles or young adults, mostly college and high school students. They uniformly show that delinquent or criminal acts are committed by people at all levels of society. Most people admit to relatively petty delinquent acts, but many report larcenies, auto thefts, burglaries, and assaults of a more serious nature.

One of the few studies of this type dealing with criminal behavior by adults was a sample of almost 1,700 persons, most of them from the State of New York. In this study, 1,020 males and 670 females were asked which of 49 offenses they had committed. The list included felonies and misdemeanors, other than traffic offenses, for which they might have been sentenced under the adult criminal code.

Ninety-one percent of the respondents admitted they had committed one or more offenses for which they might have received jail or prison sentences. Thirteen percent of the males admitted to grand larceny, 26 percent to auto theft,

147

and 17 percent to burglary. Sixty-four percent of the males and 27 percent of the females committed at least one felony for which they had not been apprehended. Although some of these offenses may have been reported to the police by the victims and would thus appear in official statistics as "crimes known to the police," these offenders would not show up in official arrest statistics.

Such persons are part of the "hidden" offender group. They evidently at one time or another found themselves in situations that led them to violate the criminal law. However, most people do not persist in committing offenses. For many the risk of arrest and prosecution is deterrence enough, while others develop a stake in a law-abiding way of life in which their youthful "indiscretions" no longer have a place.

What is known today about offenders is confined almost wholly to those who have been arrested, tried, and sentenced. The criminal justice process may be viewed as a large-scale screening system. At each stage it tries to sort out the better risks to return to the general population. The further along in the process that a sample of offenders is selected, the more likely they are to show major social and personal problems.

From arrest records, probation reports, and prison statistics a "portrait" of the offender emerges that progressively highlights the disadvantaged character of his life. The offender at the end of the road in prison is likely to be a member of the lowest social and economic groups in the country, poorly educated and perhaps unemployed, unmarried, reared in a broken home, and to have a prior criminal record. This is a formidable list of personal and social problems that must be overcome in order to restore offenders to law-abiding existence. Not all offenders, of course, fit this composite profile, as a more detailed examination of the arrest, probation, and prison data reveals.

ARREST DATA ON OFFENDERS

National arrest statistics, based on unpublished estimates for the total population, show that when all offenses are considered together the majority of offenders arrested are white, male, and over 24 years of age. Offenders over 24 make up the great majority of persons arrested for fraud, embezzlement, gambling, drunkenness, offenses against the family, and vagrancy. For many other crimes the peak age of criminality occurs below 24.

The 15-to-17-year-old group is the highest for burglaries, larcenies and auto theft. For these three offenses, 15-year-

148

olds are arrested more often than persons of any other age with 16-year-olds a close second. For the three common property offenses the rate of arrest per 100,000 persons 15 to 17 in 1965 was 2,467 as compared to a rate of 55 for every 100,000 persons 50 years old and over. For crimes of violence the peak years are those from 18 to 20, followed closely by the 21 to 24 group. Rates for these groups are 300 and 297 as compared with 24 for the 50-year-old and over group.

One of the sharpest contrasts of all in the arrest statistics on offenders is that between males and females. Males are arrested nearly seven times as frequently as females for Index offenses plus larceny under $50. The rate for males is 1,097 per 100,000 population and the corresponding rate for females is 164. The difference is even greater when all offenses are considered.

The differences in the risks of arrest for males and females seem to be diminishing, however. Since 1960 the rate of arrest for females has been increasing faster than the rate for males. In 1960 the male arrest rate for Index offenses plus larceny under $50 was 926 per 100,000 and in 1965 it was 1,097, an increase in the rate of 18 percent. However, the female rate increased by 62 percent during this same period, from 101 per 100,000 females to 164. Most of the increase was due to the greatly increased rate of arrest of women for larcenies. The larceny arrest rate for women increased 81 percent during this same period in marked contrast to an increase of 4 percent for aggravated assault, the next highest category of arrest for women among these offenses.

The factor of race is almost as important as that of sex in determining whether a person is likely to be arrested and imprisoned for an offense. Many more whites than Negroes are arrested every year but Negroes have a significantly higher rate of arrest in every offense category except certain offenses against public order and morals. For Index offenses plus larceny under $50 the rate per 100,000 Negroes in 1965 was four times as great as that for whites (1,696 to 419).

In general, the disparity of rates for offenses of violence is much greater than comparable differences between the races for offenses against property. For instance, the Negro arrest rate for murder is 24.1 compared to 2.5 for whites, or almost 10 times as high. This is in contrast to the difference between Negroes and whites for crimes against property. For example, the rate of Negro arrest (378) for burglary is only about 3½ times as high as that for whites (107). The statistics also show that the difference between the white and Negro arrest

149

rates is generally greater for those over 18 years of age than for those under 18. Negroes over 18 are arrested about 5 times as often as whites (1,684 to 325). In contrast, the ratio for those under 18 is approximately three to one (1,689 to 591).

The differences between the Negro and white arrest rates for certain crimes of violence have been growing smaller between 1960 and 1965. During that period, considering together the crimes of murder, rape, and aggravated assault, the rate for Negroes increased 5 percent while the rate for whites increased 27 percent. In the case of robbery, however, the white rate increased 3 percent while the Negro rate increased 24 percent. For the crimes of burglary, larceny, and auto theft the Negro rate increased 33 percent while the white rate increased 24 percent.

Many studies have been made seeking to account for these differences in arrest rates for Negroes and whites. They have found that the differences become very small when comparisons are made between the rates for whites and Negroes living under similar conditions. However, it has proved difficult to make such comparisons, since Negroes generally encounter more barriers to economic and social advancement than whites do. Even when Negroes and whites live in the same area the Negroes are likely to have poorer housing, lower incomes, and fewer job prospects. The Commission is of the view that if conditions of equal opportunity prevailed, the large differences now found between the Negro and white arrest rates would disappear.

PROBATION DATA ON OFFENDERS

Arrest statistics supply only a limited amount of information about offenders. More detailed descriptions can be obtained from the probation records maintained by the courts. An illustration of what such records reveal is provided in a report by the Stanford Research Institute to the President's Commission on Crime in the District of Columbia. The study examined the background characteristics contained in the probation records of a sample of 932 felons convicted during the years 1964 and 1965 in Washington, D.C.

Among those offenders for whom income information was available, 90 percent had incomes of less than $5,000. At the time of the 1960 census, 56 percent of the adult population in Washington earned less than $5,000. The highest median incomes were found among those who had been convicted of forgery, fraud, and embezzlement. Of the sample, 78 percent were Negroes, as contrasted with an estimated 61 percent of Negroes in the population of Washington. The median age of arrest was 29.2 years, and approximately three-fourths of the sample was between 18 and 34 years, a proportion very much higher than that for the same age group in the general population of the District. Adult criminal records were found in 80 percent of the cases. More than half, 52 percent, had six or more prior arrests and 65 percent had previously been confined in some type of juvenile or adult institution.

The picture that emerges from this data is of a group of young adult males who come from disorganized families, who have had limited access to educational and occupational opportunities, and who have been frequently involved in difficulties with the police and the courts, both as juveniles and adults.

PRISON DATA ON OFFENDERS

An even more disadvantaged population can be identified from the characteristics of prisoners tabulated in the 1960 U.S. Census of Population. Every 10 years, the census lists the characteristics of persons in custodial institutions, including Federal and State prisons and local jails and workhouses. These tabulations show the median years of school completed for the State and Federal prison and reformatory population is 8.6 years, in contrast to 10.6 years for the general population in the country. It also shows that 23.9 percent of the offenders were laborers, compared to 5.1 percent in the total population. Only 5.8 percent of the offender population engaged in high status occupations, such as professional, technical work, manager, official, proprietor, and similar groupings, compared to 20.6 percent of the general population. Prisoners are also much more likely to be unmarried than other males 14 or over in the general population. Only 31.1 percent of the prisoners are married compared to 69.1 percent of males generally. The comparable rates for single status are 43.7 percent and 25.1 percent, and for separated, widowed and divorced, 24.6 and 7.2.

RECIDIVISM

The most striking fact about offenders who have been convicted of the common serious crimes of violence and theft is how often how many of them continue committing crimes. Arrest, court, and prison records furnish insistent testimony to the fact that these repeated offenders constitute the hard core of the crime problem. One of the longest and most pains-taking followup studies was conducted by Sheldon and Eleanor Glueck on a sample of 510 Massachusetts reformatory inmates released between 1911 and 1922. It showed that 32 percent of the men who could be followed over a 15-year period repeatedly committed serious crimes during this period, and many others did so intermittently.

A recent study of adults granted probation by 56 of the 58 county courts in California from 1956 to 1958 showed that by the end of 1962, 28 percent of the more than 11,000 probationers had been taken off probation because almost half of them had committed new offenses, and others had absconded or would not comply with regulations. Because judges select the better risks for probation, one would expect that men discharged or paroled from prison would be more likely to commit further crimes, and the facts show that they do. A California study of parolees released from 1946 through 1949 found that 43 percent had been reimprisoned by the end of 1952; almost half for committing further felonies and the rest (almost one-third of whom were thought also to have committed further felonies) for other parole violations.

A review of a number of such studies in the various States and in the Federal prison system leads to the conclusion that despite considerable variation among jurisdictions, roughly a third of the offenders released from prison will be reimprisoned, usually for committing new offenses, within a 5-year period. The most frequent recidivists are those who commit such property crimes as burglary, auto theft, forgery, or larceny, but robbers and narcotics offenders also repeat frequently. Those who are least likely to commit new crimes after release are persons convicted of serious crimes of violence—murder, rape, and aggravated assault.

These findings are based on the crimes of released offenders that officials learn about. Undoubtedly many new offenses are not discovered. Furthermore released offenders continue to come to the attention of the police, even though not always charged or convicted for new offenses. A 2-year followup by the UCR of the arrest records of 6,907 offenders released from the Federal system between January and June 1963 shows that 48 percent had been arrested for new offenses by June 1965. Complete figures on the percent convicted are not available.

Studies made of the careers of adult offenders regularly show the importance of juvenile delinquency as a forerunner of adult crime. They support the conclusions that the earlier a juvenile is arrested or brought to court for an offense, the more likely he is to carry on criminal activity into adult life; that the more serious the first offense for which a juvenile is arrested, the more likely he is to continue to commit serious crimes, especially in the case of major crimes against property; and that the more frequently and extensively a juvenile is processed by the police, court, and correctional system the more likely he is to be arrested, charged, convicted, and imprisoned as an adult. These studies also show that the most frequent pattern among adult offenders is one that starts with petty stealing and progresses to much more serious property offenses—a process of escalation that is described more fully in chapter 11 of this report.

THE PROFESSIONAL CRIMINAL

Professional criminals think of themselves as very different from the habitual, amateur offenders whose persistent criminality resembles their own, but who do not have the skills or contacts to make a good living at crime in comparative safety from the law. Professional criminals engage in a wide variety of common law property offenses, including those involving the use of force or its threat and those in which the stealing is accomplished by stealth or by manipulating the victim. They spend their full time and their full energies on crimes. Often they may be hired to do special jobs by the established figures in the world of organized crime, but they are not regarded as permanently a part of that world.

A pilot study of professional crime in four cities sponsored by the Commission found that the way the professional criminal spends his time varies with his standing in the profession. The small-time professional spends virtually all of his time directly engaged in crime. He develops criminal opportunities, sells goods he has stolen, or procures tools or equipment needed for his next "job." It is an active but relatively planless life of crime on a day-by-day basis.

The more successful professional criminals spend a greater proportion of their time on planning and other preparation. A single promising "caper" can take weeks or months to plan and execute. But this calculation pays off in higher "scores" and lower risks of arrest. The most successful professional gangs even employ specialists to develop criminal prospects for them.

Although all professionals probably are more technically competent than most, if not all, habitual or amateur criminals, they differ widely in their professional abilities. At one end of the spectrum are the big-time jewel thieves and the

153

"big con" men who manipulate wealthy victims into parting with hundreds of thousands of dollars. At the other are the petty thieves, "short con" operators, pickpockets, and shoplifters.

The Commission's study found that professional criminals, particularly the less successful, generally do not operate in the same groups or gangs over sustained periods. Different technical skills are needed for different crimes and circumstances. To meet this fluctuating need for skills there is an "employment" system operating out of the bars and restaurants that professional criminals habituate. These places serve as job placement centers.

Even professional crime is a risky business. The Commission's study found that the professional criminal's need for ready capital often opens him to severe exploitation by loansharks. Most often this problem arises as a consequence of an arrest. To meet the cost of the premium for his bond and initial legal fees he must engage in more frequent criminal activity, often more risky than his ordinary line of work. If rearrested he will have additional costs, and this pattern may be repeated many times over before the professional is brought to trial.

Professional crime could not exist except for two essential relationships with legitimate society: The "fence" and the "fix." These are the mutually profitable arrangements between professional criminals and members of legitimate society. The fence arranges the redistribution of stolen goods; the fix gives the professional criminal sufficient immunity from law enforcement agencies to enable him to practice his profession with reasonable safety.

The professional thief aims to sell stolen goods. Although professional thieves often retail their own stolen wares, many sell to receivers of stolen goods, who resell them. Sale to a fence may cost the thief 75 percent of the value of the goods, but it reduces the risk of their being stolen from him or of his being arrested with them in his possession. He also avoids the risks involved in the retail process. In addition, large quantities of goods, goods that are perishable or otherwise quickly lose their value, and goods for which there is a specialized demand, require a division of labor and level of organization beyond the capacity of an individual thief.

Fencing takes care of one problem of the professional criminal, but the fix is even more important to him. The professional's connections and the problems to be solved determine whether he deals directly with the official himself, uses an attorney as an intermediary or deals with the local fixer who has political connections and may be tied in with organized crime. Provided he can pay the price, the professional is often able to purchase excellent protection.

Professional crime ordinarily uses cash as the bribe, but sometimes a case may be fixed on credit or as a favor. Often professional criminals offer enforcement authorities testimony or information in return for a dismissed or reduced charge. This may be a "fix" in the criminal view, but to law enforcement it is an indispensable and legitimate means of combatting crime.

Unquestionably professional criminals, because they work regularly at crime, account for a large share of thefts, particularly the costly thefts, that occur. The control of this type of criminality requires new forms of police intelligence operations, which some police departments are beginning to develop. Furthermore, this type of work needs to be supplemented by much more intensive research on professional criminality as a way of life.

"WHITE-COLLAR" OFFENDERS AND BUSINESS CRIME

Inevitably, crimes reflect the opportunities people have to commit them. Whether a person has access to a criminal opportunity or not depends very much on who he is, what work he does and where he lives. Most of the crimes discussed in this report, those that have most aroused the public, are the common crimes of violence or theft that threaten people in the streets and in their homes. These are the crimes that are the easiest for the poor and the disadvantaged to commit; they are the crimes they do commit as the arrest statistics and the information about offenders on probation, parole, or in prison clearly disclose. They also are the crimes that make up the greatest part of the cases processed by the higher criminal courts.

However, there is another set of crimes that are connected with the occupational positions people have. They are committed in the course of performing the activities of particular occupations and exist as opportunities only for people in those occupations. Within this great reservoir of actual and potential crimes, the rather vague term "white-collar crime" is now commonly used to designate those occupational crimes committed in the course of their work by persons of high status and social repute. It thus differentiates these offenders and their crimes from those committed by low-status or disreputable persons.

The "white-collar" criminal is the broker who distributes

155

fraudulent securities, the builder who deliberately uses defective material, the corporation executive who conspires to fix prices, the legislator who peddles his influence and vote for private gain, or the banker who misappropriates funds in his keeping. Arrest, court, or prison statistics furnish little information about the frequency and distribution of these offenses or about the characteristics of these offenders. The reason is that they are only rarely dealt with through the full force of criminal sanctions. This is an area of criminal activity where the standards of what is right and what is wrong are still evolving, and where society is still testing the effectiveness of less drastic sanctions for controlling undesirable conduct on the part of individuals or corporations. The newness, complexity and difficulties of control of many aspects of the "white-collar" crime problem can be seen most clearly when the offender is not an individual but a corporation.

During the last few centuries economic life has become vastly more complex. Individual families or groups of families are not sulf-sufficient; they rely for the basic necessities of life on thousands or even millions of different people, each with a specialized function, many of whom live hundreds or thousands of miles away. The manufacture and distribution of goods and the provision of services at low cost and high quality has resulted in giant business enterprises with billions of dollars in assets and in unions with hundreds of thousands of members.

Until the late 19th century, the economic life of this country was largely unregulated. At that time, the depredations of the "robber barons" made clear that business enterprise had to be regulated in order to protect not only the public but business itself. Regulations also became necessary for other purposes: to raise standards of health and safety, to stabilize prices in wartime, to assist the poor and ignorant to obtain decent housing and other necessities, and to maintain the economy at a high level of production.

And so today virtually every aspect of business life is regulated in some way. There are antitrust laws, food-and-drug laws, safety and health laws, licensing provisions for numerous kinds of businesses, housing codes, and a multitude of other regulatory statutes. Some of them, like the antitrust laws, are sometimes enforced through criminal sanctions. The defendant is tried in a criminal court under criminal rules of procedure and, if an individual, can be sentenced to imprisonment or a fine, or, if a corporation, to a fine. Less serious violations, of housing codes for example, are minor offenses handled in the lower courts and punished usually by small

156

fines. On the other hand, many regulatory laws, such as some labor laws, are enforced by administrative agencies outside the criminal system. Typically, the agency holds a hearing and, if a violation is found, either itself imposes or asks the courts to impose an administrative remedy. This remedy might be an order to abandon an improper practice or suspension of a license. Frequently, such remedies are enforced by court injunction. Noncompliance with administrative or court orders may be a violation of the criminal law. While there is considerable debate as to what regulatory laws should be deemed criminal in nature the crucial fact is that these laws are violated on a vast scale, sometimes in deliberate disregard of the law, sometimes because businessmen, in their effort to come as close to the line between legality and illegality as possible, overstep it.

It is impossible to ascertain even approximately the amount of business crime because it is almost certain that only a small proportion of it is detected. However, its pervasiveness is suggested by two studies. Edwin H. Sutherland examined decisions of the courts and regulatory commissions under the antitrust, false advertising, patent, copyright, and labor laws as they applied to 70 of the Nation's largest corporations over their history averaging approximately 45 years. He found that 980 adverse decisions had been rendered against these corporations. Every one of the 70 corporations had at least 1 decision against it; 98 percent of the 70 corporations had 2 or more decisions against them; 90 percent had 4 or more decisions against them. About 60 percent of the 70 corporations had been convicted by criminal courts; the average number of convictions per corporation was 4. Another study examined black-market violations during World War II. It indicated that approximately 1 in every 15 of the 3 million business concerns in the country had serious sanctions imposed on them for violations of price regulations. The evidence suggested further that the total volume of violations was much larger than was indicated by officially imposed sanctions.

Business crime imposes three kinds of costs on society. First, physical injury or even death can come from tainted foods and harmful drugs sold in violation of the Pure Food and Drug Act, foods sold in violation of local health laws, and various violations of safety laws and housing codes.

Second, financial losses are produced, for example, by the marketing of worthless, defective, or injurious products in violation of Post Office Department regulations, by frauds that violate the rules of the Securities and Exchange Commission, and by the sale of goods based on misrepresentation in advertising. The price-fixing by 29 electrical equipment companies alone probably cost utilities, and therefore, the public, more money than is reported as stolen by burglars in a year.

Third, as serious as the physical and financial costs of corporate crime may be, it is probable that they are less serious than the damage it does to the Nation's social, economic, and political institutions. Restraint of trade tends to undermine the principles of free enterprise that the antitrust laws are intended to protect. For example, the damage from the price-fixing conspiracy in the electrical equipment industry was not limited to the direct extra costs imposed. As Judge T. Cullen Ganey declared in sentencing the defendants: "This is a shocking indictment of a vast section of our economy, for what is really at stake here is the survival of the kind of economy under which this country has grown great, the free enterprise system."

Serious erosion of morals accompanies violations of this nature. It is reasonable to assume that prestigious companies that flout the law set an example for other businesses and influence individuals, particularly young people, to commit other kinds of crime on the ground that everyone is taking what he can get. If businessmen who are respected as leaders of the community can do such things as break the antitrust laws or rent dilapidated houses to the poor at high rents, it is hard to convince the young that they should be honest.

Reducing the scope of business crime is peculiarly difficult. The offenses are often extremely hard to detect, especially since there is often no victim but the general public, or at least victims do not know that they have been victimized. Merely determining whether or not an offense has been committed frequently involves extremely complicated factual investigation and legal judgment.

Perhaps most important, the public tends to be indifferent to business crime or even to sympathize with the offenders when they have been caught. As one executive convicted and sentenced to jail in the electrical equipment conspiracy said: "On the bright side for me personally have been the letters and calls from people all over the country, the community, the shops and offices here, expressing confidence in me and support. This demonstration has been a warm and humbling experience for me." It is unlikely that a convicted burglar would receive such letters and calls.

The Commission has not been able to investigate in detail the many different kinds of business crime and anti-social conduct and so it cannot recommend specific measures for coping with them. This would require separate analysis of virtually every aspect of the American economy and its regulatory laws. However, it is clear that such studies are needed to improve enforcement of statutes governing many kinds of business practice. The studies should conduct research into the scope of illegal and immoral conduct; consider noncriminal sanctions to deal with it; propose methods for strengthening administrative agencies; explore the need for higher penalties, including both fines and jail sentences, for serious violations; and discover whether new substantive law is needed to deal with harmful activity that is not, or may not, now be illegal.

Most important, however, it is essential that the public becomes aware of the seriousness of business crime. Without such awareness and the resulting demands for action, legislatures, courts, and administrative agencies will continue, as is now usually the case, to treat business offenses as relatively minor mistakes. The laws relating to business activities should be enforced as vigorously as those relating to the more traditional forms of crime.

PUBLIC ATTITUDES TOWARDS CRIME AND LAW ENFORCEMENT

What America does about crime depends ultimately upon how Americans see crime. The government of a free society can act only in response to the desires of the governed. This is true in general and in detail. The Nation's overall effort against crime will be only as intense as the public demands that it be. The lines along which the Nation takes specific action against crime will be those that the public believes to be the necessary ones.

A chief reason that this Commission was organized was that there is widespread public anxiety about crime. In one sense, this entire report is an effort to focus that anxiety on the central problems of crime and criminal justice. A necessary part of that effort has been to study as carefully as possible the anxiety itself. The Commission has tried to find out precisely what aspects of crime Americans are anxious about, whether their anxiety is a realistic response to actual danger, how anxiety affects the daily lives of Americans, what actions against crime by the criminal justice system and the government as a whole might best allay public anxiety. It included questions about attitudes toward crime and law enforcement in the surveys of victimization it made, and it looked hard, as well, at those national opinion polls that asked questions about crime.

Before setting forth the results of these studies and discussing the conclusions that might be drawn from them, the Commission must make one general comment. There is reason to be alarmed about crime. In fact just because crime is alarming, those discussing it—and many people must discuss it often if it is ever to be controlled—have an obligation to be cool, factual, and precise. Thoughtless, emotional, or self-serving discussions of crime, especially by those who have the public's attention and can influence the public's thinking, are an immense disservice. They do not and cannot lead to significant action against crime. They can, and sometimes do, lead to panic.

PUBLIC CONCERN ABOUT CRIME

The public sees crime as one of the most serious of all domestic problems. The Commission's NORC survey asked citizens to pick from a list of six major domestic problems the one they were paying the most attention to. As table 16

Table 16.—Most Important Domestic Problem by Race and Income

Domestic problem	Percent white		Percent nonwhite	
	Under $6,000	Over $6,000	Under $6,000	Over $6,000
Poverty	9	5	7	8
Inflation	15	17	4	4
Education	12	19	23	21
Crime	27	22	19	22
Race relations	29	34	32	38
Unemployment	8	3	15	7
Total	100	100	100	100
Number	(3,925)	(6,461)	(1,033)	(462)

SOURCE: NORC survey.

shows, crime was second to race relations as the most frequently mentioned problem, except in the case of nonwhites with annual incomes less than $6,000; they placed education second and crime third.

Crime is linked to other social problems by many people. In a 1964 Harris survey more people attributed increased

160

crime in their neighborhood to "disturbed and restless teenagers" than to any other cause. A part of the crime problem that especially worries people is juvenile delinquency. A typical finding was reported by a Gallup poll in 1963. When persons were asked to name the top problems in their community from a list of 39 problems, "juvenile delinquency" was the second most frequent selection—exceeded only by complaints about local real estate taxes. Also related to the problems of youth was a third frequently chosen problem—the need for more recreation areas.

However, people are more inclined to think of crime in moral than in social terms. An August 1965 Gallup poll that asked people what they thought was responsible for the increase of crime found that most of the reasons people mentioned had to do directly with the moral character of the population rather than with changes in objective circumstances or with law enforcement. Over half of the answers fitted under the category "family, poor parental guidance." About 6 percent of the answers gave "breakdown of moral standards." A variety of other directly moral causes were given in addition, such as: "People expect too much," "people want something for nothing," and "communism." Relatively few (12 percent) of the responses cited objective conditions such as "unemployment," "poverty," "the automobile," or "the population explosion."

Public concern about crime is mounting. National polls by Harris and Gallup show that the majority of people think the situation in their own communities is getting worse, that a substantial minority think the situation is staying about the same, and that almost no one thinks the situation is improving. A Gallup survey in April 1965 showed that this pessimistic view of the crime trend was held by men and women of all ages, incomes, and degrees of education in all parts of the country. In July 1966, Harris surveys reported that in each recent year there has been an increase over the year before in the percent of persons worried about their personal safety on the streets.

PERSONAL FEAR OF CRIME

Perhaps the most intense concern about crime is the fear of being attacked by a stranger when out alone. One-third of Americans feel unsafe about walking alone at night in their own neighborhoods, according to the NORC survey. As one would expect, the percentage of people feeling unsafe at night on the street is, according to an April 1965 Gallup survey, higher in larger cities than in smaller ones and higher in cities than in rural areas.

Recently studies have been undertaken to develop an index of delinquency based on the seriousness of different offenses. They have shown that there is widespread public consensus on the relative seriousness of different types of crimes and these rankings furnish useful indicators of the types of crime that the public is most concerned about. Offenses involving physical assaults against the person are the most feared crimes and the greatest concern is expressed about those in which a weapon is used.

A further index of the public concern about crime may be found in attitudes toward reporting crime when it occurs. Whether one reports a crime or not involves in many cases an assessment of the significance of the event to one's self or others. The results from the victim surveys indicate that the reporting of crime varies directly with a rough scale of seriousness of the offense in the public view. Other than vehicle theft, the crimes that are likely to be reported most frequently are crimes of violence, particularly those that cause great physical harm or psychological shock. Such acts as petty larceny, malicious mischief, and fraud, though the most frequent offenses as a group, are also considered the least serious and are the least likely to be reported to the police.

Fear of crime makes many people want to move their homes. In the four police precincts surveyed for the Commission in Boston and Chicago, 20 percent of the citizens wanted to move because of the crime in their neighborhoods, and as many as 30 percent wanted to move out of the highest crime rate district in Boston.

Fear of crime shows variations by race and income. In the survey in Washington, the Bureau of Social Science Research put together an index of anxiety about crime. It found that Negro women had the highest average score, followed by Negro men, white women, and white men. Anxiety scores were lower at the higher income levels for both Negroes and whites.

Fear of crime is not always highest in the areas where official crime rates are highest or where rates of victimization based on the survey findings are highest. For example, the BSSR Washington study found that the average level of concern with crime in a predominately Negro police precinct that has one of the highest crime rates in the city, according to police data, was lower than it was in another Negro precinct that had a very low rate relative to the first.

The surveys uniformly show that people feel safer in their

own neighborhoods even if they actually have a higher crime rate than other areas. For example, the national survey revealed that crime is seen as a problem most characteristic of other places. Sixty percent of those questioned compared their own neighborhoods favorably to other parts of their communities with regard to the likelihood that their homes would be broken into. Only 14 percent thought their own neighborhoods were more dangerous. Similarly, two-thirds of the respondents said they felt safe walking alone after dark if they were in their own neighborhoods. On the other hand, when persons interviewed were asked whether there were places outside their neighborhoods where they would not feel personally safe, 53 percent said there were, and almost one-third of these respondents said they never go there.

A tendency to see the risk of victimization as greater in another neighborhood than one's own was also found among residents in high crime rate precincts by the BSSR survey in Washington. The surveys in Boston and Chicago showed that 73 percent of the respondents thought their own neighborhoods were very safe or average compared to other neighborhoods in relation to the chances of getting robbed, threatened, beaten up, or anything of that sort.

The NORC survey asked people whether there have been times recently when they wanted to go somewhere in town but stayed at home instead, because they thought it would be unsafe to go there. Sixteen percent of the respondents said that they had stayed home under these conditions. This type of reaction showed marked variation with race; one out of every three Negro respondents had stayed home as contrasted with one in eight whites.

People also take special measures at home because of the fear of unwanted intruders. The national survey showed that 82 percent of the respondents always kept their doors locked at night and 25 percent always kept their doors locked even in the daytime when the family members were at home. Twenty-eight percent kept watchdogs and 37 percent said they kept firearms in the house for protection, among other reasons.

The special city surveys disclosed that a substantial number of people take other measures to protect themselves from crime. In Boston and Chicago 28 percent had put new locks on their doors primarily, as one might expect, because they had been victimized or were worried about the high crime rate in the area. Another 10 percent had put locks or bars on their windows; this occurred primarily in the highest crime rate areas. Nine percent said they carried weapons, usually knives, when they went out, and this figure rose to 19 percent in the highest crime rate district in Boston.

The close relationship between worry about crime and the taking of strong precautionary measures is further demonstrated by the results from the national survey. Respondents were asked how much they worried about being victimized by robbery or burglary and their responses were related to their tendency to take strong household security measures. Persons worried about both burglary and robbery are most likely to take such precautions, about 50 percent more likely than those who are worried about neither.

Perhaps the most revealing findings on the impact of fear of crime on people's lives were the changes people reported in their regular habits of life. In the high-crime districts surveyed in Boston and Chicago, for example, five out of every eight respondents reported changes in their habits because of fear of crime, some as many as four or five major changes. Forty-three percent reported they stayed off the streets at night altogether. Another 21 percent said they always used cars or taxis at night. Thirty-five percent said they would not talk to strangers any more.

One of the most curious findings of the surveys was that fear of crime is less closely associated with having been a victim of crime than might be supposed. The national survey showed that victims tended to have somewhat more worry about burglary or robbery. This was true for both males and females as can be seen in table 17. However, females,

Table 17.—Concern of Victims and Nonvictims About Burglary or Robbery

[In percentages]

Worry about burglary or robbery	Victim	Nonvictim
Males:		
Worried	69	59
Not worried	31	41
	100	100
Number of males	(1,456)	(3,930)
Females:		
Worried	84	77
Not worried	16	23
	100	100
Number of females	(2,399)	(6,189)

Source: NORC survey.

164

whether they had been victimized or not, were more concerned about their safety than males. Furthermore, other data show that recent experience of being a victim of crime did not seem to increase behavior designed to protect the home. Almost identical proportions, 57 percent of victims and 58 percent of nonvictims, took strong household security measures.

In its Washington study BSSR found similar results. An index of exposure to crime was developed based on having personally witnessed offenses or on whether one's self or one's friends had been victimized. Scores on this index, in general, were not associated with responses to a variety of questions on attitudes toward crime and toward law enforcement that respondents were asked. Nor did exposure to crime appear to determine the anxiety about crime manifested in the interviews. The one exception appeared in the case of the Negro male. Negro men showed a tendency to be influenced in their attitudes and behavior by their actual exposure to crime.

CONCLUSIONS

The Commission cannot say that the public's fear of crime is exaggerated. It is not prepared to tell people how fearful they should be; that is something each person must decide for himself. People's fears must be respected; certainly they cannot be legislated. Some people are willing to run risks that terrify others. However, it is possible to draw some general conclusions from the findings of the surveys.

The first is that the public fears most the crimes that occur least often, crimes of violence. People are much more tolerant of crimes against property, which constitute most of the crimes that are committed against persons or households or businesses. Actually, the average citizen probably suffers the greatest economic loss from crimes against business establishments and public institutions, which pass their losses on to him in the form of increased prices and taxes. Nevertheless, most shoplifters never get to court; they are released by the store managers with warnings. Most employees caught stealing are either warned or discharged, according to the reports of businesses and organizations in the Commission's survey in three cities.

Second, the fear of crimes of violence is not a simple fear of injury or death or even of all crimes of violence, but, at bottom, a fear of strangers. The personal injury that Americans risk daily from sources other than crime are enormously greater. The annual rate of all Index offenses involving either violence or the threat of violence is 1.8 per 1,000 Americans. This is minute relative to the total accidental injuries calling for medical attention or restricted activity of 1 day or more, as reported by the Public Health Service. A recent study of emergency medical care found the quality, numbers, and distribution of ambulances and other emergency services severely deficient, and estimated that as many as 20,000 Americans die unnecessarily each year as a result of improper emergency care. The means necessary for correcting this situation are very clear and would probably yield greater immediate return in reducing death than would expenditures for reducing the incidence of crimes of violence. But a different personal significance is attached to deaths due to the willful acts of felons as compared to the incompetence or poor equipment of emergency medical personnel.

Furthermore, this chapter has noted that most murders and assaults are committed by persons known to the victim, by relatives, friends, or acquaintances. Indeed on a straight statistical basis, the closer the relationship the greater the hazard. In one sense the greatest threat to anyone is himself, since suicides are more than twice as common as homicides.

Third, this fear of strangers has greatly impoverished the lives of many Americans, especially those who live in high-crime neighborhoods in large cities. People stay behind the locked doors of their homes rather than risk walking in the streets at night. Poor people spend money on taxis because they are afraid to walk or use public transportation. Sociable people are afraid to talk to those they do not know. In short, society is to an increasing extent suffering from what economists call "opportunity costs" as the result of fear of crime. For example, administrators and officials interviewed for the Commission by the University of Michigan survey team, report that library use is decreasing because borrowers are afraid to come out at night. School officials told of parents not daring to attend PTA meetings in the evening, and park administrators pointed to unused recreation facilities. When many persons stay home, they are not availing themselves of the opportunities for pleasure and cultural enrichment offered in their communities, and they are not visiting their friends as frequently as they might. The general level of social interaction in the society is reduced.

When fear of crime becomes fear of the stranger the social order is further damaged. As the level of sociability and mutual trust is reduced, streets and public places can indeed become more dangerous. Not only will there be fewer people abroad but those who are abroad will manifest a fear of and a lack of concern for each other. The reported incidents of bystanders indifferent to cries for help are the logical consequence of a reduced sociability, mutual distrust and withdrawal.

However, the most dangerous aspect of a fear of strangers is its implication that the moral and social order of society are of doubtful trustworthiness and stability. Everyone is dependent on this order to instill in all members of society a respect for the persons and possessions of others. When it appears that there are more and more people who do not have this respect, the security that comes from living in an orderly and trustworthy society is undermined. The tendency of many people to think of crime in terms of increasing moral deterioration is an indication that they are losing their faith in their society. And so the costs of the fear of crime to the social order may ultimately be even greater than its psychological costs to individuals.

Fourth, the fear of crime may not be as strongly influenced by the actual incidence of crime as by other experiences with the crime problem generally. For example, the mass media and overly zealous or opportunistic crime fighters may play a role in raising fears of crime by associating the idea of "crime" with a few sensational and terrifying criminal acts. Past research on the mass media's connection with crime has concentrated primarily on depictions and accounts of violence in the mass media as possible causes of delinquency and crime. Little attention has thus far been given to what may be a far more direct and costly effect—the creation of distorted perceptions of the risk of crime and exaggerated fears of victimization.

The greatest danger of an exaggerated fear of crime may well reside in the tendency to use the violent crime as a stereotype for crimes in general. For example, there may be a significant interplay between violence and the mass media and the reporting of general crime figures. Publicity about total crime figures without distinguishing between the trends for property crime and those for crimes against persons may create mistaken ideas about what is actually happening. If burglaries and larcenies increase sharply while violent crimes decrease or remain stable, the total figures will follow the property crime figures, since crimes against property are more than four-fifths of the total. Yet under these conditions people may interpret the increases in terms of the dominant stereotype of crimes of violence, thus needlessly increasing their fears. They may not only restrict their activities out of an exaggerated fear of violence but may fail to protect themselves against the more probable crimes. The fact is that most people experience crime vicariously through the daily press, periodicals, novels, radio and television, and often the reported experiences of other persons. Their fear of crime may be more directly related to the quality and the amount of this vicarious experience than it is to the actual risks of victimization.

The Commission believes that there is a clear public responsibility to keep citizens fully informed of the facts about crime so that they will have facts to go on when they decide what the risks are and what kinds and amounts of precautionary measures they should take. Furthermore, without an accurate understanding of the facts, they cannot judge whether the interference with individual liberties which strong crime control measures may involve is a price worth paying. The public obligation to citizens is to provide this information regularly and accurately. And if practices for disseminating information give wrong impressions, resources should be committed to developing more accurate methods.

Finally, public concern about crime need not have only the adverse effects that have been described so far. It can be a powerful force for action. However, making it one will not be easy. The Commission's Washington survey asked people whether they had ever "gotten together with other people around here, or has any group or organization you belong to met and discussed the problem of crime or taken some sort of action to combat crime." Only about 12 percent answered affirmatively, although the question was quite broad and included any kind of group meeting or discussion. Neither did most persons believe that they as individuals could do anything about crime in their own neighborhoods. Only slightly over 17 percent thought that they could do either a lot or just something.

Most people feel that the effort to reduce crime is a responsibility of the police, the courts and perhaps other public agencies. This was even true to some extent of administrators and officials of public agencies and utilities who were interviewed in the three city precinct surveys. However, when these officials were pressed they were able to think of many ways in which their organizations might help reduce crime, such as cooperating to make law enforcement easier, donating and helping in neighborhood programs, providing more and better street lighting, creating more parks with recreational programs, furnishing more youth programs and adult education, and promoting integration of work crews and better community relations programs.

Every American can translate his concern about, or fear of, crime into positive action. Every American should. The succeeding chapters of this report will endeavor to show how.

Chapter 3

Juvenile Delinquency and
Youth Crime

AMERICA'S BEST HOPE for reducing crime is to reduce juvenile delinquency and youth crime. In 1965 a majority of all arrests for major crimes against property were of people under 21, as were a substantial minority of arrests for major crimes against the person. The recidivism rates for young offenders are higher than those for any other age group. A substantial change in any of these figures would make a substantial change in the total crime figures for the Nation.

One of the difficulties of discussing the misconduct, criminal or not, of young people is that "juvenile" and "youth" are not precise definitions of categories of people. People are legally juveniles in most States until they pass their 18th birthdays, but in some States they stop being juveniles after they turn 16 or remain juveniles until they turn 21. The problems and behavior patterns of juveniles and youths often are similar.

FACTS ABOUT DELINQUENCY

To prevent and control delinquency, we must first know something about the nature of delinquency and the dimensions of the problem. We need to know how serious delinquency is. How much of it is there? How many of our youth are involved? What sorts of illegal acts do they commit? What have the trends in delinquency been in the past, and what can we expect in the future? We also need knowledge about the people who become delinquent—information such as where most delinquents live and under what economic conditions.

But we are severely limited in what we can learn today. The only juvenile statistics regularly gathered over the years on a national scale are the FBI's Uniform Crime Reports, based on arrest statistics, and the juvenile court statistics of the Children's Bureau of the U.S. Department of Health, Education, and Welfare, based on referrals of juveniles from a variety of agencies to a sample of juvenile courts. These reports can tell us nothing about the vast number of unsolved offenses, or about the many cases in which delinquents are dealt with informally instead of being arrested or referred to court. Supplementing this official picture of delinquency are self-report studies, which rely on asking selected individuals about their delinquent acts. While efforts are made to insure the validity of the results by such means as guaranteeing anonymity, and verifying results with official records and unofficial checks, such studies have been conducted only on a local and sporadic basis, and they vary greatly in quality.

Clearly, there is urgent need for more and better information. Nonetheless, enough is available to give some of the rough outlines of juvenile delinquency in the United States.

SERIOUSNESS OF THE DELINQUENCY PROBLEM

Volume. Enormous numbers of young people appear to be involved in delinquent acts. Indeed, self-report studies reveal that perhaps 90 percent of all young people have committed at least one act for which they could have been brought to juvenile court. Many of these offenses are relatively trivial—fighting, truancy, running away from home. Statutes often define juvenile delinquency so broadly as to make virtually all youngsters delinquent.

Even though most of these offenders are never arrested or referred to juvenile court, alarming numbers of young people are. Rough estimates by the Children's Bureau, supported by independent studies, indicate that one in every nine youths—one in every six male youths—will be referred to juvenile court in connection with a delinquent act (excluding traffic offenses) before his 18th birthday.

Youth is apparently responsible for a substantial and disproportionate part of the national crime problem. Arrest statistics can give us only a rough picture—probably somewhat exaggerated since it is likely that juveniles are more easily apprehended than adults. In addition, it may be that juveniles act in groups more often than adults when committing crimes, thus producing numbers of juvenile arrests out of proportion with numbers of crimes committed. But even with these qualifications, the figures are striking. FBI figures reveal that of all persons arrested in 1965 (not counting traffic offenders) about 30 percent were under 21 years of age, and about 20 percent were under 18 years of age. Arrest rates are highest for persons aged 15 through 17, next highest for those aged 18 through 20, dropping off quite directly with increases in age, as table 1 indicates.

Table 1.—Arrest Rates for Different Age Groups—1965

[Rates per 100,000 population]

Age groups	Arrest rates for all offenses (excluding traffic)	Arrest rates for willful homicide, forcible rape, robbery, aggravated assault	Arrest rates for larceny, burglary, motor vehicle theft
11 to 14	3,064.4	71.0	1,292.3
15 to 17	8,050.0	222.8	2,467.0
18 to 20	7,539.6	299.8	1,452.0
21 to 24	6,547.2	296.6	833.7
25 to 29	5,366.9	233.6	506.7
30 to 34	5,085.8	177.5	354.4
35 to 39	4,987.4	132.5	260.4
40 to 44	4,675.3	94.0	185.4
45 to 49	4,102.0	65.3	131.9
50 and over	1,987.4	24.2	55.2
Overall rate	3,349.9	99.9	461.5

SOURCE: FBI, Uniform Crime Reports Section, unpublished data. Estimates for total U.S. population.

The picture looks even worse if attention is directed to certain relatively serious property crimes—burglary, larceny, and motor vehicle theft. The 11- to 17-year-old age group, representing 13.2 percent of the population, was responsible for half of the arrests for these offenses in 1965 (table 2). Table 1 shows that the arrest rates for these offenses are much higher for the 15- to 17-year-olds than for any other age group in the population. But not all of the acts included within these categories are equally serious. Larceny includes thefts of less than $50, and most motor vehicle thefts are for the purpose of securing temporary transportation and do not involve permanent loss of the vehicle. Moreover, although juveniles account for more than their share of arrests for many serious crimes, these arrests are a small part of all juvenile arrests. Juveniles are most frequently arrested or referred to court for petty larceny, fighting, disorderly conduct, liquor-related offenses, and conduct not in violation of the criminal law such as curfew violation, truancy, incorrigibility, or running away from home.

It is an older age group—beyond the jurisdiction of almost all juvenile courts—that has the highest arrest rate for crimes of violence. The 18- to 24-year-old group, which represents only 10.2 percent of the population, accounts for 26.4 percent of the arrests for willful homicide, 44.6 percent of the arrests for rape, 39.5 percent of the arrests for robbery, and 26.5 percent of the arrests for aggravated assault (table 2).

Table 2.—Percent of Arrests Accounted for by Different Age Groups—1965

[Percent of total]

	Persons 11–17	Persons 18–24	Persons 25 and over
Population	13.2	10.2	53.5
Willful homicide	8.4	26.4	65.1
Forcible rape	19.8	44.6	35.6
Robbery	28.0	39.5	31.4
Aggravated assault	14.2	26.5	58.7
Burglary	47.7	29.0	19.7
Larceny (includes larceny under $50)	49.2	21.9	24.3
Motor vehicle theft	61.4	26.4	11.9
Willful homicide, rape, robbery, aggravated assault	18.3	31.7	49.3
Larceny, burglary, motor vehicle theft	50.5	24.7	21.2

SOURCE: FBI, Uniform Crime Reports Section, unpublished data. Estimates for total U.S. population.

Trends. In recent years the number of delinquency arrests has increased sharply in the United States, as it has in several Western European countries studied by the Commission. Between 1960 and 1965, arrests of persons under 18 years of age jumped 52 percent for willful homicide, rape, robbery, aggravated assault, larceny, burglary and motor vehicle theft. During the same period, arrests of persons 18 and over for these offenses rose only 20 percent. This is explained in large part by the disproportionate increase in the population under 18 and, in particular, the crime-prone part of that population —the 11- to 17-year-old age group.

Official figures may give a somewhat misleading picture of crime trends. Over the years there has been a tendency toward more formal records and actions, particularly in the treatment of juveniles. In addition, police efficiency may well have increased. But, considering other facts together with the official statistics, the Commission is of the opinion that juvenile delinquency has increased significantly in recent years.

The juvenile population has been rising, and at a faster rate than the adult population. And an increasing proportion of our society is living in the cities where delinquency rates have always been highest. These trends and the increase in the total volume of crime that they appear to foretell are testimony enough that programs for the prevention and control of delinquency deserve our full attention.

WHO THE DELINQUENTS ARE

Almost all youths commit acts for which they could be arrested and taken to court. But it is a much smaller group that ends up being defined officially as delinquent.

Official delinquents are predominantly male. In 1965 boys under 18 were arrested five times as often as girls. Four times as many boys as girls were referred to juvenile court.

Boys and girls commit quite different kinds of offenses. Children's Bureau statistics based on large-city court reports reveal that more than half of the girls referred to juvenile court in 1965 were referred for conduct that would not be criminal if committed by adults; only one-fifth of the boys were referred for such conduct. Boys were referred to court primarily for larceny, burglary, and motor vehicle theft, in order of frequency; girls for running away, ungovernable behavior, larceny, and sex offenses.

Delinquents are concentrated disproportionately in the cities, and particularly in the larger cities. Arrest rates are next highest in the suburbs, and lowest in rural areas.

Delinquency rates are high among children from broken homes. They are similarly high among children who have numerous siblings.

Delinquents tend to do badly in school. Their grades are below average. Large numbers have dropped one or more classes behind their classmates or dropped out of school entirely.

Delinquents tend to come from backgrounds of social and economic deprivation. Their families tend to have lower than average incomes and social status. But perhaps more important than the individual family's situation is the area in which a youth lives. One study has shown that a lower class youth has little chance of being classified as delinquent if he lives in an upper class neighborhood. Numerous studies have revealed the relationship between certain deprived areas—particularly the slums of large cities—and delinquency.

It is inescapable that juvenile delinquency is directly related to conditions bred by poverty. If the Fulton County census tracts were divided into five groups on the basis of the economic and educational status of their residents, we would find that 57% of Fulton County's juvenile delinquents during 1964 were residents of the lowest group which consists of the principal poverty areas of the City of Atlanta. Only 24% of the residents of the county lived within these tracts. Report of the Atlanta Commission on Crime and Juvenile Delinquency, *Opportunity for Urban Excellence* (1966), p. 24.

Thus Negroes, who live in disproportionate numbers in slum neighborhoods, account for a disproportionate number of arrests. Numerous studies indicate that what matters is where in the city one is growing up, not religion or nationality or race. The studies by Shaw and McKay, discussed under "Crime and the Inner City," in chapter 2, followed a number of different national groups—Germans, Irish, Poles, Italians —as they moved from the grim center of the city out to better neighborhoods. They found that for all groups the delinquency rates were highest in the center and lowest on the outskirts of the city.

There is no reason to expect a different story for Negroes. Indeed, McKay found Negro delinquency rates decreasing from the center of the city outward, just as they did for earlier migrant groups. And when delinquency rates of whites and Negroes are compared in areas of similar economic status, the differences between them are markedly reduced. But for Negroes, movement out of the inner city and absorption into America's middle class have been much slower and more difficult than for any other ethnic or racial group. Their attempts to move spatially, socially, economically have met much stiffer resistance. Rigid barriers of residential segregation have prevented them from moving to better neighborhoods as their desire and capacity to do so have developed, leading to great population density and to stifling overcrowding of housing, schools, recreation areas. Restricted access to jobs and limited upward mobility in those jobs that are available have slowed economic advance.

It is likely that the official picture exaggerates the role played by social and economic conditions, since slum offenders are more likely than suburban offenders to be arrested and referred to juvenile court. In fact, recent self-report studies reveal suburban and middle-class delinquency to be a more significant problem than was once assumed. But there is still no reason to doubt that delinquency, and especially the most serious delinquency, is committed disproportionately by slum and lower-class youth.

A balanced judgment would seem to be that, while there is indeed unreported delinquency and slower resort to official police and court sanctions in middle-class areas than in the central sectors of our cities, there is also an absolute difference in the amount and types of crimes committed in each area. In short, the vast differences represented in official statistics cannot be explained by differential police or court action toward children of varying backgrounds. There are, in fact, real differences leading to more frequent assaults, thefts, and breaking and entering offenses in lower socioeconomic areas of our urban centers. Wheeler and Cottrell, *Juvenile Delinquency—Its Prevention and Control* (Russell Sage Foundation 1966), pp. 12–13.

UNDERSTANDING AND PREVENTING JUVENILE DELINQUENCY

FOCUSING PREVENTION

In the last analysis, the most promising and so the most important method of dealing with crime is by preventing it —by ameliorating the conditions of life that drive people to commit crimes and that undermine the restraining rules and institutions erected by society against antisocial conduct. The Commission doubts that even a vastly improved criminal justice system can substantially reduce crime if society fails to make it possible for each of its citizens to feel a personal stake in it—in the good life that it can provide and in the law and order that are prerequisite to such a life. That sense of stake, of something that can be gained or lost, can come only through real opportunity for full participation in society's life and growth. It is insuring opportunity that is the basic goal of prevention programs.

Our system of justice holds both juveniles and adults who violate the law responsible for their misconduct and imposes sanctions on them accordingly, even though the level of responsibility may be lower for juveniles than for adults. Society thereby obligates itself to equip juveniles with the means —the educational and social and cultural background, the personal and economic security—to understand and accept responsibility.

Clearly it is with young people that prevention efforts are most needed and hold the greatest promise. It is simply more critical that young people be kept from crime, for they are the Nation's future, and their conduct will affect society for a long time to come. They are not yet set in their ways; they are still developing, still subject to the influence of the socializing institutions that structure—however skeletally—their environment: Family, school, gang, recreation program, job market. But that influence, to do the most good, must come before the youth has become involved in the formal criminal justice system.

Once a juvenile is apprehended by the police and referred to the Juvenile Court, the community has already failed; subsequent rehabilitative services, no matter how skilled, have far less potential for success than if they had been applied before the youth's overt defiance of the law. Report of the President's Commission on Crime in the District of Columbia (1966), p. 733.

One way of looking at delinquency is in the context of the "teenage culture" that has developed in America since the end of the Second World War. In America in the 1960's, to perhaps a greater extent than in any other place or time, adolescents live in a distinct society of their own. It is not an easy society to understand, to describe, or, for that matter, to live in. In some ways it is an intensely materialistic society; its members, perhaps in unconscious imitation of their elders, are preoccupied with physical objects like clothes and cars, and indeed have been encouraged in this preoccupation by manufacturers and merchants who have discovered how profitable the adolescent market is. In some ways it is an intensely sensual society; its members are preoccupied with the sensations they can obtain from surfing or drag racing or music or drugs. In some ways it is an intensely moralistic society; its members are preoccupied with independence and honesty and equality and courage. On the whole it is a rebellious, oppositional society, dedicated to the proposition that the grownup world is a sham. At the same time it is a conforming society; being inexperienced, unsure of themselves, and, in fact, relatively powerless as individuals, adolescents to a far greater extent than their elders conform to common standards of dress and hair style and speech, and act jointly, in groups—or gangs.

Adolescents everywhere, from every walk of life, are often dangerous to themselves and to others. It may be a short step from distrusting authority to taking the law into one's own hands, from self-absorption to contempt for the rights of others, from group loyalty to gang warfare, from getting "kicks" to rampaging through the streets, from coveting material goods to stealing them, from feelings of rebellion to acts of destruction. Every suburban parent knows of parties that have turned into near riots. Every doctor knows how many young unmarried girls become pregnant. Every insurance company executive knows how dangerously adolescent boys drive. Every high school principal is concerned about the use of marihuana or pep pills by his students. Every newspaper reader knows how often bands of young people of all kinds commit destructive and dangerous acts.

Other than that it appears to be increasing, little is known as yet about delinquency among the well to do. Its causes, to the extent that they are understood, are of a kind that is difficult to eliminate by any program of social action that has yet been devised. The weakening of the family as an agent of social control; the prolongation of education with its side effect of prolonging childhood; the increasing impersonality of a technological, corporate, bureaucratic society; the radical changes in moral standards in regard to such matters as sex and drug use—all these are phenomena with which the Nation has not yet found the means to cope.

Delinquency in the slums, which, as has been shown, is a disproportionately high percentage of all delinquency and includes a disproportionately high number of dangerous acts, is associated with these phenomena, of course. Both figures and observation clearly demonstrate, however, that it is also associated with undesirable conditions of life. Among the many compelling reasons for changing the circumstances of inner-city existence, one of the most compelling is that it will prevent crime.

The inner city has always been hard on whoever is living in it. The studies by Shaw and McKay described above show dramatically that it is in the inner city that delinquency rates have traditionally been highest, decade after decade and regardless of what population group is there. And besides delinquency rates, the other familiar statistical signs of trouble—truancy, high unemployment, mental disorder, infant mortality, tuberculosis, families on relief—are also highest in the inner city. Life is grim and uncompromising in the center of the city, better on the outskirts. As the members of each population group gain greater access to the city's legitimate social and economic opportunities and the group moves outward, rents are higher, more families own their own homes, the rates of disease and dependency—and delinquency—drop.

But in the inner city, now occupied by a different group,

177

the rate of delinquency remains roughly the same, regardless of race, religion, or nationality. That strikingly persistent correlation, coupled with the fact, pointed out above, that the inner city is for its present Negro inhabitants more of a trap than a way station, emphasizes the urgency of intensifying efforts to improve in the inner city the institutions that elsewhere serve to prevent delinquency.

Attempts to concentrate prevention efforts on those individuals most seriously in need of them has led to increased interest in methods for predicting who will become a delinquent. Some attempts have been at least partly successful, and such attempts should certainly be pursued. It may eventually prove possible to predict delinquency specifically with a high degree of accuracy and to design programs that can prevent the predictions from coming true. But if we could now predict with accuracy who would be delinquent, our present knowledge and experience still would not carry us far in designing effective preventive programs for individuals. And inherent in the process of seeking to identify potential delinquents are certain serious risks—most notably that of the self-fulfilling prophecy.

Even if we could identify in advance and deal with those individuals most likely to become delinquent, that would hardly be a sufficient substitute for general shoring up of socializing institutions in the slums. For the fact of the matter is that, whether or not the result in any given case is delinquency, society is failing slum youth. Their families are failing. The schools are failing. The social institutions generally relied on to guide and control people in their individual and mutual existence simply are not operating effectively in the inner city. Instead of turning out men and women who conform to the American norm at least overtly, at least enough to stay out of jail, the slums are producing the highest rates of crime, vice, and financial dependence. By failing these men and women and, most important, these young people, society wounds itself in many ways. There is the sheer cost of crime—billions of dollars every year spent on apprehending and adjudicating and treating offenders. There are the lives forfeited, the personal injuries suffered, the inconveniencing and sometimes irremediable loss and destruction of property. But all of those together are less significant than the loss of individual initiative, of productivity, of a basis for pride in and a sense of participation in society. And whether or not society is tangibly injured by crime, inevitably it is diminished by the loss of a member's potential contribution.

Perhaps we cannot be sure that it is the slum family that is

178

failing to instill the values accepted by society, or the slum school that is failing to impart the capabilities for livelihood. But it is on such institutions that we depend, and so it is to them we turn when we wish to change the way people live their lives. And because of our dependence on these social institutions to shape individuals and, through individuals, the face of the Nation, we must ask even more of the slum's institutions than of their middle- and upper-class counterparts. The family must instill strength against the larger society's harshness. The school must reach out and rescue those lacking families. Job skills must be developed and employment opportunities broadened.

In sum, our society has for too long neglected the conditions of life in the inner-city slum. The past several years have seen unprecedented recognition of the gravity of those conditions and commitment of resources to their amelioration. But if we fail to devote, in the future, even more money and people and energy and concern to the problems of our inner cities, we must be willing to pay the price—a price already high and mounting.

Crime is only part of that price. But the importance of ameliorating social conditions in order to prevent crime is not to be minimized. Each day additional law-abiding citizens turn their backs on the city; fear for personal safety—fear of crime—is a major reason. As they leave, the city changes; the quality of city life deteriorates; the crime problem worsens, hurting people not only by forcing them to narrow their lives out of apprehensiveness but also by the most direct and incompensable of injuries to their person and property—the circle continues around.

It is neither appropriate nor possible for this Commission to specify or select among the many possible ways of helping to break that circle. The time has been much too short; the Commission's experience cannot compare with that of the dedicated educators, social scientists, community workers, program planners already struggling with these discouragingly complex and intractable concerns. What is imperative is for this Commission to make clear its strong conviction that, before this Nation can hope to reduce crime significantly or lastingly, it must mount and maintain a massive attack against the conditions of life that underlie it.

SLUMS AND SLUM DWELLERS

The slums of virtually every American city harbor, in alarming amounts, not only physical deprivation and spiritual despair but also doubt and downright cynicism about the relevance of the outside world's institutions and the sincerity of efforts to close the gap. Far from ignoring or rejecting the goals and values espoused by more fortunate segments of society, the slum dweller wants the same material and intangible things for himself and his children as those more privileged. Indeed, the very similarity of his wishes sharpens the poignancy and frustration of felt discrepancies in opportunity for fulfillment. The slum dweller may not respect a law that he believes draws differences between his rights and another's, or a police force that applies laws so as to draw such differences; he does recognize the law's duty to deal with lawbreakers, and he respects the policeman who does so with businesslike skill and impartiality. Living as he does in a neighborhood likely to be among the city's highest in rates of crime, he worries about and wants police protection even more than people living in the same city's safer regions. He may not have much formal education himself, or many books in his house, and he may hesitate to visit teachers or attend school functions, but studies show that he too, like his college-graduate counterpart, is vitally interested in his children's education. And while some inner-city residents, like some people everywhere, may not be eager to change their unemployed status, it is also true that many more of them toil day after day at the dullest and most backbreaking of society's tasks, traveling long distances for menial jobs without hope of advancement. Very likely his parents (or he himself) left home—the deep South, or Appalachia, or Mexico, or Puerto Rico—looking for a better life, only to be absorbed into the yet more binding dependency and isolation of the inner city.

The children of these disillusioned colored pioneers inherited the total lot of their parents—the disappointments, the anger. To add to their misery, they had little hope of deliverance. For where does one run to when he's already in the promised land? Claude Brown, *Manchild in the Promised Land* (1965), p. 8.

A sketch drawn from the limited information available shows that disproportionately the delinquent is a child of the slums, from a neighborhood that is low on the socio-economic scale of the community and harsh in many ways for those who live there. He is 15 or 16 years old (younger than his counterpart of a few years ago), one of numerous children—perhaps representing several different fathers—who live with their mother in a home that the sociologists call fe-

180

male-centered. It may be broken; it may never have had a resident father; it may have a nominal male head who is often drunk or in jail or in and out of the house (welfare regulations prohibiting payment where there is a "man in the house" may militate against his continuous presence). He may never have known a grownup man well enough to identify with or imagine emulating him. From the adults and older children in charge of him he has had leniency, sternness, affection, perhaps indifference, in erratic and unpredictable succession. All his life he has had considerable independence, and by now his mother has little control over his comings and goings, little way of knowing what he is up to until a policeman brings him home or a summons from court comes in the mail.

He may well have dropped out of school. He is probably unemployed, and had little to offer an employer. The offenses he and his friends commit are much more frequently thefts than crimes of personal violence, and they rarely commit them alone. Indeed, they rarely do anything alone, preferring to congregate and operate in a group, staking out their own "turf"—a special street corner or candy store or poolroom—and adopting their own flamboyant title and distinctive hair style or way of dressing or talking or walking, to signal their membership in the group and show that they are "tough" and not to be meddled with. Their clear belligerence toward authority does indeed earn them the fearful deference of both adult and child, as well as the watchful suspicion of the neighborhood policeman. Although the common conception of the gang member is of a teenager, in fact the lower class juvenile begins his gang career much earlier, and usually in search not of coconspirators in crime but of companionship. But it is all too easy for them to drift into minor and then major violations of the law.

That is not to suggest that his mother has not tried to guide him, or his father if he has one or an uncle or older brother. But their influence is diluted and undermined by the endless task of making ends meet in the face of debilitating poverty; by the constant presence of temptation—drugs, drinking, gambling, petty thievery, prostitution; by the visible contrast of relative affluence on the other side of town.

The Physical Environment. It is in the inner city that the most overcrowding, the most substandard housing, the lowest rentals are found. Farther out in the city, more families own their own homes; presumably more families are intact and stable enough to live in those homes and more fathers are employed and able to buy them. The inevitable influence of slum living conditions on juvenile behavior need not be translated into sociological measurements to be obvious to the assaulted senses of the most casual visitor to the slum. Nor does the child who lives there fail to recognize—and reject —the squalor of his surroundings:

Well, the neighborhood is pretty bad, you know. Trash around the street, stuff like that and the movies got trash all in the bathroom, dirty all over the floors. Places you go in for recreation they aren't clean like they should be, and some of the children that go to school wear clothes that aren't clean as they should be. Some of them, you know, don't take baths as often as they should. Well, my opinion is * * * it's not clean as it should be and if I had a chance, if my mother would move, I would rather move to a better neighborhood. [16-year-old boy.]

It's sort of small. * * * It's something like a slum. Slum is a place where people hang out and jest messy, streets are messy, alleys are messes and a lot of dirty children hang around there. I would say it is a filthy place. [12-year-old boy.]

What the inner-city child calls home is often a set of rooms shared by a shifting group of relatives and acquaintances—furniture shabby and sparse, many children in one bed, plumbing failing, plaster falling, roaches in the corners and sometimes rats, hallways dark or dimly lighted, stairways littered, air dank and foul. Inadequate, unsanitary facilities complicate keeping clean. Disrepair discourages neatness. Insufficient heating, multiple use of bathrooms and kitchens, crowded sleeping arrangements spread and multiply respiratory infections and communicable diseases. Rickety, shadowy stairways and bad electrical connections take their accidental toll. Rat bites are not infrequent and sometimes, especially for infants, fatal. Care of one's own and respect for others' possessions can hardly be inculcated in such surroundings. More important, home has little holding power for the child —it is not physically pleasant or attractive; it is not a place to bring his friends; it is not even very much the reassuring gathering place of his own family. The loss of parental control and diminishing adult supervision that occur so early in the slum child's life must thus be laid at least partly at the door of his home.

The physical environment of the neighborhood is no better. In the alley are broken bottles and snoring winos—homeless, broken men, drunk every day on cheap wine. ("There are a whole lot of winos who hang around back in the alley there. Men who drink and lay around there dirty, smell bad. Cook stuff maybe. Chase you * * *." [13-year-old.]) Yards, if there are any, are littered and dirty ("* * * and the yard ain't right. Bottles broke in the yard, plaster, bricks, baby carriages all broken up, whole lot of stuff in people's yards." [14-year-old describing his home.]) The buildings are massive sooty tenements or sagging row houses. ("I don't like the way those houses built. They curve * * * I don't like the way they look * * *. They make the street look bad." [13-year-old.])

On some stoops, apparently able-bodied men sit passing away the time. On others children scamper around a grandmother's knees; they have been on the streets since early morning, will still be there at dusk. The nearest playground may be blocks away across busy streets, a dusty grassless plot. ("There ain't no recreation around. There was a big recreation right across the street and they tore it down. * * * [T]hey just closed it up—instead of building a road they put up a parking lot. * * * There ain't enough playgrounds, and if you go down to the railroad station, there is a big yard down there, * * * cops come and chase us off. * * *" [14-year-old boy.] Harlem, for example, although it borders on and contains several major parks,

*is generally lacking in play space * * *. [A]bout 10 percent of the area consists of parks and playgrounds, compared to over 16 percent for New York City as a whole. The total acreage of 14 parks and playgrounds is not only inadequate, but all the parks are esthetically and functionally inadequate as well. * * * For many of the children, then, the streets become play areas, and this, coupled with the heavy flow of traffic through the community, results in a substantially higher rate of deaths due to motor vehicles among persons under 25 (6.9 per 100,000 compared to 4.2 per 100,000 for all of New York City). Youth in the Ghetto* (Harlem Youth Opportunities Unlimited, Inc., 1964), pp. 100–101.

In addition to actual dangerousness, lack of recreation facilities has been shown to be linked to negative attitudes toward the neighborhood and those attitudes in turn to repeated acts of delinquency.

Overcrowding alone is an obstacle to decent life in the

slum. In central Harlem, the population density is approximately 66,000 people for every square mile—a rate at which all the people in the Nation's 12 largest cities would fit inside the city limits of New York. Even apart from its effects on the soul, such packing has obvious implications for the crime rate. Some crime is a kind of collision; when so many people are living and moving in so small a space, the probability of collisions can only increase. Crowding has a harmful effect on study habits, attitudes toward sex, parents' ability to meet needs of individual children; clearly, crowding intensifies the fatigue and irritability that contribute to erratic or irrational discipline.

Many of the people and activities that bring slum streets and buildings to life are unsavory at best. Violence is commonplace:

*When I first started living around here it was really bad, but I have gotten used to it now. Been here 2 years. People getting shot and stuff. Lots of people getting hurt. People getting beat up * * *. Gee, there's a lot of violence around here. You see it all the time * * *.* [14-year-old boy.]

Fighting and drunkenness are everyday matters:

*Sometime where I live at people be hitting each other, fighting next door. Then when they stop fighting then you can get some sleep * * *.* [15-year-old boy.]

Drinking, cussing, stabbing people, having policemen running all around mostly every day in the summertime. [14-year-old.]

Drug addiction and prostitution are familiar. The occupying-army aspects of predominantly white store ownership and police patrol in predominantly Negro neighborhoods have been many times remarked; the actual extent of the alienation thereby enforced and symbolized is only now being generally conceded.

THE FAMILY

Too frequently the combination of deprivation and hazard that characterizes the slums—a test by fire for the most cohesive of families—must be confronted in the slum by a family that lacks even minimal material and intangible supports.

The family is the first and most basic institution in our society for developing the child's potential, in all its many aspects: Emotional, intellectual, moral, and spiritual, as well as physical and social. Other influences do not even enter the child's life until after the first few highly formative years. It is within the family that the child must learn to curb his desires and to accept rules that define the time, place, and circumstances under which highly personal needs may be satisfied in socially acceptable ways. This early training—management of emotion, confrontation with rules and authority, development of responsiveness to others—has been repeatedly related to the presence or absence of delinquency in later years. But cause-and-effect relationships have proved bewilderingly complex, and require much more clinical experience and systematic research.

Research findings, however, while far from conclusive, point to the principle that whatever in the organization of the family, the contacts among its members, or its relationships to the surrounding community diminishes the moral and emotional authority of the family in the life of the young person also increases the likelihood of delinquency.

The following discussion draws upon the extensive—though not by any means exhaustive—work already done by numerous researchers.

Family Membership. If one parent (especially the father of a son) is absent, if there are many children, if a child is in the middle in age among several siblings—such family arrangements tend to reduce parental control and authority over children and consequently increase vulnerability to influences toward delinquent behavior.

Besides the basic membership of the family, relations among the members also appear significant in determining the strength of familial influence. It has been shown that deep unhappiness between parents increases the likelihood that the children will commit delinquent acts and that children reared in happy homes are less delinquent than those from unhappy homes. Apparently marital discord tends to expose the child to delinquent influences, perhaps by outright rejection or neglect or by undercutting his respect for his parents and so the force of their authority.

Discipline. The discipline associated with the loose organization and female focus that characterize many inner-city families has also been related by social scientists to the development of what has been termed "premature autonomy" and to consequent resentment of authority figures such as policemen and teachers. Often child-rearing practices are either very permissive or very stern—the latter reinforced physically. In the first instance, the child is on his own, in charge of his own affairs, from an early age. He becomes accustomed to making decisions for himself and reacts to the direction or demands of a teacher or other adult as to a challenge of his established independence. Strictness is not objectionable in itself, when it is seen as fairminded and well meant. But where strictness amounts simply to control by force, the child harbors resentment until the day when he can successfully assert physical mastery himself; rather than a learning and shaping process, discipline for him is a matter of muscle:

My father don't get smart with me no more. He used to whup me, throw me downstairs, until I got big enough to beat him. The last time he touch me, he was coming downstairs talking some noise about something. I don't know what. He had a drink, and he always make something up when he start drinking. He was trying to get smart with me, so he swung at me and missed. I just got tired of it. I snatched him and threw him up against the wall, and then we started fighting. My sister grabbed him around the neck and started choking him. So I started hitting him in the nose and everything, and around the mouth. Then he pushed my mother and I hit him again. Then he quit, and I carried him back upstairs. Next morning he jump up saying, "What happened last night? My leg hurts." He made like he don't know what had happened. And ever since then, you know, he don't say nothing to me.

An inconsistent mixture of permissiveness and strictness has also been found in the backgrounds of many delinquents. Many inner-city parents express at once a desire to keep track of their children, and keep them out of trouble, and a resignation to their inability to do so.

(How do you handle Melvin when he gets into trouble?) Well, we figure that weekends are the main times he looks forward to—parties and going out. So we'd say, "You can't go out tonight." You know, we'd try to keep him from something he really wanted to do. But he usually goes out anyway. Like one night we was watching TV, and Melvin said he was tired and went to bed. So then I get a phone call from a lady who wants to know if Melvin is here because her son is with him. I said, "No, he has gone to bed already." She says, "Are you sure?" I said, "I'm pretty sure." So I went downstairs and

186

I peeked in and saw a lump in the bed but I didn't see his head. So I took a look and he was gone. He came home about 12:30, and we talked for a while. (What did you do?) Well, I told him he was wrong going against his parents like that, but he keeps sneaking out anyway. (What does your husband do about it?) Well, he don't do much. I'm the one who gets upset. My husband, he'll say something to Mel and then he'll just relax and forget about it. (Husband and wife laugh together.) There's little we can do, you know. It's hard to talk to him cause he just go ahead and do what he wants anyway.

Such vacillations may be virtually inevitable where the man of the house is sometimes or frequently absent, intoxicated, or replaced by another; where coping with everyday life with too many children and too little money leaves little time or energy for discipline; or where children have arrived so early and unbidden that parents are too immature not to prefer their own pleasure to a child's needs. Nevertheless, erratic discipline may engender anxiety, uncertainty, and ultimately rebellion in the child.

Parental Affection or Rejection. More crucial even than mode of discipline is the degree of parental affection or rejection of the child. Perhaps the most important factor in the lives of many boys who become delinquent is their failure to win the affection of their fathers. It has been suggested that delinquency correlates more with the consistency of the affection the child receives from both parents than with the consistency of the discipline. It has also been found that a disproportionately large number of aggressive delinquents have been denied the opportunity to express their feelings of dependence on their parents.

Identification Between Father and Son. Several recent studies focusing on identification between a boy and his father have tried to determine the conditions under which a boy is more likely to be attracted to his father, on the assumption that such attraction provides a basis upon which parental discipline can inculcate youthful self-control. Unemployment has been found to weaken a father's authority with his family, especially over adolescent children for whom he is unable to provide expected support. Children also appear less likely to identify with fathers if their discipline is perceived as unfair. The strong influence of the father over his son, for good or for ill, is also very significant. When father-son and mother-son relationships are compared, the father-son relationships appear more determinative in whether or not delinquent behavior develops.

Family Status in the Community. The capacity of parents to maintain moral authority over the conduct of their children is affected not only by the family's internal structure and operation but also by the relationships that the family maintains with the community and the role of the family itself in modern life. There seems to be a direct relationship between the prestige of the family in the community and the kind of bond that develops between father and son. Respected family status increases the strength of parental authority and seems to help insulate the child from delinquency.

In inner-city families one or more of the detrimental factors discussed above is particularly likely to be present. Many families are large. Many (over 40 percent according to some estimates) are fatherless, always or intermittently, or involve a marital relationship in which the parties have and communicate to their offspring but little sense of permanence. And the histories of delinquents frequently include a large lower class family broken in some way.

Directions for Change. The factors and relationships identified above—number of children, absence of father, consistency of discipline, family status in the community, and others —are not susceptible of direct intervention by public programs. It is nevertheless inescapable that the family is a vital component in any consideration of delinquency and delinquents.

Given the need to make families function better and the impossibility of affecting them directly, the obligation and objective of our society must be to develop and provide the environment and the resources and opportunities through which families can become competent to deal with their own problems. Better housing, better recreation facilities, increased employment opportunities, assistance in family planning, increased opportunities to function as a family unit rather than as a divergent collection of autonomous beings—all these can create the independence and security that are prerequisite if relationships within the family are to be a source of strength.

Thus efforts to reduce unemployment and to provide more and better housing should be expanded. Consideration should be given various proposals for augmenting inadequate family income. Assistance in family planning must be readily accessible to all.

188

The family should be encouraged to see itself as a functioning unit. Communities should develop opportunities for participation by all the members of the family in both leisure time and community improvement activities, especially ones that provide possibilities for communication among generations. Schools should be encouraged and enabled to develop programs and services for families and to identify children's problems early and work with their families at solving them.

Even under the best of circumstances, however, many family problems will remain. Counseling and therapy provide one promising method of dealing with complex emotional and psychological relationships within the family and should be made easily available. Credit unions in neighborhood centers, visiting homemaker helpers, and instruction on marketing and other household skills are promising developments.

Ultimately, it is the strengths of its individual members, the nature of its physical surroundings, the secureness of its place in the community that will determine the family's intricate and largely unpredictable interrelationships. Thus whatever helps each member realize his own potential, whatever makes living and playing cleaner and safer, whatever insures the family a participating place among friends and neighbors in the community—those are the things that will give the family the resources it must have to help young people find their way in the outside world.

The Commission recommends:

Efforts, both private and public, should be intensified to:

Reduce unemployment and devise methods of providing minimum family income.

Reexamine and revise welfare regulations so that they contribute to keeping the family together.

Improve housing and recreation facilities.

Insure availability of family planning assistance.

Provide help in problems of domestic management and child care.

Make counseling and therapy easily obtainable.

Develop activities that involve the whole family together.

YOUTH IN THE COMMUNITY

The typical delinquent operates in the company of his peers, and delinquency thrives on group support. It has been estimated that between 60 and 90 percent of all delinquent acts are committed with companions. That fact alone makes youth groups of central concern in consideration of delinquency prevention.

It is clear that youth groups are playing a more and more important part in the transition between childhood and adulthood. For young people today that transition is a long period of waiting, during which they are expected to be seriously preparing themselves for participation at some future date in a society that meanwhile provides no role for them and withholds both the toleration accorded children and the responsibilities of adults. Some young people, however, lack the resources for becoming prepared; they see the goal but have not the means to reach it. Others are resentful and impatient with the failure of their stodgy elders to appreciate the contributions they feel ready to make. Many, slum dwellers and suburbanites both, feel victimized by the moral absolutes of the adult society—unexplained injunctions about right and wrong that seem to have little relevance in a complex world controlled by people employing multiple and shifting standards. Youth today accuse those ahead of them of phoniness and of failure to define how to live both honorably and successfully in a world that is changing too rapidly for anyone to comprehend.

The very rapidity of that change is making it ever more difficult for young people to envision the type of work they might wish to commit themselves to, more difficult for them to find stable adult models with whom to identify. To fill the vacuum, they turn increasingly to their own age mates. But the models of dress and ideal and behavior that youth subcultures furnish may lead them into conflict with their parents' values and efforts to assert control. It has been suggested that, besides being more dependent on each other, youth today are also more independent of adults; parents and their young adolescents increasingly seem to live in different and at times antagonistic worlds. That antagonism sometimes explodes in antisocial acts.

Most of the youngsters who rebel at home and at school seek security and recognition among their fellows on the street. Together they form tightly knit groups in the decisions of which they are able to participate and the authority of which they accept as virtually absolute. Their attitudes, dress, tastes, ambitions, behavior, pastimes are those of the group.

While the members are still young—before and during their early teens—such groups engage with apparent abandon and indifference in whatever seems like fun, delinquent and nondelinquent. Only some of what they do is seriously violent or destructive. Frequently, however, adults see even their minor misdeeds as malicious and defiant and label the actors troublemakers. The affixing of that label can be a momentous occurrence in a youngster's life. Thereafter he may be watched; he may be suspect; his every misstep may be seen as further evidence of his delinquent nature. He may be excluded more and more from legitimate activities and opportunities. Soon he may be designated and dealt with as a delinquent and will find it very difficult to move onto a law-abiding path even if he can overcome his own belligerent reaction and negative self-image and seeks to do so.

Being labeled a troublemaker is a danger of growing up in suburbia as well as in the slums, but the suburbs are more likely to provide parental intervention and psychiatrists, pastors, family counselors to help the youth abandon his undesirable identity. It is much harder for the inner-city youth to find alternatives to a rebel role. Thus it is in the slums that youth gangs are most likely to drift from minor and haphazard into serious, repeated, purposeful delinquency.

It is in the slums, too, that young people are most likely to be exposed to the example of the successful career criminal as a person of prestige in the community. To a population denied access to traditional positions of status and achievement, a successful criminal may be a highly visible model of power and affluence and a center of training and recruitment for criminal enterprise.

Johnny D. * * * was about the hippest cat on Eighth Avenue * * *. He was a man * * * 21 * * *. Johnny D. had been in jail since he was 17 * * *. Johnny did everything. He used to sell all the horse [heroin] in the neighborhood * * *. Everybody used to listen when he said something. It made sense to listen—he was doing some of everything, so he must have known what he was talking about * * *. He sure seemed to know a lot of things. Johnny just about raised a lot of the cats around there * * *. Claude Brown, *Manchild in the Promised Land* (1965), pp. 104, 108–109.

Delinquent gangs are commonly blamed for much of the street crime that presently alarms the Nation. In fact, however, according to a detailed 2-year study, recently completed, of the 700 members of 21 delinquent gangs, gang violence against persons is less frequent, less violent, and less uncontrolled than is generally believed. Only 17 percent of all the offenses recorded by observers included an element of violence, and about half of the violent offenses were committed against rival gang members. Much gang violence, in other words, appears to occur not against strangers but in attempts to achieve or preserve individual or gang status or territory.

Many cities have sent youth workers into the streets to befriend gang boys and dissuade them from fighting. Street workers have often succeeded in their immediate objective of averting gang violence, but, with little more permanent to offer than bus trips and ball games, they have rarely managed to convert boys from total gang involvement to more socially acceptable pursuits. Indeed, there are indications that street work has in some places had negative effects by creating a vacuum too likely to be filled by such destructive activities as using narcotics. Yet even the hard core delinquent whose gang is his life continues to share the conventional American belief that work and education are the right ways to get ahead in the world.

Directions for Change. The adherence of youth to the norms and values of legitimate society provides a natural starting place for preventive programs. Although young people, especially young rebels, may resist lectures, appeals, even handouts, they respond to opportunities for responsible involvement. Their participation in community activities should be actively sought. They can help operate community centers, plan neighborhood organization and improvement efforts, develop programs that will attract other youth; among other benefits, their participation will improve communication between the generations. They can run youth centers of their own. Encouraging them to participate in civil rights and political activities will engage their immediate energies and at the same time inform and enlist them for more long-term commitment.

The immediate need is to tide the youth over the most dangerous age—the age at which adolescent frustration may combine with inner-city alienation so that he strikes out at society. The more basic need, however, is to give him a reason to care about what happens to his world—a stake in a healthy society. Thus the ideal program absorbs his immediate attention and also improves his chances of finding satisfying work, or participating in community activities, or better understanding the workings of his government or the law. An example is recruitment of youth as paid aides to the police, to probation officers, in clinics. Such programs have the double value of giving young people immediate employment and a stake in their community and at the same time training them for a regular position in the future. The community service officer position on police forces, proposed in chapter 4, provides an excellent opportunity for young men to put their knowledge of their city to gainful use while acquiring the skills for advancement in police work.

Agencies should be established that provide easily accessible information, guidance, and services for youth. These agencies should refer young people to remedial education or job training or recreation or other similar programs as appears appropriate in the given case. They should provide such programs in communities where they do not already exist. They should make counseling, advice, assistance in finding a job readily available. The service coordinating and providing Youth Services Bureau proposed later in this chapter should accept both youths who are referred to it and those who come in on their own. Small residential centers have proved successful in a number of communities in steering youth away from incipient trouble by providing more supervision than they get at home, yet in an atmosphere that is not institutional or coercive.

Many organizations already exist that have as one of their aims—if not the major one—the provision of programs for young people. Perhaps most universal are religious institutions, many of which offer a wide variety of services ranging from individual counseling to group activities, from traditional religious instruction and worship to outward looking community improvement efforts. Boys' Clubs, Scout and Campfire groups, fraternal organizations, Y's, settlement houses, and many private and semiprivate social agencies too have served over the years as refuges for and rescuers of young people. Too frequently, however, limited resources and restrictive policies have forced such organizations to exclude difficult delinquents and older, alienated adolescents. These groups have a vital role in making available the diversified activities and sources of assistance youth need; it is essential that they expand their work in this field and seek ways of extending it to all young people.

The Commission recommends:

Efforts, both private and public, should be intensified to:

Involve young people in community activities.

Train and employ youth as subprofessional aides.

193

Establish Youth Services Bureaus to provide and coordinate programs for young people.

Increase involvement of religious institutions, private social agencies, fraternal groups, and other community organizations in youth programs.

Provide community residential centers.

DELINQUENCY AND THE SCHOOL

The complex relationship between the school and the child varies greatly from one school system to another. The process of education is dramatically different in the slum than in the middle-class suburb. The child and the problems he brings to school are different. The support for learning that he receives at home and in his neighborhood is different. The school systems themselves are very different. The slum school faces the greatest obstacles with the least resources, the least qualified personnel, the least adequate capability for effective education.

The school, unlike the family, is a public instrument for training young people. It is, therefore, more directly accessible to change through the development of new resources and policies. And since it is the principal public institution for the development of a basic commitment by young people to the goals and values of our society, it is imperative that it be provided with the resources to compete with illegitimate attractions for young people's allegiance. Anything less would be a serious failure to discharge our Nation's responsibility to its youth.

The Commission recognizes that many in the field of education have identified the shortcomings of slum schools. The Commission recognizes too that in many places efforts are being made to improve various aspects of schools. But as a general matter our society has not yet been willing to devote resources sufficient for the radical changes necessary.

Recent research has related instances of delinquent conduct to the school-child relationship and to problems either created or complicated by schools themselves. First, in its own methods and practices, the school may simply be too passive to fulfill its obligations as one of the last social institutions with an opportunity to rescue the child from other forces, in himself and in his environment, which are pushing him toward delinquency. Second, there is considerable evidence that some schools may have an indirect effect on delin-

194

quency by the use of methods that create the conditions of failure for certain students. Mishandling by the school can lower the child's motivation to learn. It can aggravate his difficulty in accepting authority and generate or intensify hostility and alienation. It can sap the child's confidence, dampen his initiative, and lead him to negative definitions of himself as a failure or an "unacceptable" person.

Some schools, particularly in the poorest areas, are unable to deal with children who are neither ready nor able to learn. Asserting demands for performance that the child cannot meet, the frustrated teacher may become hostile and the child indifferent, apathetic, or hostile in turn. If the child is also rebelling at home, the effect is more immediate and the confrontation becomes intolerable to all. The too-usual result is that the child turns to other things that have nothing to do with academic learning, and the school finds a way to ignore him or push him out so the rest of its work can continue.

The following discussion attempts to identify ways in which some schools may be contributing directly or indirectly to the behavior problems of children and to assess the capacity of schools to prevent and manage such problems. In formulating its recommendations, the Commission has had the benefit of advice and assistance from the Office of Education in the Department of Health, Education, and Welfare.

The Educationally Handicapped Child. Children enter the school system already shaped by their earlier experiences—many of them already handicapped in their potential for educational achievement. The educational handicaps that seem most closely related to delinquency appear in the slum child.

He comes from a home in which books and other artifacts of intellectual accomplishment are rare. His parents, while they care about his education, are themselves too poorly schooled to give him the help and encouragement he needs. They have not had the time—even had they the knowledge —to teach him basic skills that are milestones painlessly passed by most middle-class youngsters: telling time, counting, saying the alphabet, learning colors, using crayons and paper and paint. He is unaccustomed to verbalizing concepts or ideas. Written communication may be rare in his experience.

It is sometimes assumed that the parents of children in slum neighborhoods do not value education. In fact, there is persuasive evidence of their commitment to an adequate education for their children. Similarly, the youngsters themselves care a great deal about education. Indeed, there are indications that Negro and lower-income students place a higher value on education than do white and higher-income ones.

But whether he and his parents value education or not, the tide of life soon begins to run against success in school for the child from the ghetto. Sordid surroundings, harsh or missing discipline, having to fight for what he wants, and taking over (far too soon) control of his own comings and goings —all adversely affect the odds against him. To some extent, of course, these problems are also encountered in the middle-class school, but there they are usually less extreme, and there is a greater likelihood of useful assistance through counseling, guidance, special tutoring, or some other form of individual help.

The Slum School. The manner in which the school system responds to the educational problems that the child brings with him is of extraordinary importance. It must be able to recognize these problems and to direct a battery of resources toward them.

Stimulated by the poverty program, recent and extensive studies have been made of the educational problems of children reared in slum communities. It has been clearly demonstrated that the educational system in the slums is less well equipped than its nonslum counterpart to deal with the built-in learning problems of the children who come to it. Schools in the slums have the most outdated and dilapidated buildings, the fewest texts and library books, the least experienced full-time teachers, the least qualified substitute teachers, the most overcrowded classrooms, and the least developed counseling and guidance services in the Nation.

The inadequacies of facilities and teaching resources are aggravated by the slum school's increasing segregation, both racial and economic. Despite efforts to combat and prevent segregation, central cities are growing increasingly nonwhite and poor, suburban areas increasingly white and affluent. Educational achievement is generally lower among nonwhite lower income students, and so racial and economic segregation in the schools has the circular effect of exposing nonwhite lower income students to inferior examples of educational achievement. There is substantial evidence that the achievements and aspirations of students are strongly related to the educational backgrounds and performances of other students in their school, and that nonwhite lower income students do better when placed in mixed or middle class schools. Chief Justice Warren enunciated one destructive effect of racial segregation in *Brown* v. *Board of Education of Topeka*, the landmark school desegregation decision:

> To separate them from others of similar age and qualifications solely because of their race generates a feeling of inferiority as to their status in the community that may affect their hearts and minds in a way unlikely ever to be undone. Social and economic separation compound the educational obstacles of racial segregation in many schools today.

The deficiencies of the slum school are further aggravated by a widespread belief that the intellectual capability of most slum children is too limited to allow much education. As a result standards are lowered to meet the level the child is assumed to occupy. Frequently the chance to stimulate latent curiosity and excitement about learning is irretrievably lost, and the self-fulfilling prophecy of apathy and failure comes true.

It is increasingly apparent that grouping procedures often operate in this way. Children with educationally deprived backgrounds are often grouped on the basis of achievement or "ability" tests with built-in cultural biases. The assumption is then made that these children lack ability, and standards are lowered accordingly. Thus, while grouping methods are designed to help tailor curriculum to individual needs and abilities, and while such methods could be valuable in channeling efforts to help educationally deprived children make up for lack of preparation, too frequently they are administered with a rigidity and oversimplification that intensify rather than ameliorate the slum child's learning problems.

These problems are further reinforced by the lack of relationship between the instructional material usually provided by slum schools and the social, economic, and political conditions of living in the slums. To the youngster, the instruction seems light years away from the circumstances and facts of life that surround him every day. The following comments of a former delinquent are illuminating:

> It wasn't interesting to me, I liked the science books but I didn't dig that other stuff. Dick and Jane went up the hill to fetch a pail of water and all that crap. Mary had a little lamb. Spot jumped over the fence. See Spot jump over the fence. * * * I say, ain't this the cutest little story. And I took the book one day and shoved it straight back to the teacher and said I ain't going to read that stuff.

197

When I took the test I think I was four point something so I was real low in English, but I mostly got all my English listening in the streets, from listening to people. I didn't pick up my English mostly from school. (Can you read now?) I can read something that I am really interested in.

(Going back to junior high, what kind of things would you have liked to read, that would have made you interested?) Well, I could see Dick and Jane when I was in elementary school, but in junior high school I was ready to know about life, about how it really is out there. In elementary school it's painted like it is beautiful, everything is beautiful. (In a singsong.) Get your education and you can go somewhere. I didn't want to hear that no more, because I had seen my brother go through the same thing. He quit school, he ain't making it. So I wanted to know, okay how can I get somewhere if I go to school. How is life in general? How is the government ran? What's in the government right now that makes it hard for young people that graduate from high school to get somewhere? Why is it that people are fighting each other in the United States? Why is it that people can't communicate with each other? Society in general—what is it that society has said that we have to follow? How is the police structure set up? Why is the police hard on youth?

These are all the things I would have loved to learn in school. (Is that the way you think now or the way you thought then?) I used to want to know about the government. How it was structured. I wanted to learn how it was run—really. Back then I didn't know people were marching for their rights. I didn't know about that. (When did you find out?) In the streets.

The slum child often feels a similar lack of relationship between school and his future in the adult world:

(What kind of school program were you doing? Vocational education?) Yeah, vocational training. (Did that prepare you for a job?) It was supposed to prepare me for a job but it didn't. (Did you try to get a job?) Yeah, I tried to get a job. The men said I wasn't qualified. (Did you think while you were in school that you would get a job?) That's right—that's why I stayed in school so I could get a job upon completion of high school because they put so much emphasis on getting a high school diploma. "If you get a high school diploma, you can do this and you can do this, without it you can't do *this." And I got one and I still can't do nothing. I can't get a job or nothing after I got one.* [Ex-delinquent.]

There is evidence that many students become disillusioned earlier than this young man. Many students who are not taking college preparatory work seem to believe that regardless of their efforts or achievement, the system will not come through with anything but low status, low paying jobs after high school. Present tasks and demands of the school therefore have little meaning or payoff. That problem, to be sure, lies not only in the schools' failure to prepare students adequately for the future, but also in the absence of adequate and equal employment opportunity. The U.S. Department of Labor has shown that a Negro high school graduate has a greater chance of being unemployed than a white high school dropout—a subject dealt with in greater detail below.

Too often, as a result of the virtual absence of relation between it and the life he is living or will live, the school cannot hold the slum child's interest. It is boring, dull, and apparently useless, to be endured for awhile and then abandoned as a bad deal.

Failure in School and Delinquency: The Downward Spiral of Failure. When the school system is not adequately equipped to meet the early learning problems a child brings to school with him, a cycle of deterioration and failure may be set in motion. As the youngster is "promoted" from grade to grade to keep him with his age mates but before he has really mastered his tasks, failure becomes cumulative. While he may have been only half a year behind the average in fourth grade, for example, recent evidence shows that the achievement gap may widen to three-quarters of a year by sixth grade and to one-and-one-quarter years by eighth grade.

The school failure, especially if he has developed a tough, indifferent facade, may give the impression that he does not care about his conspicuous failure to "make out" in school. In fact he probably cares a great deal, and even if the academic failure itself does not much matter to him, the loss of others' esteem does. He finds himself labeled a slow learner or a "goof-off." The school typically reacts to his failure with measures that reinforce his rejection: by assigning him to a special class for slow students, by excluding him from participation in extracurricular activities, by overlooking him in assigning prestigious school tasks and responsibilities.

The child, in self-defense, reacts against the school, perhaps openly rebelling against its demands. He and others like him seek each other out. Unable to succeed in being educated, they cannot afford to admit that education is important. Unwilling to accept the school's humiliating evaluation of them, they begin to flaunt its standards and reject its long-range goals in favor of conduct more immediately gratifying.

That conduct may not at first be seriously delinquent, but it represents a push toward more destructive and criminal patterns of behavior. Moreover, it takes forms, such as repeated truancy, that end hope of improved academic achievement. It may lead to dropping out of school.

There is mounting evidence that delinquency and failure in school are correlated. For example, in comparison of a group of "A" and "B" students with a group of "C" and "D" ones (both working and middle class), the "C" and "D" ones were seven times more likely to be delinquent; boys from blue-collar backgrounds who failed in school have been found to be delinquent almost seven times more often than those who did not fail.

It is of course difficult if not impossible to separate the part played by some schools from the innumerable other forces that may be related to the development of delinquent behavior. But both common sense and data such as these support the view that the high degree of correlation between delinquency and failure in school is more than accidental.

School Response to Behavior Problems. Student misbehavior is a real and urgent problem in many slum schools. Much youthful obstreperousness is best understood as a process of "testing" those in authority and demonstrating—partly for the benefit of peers—one's toughness and masculinity. For many inner-city children, the teacher represents the first real challenge to their independence. While middle-class children, accustomed to the close supervision of parents or parent substitutes, defer almost automatically to the authority of the teacher, the slum child arrives at school in the habit of being his own master and is not about to surrender his autonomy upon demand.

The way in which the school responds to early signs of misbehavior may have a profound influence in either diverting the youngster from or propelling him along the path to a delinquent career. Not all teachers have trouble with "difficult" youngsters. Some, especially sensitive to what lies behind insolence and disobedience, adopt a firm but positive attitude that allows the task of learning to be carried on, if not always under placid conditions.

Like my Civics teacher, he understand all the students. He know we like to play. Like, you know, he joke with us for about the first fifteen minutes and then, you know, everybody gets settled down and then they want to do some work. He got a good sense of humor and he understand. [Gang member, 17 years old.]

Other teachers simply submit, ignoring as best they can commotions and disruptions of classroom routine—an alternative that avoids head-on conflict with autonomy-seeking youth but at the same time deprives them of instruction even when they choose to accept it.

Like this one stud, man, he don't try to help us at all. He just goes on rapping (talking) to the poopbutts (squares), and when we ask a question he don't even pay no attention. I don't think that's fair. We there trying to learn just like anybody else! (All the time?) Well, sometimes. [Teenage gang member.]

Many teachers, on the other hand, assume a right to unquestioning obedience. There results a sometimes ceaseless conflict between teacher and child. The child's assertions of autonomy are dealt with by the teacher, and eventually the school administration, as misbehavior, and sanctioned in a variety of ways. By labeling the youth a troublemaker and excluding him from legitimate activities and sources of achievement, the sanctions may reinforce his tendency to rebel and resist the school's authority. Nor is it easy for him to reform; grades lowered for misconduct, the stigma of assignment to a special class, and records of misbehavior passed on both formally and informally from teacher to teacher make his past difficult to live down. The conception he forms of himself as an outsider, a nonconformer, is of particular importance. With no other source of public recognition, such negative self-images become attractive to some young people, and they begin to adapt their behavior to fit the labels applied to them. A process of defining and communicating a public character occurs, and some young people in a sense cooperate in actually becoming the delinquents they are said to be.

Directions for Change.   The slum student typically comes to school with a number of problems not shared by his middle-class counterpart, and the school that is faced with these problems has fewer resources than its middle-class counterpart to cope with them. It is therefore not surprising that the slum school has so often failed in the task of educating the slum child, a failure that relates in different and complex ways to delinquency.

Society should of course devote to slum schools the resources necessary to make them as well equipped and staffed as schools in other areas. But if we expect slum schools to succeed in their task of education, we must give them additional resources so that they can attempt to compensate, insofar as possible, for various handicaps suffered by the slum child—to rescue him from his environment.

Vast resources are required to improve the quality of teachers and facilities in slum schools. Efforts must be made to attract more and better teachers. Teachers' colleges must provide training, including internships, for working and disadvantaged children, as they already do for the mentally and physically handicapped. Incentives—financial, status, intellectual—must be provided to offset the dangers and discouragements of working in slum areas. Programs such as the National Teacher Corps seem useful for bringing new ideas and teaching methods into disadvantaged schools. There must be building programs to replace and improve deteriorated schools and to accommodate rapidly growing youth populations. Funds are needed for new equipment, for textbooks and library facilities.

Present efforts to combat school segregation along racial and economic lines, and the housing segregation that underlies it, must be continued and expanded. To the extent that school desegregation introduces inner-city children to the better schools outside the slums or accomplishes real improvement in slum schools, it would insure at least the allocation of comparable resources to the education of nonwhite lower-class children, as well as giving them the educational advantage of contact with children at higher levels of preparation and performance. And while school integration imposed in advance of residential desegregation in theory could subject as many nonslum children to inadequate slum schools as it exposed slum children to good nonslum schools, in fact the influence on school policy generally exercised by middle-class parents would most likely result in rapid upgrading of poor schools to which their children had been sent.

The Commission recommends:

In order that slum children may receive the best rather than the worst education in the Nation, efforts, both private and public, should be intensified to:

Secure financial support for necessary personnel, buildings, and equipment.

Improve the quality and quantity of teachers and facilities in the slum school.

Combat racial and economic school segregation.

There are numerous ways in which schools must adapt themselves to the particular needs of the disadvantaged child. They must, for example, learn to cope with the child who arrives at school inadequately prepared for education. Instead of assuming that the child is stupid and lowering expectations for his achievement, schools must help the child make up for the preparation he has missed. That is the goal of the early childhood education programs, involving both preschool and primary grades, already instituted in some schools; the preschool Head Start programs sponsored by the Office of Economic Opportunity have provided impetus for this effort on a nationwide scale. And better methods must be found for determining the innate ability of children and for encouraging each to achieve his full potential.

It is also important that schools learn to understand and control the child who arrives at school accustomed to autonomy and averse to assertions of authority. New methods of dealing with behavior problems are needed that avoid labeling the child a troublemaker, excluding him from his group and from legitimate activities, and reinforcing misbehavior patterns.

Flexible school administrative arrangements would make it possible to assign difficult students to regular classes taught by teachers who are particularly successful with such students. Teacher seminars would enable those teachers to share their insights with their fellows. Roving teams of consultants have been trained to work with teachers, parents, relatives, friends—anyone who can be taught to help children who are "acting up" in school. A number of experimental methods of dealing with misbehavior problems show promise. Some give added responsibilities to problem children: Mobilization for Youth employed older students, many of whom were delinquents, to tutor younger students. Other programs have improved school performance and reduced misbehavior in class with group techniques that encourage peer group control of members. A few schools have initiated and had favorable experience with efforts to detect delinquent tendencies at the elementary school level and to deal with them in a variety of ways, including special inservice training for teachers, special counselors and social services, incentive and reward systems for pupils, and cooperative work with parents.

When it is necessary to impose sanctions on the difficult child and separate him from his fellows, perhaps in a special class, it is important that he not be simply pushed out and neglected. Instead special resources should be devoted to helping him, special counseling and guidance services should be available, and channels should be kept open so that, where feasible, he can again become part of the regular student body.

In order to gain and keep the slum child's interest, schools must try to relate curriculum content and material to conditions of life in the slums. Reading and subject matter must not be limited to people, places, and situations that have no meaning for the slum child. Schools should address the problems and issues in his real world: poverty, disease, drug addiction, unemployment, police relations, discrimination, civil rights. One effort already made in this direction is development of primers that picture slum children and use vocabulary recognizable to them. Another is the designing, by Hunter College in New York, of new curricula for inner-city schools.

The Commission recommends:

In order that schools may better adapt to the particular educational problems of the slum child, efforts, both private and public, should be intensified to:

Help slum children make up for inadequate preschool preparation.

Deal better with behavior problems.

Relate instructional material to conditions of life in the slums.

There are numerous other ways in which the school can and should adapt to the needs of the slum child. Where families cannot provide a place and time for study because of crowded housing, or where they do not because of lack of interest, schools can make their facilities available. Where family and community offer little opportunity for recreation, schools can offer their personnel, buildings, and equipment to fill the void. Where family and community health care is inadequate, schools can provide supplemental services.

Schools should assume a greater responsibility for preparing students for the future. They should help raise the aspirations and expectations of those students capable of higher education and should prepare them for it. This is the objective of the Upward Bound programs sponsored by the Office of Economic Opportunity. Present programs for students not headed for college should also be reviewed and revised. Vocational training programs removed from industry often provide highly unrealistic training, and often it is for obsolete jobs. Schools should concern themselves with job placement for their graduates; it is already common for colleges to have placement offices and for industry to recruit directly from college.

The Commission recommends:

In order that schools may better prepare students for the future, efforts, both private and public, should be intensified to:

Raise the aspirations and expectations of students capable of higher education.

Review and revise present programs for students not going to college.

Further develop job placement services in schools.

Finally, it must be clearly recognized that the schools cannot solve the basic problems of education in isolation from the community, especially the family. Slum schools must become more aware of the community's requirements and develop a greater sensitivity to the expectations and educational objectives that parents hold for their children. And parents must become more involved in their children's education and more committed to its success, so that they can be more effective advocates of education at home. One approach has been the establishment of school-community advisory panels that have access to information about educational, vocational, curricular, and behavorial problems in the school. Their function is to suggest improvements in these areas. Some programs have employed parents and others as teacher aides. Some communities have greatly increased parental and community contact with the school by experimenting with the community school concept, through which the school remains open morning and night during the entire year and accommodates a variety of community activities, utilizing many local persons in planning and operating roles.

The Commission recommends:

In order that schools may become more responsive to community needs and parental expectations, efforts, both private and public, should be intensified to develop cooperation between schools and their communities.

DELINQUENCY AND EMPLOYMENT

Growing up properly is difficult at best, but manageable with help at times of critical need. To become a fully functional adult male, one prerequisite is essential: a job. In our society a person's occupation determines more than anything else what life he will lead and how others will regard him. Of course other important factors—family, wealth, race, age—exert significant influence on his future. But for most young men, it is securing jobs consistent with their aspirations that is crucial, that provides a stake in the law-abiding world and a vestibule to an expanding series of opportunities: To marry, to raise a family, to participate in civic affairs, to advance economically and socially and intellectually.

Getting a good job is harder than it used to be for those without preparation. To be a Negro, an 18-year-old, a school dropout in the slums of a large city is to have many times more chance of being unemployed than has a white 18-year-old high school graduate living a few blocks away. Poorly educated, untrained youth from 16 to 21 years of age are becoming the Nation's most stubborn employment problem, especially in the large cities. Our current economy simply does not need the skills and personal attributes they have to offer.

Youth and the Labor Market of the Future. Between 1960 and 1970 the available labor force is expected to rise by more than 1.5 million persons a year, an average annual increase nearly 50 percent greater than that which occurred during the first half of the 1960's and almost double that of the 1950's. Young workers, aged 14 to 24, will constitute nearly half (about 45 percent) of this increase.

One sign of greater difficulties ahead is the rising ratio of nonwhite workers joining the labor force—the workers who suffer most from lack of adequate education and training, shortage of unskilled jobs, and discriminatory barriers to em-

206

ployment. Between 1965 and 1970, the number of nonwhite youth reaching 18 will increase by 20 percent over the 1965 level. During the same period, the white population in the same age group will actually decrease, and will not regain the 1965 figure of 3.3 million until 1970. During the 5-year period after that, the number of nonwhite 18-year-olds will again increase by 20 percent while the number of white 18-year-olds will increase by only 10 percent.

And young people compose the category of workers with the highest unemployment rate. In 1965 the average unemployment rates for youth between 16 and 24 decreased somewhat from the peak reached in 1963. But the unemployment rate of youth aged 16 to 21 was over 12.5 percent, two and one-half times that for all workers. The 1.1 million young people unemployed represented, therefore, one-third of the jobless workers in the country, and for them the familiar syndrome—minority group member, school dropout, unemployed—holds stubbornly true. Of the 26 million young people who will enter the labor force during the 1960's, an estimated 25 percent will not have completed high school. Only 45 percent will be high school graduates. Only 26 percent will have graduated from or even attended college.

Employment and Employability. Any young person meets a number of problems when he sets out to find a job. He must learn where and how to look, decide what to look for, and finally, make himself acceptable. If he is a school dropout or has a delinquency record, those problems are significantly more serious.

It is commonplace today to observe that educational preparation is increasingly required for getting and holding a steady job. One would expect, therefore, that dropping out of school and being unemployed might be related to each other. Undereducated youngsters are eligible only for unskilled jobs; it is hard for them to get information about the local job market; they lack prior work experience. Most of them, consequently, do not in any real sense choose a job. Rather, they drift into one. And since such jobs rarely meet the aspirations that applicants bring with them, frustration typically results.

The search for a job may be even more discouraging when the young person has a delinquency record. There is evidence that many employers make improper use of records. A juvenile's adjudication record is required by the law of most jurisdictions to be private and confidential; in practice the confidentiality of these records is often violated. The employment application may require the applicant to state whether he was ever arrested or taken into custody, or employers may ask juvenile applicants to sign waivers permitting the court to release otherwise confidential information.

Many employers also inquire as to all arrests, whether or not a conviction resulted. About 75 percent of the employment agencies sampled in a recent study of employment practices in the New York City area stated that they ask applicants about arrest records and, as a matter of regular procedure, do not refer any applicant with a record, regardless of whether the arrest was followed by conviction. The standard U.S. Government employment application form (Form 57) has just recently been modified to ask for information concerning only those arrests that were followed by conviction, rather than all arrests as previously. The fact that the majority of slum males (estimates vary from 50 to 90 percent) have some sort of arrest record indicates the magnitude of this problem.

The delinquency label may preclude membership in labor unions or participation in apprenticeship training. Licensing requirements for some occupations, such as barbering and food service, may act as a bar to entry for those with a record of delinquent conduct.

The Effect of Unemployment. It does not take the slum youth long to discover the gap between what he had hoped for and thought he was entitled to as an American and what actually awaits him; and it is a bitter as well as an oft repeated experience. So he looks for some other way out.

The career decisions of these youths, and the reasons for them, are varied; many are not really decisions at all. Some find their way back to school or into a job training program. Some drift among low paying jobs. Those who have good connections with organized criminal enterprises may feel few restraints against following a career that, although illegitimate, is relatively safe and lucrative; they have seen many others thrive on the proceeds of vice, and it will not be hard for them to persuade themselves that the steady demand for illicit goods and services justifies providing them. Others try theft; some become good enough at it to make it their regular livelihood; others lack aptitude or connections and become failures in the illegal as well as the legal world—habitués of our jails and prisons. Finally, there are those who give up, retreat from conventional society, and search for a better world in the private fantasies they can command from drink and drugs.

The Transmission of Poverty From One Generation to the Next. Lack of educational preparation, an economy that does not need the young, availability of illicit "jobs," the effect of having an arrest record—all these decrease the slum youth's employment opportunities and increase his chances of becoming or continuing delinquent. Basic to the economics of delinquency is the transmission of poverty across the generations. Today, for the 18-year-old, employment is hard to find. What chance has a slum-dwelling 6-year-old to break out of the cycle of poverty? Individual initiative may be important in determining an individual's destiny, but it is the economic and social forces shaping the way children are brought up, their preparation for adulthood by public institutions, their chances for self-improvement that perpetuate poverty.

The neighborhood in which the 6-year-old has been growing up is disorganized and has a high rate of delinquency. His father may be struggling to support a large family on a low wage or, jobless, may have left or deserted his family. Chronic dependency of families is further reinforced by the failure of welfare laws to provide economic incentives for fathers to remain in the home.

The 6-year-old now enters school. Although his parents value education, they realistically enough have little expectation that he will advance very far, and they have neither time nor skill to aid him. The slum school, as discussed above, is incapable of picking up the burden. He leaves school, or is pushed out at age 16, educationally unprepared, often already with an arrest record. He marries early or fathers illegitimate children. The cycle continues.

In earlier times, when musclepower was enough to earn a living, his slum-dwelling predecessors could with less difficulty break out of the cycle of poverty. A better job meant a chance to move into a better neighborhood. The better neighborhood was less crowded, had better schools, better social services. The poverty circle was broken, and, as shown by studies like McKay's, described above, delinquency rates were concomitantly reduced. The new American "immigrants" have much greater difficulty escaping the city's high-delinquency areas. They are confined there by the new economics of the job market and the old coin of racial prejudice. The ghettos expand, the citizen fears crime, the summer brings riots, and no less than the future of America's cities is threatened.

Directions for Change. Reducing unemployment and underemployment is imperative both to enable every adult to make a decent living, with all its accompanying bulwarks against criminality, and to interrupt the poverty and disadvantage that unemployment and financial dependence pass on from generation to generation. Real improvement requires not only equipping potential workers with the skills to hold existing jobs but also making jobs available where none now exist.

No need is more obvious than to prepare youth for the jobs that are available. Programs are already in progress or being developed through the cooperative efforts of the Department of Labor, the Office of Education in the Department of Health, Education, and Welfare, and the Office of Economic Opportunity to ready young people for employment through training, counseling, and remedial education, and then to place them. These efforts should be expanded. Particularly they should be provided with resources enabling devotion of substantial attention to youths who have already demonstrated proneness to antisocial conduct.

For out-of-school youth, who as demonstrated above are at a special disadvantage on the job market, programs such as those authorized by the Department of Labor's Manpower Development and Training Act and the Labor-sponsored Youth Opportunity Centers are particularly important. For those young people still in school, it is essential that schools seek ways of equipping them for work. Vocational training programs should be reexamined; as pointed out above, many are obsolete or impractical. Means should be developed that enable students to combine academic education, vocational training, and on-the-job experience, for purposes of both immediate financial assistance and future employment; the Neighborhood Youth Corps is a promising beginning. Schools should further develop their placement activities, for part-time jobs for youth still in school as well as for more permanent employment upon graduating from or leaving school.

Besides government and the schools, labor organizations and industry must also become engaged in the effort to make youth employable. The youth training program sponsored by the National Association of Manufacturers provides an example of what can be done by industry, to the mutual benefit of industry and youth.

Too frequently youth, even those qualified for existing jobs, lack easy access to job information. Typically, especially among inner-city young people who may feel alienated from regular methods of seeking employment, employment opportunity news travels chiefly by word of mouth; in areas where unemployment is already prevalent, such information is likely to be sparse. The Youth Opportunity Centers sponsored by the Department of Labor are one method of meeting this problem; others should be sought.

As discussed above, it is not only inadequate preparation that stands between young people and gainful employment, but also such special barriers as discrimination against nonwhites, exclusion on the basis of an arrest record, the existence of unnecessary requirements for many jobs. Fair employment practices and laws exist in many places; enforcement of them must be diligent and strict. Steps should be taken to eliminate discrimination in, and better regulate, the use of arrest information—often unsupported by information on the disposition of the charge—in employment decisions. This is particularly important with respect to juvenile records, which may reflect adolescent habits abandoned by the time employment is being sought. It is also critical in the inner city, where the arrest rate is generally high and where an arrest record frequently combines with undereducation and minority group membership and gravely compounds the difficulties of finding work. One possible solution is illustrated by the experimental Department of Labor program for bonding persons whose police record would otherwise bar them from obtaining the personal bond required by many jobs.

Employment specialists have had considerable success in persuading employers to reexamine their requirements for given positions and to hire on a trial basis otherwise satisfactory candidates who lack some nonessential qualification. Employers must themselves take the initiative in such reconsideration. Employers must also, however, be willing simply to take a chance, where it is not an unduly dangerous one— a youth with a minor record, for instance, or one who is generally able but undertrained.

Finally, the job market itself must be expanded. Jobs must be created as well as made more easily available. The poverty program is a prime example. It has brought into existence jobs that did not exist before and that can be done by persons who would otherwise have great difficulty in finding work because of a criminal record or lack of education. Besides poverty and other community development programs, a particularly promising area for employment of people with special employment difficulties is that of the human services—police and probation aides, medical assistants, teacher helpers. Such positions have the advantage of providing opportunity to advance through inservice training and on-the-job experience as well as immediate employment for persons with little education or training. It is particularly important that new sources

211

of employment include such opportunities. One recent suggestion is that a youth service corps be formed patterned after the Peace Corps and VISTA (Volunteers In Service To America, the domestic peace corps), which would appeal especially to the older youth who present the most serious unemployment problem and which would include training and advancement within the corps leading to the possibility of a community service or government career.

The Commission recommends:

Efforts, both private and public, should be intensified to:

Prepare youth for employment.

Provide youth with information about employment opportunities.

Reduce barriers to employment posed by discrimination, the misuse of criminal records, and maintenance of rigid job qualifications.

Create new employment opportunities.

THE JUVENILE JUSTICE SYSTEM

All three parts of the criminal justice system—police, courts, and corrections—have over the years developed special ways of dealing with children and young people. Many police departments have sought to develop specialists skilled at the difficult decisions that must be made about the many young people with whom the police have contact. Officers have organized and participated in athletic and other programs to help improve police relations with youth and enrich life in the community. Corrections systems have established separate institutions for juveniles and have emphasized probation over institutionalization for juveniles more than they have for adults. The juvenile court—even where it shares its judge with other tribunals or is not physically distinct—has a philosophy and procedures of its own and markedly unlike those of the adult criminal court.

Although its shortcomings are many and its results too often disappointing, the juvenile justice system in many cities is operated by people who are better educated and more highly skilled, can call on more and better facilities and services, and has more ancillary agencies to which to refer its clientele than its adult counterpart. Yet the number of cases referred to juvenile courts continues to grow faster than the juvenile population, the recidivism rate continues to increase, and while there are no figures on how many delinquents

212

graduate to become grownup criminals, it is clear that many do. This part of chapter 3 deals with ways in which the juvenile justice system can be made more effective and more fair.

THE POLICE: INITIAL CONTACT POINT WITH THE JUVENILE JUSTICE SYSTEM

Whether or not a juvenile becomes involved in the juvenile justice system usually depends upon the outcome of an encounter with the police. Such encounters are frequent, especially in the crowded inner city.

Some of them grow out of a criminal act of significant proportions: The juveniles have been caught in the act, or are being sought, or there is reason to believe that they answer the description given by a complainant. In such instances, the contact is very likely to lead to further processing by the juvenile justice system.

On the other hand, many encounters are based on a relatively minor violation, or not on a specific crime at all but on the policeman's sense that something is wrong. He may suspect that a crime has happened or is about to happen. Or he may believe the juvenile's conduct is offensive, insolent, or in some other way improper. On such occasions, the policeman has a relatively great range of choices. He can pass by. He can stop for a few words of general banter. He can ask the juveniles their names, where they live, where they are going. He can question them about what has been happening in the neighborhood. He can search them, order them to disperse or move on, check with the station for records and recent neighborhood offenses. He can send or take them home, where he may warn their parents to keep them off the street. Suspicion, even perhaps without very specific grounds for it, may on occasion lead him to bring them in to the station for further questioning or checking.

In any given encounter the policeman's selection among alternatives may vary considerably among departments and among individual officers. It is governed to some extent by departmental practice, either explicitly enunciated or tacitly understood. Such policies are difficult to evolve—indeed, in many instances they could not be specific enough to be helpful without being too rigid to accommodate the vast variety of street situations. Nevertheless, it is important that, wherever possible, police forces formulate guidelines for policemen in their dealings with juveniles.

Besides the nature of the situation and departmental policy, however, police-juvenile encounters are shaped by other, less tangible forces.

One such influence is the character of the police force as a whole. In a recent field study of two police forces—one putting particularly great emphasis on education and training, merit promotions, centralized control; the second relying more heavily on organization by precinct, seniority, on-the-job experience—significant differences were found between the two in handling delinquents. In the first city, the one with the more professionalized force, rates of both processing (police contact not amounting to arrest but requiring the police officer to make an official record) and arrest (formal police action against the juvenile either by ordering him to appear before a court official or by taking him into custody) were more than 50 percent higher than those in the second city. In other words, meetings between policemen and juveniles had formal, official, recorded consequences much more frequently in the first city, with its more highly trained and impersonal police force, than in the second. At the conclusion of his study on the police the researcher, noting how little is known about the actual effects on juveniles of different handling methods, speculates about the various arguments that might be made:

*The training of a police force apparently alters the manner in which juveniles are handled. The principal effect of the inculcation of professional norms is to make the police less discriminatory but more severe * * *. Plausible arguments can be advanced * * * to the effect that certain, swift punishment (in this case, certain, swift referral to a court agency) is an excellent deterrent to juvenile crime. Youths are impressed early, so the argument might go, with the seriousness of their offense and the consequences of the actions. Equally plausible arguments can no doubt be adduced to suggest that arresting juveniles—particularly first offenders—tends to confirm them in their deviant behavior; it gives them the status, in the eyes of their gang, of "tough guys" who have "been downtown" with the police; it throws them into intimate contact with confirmed offenders, where presumably they become "con-wise" and learned in the tricks of the thievery trade; and (somewhat contradictory) since sentencing is rarely severe, it gives them a contempt for the sanctions available to society.* James Q. Wilson in *The Police,* Bordua, ed. (1967).

The reactions and attitudes of individual officers are also influential when they are dealing with juveniles. As numerous observers and students of police work have pointed out, a policeman in attempting to solve crimes must employ, in the absence of concrete evidence, circumstantial indicators to link specific crimes with specific people. Thus policemen may stop Negro and Mexican youths in white neighborhoods, may suspect juveniles who act in what the policemen consider an impudent or overly casual manner, and may be influenced by such factors as unusual hair styles or clothes uncommon to the wearer's group or area. Naturally, the adolescents involved are aware of such police distinctions. They are at a notoriously sensitive age and are ready to see themselves as victims of police harassment. In the words of one boy: "Them cops is supposed to be out catching *criminals*. They ain't paid to be looking after my hair!" When boys are actually stopped by policemen, their own attitudes and their demeanor appear often to play a part in what happens next. Some observers have suggested that those who act frightened, penitent, and respectful are more likely to be released, while those who assert their autonomy and act indifferent or resistant run a substantially greater risk of being frisked, interrogated, or even taken into custody.

Informal street handling of juveniles creates conflicts that are extremely difficult to resolve. Juveniles commit large numbers of offenses. Some of the circumstances that lead policemen to suspect given juveniles often do stem from criminal conduct. The policeman's dependence upon the sort of information juveniles provide in informal encounters is real and unlikely to be satisfied elsewhere.

On the other hand, abuse of authority—real or imagined —may seriously impair young people's respect for constituted authority and produce deep resentment. Informal investigatory police encounters with juveniles are inevitable, but it is of the utmost importance that juveniles receive treatment that is neither unfair nor degrading.

The Commission recommends:

To the greatest feasible extent, police departments should formulate policy guidelines for dealing with juveniles.

All officers should be acquainted with the special characteristics of adolescents, particularly those of the social, racial, and other specific groups with which they are likely to come in contact.

Custody of a juvenile (both prolonged street stops and sta-

215

tionhouse visits) should be limited to instances where there is objective, specifiable ground for suspicion.

Every stop that includes a frisk or an interrogation of more than a few preliminary identifying questions should be recorded in a strictly confidential report.

THE JUVENILE COURT AND RELATED AGENCIES

Juvenile courts are judicial tribunals that deal in special ways with young people's cases. They exist in all jurisdictions. Their cases include delinquency (both conduct in violation of the criminal code and truancy, ungovernability, and certain conduct illegal only for children), neglect, and dependency. The juveniles with whom they deal are those below a designated age, usually between 16 and 21; court authority over the child extends until he reaches his majority. They differ from adult criminal courts in a number of basic respects, reflecting the philosophy that erring children should be protected and rehabilitated rather than subjected to the harshness of the criminal system. Thus they substitute procedural informality for the adversary system, emphasize investigation of the juvenile's background in deciding dispositions, rely heavily on the social sciences for both diagnosis and treatment, and are committed to rehabilitation of the juvenile as the predominant goal of the entire system.

Studies conducted by the Commission, legislative inquiries in various States, and reports by informed observers compel the conclusion that the great hopes originally held for the juvenile court have not been fulfilled. It has not succeeded significantly in rehabilitating delinquent youth, in reducing or even stemming the tide of delinquency, or in bringing justice and compassion to the child offender. To say that juvenile courts have failed to achieve their goals is to say no more than what is true of criminal courts in the United States. But failure is most striking when hopes are highest.

One reason for the failure of the juvenile courts has been the community's continuing unwillingness to provide the resources—the people and facilities and concern—necessary to permit them to realize their potential and prevent them from acquiring some of the undesirable features typical of lower criminal courts in this country. In some jurisdictions, for example, the juvenile court judgeship does not have high status in the eyes of the bar, and while there are many juvenile court judges of outstanding ability and devotion, many are not. One crucial presupposition of the juvenile court philosophy—a mature and sophisticated judge, wise and well versed in law and the science of human behavior—has proved in

216

fact too often unattainable. A recent study of juvenile court judges in the United States revealed that half had no undergraduate degree; a fifth had received no college education at all; a fifth were not members of the bar. Almost three-quarters devote less than a quarter of their time to juvenile and family matters, and judicial hearings often turn out to be little more than attenuated interviews of 10 to 15 minutes' duration.

Similarly, more than four-fifths of the juvenile judges polled in a recent survey reported no psychologist or psychiatrist available to them on a regular basis—over half a century after the juvenile court movement set out to achieve the coordinated application of the behavioral and social sciences to the misbehaving child. Clinical services to diagnose and to assist in devising treatment plans are the exception, and even where they exist, the waiting lists are so long that their usefulness is more theoretical than real.

The dispositional alternatives available even to the better endowed juvenile courts fall far short of the richness and the relevance to individual needs envisioned by the court's founders. In most places, indeed, the only alternatives are release outright, probation, and institutionalization. Probation means minimal supervision at best. A large percentage of juvenile courts have no probation services at all, and in those that do, caseloads typically are so high that counseling and supervision take the form of occasional phone calls and perfunctory visits instead of the careful, individualized service that was intended. Institutionalization too often means storage—isolation from the outside world—in an overcrowded, understaffed security institution with little education, little vocational training, little counseling or job placement or other guidance upon release. Intermediate and auxiliary measures such as halfway houses, community residential treatment centers, diversified institutions and programs, intensive community supervision have proved difficult to establish.

But it is by no means true that a simple infusion of resources into juvenile courts and attendant institutions would fulfill the expectations that accompanied the court's birth and development. There are problems that go much deeper. The failure of the juvenile court to fulfill its rehabilitative and preventive promise stems in important measure from a grossly overoptimistic view of what is known about the phenomenon of juvenile criminality and of what even a fully equipped juvenile court could do about it. Experts in the field agree that it is extremely difficult to develop successful methods for preventing serious delinquent acts through rehabilitative

217

programs for the child. What research is making increasingly clear is that delinquency is not so much an act of individual deviancy as a pattern of behavior produced by a multitude of pervasive societal influences well beyond the reach of the actions of any judge, probation officer, correctional counselor, or psychiatrist.

The same uncritical unrealistic estimates of what is known and can be done that make expectation so much greater than achievement also serve to justify extensive official action and to mask the fact that much of it may produce more harm than good. Official action may actually help to fix and perpetuate delinquency in the child through a process in which the individual begins to think of himself as delinquent and organizes his behavior accordingly. That process itself is further reinforced by the effect of the labeling upon the child's family, neighbors, teachers, and peers, whose reactions communicate to the child in subtle ways a kind of expectation of delinquent conduct. The undesirable consequences of official treatment are maximized in programs that rely on institutionalizing the child. The most informed and benign official treatment of the child therefore contains within it the seeds of its own frustration and itself may often feed the very disorder it is designed to cure.

The limitations, both in theory and in execution, of strictly rehabilitative treatment methods, combined with public anxiety over the seemingly irresistible rise in juvenile criminality, have produced a rupture between the theory and the practice of juvenile court dispositions. While statutes, judges, and commentators still talk the language of compassion and treatment, it has become clear that in fact the same purposes that characterize the use of the criminal law for adult offenders —retribution, condemnation, deterrence, incapacitation—are involved in the disposition of juvenile offenders too. These are society's ultimate techniques for protection against threatening conduct; it is inevitable that they should be used against threats from the young as well as the old when other resources appear unavailing. As Professor Francis Allen has acutely observed:

In a great many cases the juvenile court must perform functions essentially similar to those exercised by any court adjudicating cases or persons charged with dangerous and disturbing behavior. It must reassert the norms and standards of the community when confronted by seriously deviant conduct, and it must protect the security of the community by such measures as it has at its disposal, though the available means may be unsatisfactory when viewed either from the stand-point of the community interest or to the welfare of the child. Allen, *The Borderland of Criminal Justice* (1964), p. 53.

The difficulty is not that this compromise with the rehabilitative idea has occurred, but that it has not been acknowledged. Juvenile court laws and procedures that can be rationalized solely on the basis of the original optimistic theories endure as if the vitality of those theories were undiluted. Thus, for example, juvenile courts retain expansive grounds of jurisdiction authorizing judicial intervention in relatively minor matters of morals and misbehavior, on the ground that subsequent delinquent conduct may be indicated, as if there were reliable ways of predicting delinquency in a given child and reliable ways of redirecting children's lives. Delinquency is adjudicated in informal proceedings that often lack safeguards fundamental for protecting the individual and for assuring reliable determinations, as if the court were a hospital clinic and its only objective were to discover the child's malady and to cure him.

The Commission does not conclude from its study of the juvenile court that the time has come to jettison the experiment and remand the disposition of children charged with crime to the criminal courts of the country. As trying as are the problems of the juvenile courts, the problems of the criminal courts, particularly those of the lower courts that would fall heir to much of the juvenile court jurisdiction, are even graver; and the ideal of separate treatment of children is still worth pursuing. What is required is rather a revised philosophy of the juvenile court, based on recognition that in the past our reach exceeded our grasp. The spirit that animated the juvenile court movement was fed in part by a humanitarian compassion for offenders who were children. That willingness to understand and treat people who threaten public safety and security should be nurtured, not turned aside as hopeless sentimentality, both because it is civilized and because social protection itself demands constant search for alternatives to the crude and limited expedient of condemnation and punishment. But neither should it be allowed to outrun reality. The juvenile court is a court of law, charged like other agencies of criminal justice with protecting the community against threatening conduct. Rehabilitation of offenders through individualized handling is one way of providing protection, and appropriately the primary way in dealing with children. But the guiding consideration for a court of law that deals with threatening conduct is nevertheless protection of the community. The juvenile court, like other courts, is therefore obliged to employ all the means at hand, not excluding incapacitation, for achieving that protection. What should distinguish the juvenile from the criminal courts is their greater emphasis on rehabilitation, not their exclusive preoccupation with it.

This chapter outlines a series of interlocking proposals aimed at what the Commission believes are basic deficiencies in the system of juvenile justice. Those concerning early stages in police handling of juveniles have already been set forth. The essence of those relating to the juvenile court and institutions closely connected with it is as follows:

☐ The formal sanctioning system and pronouncement of delinquency should be used only as a last resort. In place of the formal system, dispositional alternatives to adjudication must be developed for dealing with juveniles, including agencies to provide and coordinate services and procedures to achieve necessary control without unnecessary stigma. Alternatives already available, such as those related to court intake, should be more fully exploited.

☐ The range of conduct for which court intervention is authorized should be narrowed.

☐ The cases that fall within the narrowed jurisdiction of the court and filter through the screen of pre-judicial, informal disposition modes would largely involve offenders for whom more vigorous measures seem necessary. Court adjudication and disposition of those offenders should no longer be viewed solely as a diagnosis and prescription for cure, but should be frankly recognized as an authoritative court judgment expressing society's claim to protection. While rehabilitative efforts should be vigorously pursued in deference to the youthfulness of the offenders and in keeping with the general commitment to individualized treatment of all offenders, the incapacitative, deterrent, and condemnatory purposes of the judgment should not be disguised. Accordingly, the adjudicatory hearing should be consistent with basic principles of due process. Counsel and evidentiary restrictions are among the essential elements of fundamental fairness in juvenile as well as adult criminal courts.

Pre-Judicial Disposition Outside the Court. It is a salient characteristic of the American criminal law system that substantial numbers of those who, on the basis of facts known to

220

the authorities, could be dealt with by the formal machinery of justice are in fact disposed of otherwise. Chapter 5 on the courts includes discussion of nonjudicial disposition of adult offenders. The pressures and policies responsible for development of pre-judicial dispositions in the juvenile system are in part the same as those that have led to the use of alternatives to the adult criminal process. The felt overseverity of the formal process in the circumstances of the particular case, the broad reach of the definition of the forbidden conduct beyond what is appropriately dealt with by the criminal or juvenile justice system, and the sheer volume of workload are among the most important considerations.

Informal and discretionary pre-judicial dispositions already are a formally recognized part of the process to a far greater extent in the juvenile than in the criminal justice system. The primacy of the rehabilitative goal in dealing with juveniles, the limited effectiveness of the formal processes of the juvenile justice system, the labeling inherent in adjudicating children delinquents, the inability of the formal system to reach the influences—family, school, labor market, recreational opportunities—that shape the life of a youngster, the limited disposition options available to the juvenile judge, the limitations of personnel and diagnostic and treatment facilities, the lack of community support—all of these factors give pre-judicial dispositions an especially important role with respect to juveniles.

Consequently, the informal and pre-judicial processes of adjustment compete in importance with the formal ones and account for a majority of juvenile dispositions. They include discretionary judgments of the police officer to ignore conduct or warn the child or refer him to other agencies; "station adjustment" by the police, in which the child's release may be made conditional on his complying with designated limitations on his conduct; the planned diversion of alleged delinquents away from the court to resources within the school, clinic, or other community facilities, by such groups as mental health, social, and school guidance agencies; pre-judicial dispositions, at the intake stage of the court process, by probation officers or sometimes judges exercising a broad screening function and selecting among alternatives that include outright dismissal, referral to another community agency for service, informal supervision by the probation staff, detention, and filing a petition for further court action. In many courts the court intake process itself disposes of the majority of cases.

There are grave disadvantages and perils, however, in that

vast continent of sublegal dispositions. It exists outside of and hence beyond the guidance and control of articulated policies and legal restraints. It is largely invisible—unknown in its detailed operation—and hence beyond sustained scrutiny and criticism. Discretion too often is exercised haphazardly and episodically, without the salutary obligation to account and without a foundation in full and comprehensive information about the offender and about the availability and likelihood of alternative dispositions. Opportunities occur for illegal and even discriminatory results, for abuse of authority by the ill-intentioned, the prejudiced, the overzealous. Irrelevant, improper considerations—race, nonconformity, punitiveness, sentimentality, understaffing, overburdening loads—may govern officials in their largely personal exercise of discretion. The consequence may be not only injustice to the juvenile but diversion out of the formal channels of those whom the best interests of the community require to be dealt with through the formal adjudicatory and dispositional processes.

Yet on balance, it is clear to the Commission that informal pre-judicial handling is preferable to formal treatment in many cases and should be used more broadly. The possibilities for rehabilitation appear to be optimal where community-based resources are used on a basis as nearly consensual as possible. The challenge is to obtain the benefits of informal pre-judicial handling with a minimum of its attendant evils. The following recommendations are offered to that end.

(a) Pre-Judicial Handling by the Police. The police should promptly determine which cases are suitable for pre-judicial disposition. Where there are juvenile specialists, they should be present at the stationhouse for as many hours of the day as possible and available on call when absent, to facilitate speedy pre-judicial decisions. The police should have written standards for release, for referral to nonjudicial sources, and for referral to the juvenile court. The standards should be sent to all agencies of delinquency control and should be reviewed and appraised jointly at periodic intervals. They should be made the basis for inservice training that would consider, besides the decision-making duties of the police, materials pertinent to increasing understanding of juvenile behavior and making more effective use of nonjudicial community resources.

In cases where information on the child is needed, it should be sought through home visits as well as from official records, and the police should be aided, or replaced, by paid case aides drawn from the neighborhood within the police district and selected for their knowledge of the community and their ability to communicate easily with juveniles and their families.

In addition to outright referral to nonjudicial agencies the police should have the option to refer directly to the juvenile court specified classes of cases, including those of more serious offenders, repeated offenders for whom other and persistent redirecting efforts had failed, and certain parole and probation violators. The police should not undertake to redirect juveniles by such means as conducting quasi-judicial hearings or imposing special duties or personal obligations.

Police practices following custody thus should continue as at present but with two significant changes: Cases deemed suitable for adjustment would be referred to a youth-serving agency within a neighborhood service center (the Youth Services Bureau proposed herein and described in detail subsequently), and the categories of cases that could be referred by the police directly to juvenile court would be restricted. Exercise of discretion to release outright would be encouraged, as now, so that minor offenses not apparently symptomatic of serious behavior problems could be dismissed at the earliest stage of official handling, and even more serious offenses could be adjusted by referral to a Youth Services Bureau or other organization if, in the judgment of the police, there was no immediate threat to public safety.

The Commission recommends:

Police forces should make full use of the central diagnosing and coordinating services of the Youth Services Bureau. Station adjustment should be limited to release and referral; it should not include hearings or the imposition of sanctions by the police. Court referral by the police should be restricted to those cases involving serious criminal conduct or repeated misconduct of a more than trivial nature.

(b) Community Agencies. There should be expanded use of community agencies for dealing with delinquents nonjudicially and close to where they live. Use of community agencies has several advantages. It avoids the stigma of being processed by an official agency regarded by the public as an arm of crime control. It substitutes for official agencies organizations better suited for redirecting conduct. The use of locally sponsored or operated organizations heightens the community's awareness of the need for recreational, employment, tutoring, and other youth development services. Involvement of local residents brings greater appreciation of the complexity of delinquents' problems, thereby engendering the sense of

223

public responsibility that financial support of programs requires.

Referrals by police, school officials, and others to such local community agencies should be on a voluntary basis. To protect against abuse, the agency's option of court referral should terminate when the juvenile or his family and the community agency agree upon an appropriate disposition. If a departure from the agreed-upon course of conduct should thereafter occur, it should be the community agency that exercises the authority to refer to court. It is also essential that the dispositions available to such local organizations be restricted. The purpose of using community institutions in this way is to help, not to coerce, and accordingly it is inappropriate to confer on them a power to order treatment or alter custody or impose sanctions for deviation from the helping program.

Those recommendations could be put into effect in the near future, with existing organizations. Long-term recommendations for enhanced use of community service agencies, however, would require the creation of new social institutions. An essential objective in a community's delinquency control and prevention plan should therefore be the establishment of a neighborhood youth-serving agency, a Youth Services Bureau, with a broad range of services and certain mandatory functions. Such an agency ideally would be located in a comprehensive community center and would serve both delinquent and nondelinquent youths. While some referrals to the Youth Services Bureau would normally originate with parents, schools, and other sources, the bulk of the referrals could be expected to come from the police and the juvenile court intake staff, and police and court referrals should have special status in that the Youth Services Bureau would be required to accept them all. If, after study, certain youths are deemed unlikely to benefit from its services, the Bureau should be obliged to transmit notice of the decision and supporting reasons to the referral source. A mandate for service seems necessary to insure energetic efforts to control and redirect acting-out youth and to minimize the substantial risk that this population, denied service by traditional agencies, will inevitably be shunted to a law enforcement agency.

A primary function of the Youth Services Bureau thus would be individually tailored work with troublemaking youths. The work might include group and individual counseling, placement in foster homes, work and recreational programs, employment counseling, and special education (remedial, vocational). It would be under the Bureau's direct control either through purchase or by voluntary agreement with other community organizations. The most significant feature of the Bureau's function would be its mandatory responsibility to develop and monitor a plan of service for a group now handled, for the most part, either inappropriately or not at all except in time of crisis.

It is essential that acceptance of the Youth Services Bureau's services be voluntary; otherwise the dangers and disadvantages of coercive power would merely be transferred from the juvenile court to it. Nonetheless, it may be necessary to vest the Youth Services Bureau with authority to refer to the court within a brief time—not more than 60 and preferably not more than 30 days—those with whom it cannot deal effectively. In accordance with its basically voluntary character, the Youth Services Bureau should be required to comply with the parent's request that a case be referred to juvenile court.

In many communities there may already exist the ingredients of a Youth Services Bureau in the form of community or neighborhood centers and programs for juveniles. All communities should explore the availability of Federal funds both for establishing the coordinating mechanisms basic to the Youth Services Bureau's operation and for instituting the programs that the community needs.

The Commission recommends:

Communities should establish neighborhood youth-serving agencies—Youth Services Bureaus—located if possible in comprehensive neighborhood community centers and receiving juveniles (delinquent and nondelinquent) referred by the police, the juvenile court, parents, schools, and other sources.

These agencies would act as central coordinators of all community services for young people and would also provide services lacking in the community or neighborhood, especially ones designed for less seriously delinquent juveniles.

The Juvenile Court. (a) Intake—Pre-Judicial Disposition In Court. Pre-judicial disposition is no newcomer to the juvenile court. Some courts today, as noted above, dispose of more than half the cases referred to them by means short of adjudication. It is in the court, therefore, where problems of lack of accurate, up-to-date information about needs and alternatives; lack of coordination among available services; and lack of systematic ways to bring the juvenile and the service together are particularly acute.

To meet those difficulties, the court intake function of pre-judicial disposition should be more systematically employed and more formally recognized and organized. Written guides and standards should be formulated and imparted in the course of inservice training. Staff resources should be augmented where necessary to keep abreast of service opportunities and programs in the community and to make inquiries into the backgrounds of juveniles sufficiently comprehensive to select intelligently among alternatives. Overly informal methods of control (such as informal probation with filing of a petition as the penalty for violation), subject as they are to abuse, should be abandoned in favor of institutionalized non-adjudicatory disposition.

More specifically, the Commission commends to the attention of juvenile courts the preliminary conference recently adopted by both New York and Illinois, through which voluntarily attended discussions among court personnel, juvenile, parents, complainants, and other involved parties are used to resolve grievances without adjudication. Safeguards essential to such a procedure are that it occur within a specifically limited time, to eliminate the indirect coercion of an indefinite threat that a petition will be filed at some later date, and that use of statements made at the conference be inadmissible in subsequent court proceedings.

The Commission recommends:

Juvenile courts should make fullest feasible use of preliminary conferences to dispose of cases short of adjudication.

Another method of employing the arbitrating and treating authority of the juvenile court without the disadvantages of adjudication is the consent decree. Consent decree negotiations, too, would be conducted by intake officers and would involve the juvenile and his parents and lawyer (the presence of whom, unless waived, would be required) and a probation officer assigned to the case. The consent decree would be embodied in writing and attested to by the parties and would be effective only upon approval of its terms by the juvenile court judge. It would prescribe a treatment plan but could not commit to an institution. Its duration would be limited, preferably to a year. Negotiations would be subject to the same protections as the preliminary conference procedure. If negotiations failed or the consent decree were violated, the same possibilities—dismissal, referral to a nonjudicial agency, and filing of a petition—would be available as were available prior to the decree. In case of violation of the consent decree, the charge would be the one that initially gave rise to the proceedings. Violation of the decree would be relevant only to disposition.

The Commission recommends:

Juvenile courts should employ consent decrees wherever possible to avoid adjudication while still settling juvenile cases and treating offenders.

(b) Legislative Standards for Juvenile Court Intervention. A hallmark of the juvenile court has traditionally been the inclusion in its jurisdiction of a very diverse group, sometimes characterized as children in trouble—whether the trouble consists of youthful criminality, truancy or other conduct wrong only for children, or a parent's inadequacy or abusiveness. The basic philosophy of the juvenile court was considered antithetical to narrow, restrictively specific jurisdictional requisites, and so they were discarded in favor of all-encompassing formulations intended to bring within the court's jurisdiction virtually every child in need of help, for whatever reason and however the need was manifested. To the chancery court's traditional clientele of neglected children was added the category of underage criminal lawbreakers, who were, however, not to be designated or considered as such and toward whom, despite their considerably more threatening behavior, the judicial attitude was to be equally solicitous. In accordance with the protective and rehabilitative theories of the juvenile court, the definition of conduct making one eligible for the category of delinquency was not limited by conduct criminal for adults but rather amounted virtually to a manual of undesirable youthful behavior. And in addition to enforcing the penal law, the commonly accepted standards of conduct for youth, and the basic obligations of parents to children, the juvenile court also undertook to reinforce the duties owed parents and schools by children. Thus truancy was included among the bases for juvenile court jurisdiction, as was a catch-all state variously called incorrigibility, ungovernability, uncontrollability, or simply "beyond control," which basically means defying parental authority.

The rationale for this comprehensive array of jurisdictional pegs generally emphasized the growth of social as opposed to legalistic justice and the new efforts to bring the law out of isolation and into partnership with the ascending social and behavioral sciences. The juvenile court was to arrest the development of incipient criminals by detecting them early and uncovering and ameliorating the causes of their disaffection.

Experience of over half a century with juvenile courts has taught us that these aspirations were greatly overoptimistic and chimerical. The court's wide-ranging jurisdiction thus has often become an anachronism serving to facilitate gratuitous coercive intrusions into the lives of children and families. Recent legislative revisions in several States, including California, Illinois, and New York, have significantly restricted the court's jurisdictional bases.

The Commission recommends:

The movement for narrowing the juvenile court's jurisdiction should be continued.

Specifically, the Commission recommends as follows:

Any act that is considered a crime when committed by an adult should continue to be, when charged against a juvenile, the business of the juvenile court.

The conduct-illegal-only-for-children category of the court's jurisdiction should be substantially circumscribed so that it ceases to include such acts as smoking, swearing, and disobedience to parents and comprehends only acts that entail a real risk of long-range harm to the child, such as experimenting with drugs, repeatedly becoming pregnant out of wedlock, and being habitually truant from school. Serious consideration, at the least, should be given to complete elimination of the court's power over children for noncriminal conduct.

Traffic violations by juveniles should be dealt with by traffic courts, except for serious offenses such as vehicular homicide and driving while under the influence of alcohol or drugs.

The neglect jurisdiction of the juvenile court should be retained since it involves conflicts between the parents' right to custody and the child's physical and mental well-being.

Dependency jurisdiction should be abolished since such cases involve inability rather than willful failure to provide properly for children and can adequately and more appropriately be dealt with by social, nonjudicial agencies.

Careful consideration should be given proposals to create family courts that, by dealing with all intrafamily matters

228

including those now generally handled by juvenile courts, would provide one means of achieving the consistency and continuity of treatment now too often undercut by fragmented jurisdiction.

(c) Procedural Justice for the Child. The original humanitarian philosophy of the juvenile court was believed to require a significant change in the manner in which courts determined which children to deal with and how to deal with them. The formalities of criminal procedure were rejected on the ground that they were not needed in juvenile court proceedings and that they would be destructive of the goals of those proceedings. In their place was to be substituted a wholly informal and flexible procedure under which, by gentle and friendly probing by judge, social worker, parent, and child, the roots of the child's difficulties could be exposed and informed decisions made as to how best to meet his problems. Informality in both procedure and disposition thus became a basic characteristic of juvenile courts.

In recent years, however, there has been a mounting reaction against this commitment to informality, stemming principally from profound concern about the potential arbitrariness and unfettered judicial discretion in dealing with human lives that informality establishes. This reaction is only one manifestation of much broader concern about protection of the rights of persons threatened with State intervention in their daily lives, particularly insofar as those who are involved live in poverty at the margin of American life and have not in the past had full protection. But there are special considerations applicable to the juvenile court that are of immediate importance.

First, efforts to help and heal and treat, if they are to have any chance of success, must be based upon an accurate determination of the facts—the facts of the conduct that led to the filing of the petition and also the facts of the child's past conduct and relationships. The essential attributes of a judicial trial are the best guarantee our system has been able to devise for assuring reliable determinations of fact.

Second, we are committed to the value of individual self-determination and freedom. The fact that the State's motives are beneficent and designed to provide what, at least in its view, the child and its parents need, should not be allowed to obscure the fact that in taking a child from his parents or placing him in an institution or even subjecting him to probation and supervision, the State is invoking its power to interfere with the lives of individuals as they choose to lead them.

229

Third, as was developed earlier in this chapter, it has proved to be true for a variety of reasons that the promise of the juvenile courts to help the child, to rehabilitate him, to lead him into a healthy and constructive life has not been kept. This has been partly because of lack of community support; but as was observed above, it has in addition been because of considerations beyond society's power to alter. Therefore, the major rationale for the withdrawal of procedural safeguards ceases to exist. The point was made recently by the U.S. Supreme Court, which observed:

There is evidence, in fact, that there may be grounds for concern that the child receives the worst of both worlds: that he gets neither the protections accorded to adults nor the solicitous care and regenerative treatment postulated for children. Kent v. United States, 383 U.S. 541 (1966).

Fourth, in point of fact, the welfare and the needs of the child offender are not the sole preoccupation of the juvenile court, which has the same purposes that mark the criminal law. To the extent that this is so, the justification for abandoning the protective procedural guarantees associated with due process of law disappears.

Fifth, there is increasing evidence that the informal procedures, contrary to the original expectation, may themselves constitute a further obstacle to effective treatment of the delinquent to the extent that they engender in the child a sense of injustice provoked by seemingly all-powerful and challengeless exercise of authority by judges and probation officers.

These challenges to the departure from procedural regularity in the juvenile courts make the case for bringing juvenile court procedures into closer harmony with our fundamental commitments to due process of law. What is entailed is not abandonment of the unique qualities of the juvenile court or adoption of the precise model of the criminal trial but rather accommodation of the dual goals of due process and welfare by instituting procedures permitting the court effectively to pursue humane and rehabilitative aims within the framework of a system that recognizes the indispensability of justice to any coercive governmental venture into the lives of individuals. Many of the issues here considered are raised by the case of *Gault v. United States,* now pending before the U.S. Supreme Court. Any procedural formulations and alterations must of course conform with its decision.

Counsel. The Commission believes that no single action

holds more potential for achieving procedural justice for the child in the juvenile court than provision of counsel. The presence of an independent legal representative of the child, or of his parent, is the keystone of the whole structure of guarantees that a minimum system of procedural justice requires. The rights to confront one's accusers, to cross-examine witnesses, to present evidence and testimony of one's own, to be unaffected by pre-judicial and unreliable evidence, to participate meaningfully in the dispositional decision, to take an appeal have substantial meaning for the overwhelming majority of persons brought before the juvenile court only if they are provided with competent lawyers who can invoke those rights effectively. The most informal and well-intentioned of judicial proceedings are technical; few adults without legal training can influence or even understand them; certainly children cannot. Papers are drawn and charges expressed in legal language. Events follow one another in a manner that appears arbitrary and confusing to the uninitiated. Decisions, unexplained, appear too official to challenge. But with lawyers come records of proceedings; records make possible appeals which, even if they do not occur, impart by their possibility a healthy atmosphere of accountability.

Fears have been expressed that lawyers would make juvenile court proceedings adversary. No doubt this is partly true, but it is partly desirable. Informality is often abused. The juvenile courts deal with cases in which facts are disputed and in which, therefore, rules of evidence, confrontation of witnesses, and other adversary procedures are called for. They deal with many cases involving conduct that can lead to incarceration or close supervision for long periods, and therefore juveniles often need the same safeguards that are granted to adults. And in all cases children need advocates to speak for them and guard their interests, particularly when disposition decisions are made. It is the disposition stage at which the opportunity arises to offer individualized treatment plans and in which the danger inheres that the court's coercive power will be applied without adequate knowledge of the circumstances.

Fears also have been expressed that the formality lawyers would bring into juvenile court would defeat the therapeutic aims of the court. But informality has no necessary connection with therapy; it is a device that has been used to approach therapy, and it is not the only possible device. It is quite possible that in many instances lawyers, for all their commitment to formality, could do more to further therapy for their clients than can the small, overworked social staffs of the courts. A lawyer—especially a poverty program or legal aid lawyer or other practitioner specializing in criminal matters—is often familiar with the various rehabilitative and preventive programs and organizations available in his community. He might already know the youngster's family or neighborhood. Thus he often would be, in other words, in a position to assist the court in developing a plan of disposition and treatment appropriate for the individual juvenile and, more important, in seeing that it is carried out: in making the appointments and taking the other specific steps that the press of business may force the probation officer to leave to the reluctant child or his bewildered parents. There are not nearly enough lawyers now with the skills to perform this role, but the fact that there are some argues that there could be more if there were more calls for their services. To suggest that lawyers perform these tasks is not to suggest that they become social workers. It is to suggest that in many instances lawyers can, and do, perform services for their clients that go beyond formal court representation.

The Commission believes it is essential that counsel be appointed by the juvenile court for those who are unable to provide their own. Experience under the prevailing systems in which children are free to seek counsel of their choice reveals how empty of meaning the right is for those typically the subjects of juvenile court proceedings. Moreover, providing counsel only when the child is sophisticated enough to be aware of his need and to ask for one or when he fails to waive his announced right are not enough, as experience in numerous jurisdictions reveals.

The Commission recommends:

Counsel should be appointed as a matter of course wherever coercive action is a possibility, without requiring any affirmative choice by child or parent.

Adjudication and Disposition. Perhaps the height of the juvenile court's procedural informality is its failure to differentiate clearly between the adjudication hearing, whose purpose is to determine the truth of the allegations in the petition, and the disposition proceeding, at which the juvenile's background is considered in connection with deciding what to do with him. In many juvenile courts the two questions are dealt with in the same proceeding or are separated only in the minority of cases in which the petition's allegations are at

232

issue. Even where adjudication and disposition are dealt with separately, the social reports, containing material about background and character that might make objective examination of the facts of the case difficult, are often given to the judge before adjudication. Practices vary on disclosure of social study information to the juvenile and his parents and lawyer, if he has one.

Bifurcating juvenile court hearings would go far toward eliminating the danger that information relevant only to disposition will color factual questions of involvement and jurisdictional basis for action.

The Commission recommends:

Juvenile court hearings should be divided into an adjudicatory hearing and a dispositional one, and the evidence admissible at the adjudicatory hearing should be so limited that findings are not dependent upon or unduly influenced by hearsay, gossip, rumor, and other unreliable types of information.

To minimize the danger that adjudication will be affected by inappropriate considerations, social investigation reports should not be made known to the judge in advance of adjudication. As is recommended for adult presentence reports, in the absence of compelling reason for nondisclosure of special information, those facts in the social study upon which the judge relies in making the disposition decision should be disclosed to the child, his parents, or his lawyer.

Notice. The unfairness of too much informality is also reflected in the inadequacy of notice to parents and juveniles about charges and hearings.

The Commission recommends:

Notice should be given well in advance of any scheduled court proceeding, including intake, detention, and waiver hearings, and should set forth the alleged misconduct with particularity.

Detention. Detention appears to be far too routinely and frequently used for juveniles both while they are awaiting court appearance and during the period after disposition and before institution space is available. In theory a juvenile is detained only when no suitable custodian can be found or when there appears to be a substantial risk that he will get into more trouble or hurt himself or someone else before he can be taken to court. A study for the Commission found, however, that in 1965 two-thirds of all juveniles apprehended were admitted to detention facilities and held there an average of 12 days at a total cost of more than $53 million. Furthermore, for nearly half the Nation's population there is no detention facility except the county jail, and many of the jails used for children are unsuitable even for adult offenders.

The Commission recommends:

Adequate and appropriate separate detention facilities for juveniles should be provided.

For children for whom detention is made necessary only by the unavailability of adequate parental supervision, there should be low-security community residential centers and similar shelters.

The Commission recommends:

Legislation should be enacted restricting both authority to detain and the circumstances under which detention is permitted.

Such legislation should require that only the probation officer be authorized to detain, except for those periods of time between the beginning of police custody and the arrival of a probation officer; that detention pending a detention hearing be restricted to situations in which it is clearly necessary for the child's protection or to keep him in the jurisdiction; that a detention hearing be required within no more than 48 hours of initial detention; and that the judge be required to release the juvenile when a detention hearing shows that the probation officer was without authority to order the initial detention.

Confidentiality of Court Records. Confidentiality of juvenile court records, both legal and social, is a particularly difficult issue. Privacy of proceedings and secrecy of information are basic to the court's objectives of avoiding stigma and improving rather than worsening the juvenile offender's chances to succeed in society. And the fact that damaging information is to be recorded only in the interest of assisting the juvenile is advanced to justify elimination of the check on

234

court action that publicity would provide. In practice, however, while most juvenile courts bar or restrict attendance of uninvolved persons and limit that which may be publicly reported, the confidentiality of records is far from complete.

Employers, schools, social agencies have an understandable interest in knowing about the record of a juvenile with whom they have contact. On the other hand, experience has shown that in too many instances such knowledge results in rejection or other damaging treatment of the juvenile, increasing the chances of future delinquent acts.

The Commission believes that legal reports should be available only to official agencies of criminal justice except when the juvenile court judge is satisfied that the information will not be used against the juvenile's interest. Social reports—which often contain the most personal of information and may incorporate the investigator's subjective interpretations —should be available only on a strictly limited basis to those agencies that need and will use the information for the same purpose for which it was originally gathered. Thus, social reports would be available only to agencies such as criminal court probation departments, mental health clinics, social agencies dealing with the delinquent.

The above recommendations on procedure must be seen as part of a whole pattern of recommendations concerning the juvenile court, particularly those with respect to pre-judicial handling and standards for legislative intervention. The major impact of these proposals would be to deemphasize adjudication as the primary method for dealing with difficult children. Most of those who did filter through to adjudication would be youths who had already proved resistant to helping services or whose conduct was so repetitive or so clearly dangerous to the community that no other alternative seemed feasible. A schematic representation of the proposed system appears on page 89.

The Commission strongly believes that all of these proposals will improve the effectiveness and the fairness of the juvenile justice system. But the fairest and most effective method for determining what treatment is needed cannot guarantee the availability of that treatment. In the last analysis, therefore, it is developing and establishing treatment methods and programs that must particularly engage the immediate and continuing efforts of communities concerned about juvenile delinquency and youth crime.

235

CONCLUSION

Society's efforts to control and combat delinquency may be seen as operating at three levels.

The first and most basic—indeed, so basic that delinquency prevention is only one of the reasons for it—involves provision of a real opportunity for everyone to participate in the legitimate activities that in our society lead to or constitute a good life: education, recreation, employment, family life. It is to insure such opportunity that schools in the slums must be made as good as schools elsewhere; that discrimination and arbitrary or unnecessary restrictions must be eliminated from employment practices; that job training must be made available to everyone; that physical surroundings must be reclaimed from deterioration and barrenness; that the rights of a citizen must be exercisable without regard to creed or race.

The pursuit of these goals is not inconsistent with the need to strengthen the system of juvenile justice. Some young offenders are dangerous repeaters, responsible for holdups, muggings, aggravated assaults—the crimes that frighten people off the streets. Others, while less threatening, have already shown themselves resistant to non-coercive rehabilitating efforts. Dealing with these youths so as to protect society requires—at least at this point in our understanding of human behavior—custody, adjudication of fact, imposition of sanction. Those measures depend upon an effective, efficient system of juvenile justice. Swift apprehension, thorough investigation, prompt disposition—carried out by persons carefully selected and trained for their functions should maximize the system's deterrent impact and the respect accorded the law it upholds. Insofar as the juvenile justice system does deal with delinquency, its dealings should be characterized by these attributes.

Further, the system should operate with all the procedural formality necessary to safeguard adequately the rights that any person has when he is subject to the application of coercive power. Juveniles should be represented by counsel; they should be able to confront those complaining of their conduct; their fate should not be determined by hearsay or gossip. They should not be unnecessarily detained.

Between these two aspects of delinquency control—the first relevant to all young people, the second reserved for those who appear to need the coercive authority of the court— there is a third: response to the special needs of youths with special problems. They may already have delinquency rec-

Proposed Juvenile Justice System

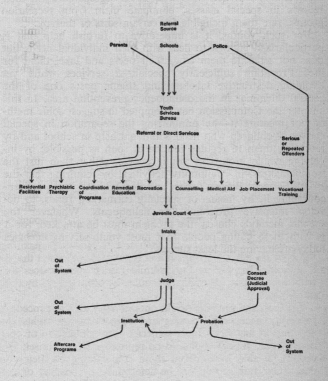

ords. They may be delinquent but not seriously so. They may be law-abiding but alienated and uncooperative in making use of education or employment or other opportunities. They may be behavior or academic problems in school, or misfits among their peers, or disruptive in recreation groups. Whatever the nature or degree of the difficulty, today they are all too likely to be excluded by most agencies and institutions, which find these youngsters, whom ostensibly they exist to help, in fact more than their limited resources can manage. They may restrict the participation of such youths in extracurricular school activities, keep them segregated from their fellows in special classes, eliminate them from recreation groups, rate them ineligible for certain sorts of therapy.

For such youths, it is imperative to furnish help that is particularized enough to deal with their individual needs but does not separate them from their peers and label them for life. Providing sufficiently specialized services while yet avoiding destructive labeling and stigma poses one of the central dilemmas in the delinquency prevention area. In this chapter the Commission has attempted to suggest some methods of meeting it—by minimizing the separation in special classes of children who need additional help in school and by returning them to regular routine as soon as possible; by involving whole groups of young people, rather than just the troublemakers, in community activities; by requiring that the Youth Services Bureau accept and deal with all youth and encouraging it, by means of specially earmarked funds, to develop intensive programs for delinquents. Whatever the specific methods chosen, the problem must be attacked, for it is with these young people that most youth-serving agencies today are having the least success.

Chapter 4

The Police

THE POLICE—some 420,000 people working for approximately 40,000 separate agencies that spend more than $2½ billion a year—are the part of the criminal justice system that is in direct daily contact both with crime and with the public. The entire system—courts and corrections as well as the police—is charged with enforcing the law and maintaining order. What is distinctive about the responsibility of the police is that they are charged with performing these functions where all eyes are upon them and where the going is roughest, on the street. Since this is a time of increasing crime, increasing social unrest and increasing public sensitivity to both, it is a time when police work is peculiarly important, complicated, conspicuous, and delicate.

"Police work" is a phrase that conjures up in some minds a dramatic contest between a policeman and a criminal in which the party with the stronger arm or the craftier wit prevails. To be sure, when a particularly desperate or guileful criminal must be hunted down and brought to justice, there are heroic moments in police work.

The situations that most policemen deal with most of the time are of quite another order, however. Chapters 2 and 3 of this report have shown that much of American crime, delinquency, and disorder is associated with a complex of social conditions: Poverty, racial antagonism, family breakdown, or the restlessness of young people. During the last 20 years these conditions have been aggravated by such profound social changes as the technological and civil rights revolutions, and the rapid decay of inner cities into densely packed, turbulent slums and ghettos.

It is in the cities that the conditions of life are the worst, that social tensions are the most acute, that riots occur, that crime rates are the highest, that the fear of crime and the demand for effective action against it are the strongest. It is in the cities that a large proportion of American policemen work and that a large proportion of police money is spent. Though there are 40,000 separate law enforcement agencies in the Nation, 55 of them, the police departments of the cities of more than 250,000 population, employ almost one-third of all police personnel. Policing a city of more than one million population costs $27.31 per resident per year; policing a city of less than 50,000 costs less than one-third as much, or $8.74.

A great majority of the situations in which policemen intervene are not, or are not interpreted by the police to be, criminal situations in the sense that they call for arrest with its possible consequences of prosecution, trial, and punishment. This is not to say that the police intervene in these situations mistakenly. Many of them are clear public nuisances that the community wants stopped: Radios blaring or dogs barking at 3 o'clock in the morning, more or less convivial groups obstructing sidewalks, or youths throwing snowballs at passing motorists.

Many situations involve people who need help whether they want it or not: Helpless drunks out in freezing weather, runaway boys who refuse to go home, tourists in search of exciting night life in a dangerous neighborhood. Many of them involve conduct that, while unlawful, cannot be prevented or deterred to any great degree by means now at the disposal of the criminal justice system: Using narcotics, prostitution, gambling, alcoholism. Many situations, whether or not they involve unlawful conduct, may be threatening: A sidewalk orator exercising the right of free speech in the midst of a hostile crowd, a midnight street corner gathering of youths whose intentions are questionable, an offer by a belligerent drunk to lick any man in the house.

All of these situations could involve the violation of some ordinance or statute. All of them could lead to a serious breach of public order, or for that matter to a serious crime. Much of police work is seeing to it they do not lead to this extreme. This means becoming involved in the most intimate, personal way with the lives and problems of citizens of all kinds.

It is hard to overstate the intimacy of the contact between

the police and the community. Policemen deal with people when they are both most threatening and most vulnerable, when they are angry, when they are frightened, when they are desperate, when they are drunk, when they are violent, or when they are ashamed. Every police action can affect in some way someone's dignity, or self-respect, or sense of privacy, or constitutional rights. As a matter of routine policemen become privy to, and make judgments about, secrets that most citizens guard jealously from their closest friends: Relationships between husbands and wives, the misbehavior of children, personal eccentricities, peccadilloes and lapses of all kinds. Very often policemen must physically restrain or subdue unruly citizens.

A common kind of situation that illustrates the complexity, delicacy—and frustration—of much police work is the matrimonial dispute, which police experts estimate consumes as much time as any other single kind of situation. These family altercations often occur late at night, when the only agency available to people in trouble is the police. Because they occur late at night, they can disturb the peace of a whole neighborhood. And, of course, they can lead to crime; in fact, they are probably the single greatest cause of homicides. Yet the capacity of the police to deal effectively with such a highly personal matter as conjugal disharmony is, to say the least, limited. Arresting one party or both is unlikely to result in either a prosecution or a reconciliation. Removing one of the parties from the scene, an expedient the police often resort to, sometimes by using force, may create temporary peace, but it scarcely solves the problem. An order to see a family counselor in the morning is unenforceable and more likely to be ignored than obeyed. And mediating the difficulty of enraged husbands and wives ad hoc is an activity for which few policemen—or people in any other profession— are qualified by temperament or by training. Again no statistics are available, but there is a strong impression in police circles that intervention in these disputes causes more assaults on policemen than any other kind of encounter.

Since police action is so often so personal, it is inevitable that the public is of two minds about the police: Most men both welcome official protection and resent official interference. Upon the way the police perform their duties depends to a large extent which state of mind predominates, whether the police are thought of as protectors or oppressors, as friends or enemies. Yet policemen, who as a rule have been well trained to perform such procedures as searching a person for weapons, transporting a suspect to the stationhouse, taking fingerprints, writing arrest reports, and testifying in court, have received little guidance from legislatures, city administrations, or their own superiors, in handling these intricate, intimate human situations. The organization of police departments and the training of policemen are focused almost entirely on the apprehension and prosecution of criminals. What a policeman does, or should do, instead of making an arrest or in order to avoid making an arrest, or in a situation in which he may not make an arrest, is rarely discussed. The peacekeeping and service activities, which consume the majority of police time, receive too little consideration.

Finally, more than public attitudes toward the police and, by extension, toward the law, are influenced by the way any given policeman performs his duties. Every Supreme Court decision that has redefined or limited such important and universal police procedures as search and seizure, interrogation of suspects, arrest, and the use of informants has been a decision about the way a specific policeman or group of policemen handled a specific situation. Most of the recent big-city riots were touched off by commonplace street encounters between policemen and citizens. In short, the way any policeman exercises the personal discretion that is an inescapable part of his job can, and occasionally does, have an immediate bearing on the peace and safety of an entire community, or a long-range bearing on the work of all policemen everywhere.

THE LAW ENFORCEMENT FUNCTION OF THE POLICE

In society's day-to-day efforts to protect its citizens from the suffering, fear, and property loss produced by crime and the threat of crime, the policeman occupies the front line. It is he who directly confronts criminal situations, and it is to him that the public looks for personal safety. The freedom of Americans to walk their streets and be secure in their homes —in fact, to do what they want when they want—depends to a great extent on their policemen.

But the fact that the police deal daily with crime does not mean that they have unlimited power to prevent it, or reduce it, or deter it. The police did not create and cannot resolve the social conditions that stimulate crime. They did not start and cannot stop the convulsive social changes that are taking place in America. They do not enact the laws that they are required to enforce, nor do they dispose of the criminals they arrest. The police are only one part of the criminal justice system; the criminal justice system is only one part of the government; and the government is only one part of society. Insofar as crime is a social phenomenon, crime prevention is the responsibility of every part of society. The criminal process is limited to case by case operations, one criminal or one crime at a time.

But in order to work effectively, the police should—and all too often do not—recognize crime as a broader phenomenon. They should—and sometimes do—observe its ebbs and flows, accumulate information about what crimes most commonly occur where and when, what kinds of people are most likely to be criminals or victims of crime, or how criminals of different sorts go about their business. However, when that has been said, the fact remains that the mission of the police is not to remove the causes of crime, but to deter crime, and to deal with specific criminals whoever they are, and with specific crimes whenever, wherever and however they occur. Moreover, they perform this mission under a variety of restrictions, some of them within their power to alter, some of them not.

THE LEGAL POWERS OF THE POLICE

The struggle to maintain a proper balance between effective law enforcement and fairness to individuals pervades the entire criminal justice system. It is particularly crucial and apparent in police work because, as has been noted, every police action can impinge directly, and perhaps hurtfully, on a citizen's freedom of action.

To maintain public order, policemen, as a matter of routine, issue such orders as "cut down the noise" and "stand back." Such exercise of police power offers no fundamental threat to individual freedom, and is accepted as reasonable by the public and the courts alike. Policemen, as a part of their crime prevention and solution duties, stop citizens on the street, inquire into their business and, if necessary, detain them for brief questioning. The police consider this power to be essential, and they assume that they have the legal right to exercise it.

But standard police procedures that are more intrusive have, during the last 30 years, been increasingly circumscribed by court rulings. Personal and property searches and the seizure of the evidence they yield, the use of informants, the arrest of demonstrators, and stationhouse detention and questioning of suspects have been more and more rigorously measured by the courts against the constitutional standards of due process, right to counsel, probable cause, privilege against self-incrimination, prompt presentment in court, and the rights of free speech and peaceable assembly. Issues that are now under court review, and probably will be for many years to come, are the temporary detention of suspects for questioning on the street, the entry of undercover policemen in suspect premises and electronic surveillance—all of which are practices the police consider essential as either general or specific law enforcement techniques.

It is evident that every restriction that is placed on police procedures by the courts—or anyone else—makes deterring or solving crimes more difficult. However, it is also evident that police procedures must be controlled somehow. In 1931, the Wickersham Commission reported that the extraction of confessions through physical brutality was a widespread, almost universal, police practice. During the next several years the Supreme Court issued a number of rulings that excluded such confessions as admissible evidence in court. There can be no doubt that these rulings had much to do with the fact that today the third degree is almost nonexistent. No one can say just how much the third degree helped law enforcement in deterring or solving crimes, but even if it helped considerably few Americans regret its virtual abandonment by the police.

America's form of government, its laws and its Constitution, all express the desire to maintain the maximum degree of individual liberty consistent with maintenance of social order. The process of striking this balance is complex and delicate. An example is the "probable cause" standard that governs arrest. Probable cause does not insure that no innocent man ever will be arrested, but it does restrict police actions that are arbitrary or discriminatory or intuitive. At the same time, it is far less restrictive than the standard that governs conviction in court—"proof beyond a reasonable doubt." If the police had to abide by that standard before making an arrest, law enforcement would be an all but impossible job.

In any case, although the courts can review police actions, and do review them more than they once did, most police actions are not so reviewed. Those that do not lead to arrest and prosecution almost never are reviewed for the simple reason that, short of a civil suit against the police by a citizen, there is no court machinery for reviewing them.

Nevertheless many police officers and citizens believe that recent judicial interpretations of the Constitution and various statutes have unduly and inappropriately inhibited the work of the police and so have made it harder for police to protect the public. Part of this feeling stems, no doubt, from the

244

sharp contrast between the tense, fast-moving situations in which policemen are called upon to make split-second decisions, and the calm that prevails in the appellate courts while lawyers and judges argue the merits of those decisions, after having searched lawbooks for apposite precedents.

Another part of it results from the fact that many of those court decisions were made without the needs of law enforcement, and the police policies that are designed to meet those needs, being effectively presented to the court. If judges are to balance accurately law enforcement needs against human rights, the former must be articulated. They seldom are. Few legislatures and police administrators have defined in detail how and under what conditions certain police practices are to be used. As a result, the courts often must rely exclusively on intuition and common sense in judging what kinds of police action are reasonable or necessary, even though their decisions about the actions of one police officer can restrict police activity in the entire Nation.

These problems are illustrated by the recent U.S. Supreme Court decision in the case of *Miranda* v. *Arizona,* which prohibited, by a 5-to-4 decision, the questioning of a suspect in custody unless counsel is present, or the suspect expressly waives his right to counsel. The majority of the Court, after studying police manuals and textbooks that describe how confessions are best obtained, concluded that interrogation in the isolated setting of a police station constituted informal compulsion to confess. It concluded further that the need for confessions is overestimated by the police. The minority felt that a good many guilty defendants would never be convicted because of the Court's decision voiding police practices, which only 8 years previously had been found constitutional by the Court. Neither the majority nor the minority had much solid data to go on. Only recently has research commenced to assess the police need for confessions and the possibilities of establishing rules under which stationhouse questioning would be permissible.

The Commission believes that it is too early to assess the effect of the *Miranda* decision on law enforcement's ability to secure confessions and to solve crimes. But this and other decisions do represent a trend toward findings by the judiciary that previously permitted police practices are unconstitutionally offensive to the dignity and integrity of private citizens. The need for legislative and administrative policies to guide police through the changing world of permissible activity is pressing. Even such a detailed, prescriptive opinion as *Miranda* failed to provide the police with a complete set of rules governing in-custody interrogation. As noted in Justice White's dissenting opinion:

[The] decision leaves open such questions as whether the accused was in custody, whether his statements were spontaneous or the product of interrogation, whether the accused has effectively waived his rights, and whether nontestimonial evidence introduced at trial is the fruit of statements made during a prohibited interrogation, all of which are certain to prove productive of uncertainty during investigation and litigation during prosecution * * *

The majority of the Court did note that the interrogation methods prescribed in the decision could be replaced by others devised by legislators and administrators as long as each accused was apprised of his right to silence and afforded continuous opportunity to exercise that right. Courts always will have the final word as to constitutional limitations upon police action, of course. But legislators, and the police themselves, by not waiting for judicial prodding, can affect the nature and result of court review. They can establish through empirical research what the needs of law enforcement are, and they can enumerate policies and prescribe practices that meet those needs.

If the present trend continues, it is quite likely that some current investigative practices and procedures thought by police to be proper and effective will be held to be unconstitutional or subjected to restrictive rules. Whether this happens will depend in some measure upon whether the police, first, can develop policies that differentiate the proper from the improper use of particular investigative practices, and whether, second, they can insure through proper supervision that individual officers are held to those policies. In an equally large measure, State legislatures are responsible for establishing police policy. As the New Republic recently observed: "The community acting through its elected representatives must decide and state precisely what it wants the police to do, not simply admonishing them for disobeying indistinct or nonexistent commands."

The Commission feels compelled to comment upon two investigative practices that are particularly clouded in controversy and that law enforcement officials believe are crucial. One of them is wiretapping and electronic eavesdropping. The state of the law in this field is so thoroughly confused that no policeman, except in States that forbid both practices totally, can be sure about what he is allowed to do. This situa-

246

ation, and the Commission's proposals for clarifying it, are discussed at some length in Chapter 7.

The other issue involves the basic police practice of stopping suspects, detaining them for brief questioning on the street and, for the policeman's self-protection, "frisking" them for weapons. Commission observers of police street-work in high-crime neighborhoods of some large cities report that 10 percent of those frisked were found to be carrying guns, and another 10 percent were carrying knives. If the police were forbidden to stop persons at the scene of a crime, or in situations that strongly suggest criminality, investigative leads could be lost as persons disappeared into the massive impersonality of an urban environment. Yet police practice must distinguish carefully between legitimate field interrogations and indiscriminate detention and street searches of persons and vehicles.

The Commission recommends:

State legislatures should enact statutory provisions with respect to the authority of law enforcement officers to stop persons for brief questioning, including specifications of the circumstances and limitations under which stops are permissible.

Such authority would cover situations in which, because of the limited knowledge of a policeman just arriving at the scene, there is not sufficient basis for arrest. Specific limitations on the circumstances of a stop, the length of the questioning, and the grounds for a frisk would prevent the kind of misuse of field interrogation that, the Commission study also indicated, occurs today in a substantial number of street incidents in some cities. As discussed in a later section, such statutes should be implemented by the creation by police administrators of specific guidelines for police action on the street. A balance between individual rights and society's need for protection from crimes can be struck most properly through this combination of legislative and administrative action. Court review then proceeds under more enlightening circumstances.

The Commission notes that the U.S. Supreme Court will review this term at least two cases bearing on police authority to stop persons. Of course, any legislation and administrative rules must be consistent with court rulings on this issue.

THE OPERATIONAL PROBLEMS OF LAW ENFORCEMENT

PATROL

The heart of the police law enforcement effort is patrol, the movement around an assigned area, on foot or by vehicle, of uniformed policemen. In practically every city police department at least one-half of the sworn personnel perform their duties in uniform on the street. Patrol officers are not, of course, mere sentries who make their rounds at a fixed pace on a fixed schedule. They stop to check buildings, to investigate out-of-the-way occurrences, to question suspected persons, to converse with citizens familiar with local events and personalities. If they are motorized, they spend much of their time responding to citizen complaints and the reports of crime that are relayed to them over their radios.

There can be no doubt that large numbers of visible policemen are needed on the streets. For example, a Commission analysis showed that 61.5 percent of over 9,000 major crimes against the person—including rapes, robberies, and assaults —in Chicago over a 6-month period occurred on the streets or in other public premises. Moreover, there have been a number of demonstrations that increasing the patrol force in an area, through use of special tactical patrols, causes a decline in crimes directed at citizens walking the streets in the heavily patrolled area. The number of crimes committed in the New York subways also declined by 36.1 percent last year after a uniformed transit patrolman was assigned to every train during the late night hours.

Although all police experts agree that patrol is an essential police activity, the problem of how many policemen, under what orders and using what techniques, should patrol which beats and when, is a complicated, highly technical one. A principal purpose of patrol is "deterrence": discouraging people who are inclined to commit crimes from following their inclinations. Presumably, deterrence would best be served by placing a policeman on every corner. Street crimes would be reduced because of the potential criminal's fear of immediate apprehension. Even indoor crimes, such as burglary, might be lessened by the increased likelihood of detection through a massive police presence. But few Americans would tolerate living under police scrutiny that intense, and in any case few cities could afford to provide it.

An adequate number of policemen must be available and must be deployed in the most efficient, effective manner possible. On the theory that the widest patrol coverage is the most deterrent coverage, police have only recently begun to devise systematic ways of obtaining this coverage in the most economical fashion and at the times of day and night when it is most needed. However, resources and talent for proper research have not been devoted in any great extent to discovering and analyzing the relationship between police patrol and deterrence. There have been few scientifically controlled experiments concerning deterrent effects of various patrol techniques. One line for such experimenting on the effects of deploying varying numbers of policemen, suggested by the Science and Technology Task Force, is described in chapter 11.

There are a multitude of questions about deterrence that the police, in the present state of knowledge, simply cannot answer. One set of questions concerns the extent to which crimes of various kinds can be deterred. Common sense would seem to suggest that crimes like homicide, which are typically committed in moments of high emotion, are less likely to be deterred by fear of arrest and punishment than crimes like burglary, which typically arise from premeditation and calculation. But little or no research into this subject has been done.

Another set of questions concerns the extent to which various kinds of people can be deterred from crime. Once again, on the basis of guesswork, it can be maintained that youths are harder to deter than older people because they tend to be more hotheaded, or that people with criminal histories are harder to deter than those who have none because the social stigma of being arrested has already been imposed on them. Once again, there are no data to confirm or refute such theories.

A third set of questions concerns where and when what kinds of crimes are most likely to occur. Clearly such knowledge is needed if the police are to look for the right things in the right places at the right times. A number of big-city police departments do have fairly ambitious programs of crime analysis, but they are too recent for meaningful evaluation. The departments must have the aid of representatives of academic disciplines—such as operations analysts, criminologists and other social scientists—before crime trend prediction can be fully developed and usefully related to day to day changes in patrol concentrations and planning for long-range patrol needs.

A final set of questions concerns the extent to which different patrol techniques result in arrests and lead to the fear of arrest. There has been a good deal of discussion in police circles about foot patrol versus motor patrol, one-man patrol versus two-man patrol, fixed patrol versus fluid patrol, whether or not to use detectives on patrol, and other such technical matters. Lack of knowledge about deterrence has meant that many of these operational patrol decisions have been made on the basis of guesswork or logic, rather than on facts.

Perhaps the best proof that much remains to be discovered about police work is that the ratios of policemen per thousand residents in cities of over 500,000 population range from 1.07 to 4.04, while the incidence of reported crime in those cities shows no such gross differences. One part of the explanation for such a disparity is that the size and physical characteristics of a city, its geographic location, and its population mix are factors in determining police needs. However, another part is that there is no consensus among chief administrators about many aspects of the how, what, and when of police patrol.

INVESTIGATION

When patrol fails to prevent a crime or apprehend the criminal while he is committing it, the police must rely upon investigation. Every sizable department has a corps of investigative specialists—detectives—whose job is to solve crimes by questioning victims, suspects, and witnesses, by accumulating physical evidence at the scene of the crime, and by tracing stolen property or vehicles associated with the crime. In practically every department the caseloads carried by detectives are too heavy to allow them to follow up thoroughly more than a small percentage of the cases assigned them. In other words, a great many cases are unsolved by default—or, at least, time will not permit a determination of whether or not they are solvable. The effects of this condition go far beyond lack of redress for many victims of crime.

A Commission survey of the reasons citizens give for not reporting crimes to the police shows that the number one reason is the conviction that the police cannot do anything. If this impression of the ineffectiveness of the police is widely held by the public, there is every reason to believe that it is shared by criminals and would-be criminals. Under such circumstances, "deterrence" is, to say the least, not operating as well as it might.

In the present state of police knowledge and organization many crimes are, in fact, not solvable. In the great majority of cases, personal identification by a victim or witness is the *only* clue to the identity of the criminal. The Commission analyzed 1,905 crimes reported during January of 1966 in Los Angeles, which has a notably well-trained and efficient police department. The police were furnished a suspect's name in 349 of these cases, and 301 were resolved either by arrest or in some other way—either the victim would not prosecute, subsequent investigation disclosed that the reported crime was not actually a crime, or a prosecutor declined to press the case. Of the 1,375 crimes for which no suspect was named, only 181 cases were cleared. Since crimes against the person are more likely to be named-suspect crimes than crimes against property, it is natural that a much higher proportion of them are solved. In 1965, 78 percent of reported serious crimes against property were never solved.

An increase in the number of investigative personnel would permit a wider search for possible witnesses to a crime and thus increase the number of cases in which suspects are named. However, insufficient manpower is not the only impediment to effective investigation. Scientific crime detection, popular fiction to the contrary notwithstanding, at present is a limited tool. For example, single fingerprints can be used for positive identification when compared to those of a named suspect, but they are of limited utility when there are no suspects. There is no practical method for classifying and searching single latent fingerprints by a manual search of local, State, or national files. Overcoming this difficulty is a major, long-range technological problem that is discussed in chapter 11.

Moreover, there is a shortage of policemen who are skilled in the collection, analysis and preservation of evidence. Only the biggest and best-run departments have personnel with sufficient technical training to search a crime scene effectively and have laboratory facilities to make use of the fruits of such searches. By and large, the most productive kinds of criminal investigation today are first, questioning a person who may have some knowledge of the identity of a criminal and, second, tracing stolen property.

Successful crime solution also depends on good patrol work. The Los Angeles study, admittedly conducted on a very small scale, bears this out. Nine-tenths of the arrests were made by patrolmen rather than by detectives, although a quarter of the patrolmen's arrests were on the basis of leads provided by detectives who conducted followup investigations.

There appears to be a correlation between crime solution and the time it takes for patrol officers to respond to a call. The average response time in cases in which arrests were made was 4.1 minutes; in cases in which arrests were not made it was 6.3 minutes. The Los Angeles study further shows that almost 36 percent of all arrests were made within one-half hour of the commission of the crime; more than 48 percent were made within 2 hours.

What these figures suggest to the Commission is that rapid arrival by the police at the scene of a crime is of sufficient importance that ways should be found of getting persons with investigative expertise to crime scenes with the greatest possible rapidity—before crimes, in police terms, are "cold." The new division of police functions that is proposed in a later section of this chapter has this as one of its aims.

THE COMMUNITY-SERVICE FUNCTION OF THE POLICE

In the course of inquiring into police activities, the Commission encountered many differences of opinion among police administrators as to whether the primary police responsibility of law enforcement is made easier or more difficult by the many duties other than enforcing the law that policemen ordinarily perform. Policemen, in large numbers, direct and control traffic. Policemen watch the polls on election day, escort important visitors in and out of town, license taxicabs and bicycles, and operate animal shelters. Policemen assist stranded motorists, give directions to travelers, rescue lost children, respond to medical emergencies, help people who have lost their keys unlock their apartments. It is easy to understand why the police traditionally perform such services. They are services somebody must perform, and policemen, being ever present and mobile, are logical candidates. Since much of a uniformed patrolman's time is spent on simply moving around his beat on preventive patrol, it is natural for the public to believe that he has the time to perform services. Moreover, it is natural to interpret the police role of "protection" as meaning protection not only against crime but against other hazards, accidents or even discomforts of life.

Those who believe that policemen should be relieved of all duties not directly relevant to enforcing the law have a number of arguments: That full-time service duties—traffic direc-

252

tion and so forth—are a waste of the time and the skills of people who have been specifically trained for fighting crime; that every minute a patrolman spends off patrol is a minute during which a crime that he might have deterred may be committed; that a patrolman busy on a service call is out of communication with superiors who may want him for an emergency call; that the only way policemen can become the crime specialists they should be is by concentrating exclusively during every working hour on crime; that the routine performance of trivial duties discourages able men from entering police work and drives other able men out of it.

The opposing arguments are that traffic officers often do deter crimes or solve them by virtue of their presence and availability; that answering service calls stimulates public esteem for and cooperation with the police, helps familiarize policemen with the community and furnishes investigative leads to alert and intelligent officers; that opportunities to be friendly and useful are psychologically valuable to men who spend much of their time dealing with the seamy side of life.

The Commission has had difficulty in analyzing these arguments empirically. Police department records rarely reveal what proportion of working time policemen spend on what activities—preventive patrol, answering service calls, investigating crimes, appearing in court, writing reports, directing traffic and so forth. In the absence of conclusive proof to the contrary, the Commission believes that the performance of many of the nonenforcement duties by the police helps them to control crime, and that radically changing the traditional police role would create more problems than it would solve —including the problem of finding other people to perform the indispensable services the police would be excused from performing.

However, the community should take a hard look at such police assignments as running the dog pound, tax collection, licensing, jail duty or chauffeur duty, which are related neither to law enforcement nor to performing essential community services on the streets. Meanwhile, police administrators and other municipal officials should try to arrive at precise answers to such questions as the extent of the contribution to law enforcement made by traffic policemen, the kind of patrolling that demonstrably deters crime, the nature of the services the community demands of its police—in short how policemen should be spending their time. These questions cannot be answered definitively today.

The community's study of the role of the police should cover additional ground. It should examine whether it is desirable, or possible, for the police to devote more time than they now generally do to protecting the community against social injustices. Some of these injustices which are criminal, such as loan sharking and consumer frauds, are already police business, although they are more commonly of a sort dealt with by headquarters squads or investigators working for a district attorney then by uniformed patrolmen.

Others are not police business, but perhaps should be. Policemen are uniquely situated to observe what is happening in the community. They are in constant contact with the conditions associated with crime. They see in minute detail situations that need to be and can be corrected. If a park is being badly maintained, if a school playground is locked when it is most needed, if garbage goes uncollected, if a landlord fails to repair or heat his building, perhaps the police could make it their business to inform the municipal authorities of these derelictions. In this way, police would help to represent the community in securing services to which it is entitled.

In large measure the answer to these questions depends on whether such new activities could be performed without enormous increases in police personnel. In this chapter a recommendation is made for the creation of a new kind of officer, a "community service officer," who might be in a position to assume many of these tasks. The Commission is inclined to think that broadening the role of the police in this fashion would not distract the police from law enforcement. On the contrary it would contribute to law enforcement by making the police more active and more valued members of the community. Any course of action that might enhance the community's respect for and sense of identity with the police deserves thorough consideration.

In this connection, it appears desirable to consider also how police departments, as well as individual policemen, can broaden their roles. One suggestion that the Commission believes merits attention is the creation of municipal planning boards on which police community-planning experts would sit, along with representatives of other city departments. The work of such city departments as those dealing with housing, parks, welfare, and health are all related to crime; and often such departments have law enforcement functions. Also, community planning is needed since it has a direct bearing on crime, and therefore on police business. The police often have knowledge on such subjects as where and how to build parks, schools, housing, and commercial developments, and as to the effects on the community of urban renewal and the relocation of population—neighborhood conditions to which municipal attention should be directed.

The Commission recommends:

The police should formally participate in community planning in all cities.

THE POLICE IN THE COMMUNITY

Carrying out with proper efficiency and discretion the complicated law enforcement and community-service tasks the police are expected to perform is a formidable assignment under the best of circumstances: When the public sympathizes and cooperates with the police. Those circumstances do exist to a considerable extent in most rural, smalltown and suburban communities, and in many big-city neighborhoods. The chief limitations on police work in those places are the talents and skills of policemen and police administrators, and the funds, equipment, and facilities available to them. In city slums and ghettos, the very neighborhoods that need and want effective policing the most, the situation is quite different. There is much distrust of the police, especially among boys and young men, among the people the police most often deal with. It is common in those neighborhoods for citizens to fail to report crimes or refuse to cooperate in investigations. Often policemen are sneered at or insulted on the street. Sometimes they are violently assaulted. Indeed, everyday police encounters in such neighborhoods can set off riots, as many police departments have learned.

This is the problem that is usually—and politely—referred to as "police-community relations." It is overwhelmingly a problem of the relations between the police and the minority-group community, between the police and Negroes, Puerto Ricans, and Mexican-Americans. It is as serious as any problem the police have today.

Of course, to say that there is much distrust of the police among members of minority groups is not to say that all members of minority groups distrust the police, or to imply that only members of minority groups distrust the police. A survey of public attitudes toward the police conducted, at the Commission's request, by the National Opinion Research Center shows, naturally enough, a spectrum of opinion. However, the differences in attitude by race are striking. Twenty-three percent of all white people thought that the police were

255

National Opinion Research Center Poll : Affirmative Answers

Do police do "excellent" job?

White ——— 23%

Non-White ——— 15%

Are police "almost all honest"?

White ——————————— 63%

Non-White ———— 30%

Do police do "poor" job?

White ——— 7%

Non-White ——— 16%

Are police "almost all corrupt"?

White —— 1%

Non-White —— 10%

doing an "excellent" job of enforcing the law, while only 15 percent of nonwhites held that view. At the opposite end of the scale, 7 percent of whites thought the police were doing a "poor" job, as contrasted with 16 percent of nonwhites. Roughly the same kind of response was obtained to a question about how well the police protect citizens.

With the questions, "How good a job do the police do on being respectful to people like yourself?" and "Do you think the police around your neighborhood are almost all honest, mostly honest, with a few who are corrupt, or are they almost all corrupt?", the difference in response by race was more than striking. It was startling. Sixty-three percent of whites and 30 percent of nonwhites thought the police were "almost all honest." One percent of whites and 10 percent of nonwhites thought the police were "almost all corrupt."

It may be paradoxical that the same people who are most victimized by crime are most hostile to the police, but it is not remarkable. In view of the history of race relations in America and of the ghetto conditions in which most minority-group members live, doubt about American ideals and resentment against authority are to be expected among Negroes, Puerto Ricans, and Mexican-Americans. No doubt the police are condemned by the nature of their work to bear the brunt of such feelings.

However, this is not the heart of the police-community relations problem. Throughout the country minority-group residents have grievances not just against society as a whole, but specifically against the police. Commission observers watched policemen work in minority-group neighborhoods in a number of major cities, and the Commission has studied the findings of those who have made observations in many other cities. These observations indicate that any generalization about how "policemen" treat "minority-group members," or vice versa, is almost sure to be misleading. For example, one Commission study conducted in a few cities showed that most policemen treat minority-group citizens in a nondiscriminatory manner, and received at least as much cooperation and courtesy from Negroes as from whites.

However, Commission studies also showed, and in this finding responsible police officials concur, that too many policemen do misunderstand and are indifferent to minority-group aspirations, attitudes, and customs, and that incidents involving physical or verbal mistreatment of minority-group citizens do occur and do contribute to the resentment against police that some minority-group members feel.

Citizen hostility toward the police is every bit as disruptive of peace and order, of course, as police indifference to or mistreatment of citizens. It is so obvious as almost to be a truism that ghetto residents will not obtain the police protection they badly want and need until policemen feel that their presence is welcome and that their problems are understood. However, in the effort to achieve this state of affairs, the duty of taking the initiative clearly devolves on the police, both because they are organized and disciplined and because they are public servants sworn to protect every part of the community. It is an urgent duty. Social tensions are growing and crime rates are mounting. Police agencies cannot preserve the public peace and control crime unless the public participates more fully than it now does in law enforcement. Bad community feeling does more than create tensions and engender actions against the police that in turn may embitter policemen and trigger irrational responses from them. It stimulates crime.

The Commission believes that a police-community relations program is one of the most important functions of any police department in a community with a substantial minority population. It believes further that such programs must be organized and administered in accordance with certain principles:

□ A community-relations program is not a *public*-relations program to "sell the police image" to the people. It is not a set of expedients whose purpose is to tranquilize for a time an angry neighborhood by, for example, suddenly promoting a few Negro officers in the wake of a racial disturbance. It is a long-range, full-scale effort to acquaint the police and the community with each other's problems and to stimulate action aimed at solving those problems.

□ Community relations are not the exclusive business of specialized units, but the business of an entire department from the chief down. Community relations are not exclusively a matter of special programs, but a matter that touches on all aspects of police work. They must play a part in the selection, training, deployment, and promotion of personnel; in the execution of field procedures; in staff policymaking and planning; in the enforcement of departmental discipline; and in the handling of citizens' complaints.

□ The needs of good community relations and of effective law enforcement will not necessarily be identical at all times.

For example, restricting the way field interrogations are carried out could lead, in the short run, to apprehending fewer criminals; imposing harsh penalties on officers who verbally abuse minority-group citizens could temporarily depress departmental morale. Moreover, professionalization of the police has meant, to a considerable extent, improving efficiency by such methods as decreasing the number of officers on foot patrol, reducing the number of precinct stations and insisting that patrol officers spend more time on law enforcement duties and less on maintaining relations with citizens on the street. A result of this has been a lessening of the informal contacts between policemen and citizens. Conflicts of this sort are not easy to resolve, but the attempt must be made. While immediate law enforcement considerations may take precedence, it should be remembered that sound community relations are, in the long run, essential to effective law enforcement.

□ Improving community relations involves not only instituting programs and changing procedures and practices, but re-examining fundamental attitudes. The police will have to learn to listen patiently and understandingly to people who are openly critical of them or hostile to them, since those people are precisely the ones with whom relations need to be improved. Quite evidently, it is not easy for a man who was brought up to obey the law and to respect law enforcement officers to maintain his poise and equanimity when he is denounced, sneered at, or threatened. However, policemen must do just that if police-citizen relationships on the street are to become person-to-person encounters rather than the black-versus-white, oppressed-versus-oppressor confrontations they too often are.

□ The police must adapt themselves to the rapid changes in patterns of behavior that are taking place in America. This is a time when traditional ideas and institutions are being challenged with increasing insistence. The poor want an equal opportunity to earn a share of America's wealth. Minority groups want a final end put to the discrimination they have been subjected to for centuries. Young people, the fastest growing segment of the population, have more freedom than they ever have had. The police must be willing and able to deal understandingly and constructively with these often unsettling, even threatening, changes.

The Commission recommends:

Police departments in all large communities should have

259

community-relations machinery consisting of a headquarters unit that plans and supervises the department's community-relations programs. It should also have precinct units, responsible to the precinct commander, that carry out the programs. Community relations must be both a staff and a line function. Such machinery is a matter of the greatest importance in any community that has a substantial minority population.

A staff community-relations unit should be commanded by a high-ranking officer who is responsible directly to the chief and who sits on the departmental policymaking board that is proposed later in this chapter. This unit should have a voice in departmental decisions about recruiting, training, promotion, internal discipline, and field operations. It should be actively involved in departmental planning with respect to demonstrations and riots. It should represent the department in dealing with city-wide civil rights and minority-group organizations. It should conduct continuing research into citzens' attitudes toward, or conflicts with, the police, and evaluate the department's performance in the light of its findings. It should plan and supervise the work of the precinct units, and formulate the community-relations responsibilities and duties of all the department's officers and officials. In short, community-relations work should have the same high status, the same strong support from the chief and the same access to needed resources of manpower, equipment, and money as any other essential police function. According high departmental status to the community-relations operation, as has been done in San Francisco and a number of other departments, has been an important ingredient in the success of programs in those cities.

In the precincts, the units, headed by a lieutenant or, at least, a sergeant, should maintain contacts with neighborhood groups of all kinds, advise the commander about community-relations problems and policies, help individual officers solve problems, conduct rollcall training in community-relations subjects, and provide the headquarters unit with information about neighborhood advisory committees that would meet regularly with precinct officials to discuss problems of conflict between the police and the community. If such subjects as the use of stop-and-frisk or police policies toward juveniles were openly and fully discussed by representatives of the police and the community, much misunderstanding and mutual antipathy could be avoided. It should be possible for the police to consult with community representatives about the

260

most advantageous ways of achieving certain law enforcement objectives. The St. Louis Police Department has been a pioneer in organizing such advisory committees, and a number of other departments have followed its example.

The Commission recommends:

In each police precinct in a minority-group neighborhood there should be a citizens' advisory committee that meets regularly with police officials to work out solutions to problems of conflict between the police and the community. It is crucial that the committees be broadly representative of the community as a whole, including those elements who are critical or aggrieved.

PERSONNEL CONSIDERATIONS

Two general conditions with respect to police personnel must be met before any department can hope to do effective community-relations work. One is that there be a sufficient number of minority-group officers at all levels of activity and authority. The other is that all officers be thoroughly aware of, and trained in, community-relations problems. They should hold to high standards of fairness and coolness in their behavior toward citizens. Many of the recommendations that will be made in this chapter's sections on "Police Personnel" and "Police Organization, Management, and Field Operations" are specifically designed to achieve these objectives. However, some discussion of the problems is warranted here.

A department can show convincingly that it does not practice racial discrimination by recruiting minority-group officers, by assigning them fairly to duties of all sorts in all kinds of neighborhoods, and by pursuing promotion policies that are scrupulously fair to such officers. If there is not a substantial percentage of Negro officers among the policemen in a Negro neighborhood, many residents will reach the conclusion that the neighborhood is being policed, not for the purpose of maintaining law and order, but for the purpose of maintaining the ghetto's status quo. They may draw the same conclusion if most or all of a department's Negro officers are assigned to patrol Negro neighborhoods, and are rarely seen in white neighborhoods or performing such duties as criminal investigation or staff work, or teamed in two-man patrols with white officers. And such policies as not entrusting Negro officers with command on the "practical" ground that white officers will not take orders from Negroes will not go unnoticed in the community. These policies are also likely to prove, in the long run, extremely impractical. Inducing qualified young men from minority groups to enter police work is not easy in view of the distrust for the police felt by members of minority groups, and especially by young men. However, it is essential, and some suggestions about how it can be done are made later in this chapter. In addition to what the police themselves can do, it is vitally important that leaders in the Negro community support and encourage young Negroes to consider police careers.

Somewhat easier to achieve is the adjustment of screening and training programs so that community-relations considerations are emphasized in them. Background investigations of and oral interviews with police candidates, and careful scrutiny of recruits during their probationary period, can do much to insure that prejudiced or unstable officers are not added to or retained in the force. Community-relations subjects, such as the psychology of prejudice, the background of the civil rights movement and history of the Negro in the United States should be emphasized in both recruit and in-service training programs. In addition, the community-relations implications of law enforcement practices like field interrogations and "saturation" patrolling should be stressed in courses dealing with field techniques. All commanding and staff officers should be especially trained in community relations, and the community relations performance of an officer should play a major part in the evaluation of his fitness for promotion.

The Commission recommends:

It should be a high-priority objective of all departments in communities with a substantial minority population to recruit minority-group officers, and to deploy and promote them fairly. Every officer in such departments should receive thorough grounding in community-relations subjects. His performance in the field of community relations should be periodically reviewed and evaluated.

POLICE CONTACTS WITH CITIZENS

A community's attitude toward the police is influenced most by the actions of individual officers on the streets. No

262

community-relations or recruiting or training program will avail if courteous and coolheaded conduct by policemen in their contacts with citizens is not enforced. Commission observers in high-crime neighborhoods in several cities have seen instances of unambiguous physical abuse: officers striking handcuffed suspects, for example. They have heard verbal abuse. They have heard much rudeness. They have reported that officers too seldom use polite forms of address to members of minority groups or juveniles. If officers are under orders to use polite forms of address, they may use them sarcastically or sneeringly. Commission observers have seen a certain amount of harassment in the use of such orders as "move on" and "break it up." They have found that the enforcement of minor ordinances such as, for example, those against drinking in public, is sometimes discriminatory. They have found that in some instances high-crime neighborhoods are used as "punishment" assignments for ineffective or misbehaving officers.

These observers also have found that most officers handle their rigorous work with considerable coolness. They have found that there is no pronounced racial pattern in the kind of behavior just described; the most discernible tendency is for officers, regardless of race, to treat "blue collar" citizens, regardless of race, in such a fashion. However, all such behavior is obviously and totally reprehensible, and when it is directed against minority-group citizens it is particularly likely to lead, for quite obvious reasons, to bitterness in the community. The Commission does not underestimate the provocation that officers must endure in high-crime neighborhoods, nor the physical danger they often run. But as O. W. Wilson, now the Chicago police superintendent, wrote in his book, "Police Administration":

*The officer * * * must remember that there is no law against making a policeman angry and that he cannot charge a man with offending him. Until the citizen acts overtly in violation of the law, he should take no action against him, least of all lower himself to the level of the citizen by berating and demeaning him in a loud and angry voice. The officer who withstands angry verbal assaults builds his own character and raises the standards of the department.*

All responsible police officials subscribe to those views, and departments have regulations prescribing decorous and courteous behavior by its members, although in many departments the regulations are too unspecific. In many places where such regulations are violated with any frequency, the reason is likely to be an insufficiently effective system of internal discipline. This problem is discussed in more detail later in this chapter.

THE GRIEVANCES OF CITIZENS

The best way to deal with police misconduct is to prevent it by effective methods of personnel screening, training, and supervision. A department that clearly articulates its community-relations policies and holds its members to them should receive a minimum of complaints from citizens. However, there will always be some citizen complaints, warranted, and unwarranted, about treatment by the police. How such complaints should be handled has been the subject of perhaps the fiercest of the many controversies about the police that have raged in recent years.

Formal machinery within every police department for the investigation of complaints against police activity or employees is an absolute necessity. It is also important that the complainant be personally informed of the results of the investigation and the disposition of the complaint. Every large department has machinery of some kind for dealing with charges of misconduct by its members, whether those charges originate inside or outside of the department. It typically consists of a board of high-ranking officers or, in some cases, nonsworn departmental officials, that investigates the facts of alleged dereliction and makes a recommendation to the departmental administrator. He properly has the authority and responsibility to take disciplinary action. When this kind of machinery is fully and fairly used it succeeds both in disciplining misbehaving officers and deterring others from misbehaving.

If the complainant remains dissatisfied with the disposition of the case, there are other avenues of appeal outside of the police agency: The local prosecutor; the courts; elected officials such as councilmen, or the mayor; the States' attorney general; the U.S. Department of Justice; and various civil rights or human relations commissions. While all of these are traditional institutions of legal redress they are frequently too formal, awesome, or geographically far removed from the often bewildered citizen. Some of them lack the machinery or resources to process grievances. Some can take action only if a criminal law has been violated. But many of the grievances that constitute acts of misconduct will not qualify as a basis for criminal action.

264

In going beyond the established legal procedures, the Commission finds it unreasonable to single out the police as the only agency that should be subject to special scrutiny from the outside. The Commission, therefore, does not recommend the establishment of civilian review boards in jurisdictions where they do not exist, solely to review police conduct. The police are only one of a number of official agencies with whom the public has contact, and in some cases, because they are the most visible and conspicuous representatives of local government, they may be the focus of more attention than they deserve. Incompetence and mistreatment by housing, sanitation, health, and welfare officials can be as injurious to citizens as mistreatment by the police and should be equally subject to public scrutiny. These officials, like policemen, are public servants. In view of the increasing involvement of government officials in the lives of citizens, adequate procedures for the consideration of such individual grievances as citizens may have against such officials are essential to effective government. So far as possible, it is desirable that such procedures be established within the governmental agency involved. To the extent such procedures are ineffective or fail to inspire general public confidence including the confidence of those who may have legitimate grievances, further recourse is essential. The form that such further recourse should take is dependent on local needs and governmental structure.

The Commission recommends:

Every jurisdiction should provide adequate procedures for full and fair processing of all citizen grievances and complaints about the conduct of any public officer or employee.

THE DEVELOPMENT OF GUIDELINES FOR POLICE ACTION

In view of the importance, complexity, and delicacy of police work, it is curious that police administrators have seldom attempted to develop and articulate clear policies aimed at guiding or governing the way policemen exercise their discretion on the street. Many police departments have published "general order" or "duty" or "rules, regulations, and procedures" manuals running to several hundred pages. They deal extensively, and quite properly, with the personal conduct of officers on and off duty, with uniform and firearms regulations, with the use of departmental property, with court appearances by officers, with the correct techniques of approaching a building in which a burglary may be in progress. They instruct an officer about taking a suspect into custody and transporting him to the station, or about dealing with sick or injured persons, or about handling stray dogs, or about cooperating with the fire department, or about towing away abandoned automobiles—with, in short, dozens of situations in which policemen commonly, or uncommonly, find themselves. What such manuals almost never discuss are the hard choices policemen must make every day: whether or not to break up a sidewalk gathering, whether or not to intervene in a domestic dispute, whether or not to silence a street-corner speaker, whether or not to stop and frisk, whether or not to arrest. Yet these decisions are the heart of police work. How they are made determines to a large degree the safety of the community, the attitude of the public toward the police and the substance of court rulings on police procedures.

No doubt there are several reasons for the failure of the police to set forth consistent law enforcement policies. One is that it is an extremely hard thing to do. For example, defining the amount of objectively based suspicion that justifies a "stop," in such a way that the definition will be of some help to a patrolman on his beat, takes much thought and much expertise. However, it is by no means impossible. The bulletin of the New York State Combined Council of Law Enforcement Officials affords the patrolman practical guidance for his actions, including examples, factual variables, and guiding principles. In effect, this carries a New York "stop and frisk" statutory provision into the street situations in which it is administered. The administrative guidance supplements the general legislative policy.

Another reason that law enforcement policies are seldom stated is that many of them would turn out to be, if clearly set forth, highly controversial. For example, if the police announced publicly that nondisorderly drunks would be arrested only if they had no home to go to, they might be accused of discriminatory treatment.

Probably the most pervasive reason that the police do not articulate policy formally is that they usually do not realize that they make policy informally every day. The police are not accustomed to thinking of themselves as employees of an agency that much more often enforces laws administratively than by invoking the formal criminal process through arrest. Yet a decision by a policeman to order a sidewalk gathering to "break it up," or to take a delinquent youth home rather than arrest him, or to "cool off" a drunk in a precinct lockup rather than formally charge him, is an administrative decision. Not only should policemen be guided by departmental policy in the making of such delicate decisions, but the people who will be affected by these decisions—the public—have a right to be apprised in advance, rather than ex post facto, what police policy is.

The Commission recommends:

Police departments should develop and enunciate policies that give police personnel specific guidance for the common situations requiring exercise of police discretion. Policies should cover such matters, among others, as the issuance of orders to citizens regarding their movements or activities, the handling of minor disputes, the safeguarding of the rights of free speech and free assembly, the selection and use of investigative methods, and the decision whether or not to arrest in specific situations involving specific crimes.

The issuance of orders to individuals regarding their movements, activities, and whereabouts relates particularly to the common police practice of ordering many street gatherings to "break it up" and "move on." Considerations that might govern the issuance of such orders are the time of day, the amount of disturbance the gathering is causing, whether or not the members are intoxicated, whether or not they are unduly obstructing traffic, and whether or not they are people known to the police as offenders or troublemakers.

Also involved are cultural considerations that are more complex. Some people ordinarily conduct their social lives on the street, particularly if they live in neighborhoods where the housing is dilapidated and overcrowded and where there are few parks or other recreational facilities. Breaking up such groups, rather than contributing to public order, is likely to have the reverse effect. Moreover, formulating and executing policy in this field could make the police more conscious of neighborhood problems and could, therefore, make the police more effective servants of the community.

Handling minor disputes is an activity that is regarded as of small importance by most police administrators. Yet it occupies a great deal of the time of many policemen. To the disputants themselves, who are more often than not law-abiding citizens, the manner in which the police intervene in their affairs is a matter of great importance. Disputes, particularly domestic disputes, as discussed earlier, are a subject about which it would be difficult to formulate policy without first engaging in considerable research. The police should seek to accumulate information about families that cause repeated disturbances, to discover whether certain kinds of disturbances are more likely than others to lead to serious assaults or to homicides, to compile statistics on the typical effects of having one of the parties swear out a complaint against the other, to become familiar with the social-service agencies, if any, to which troubled families can be referred. For the police to mediate, arbitrate or suppress each dispute that they encounter as if it were unique—or as if all disputes were alike—contributes little, in the long run, either to law enforcement or to community service.

Chapter 3 has discussed at some length the intimate street relationships between policemen and juveniles. Because juveniles frequent the streets so much, because they are usually in groups, because they are sensitive to real or imagined slights, and because the line between natural and relatively harmless conduct and threatening or injurious behavior is often hard to draw, the police must exercise great discretion in dealing with them. Clear police policies about ways of handling various juvenile situations would be of great help to policemen on the street. There is a trend toward articulating policy about this part of police work. For example, the Chicago Police Department has issued a particularly lucid set of prescriptions for dealing with juveniles.

Safeguarding the rights of free speech and free assembly has become in recent years an increasingly important police duty, and one that can, on occasion, divert large numbers of police from patrol or investigative duties. During 1 month in Philadelphia, for example, there were 15 major demonstrations that needed police protection or at least police presence. This figure does not include dozens of street corner meetings and other minor forms of propagandizing or protest—each of which required the continuous attention of at least one policeman, while it was underway. These demonstrations were either for or against police brutality, a strike of California grape pickers, the Pennsylvania divorce laws, rock and roll music, slum landlords, draft classification examinations, black power, a movie about the Battle of the Bulge, a "rape sentencing" bill, equal rights for homosexuals, low wages at a convalescent home, more post office promotions for Negroes, and the war in Vietnam.

Policing demonstrations is a particularly sensitive job, not only because of the occasional difficulty in distinguishing between the legitimate exercise of constitutional rights, and trespass or incitement to riot, but because policemen have views

Formulation and Execution of Police Policy

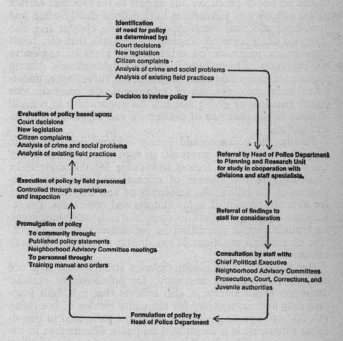

Identification
of need for policy
as determined by:
Court decisions
New legislation
Citizen complaints ·
Analysis of crime and social problems
Analysis of existing field practices

Decision to review policy

Evaluation of policy based upon:
Court decisions
New legislation
Citizen complaints
Analysis of crime and social problems
Analysis of existing field practices

Execution of policy by field personnel
Controlled through supervision
and inspection

Promulgation of policy
To community through:
Published policy statements
Neighborhood Advisory Committee meetings
To personnel through:
Training manual and orders

Referral by Head of Police Department
to Planning and Research Unit
for study in cooperation with
divisions and staff specialists.

Referral of findings to
staff for consideration

Consultation by staff with:
Chief Political Executive
Neighborhood Advisory Committees
Prosecution, Court, Corrections, and
Juvenile authorities

Formulation of policy by
Head of Police Department

of their own about the issues that are being vociferously debated. When spontaneous or surprise demonstrations take place the policemen on the scene have to decide rapidly whether to protect the demonstrators or to put an end to the demonstration in order to keep order. In such situations they especially need the guidance of clear policies about which ways of demonstrating are permissible and which are unlawful.

The selection of investigative methods is probably the most important field in which police policy is needed. This chapter has already discussed the restrictions that the courts have placed on police practices, due in part to the fact that neither police officials nor legislatures have defined clearly when and how those practices were appropriate. The chapter has also discussed the effects on community relations that can result from police insistence on using certain kinds of aggressive law enforcement techniques in certain neighborhoods. Among police procedures that need definition are surveillance, undercover techniques, the use of informants, the common vice squad practices of giving suspects the opportunity to commit offenses in the presence of policemen, and especially field interrogation.

Finally, the police should openly acknowledge that, quite properly, they do not arrest all, or even most, offenders they know of. Among the factors accounting for this exercise of discretion are the volume of offenses and the limited resources of the police, the ambiguity of and the public desire for nonenforcement of many statutes and ordinances, the reluctance of many victims to complain and, most important, an entirely proper conviction by policemen that the invocation of criminal sanctions is too drastic a response to many offenses.

But while the Commission believes strongly that it is not only appropriate, but necessary, for policemen to exercise discretion about arrests, it also believes that it is both inappropriate and unnecessary for the entire burden of exercising this discretion to be placed on individual policemen in tumultuous situations. It is incumbent on police departments to define as precisely as possible when arrest is a proper action and when it is not.

THE POTENTIAL BENEFITS OF POLICE POLICYMAKING

Some of the advantages the police would gain by taking the responsibility for formulating guidelines are readily apparent and have been indicated above. It would bring the important street decisions, now made only by patrolmen, up to the level of the chief administrator and his staff, who would formulate policy much in the way a board of directors serves a corporation. This would remove from individual policemen some of the burden of having to make important decisions ad hoc, in a matter of seconds. It would create a body of standards that would help make the supervision and evaluation of the work of individual policemen consistent. It would help courts understand the issues at stake when police procedures are challenged and lessen the likelihood of inappropriate judicial restrictions being placed on police work. Police administrators would then have more freedom to meet the changing needs of law enforcement.

Other advantages would be less immediate but no less important. A commitment to policymaking by the police would compel them to inquire far more deeply than they have so far into both the social and the technical aspects of law enforcement. It would force the police to ponder the nature of deterrence and the best ways of achieving it. It would suggest experiments with various techniques of patrol and investigation, and indicate the kinds of equipment and management systems that might make police work more efficient, including, perhaps, a computerized data bank of policy information that would permit instant response to queries by line officers and their supervisors. Policymaking would result in a codification of police expertise that could be used in training programs and that would be available to all policemen everywhere. It would involve the police in the programs of social betterment to which the community as a whole is dedicated. It would, in short, do much to professionalize police work in the most meaningful sense of the word.

Finally, recognition by the police and by the community that policymaking is a legitimate and essential part of the police function would tend to involve the rest of the community in law enforcement in a more helpful way. Mayors and city councils are nominally possessed of the ultimate responsibility for police work, but it is difficult for them to exercise their powers to influence police policy when that policy is informal and inexplicit. By the same token, prosecutors and judges find it difficult to evaluate how well the police are doing their job and to help them do it better when police policy is unexpressed. Legislatures will be unable to make informed statutory policy in the law enforcement field until the police articulate their problems and their needs. The citizen grievance procedures and the neighborhood advisory committees that have been recommended in this chapter's section on community relations could be helpful to the police in the formulation and evaluation of policy. The Commission has found that a certain kind of isolation from many currents of community life is a serious police problem. The Commission can imagine no better way for the police to end that isolation, which inhibits both law enforcement and service to the community, than by the police taking the responsibility for formulating policy and discussing it with the community.

POLICE PERSONNEL

There is impressive evidence that in many cities there are too few policemen. The current police-population ratio of 1.7 policemen per thousand citizens obscures the many differences from city to city and region to region. Even the big-city ratio of 2.3 per thousand is misleading, for in San Diego there are 1.07 policemen per thousand citizens and in Boston 4.04.

There appears to be no correlation between the differing concentrations of police and the amount of crime committed, or the percentage of known crimes solved, in the various cities.

At the same time it is apparent that, nationwide, the number of police has not kept pace with the relocation of the population and the attendant increases in crime and police responsibility. Later in this chapter the Commission recommends, in order to increase the effectiveness of the police, adding community service officers and staff specialists. That means additional personnel, and when these new requirements are added to the existing vacancies in departments throughout the country, it is apparent that more police are needed and that municipalities must face up to the urgency of that need and provide the resources required to meet it if crime is to be controlled. But mere addition of manpower without accompanying efforts to make the best use of existing personnel strength might serve only to aggravate the problem of inefficiency. In many departments police personnel are being wasted on trivial duties. In others, increased investment in staff work or more sophisticated equipment would do more to improve police work than investment in more men. Switching from two-man to one-man patrol cars would in some instances free large numbers of policemen for added patrol or investigative duties.

The Commission recommends:

Each municipality, and other jurisdiction responsible for law enforcement, should carefully assess the manpower needs of its police agency on the basis of efficient use of all its personnel and should provide the resources required to meet the need for increased personnel if such a need is found to exist.

The police personnel need that the Commission has found to be almost universal is improved *quality*. Generally, law enforcement personnel have met their difficult responsibilities with commendable zeal, determination, and devotion to duty. However, Commission surveys reflect that there is substantial variance in the quality of police personnel throughout the United States. The recommendations that have been made earlier in this chapter about community relations and policy-making, and the ones made later about organization and management, are predicated on the sharp improvement of the quality of police personnel from top to bottom. The Commission believes that substantially raising the quality of police personnel would inject into police work knowledge, expertise, initiative, and integrity that would contribute importantly to improved crime control.

The word "quality" is used here in a comprehensive sense. One thing it means is a high standard of education for policemen. Police work always will demand quick reflexes, law enforcement know-how and devotion to duty, but modern police work demands much more than that, as this chapter has shown. A policeman today is poorly equipped for his job if he does not understand the legal issues involved in his everyday work, the nature of the social problems he constantly encounters, the psychology of those people whose attitudes toward the law differ from his. Such understanding is not easy to acquire without the kind of broad general knowledge that higher education imparts, and without such understanding a policeman's response to many of the situations he meets is likely to be impulsive or doctrinaire. Police candidates must be sought in the colleges, and especially among liberal arts and social science students.

"Quality" also means personnel who represent all sections of the community that the police serve. It scarcely needs stating that a college education does not guarantee that its recipient will be able to deal successfully with people whose ways of thought and action are unfamiliar to him. As this chapter has also shown, lack of understanding of the problems and

273

behavior of minority groups is common to most police departments and is a serious deterrent to effective police work in the often turbulent neighborhoods where those groups are segregated. And the relationship between the police and the community is so personal that every section of the community has a right to expect that its aspirations and problems, its hopes and fears, are fully reflected in its police. A major, and most urgent, step in the direction of improving police-community relations is recruiting more, many more, policemen from minority groups.

There are major obstacles to the recruitment of both kinds of personnel. College graduates are likely to be deterred from a police career by the fact that it traditionally and almost universally starts at the bottom. A young man enters a police department as a uniformed patrolman and serves in that capacity for a considerable period of time—rarely less than 2 years and more often 4 or 5—before becoming eligible for promotion. The knowledge and skill that college education can provide must receive recognition at the entry level, through pay, rating, and an immediate opportunity to do interesting work before massive numbers of college graduates will be attracted to the police.

On the other hand, recruitment from minority groups will be all but impossible in the immediate future if rigid higher education entry standards are instituted for all police jobs. According to a 1966 census report, 78 percent of all white males between the ages of 20 and 24 have completed at least 4 years of high school while only 53 percent of nonwhite males have. In the 18-to-19 year age group the gap is somewhat greater: 63 percent of white and 37 percent of nonwhite males have completed high school.

Seventy percent of all police departments require a police candidate to have a high school diploma. From the point of view of recruiting college graduate and minority group personnel of the requisite quality, this standard is both too low and too high. In the Commission's view, a promising way to attract better personnel, to utilize them more effectively in controlling crime, and to gain greater understanding of community problems is to allow police candidates to enter departments at three levels of qualification, competence, responsibility, and pay.

The Commission recommends:

Basic police functions, especially in large and medium sized urban departments, should be divided among three kinds of

officers, here termed the "community service officer," the "police officer," and the "police agent."

To enter a police department as a police agent would require considerable educational attainment—at least 2 years of college work and preferably a baccalaureate degree in the liberal arts or social sciences. The job of agent would also be open to officers who could not make an academic showing of that kind but who have shown their capability for imaginative and responsible police work. In every department today there are many patrolmen and detectives who could qualify immediately as agents. The agent would do whatever basic police jobs were the most complicated, sensitive, and demanding. He might be a juvenile officer or a community-relations officer. He might be in uniform patrolling a high-crime or restless neighborhood. He might be a career specialist in narcotics, or robbery, or homicide investigation. He might have staff duties. He would be the most knowledgeable and responsible member of a police team, and would guide and advise the CSO's and officers with whom he worked. He would be encouraged to develop innovative procedures and techniques. He would require minimum supervision.

The police officer would perform the police duties of enforcing laws and investigating those crimes that can be solved by immediate followup investigations or are most likely to have suspects close to the crime scene. He would respond to selected called-for services, perform routine patrol, render emergency services, enforce traffic regulations, and investigate traffic accidents. In addition to these responsibilities, the police officer would be an integral part of the team policing plan, working in concert with police agents and CSO's in solving crimes and meeting other police problems. If he desired to do so he would be helped by the department to qualify as a police agent.

The Commission visualizes the CSO as a young man, typically between the ages of 17 and 21, with the aptitude, integrity and stability necessary to perform police work. A CSO would be, in effect, an apprentice policeman—replacing the present police cadet. He would work on the street under close supervision, and in close cooperation with the police officer and police agent. He would not have full law enforcement powers or carry arms, neither would he perform only clerical duties, as many police cadets do today. He would be a uniformed member of the working police who performs certain

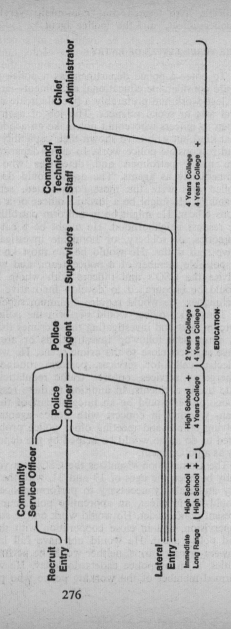

Career Development and Educational Standards

Recruit Entry	Community Service Officer	Police Officer	Police Agent	Supervisors	Command, Technical Staff	Chief Administrator

	Immediate	Long Range
Lateral Entry	High School + −	High School + −
	High School +	2 Years College
	4 Years College	4 Years College
		4 Years College
		4 Years College

EDUCATION

276

service and investigative duties on the street. He would maintain close contact with the juveniles in neighborhoods where he works. He might be available in a neighborhood storefront office or community service center and might use a radio-dispatched scooter to move around the community. He would perform the service duties discussed earlier in this chapter that inner-city residents need so badly and that law enforcement officers have so little time to perform. He would be an integral part of the police teams that will be described later in this chapter.

A young man might be accepted as a CSO despite a minor offense record; otherwise it might be difficult to recruit members of minority groups for this position since Commission studies show that, for the reasons discussed in chapters 2 and 3, it is more likely than not that a Negro youth who grows up in a slum will have such a record. He would be expected to qualify as rapidly as possible for the positions of officer or agent. Under the sponsorship and at the expense of the department, he would continue his studies to that end. When he qualified, he would be promoted as soon as an opening occurred.

This new division of functions should increase the attractiveness of police work by making it possible for a college graduate to assume the responsible position of agent after a brief internship but without long prior service as a patrol officer, and for officers and CSO's to become agents as soon as they qualify and vacancies exist. The opportunity to continue with education at the expense of and with the help of a police department would surely increase the attractiveness of police work to members of minority groups—or to any young men who are unable to further themselves because of insufficient schooling. Creating the positions of CSO and agent might do much to solve the manpower problems of those departments that have them, and might be, as well, the fastest way of recruiting large numbers of well-qualified and experienced minority-group officers. However, it is important to add in the latter connection, that every department should strengthen its efforts to recruit minority-group police officers and agents who do not need to go through the CSO phase. A department that admits minority-group personnel only at the CSO level will merit the charge that it is practicing a subtle kind of discrimination.

ATTRACTING RECRUITS

As this report is being written, approximately two-thirds of the police departments in medium-sized and big cities are below their authorized personnel strength. On a national average, cities are 10 percent below strength. This is not due principally to a shortage of police candidates, but to a shortage of successful ones. Between 1956 and 1961 success rates on entry examination decreased from 30 to 22 percent on a national average. The Los Angeles Department, which has set high standards and maintains them rigorously, accepted less than 3 percent of applicants in 1965. At the same time as applicants' success rates are declining, retirement rates are threatening to rise. This is chiefly because the most rapid modern increase in the size of police departments occurred just after the end of the Second World War, and 20 years is the typical—though by no means universal—period of service that a police department requires of its officers before they become eligible for pensions. To cite Los Angeles again, in 1967 no less than 41 percent of the force will be eligible for retirement. Taking into account the 5.4 percent rate at which officers have left the service for all reasons (retirement, resignation, disability, dismissal, death) over the last 5 years, the present authorized strength of the Nation's departments, and the fact that each year the authorized strength rises by about 3 percent, the Commission calculates that bringing all departments up to 1967 authorized strength will take 50,000 new policemen.

Two kinds of places that the police for the most part have ignored are the Nation's college campuses and its innercity neighborhoods. However, recruitment in these places will not be successful unless police departments recruit much more actively than they now ordinarily do. Recruiting officers must set up recruiting stations, address clubs and civic groups, advertise, answer questions, make it known far and wide that police work has many attractions and opportunities. They should help to organize and participate actively in regional or statewide recruiting programs. Brief notices in civil-service journals about forthcoming examinations, or routine press releases will not attract college graduates, members of minority groups, or for that matter other kinds of high-quality candidates in sufficient number.

The Commission recommends:

Police departments should recruit far more actively than they now do, with special attention to college campuses and innercity neighborhoods.

The standards police departments typically require police candidates to meet fall under several headings. Every department has detailed and rigidly enforced physical standards. Many departments insist on prior residence in the community for a given length of time. Every department demands "good moral character," but many departments do no investigating beyond a personal interview and a check on whether or not the candidate has an arrest record. Some departments give psychological tests and many do not. Only about one-quarter of local departments attempt to screen candidates for emotional fitness. More than 70 percent of departments require a high school diploma, as has been noted; fewer than two dozen of the Nation's 40,000 police agencies require college credits.

From the point of view of securing recruits of the proper quality, some of these standards are too rigid, some are too lax. The Commission believes strongly that it should be the long-range goal of all departments to raise their educational standards.

The Commission recommends:

The ultimate aim of all police departments should be that all personnel with general enforcement powers have baccalaureate degrees.

Beyond question it will take many years for a reform this sweeping to be fully implemented. It never will be implemented if a strong movement toward it does not begin at once. It should be possible, for example, for every department to insist immediately that all recruits, except community service officers, have both a high school diploma and a demonstrated ability, measured by appropriate tests, to do college work. Those departments that put into effect the division of police functions that the Commission has proposed should immediately require agent candidates to have completed 2 years of college. As the supply of qualified police candidates increases, the standards can be raised step by step until the goal of a baccalaureate degree for all policemen is reached. No doubt many police administrators will, at first glance, consider this recommendation of the Commission so radical as to be unattainable. Let them consider the fact that the median education level for all policemen in the United States is

12.4 years, which indicates that many policemen already have done some college work. It is this trend that the Commission believes should be sharply accelerated.

Clearly, if college degrees for police officers are a long-range objective, they must be a short-range objective for police supervisors and administrators, and an immediate objective for chiefs.

The Commission recommends:

Police departments should take immediate steps to establish a minimum requirement of a baccalaureate degree for all supervisory and executive positions.

The long-range objective for high-ranking officers should be advanced degrees in the law, sociology, criminology, police or public administration, business management, or some other appropriate specialty.

Of equal importance with his education is a police candidate's aptitude for the job: His intelligence, his moral character, his emotional stability, his social attitudes. The consequences of putting on the street officers who, however highly educated, are prejudiced, or slow witted, or hot tempered, or timid, or dishonest are too obvious to require detailed discussion. Thorough personal screening of police candidates is a clear necessity. The amount of thoroughness with which local departments screen candidates varies enormously. Some departments screen quite sketchily; others, including those in many of the biggest cities, make in-depth background investigations, administer intelligence tests and interview candidates exhaustively. However, it is fair to say that even the most thorough departments do not evaluate reliably the personal traits and characteristics that contribute to good police work, not because they lack the desire to do so but because a technique for doing so does not exist. Clearly this is a field in which intensive research is needed.

The Commission recommends:

Until reliable tests are devised for identifying and measuring the personal characteristics that contribute to good police work, intelligence tests, thorough background investigations and personal interviews should be used by all departments as absolute minimum techniques to determine the moral character and the intellectual and emotional fitness of police candidates.

No doubt many police administrators will think it odd of the Commission to recommend the raising of any standards at all at a time when so many departments are below authorized strength. The Commission has considered this question with care. It has found, first, by observing closely those few departments that now approach the standards that are being proposed, that high-quality personnel far outperform personnel selected according to traditional standards; there are many places where, if an either/or choice had to be made between raising recruitment standards and reaching authorized strength, the prudent choice in terms of performance would be to raise the standards. It has found, second, that most of those departments that have already instituted high standards have had no unusual trouble remaining at authorized strength because of the attractiveness of working in such departments. It has found, third, that most departments have had no experience with mounting vigorous recruitment programs and owe it to themselves to attempt such programs.

Furthermore, some police recruitment standards are too rigid. The traditional standards relating to age, height, weight, visual acuity, and prior residence in the community are deterrents to the recruitment of able personnel. Most departments insist that a recruit be between 21 and 35. Both limits are arbitrary, and the lower one undoubtedly keeps out of police work many young men, who are unwilling to wait 2 or 3 years after graduating from high school to begin their careers. As police departments put into effect the recommendations for educational standards that have been described above, this will become less of a problem, of course. Meanwhile many communities, including such large cities as Chicago, Minneapolis, and Dallas, have lowered the minimum age without ill effects. That raising the maximum age is equally appropriate is indicated by the fact that the Federal Bureau of Investigation accepts candidates up to the age of 41.

The typical physical requirements for recruits are a 150- to 250-pound weight range, a height minimum of 5 feet 8 or 9 inches and at least 20–40 vision. These limits, too, are arbitrary. A man with 20–100 vision, correctable to 20–20, can be licensed as a commercial pilot. Successful athletes come in all sizes. Particularly in cities where there is a large Puerto Rican population, the height and weight restrictions keep out of police work men who are badly needed. Prior residency requirements typically demand that a man live in a community for at least 6 months before becoming eligible for police work. These are probably the most restrictive requirements of all, for they prevent many police departments from searching for recruits; they prevent many young men from small rural communities from embarking on police careers; they prevent, to give a particularly vivid example of their questionable logic, young men who have put in a period of service in the military police from continuing in police work in civilian life.

The Commission recommends:

Police departments and civil service commissions should reexamine and, if necessary, modify present recruitment standards on age, height, weight, visual acuity, and prior residence. The appointing authority should place primary emphasis on the education, background, character and personality of a candidate for police service.

POLICE SALARIES

The new division of functions also dictates a reexamination of police salary scales, which in most cases are now too low to attract the best qualified recruits, or to keep the best qualified policemen. In small cities the median annual pay for a patrolman is $4,600; in large cities it is $5,300. Typically, the maximum salary for nearly all positions is less than $1,000 over the starting salary. On the other hand, a special agent of the Federal Bureau of Investigation begins at $8,421 a year and, if he serves long enough and well enough, can reach, without promotion to a supervisory position, $16,905. No doubt a salary scale that high is out of the question at the present time in many cities, especially small ones. However, every city should regard it as a standard against which to measure its own potential for attracting able recruits. And every city, even those unable to raise starting minimum salaries for policemen should earnestly consider raising the maximums substantially so that police careers will offer long-term financial inducements. Some big cities should be able to match the FBI's scale for the position of agent immediately, or in the near future. An officer's salary might be $1,000 a year less. A community service officer should receive at least $5,000 a year.

The Commission recommends:

Police salaries must be raised, particularly by increasing maximums. In order to attract college graduates to police service, starting and maximum salaries must be competitive with

other professions and occupations that seek the same graduates.

In many cities, police salaries are tied to the salaries of other municipal employees, most often those of firemen. This practice often aggrieves both policemen and firemen, and sometimes provokes hot debates about which kind of public servant has the most arduous or perilous job and should therefore be the better paid. The Commission has no intention of involving itself in such a dispute, but it does believe that identical pay scales for employees with widely differing functions are unfair and unwise.

The Commission recommends:

Salary proposals for each department within local government should be considered on their own merits and should not be joined with the demands of other departments within a city.

PROMOTION AND LATERAL ENTRY

Able recruits may be the most pressing police personnel need, but it is not the only one. Better personnel are needed throughout most departments. Traditional procedures often inhibit the rapid promotion of able officers into supervisory or command positions. As has already been mentioned, patrolmen must serve a considerable number of years, usually at least 4 to 5, before becoming eligible for promotion. In addition, promotions are made, more often than not, from a civil service "list" that is compiled on the exclusive basis of grades scored on technical written examinations. A list arrived at in such a fashion takes no account of the evaluation of individual officers by their superiors, of the special qualifications of certain officers for certain jobs, of the performance records of officers and the awards and commendations (or reprimands) they have received.

The Commission recommends:

Promotion eligibility requirements should stress ability above seniority. Promotion "lists" should be compiled on the basis not only of scores on technical examinations but on prior performance, character, educational achievement and leadership potential.

Most police departments today do not permit "lateral entry" into command or staff positions by officers from other departments, or by civilians. This is partly because of civil service regulations that have rigid promotion and prior residence provisions, partly because police pension rights are not movable from department to department, partly because of a traditional police resistance to "outsiders." One consequence is that America's police personnel are virtually frozen into the departments in which they started. An officer whose special skills are in oversupply in his own department cannot move to a department where those skills are in demand. An officer who seeks to improve his situation by moving from a small department where opportunities for advancement are few to a large department where they are numerous cannot do it, nor can a city officer who would like to work in a small community follow his inclinations. A department that cannot fill important jobs adequately from its own ranks is precluded from seeking experienced officers elsewhere.

Even more damaging to the effectiveness of police work is the failure to use civilian manpower where it is needed. Eleven percent of America's police personnel is civilian, but the great majority of civilians work as maintenance men, clerks or stenographers, or enforce parking regulations. It is to police staff work that civilians can make the greatest contribution. Communications, records, information retrieval, research, planning, and laboratory analysis are vital parts of police work that, as often as not, could be performed better by civilians with specialized training than by sworn law enforcement officers. And at higher administrative levels, there is a great need for the development of police careerists with professional qualifications in the law, in psychology, in sociology, in systems analysis, and in business management.

The Commission recommends:

Personnel to perform all specialized police functions not involving a need for general enforcement powers should be selected for their talents and abilities without regard to prior police service. Professional policemen should have the same opportunities as other professionals to seek employment where they are most needed. The inhibitions that civil service regulations, retirement plans and hiring policies place on lateral entry should be removed. To encourage lateral movement of police personnel, a nationwide retirement system should be devised that permits the transferring of retirement credits.

Spurred by the Federal Bureau of Investigation, which dramatized the need, set standards, devised techniques and provided personnel for police training, the police have made great strides in the past 30 years in widespread institution of formal recruit training programs. In 70 percent of the cities over 500,000 population, new recruits receive at least 8 weeks' training. However, many courses are unsophisticated and incomplete. Instruction is often limited to "how to do" and there is far too little discussion of fundamental principles. The legal limitations on street policing and the proper use of discretion are rarely stressed. Recruits receive too little background in the nature of the community and the role of the police; in two large departments that offer over 10 weeks of training, less than 2 days are devoted to police-minority group relations. Civilian instructors are seldom employed to teach nontechnical or specialized subjects—the criminal law, sociology, the history of the civil rights movement. Only a small percentage of departments combine classroom work with formal field training that would acquaint recruits with everyday street problems. New educative techniques are seldom used in police academies.

The Commission recommends:

All training programs should provide instruction on subjects that prepare recruits to exercise discretion properly, and to understand the community, the role of the police, and what the criminal justice system can and cannot do. Professional educators and civilian experts should be used to teach specialized courses—law and psychology, for example. Recognized teaching techniques such as problem-solving seminars should be incorporated into training programs.

Recruit training programs at least exist in every big city; small rural departments often provide recruits with no training at all. By and large this is a question of money. Training programs are expensive, and they cannot be provided on a local basis for two or three officers at a time. There is a great need for regional police academies, financed with State or Federal funds, to train recruits from small departments. Until such academies are organized, big-city recruit programs might well make room for a certain number of trainees from smaller departments.

The Commission recommends:

Formal police training programs for recruits in all departments, large and small, should consist of an absolute minimum of 400 hours of classroom work spread over a 4- to 6-month period so that it can be combined with carefully selected and supervised field training.

Although most departments have probationary periods for police recruits, over two-thirds limit the time to 6 months or less, and few departments effectively use the probationary process. As the performance of each officer becomes more crucial to maintenance of social order, probation period observation and rating increases in importance. The limited ability of initial screening procedures to test personality and temperament makes close and systematized observation of new patrolmen imperative. Sometimes probation evaluation is negated by the chief administrator's lack of authority to dismiss those who perform marginally and unsatisfactorily, and civil service requirements are sometimes unduly restrictive.

The Commission recommends:

Entering officers should serve probation periods of, preferably, 18 months and certainly no less than 1 year. During this period the recruit should be systematically observed and rated. Chief administrators should have the sole authority of dismissal during the probation period and should willingly exercise it against unsatisfactory officers.

INSERVICE TRAINING AND EDUCATION

Training needs continue throughout a policeman's career. Laws and procedures change. Policies are redefined. Techniques are improved. These developments must be brought to policemen at all levels of responsibility. Most existing programs rely on bulletins or short sessions of instruction at roll-call. Such techniques are effective only as supplements to annual periods of intensive training during which officers are relieved from their ordinary duties for several days of study. Very few departments have such programs. Very few, furthermore, actively encourage their personnel to continue their studies outside the department by making educational achievement a pathway to rapid promotion, by granting leaves of absence, by helping to pay tuition bills. Very few departments make training in legal, administrative, or business skills a prerequisite for advancement into supervisory positions.

The Commission recommends:

Every general enforcement officer should have at least 1 week of intensive inservice training a year. Every officer should be given incentives to continue his general education or acquire special skills outside his department.

POLICE ORGANIZATION, MANAGEMENT AND FIELD OPERATIONS

The problems to be discussed under this heading are necessarily the problems of city police departments. In a department of less than, say, 50 men, the problems of staff work, chains of command, deployment of forces, and so forth, are seldom complicated. In New York's 28,000-man department they are much more complicated than the organization and management problems of a big corporation. The Commission discussed organization and management with 4 separate advisory panels and over 250 representatives of police forces and professional organizations; these discussions were supplemented by a review of police literature, textbooks, and consultant reports, covering the organization and management of 75 police departments. An outside study performed for the Commission involved even more extensive contacts.

Each study and every expert agreed that, with some notable exceptions, city police forces are not well organized and managed. The same two failures were cited universally as the crucial ones: The failure to develop career administrators, and the failure to use the techniques and acquire the resources that experts on the subject prescribe.

No one with whom the Commission consulted made a dramatic new proposal or recommendation, but the fact that most departments have not adopted recognized principles of organization and management is, in and of itself, significant. Since proper organization and management is a prerequisite for implementation of most of the other recommendations in this chapter, the Commission believes that adoption in practice of the recognized principles of good organization and management is a matter of great urgency. In addition, research into and experimentation with this aspect of police work are not only, under the circumstances, clearly called for, but likely to produce important results.

The Commission recommends:

Each State, through its commission on police standards (discussed later in the chapter), should provide financial and technical assistance to departments to conduct surveys and make recommendations for improvement and modernization of their organization, management, and operations.

For police organization, as for large-scale organization of any kind, the heart of the matter is central control. This simple basic principle has extremely complex and practical implications. Organizationally, it implies that a chief administrator has available to him the advice of staff experts in a variety of subjects, that a sufficient number of middle managers are provided for to insure that authority can be delegated without being dissipated, and that the lines of communication between the chief administrator and the street are kept unobstructed. Administratively it implies policymaking and planmaking, and the kind of supervision that guarantees that policies and plans are understood and carried out by every member of the department. Operationally it implies that such activities as communications and deployment of forces are carried out not on a precinct-by-precinct but on a citywide basis, and that countless kinds of records a department, or a regional or State agency must keep (alphabetical name index files, intelligence files, modus operandi files, wanted criminals files, stolen property files and many more) are easily accessible to all members of the department who need them. Overall it implies the maintenance of departmental integrity by providing that governmental control over the department is exercised only by top-level executives through top-level enforcement officials, and not by neighborhood politicians through precinct officials.

DEPARTMENTAL STAFF

In recent years there has been a growing recognition in city departments, particularly those in the biggest cities, that police work on the street, to be effective, must be supported by strong staff services. Increasing crime and disorder have led to increasing awareness by the police of the importance of crime analysis, research and planning. In order to attract the able recruits they need and to train them properly, many departments have begun strengthening the personnel sections of their staffs. Staff inspection and internal investigation have also received more and more attention as the importance of insuring good performance and rooting out misconduct has become more and more apparent. However, only a few departments as yet have made community relations a staff activity, and even fewer as yet have recognized the necessity for legal advisers as departmental staff members. And as a general proposition, it is fair to say that police staff work almost everywhere, and especially in medium-sized cities, is given far less attention than it needs and deserves.

A police force cannot be effective if it is administered on a day-to-day or crisis-to-crisis basis. It needs plans: contingency plans about, for example, how to handle a visit by the President or how to capture an armed desperado holed up in an apartment; operational plans about how to deploy men in various neighborhoods at various times of day or how to deal with the problem of apartment burglaries; long-range plans about improving the quality of personnel, installing new equipment or controlling widespread vice activities; budgetary plans, community-relations plans, technological plans, plans of many other kinds. It needs not only to develop new plans but to review continually the operation of plans already in effect and to amend them or discard them when necessary. To do this kind of planning to best advantage, a department must first engage in research and analysis. Crime trends, long-range and short-range, must be studied, as well as the social conditions associated with them. Experimental projects must be devised to test novel police techniques on a limited scale and under controlled conditions. Such departments as Chicago, St. Louis, and Los Angeles already have good sized, expertly staffed research, analysis and planning units, but even in those places, it can be said, the enormous possibilities of this kind of police staff work are still largely unexplored.

Of 276 municipal departments that responded to a 1965 survey of the police by the National League of Cities, only 14 reported that they employed legal advisers, and 6 of those reported that the employment was on a part-time basis. Yet the need for continuing legal advice within a department has long been recognized by authorities on the police, and in any case should now be evident to everyone in view of the great interest in police practices the courts are evincing. The duties of a police legal adviser should be, of course, far more extensive than just advising the police, generally or specifically, about permissible field procedures. He could impart to training programs and to duty manuals more legal sophistication

289

than they ordinarily possess today. He could be a useful liaison between police officials and prosecutors. He could do important work in legislative drafting and lobbying, in community relations and in the department's relationship with other municipal agencies. He could be an extremely helpful participant in departmental inquiries into misconduct by officers and in such proceedings as might be taken against misbehaving officers.

The Commission recommends:

Every medium- and large-sized department should employ a skilled lawyer full time as its legal adviser. Smaller departments should arrange for legal advice on a part-time basis.

Little need be said here about staff personnel units; in view of the recommendations about greatly expanded recruitment and training programs that have already been made in this chapter, the importance of such units should be evident. Community relations units have already been discussed. As for the staff functions of inspection and internal investigation, they raise the enormously important question of how police misconduct can most effectively be controlled, and will therefore be discussed in some detail below.

The Commission recommends:

Police departments must take every possible step to implement the guiding organizational principle of central control. Specialist staff units for such matters as planning, research, legal advice, and police personnel should include persons trained in a variety of disciplines and should be utilized to develop and improve the policies, operations, and administration of each police function.

There is one final, crucial point about staff to be made. The kind of policymaking that this chapter described earlier is clearly impossible without expert police staff work. Making policy depends on research and analysis and on legal knowledge. Carrying out policy depends on planning, training and efficient supervision.

The Commission recommends:

Every department in a big or medium-sized city should organize key ranking staff and line personnel into an adminis-

trative board similar in function to a corporation's board of directors, whose duty would be to assist the chief and his staff units in developing, enunciating and enforcing departmental policies and guidelines for the day-to-day activities of line personnel.

CONTROLLING POLICE MISCONDUCT

There is no profession whose members are more frequently tempted to misbehave, or provided with more opportunities to succumb to temptation, than law enforcement. The opportunities arise, on the whole, from the simple physical fact that policemen generally work alone or in pairs, out of sight of their colleagues and superiors. The temptations are more various and complicated. A chief one is that many people want to do things the law forbids, or do not want to do things the law demands, and are willing to pay money to, or do favors for, policemen for not enforcing laws. Another is that policemen often are subjected to kinds of verbal abuse, or even to physical indignities, that provoke a desire to respond in kind. A complicating factor is that because policemen are not only public servants, but sworn upholders of the law, they are expected to conduct themselves with more honor and more restraint than most other citizens. Businessmen commonly accept Christmas presents, or theater tickets, or expensive lunches, from the comparative strangers they do business with; policemen must not. An ordinary citizen walking down the street is not held accountable if he replies insultingly to insults addressed to him; a policeman is.

There is, of course, no possible way of calculating, or even of guessing, how much police misconduct there is in America. Policemen are no more likely than citizens of any other kind to misbehave in front of audiences. The Commission believes that the corruption at all levels and the widespread use of physical coercion that prevailed in many police departments during the era of Prohibition is largely a thing of the past. It is quite sure that almost all departments are headed by honest and honorable officials, and that the large majority of working policemen at all levels of authority conduct themselves honestly and honorably.

However, the Commission does have evidence from its own studies and from police officials themselves, that in some cities a significant percentage of policemen assigned to high-crime areas do treat citizens with disrespect and, sometimes, abuse them physically. It further has knowledge that in these same areas some policemen are accepting bribes from motorists and storekeepers, stealing from burglarized premises or from drunks and receiving kickbacks from tow-truck operators. And it is a matter of public record that in some cities, at this or that time, certain policemen and police officials—and other public officials as well—have protected bookmakers, prostitutes, and narcotics pushers, have operated burglary rings, have favored politicians or other people with "pull," and have acted in concert with leaders of organized crime.

In one important respect, the issue is not how many dishonest or brutal officers there are, but whether there are any at all. A small number of such officers can destroy confidence in the police, confidence that takes many years to rebuild even when the misbehavior has been promptly weeded out. Moreover, even a small amount of misconduct can undermine the morale and discipline of a department. Cliques can grow up that thrive on secrecy and resist reform. Well-behaved officers become corrupted by the mores of their environment, especially by the unspoken rule that often prevails in such situations: an officer must not "inform" on his colleagues. And of course, law enforcement suffers. A police department with a reputation for unfairness cannot promote justice. A police department with a reputation for dishonesty cannot combat crime effectively.

The blame for corruption is often shared by the community as a whole. Poor pay can tempt an officer to accept small favors that eventually bind him to corrupt practices. Widespread racial prejudice, publicly expressed, can make it difficult for an officer to control his own conduct. In some communities there is petty political interference with such things as shift assignment and promotions. A lack of policy about the enforcement of antivice laws, for example, and poor supervision give him too much room for ill-conceived and extemporaneous exercise of discretion. He has daily contact with gamblers and other representatives of organized crime, whom the community prefers to believe are not wrongdoers. Under orders to clean up his beat and without specific guidance as to how to do so under existing legal constraints, he often justifies his derelictions of duty by telling himself that they are the system's fault, not his. He may see gross corruption or political fixing of cases in the prosecutor's office or in the courts. Many times the dishonest officer is merely reflecting the ambivalent standards of his community. An ordinary man, he is expected to resist these extraordinary pressures.

Nonetheless, police experts agree that every police department has a direct and nontransferable responsibility for enforcing proper conduct by its members. There are several ways of doing this; some already have been discussed. If the chief administrator's commitment to fulfilling these internal enforcement responsibilities is made clear by actions as well as words, police misbehavior is deterred. The development and enunciation of detailed police policies would set standards for both performance and supervision. Better screening and training of police recruits would help insure that only men of high character are given a policeman's great responsibilities. The removal of political pressures from subordinate police officials would make discriminatory law enforcement more difficult. The assignment of the best, rather than the worst, officers to ghetto neighborhoods is a clear necessity.

Some police departments have organized strong internal investigation units to enforce honest behavior by policemen. They have been sparingly used by most police departments to insure respectful behavior toward citizens by policemen, except when charges of flagrant brutality are made. From the point of view of police-community relations, it is extremely important that policemen be held to account for rudeness and disrespect as well. If internal investigation units are not well enough manned to add this essential duty to the ones they already have, they should be given more men. Furthermore, it should be definite departmental policy to assign minority-group officers to internal investigations, especially since it appears that it is in the ghettos that policemen most frequently misbehave.

Most of the existing internal investigation units operate by the case method—tracking down and bringing to book individual officers who misbehave. However, they should be essentially a deterrent or preventive operation. This means identifying the problems that cause police misconduct and the neighborhoods or situations in which such misconduct is most likely to occur; devising procedures that will help solve the problems; patrolling and scrutinizing the neighborhoods, and keeping track of the situations. Ways must be found to rid police mores of the pervasive feeling that an allegation of misconduct against one officer is an attack upon the entire police force and that to report a corrupt fellow officer is a detriment, rather than a benefit, to the department. Finally, an internal investigation unit should be responsible to a department's chief and to him alone. By these means it should be possible to bring police misconduct to an irreducible minimum.

The Commission recommends:

Every department, regardless of size, should have a comprehensive program for maintaining police integrity and every medium- and large-sized department should have a well-manned internal investigation unit responsible only to the chief administrator. The unit should have both an investigative and preventive role in controlling dishonest, unethical, and offensive actions by police officers.

COMMUNICATIONS AND INFORMATION RETRIEVAL

Because the members of a police force are so widely dispersed when they are at work the efficiency of police communications systems is crucial. Rapid response to emergency calls, which this chapter has shown to be an important factor in crime solution, depends on good communications. So does effective, continuing supervision of policemen on the streets. The ability of an individual officer to make decisions accurately is enormously increased if he can consult in a matter of seconds with his superiors, or can receive prompt information from the department's records division about such matters as whether a particular man or car is wanted, whether a piece of property is listed as stolen, whether a modus operandi is typical of a person he suspects of having committed a crime. All these activities depend not only on communications but on the ability of the department to retrieve information from its records rapidly.

Communications and information retrieval are enormously complicated technological problems, which are discussed in considerable detail in chapter 11 of this report. How complicated they are is illustrated by some of the facts about the model central communications system installed by the Chicago Police Department in 1961. It controls more than 1,400 vehicles covering 224 square miles and serving more than 3,500,000 people; it utilizes 27 radio frequencies and requires more than 300 people to operate; it cost $2 million. In the opinion of the Chicago police it was an investment that was well worth making. A second urgent communications need is cigarette-pack-sized, transmitting-and-receiving radio equipment that foot patrolmen and investigators can carry easily, and that motorized patrolmen can make use of when they leave their cars. For radio communications of these kinds to be effective, more radio frequencies will have to be made available to the police in most cities. This problem, too, is discussed in chapter 11.

PATROL ALLOCATION AND TECHNIQUES

Early in the work of the Commission, its Chairman, then Attorney General of the United States, asked 2,100 law enforcement agencies and 125 colleges offering police science courses to report any new police techniques for preventing or solving crimes that had come to their attention. Many of the 414 replies from police agencies and 33 replies from colleges described field procedures that were being tried for the first time by some agency or in some area. None of them described field procedures that could be said to be completely original.

Preventive patrol—the continued scrutiny of the community by visible and mobile policemen—is universally thought of as the best method of controlling crime that is available to the police. However, the most effective way of deploying and employing a department's patrol force is a subject about which deplorably little is known. Evaluation of differing methods of patrol depends on trying out those methods over long periods of time and calculating the changes in crime rates and solution rates that the changes in patrol techniques have produced. This sort of research has scarcely begun in America, partly because few police departments have the funds or the personnel to devise, develop, and test innovative procedures. The reluctance to abandon traditional methods of operation in favor of untested, and therefore potentially unsuccessful, ones has also delayed research into new methods.

If the Commission has an overall recommendation in the field of police operations, it is that research, in the form of operational experiments that are scientifically observed and evaluated, be conducted by departments in conjunction with universities, research centers, and other private organizations. Meanwhile it is useful to mention some of the promising developments in field operations that were reported to the Commission.

Scientific efforts to maximize the crime-control use of existing personnel have commenced in several cities. Crime trends are observed from month to month, by time of day and by location within the community, and beat boundaries altered accordingly. Through the use of computers and crime analysis units, a few large departments have radically altered traditional assignments and changed patrol allocation as often as hour to hour.

Other cities have experienced success with special procedures adapted to unusual crime situations. In some of the larger departments, concentrations of street crime have been met by "tactical forces"—mobile patrol forces working out of headquarters—which are deployed in different areas of the city at different times.

Another tactic being used is the creation of a fourth shift which serves during most of the regular evening and the beginning of the early morning shifts. These programs get more men on the street at the times when and in the places where unusually serious outbreaks of crime have taken place.

The lack of knowledge about the effectiveness of different types of patrol is betrayed by the absence of consistent patrol practices. All but four of 37 cities of between 300,000 and 1 million population have walking beats for patrolmen, but the number varies from 2 in Birmingham and Phoenix to 434 in Baltimore. In congested business districts and in those high-crime neighborhoods where the streets are almost always crowded there are a number of advantages to foot patrol, on both law enforcement and community relations grounds, despite its expense. Otherwise, in view of the limited area that foot patrolmen can cover, the expense involved does not seem to justify foot patrol. The extreme mobility and coverage provided by motor patrol compels its use, despite losses in neighborhood contact. Resumption of such contact would occur through the proposed community service officers in the precincts.

In motor patrol assignment, controversy as to whether cars should have one or two men is gradually being resolved in favor of one-man cars. From 1946 to 1964, the percentage of large cities utilizing only two-man cars dropped from 62 to 20 percent. The percentage of all cities using one-man cars exclusively rose from 18 to 41 percent. Almost one-half of the smaller cities employ one-man cars only. Since salaries consume about 90 percent of police budgets, one-man cars cut per-car expenditures almost in half, which means that a police department can put almost twice as many one-man cars on the streets as two-man cars.

Several cities have successfully used scooters and bicycles for patrol. They are peculiarly adapted to urban street conditions and do provide intimate contact with the neighborhood.

There are a number of other law enforcement techniques that have been tried out in various places and might prove useful in others. The use of dogs is one. Only 1 canine corps unit existed in 1957; now about 200 cities have an aggregate of 500 man-dog teams. These are particularly effective for antiburglary patrol in industrial and commercial areas and for building searches. Research is proceeding on the use of dogs for drug detection. However, the use of dogs for routine patrol, especially in minority-group neighborhoods, tends to antagonize the community and may do more harm than good.

Several departments report success with special surveillance operations. For example, one sheriff employed a 10-man surveillance squad for 4 months in a concentrated attack on known professional criminals. During this period, 127 major arrests cleared 236 serious offenses and resulted in the recovery of property valued at $300,000.

Surveillance from rooftops in high-crime areas has also been successful. So has the use of "decoy autos" planted by the department and set to emit a radio signal when stolen. Such autos are equipped with ignition cutoff systems, which stop the engine after the thief has driven a short distance.

Photographic installations in banks, stores, homes, schools, and check-cashing areas have also provided convincing evidence against the perpetrators of crime.

Prearranged blockade plans and observation points rationally devised by geographic area have been effectively established in many communities.

Special techniques involving helicopter patrol, antivandalism and burglar alarms, simultaneous broadcast networks and closed circuit television are also being explored.

TEAM POLICING

In almost all large police departments there is a considerable amount of organizational fragmentation. Traditionally and almost universally, patrol and investigative forces have separate lines of command and tend to be isolated from one another; often they keep separate sets of records; frequently they work different shifts or are based in different places so that there is a minimum of contact between patrolmen and detectives. In addition, investigators are more often than not divided at both headquarters and precinct levels into squads —vice, robbery, burglary, fraud, homicide, and so forth— that may themselves keep separate records, use separate informants and remain more or less isolated from each other in other ways.

At both the staff and the field levels, this overseparation of functions, or overspecialization, can have undesirable results. When intelligence is not centralized and coordinated, staff planning for the purpose of either apprehending specific criminals, or solving crime problems such as, for example, an outbreak of burglaries in some neighborhood, is almost impossible. When lines of command are kept rigidly separate, it is difficult to bring the full resources of a department to bear on crime solution.

The agent-officer-community service officer recommendation made earlier in this chapter has not only the improvement of the quality of police personnel as its objective, but also a change in the way the police work in the field. The concept, which might be called "team policing," is that all police work, both patrol and criminal investigation, in a given number of city blocks should be under unified command. A "field supervisor" would have under his command a team of agents, officers, and community service officers. The team would meet at the beginning of a tour of duty and receive a briefing on the current situation in the neighborhood—what crimes were unsolved, what suspects were wanted for questioning, what kinds of stolen goods to look out for, what situations were potentially troublesome, and so forth. On this basis the members would be assigned to specific areas or duties. If conditions warranted it, agents might be assigned to patrol and wear uniforms or plainclothes officers might be assigned to investigation. Community service officers might be delegated to help either. In specific investigations or incidents, agents would be given authority over the actions of CSOs and officers. If the conditions in the area changed during the tour, if a major crime was committed or a major disorder erupted, the assignments could be promptly changed by the field supervisor.

Obviously, this proposal does not envision the abandonment of special duties or special squads. An agent serving as a narcotics, or juvenile, or community-relations specialist, for example, would almost always cover a territory policed by several teams, and would be moved into other work only in emergencies. There would still be a need for squads of officers with special knowledge of certain kinds of crime.

The Commission recommends:

Police departments should commence experimentation with a team policing concept that envisions those with patrol and investigative duties combining under unified command with flexible assignments to deal with the crime problems in a defined sector.

The Commission believes that team policing would result

in both increased crime solution, and the most advantageous use of the time and talents of all policemen. It wishes to stress, furthermore, that experiments with team policing are not dependent on the agent-officer-CSO division of functions. They could easily be conducted with existing personnel.

CRIME SCENE SEARCH AND LABORATORY WORK

The Commission has found that the police are not making the most of their opportunities to obtain and analyze physical evidence. They are handicapped by technical lacks. There is a very great lack in police departments of all sizes of skilled evidence technicians, who can be called upon to search crime scenes not merely for fingerprints, but for potentially telltale evidence like footprints, hairs, fibers, or traces of blood or mud. In one 2,000-man force, for example, there are only 2 technicians on each shift. More often than not, perhaps, such evidence would not lead directly to the identification of a criminal about whom nothing else is known, but it might help greatly to establish a case for or against a suspect. The two chief reasons for the lack of skilled technicians are that few persons with the requisite science education have been recruited into police operations, and that few training programs for evidence technicians have so far been developed.

The undeveloped state of training in this field also accounts for the fact that many patrolmen and detectives have no more than a rudimentary idea of how to search the scene of a crime. The absence of adequate laboratory facilities to analyze physical evidence is most acutely felt by smaller departments; most big-city departments have, or have access to, good laboratories. The establishment of State or regional training programs and crime laboratories is discussed later in this chapter.

In any case, the Commission strongly believes that it should be an important goal of the police to develop the capacity to make a thorough search of the scene of every serious crime and to analyze evidence so discovered.

RIOT CONTROL

One of the most hazardous and frustrating tasks in policing today is the control of riots. Members of the Commission staff studied the police handling of riots in some detail; they consulted with local police and State National Guard officials, and convened a 2-day conference that discussed this problem. They turned over the knowledge they obtained and the conclusions they reached to the Federal Bureau of Investigation, which, pursuant to presidential order, is responsible for the training of local police in this field.

The Commission found that most large city departments have developed plans and expertise in this aspect of police work; but that smaller departments yet have much to learn. Certain principles are especially important.

Demonstrations should not be confused with riots. Police must not react to disorder in the course of demonstrations too quickly or with too much force. Furthermore, they would be greatly helped in their task of preserving order and protecting constitutional rights if the leaders of protesting or demonstrating groups discussed, in advance with the police, the appropriate times and places for demonstrations and methods of demonstrating. On the other hand, strong law enforcement responses in a true riot situation must occur rapidly, on the basis of advance planning and operational coordination.

Advance planning is a necessity and must be conducted jointly between the police and local, State, and Federal governments. Too few departments have held the drills and rehearsals that disclose in advance deficiencies in planning, communications, coordination and chain of command. Procedures for calling in the National Guard and allocating command responsibility must be worked out prior to riotous situations.

The tactics chosen at the beginning of disorder may well be the crucial factor in controlling a riot. The kinds and extent of police force employed, and equipment involved, must be thought out well in advance, taught to personnel through training and constantly reassessed. Procedures for the acquisition and channeling of intelligence must be established so that information is centralized and disseminated to those who need it.

Like any kind of crime, riots are best controlled by prevention. This of course involves maintaining proper police conduct, but the most important element in prevention is a city government's awareness of and response to the frustrations of the community.

FIREARMS USE POLICY

In most cities police officers receive too little guidance as to when firearms may be drawn and used. Recruit and inservice training should keep officers continually alert to the legal and moral aspects of the use of firearms.

The Commission recommends:

A comprehensive regulation should be formulated by every chief administrator to reflect the basic policy that firearms may be used *only* when the officer believes his life or the life of another is in imminent danger, or when other reasonable means of apprehension have failed to prevent the escape of a *felony* suspect whom the officer believes presents a serious danger to others.

COORDINATION AND POOLING OF POLICE SERVICES

The machinery of law enforcement in this country is fragmented, complicated and frequently overlapping. America is essentially a nation of small police forces, each operating independently within the limits of its jurisdiction. The boundaries that define and limit police operations do not hinder the movement of criminals, of course. They can and do take advantage of ancient political and geographic boundaries, which often give them sanctuary from effective police activity.

Nevertheless, coordination of activity among police agencies, even when the areas they work in are contiguous or overlapping, tends to be sporadic and informal, to the extent that it exists at all. This serious obstacle to law enforcement is most apparent in the rapidly developing urban areas of the country, where the vast majority of the Nation's population is located and where most crimes occur. In 1960, almost 117 million people, about 70 percent of our population, resided in America's 18,000 cities. Of these, almost 113 million persons, 63 percent of our population, resided in the 212 areas designated by the Bureau of the Census as Standard Metropolitan Statistical Areas. According to FBI reports, approximately 83 percent of the Part I crimes committed in the United States in 1965 were committed in these SMSA's. These 212 sprawling, metropolitan areas comprise 313 counties and 4,144 cities, each of which has its own police force. The majority of these departments are small and have only limited facilities and services. Thus, the responsibility for dealing with most of the serious crime in this country is diffused among a multitude of independent agencies that have little contact with neighboring forces.

The Commission believes that the principal method of improving enforcement outside of the large cities is the coordination or pooling of police services. Coordination involves an agreement between two or more jurisdictions to perform certain services jointly; usually one of the jurisdictions will provide one or more services for the others. Pooling occurs when local government jurisdictions consolidate by merging one jurisdiction, or a function thereof, with another jurisdiction, or function thereof. Coordination is the more feasible form of law enforcement cooperation because there are fewer political or legal obstacles to achieving it.

In studying how coordination or pooling might improve the quality of law enforcement, the Commission was guided by two assumptions. First, some pooling could take place without jeopardizing the independence of local government. Second, it is desirable to preserve as much local governmental control as is consistent with increasing the quality and quantity of police service. The Commission further believes that the cost of any program resulting from the coordination or pooling of police services should be allocated on an equitable basis and that it is important to the success of any joint program that it involve the political leadership, as well as the law enforcement officials, of the communities involved.

STAFF SERVICES

Staff services of law enforcement agencies are those nonline functions and activities that help develop departmental personnel, assist the departments to perform their basic police responsibilities effectively, and provide meaningful, internal controls. Included in staff services are recruitment, selection and training of personnel, planning, organized crime intelligence, purchasing, public information, internal investigation, and staff inspection. All but the last two functions can be performed more efficiently and with improved quality through joint action.

Personnel and Planning. Many police agencies lack the necessary resources for recruiting and selecting qualified personnel and for providing the training needed at all levels of service. The Commission believes that police activities related to personnel should be organized on the basis of areas large enough to support good programs. Police agencies will benefit from joint recruitment, selection, and training programs. The State should participate in the programs through setting standards, assisting departments in coordinating recruitment programs, and making training facilities available.

302

Although the fulfillment of police responsibilities depends upon the effective use of manpower, relatively few departments possess the resources and capabilities for providing the sound, continuous planning essential for assigning personnel and evaluating police effectiveness. A statewide body for police administration service, such as exists in New York State, or as is proposed in the discussion of standards councils below, could serve as a clearinghouse of information relative to administrative and operational problems, needs and suggested solutions. States should provide modus operandi files and related services, which have been found useful in Michigan and California, thereby providing police agencies with access to areawide crime and modus operandi analyses.

Organized Crime Intelligence, Purchasing and Public Information. Organized crime intelligence should be shared among local, State, and Federal agencies to the extent possible. This is discussed more fully in chapter 7.

Police purchasing should be a function of a centralized purchasing department of a whole jurisdiction. Volume buying would lead to lower prices, and purchasing expertise would produce better equipment and better testing and inspection, as has been demonstrated in Los Angeles County, Chicago, and in Dade County, Fla.

While mainly a staff aid to the individual police administrator, public information services could be usefully coordinated in many metropolitan areas. A joint program between a central city and its suburbs, for example, could improve public information programs that involve the commuting public.

AUXILIARY SERVICES

The auxiliary services provide technical, special, or supportive services to a law enforcement agency. These include records, communications, detention, laboratory services, equipment, and buildings. In general they are the police functions best suited to pooling or coordination throughout an area. Moreover, along with training, they are the services most often performed jointly, since the cooperation relates essentially to technical matters. Another argument for joint performance of such services is that they are costly and require resources beyond the ability of most jurisdictions.

Records and Communications. Criminal records and communications systems together provide the mechanisms by which the police should be able, swiftly and efficiently, to

303

learn about crimes, to store and retrieve pertinent information, and to deploy personnel effectively. The establishment of an areawide records center is fundamental to successful police operations, particularly in metropolitan areas comprising several jurisdictions, each with its own force. The integration at an areawide records center of basic information collected by many law enforcement agencies would enable inquiring police departments to check only one source rather than several. This would eliminate duplication of effort and physical facilities, reduce the possibility of error, and reduce significantly the time needed to conduct an inquiry or search. In addition, detailed crime analysis and planning studies now needed to assist departments in deploying their forces more effectively would become feasible on an areawide basis.

An areawide communications center can improve the speed with which citizen requests for service are answered. Duplication of expensive communications facilities can be greatly reduced and existing facilities utilized more effectively. By integrating and centralizing communications facilities where this is practical, many problems arising out of the limited number of radio frequencies available for police operations would be mitigated if not eliminated. In this connection, the States should serve as a coordinating agency and assist law enforcement agencies in realizing the benefits that would result from pooling and consolidating records and communications systems.

The Commission recommends:

States should assume responsibility for assuring that areawide records and communications needs are provided.

Detention. Chapter 6 of this report discusses in some detail the problem of local jails, which in many communities are administered by police agencies. Because a jail is generally situated in the midst of a community, it could be the scene of significant programs designed to reintegrate offenders into the community. However, the police are trained in law enforcement rather than in rehabilitation, and such programs rarely are in effect. Turning over jails to qualified correctional agencies appears to be the proper solution for this problem.

Laboratory Services. Only large departments have adequate laboratory facilities. The shortage of technicians and equipment usually means that city laboratories are unable to help neighboring jurisdictions. An outstanding exception to this,

304

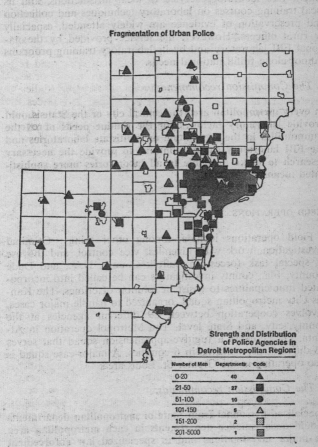

Fragmentation of Urban Police

**Strength and Distribution
of Police Agencies in
Detroit Metropolitan Region:**

Number of Men	Departments	Code
0-20	40	▲
21-50	27	■
51-100	10	●
101-150	6	△
151-200	2	▨
201-5000	1	▩

and an indication of what can be accomplished locally, is the Chicago Police Department laboratory, which renders expert free service to 140 neighboring jurisdictions in addition to free training about crime scene search. The FBI provides excellent free laboratory service to local jurisdictions, and its local training courses on laboratory techniques and collection and preservation of evidence are widely attended, especially by rural officers. However, the service provided by the national FBI laboratory and by its laboratory training programs cannot alone fulfill national needs.

The Commission recommends:

In every metropolitan area the central city or the State should provide laboratory facilities for the routine needs of all the communities in the area. State or multistate laboratories and the FBI laboratory should continue to provide the necessary research to make available to all laboratories more sophisticated means of analysis.

FIELD OPERATIONS

Field operations include, among other things: Criminal investigation, work with juveniles, vice control, and the use of special task forces. In Suffolk County, N.Y., and Dade County, Fla., county investigators can be called into incorporated municipalities to assist in solution of crimes. The Kansas City metropolitan squad, organized to handle major cases, involves cooperation between 29 different agencies at the county, city, and State level. The Metropol operation in Atlanta, Ga., created a fugitive-apprehension squad that serves 38 different departments in 6 counties. A major-case squad is also operating in the Greater St. Louis area.

The Commission recommends:

Specialized personnel from State or metropolitan departments should assist smaller departments in each metropolitan area on major investigations and in specialized law enforcement functions.

Trained investigators from large departments could be provided to small departments for followup investigations, and officers in the small departments could be trained by them in methods of handling preliminary investigations. Regional squads, manned by qualified officers from each or any of a region's jurisdictions, should be formed to solve major crimes, investigate a series of crimes committed by the same suspect in different communities within a region, apprehend fugitives, and create blockade plans.

In juvenile work, specialists from large departments should train officers in small departments in handling juveniles and should provide operational aid in matters beyond the capacity of the smaller jurisdiction. Areawide associations of juvenile officers should discuss common problems and develop optimum field procedures.

In vice operations, small departments should be able to call in State or county officers. Large city departments should brief the surrounding community police agencies about areawide vice and crime conditions except when there is reason to believe corruption exists in a local department. Action that might be taken in such cases is discussed in chapter 7.

Mutual-aid agreements should be made among jurisdictions so that one department can borrow sufficient personnel from other departments for special needs, such as policing public events, riots, and civil disasters and providing undercover personnel for vice investigations. Enabling legislation should give the borrowed officers the power of arrest and afford them the privileges and immunities possessed by officers in the borrowing jurisdiction. Special tactical operations in multijurisdictional crime situations could also be established.

CONSOLIDATION OR POLICING AGREEMENTS

The ultimate form of jurisdictional consolidation is metropolitan government, a complete political merger of a city and its suburbs. This has happened in only one place in the country—Nashville-Davidson County, Tenn. Obviously pooled law enforcement is only one, and not the chief, purpose of a political reform that basic in nature. The Commission can only note, in this connection, that police performance and public support of the police in Davidson County have improved sharply since the merger. Annexation by a city of surrounding territory, for equally broad reasons, can also improve law enforcement in the annexed areas.

Leaving aside such sweeping reforms, there are ways in which law enforcement activities can be pooled without necessarily affecting other governmental functions. Two of the most promising are contract law enforcement and county subordinate service districts.

307

Contract Law Enforcement. This is an arrangement that authorizes one governmental jurisdiction to furnish some or all of its police services to another jurisdiction for a fee, thus broadening the geographical area for handling common functions. California, where 500 such intergovernmental agreements exists, is the only State that now employs these contracts on a widespread basis. In Los Angeles County, for example, the sheriff provides complete police service to 29 of the 77 municipalities.

Contract law enforcement is one of the least complicated ways to achieve pooling of law enforcement services. Although the usual method is county-to-city service, provisions exist in the Nation for city-to-county service and State-to-city service.

Subordinate Service Districts. This pooling arrangement is unique, in that county police operate in incorporated as well as in unincorporated areas. Towns, villages, and boroughs vote to cede law enforcement functions to the county, and their citizens pay a special tax. Although other elements of local government retain their independence, subordinate police service districts institute a contiguous policing jurisdiction that guarantees a consistently higher level of police service. The best examples of this are in Nassau and Suffolk Counties, Long Island, N.Y.

The Commission recommends:

Each metropolitan area and each county should take action directed toward the pooling, or consolidation, of police services through the particular technique that will provide the most satisfactory law enforcement service and protection at lowest possible cost.

OBSTACLES TO COORDINATION AND POOLING

To obtain either pooling or coordination of law enforcement, most States must amend their constitutions and statutes. Without special legislation permitting cooperation, 28 States must comply with home rule provisions that block the exercise of power beyond the limits of a particular jurisdiction. Sheriffs, for example, are usually constitutional officers whose common-law powers cannot be removed or restricted without amending State constitutions. Most law enforcement officers are restricted by provisions that prohibit dual office-holding and bar officers in one jurisdiction from serving in another without appropriate enabling legislation. Even county governments normally have only the powers specifically awarded to them by a State constitution.

More than one-half of the States do have legislation permitting intergovernmental agreements, but these are limited mostly to particular situations and do not cover law enforcement pooling. The model act of the Council of State Governments provides for joint or cooperative activities, as to any existing power of local government, but this act has been adopted in substance by only six States. What makes the statutory and constitutional obstacles to coordination and consolidation so difficult to overcome is the reluctance of citizens to remove them by vote. This is often due to local pride, fear of higher taxes, or the unwillingness of citizens to take on problems that their community does not have but that neighboring communities do. Most city-county pooling proposals have been defeated at the polls. Citizens must be made aware that in many cases the partial consolidation of police service can result in vastly improved law enforcement for essentially the same cost.

IMPLEMENTATION THROUGH STATE COMMISSIONS ON POLICE STANDARDS

Properly constituted and empowered, a State commission on police standards can be an effective vehicle for improving law enforcement. Without removing control from local agencies, such a commission can be of great assistance in establishing adequate personnel selection standards, establishing and strengthening training procedures, certifying qualified police officers, coordinating recruitment and improving the organization and operations of local departments through surveys. They could also conduct or stimulate research, provide financial aid to participating governmental units and make inspections to determine whether standards are being adhered to. A number of States now have commissions or councils, but most of them do not have the power either to establish mandatory standards or to give local departments money to help them comply. This lack of power weakens them seriously.

The Commission recommends:

Police standards commissions should be established in every State, and empowered to set mandatory requirements and to

give financial aid to governmental units for the implementation of standards.

Chapter 13 of this report proposes the establishment of State and local planning bodies to upgrade criminal justice. Police standards commissions, appointed by governors and consisting of leading law enforcement officials and perhaps a few laymen from various parts of each State, could serve in conjunction with such groups. The task of the commissions should not be conceived in narrow terms. The setting of minimum standards must be done with sufficient imagination and flexibility to avoid the rigidity that now characterizes recruitment criteria in most departments. They must lead the effort to help reform civil service requirements when they are restrictive, and to develop and implement better methods for screening the personality and attitudes of applicants and assessing their performance on duty.

In training, the commission could marshal the talents of police science curriculum experts to improve basic training and continuing training programs. They could stimulate the development of a wider selection of course materials, and they might sponsor programs to train instructors in important subjects such as community relations and control of riots, or in better methods of teaching. Programs that meet standards should be certified, and attendence at certified programs required.

State commissions could be an effective voice in promoting greater coordination among law enforcement agencies, among agencies within the administration of justice, with community groups, and with other units of government.

Perhaps most important, State commissions could initiate the research that must continually test, challenge, and evaluate professional techniques and procedures in order to keep abreast of social and technical change. And though the task is difficult, they could help develop within the ranks of law enforcement the vision, inventiveness, and leadership that is necessary to meet the complex challenges facing the police of our cities.

Chapter 5

The Courts

THE CRIMINAL COURT is the central, crucial institution in the criminal justice system. It is the part of the system that is the most venerable, the most formally organized, and the most elaborately circumscribed by law and tradition. It is the institution around which the rest of the system is in large measure responsible. It regulates the flow of the criminal process under governance of the law. The activities of the police are limited or shaped by the rules and procedures of the court. The work of the correctional system is determined by the court's sentence.

Society asks much of the criminal court. The court is expected to meet society's demand that serious offenders be convicted and punished, and at the same time it is expected to insure that the innocent and the unfortunate are not oppressed. It is expected to control the application of force against the individual by the State, and it is expected to find which of two conflicting versions of events is the truth. And so the court is not merely an operating agency, but one that has a vital educational and symbolic significance. It is expected to articulate the community's most deeply held, most cherished views about the relationship of the individual and society. The formality of the trial and the honor accorded the robed judge bespeak the symbolic importance of the court and its work.

Here, at the beginning of the Commission's examination of the court and its work, it is important to discuss some fundamental aspects of the criminal process that determine what the court can and cannot do and, in many important respects, what the entire system of criminal justice can and cannot do.

The criminal process is determined by the U.S. and State constitutions, by statute, by practice, and by court decision—all of which are built upon the model of the English common law. These basic sources of law give structure to the process and limit its methods.

Some constitutional limitations on the criminal court are based on principles common to most civilized criminal systems. One is that criminal penalties may be imposed only in response to a specific act that violates a preexisting law. The criminal court cannot act against persons out of apprehension that they may commit crimes, but only against persons who have already done so. In other words, the court is primarily an institution for dealing with specific criminal acts that already have taken place; only insofar as its handling of criminals can be cautionary or rehabilitative can it deal with future criminality.

Furthermore, the basic procedures of the criminal court must conform to concepts of "due process" that have grown from English common law seeds. A defendant must be formally notified of the charge against him and must have an opportunity to confront witnesses, to present evidence in his own defense, and to have this proof weighed by an impartial jury under the supervision of an impartial judge. In addition, due process has come to incorporate the right of a defendant to be represented by an attorney. Unquestionably adherence to due process complicates, and in many instances handicaps, the work of the courts. They could be more effiicent—in the sense that the likelihood and speed of conviction would be greater—if the constitutional requirements of due process were not so demanding. But the law rightly values due process over efficient process. And by permitting the accused to challenge its fairness and legality at every stage of his prosecution, the system provides the occasion for the law to develop in accordance with changes in society and society's ideals.

The system also imposes limitations on how the prosecution may prove its case against one accused of crime. It must establish guilt beyond a reasonable doubt without compelling the accused to produce evidence or give testimony. The defendant can refuse to explain his actions and can refuse to respond to the testimony against him; he cannot be penalized for doing so. No statement or confession he makes after his arrest can be used against him, unless it has been made voluntarily, with knowledge that he could have remained silent if he had chosen to do so, and in circumstances that made it possible for him to exercise that choice freely. He cannot be required by court order or subpoena to produce private papers or other personal property that might incriminate him.

In the Federal system, as well as in many States, the existing rule, now the subject of reconsideration by the Supreme Court, is that search warrants may be used only to seize contraband or the fruits or instrumentalities of crime. In the words of a Supreme Court decision:

*[T]hey may not be used as a means of gaining access to a man's house or office and papers solely for the purpose of making search to secure evidence to be used against him in a criminal or penal proceeding * * *. Gouled* v. *United States,* 255 U.S. 298, 309 (1921).

If evidence is seized illegally, it cannot be used in court.

These limitations on proof of guilt are not universal; many countries operate effective and humane criminal systems without putting so great a burden on the prosecution. America's adherence to these principles not only demands complex and time-consuming court procedures but also in some cases forecloses the proof of facts altogether. Guilty criminals may be set free because the court's exclusionary rules prevent the introduction of a confession or of seized evidence. Crimes may never even be detected because restrictions on the methods of investigation insulate criminal conduct from the attention of the police.

Nevertheless these limitations on prosecution are the product of two centuries of constitutional development in this country. They are integral parts of a system for balancing the interests of the individual and the state that has served the Nation well.

SUBSTANTIVE CRIMINAL LAW

The substantive criminal law—the statutes and ordinances that the criminal justice system is called upon to enforce—forbids acts of many different kinds and degrees of injuriousness. A major part of it is a set of universally accepted prohibitions against such dangerous and frightening acts as homicide, rape, assault, and robbery. The place of these offenses in the criminal code is clear, and society rightly expects the criminal process to protect against them.

However, defining, grading, and fixing levels of punishment for these serious offenses, as well as for other conduct made punishable by the criminal code, is persistently difficult. Many common offenses have ancient antecedents, yet age has not contributed to the clarity of their definitions. In other instances new situations strain familiar definitions.

Criteria for distinguishing greater and lesser grades and degrees of crime also are in need of reexamination. They frequently determine the severity of the punishment, an issue that can be more significant in a particular case than the question of whether the defendant's conduct was criminal.

About 30 States and the Federal Government are taking a fresh look at their substantive criminal codes and are considering revising them. The American Law Institute has given impetus to this effort through its Model Penal Code, produced after a decade of sustained labor. The model code offers a thoughtful and comprehensive reexamination of the substantive criminal law, and it has proven to be a sound guide to criminal code reform.

It is not only vital that a criminal code define and grade offenses in a rational manner, but that the courts enforce it in rational ways. Before the criminal courts come many offenders who are marginal in the sense that, although they are guilty of serious offenses as defined by the penal code, they may not be habitual and dangerous criminals. It is not in the interest of the community to treat marginal offenders as hardened criminals, nor does the law require that the courts do so. Framing statutes that identify and prescribe for every nuance of human behavior is impossible; a criminal code has no way of describing the difference between a petty thief who is on his way to becoming an armed robber and a petty thief who succumbs once to a momentary impulse.

Making such distinctions is vital to effective law enforcement. Therefore the law gives wide latitude to police and prosecutors in making arrests and in bringing charges, judges in imposing penalties, and correctional authorities in determining how offenders shall be treated in prison and when they shall be released on parole. The law, in short, makes prosecutors, judges, and correctional authorities personally responsible for dealing individually with individual offenders, for prescribing rigorous treatment for dangerous ones, and for giving an opportunity to mend their ways to those who appear likely to do so. On the quality of the court and its officers depend both the individual's future and the general safety.

In terms of volume most of the cases in the criminal courts consist of what are essentially violations of moral norms or instances of annoying behavior, rather than of dangerous crime. Almost half of all arrests are on charges of drunkenness, disorderly conduct, vagrancy, gambling, and minor sexual violations.

Such behavior is generally considered too serious to be ignored, but its inclusion in the criminal justice system raises questions deserving examination. For one thing the investigation and prosecution of such cases ties up police and clogs courts at the expense of their capacity to deal with more threatening crimes. Moreover, to the extent that these offenses involve willing victims, their detection often requires a kind of enforcement activity that is degrading for the police and raises troublesome legal issues for the courts.

In some cities the enforcement of these laws has been unhappily associated with police, prosecutor, and court venality and corruption, which in turn have led to a general decline in respect for the law. Arrest, conviction, and jail or probation rarely reform persons who engage in these kinds of behavior, nor do they appear to deter potential violators. And continued reliance on criminal treatment for such offenders may blunt the community's efforts to find more appropriate programs to deal with the alcoholic, the homeless man, the compulsive gambler, or the sexual deviant.

At the heart of some of the predicaments in which the criminal law finds itself has been too ready acceptance of the notion that the way to deal with any kind of reprehensible conduct is to make it criminal. There has been widespread scholarly debate in recent years on the extent to which conduct that does not produce demonstrable harm to others, but is generally considered abhorrent or immoral, should be made criminal. Some argue that lowering the criminal bars against such behavior might be understood as a license to engage in it. Others maintain that the limited tool of the criminal law will work better against the most dangerous and threatening kinds of crime if it is confined to the kinds of crime it can deal with most effectively. Beyond recognizing that criminality and immorality are not identical, the Commission has not found itself in a position to resolve this issue. However, it does urge the public and legislatures, when code reform is being considered, to weigh carefully the kinds of behavior that should be defined as criminal.

CRIMINAL PROCEDURES

Even within their limitations the courts do not work perfectly, and never have. Hamlet considered "the law's delay" to be as deplorable a feature of the human scene as "the pangs of mispriz'd love," and the works of Charles Dickens are crammed with descriptions of the law's abuses, from the bumbling beadle in "Oliver Twist" to the unwieldy English Chancery in "Bleak House." For as long as judges have had the power to determine sentences, there have been individual judges who have misused that power by sentencing too leniently or too severely. For as long as money bail has been used to insure that defendants appear for trial, it has discriminated against poor defendants. For as long as defense counsel have had the right to question and test the criminal process, some defense counsel have resorted to obfuscation and chicanery. Courts can be only as effective and just as the judges and prosecutors, counsel and jurors who man them. Protecting the courts against misuse, abuse, or simple operational inefficiency has always been a hard and urgent problem.

It is an especially hard and urgent problem today, for in some respects American courts have not kept abreast of American social and economic changes. The Nation's court system was designed originally for small, rural communities. The basic unit of court organization in most States remains the county, and about two-thirds of the counties in this country still are predominantly rural in nature. But most Americans live in an urban environment, in large communities with highly mobile populations that are being subjected to particular stress. It is the urban courts that particularly need reform.

In a rural community the parties involved in a criminal case, the offender, the victim, the attorneys, the judge, and the jury, often know each other. What the trial does is to develop specific facts about the offense. In a city or large suburban community the parties in a case are likely to be strangers. One result is that prosecutors and judges seldom know anything at all about a defendant's background, character, or way of life either at first hand or by hearsay. Moreover, information of crucial importance to a magistrate when he fixes bail, to a prosecutor when he decides upon a charge, to a trial judge when he passes sentence is not always easy to obtain. Gathering such data requires trained personnel using time-consuming procedures. In city and suburban courts today these personnel and procedures are not adequate.

The problem of courts and prosecutors in densely populated cities goes further than the difficulty of obtaining information about an individual defendant. The populations of many cities are made up of groups that have little understanding of each other's ways. The law and court procedures are not understood by, and seem threatening to, many defendants, and many defendants are not understood by, and seem threatening to, the court and its officers. Even such simple matters as dress, speech, and manners can be misinterpreted. A prosecutor or judge with a middle-class background and attitude, confronted with a poor, uneducated defendant, may often have no way of judging how the defendant fits into his own society or culture. He can easily mistake a certain manner of dress or of speech, alien or repugnant to him, but ordinary enough in the defendant's world, as an index of moral worthlessness. He can mistake ignorance or fear of the law as indifference to it. He can mistake the defendant's resentment against the social evils he lives with as evidence of criminality. Or conversely, he can be led to believe by neat dress, a polite and cheerful mannner, and a show of humility that a dangerous criminal is merely an oppressed and misunderstood man.

There is a great need in the city courts for dedicated and sophisticated defense counsel who can contribute to the court's and the prosecution's understanding of the defendant and the defendant's understanding of the system. There is a great need for probation officers with thorough training and reasonable caseloads who can prepare searching presentence reports and effectively supervise those offenders who are sentenced to probation. And there is a great need for judges and prosecutors to become more knowledgeable about life in the communities from which many defendants come. These needs have not been adequately met in most city courts.

The final and most serious problem of urban and suburban courts is the enormous volume of the crime and delinquency cases that come before them. The traditional methods of court administration have not been equal to managing huge caseloads. Law enforcement effectiveness is lost as courts are unable to deal properly with the defendants brought into them. Sometimes cases are—and must be—heard and disposed of in a matter of minutes; in the common categories of drunkenness and vagrancy, they may be heard and disposed of in seconds. The reverse side of this situation is that defendants who demur and demand a more deliberate examination of their cases often have weeks to wait—in jail if they cannot post bail—before the court can find time for them.

Partly in order to deal with volume, many courts have routinely adopted informal, invisible, administrative procedures for handling offenders. Prosecutors and magistrates dismiss cases; as many as half of those who are arrested are dismissed early in the process. Prosecutors negotiate charges with defense counsel in order to secure guilty pleas and thus

avoid costly, time-consuming trials; in many courts 90 percent of all convictions result from the guilty pleas of defendants rather than from trial. Much negotiation occurs without
any judicial consideration of the facts concerning an offender
or his offense. These circumstances create important problems that the courts generally have not recognized or dealt
with effectively.

THE LOWER COURTS

In many big cities the congestion that produces both undue
delay and unseemly haste is vividly exemplified in the lower
courts—the courts that dispose of cases that are typically
called "misdemeanors" or "petty offenses," and that process
the first stages of felony cases. The importance of these courts
in the prevention or deterrence of crime is incalculably great,
for these are the courts that process the overwhelming majority of offenders. Although the offenses that are the business
of these lower courts may be "petty" in respect to the amount
of damage they do and the fear they inspire, their implication
can be great. Hardened habitual criminals do not suddenly
and unaccountably materialize. Most of them committed, and
were brought to book for, small offenses before they began to
commit big ones. This does not suggest, of course, that everyone who commits a small offense is likely to commit a big
one.

The criminal justice system has a heavy responsibility, particularly in cities where so many men are so nearly anonymous and where the density of population and the aggrava-
tion of social problems produce so much crime of all kinds,
to seek to distinguish between those offenders who are dangerous or potentially dangerous and those who are not. It has
an additional responsibility to prevent minor offenders from
developing into dangerous criminals. It is a responsibility that
the system is in some ways badly equipped to fulfill.

The Commission has been shocked by what it has seen in
some lower courts. It has seen cramped and noisy courtrooms, undignified and perfunctory procedures, and badly
trained personnel. It has seen dedicated people who are frustrated by huge caseloads, by the lack of opportunity to examine cases carefully, and by the impossibility of devising
constructive solutions to the problems of offenders. It has seen
assembly line justice.

A central problem of many lower courts is the gross disparity between the number of cases and the personnel and facilities available to deal with them. For example, until legisla-

tion last year increased the number of judges, the District of Columbia Court of General Sessions had four judges to process the preliminary stages of more than 1,500 felony cases, 7,500 serious misdemeanor cases, and 38,000 petty offenses and an equal number of traffic offenses per year. An inevitable consequence of volume that large is the almost total preoccupation in such a court with the movement of cases. The calendar is long, speed often is substituted for care, and casually arranged out-of-court compromise too often is substituted for adjudication. Inadequate attention tends to be given to the individual defendant, whether in protecting his rights, sifting the facts at trial, deciding the social risk he presents, or determining how to deal with him after conviction. The frequent result is futility and failure. As Dean Edward Barrett recently observed:

Wherever the visitor looks at the system, he finds great numbers of defendants being processed by harassed and overworked officials. Police have more cases than they can investigate. Prosecutors walk into courtrooms to try simple cases as they take their initial looks at the files. Defense lawyers appear having had no more than time for hasty conversations with their clients. Judges face long calendars with the certain knowledge that their calendars tomorrow and the next day will be, if anything, longer, and so there is no choice but to dispose of the cases.

Suddenly it becomes clear that for most defendants in the criminal process, there is scant regard for them as individuals. They are numbers on dockets, faceless ones to be processed and sent on their way. The gap between the theory and the reality is enormous.

Very little such observation of the administration of criminal justice in operation is required to reach the conclusion that it suffers from basic ills.

There are judges, prosecutors, defense attorneys, and other officers in the lower courts who are as capable in every respect as their counterparts in the more prestigious courts. The lower courts do not attract such persons with regularity, however. Judging in the lower courts is often an arduous, frustrating, and poorly paid job that wears down the judge. It is no wonder that in most localities judges in courts of general jurisdiction are more prominent members of the community and better qualified than their lower court counterparts.

In some cities lower court judges are not even required to be lawyers.

In a number of jurisdictions the State is represented in the lower court not by the district attorney but by a special prosecutor or by a police officer. Part-time attorneys are sometimes used as prosecutors to supplement police officers. In jurisdictions where assistant district attorneys work in the lower courts, they usually are younger and less experienced men than the staff of the felony court. The shift of a prosecutor from a lower court to a felony trial court is generally regarded as a promotion. Movement back to the lower courts by experienced men is rare. As a result there often is inadequate early screening of cases that are inappropriate for prosecution, lack of preparation for trials or negotiated pleas, and little prosecutor control over the proceedings. These inadequacies add to the judge's burdens and increase the likelihood of inadequate attention by the judge to the processes of adjudication and the goals of disposition.

In many lower courts defense counsel do not regularly appear, and counsel is either not provided to a defendant who has no funds; or, if counsel is appointed, he is not compensated. The Commission has seen, in the "bullpens" where lower court defendants often await trial, defense attorneys demanding from a potential client the loose change in his pockets or the watch on his wrist as a condition of representing him. Attorneys of this kind operate on a mass production basis, relying on pleas of guilty to dispose of their caseload. They tend to be unprepared and to make little effort to protect their clients' interests. For all these shortcomings, however, these attorneys do fill a need; defendants probably are better off with this counsel than they would be if they were wholly unrepresented.

In most jurisdictions there is no probation service in the lower courts. Presentence investigations are rare, although the lower courts can and do impose sentences as long as several years' imprisonment. While jail sentences of 1, 2, or 3 months are very common, probation appears to be used less frequently than it is for presumably more serious offenses in the same jurisdictions.

Every day in large cities hundreds of persons, arrested for being drunk or disorderly, for vagrancy or petty gambling, for minor assaults or prostitution, are brought before the petty offense part of lower courts. In some cities these defendants are stood in single file and paraded before the judge. In others, 40 or 50 or more people are brought before the bench as a group. Almost all plead guilty and sentence is

320

imposed in such terms as "30 days or $30." A large part of the jail population in many cities is made up of persons jailed in default of the payment of a fine. The offender subjected to this process emerges from it punished but unchanged. He returns to the streets, and it is likely that soon the cycle will be repeated in all its futility.

Those few cases in which the defendant demands a trial may be inordinately delayed by the unavailability of judges to try cases. One result of this can be that witnesses, who are grossly undercompensated at rates as low as 75 cents a day, become weary and disappear. The courthouse in which the lower court sits is likely to be old, dirty, and extremely overcrowded. Witnesses, policemen, lawyers, and defendants mill around halls and courtrooms. Office facilities for clerks and prosecutors are commonly inadequate.

Study commissions have pointed out the scandal of the lower criminal courts for over a century. More than 30 years ago the Wickersham Commission concluded that the best solution to the problem would be the abolition of these courts. The Commission agrees. While the grading of offenses as felonies, misdemeanors, and petty offenses is an appropriate way of setting punishments, is dictated by history and constitutional provisions, and is necessary for such procedural purposes as grand jury indictment and jury trial, the Commission doubts that separate judicial systems are needed to maintain these distinctions. A system that treats defendants who are charged with minor offenses with less dignity and consideration than it treats those who are charged with serious crimes is hard to justify. The unification of these courts and services may provide a sound way to bring about long overdue improvement in the standards of the lower courts. Existing differences in punishment, right to grand jury indictment and jury trial, and the like should be retained unchanged, but all criminal cases should be tried by judges of equal status under generally comparable procedures.

The Commission recommends:

Felony and misdemeanor courts and their ancillary agencies —prosecutors, defenders, and probation services—should be unified.

As an immediate step to meet the needs of the lower courts, the judicial manpower of these courts should be increased and their physical facilities should be improved so

that these courts will be able to cope with the volume of cases coming before them in a dignified and deliberate way.

Prosecutors, probation officers, and defense counsel should be provided in courts where these officers are not found, or their numbers are insufficient.

The rural counterpart of the lower criminal court is the justice of the peace, who continues to exercise at least some criminal jurisdiction in 35 States. In a majority of these States his compensation is fixed by a fee assessed against the parties. In at least three States justices of the peace receive a fee only if they convict a defendant and collect from him, a practice held unconstitutional 40 years ago by the Supreme Court. The dangers of the fee system are illustrated by reports that police receive kickbacks from justices of the peace for bringing cases to them. A justice who regularly rules for the defendant is likely to find that he does not receive cases or fees. In more than 30 States justices of the peace are not required to be lawyers, and the incompetence with which many perform their judicial functions has long been reported.

In recent years a number of States have moved to reform the justices' courts. Illinois has abolished some 4,000 fee-system courts and replaced them with circuit courts aided by 207 salaried magistrates. In 1961 Connecticut and Maine replaced justices with professional judges. Delaware, Florida, and North Carolina have taken steps against the fee system. New York, Mississippi, and Iowa have sought to attack the problem by requiring justices to take training courses.

Careful consideration should be given to total abolition of these offices and the transfer of their functions to district or circuit judges who have full-time professional standing. In States where it is decided to retain the office, all justices of the peace should be placed under central State administration and supervision; they should be made accountable to a State judicial officer and be required to maintain records of their activities. Justices should be salaried and all fines and fees should go to the State treasury. The fee system should be replaced and local government foreclosed from considering criminal justice a prime source of revenue. All justices should be required to be fully trained in the law and in their duties, and their level of competence should be maintained by continuing training.

The large number of justices in many States impedes reform. In many places positions are unfilled or the incumbent is inactive and performs little judicial business. Where they are retained, States should substantially reduce the number of justices.

The U.S. Senate Judiciary Committee is considering legislation to reform the office of U.S. commissioner, a position comparable to the justices of the peace in the State court systems. Commissioners possess authority to issue arrest and search warrants, arraign defendants on complaints, fix bail, hold preliminary hearings in felony cases, and in certain Federal reservations to try petty offenses. There are approximately 700 commissioners throughout the country, barely 1 percent of whom could be considered full-time officers. About one-third are not attorneys, yet there is no existing training program. With the exception of a few commissioners who serve in national parks, commissioners are compensated on a fee basis. As in the case of State justices of the peace the choice appears to be either to abolish the office and transfer its functions to professional full-time judges, as has been done in a U.S. District Court in Michigan, or to improve the quality and increase the responsibilities of these officers, placing them on a salary basis and training them for the job.

The Commission recommends:

The States and Federal Government should enact legislation to abolish or overhaul the justice of the peace and U.S. commissioner systems.

THE INITIAL STAGES OF A CRIMINAL CASE

The criminal process disposes of most of its cases without trial. Chapter 4 discusses the frequent use by policemen of their discretion not to arrest certain offenders. Prosecutors exercise discretion in a similar fashion. They do not charge all arrested suspects, they frequently have wide choices of what offense they will charge, and they often move to dismiss charges they have already made. Beyond this the overwhelming majority of cases are disposed of by pleas of guilty. Often those pleas are the result of negotiations between prosecutors and defendants or their attorneys. Guilty pleas may be obtained in exchange for a reduction of charges or for agreed-upon sentencing recommendations. In many instances it is the prosecutor who, in effect, determines or heavily influences the sentence a defendant receives.

Much of the criminal process is administrative rather than judicial. There are good reasons for this. The most readily apparent is the enormous number of cases that come into the process, especially in the Nation's metropolitan areas. If a substantial percentage of them were not dropped or carried to negotiated conclusions administratively, justice would be not merely slowed down; it would be stopped. A second reason is that the facts in most cases are not in dispute. The suspect either clearly did or clearly did not do what he is accused of having done. In these cases a trial, which is a careful and expensive procedure for determining disputed facts, should not be needed.

Finally, subjecting all offenders to the full criminal process is inappropriate. It is inappropriate because, as already noted, the substantive criminal law is in many respects inappropriate. In defining crimes there is no way to avoid including some acts that fall near the line between legal and illegal conduct, thus including some offenders who violate the law under circumstances that do not seem to call for the invocation of criminal sanctions. It is inappropriate because placing a criminal stigma on an offender may in many instances make him more, rather than less likely to commit future crimes. It is inappropriate because effective correctional methods for reintegrating certain types of offenders into their communities often are either not available or are unknown. As Judge Charles Breitel has written—

If every policeman, every prosecutor, every court, and every post-sentence agency performed his or its responsibility in strict accordance with rules of law, precisely and narrowly laid down, the criminal law would be ordered but intolerable.

Because many important decisions are, and must be, made in that part of the criminal process that is essentially administrative—outside the formal court procedures—it is essential that administrative procedures be visible and structured. Today many administrative decisions are made hastily and haphazardly. Most of them are made on the basis of insufficient information about the offense, the offender, his needs, or the community and correctional treatment programs that are available to him. They often are made visibly, unguided by explicit statutes, judicial rules, or administrative policies, and are not subjected to public, or in most cases judicial, scrutiny.

When such decisions are made before the charge, defense counsel are seldom involved. When guilty pleas are negotiated, there is often a pretense in court that they have not been. There is no way of knowing how many decisions have been made accurately and how many inaccurately, how many dangerous offenders have been treated with excessive leniency, how many marginal ones with excessive harshness. Since these decisions are rarely arrived at on the basis of carefully worked out policies or by the use of systematic procedures and are rarely reviewed more than perfunctorily after they have been made, it is surely safe to assume that many mistakes are made.

This section discusses ways in which the wholly desirable objectives of early diversion of some cases from the criminal process, and disposition of many cases through a broader range of alternatives in the criminal process, can be reached fairly, efficiently and openly in the pretrial stage. Three particularly important events take place during the pretrial stage: the conditions under which a defendant may be released pending trial are set by a magistrate; a specific charge against the defendant is made, usually by a prosecutor; and a plea of guilty or not guilty is entered by the defendant.

PRETRIAL RELEASE

One-half or more of the defendants who are brought into a police or magistrate's court are released or convicted and sentenced within 24 hours of their arrest. The cases of the remainder, including all those against whom the accusation of a serious crime can be maintained, await final disposition for days or weeks or sometimes months, depending on the prosecutor's caseload, the gravity and complexity of the case, and the condition of the calendar in the court that will hear it.

The magistrate is empowered to decide whether or not such defendants will be released pending trial. The importance of this decision to any defendant is obvious. A released defendant is one who can live with and support his family, maintain his ties to his community, and busy himself with his own defense by searching for witnesses and evidence and by keeping in close touch with his lawyer. An imprisoned defendant is subjected to the squalor, idleness, and possibly criminalizing effects of jail. He may be confined for something he did not do; some jailed defendants are ultimately acquitted. He may be confined while presumed innocent only to be freed when found guilty; many jailed defendants, after they have been convicted, are placed on probation rather than imprisoned. The community also relies on the magistrate for protection when he makes his decision about releasing a defendant. If a released defendant fails to appear for trial, the law is flouted. If a released defendant commits crimes, the community is endangered.

The device that is used in most magistrates' courts to resolve these complicated issues is money bail in an amount fixed by the magistrate; a defendant without access to that amount of money is remanded to jail. The ordinary method defendants use to furnish bail is to pay a fee, commonly from 5 to 10 percent of the full amount of the bail, to a bail bondsman, who posts a bond for the full amount with the court. By and large, money bail is an unfair and ineffective device. Its glaring weakness is that it discriminates against poor defendants, thus running directly counter to the law's avowed purpose of treating all defendants equally. A study in New York, where the bondsman's fee is 5 percent, showed that 25 percent of arrested persons were unable to furnish bail of $500—i.e., raise $25; 45 percent failed at $1,500; 63 percent failed at $2,500. A massive side effect of money bail is that it costs taxpayers millions of dollars a year. A community spends from $3 to $9 a day to house, feed, and guard a jailed defendant.

Beyond this, evaluating a defendant's reliability in terms of dollars is so difficult that, perhaps inevitably, most jurisdictions have come to use what might be called a standard crime-pricing system. On the theory that the likelihood of a defendant's appearance depends on the size of the penalty he faces and therefore on the seriousness of a charge against him, bail rates are often preordained by stationhouse or judicial schedules: so and so many dollars for such and such a crime. The effect of standard rates and their disparity from place to place is to leave out of consideration not only the important question of a defendant's financial means but also the equally important one of his background, character, and ties to the community.

Although bail is recognized in the law solely as a method of insuring the defendant's appearance at trial, judges often use it as a way of keeping in jail persons they fear will commit crimes if released before trial. In addition to its being of dubious legality, this procedure is ineffective in many instances. Professional criminals or members of organized criminal syndicates have little difficulty in posting bail, although, since crime is their way of life, they are clearly dangerous.

If a satisfactory solution could be found to the problem of the relatively small percentage of defendants who present a significant risk of flight or criminal conduct before trial, the Commission would be prepared to recommend that money bail be totally discarded. Finding that solution is not easy. Empowering magistrates to jail defendants they believe to be dangerous might well create more of a problem than the imposition of money bail, in the light of the difficulty of predicting dangerousness. Such a system also might raise issues under State and Federal constitutional grants of a right to bail, issues that have not been determined by the Supreme Court.

A partial solution for the problem would be to provide an accelerated trial process for presumably high-risk defendants. In Philadelphia, for example, a special calendar for defendants charged with crimes of violence has recently been set up; such defendants are to come to trial no more than 30 days after indictment. It is still too early to know whether and how much this lessens the likelihood that released defendants will commit dangerous acts, but other studies have shown that the risks are closely related to the length of time that elapses before trial. The use of conditions and restrictions short of detention to control potentially dangerous persons may provide an adequate and more clearly permissible approach and should be tried.

In any case, money bail should be imposed only when reasonable alternatives are not available. This presupposes an information-gathering technique that can promptly provide a magistrate with an array of facts about a defendant's history, circumstances, problems, and way of life. The Vera Institute of Justice in New York has been a pioneer in devising such a technique. The Institute prepared a short standard form on which pertinent facts about a defendant were entered. Employees of the criminal court's probation department now question defendants as they await their appearance before the judge, and fill out the form. Often they check by telephone the facts they are given with the defendant's family or neighbors or employer. The entire procedure can take as little as 20 minutes, and by the time the defendant makes his court appearance, the judge knows enough about him to make an informed decision about whether bail is appropriate or whether the defendant can be released on his own recognizance, that of a member of his family, or his lawyer's. Since the Vera Institute established this approach, more than a hundred other jurisdictions have adopted the same or similar techniques.

The Commission recommends:

Bail projects should be undertaken at the State, county, and local levels to furnish judicial officers with sufficient information to permit the pretrial release without financial condition of all but that small portion of defendants who present a high risk of flight or dangerous acts prior to trial.

327

The Federal Bail Reform Act of 1966 may serve as a helpful guide for States considering comprehensive legislation. The act states a presumption in favor of the release of defendants upon their promise to return, or on an unsecured bond. Judges are authorized to place nonmonetary conditions upon release, such as assigning the defendant to the custody of a person or organization to supervise him, restricting his travel, association or place of abode, or placing him in partial custody so that he may work during the day and be confined at night.

The act contemplates the gathering and consideration by the judge of information concerning the bail risk presented and provides rational standards against which the facts may be measured. Procedures are established for the speedy review and appeal of bail decisions. Special provisions for capital cases and bail for convicted persons pending appeal permit the judge to consider explicitly the dangerousness of the person in deciding whether to release the offender. The criminal penalties for a defendant's failure to appear also are strengthened by the act.

The Commission recommends:

Each State should enact comprehensive bail reform legislation after the pattern set by the Federal Bail Reform Act of 1966.

A number of recent projects have sought to gain the speedy release of arrested persons and, in limited classes of cases, to dispense with the arrest altogether by use of a summons or citation. Early release and summons projects reduce the time between arrest and release, avoiding the situation in some cities where several days may pass after arrest before a defendant gets before a judge who sets bail. Since 1964 the New York Police Department with the assistance of the Vera Institute of Justice has operated a stationhouse summons project for relatively minor criminal cases (simple assault, petty larceny, malicious mischief) which is to be expanded to major misdemeanors and some felonies.

This project, which has been followed in other cities, does not eliminate arrest. Rather, the arrested person is brought to the precinct station where, after identification, booking, search, questioning, and fingerprinting, his community ties are investigated, much as they might be for purposes of bail. If the defendant is found to be a good risk, the precinct officer is authorized to release him with a citation or summons directing him to appear in court at a later date. In addition to the advantages of bail reform, this procedure saves substantial police time and has shown economies in the operation of lockup and detention facilities.

Beyond stationhouse release there has been an effort to displace arrest in appropriate cases by greater use of summons or citations by police in the street. This procedure, now frequently used for traffic or administrative violations, has been expanded to certain minor offenses that do not call for booking and in-custody investigation. An experimental project in Contra Costa County, Calif., suggests the potential of this procedure. Using a computer-based police identification network, an officer can find out in a minute or less whether the defendant is wanted for another crime, and he can decide on that basis whether to use summons rather than arrest for minor offenses. This procedure has permitted the broader use of the summons in cases of petty theft, breach of the peace, minor assault, and other offenses, when the defendant can properly identify himself.

The Commission recommends:

Each community should establish procedures to enable and encourage police departments to release, in appropriate classes of cases, as many arrested persons as possible promptly after arrest upon issuance of a citation or summons requiring subsequent appearance.

THE DIVERSION OF CASES BEFORE CHARGE

The limited statistics available indicate that approximately one-half of those arrested are dismissed by the police, a prosecutor, or a magistrate at an early stage of the case. Some of these persons are released because they did not commit the acts they were originally suspected of having committed, or cannot be proved to have committed them, or committed them on legally defensible grounds. The police can arrest on "probable cause," while conviction requires proof "beyond a reasonable doubt." Therefore, some justified arrests cannot lead to prosecution and conviction.

However, others who are released probably did commit the offenses for which they were arrested. In some instances offenders who could and should be convicted are released simply because of an overload of work, or inadequate investigation in the prosecutor's office. In other cases the police, or more often prosecutors, have exercised the discretion that is traditionally theirs to decline to prosecute offenders whose conduct appears to deviate from patterns of law-abiding conduct, or who present clear medical, mental, or social problems that can be better dealt with outside the criminal process than within it. First offenders are often dealt with in this way. So are persons whose offenses arise from drinking or mental problems, if the offenses are minor. So are many cases of assault or theft within families or among friends, of passing checks with insufficient funds, of shoplifting when restitution is made, of statutory rape when both boy and girl are young, of automobile theft by teenagers for the purpose of joyriding.

The Commission regards the exercise of discretion by prosecutor as necessary and desirable. However, it has found that more often than not prosecutors exercise their discretion under circumstances and in ways that make unwise decisions all too likely. The haste and tumult of the lower courts in large cities have been described. In addition to having generally unfavorable working conditions, prosecutors suffer from several other handicaps.

One is the lack of sufficient information on which to base their decisions. A prosecutor who bases his estimate of the provability of a case on a one-page police report can easily dismiss strong cases and press cases that ultimately prove to have little foundation. A prosecutor with no background information about an offender can easily mistake a dangerous person with a plausible manner or story for a marginal offender. Or, in the absence of background information, he can operate on rule-of-thumb policies—for example, all family assault cases should be dismissed, or all automobile theft cases should be prosecuted. A prosecutor with little knowledge of the treatment programs and facilities in the community can either dismiss or prosecute a case that might better be referred to another agency.

Another want, particularly felt by young, inexperienced assistants in large offices, is the lack of clearly stated standards to guide them in making decisions. Standards should pertain to such matters as the circumstances that properly can be considered mitigating or aggravating, or the kinds of offenses that should be most vigorously prosecuted in view of the community's law enforcement needs. In large offices where no such standards are devised and communicated, it is unlikely that assistants will charge or dismiss in the same manner.

A third deterrent to the systematic making of charge decisions is the lack of established procedures for arriving at them. Procedures, in this sense, does not mean an elaborate and cumbersome apparatus for transacting business that should be done with a considerable amount of speed and informality. It means setting forth the separate steps that a prosecutor should take before making a charge decision, and indicating when he should take them. Clearly, before a prosecutor decides whether to charge or dismiss in any case that is not elementary, he should review the case file and discover whether there is sufficient evidence to justify a charge and whether more evidence and witnesses than the police have uncovered are available. He should confer with defense counsel in doubtful cases. Prosecutors often fail to do such things not so much because they lack time as because no one requires them to. Greater involvement of court probation departments and the availability of probation officers for consultation with the prosecutor and defense counsel at this stage of the proceedings could provide this link. When discretion not to charge is exercised in felony cases, the prosecutor's disposition of the case and the underlying reasons should be reduced to writing and filed with the court.

Prosecutors deal with many offenders who clearly need some kind of treatment or supervision, but for whom the full force of criminal sanctions is excessive; yet they usually lack alternatives other than charging or dismissing. In most localities programs and agencies that can provide such treatment and supervision are scarce or altogether lacking, and in many places where they exist, there are no regular procedures for the court, prosecutors, and defense counsel to take advantage of them.

Procedures are needed to identify and divert from the criminal process mentally disordered or deficient persons. Not all members of this group are legally insane or incompetent to stand trial under traditional legal definitions. The question of how to treat such offenders cannot be satisfactorily resolved by recourse to the definitions of forensic psychiatry. While recognizing the importance of the long-standing controversies over the definitions of criminal responsibility, insanity, and competence to stand trial, the Commission does not believe it has a substantial contribution to make to their resolution. It is more fruitful to discuss, not who can be tried and convicted as a matter of law, but how the officers of the administration of criminal justice should deal with people who present special needs and problems. In common prosecutorial practice this question is, and the Commission believes should be, decided on the basis of the kind of correctional program that appears to be most appropriate for a particular

331

offender. The Commission believes that, if an individual is to be given special therapeutic treatment, he should be diverted as soon as possible from the criminal process. It believes further that screening procedures capable of identifying mentally disordered or deficient offenders as early in the process as possible can be improved by training law enforcement and court officers to be more sensitive to signs of mental abnormality and by making specialized diagnostic referral services more readily available to the police and the courts.

The Commission recommends:

Prosecutors should endeavor to make discriminating charge decisions, assuring that offenders who merit criminal sanctions are not released and that other offenders are either released or diverted to noncriminal methods of treatment and control by:

> **Establishment of explicit policies for the dismissal or informal disposition of the cases of certain marginal offenders.**

> **Early identification and diversion to other community resources of those offenders in need of treatment, for whom full criminal disposition does not appear required.**

In some communities a beginning has been made in providing alternatives other than charge or outright dismissal. In several cities the police or prosecutors conduct hearings at which the attempt is made to settle disputes, to arrange restitution or damages, to calm family quarrels, and to obtain promises to keep the peace in the future. In some places the judge participates in this process, and there are procedures to place defendants under informal probation supervision without conviction. The laws of at least five States and the provisions of the Model Sentencing Act specifically provide for such dispositions, and they appear to be used in other places without specific statutory authority.

Alternative ways of disposing of criminal cases that involve close supervision or institutional commitment without conviction, call for protections from their abuse, protections that should be roughly comparable to those of the criminal law. Experience with civil procedures for the commitment of the mentally ill, for so-called sexual psychopaths, and for similar groups demonstrates that there are dangers of such programs developing in ways potentially more oppressive than those foreclosed by the careful traditional protections of the criminal law. When the alternative noncriminal disposition involves institutionalization or prolonged or intrusive supervision of the offender in the community, the disposition should be reviewed by the court.

The effect of these recommendations might well be to alter the responsibilities of the prosecutor and defense counsel and require more effort on their part early in the case. But these procedures also would result in the early elimination of many cases from the process and thus relieve the system from some of its caseload burden without sacrificing the proper administration of justice. The additional investment of manpower and talent would not appear as great as that required to make existing practice work with equal effectiveness.

Of course, implementation of this recommendation is heavily dependent on the availability to the prosecutor, defense counsel, and the courts of adequate factual information on offenders and of appropriate facilities and programs in the community for the diagnosis and management of offenders who are diverted. Community programs are discussed in chapters 3 and 6 of this report.

THE NEGOTIATED PLEA OF GUILTY

Most defendants who are convicted—as many as 90 percent in some jurisdictions—are not tried. They plead guilty, often as the result of negotiations about the charge or the sentence. It is almost impossible to generalize about the extent to which pleas are negotiated or about the ways in which they are negotiated, so much does practice vary from jurisdiction to jurisdiction. A plea negotiation can be, and often is in a minor case, a hurried conversation in a courthouse hallway. In grave cases it can be a series of elaborate conferences over the course of weeks in which facts are thoroughly discussed and alternatives carefully explored. Most often the negotiations are between a prosecutor and defense counsel, but sometimes a magistrate or a police officer or the defendant himself is involved. In some courts there are no plea negotiations at all. There almost never are negotiations in the cases of petty offenders. And, of course, many guilty pleas are not the result of negotiations. The two generalizations that can be made are that when plea negotiations are conducted, they usually are conducted informally and out of sight, and that the issue in a plea negotiation always is how much leniency an offender will be given in return for a plea of guilty.

Through his power over the charge the prosecutor has

great influence on the sentence. Usually a prosecutor has considerable latitude as to what to charge. Some sets of facts can be characterized as either felonies or misdemeanors, or as crimes in the first, second, or third degree. Some defendants can with equal appropriateness be charged with one crime or with several related crimes. The forgery of the endorsement and the negotiation of a check may be charged as one offense; or the forging, uttering, and possession of the check may be charged as three distinct crimes. Misdemeanors typically carry lighter penalties than felonies, and misdemeanants are typically sentenced by different judges than felons. The degree of a crime determines the maximum and sometimes the minimum penalty that can be imposed, and occasionally whether an offender may be granted probation or parole. If a defendant is convicted on more than one count, a judge can decide to have the sentences run concurrently or consecutively.

A distorting aspect of charge decisions is that the prosecutor, because of lack of information and contact with defense counsel before charge, may be under pressure to make the most serious possible charge. This leaves him freedom to reduce the charge later, if the facts are not as damning as they might be, and places him in an advantageous position for negotiating with defense counsel on a plea of guilty.

Beyond the prosecutor's influence on the sentence by his power over the charge, he is, in many courts, empowered or even required to make sentencing recommendations. Much more often than not such recommendations are given great weight by judges. Sometimes prosecutors are able to see to it that specific cases come before specific judges. Since some judges habitually sentence more leniently than others, this consideration can be an important factor in plea negotiations. In some cases there is a tacit or explicit agreement by the judge to the bargain, and in extreme cases the judge may participate in its negotiation.

The negotiated guilty plea serves important functions. As a practical matter, many courts could not sustain the burden of having to try all cases coming before them. The quality of justice in all cases would suffer if overloaded courts were faced with a great increase in the number of trials. Tremendous investments of time, talent, and money, all of which are in short supply and can be better used elsewhere, would be necessary if all cases were tried. It would be a serious mistake, however, to assume that the guilty plea is no more than a means of disposing of criminal cases at minimal cost. It relieves both the defendant and the prosecution of the inevitable risks and uncertainties of trial. It imports a degree of certainty and flexibility into a rigid, yet frequently erratic system. The guilty plea is used to mitigate the harshness of mandatory sentencing provisions and to fix a punishment that more accurately reflects the specific circumstances of the case than otherwise would be possible under inadequate penal codes. It is frequently called upon to serve important law enforcement needs by agreements through which leniency is exchanged for information, assistance, and testimony about other serious offenders.

At the same time the negotiated plea of guilty can be subject to serious abuses. In hard-pressed courts, where judges and prosecutors are unable to deal effectively with all cases presented to them, dangerous offenders may be able to manipulate the system to obtain unjustifiably lenient treatment. There are also real dangers that excessive rewards will be offered to induce pleas or that prosecutors will threaten to seek a harsh sentence if the defendant does not plead guilty. Such practices place unacceptable burdens on the defendant who legitimately insists upon his right to trial. They present the greatest potential abuse when the sentencing judge becomes involved in the process as a party to the negotiations, as in some places he does.

Plea negotiations can be conducted fairly and openly, can be consistent with sound law enforcement policy, and can bring a worthwhile flexibility to the disposition of offenders. But some courts are able to deal with their caseloads without reliance on guilty pleas, and in other courts, particularly single judge courts, it may not be feasible to introduce the safeguards that are necessary for the negotiated plea system to operate fairly and effectively. The Commission's recommendations are directed primarily, therefore, to those jurisdictions where plea negotiations are ordinary occurrences. In many of those jurisdictions it is desirable for judges and prosecutors to reexamine existing practices.

Negotiations should be more careful and thorough, broader, and preferably held early in the proceedings. It does not contribute to the soundness of the practice when negotiations are held on the eve of trial or in the public atmosphere of the courtroom hallway.

Prosecutors should be available to defense counsel from the beginning of the case for the purpose of discussing the possibility of a disposition by plea of guilty. Except in the most petty cases, such discussion should be had with counsel rather than directly with the defendant. These discussions should thoroughly assess the facts underlying the prosecution's case, consider information on the offender's background and correctional needs, and explore all available correctional alternatives as well as review the charge to which the plea will be entered. To a much greater extent than at present the facilities of the probation department and other referral and diagnostic services should be available to the parties. In some instances it may be desirable to have a full presentence report prepared so the negotiating parties as well as the reviewing judge can assess the agreed disposition, although in many cases less elaborate methods of factfinding should suffice. While the emphasis should be on correctional and law enforcement considerations, the prosecutor properly may take account of the defendant's cooperation, testimony against other criminals, and similar factors.

The defendant should be able to include in the discussions, and cover within the disposition, all specific crimes, charged or not, that could be charged within the jurisdiction of the court. This discussion should involve the full and frank exchange of information, and appropriate provision should be made to insure that a defendant's statements and information disclosed are not used against him in the event of a trial. Defense counsel should painstakingly explain to the defendant the terms of the agreement and the alternatives open to him.

An obvious problem is insuring that the defendant receives from the judge the sentence he has bargained for with the prosecutor. Under existing practice the fact that negotiations have occurred is commonly denied on the record, and so is the explicit or tacit expectation that the judge will impose the agreed punishment. The Commission believes that this is undesirable and that the agreed disposition should be openly acknowledged and fully presented to the judge for review before the plea is entered. A desirable change might be that before the plea is finally entered, the judge would indicate whether the disposition is acceptable to him and will be followed. Should the judge feel the need for more information or study, the plea may be entered conditionally, and if a more severe sentence is to be imposed, the defendant should have an opportunity to withdraw his plea.

Inevitably the judge plays a part in the negotiated guilty plea. His role is a delicate one, for it is important that he carefully examine the agreed disposition, and it is equally important that he not undermine his judicial role by becoming excessively involved in the negotiations themselves. The judge's function is to insure the appropriateness of the correctional disposition reached by the parties and to guard against any tendency of the prosecutor to overcharge or to be excessively lenient.

The judge should satisfy himself and insure that the record indicates that there is a factual basis for the plea, that the defendant understands the charge and the consequences of his plea, and where there has been an agreement on sentence that the agreed disposition appears within the reasonable range of sentencing appropriateness. In cases involving dangerous offenders or career criminals, the judge should be satisfied that the agreement adequately protects the public interest.

The judge should weigh the agreed disposition against standards similar to those that would be applied on imposition of sentence after a trial: The defendant's need for correctional treatment; the circumstances of the case; the defendant's cooperation; and the requirements of law enforcement. The court should be apprised of all information concerning the offense, including appropriate investigative reports, grand jury minutes, and all information and diagnostic reports concerning the offender. If the agreed sentence appears within the reasonable range of what would be an appropriate sentence after trial, it should satisfy the need to deal effectively with the serious offender, and at the same time not be an improper inducement to the defendant to surrender his right to a trial. The judge's role is not that of one of the parties to the negotiation, but that of an independent examiner to verify that the defendant's plea is the result of an intelligent and knowing choice and not based on misapprehension or the product of coercion.

Since this approach contemplates that the judge will assess and indicate acceptance of the agreement before the plea is entered, provision must be made for those cases in which he finds the agreement unacceptable and in which the case, therefore, is set for trial. In such instances the judge's participation as arbiter at the trial would be complicated by his participation during the plea proceedings and the knowledge he obtained then. Provision should be made that when a judge rejects an agreement, trial and all further proceedings in the case are referred, if possible, to another judge. The return of the parties to the same judge with a renegotiated plea would tend to increase the likelihood of his becoming, in practical effect, a party to the negotiations.

The Commission recommends:

If a negotiated agreement to plead guilty is reached, care should be taken by prosecutor and defense counsel to state explicitly all its terms.

Upon the plea of guilty in open court the terms of the agree-

337

ment should be fully stated on the record and, in serious or complicated cases, reduced to writing.

A plea negotiation is fundamentally a negotiation about the correctional disposition of a case and is, therefore, a matter of moment to the community as well as to the defendant. If the offense is a serious one, a plea bargain should be founded on the kind of information, fully shared between the parties, that probation departments develop for presentence reports. In the District of Columbia the defender's office has an experimental project, in many respects resembling a probation service, for evaluating defendants and developing correctional plans for them. Such a service might well be one means of securing the full information that is needed in order to dispose of serious offenders effectively, as well as a means for developing the less complete information that would be adequate for arriving at dispositional decisions about minor offenders.

At the same time subtle and difficult questions are presented in some cases by an approach calling for full sharing of information. Defense counsel may well possess information adverse to his client, and the prosecutor may have erroneous information which defense counsel knows paints an unjustifiably favorable picture of his client. For example, an apparent conflict exists between the need for a frank exchange of information with the prosecutor and counsel's obligation to act only in ways favorable to his client. Obviously all exchanges of information must be explicitly authorized by the defendant and if conflicts are likely, the problem is one to be considered by defendant and counsel before consent is given. While the consent of the client simplifies some aspects of this problem, it is clear that the expansion of discovery and the sharing of information early in the case will create new professional responsibilities for both prosecutors and defense counsel. Experience may provide guides for some of the problems presented, other norms may be provided by such efforts as those of the American Bar Association redefinition of the canons of professional ethics or the consideration of the role of counsel by the ABA Special Project on Minimum Standards for the Administration of Criminal Justice.

The Commission recommends:

Prosecutors and defense counsel should in appropriate cases share information they secure independently at all points in the process when such sharing appears likely to lead to early disposition. Defender agencies should adopt programs through which background data, diagnostic information, and correctional planning for offenders can be developed early in the process.

COURT PROCEEDINGS

This chapter's emphasis on the pretrial administrative aspects of the court process does not imply that the trial is unimportant. The cases decided at trial are only a small fraction of the total of cases, but they are most important to the process because they set standards for the conduct of all cases. The trial decides the hard legal issues, and reviews and rules on claims of official abuse. Trial procedures have evolved over centuries and in general have proven that they can resolve disputed cases effectively.

Unlike the administrative proceedings in the pretrial stage, court proceedings are continually being studied by lawyers and are now receiving intensive scrutiny from other groups. The Judicial Conference of the United States sponsors continuing studies of the Federal Rules of Criminal Procedure, proposed rules of evidence in criminal cases in the Federal courts, and the habeas corpus jurisdiction of those courts. The American Bar Association, through its sections on criminal law and judicial administration and its Special Project on Minimum Standards for the Administration of Criminal Justice, is conducting broadly based studies that relate to many major areas of interest in the criminal law and court administration. The American Law Institute has sponsored intensive studies that have produced the Model Penal Code and a draft of a Model Code of Pre-Arraignment Procedure. The National Conference of Commissioners on Uniform State Laws has drafted several model State statutes dealing with problems of criminal administration.

The Commission has tried to avoid duplicating the exhaustive work of these responsible professional organizations. Later this chapter will treat some aspects of court proceedings under the headings of jurors and witnesses and court scheduling, management and organization. The discussion here will be limited to a few points of particular public concern.

THE NEWS MEDIA AND THE ADMINISTRATION OF JUSTICE

Newspaper, television, and radio reporting are essential to the administration of justice. Reporting maintains the public knowledge, review, and support so necessary for the proper functioning of the courts. Critical inquiry and reports by the media on the operation of the courts can prevent abuses and promote improvements in the administration of justice. On the other hand, a fair jury trial can be held only if the evidence is presented in the courtroom, not in the press, and jurors do not come to their task prejudiced by publicity.

Two recent cases decided by the Supreme Court have dramatized how prejudicial publicity can endanger a fair trial. In the *Sheppard* case a murder trial was turned into what one court described as a "Roman circus" by an overzealous press and an overtolerant judge. In the *Estes* case the Court found that the presence of television and still cameras in the courtroom during trial destroyed the "judicial serenity and calm" necessary for a fair trial.

While unrestrained newsgathering in the courtroom can prejudice the actual conduct of a trial, a more serious threat to fairness is release to the press by police, prosecutors, or defense counsel of inaccurate or legally inadmissible information. Increasing attention has been given to regulation by law enforcement agencies and the courts of such statements. The Department of Justice and the New York City Police Department, among others, have issued regulations and standards identifying types of information that should not be disclosed to the press in pretrial statements by law enforcement officers. Thoughtful and constructive studies by a committee of the American Bar Association Project on Minimum Standards for Criminal Justice and by the American Newspaper Publishers Association have identified the issues that must be faced in placing limitations on statements to the press.

The Commission recognizes that the guarantees of both free press and fair trial must be scrupulously preserved and that indeed each sustains the other in a most fundamental sense. To avoid abuses which might affect fair trial adversely, reasonable regulations with respect to release of information should be adopted and enforced by administrative discipline within police departments, by professional discipline with respect to prosecutors and defense counsel, and in limited instances by the courts. In addition, courts should firmly control or prohibit those newsgathering activities in the courthouse that detract from the dignity of a judicial proceeding or threaten to prejudice the fairness of a trial, while permitting legitimate, nondisruptive newsgathering.

The Commission recommends:

Police, prosecutors, bar associations, and courts should issue

340

regulations and standards as to the kinds of information that properly may be released to the news media about pending criminal cases by police officers, prosecutors, and defense counsel. These regulations and standards should be designed to minimize prejudicial statements by the media before or during trial, while safeguarding legitimate reporting on matters of public interest.

JUDICIALLY SUPERVISED DISCOVERY

The relatively informal exchanges of information between the prosecution and the defense proposed earlier in this chapter are intended primarily for the case that will be disposed of before trial, although their usefulness for the fully litigated case is apparent. In addition to such procedures, there has been, in recent years, increasing interest in and expansion of the procedures for formal discovery of evidence before trial. Over the past generation broad discovery, by examination of witnesses and evidence, has become commonplace in civil cases, but its utilization in criminal cases has been slowed by fears that pretrial disclosure of the Government's case would lead to perjury and threats to witnesses, and that undue disclosure of confidential criminal files would impede ongoing investigations. The defendant's privilege against testifying forecloses the full mutuality of discovery by both sides that exists in civil cases and could place an unfair additional burden on the prosecution.

Several States, particularly California and Minnesota, have been experimenting with expanded discovery in criminal cases. Within the year the Federal courts have adopted new rules providing freer disclosure to a defendant of his own statements; his testimony before a grand jury; medical, scientific, and expert witness reports; and tangible evidence in the possession of the Government. In California the defendant also may obtain the names and statements of witnesses upon application. In many jurisdictions, however, the right of discovery in criminal cases is extremely restricted or nonexistent.

There also has been expansion within constitutional limits of the prosecution's right to discovery of the defendant's evidence. In a number of States the defendant, by statute or rule, must disclose in advance whether he will assert particular defenses, such as insanity or an alibi, what witnesses he will call, and what physical evidence he will present. The Government in Great Britain is seeking legislation requiring the defendant to give notice of alibi defenses. Under the revised Federal rules the court may make the defendant's discovery of the Goverment's case conditional upon his own disclosure of physical evidence and scientific reports.

After a case has begun, neither the prosecutor nor defense counsel has legal power to compel the appearance of witnesses for pretrial examination. In civil cases depositions and other examinations of witnesses before trial have been widely and successfully used, but in criminal cases their use has been limited in most jurisdictions to situations in which a witness may be unavailable to testify at trial and his testimony must be preserved. Prosecutors frequently can convince witnesses to cooperate by assertion of the prestige of their office, although in some places subpoenas and grand jury process are used for these purposes without legal authority. Expanded availability of depositions would provide for both sides a legitimate method to make these examinations which are so important to proper trial preparation.

The Commission has not made a detailed study of the complex specific issues raised in framing rules of discovery in criminal cases. It commends to the States the efforts of the Judicial Conference of the United States, the American Bar Association special project, and those States that have moved forward in this area. It generally favors the expansion of pretrial discovery and depositions in criminal cases to ensure the fairness and accuracy of trial and pretrial dispositions. The Commission recognizes that in certain cases, particularly those involving the national security, espionage, organized crime, or dangerously violent offenders who might intimidate witnesses, discovery must be limited. In most cases expanded mutual discovery by the State within constitutional limits is desirable.

HABEAS CORPUS AND FINALITY

There has been a rapid growth in the number of petitions for habeas corpus and similar relief filed in the Federal courts between the 1940's, when a few hundred petitions were filed each year, and 1965 when 5,786 reached the courts. Our system is unique in the extent to which a person convicted at trial can continue to challenge his conviction in a series of appeals and collateral attacks in the nature of habeas corpus in the State and Federal courts. Frequently this procedure is the only way he can obtain judicial consideration of substantial constitutional infirmities in the process by which he was convicted. The availability of such a remedy is embodied in the Constitution and is basic to our system of law.

The vast increase in the number of petitions, including a large proportion of frivolous petitions; public exasperation about cases in which punishment is postponed, sometimes for many years, because of successive hearings; the resulting sense of friction between the State and Federal courts—all have reinforced the need for reevaluation of the use and administration of the writ. A result has been new Federal legislation and extensive studies by the Judicial Conference of the United States, the National Conference of Commissioners on Uniform State Laws, and a committee of the American Bar Association Project on Minimum Standards for Criminal Justice.

The issues raised are complex and highly technical in several respects. In large part the increase in the number of petitions for habeas corpus is a reflection of the expanding interpretation the courts have given to constitutional standards applied to the criminal process. As standards change, the number of cases in which these issues can be raised by habeas corpus grows apace. In addition, the court rules governing such petitions have been liberalized to permit greater recourse to the writ.

Finality, the conclusive end of a case, is desirable, but so is providing a man in prison or under sentence of death every opportunity to press his claim that he is wrongfully held. This is complicated by the nature of the Federal system, which in certain circumstances makes it possible for a single Federal district judge to sit in review of State court actions and decisions that have been considered and approved by the full supreme court of a State.

A partial answer to the great number of habeas corpus proceedings is the improvement of trials. This means not only insuring that constitutional rights are protected but that the protection is fully documented on the record. Judges should take pains to insure that constitutional issues present in the case are confronted and decided.

A more important partial solution lies in the improvement of State procedures for dealing with postconviction claims. Much of the criticism of current practice is based on the sense that Federal courts are becoming involved to an excessive degree in State criminal proceedings. But frequently when the Federal district court holds a hearing on such a petition, it is because there is no available procedure through which the prisoner can obtain relief in the State courts. Far fewer than half of the States now have satisfactory postconviction procedures by statute or judicial rule. Most of the remainder rely on a faulty and antiquated system of ill-defined common law remedies that fall far short of the protection available in Federal courts and of that which is constitutionally required. In a recent Supreme Court decision, Mr. Justice Brennan, after noting the considerable drop in Federal applications from State prisoners in a State that enacted a modern postconviction relief act, described succinctly the attributes of such a law:

*The procedure should be swift and simple and easily invoked. It should be sufficiently comprehensive to embrace all federal constitutional claims. * * * [I]t should eschew rigid and technical doctrines of forfeiture, waiver, or default. * *, * It should provide for full fact hearings to resolve disputed factual issues, and for compilation of a record to enable federal courts to determine the sufficiency of those hearings. * * * It should provide for decisions supported by opinions, or factfindings and conclusions of law, which disclose the grounds of decision and the resolution of disputed facts. Case v. Nebraska, 381 U.S. 336, 346 (1965).*

Another pressing need is the more frequent provision of legal counsel to prisoners seeking release on habeas corpus. Legal assistance and advice for all prisoners seeking them should be supplemented by the assignment of counsel for prisoners with substantial claims to present to the court. The assignment of counsel in appropriate cases would tend to curtail worthless petitions, since petitions an attorney refused to sign would carry less weight in court. It would also unearth worthy claims that now are not presented or clearly articulated because of the ignorance of the inmate. Programs in Kansas, Wyoming, and Pennsylvania offer models for providing legal advice in prisons through law professors and students, as well as through practicing lawyers.

The Commission recommends:

States that do not have procedures that provide adequate postconviction remedies should enact legislation or establish rules that do provide a single, simple remedy for all claims of deprivation of constitutional right. These procedures should provide for the assistance of counsel. Petitions should be decided on their merits rather than upon procedural technicalities.

344

In every jurisdiction in this country the right of the prosecution to appeal from an adverse ruling by a court is more limited than the comparable right of the defendant. The argument against retrying a man who has convinced a court of the merit of his cause has led to double jeopardy clauses in the Federal Constitution and the constitutions of 45 States. The same argument inhibits appeals that, if successful, would result in just such a retrial. But in most States and the Federal system these considerations do not forbid all appeals by the prosecution, particularly those from pretrial rulings that are made before jeopardy attaches in the constitutional sense. Developments in the law, particularly the growth of search and seizure law and exclusionary rules governing confessions, call for a reexamination of the adequacy of the prosecution's right to appeal.

Under common practice motions for the suppression of evidence are required to be made before trial when possible. These motions are likely to become more frequent as a result of recent court decisions, and in an increased number of cases the prosecution will be blocked by a pretrial order suppressing evidence or a statement. Frequently the prosecution cannot successfully proceed to trial without the suppressed evidence. Yet in only a few States does the prosecution have the right to appeal from the grant of such orders, and in the Federal courts the right to appeal applies only to narcotics cases.

Not only does the absence of a right of appeal preclude successful prosecution in many cases, including important cases involving organized crime, narcotics, and major thefts, but it has distinctly undesirable effects upon the development of law and practice. The law of search and seizure and confessions today is highly uncertain. This uncertainty is compounded by lower court rulings that restrict police conduct yet cannot be tested on appeal, and by inconsistent lower court decisions that can be resolved only on an appeal sought by the defendant.

When the prosecution is not permitted an appeal, law enforcement officers faced with restrictive rulings they feel are erroneous have available two courses, each of which is undesirable: They can follow the lower court decision and abandon the practice, in which case an authoritative decision by an appellate court never can be obtained; or they can continue the practice, hoping that in a future case a trial court will sustain it and that a defendant by appealing will give the higher court an opportunity to resolve the point. The first choice is undesirable because it results in the abandonment of what may be legitimate police practice merely because there is no way of testing it in the appellate courts. The second choice is equally undesirable for it puts the police in the position of deciding which court decisions they will accept and which they will not.

A more general right of the prosecution to appeal from adverse pretrial rulings is desirable. Controls may be needed to insure that appeals are taken only from rulings of significant importance and that the accused's right to a speedy trial is preserved by requirements of diligent processing of such appeals.

The Commission recommends:

Congress and the States should enact statutes giving the prosecution the right to appeal from the grant of all pretrial motions to suppress evidence or confessions.

IMMUNITY

A grand jury subpoena can compel the attendance of a witness and the production of books and records, but the grand jury has no power to compel a witness to testify or to inspect private books and records if their owner demurs. However, it is constitutionally permissible under proper conditions to displace a witness's privilege against self-incrimination with a grant of immunity from criminal prosecution. On the Federal level immunity is available only in prosecutions under specific statutes, such as those dealing with narcotics, antitrust, and Communications Act violations. Some States follow a similar pattern, while others have enacted general immunity statutes permitting the prosecution to grant immunity in any criminal case.

Immunity provisions are particularly necessary to secure testimony in cases of official corruption, and the special need for the power to grant immunity in organized crime cases is discussed in chapter 7.

One serious danger, in the light of court decisions with respect to the application of immunity given by one jurisdiction to prosecutions in other jurisdictions, is that the grant of immunity to a witness in one proceeding will interfere with investigations elsewhere. Since facilities for communication between elements of the Federal Government are better developed than those at State and local levels, the problem is greater in State courts and grand jury investigations. The creation of inter-agency communication procedures where none now exist and the improvement of existing procedures are most important if grants of immunity are to be intelligently made. The Attorney General or other chief law enforcement officer must be in a position to ascertain whether other investigations are pending if he is to have the perspective necessary for him to choose which investigation is most important to the overall administration of justice.

Filing with the court a notice of the grant of immunity would reduce the possibility of abuse of authority by prosecutors as well as the danger of hidden immunization for corrupt purposes.

The Commission recommends:

A general witness immunity statute should be enacted at Federal and State levels, providing immunity sufficiently broad to assure compulsion of testimony. Immunity should be granted only with the prior approval of the jurisdiction's chief prosecuting officer. Efforts to coordinate Federal, State, and local immunity grants should be made to prevent interference with concurrent investigations.

PERJURY

The criminal law must offer more effective deterrents against false statements. The integrity of the trial depends on the power to compel truthful testimony and to punish falsehood. Immunity can be an effective prosecutive weapon only if the immunized witness then testifies truthfully. Perjury statutes provide criminal penalties for false testimony under oath, but the infrequency of their use and the difficulty of securing convictions in perjury cases has limited the effectiveness of this criminal sanction.

Perjury has always been widespread; according to Pollock and Maitland's standard history of English law, "our ancestors perjured themselves with impunity." The requirements for proof in perjury cases are complicated by special common law rules of evidence, particularly the two-witness rule and its corollary, the direct evidence rule. In essence the former requires that the falsity of the testimony of the defendant charged with perjury be established by more than the uncorroborated oath of one witness, and the latter that circumstantial evidence, no matter how persuasive, will not alone support a conviction for perjury. There are, in addition to the direct evidence rule, decisions which hold that contradictory statements under oath may not be the subject matter of a perjury prosecution without additional proof of the falsity of one of the statements. Dissatisfaction has led to changes by statute in some jurisdictions; however, the common law rule prevails in Federal proceedings and in a number of States. These restrictive evidentiary rules are an unwarranted obstacle to securing legitimate perjury convictions.

There is no apparent reason for the distinction between perjury and other crimes. Sound prosecutive discretion, proof beyond a reasonable doubt to a judge and jury, and the other traditional safeguards applicable to every criminal case provide adequate protection against the unwarranted charge and conviction of perjury.

The Commission recommends:

Congress and the States should abolish the rigid two-witness and direct evidence rules in perjury prosecutions although maintaining the requirement of proving an intentional false statement.

SENTENCING POLICIES AND PROCEDURES

There is no decision in the criminal process that is as complicated and difficult as the one made by the sentencing judge. A sentence prescribes punishment, but it also should be the foundation of an attempt to rehabilitate the offender, to insure that he does not endanger the community, and to deter others from similar crimes in the future. Often these objectives are mutually inconsistent, and the sentencing judge must choose one at the expense of the others. A man who has committed murder in a moment of extreme emotion may require no correctional program and may present no significant threat to the general safety, but few judges would be likely to respond to an offense so heinous by suspending the offender's sentence or granting him probation.

The difficulty of making such important choices is compounded by the fact that a sentence is in large part a prediction. It tries to predict how an offender will behave under certain circumstances and how other potential offenders will behave. But judges do not have much predictive data to guide them. Very little is yet known about how different kinds of individuals are likely to react to correctional programs or about the deterrent effects of the criminal process. In some courts judges are not even given information that could be gathered about an offender's background and character. Wise and fair sentencing requires intuition, insight, and imagination; at present it is less a science than an art. In the final analysis good sentencing depends on good judges.

At the same time greater efforts must be made to improve our understanding of how different types of offenders respond to differing kinds of correctional treatment. The court information proposed in chapter 11 of this report would provide for the systematic gathering and analysis of sentencing and correctional data for large numbers of offenders that are necessary to improve the predictive value of the sentencing decision. This information system might provide a basis for identifying factors that are and are not particularly relevant to sentencing. Judges have only limited opportunity to observe other judges at work. More complete data on sentencing practices would enable judges to compare the sentences they impose with the way other judges have treated similar offenses or offenders and with the results of their own previous sentencing predictions.

SENTENCING STATUTES

The sometimes rigid, but more often extremely flexible framework within which a sentencing judge operates is the sentencing code, the statutory provisions that prescribe the penalties he can impose for each particular crime. In most places sentencing codes have been enacted piecemeal over many years, and the grading of offenses in terms of seriousness is replete with anomalies and inconsistencies.

The Oregon Penal Code contains 466 penalties that can be imposed for one or more of 1,413 offenses. A recent study of the Colorado statutes disclosed that a person convicted of first-degree murder must serve 10 years before becoming eligible for parole, while a person convicted of a lesser degree of the same offense must serve 15 or more years; stealing a dog is punishable by 10 years' imprisonment, while killing a dog carries a maximum of 6 months. Under Federal law, armed bank robbery is punishable by fine, probation, or any prison term up to 25 years, but in cases involving armed robbery of a post office, the judge is limited to granting probation or imposing a 25-year prison sentence.

The most obvious effect of these anomalies and inconsistencies is that sometimes judges are compelled to choose between equally unwise alternatives. In the example of armed robbery of a post office, most judges would choose probation rather than 25 years in prison for all offenders but the most desperate ones, though undoubtedly the interests both of the community and many offenders would be served if shorter prison terms were permissible. A less obvious effect is that prosecutors, surveying an inconsistent penal code, sometimes choose a charge that carries the penalty they think should be imposed rather than the charge that most accurately fits the facts of the offense. For example, the Michigan Penal Code made burglary at night so much graver an offense than burglary by day that, in the words of one big-city prosecutor, "You'd think all our burglaries occurred at high noon."

Another defect in some sentencing codes is that certain offenses carry mandatory minimum sentences of great severity and forbid the granting of probation or parole. These offenses vary from State to State, although armed robbery and the sale of narcotics are two that often are treated in this way. It sometimes happens, when a marginal offender has committed such an offense, that a judge who feels the mandatory penalty is completely inappropriate dismisses the case or acquits the offender.

A more common defect than mandatory minimums is extremely high maximums. For many offenses in most States judges are allowed to choose penalties that range from probation to prison terms of 20 to 25 years. Few other countries allow judges that much leeway, and prison sentences in America are, as a general rule, longer than those elsewhere. High maximum sentences also put a great strain on the correctional system. Parole boards frequently have broad discretion as to how much of his sentence a prisoner serves. When there is a gap of many years between the earliest possible date for granting of parole and the maximum sentence, the dangers of unfairness to individual prisoners are evident.

Finally, few sentencing codes set forth criteria for distinguishing between the occasional and the aggravated or repeated offender. A clear definition of the circumstances under which, for example, it is appropriate to impose capital punishment or an extended prison term or to grant probation would help guide sentencing judges.

About half the States are now undertaking projects to revise their penal laws and sentencing codes. Upon recommendation of President Johnson in his 1966 crime message, Congress has authorized the establishment of a special commission to study and revise the provisions of the United States Code defining and fixing the punishment for Federal crimes.

The American Law Institute in its Model Penal Code takes an imaginative and constructive approach to simplifying and standardizing the grading of offenses for sentencing purposes. It reduces all crimes to three grades of felony and two grades of misdemeanor. Each grade carries a maximum penalty, most of which are shorter than those now prevalent in the States. The maximum can be extended by the judge if the offense is an especially atrocious one or the offender is an especially dangerous one by clearly defined standards. The discretion to grant probation is allowed to the judge except in capital cases. The judge may set a minimum term of imprisonment that for all but the most serious felonies cannot exceed 3 years, and that for any felony must be for at least 1 year. Beyond these limits correctional authorities have discretion to grant parole. Under the code judges are granted flexibility to impose a sentence that fits the circumstances of a specific case, and parole boards are allowed to review reasonably soon after the correctional process has begun, the judge's prediction about how the offender will react to treatment.

The Model Penal Code also contains sentencing criteria, as does the Model Sentencing Act drafted by the Council of Judges of the National Council on Crime and Delinquency. For example, the Model Penal Code's criteria for probation, which are drawn upon heavily in the recently revised New York State penal law, declare that an offender's probable dangerousness, his need for treatment, and the seriousness of his offense are grounds for withholding probation. The code then lists 11 grounds for the granting of probation, including the relative mildness of the offense, the provocation offered the offender, the involvement of the victim in the offense, the character of the offender, and the hardship imprisonment would impose on the offender or his dependents. Both the model code and the model act seek to establish criteria identifying the persistent, habitual, or hardened criminal. Framing statutory sentencing standards is a complicated and laborious undertaking on which there still is much work to be done. Standards for many sentencing decisions cannot yet be articulated. However, it is an undertaking of great importance, and continued experimentation is likely to produce valuable results.

The Commission recommends:

States should reexamine the sentencing provisions of their penal codes with a view to simplifying the grading of offenses, and to removing mandatory minimum prison terms,

long maximum prison terms, and ineligibility for probation and parole. In cases of persistent habitual offenders or dangerous criminals, judges should have express authority to impose extended prison terms. Sentencing codes should include criteria designed to help judges exercise their discretion in accordance with clearly stated standards.

CAPITAL PUNISHMENT

As the abolition or the retention of the death penalty is being widely debated in the States, it is appropriate to point out several aspects of its administration that bear on the issue.

The most salient characteristic of capital punishment is that it is infrequently applied. During 1966 only 1 person was executed in the United States; the trend over the last 36 years shows a continual decline in the number of executions, from a high of 200 in 1935 to last year's low of one. Furthermore, all available data indicate that judges, juries, and governors are becoming increasingly reluctant to impose, or authorize the carrying out of a death sentence. Only 67 persons were sentenced to death by the courts in 1965, a decline of 31 from the previous year, and 62 prisoners were reprieved from their death sentences. In a few States in which the penalty exists on the statute books, there has not been an execution in decades.

The decline in the application of the death penalty parallels a substantial decline in public support for capital punishment. The most recent Gallup Poll, conducted in 1966, revealed that less than half of those interviewed favored retaining the death penalty. In the last 3 years, 5 States either totally abolished capital punishment or severely limited its use, thus bringing to 13 the number of States which have effectively repealed capital punishment. Great Britain experimentally suspended the death penalty for 5 years in 1965. The trend toward abolition has not been uniform, however. Capital punishment was abolished in Delaware in 1958 but restored in 1961. And in 1966 a constitutional amendment abolishing capital punishment was rejected by the voters in Colorado. In 1965 the Canadian Parliament rejected a move to abolish the death sentence.

It is impossible to say with certainty whether capital punishment significantly reduces the incidence of heinous crimes. The most complete study on the subject, based on a comparison of homicide rates in capital and noncapital jurisdictions, concluded that there is no discernible correlation between the availability of the death penalty and the homicide rate. This study also revealed that there was no significant difference between the two kinds of States in the safety of policemen. Another study of 27 States indicated that the availability of the death sentence had no effect on the rate of assaults and murders of prison guards.

Whatever views one may have on the efficacy of the death penalty as a deterrent, it clearly has an undesirable impact on the administration of criminal justice. Capital cases take longer to litigate at the trial level; the selection of a jury often requires several days, and each objection or point of law requires inordinate deliberation because of the irreversible consequences of error. In addition, the inherent sensationalism of a trial for life distorts the factfinding process and increases the danger that public sentiment will be aroused for the defendant, regardless of his guilt of the crime charged. This distortion is not restricted to the trial level. As Mr. Justice Jackson noted: "When the penalty is death * * * [appellate] judges are tempted to strain the evidence and even in close cases, the law, in order to give a doubtfully condemned man another chance."

Furthermore, the imposition of a death sentence is but the first stage of a protracted process of appeals, collateral attacks, and petitions for executive clemency. At the end of 1965 there were 331 prisoners awaiting execution in the United States, and since then this number undoubtedly has increased. These prisoners then were under sentence for an average of 30.8 months, and the average time between imposition and execution was almost 4 years. The spectacle of men living on death row for years while their lawyers pursue appellate and collateral remedies tarnishes our image of humane and expeditious justice. But no one seriously proposes to limit the right of a condemned man to have errors at his trial corrected or to obtain the mercy of the executive.

Finally there is evidence that the imposition of the death sentence and the exercise of dispensing power by the courts and the executive follow discriminatory patterns. The death sentence is disproportionately imposed and carried out on the poor, the Negro, and the members of unpopular groups.

Some members of the Commission favor the abolition of capital punishment, while other members favor its retention. Some would support its abolition if more adequate safeguards against the release of dangerous offenders were devised. All members of the Commission agree that the present situation in the administration of the death penalty in many States is intolerable for the reasons stated above.

The Commission recommends:

The question whether capital punishment is an appropriate sanction is a policy decision to be made by each State. Where it is retained, the types of offenses for which it is available should be strictly limited, and the law should be enforced in an evenhanded and nondiscriminatory manner, with procedures for review of death sentences that are fair and expeditious. When a State finds that it cannot administer the penalty in such a manner, or that the death penalty is being imposed but not carried into effect, the penalty should be abandoned.

SENTENCING PROCEDURES

Although the criminal trial on the issue of guilt is a strictly formal procedure, the determination of what is to be done with a convicted offender is often a rather informal one. A judge, when he sentences, needs facts about the offender and his offense. Both will be absent in those many instances when conviction has resulted from a plea of guilty and the court lacks, or has inadequate facilities for preparing, presentence reports. The judge then must rely on the necessarily incomplete and biased oral statements of the prosecutor, defense counsel, and defendant. Such statements may be supplemented by a "rapsheet," a 1-page record of the offender's prior criminal involvements.

In most felony courts presentence reports are prepared, but they are of uneven quality and usefulness. One almost universal problem is that the probation officers who prepare them have more work than they can effectively do. They often have as many as 100 offenders on probation to supervise, besides preparing reports. Another problem is that the pay, recruitment, and training standards for probation officers are often low, and the officers are not equipped to evaluate the information they receive in the course of their investigations.

Most misdemeanor courts do not require presentence reports. In the case of the majority of misdemeanants full field investigations by trained probation officers may not be called for. However, some relevant information should be provided to the sentencing judge, perhaps no more than is obtained by the use of the kind of short form that was described in this chapter's discussion of bail.

Many misdemeanor courts have no probation services at all. In such courts a sentence of probation is in effect an unconditional release, except that the offender can be later jailed for his offense if a violation of his probation comes to the attention of the court as the result of his being arrested on another charge. This has led to the paradoxical situation that a smaller proportion of misdemeanor offenders receive probation than do felony offenders, who have committed more serious crimes.

The Commission recommends:

All courts, felony and misdemeanor, should have probation services. Standards for the recruitment and training of probation officers should be set by the States, and the funds necessary to implement this recommendation should be provided by the States to those local courts that cannot finance probation services for themselves. All courts should require presentence reports for all offenders, whether those reports result from full field investigations by probation officers or, in the case of minor offenders, from the use of short forms.

Fairness to the defendant requires that he be given a reasonable opportunity to present information to the court and to contest the accuracy of important factual statements in the presentence report or other material presented to the court. Gossip often finds its way into presentence reports, and without disclosure there is often no way of counteracting its effects. The issue whether the presentence report itself should be disclosed to the defendant and his counsel has been the subject of considerable debate, and disclosure at the present time is generally a matter of judicial discretion, although in five States disclosure is required by statute.

In many cases information clearly could be disclosed without substantial likelihood of harm; yet there can be circumstances in which the particularly confidential nature of the source of the information may preclude its disclosure, or in which disclosure of a statement would be harmful to rehabilitation. Presentence reports sometimes rely upon the records of social, welfare, and juvenile agencies that are required to keep their records confidential; such agencies might stop providing information if disclosure were compelled. In other cases the person who provided certain information might be easily identified by the offender and, if the information is unfavorable, that person might be endangered. However, the experience of the courts where disclosure is a matter of routine indicates that such problems can be solved by the proper exercise of judicial discretion.

The Commission recommends:

In the absence of compelling reasons for nondisclosure of special information, the defendant and his counsel should be permitted to examine the entire presentence report.

Sentencing judges make important correctional decisions, but few have received training in correctional theories and practices. One technique for acquainting judges with correctional theory and with the programs and facilities that are available to treat various kinds of offenders is the judicial sentencing institute.

Judicial sentencing institutes are meetings of trial judges at which they have an opportunity to discuss, frequently with participation by correctional authorities, legal scholars, and persons from other relevant disciplines, the problems and standards for imposing sentence. A Federal program was founded with congressional authority in 1959 at a time when concern with disparity of sentencing was intensified by changes in sentencing codes that gave greater discretionary alternatives to judges. Over the past 7 years 16 institutes have been conducted, and the judges of all Federal circuits have had an opportunity to participate in at least one. The programs have varied and have dealt with such subjects as disparity, the identification of dangerous offenders, and the use of presentence reports. Often visits to correctional institutions are included during which judges become more familiar with the programs and facilities offered. Some State institutes have followed the Federal pattern. In California institutes have studied both standards for commitment to correctional institutions and the policies of the adult correctional authority in regard to term setting and parole eligibility. In other States, such as New York, the subject of sentencing is one of the items considered at a broader annual judicial meeting.

The Commission recommends:

Every State should organize and finance regular judicial institutes or conferences at which judges meet with other judges and with correctional authorities to discuss sentencing standards and learn about available correctional programs and facilities.

In 10 States sentences are fixed by juries rather than by judges. Data indicate that this is a poor practice. Jurors do not and cannot have the expertise to assess rationally the correctional needs of offenders; and juries, because of their size and their position of being half in and half out of the court system, are inappropriate recipients of sentencing information.

The extent of the failings of jury sentencing were vividly revealed in a recent survey by the Atlanta Crime Commission, which showed that in that city for some offenses first offenders received more severe sentences on the average than hardened recidivists.

The Commission recommends:

Jury sentencing in noncapital cases should be abolished.

SENTENCING DISPARITY

That different judges sentence differently is, and always has been, a major and justified complaint against the courts. Mr. Justice Jackson, when he was Attorney General of the United States, stated:

It is obviously repugnant to one's sense of justice that the judgment meted out to an offender should depend in large part on a purely fortuitous circumstance; namely, the personality of the particular judge before whom the case happens to come for disposition.

Several of the recommendations in this section of the chapter would tend to reduce disparity. The enactment of statutory criteria for sentencing, together with programs to educate judges in sentencing and correctional methods, would enable them to sentence on the basis of more uniform standards. Two devices, sentencing councils and appellate review of sentences, are particularly designed to reduce disparity.

The sentencing council consists of several judges of a multijudge court who meet periodically to discuss sentences to be imposed in pending cases. Sentencing councils are in use on a regular basis in at least three U.S. district courts. Foremost among their advantages is the opportunity they give for discussion of sentencing attitudes. From such a discussion a consensus on sentencing standards may emerge. The council provides occasion also for full consideration of available sentencing alternatives. The ultimate responsibility for determining sentence rests with the judge to whom the case is assigned, although the discussion and need to state reasons for a sentence tend to restrain the imposition of unreasonably severe or lenient sentences. The sentencing council in the U.S. District Court for the Eastern District of Michigan has produced changes from the sentencing judge's initial recommendation in slightly over 40 percent of the cases considered, and the number of cases in which sentences were made more severe was approximately equal to the number in which they were reduced.

Appellate review of sentences affords the occasion for a systematic and continuous examination of sentencing policy by an appellate court. Authority for appellate review of legally imposed sentences has been expressly granted by the legislatures of 12 States and by Congress for the military courts. In addition, the appellate courts of a few States have construed their laws to grant such authority. However, in at least 31 States and the Federal system sentencing power is vested solely with the trial judge.

Appellate review would encourage the development of uniform and considered sentencing policies within a jurisdiction. It leads both the trial court and the appellate court to give sustained and explicit consideration to the justification for particular sentences. It provides a workable means of correcting unjust and ill-considered sentences, particularly those in which the punishment imposed is grossly inappropriate. While there is room for difference of opinion as to whether the appellate court should have authority to increase as well as decrease sentences appealed by the defendant, the Commission favors such authority. A committee of the American Bar Association special project has proposed detailed standards for appellate review procedures.

The Commission recommends:

Procedures for avoiding and correcting excessive, inadequate, or disparate sentences should be devised and instituted.

OFFICERS OF JUSTICE

JUDGES

The quality of the judiciary in large measure determines the quality of justice. It is the judge who tries disputed cases and who supervises and reviews negotiated dispositions. Through sentencing the judge determines the treatment given to an offender. Through the exercise of his administrative power over his court he determines its efficiency, fairness, and effectiveness. No procedural or administrative reforms will help the courts, and no reorganizational plan will avail unless judges have the highest qualifications, are fully trained and competent, and have high standards of performance.

Selection of Judges.   Methods for the selection of judges vary from jurisdiction to jurisdiction, and some States use different methods of selection for upper court judges than for lower court judges. In 11 States judges are appointed either by the Governor or the legislature; in some of these States they are first appointed and then must run for election on their records; in 15 States they are elected without party labels, and in 19 States they are elected on a partisan basis. In a number of States there is a professional or nonpartisan screening process that develops an identified group of professionally qualified persons from which all nominations or appointments are made, or that reviews proposed nominations or appointments for professional competence. Sometimes this process is required by State constitution or statute; sometimes it is informal. Sometimes it is employed for all judges, sometimes only for certain kinds of judges. It is employed least often in the States in which judges are elected in partisan contests.

The elective process, particularly if judges are elected as candidates of political parties, has not proven an effective system for choosing persons to fill an office as removed from daily political pressures as the judiciary should be. Selection of candidates tends to be dictated to an excessive degree by party considerations and other factors unrelated to the candidates' qualifications for office, and the electoral process gives the voters little opportunity to weigh the relative abilities of the candidates. Interest in and experience with politics are qualities that may contribute to a judge's effectiveness in settling disputes and dealing with people who appear before the court. But judicial appointments should be made on grounds other than partisanship, and sitting judges should be free from political obligations. Indeed there is reason to believe that the elective method discourages the candidacy of good potential judges and sometimes subjects those who do run to undue political pressures in the performance of their office.

In general, the Commission favors the appointive method for the selection of judges over the elective method, although it recognizes that in some special situations the elective method presents advantages, especially in diverse urban communities where the election of judges may insure that all groups in the community are represented in the judiciary.

The Commission believes that far more important than the choice between elective and appointive systems, however, is the existence in the selection system of an effective procedure for the screening of potential candidates for the judiciary on the basis of their personal and professional qualifications for office. The group that performs this screening function should be established by law, should be directly responsible to the appointing authority, and should be carefully selected to insure that its membership is representative and is not drawn from an unduly narrow segment of the bar or the community.

The Commission believes that the best selection system for judges is a merit selection plan generally of the type used successfully in Missouri for some 25 years, and long supported in principle by the American Bar Association and the American Judicature Society. The Missouri type plan is now in use with a number of variations in some 10 States. Its basic approach is also embodied in the procedures used by the mayor of the city of New York to appoint criminal court judges. The Missouri plan is characterized by four elements:

1. The nomination of a panel of judicial candidates by a nonpartisan commission composed of conscientious, qualified laymen and lawyers.

2. The requirement that the executive appoint judges only from the panel submitted by the commission.

3. The review of the appointment by the voters after a short probationary term of service in which the only question is whether the judge's record warrants his retention in office.

4. Periodic review of the appointment at the end of each term of office by the voters in which the only question is whether the judge's record warrants his continued retention in office.

Another way to remove judges from undue political influence and to increase their independence is to provide lengthy tenure. Yet in a number of States the judge of major criminal trial courts must seek reelection as frequently as every 4 years. Federal judges hold office for life during good behavior, and in many States they sit to a fixed retirement age, or for a term of from 10 to 14 years. Under both of these approaches giving long tenure, generally high judicial standards have been maintained. It is important that there be liberal provisions for the dignified retirement of judges at a fixed age to ensure the continuing capacity of the judiciary.

Many States and the Federal Government have authorized the continued service of vigorous retired judges, enabling the full use of their experience while making room for the appointment of younger judges.

The Commission recommends:

Judicial tenure in major trial courts should be for a term of 10 years or more, with appropriate provisions to facilitate retirement of judges at a predetermined age.

Judicial Education. Courts, particularly the courts that try felonies, are typically both civil and criminal, and the judges in them preside over both civil and criminal cases. Naturally many judges are civil, not criminal, lawyers.

A recent survey showed that only about one-half of newly selected judges have any prior courtroom experience and that few of them have any background in criminal cases. Such judges need guidance in the conduct of trials; yet they seldom have opportunities to watch experienced judges at work and to learn from their performance. Such judges also need guidance in the substantive criminal law, in corrections and sentencing, and in administration and management.

In some States judicial conferences, seminars, and institutes have been used successfully to train sitting judges. National programs, such as those sponsored by the National College of State Trial Judges established by the American Bar Association, and the Institute for Judicial Administration have been made available for newly appointed judges. The Commission urges expansion of programs for the training of judges, investment of more effort in curriculum development, and experimentation with procedures making participation in continuing programs mandatory.

Judicial careers tend to be long. Available data indicate that they average over 25 years. For a career of such length a period of apprenticeship or preservice training appears appropriate. The Judicial Conference of the United States directs its training programs particularly at newly appointed judges, as does the National College of State Trial Judges. After election or appointment judges might well be required to spend their first months in full-time formal training programs and in sitting with experienced judges.

Control and Supervision. Long tenure for judges makes the maintenance of high standards of judicial performance crucial. It requires that there be administrative methods of dealing speedily and appropriately with judicial incompetence or misbehavior. In most States the only available methods are impeachment or recall, which are both cumbersome and far too severe to be invoked in most cases. A particular problem is excusing physically or mentally incapacitated judges from their duties without publicly humiliating them. Recently California and Texas, among other States, have set up within the judicial department commissions charged with examining judicial conduct and taking necessary action. These commissions rely heavily upon informal conferences and discussions calculated to appeal to an individual judge's sense of status and his self-motivation. In California over a 4-year period this commission has removed 26 judges and has been instrumental in the retirement or resignation of a number more, yet only one recommendation for removal was contested in the State Supreme court. The Subcommittee on Improvements in Judicial Machinery of the Senate Judiciary Committee has held hearings on proposals to create similar machinery in the Federal system, as well as to improve procedures for the compulsory retirement of physically or mentally disabled judges. In New York a Court on the Judiciary has been established to hear complaints of judicial misconduct.

The Commission recommends:

States should establish commissions on judicial conduct taking the approach used in California and Texas. States should review their statutes governing the retirement of physically or mentally incapacitated judges to insure that the judiciary can require the retirement with dignity of judges unable to bear the burdens of office.

PROSECUTORS

The prosecutor's discretion to decide what charge to bring against, and what disposition to recommend for, an offender is indicative of his crucial position in the law enforcement system. The prosecutor is particularly able to influence police operations. He affects the development of legal rules by his arguments in court. He can help bring about needed reform by pressing for changes in bail practices, for example, or in procedures for the appointment of counsel. Except for the judge he is the most influential court official.

Yet many prosecutors in this country are part-time officers. They generally are elected or selected on a partisan political basis and serve for relatively short terms. In many places the office traditionally has been a steppingstone to higher political office or the bench. Prosecutors in most places are so poorly paid that they must, and are expected to, engage in private law practice. This creates inevitable conflicts between the demands of the office and of private practice. It can lead to undesirable potential conflicts of interest in dealings with other attorneys, judges, and members of the community. As the participation of defense counsel in criminal cases grows, the need to improve the quality of the prosecution becomes increasingly urgent.

The Commission recommends:

Localities should revise salary structures so that district attorneys and assistants devote full time to their office without outside practice. The effort should be to raise the quality of the office so that highly talented lawyers will seek it. In smaller jurisdictions, where the caseload does not justify a full-time criminal prosecutor, consideration should be given to use of prosecutors representing larger districts, in place of county or town attorneys. Assistants should be hired on a nonpartisan basis.

There are real advantages in the politically oriented selection and noncareer tenure of prosecutors. They ensure that the office will be responsive to the dominant law enforcement views of the community. The elective process provides the prosecutor with an independent political base. But these same factors can interfere with the full development of the prosecutor as more than a vigorous courtroom advocate for the State. Political considerations make some prosecutors overly sensitive to what is safe, expedient, and in conformity with law enforcement views that are popular, rather than carefully thought out. In some places, including some of our largest cities, unusually able district attorneys have surmounted this pattern and have developed highly professional career offices, manned by attorneys of long experience and broad outlook, in which careful attention is given to the development of sound prosecutive policies. These examples show that the elective system can provide competent, professional prosecutors if those who control the process of selection strive for these qualities.

The training of a prosecutor is generally limited to his legal education and whatever courtroom experience he has had. While this may meet the need for the courtroom and trial aspects of the job, it does not necessarily prepare the man for his administrative and law enforcement functions. Many young assistant district attorneys are appointed without specialized knowledge of the criminal law or experience in court or in the investigative and discretionary parts of their work. The U.S. Department of Justice and the National District Attorneys Association recently have started programs to train prosecutors. Both preservice and continuing education are needed, and it will require a concerted effort by the States and localities to ensure the broadest possible participation in them.

The Commission recommends:

The Federal Government, States, and district attorneys' offices, with assistance from law schools and professional organizations, should develop curricula and programs for the preservice and inservice training of prosecutors and should require the broadest possible participation in such programs by prosecutors.

STATE COORDINATION

The office of prosecutor traditionally has been a local position. Prosecutors are elected on county, city, or district lines and in most places are effectively independent of all State and local officials. Closer communication among prosecutors' offices and greater involvement by the State government in their operations would help to raise the general level of operation toward that of the most efficient and successful offices. It would lead to more uniform policies within the State concerning both law enforcement and procedure. Personnel training, standards on the selection, tenure, compensation, and outside practice of assistants could be the subjects of statewide policies, and State assistance could more easily be made available to implement these policies.

Small local offices are unable to maintain on a continuing basis specialized manpower and technical facilities or special investigatory personnel. A State-level office could make available a pool of manpower to provide trial counsel to local offices during unusual or peak periods of activity or for unusually difficult cases. Greater State-level coordination would foster the exchange of intelligence information and provide a clearinghouse for files, records, statistics, and other data. Such an office could also become a statewide center for research in problems of criminal law administration, either through its own staff or through links with State universities

364

or law schools. A State office could develop a State plan for improved law enforcement and be a channel for Federal assistance to State criminal justice.

The concept of creating greater State government responsibility for local law enforcement, particularly prosecutors, is not a new one. The Wickersham Commission called for increased authority in the State attorney general, and in the 35 years since that recommendation some steps in this direction have been taken in a few States, notably California and Alaska.

In 1952 the American Bar Association and the National Conference of Commissioners on Uniform State Laws proposed a Model State Department of Justice Act designed to clarify and strengthen the role of the State attorney general, to encourage cooperation among law enforcement officers and to provide general supervision over prosecution within the State. The prevailing pattern, however, is that while most State attorneys general do possess some formal authority to coordinate local law enforcement activity, in most States this authority is not exercised, and even in those States where some coordination is attempted much more should be done.

Progress toward a more coherent law enforcement organization is beset by difficulties, but the need to move in this direction is compelling. County prosecutorial lines that made little sense in the 1930's often make no sense today. The growth of our enormous urban complexes transcending even county lines, the rapid mobility of the modern day criminal and the increased incidence of organized criminal activity make the need for coordination of prosecutorial efforts greater today than it was 30 years ago.

The Commission recommends:

States should strengthen the coordination of local prosecution by enhancing the authority of the State attorney general or some other appropriate statewide officer and by establishing a State council of prosecutors comprising all local prosecutors under the leadership of the attorney general.

The attorney general is the appropriate officer to assume responsibility in organizing the council, which could simply be a group which meets periodically to exchange views, although it would be preferable if it could grow to have a real policymaking function.

Creation of such a council would insure participation of local prosecutors in the State programs. Since the district attorneys are independently elected officials it would be desirable if the decisions affecting the exercise of their office were the result of collegial discussions of local prosecutors in which all participate. The council could also have the advantage of allaying the fears of local prosecutors that their authority is being subverted by a central, powerful State officer. Cooperation and implementation become less formidable problems when decisions represent the consensus of those who must carry them out at the operating level. Most important, use of the council in setting statewide standards would insure their relevance to local operating conditions. The policies set by the State officer are likely to have greater pertinence and impact on local practice if developed with the participation of a group of seasoned practitioners.

It might be the function of the attorney general's office to bring continuity of effort that a sporadically meeting council cannot and to provide a research staff to suggest areas in which statewide standards, programs and policies are needed.

DEFENSE COUNSEL

A man standing alone cannot defend himself adequately against a criminal charge. As observed many years ago by Mr. Justice Sutherland:

The right to be heard would be, in many cases, of little avail if it did not comprehend the right to be heard by counsel. Even the intelligent and educated layman has small and sometimes no skill in the science of law. If charged with crime, he is incapable, generally, of determining for himself whether the indictment is good or bad. He is unfamiliar with the rules of evidence. Left without the aid of counsel he may be put on trial without a proper charge, and convicted upon incompetent evidence, or evidence irrelevant to the issue or otherwise inadmissible. He lacks both the skill and knowledge adequately to prepare his defense, even though he have a perfect one. He requires the guiding hand of counsel at every step in the proceedings against him. Without it, though he be not guilty, he faces the danger of conviction because he does not know how to establish his innocence. Powell v. Alabama, 287 U.S. 45, 69 (1932).

This long-recognized principle is being increasingly incorporated into everyday practice. Under recent landmark decisions of the U.S. Supreme Court, particularly *Gideon v. Wainright,* all felony defendants now must be afforded counsel at trial and on appeal. Most communities have begun to provide this assistance. Under the recent decision in *Miranda* v. *Arizona,* counsel must be made available to arrested persons held in custody if the results of police questioning are to be admissible in court. Several States, including some of the most populous, have enacted statutes providing for counsel to be appointed and compensated in misdemeanor, habeas corpus, and juvenile cases. Existing programs to provide counsel through defender offices, coordinated assignment plans and neighborhood legal services are showing how the need for counsel can best be met and doubtless will lead to more and expanded programs throughout the country. Defendants are becoming more aware of the importance of counsel and quicker to demand that they be given this assistance when they are unable to secure it for themselves. The recommendations earlier in this chapter regarding precharge conference, plea negotiation and early factfinding will, if implemented, increase the number of lawyers needed. Nor does the need for a lawyer terminate after sentence, for the appellate process and the collateral proceedings that may follow it are uniquely the province of the law-trained man, able to deal with technical legal issues with an advocate's special skill.

The provision of counsel entails costs beyond the expense of paying for their services. Counsel can be expected to require that the court deal deliberatively with his client; in many respects lawyers complicate the process. A court that has been adjudging men guilty and fixing their punishments in a matter of a few minutes is unlikely to be able to continue to do so when the accused persons before it are represented by lawyers. Defense counsel will demand compliance with the rules of evidence and make motions for discovery and suppression of evidence. Sometimes they will seek delay for tactical advantages, cast doubt on a truthful witness, or challenge legitimate proof.

However, the Commission believes that the burdens counsel may impose upon the system are burdens that too long have been avoided and must be borne if there is to be an effective adversary system. The role of the defense counsel, serving as a prod, vigorously challenging existing practice, is an important benefit to the operation of the administration of justice. While in many cases the presence of a lawyer will be a factor contributing to delay, in some cases defense counsel will press the courts to early consideration of matters that eventually have to be considered, and in some instances early consideration may result in foreshortened proceedings. The costs of counsel can be minimized by firmer controls on delay and by simplified procedures; they probably cannot be eliminated. However, they are clearly worth paying.

The Commission recommends:

The objective to be met as quickly as possible is to provide counsel to every criminal defendant who faces a significant penalty, if he cannot afford to provide counsel himself. This should apply to cases classified as misdemeanors as well as to those classified as felonies. Counsel should be provided early in the proceedings and certainly no later than the first judicial appearance. The services of counsel should be available after conviction through appeal, and in collateral attack proceedings when the issues are not frivolous. The immediate minimum, until it becomes possible to provide the foregoing, is that all criminal defendants who are in danger of substantial loss of liberty shall be provided with counsel.

The criminal trial process is not the only one in which a person may be deprived of his liberty. The revocation of probation and parole presents an equal threat, and though the legal issues in such proceedings are seldom complicated, the factual issues may be. The special proceedings in the juvenile court are discussed in chapter 3 of this report. A child facing confinement in a penal institution, or other coercive treatment, is even less able to represent himself than an adult.

The Commission recommends:

Legal assistance should be provided in parole and probation revocation proceedings, in juvenile delinquency proceedings if there is a possibility of coercive disposition and in all legal processes that threaten the respondent with a substantial loss of liberty.

Methods of Providing Counsel. Two basic methods are used to provide defense counsel to the indigent in this country. In systems for assigned counsel an individual attorney is selected by the court to represent a particular defendant. Under a defender system all defendants requiring counsel are represented either by a public official, usually known as the Public Defender, or by a private agency such as a legal aid society. The majority of jurisdictions use an assigned counsel approach, although many urban courts with heavy caseloads have instituted defender systems. A number of considerations

368

may favor one or the other of these systems, and in many places there is a successful combination of the two.

There are clear disadvantages to reliance on the most common assignment system: the appointment of counsel by the judge from among lawyers he happens to know or who happens to be in the courtroom. This leads to an unfair allocation of cases and sometimes, when assigned counsel receive compensation from the state, it is seriously abused. Assignment does not have to take this form, however. Under coordinated assigned counsel systems counsel are selected by an agency using a systematic approach to insure the even and broad use of all available competent counsel. The Houston Legal Foundation sponsors a coordinated assigned counsel system that calls upon all attorneys in the county. They are assigned by means of a complex computer system to the jobs for which they are best suited: trial counsel, assisting counsel, or appellate counsel. The assignment of counsel can be coordinated with a program to train lawyers, to increase their skills, and to provide them with specialized investigative or referral assistance.

Where there is a high volume of cases, a defender's office may produce significant savings in cost and efficiency, while in rural areas an assigned counsel, part-time defender, or regional defender may be more appropriate. Use of defenders encourages specialized knowledge, while assigned counsel systems can help to broaden the participation and interest of the bar in criminal law and the operation of the courts. The National Defender Project of the National Legal Aid and Defender Association has gained substantial experience in helping communities weigh the local factors that may favor one approach or the other. The Commission recognizes the usefulness of either approach.

The Commission recommends:

All jurisdictions that have not already done so should move from random assignment of defense counsel by judges to a coordinated assigned counsel system or a defender system.

The costs of providing these services are already high and will become much higher. In all but a few States some provision exists for compensating assigned defense counsel, but in most places heavy reliance is still placed on the donated services of lawyers. Lawyers have traditionally performed these services as an obligation of their profession. The Commission hopes they will continue to, but it does not believe that donated services alone can provide a sound basis for a counsel system. Present State and local government appropriations for counsel now are less than $20 million annually, more than half of which is provided by three States. A moderate estimate of what counsel services may soon cost nationwide might well run in excess of $100 million a year.

The Commission recommends:

Each State should finance assigned counsel and defender systems on a regular and statewide basis.

An Expanded Role for Counsel. It seems likely that as counsel becomes more involved in criminal cases on a regular basis, he will be called upon to do more things. It has been noted that the criminal charge frequently is but one of the difficulties that confront persons charged under the criminal law. Lawyers participating in programs to counsel prisoners have discovered that many of those consulting them are more interested in and more in need of help with their civil law difficulties than they are with their criminal cases. Frequently they confront a whole complex of problems involving employment, housing, consumer credit, and family status. Projects in the District of Columbia have demonstrated the useful role defense counsel can play, when supported with adequate facilities, in the development of a program for the reintegration of the offender into a law-abiding community. When planned by the defense, such a program can begin before conviction and be part of the defendant's own response to the case, rather than a regimen imposed on him as a form of punishment. Many of these functions could be performed by people who are not lawyers. Defense counsel needs ready access to a number of auxiliary services resembling those available to a modern and well-equipped probation office. Referral services for medical, educational, or vocational assistance increase the potential for diagnosis and planning for the needs of the accused. Social investigation, diagnosis, and planning call for the efforts of persons from many disciplines, of which the law is but one. There is a need to expand available legal manpower, and at the same time to bring other talents into the effort.

Legal Manpower. Clearly the most vexing question in connection with increased provision of defense counsel is: Where will all the lawyers come from? It would be foolish to pretend that they will come, in sufficient numbers, from anywhere for many years. The shortage of criminal lawyers, which is already severe, is likely to become more acute in the immediate future. Some of the reasons for this shortage can be found in the very nature of criminal law practice, with its generally meagre economic rewards and limited security. Most criminal defendants can pay only a small fee, if any, and only the organized or professional criminal can provide the steady business of a prosperous civil clientele. Counsel for the defense must expect to lose more cases than he wins, not for any reason related to his legal capabilities but because, as a matter of statistics, most defendants whose cases are not dropped early in the process are in fact found guilty. Men with enough dedication and self-assurance to accept repeated defeats without coming to doubt the value of their efforts are no easier to find in the bar than anywhere else.

All but the most eminent criminal lawyers are bound to spend much of their working lives in overcrowded, physically unpleasant courts, dealing with people who have committed questionable acts, and attempting to put the best possible construction on those acts. It is not the sort of working environment that most people choose. Finally, the professional status of the criminal lawyer tends to be low. To some extent the criminal lawyer is identified unjustifiably in the public eye with the client he represents. Indeed some criminal lawyers are in fact house counsel for criminal groups engaged in gambling, prostitution, and narcotics. The reprehensible conduct of the few sometimes leads the public to see honest, competent practitioners as "mouthpieces" also. Furthermore, in nearly every large city a private defense bar of low legal and dubious ethical quality can be found. Few in number, these lawyers typically carry large caseloads and in many cities dominate the practice in routine cases. They frequent courthouse corridors, bondsmen's offices, and police stations for clients, and rely not on legal knowledge but on their capacity to manipulate the system. Their low repute often accurately reflects the quality of the services they render. This public image of the criminal lawyer is a serious obstacle to the attraction of able young lawyers, and reputable and seasoned practitioners as well, to the criminal law.

Under these circumstances it is tempting to put aside the problem of recruiting more and better criminal lawyers as an insoluble one. That, in effect, is what society has done for many years. Now it is no longer possible to do so. The movement to provide every defendant with counsel is powerful and irreversible. Furthermore, the very strength and inexorability of this movement contribute importantly to solving the manpower problem. As more defender systems are set up, more interesting jobs will be open to young men who would like to practice the criminal law as either a prelude to a career in other legal specialties or as a career in itself. Such jobs will not carry with them the "mouthpiece" stigma. As more coordinated assigned counsel systems are set up, more lawyers from other specialties will gain experience in the criminal law.

The Office of Economic Opportunity's program of neighborhood legal assistance has been valuable. A defender system like Minnesota's, which pays county defenders on a part-time basis to defend indigent clients, and allows them to represent paying clients as well, promises to be an effective way of attracting able lawyers to the criminal law.

The law schools, too, in recent years have strengthened their criminal law faculties and curricula, and have introduced undergraduate and graduate programs for involving students in criminal practice. About one-half of the law schools have developed clinical programs in which law students work for legal aid and defender agencies under the supervision of faculty and agency lawyers. In some of these programs the student's experience is drawn upon in the classroom study of criminal procedure. In at least nine States, third-year law students are permitted by law to represent indigent defendants charged with misdemeanors at trial. This provides an opportunity for law schools in those States to give their students invaluable training under proper supervision while at the same time improving the quality of representation previously available in those courts and relieving the manpower shortage. Similar programs for the use of law students in the prosecution of cases in the lower courts of Massachusetts are now being instituted by Harvard and Boston University law schools.

A summer internship program in Wisconsin provides a small number of law students with intensive working experience in penitentiaries, with parole and probation supervisors, and with metropolitan police departments. The legal problems they encounter are evaluated during a third-year criminal law seminar. Three graduate internship programs, leading to master's degrees, are used to train lawyers. Two of them concentrate on defenders and trial attorneys and the third on training police legal advisers. They are aimed at producing a group of specialists. The Commission heartily commends such programs and urges that law schools that have not yet adopted them do so.

Criminal law training for all members of the bar is particularly important because of the large number of lawyers who are called from their noncriminal practices to serve as appointed counsel. A national manual for defense attorneys, which is to be annotated for use in each State, is being prepared by the Joint Committee on Continuing Legal Education, the American College of Trial Lawyers, and the National Legal Aid and Defender Association. In some States brief training programs in criminal practice have been developed by local or State bar associations; this example might well be followed elsewhere. Another activity the organized bar could undertake with profit is to develop and promulgate standards of competence in the criminal law and of the ethics of criminal practice. The Commission urges that programs such as these, which have already been devised and are beginning to be put into effect, be greatly accelerated.

While the many existing programs represent important progress, the Commission does not believe either that they are sufficient or that they even approach all that can and must be done to provide the enormously expanded pool of criminal lawyers required to meet the country's needs.

To begin with, the financial incentives must be made much greater. Defenders are usually paid less than prosecutors, and many prosecutors are badly paid. In one of the most prestigious district attorney's offices in the country, New York County's, it takes an assistant 5 years to reach the salary he could reach after a year or so with a successful law firm. This kind of financial sacrifice is too much to ask of a talented young man with a family to support and no private means. Prosecutors' salaries should be raised, and defenders' salaries should be as high as prosecutors'.

The Commission believes that law firms and leaders of the bar have a crucial role to play in meeting the need for criminal lawyers. At present, many able and energetic law school graduates who would otherwise be interested are deterred from going into criminal work bcause they are concerned that, unless they get on the "ladder" in a successful civil practice firm early, they will not be hired by such firms or their progress in the firms will be impeded. Both because the bar as a whole has a professional obligation to strengthen criminal practice and because young men with breadth of experience can contribute greatly to the work of any firm, the Commission believes law firms should not discourage prospective association from a 2- to 5-year stint of defense or prosecution work and should be willing to grant leaves of absence to those of its young lawyers who would like to spend a period in criminal practice and then return. In addition, of

373

course, it is essential that law firms make lawyers available to handle assigned cases, or to assist a defender's office.

It seems appropriate that criminal defense work should attract a high proportion of young lawyers. Even with substantially greater governmental support, compensation in this area is unlikely to be competitive with other kinds of practice, although the experience in understanding the problems of our society, in negotiation, and in trying cases makes it attractive and valuable for young lawyers. The Commission does not believe that only lawyers with many years of criminal practice can handle important cases. The infusion of young lawyers, likely to make greater demands on the system, has already been shown to have had a healthy effect on the system's operations. And having in the successful law firms "alumni" of criminal practice will help to give the leaders of the bar a greater sense of stake in the continuing improvement of criminal administration.

To make the best use of those lawyers who are available for defense work, it is obviously desirable to seek to use persons who are not members of the bar for many of the tasks involved in defense work. This would include factual investigation and exploring such alternative forms of treatment as may be available in lieu of the defendant's running the full course of the criminal system. Residents of the poor neighborhoods, knowledgeable about the problems that are part of the background of particular criminal cases, and about the people connected with those cases, are a promising source of manpower for such jobs. A number of the Neighborhood Legal Services offices financed by the Office of Economic Opportunity are experimenting with the use of such personnel.

The Commission does not believe that these suggestions nearly exhaust the possibilities. It does believe that there is sufficient imagination and freedom of action in the American bar to devise ways, orthodox or unorthodox, for meeting the critical need for manpower in this field. Indeed, the country's estimate of the capability and responsibility of the bar may well be influenced by how well it performs this task.

COURT SCHEDULING, MANAGEMENT AND ORGANIZATION

From the beginning of the criminal process to its end, from police work to correctional work, there is a tension between efficiency—protecting the community from crime—and fairness—protecting the rights of individuals. If these opposing pulls are not kept in balance, the process tends to become either excessively arbitrary, perfunctory, and hasty or excessively deliberate, cumbersome, and dilatory. Every year both pressures are becoming stronger, and the effect of this on the courts is especially conspicuous. The volume of criminal cases is growing, and so cases have to be pushed through crowded courts. Decisions requiring intervention of defense counsel at early stages of the process are becoming more rigorous, and so the deliberation with which cases must be considered is becoming greater.

The Commission is well aware that the preponderant, though not the entire, stress of the recommendations it has made for greater participation by counsel, for more careful procedures, and for fuller information relating to precharge decisions and plea negotiations is in a direction that will slow the process down. A chief purpose of this section is to discuss ways in which the countervailing pull can be strengthened, in which the process can be kept moving in the face of rising volume.

That all too often now it does not move is clear. There are courts in which the normal lapse of time between the preliminary hearing and action by a grand jury is 3 months, and in which persons charged with serious crimes normally await trial for over a year. Such courts make a mockery of bail decisions. It is clearly unfair to a defendant to jail him for months without trial; it is clearly unfair to the community for a defendant charged with a serious crime to be at large for months without trial. Important cases are lost in such courts by attrition. Delay for the sake of delay is often in the interest of a defendant who is guilty and free on bail. If his counsel is allowed to procrastinate by making untenable motions and demanding repeated continuances, the process can be worn down to a point at which witnesses become forgetful or elusive, and the prosecutor may become so anxious to dispose of the case that he dismisses the charge or reduces it excessively in return for a plea of guilty. Such delay undermines the law's deterrent effect by demonstrating that justice is not swift and certain but slow and faltering.

In general, the courts in which these conditions exist are the overcrowded urban courts. Traditionally, the management of a court's calendar—the schedule of what cases are to be heard on a given day—is in the hands of the judge. In a court with a small caseload a judge has little difficulty in keeping track of every case and every defendant. He can remember what motions he has heard and how he ruled on them, how many continuances he has granted and for what reasons, which defendants are in jail and which are not. He

Model Timetable for Felony Cases

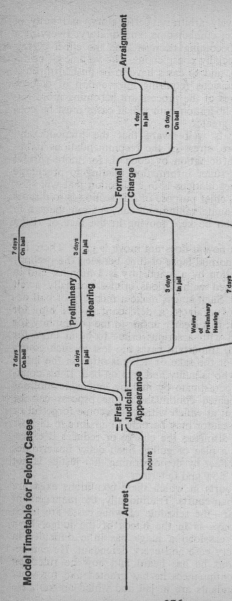

Arrest to First Judicial Appearance. Many States and the Federal courts require appearance "without unnecessary delay." Depending on the circumstances, a few hours—or less—may be regarded as "unnecessary delay." Compliance with this standard may require extension of court operating hours and the continual availability of a magistrate.

First Judicial Appearance to Arraignment. Standards here are complicated because: (a) a shorter period is appropriate for defendants in jail than for those released; (b) preliminary hearings are waived in many cases and the formality and usefulness of the hearing varies; (c) formal charge in some cases is by grand jury indictment, while in others by prosecutor's information—usually the right to indictment can be waived by the defendant; and (d) in many jurisdictions proceedings through preliminary hear-

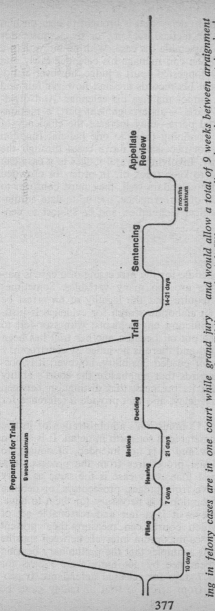

Preparation for Trial
9 weeks maximum

Filing
10 days

Hearing
7 days

Motions
21 days

Deciding

Trial

Sentencing
14-21 days

Appellate Review
5 months maximum

---

ing in felony cases are in one court while grand jury charge and subsequent proceedings are in another. While in all cases these steps should take no more than 17 days, in most cases it should be possible to accomplish them in substantially less time.

Arraignment to Trial. Many of the increasing number of motions require the judge to hear and decide factual issues. Discovery orders may require time for the assembling and screening of documents. The recommended standard would allow slightly more than 5 weeks for these steps and would allow a total of 9 weeks between arraignment and trial. Where complicated motions are not involved, the period before trial should be shortened.

Trial to Sentence. During this period a presentence investigation should be completed.

Sentence to Appellate Review. This standard is based on the time periods of the proposed Uniform Rules of Federal Appellate Procedure. Many jurisdictions would have to change existing practices concerning printing and preparation of records to meet this standard.

can resist the pressure to delay that is brought to bear on him by defense counsel for tactical reasons, or by a prosecutor who has been slow to assemble his case. With no more than a sketchy set of records he can manage his calendar fairly and efficiently. In a badly congested court a judge, however elaborate and faithfully kept his records are and however fair and efficient he is, often cannot manage his calendar. And dividing the courts into "parts"—an arraignment part, a motions part, a number of trial parts—may increase the efficiency of individual judges by confining them to one judicial function at a time, but does not necessarily move cases through the process more promptly. Involving several judges in a case can make the case harder to keep track of. In order for crowded courts to manage their calendars well, they must conform to agreed-upon standards of performance, use up-to-date administrative and technological techniques, and be subject to central supervision.

A MODEL TIMETABLE

A rigid advance schedule for the processing of a case is patently unfeasible. There are too many variables. Sometimes motions to suppress require that the legality of an arrest be examined at length; an elaborate search for evidence is justified; lawyers have conflicting engagements; witnesses fail to appear; a trial must be put off because another trial has been unexpectedly prolonged and there is no judge or courtroom.

Making allowance for needed flexibility, however, it is possible to establish standards that emphasize the court's ability to deal efficiently with its business, that distinguish between needless and necessary delay, and that provide a reference for court management.

In the report of the Commission's administration of justice task force, a model timetable is set forth in detail. It is shown in graphic form below and it is not intended, of course, to eliminate any traditional procedures from the process. It is not intended to suggest that every case is the same as every other case or to remove from judges, prosecutors, or defense counsel any of the discretion it is necessary for them to have. The Commission believes it is a fair and reasonable set of guidelines against which courts can measure their present performance. It proposes maximum intervals between specific steps in the process, for example, that the preliminary hearing follow the initial appearance by not more than 3 days for jailed defendants and 7 days for released defendants. It proposes that the period from arrest to trial of felony cases be

378

not more than 4 months and that the period from trial to appellate decision be within 5 months—that, in short, the entire process take no more than 9 months. In chapter 11 of this report an experimental computer simulation of the workload of an existing court is described. This effort indicates the feasibility of the time standards described in the model timetable and shows the usefulness of this approach as part of an analysis of court operations.

Court administrators should collect regularly reported information on the time the courts are taking to dispose of cases and should measure this experience against the standards. Delay may be met by a variety of measures including assignment of additional judges; calling extra or longer sessions of courts; special priorities for criminal cases; the public reporting of courts experiencing special delay; and, particularly when excessive delay is experienced between arraignment and trial, by the establishment of special parts and calandars in which particularly vigorous efforts may be made to deal with stalled cases. Establishment of the timetable by a court or court system can be by local rule, by calendar order, or, where rule-making power is totally lacking, by legislation.

The Commission recommends:

Courts and court systems should establish standards for the completion of the various stages of criminal cases. These standards should be designed to be within the capabilities of deliberate court consideration of cases, yet also should ensure that the disposition of cases shall be expeditious. Where existing court facilities are inadequate to enable cases to be disposed of in a reasonably short time, the need for greater resources and reform of procedures is demonstrated.

TECHNICAL MANAGEMENT

A requisite for the implementation of a timetable is that courts know at all times what the cases before them are and at what stages they are. In an age when new management techniques and business machines have revolutionized many business and government operations, the courts' business procedures have remained in most places very much like those of a former age. The use of multiple long-hand entries, cumbersome dockets, and inefficient filing and indexing systems with limited retrieval capacity persists in many courts because the volume of cases has not been so great as to cause the system to break down. Increasing urbanization has placed great new pressures upon these courts, however, and has highlighted the inadequacy and obsolescence of the business methods used.

In some of the largest cities the volume of criminal court business has reached a point at which the use of computers and automatic business machines is being instituted to maintain an orderly flow of clerical business. While there does not yet appear to be a pressing need for the use of such elaborate equipment in medium sized cities, many of their courts do need to reorganize and modernize their manual clerical methods through better forms, filing systems, and indexing and scheduling methods. Modern technical management holds promise for enabling these courts to perform their job more quickly and cheaply by improving the retrieval of information, the scheduling of cases, and the maintenance of records.

The Commission urges courts and court administrators to seek the advice and assistance of experts in business management and business machine systems in an effort to develop plans and forms for more efficient court business systems.

CENTRAL SUPERVISION AND PROFESSIONAL ADMINISTRATION

For cases to move expeditiously through a court with many judges and thousands of cases, it is necessary that all the cases and all the judges be centrally supervised. Central supervision of cases makes it possible to keep track of the status of every case, to shift cases from one judge to another according to their various caseloads, to set up special calendars for cases that inherently demand prompt action or that have fallen behind the normal schedule. Central supervision of judges makes it possible to assign judges appropriately, to set up work and vacation schedules that all judges are expected to conform to, and to press dilatory judges to act more speedily.

Of course, the supervision of calendars and judges is a judicial function. It could be performed by a court's chief justice, or by a small administrative committee of judges, or by an administrative judge appointed for this purpose. Whatever form central supervision takes, large and complicated courts need the services of professional administrators to assist the judges charged with administration. Some thirty States have provided for an administrative office to aid the judiciary by collecting judicial statistics, managing fiscal affairs, supervising court personnel, and performing duties in connection with the assignment of judges and scheduling of cases. In many of these States, however, the functions of this office are limited, and its potential has not yet been realized. By bringing men into courts with training and a primary interest in management, techniques of court management will be improved. Court administration is a developing field in which a clear understanding of techniques is evolving. There is a need for more experimentation and increased use of promising methods for ordering the business of the courts.

The Commission recommends:

States should provide for clear administrative responsibility within courts and should ensure that professional court administrators are available to assist the judges in their management functions.

JURORS AND WITNESSES

A problem closely related to the administration of the courts is the treatment of citizens whose primary contact with the criminal courts is as jurors or witnesses. For many law-abiding citizens this experience with the courts forms the basis for their impression of the fairness, sensitivity, and efficiency of the system. The successful prosecution of criminals depends upon citizens reporting crimes to the police and being willing to appear as witnesses at trial. Whether the jury system works depends on the willingness of citizens to serve. Yet in many places negative attitudes toward the administration of justice are reinforced by citizens' experiences as witnesses or jurors.

Physical facilities for waiting witnesses and jurors as a rule are inadequate or nonexistent, with the result that these persons must spend long periods standing in hallways or sitting in the back of courtrooms. Little consideration is generally given to the convenience of witnesses, who are required to appear on a number of occasions only to learn, after a long wait in court, that the case is adjourned or disposed of and that their appearance was not necessary.

Witness and juror fees are extremely modest. In one urban court witnesses receive 75 cents a day and in the Federal system jurors receive $4 a day. This economic sacrifice by wage earners and small businessmen cannot be justified as a duty of citizenship or on any other ground. Particular problems are posed by policemen who frequently are called upon as witnesses. Often they must appear on their own time, and in

381

their case delay has a direct effect upon law enforcement in the field.

The Commission recommends:

The Federal and State Governments should improve physical facilities and compensation for witnesses and jurors, expand the use of scheduling and witness call systems to reduce unnecessary appearances and waiting, and, except in cases where there is to be an immediate hearing on the arrest or charge, substitute sworn statements for the appearance of the arresting police officer at the initial court appearance.

COURT REORGANIZATION

While in some States successful court reform has created courts able to meet new demands, in many States the entire court structure continues to reflect an earlier age. There is a multiplicity of trial courts without coherent and centralized administrative management. Jurisdictional lines are unnecessarily complex and confusing. Each court and each judge within the court constitute a distinct administrative unit, moving at its own pace and in its own way. In a number of States courts not responsible to a statewide system nor subject to its management continue to be viewed as a source of local revenue, and criminal justice is seen as a profitmaking activity.

Modern management and efficiency can be promoted by putting all courts and judges within a State under a single, central administration with provision for the shifting and allocation of judicial and administrative manpower to meet changing requirements.

For this to be effective the judiciary must be given rulemaking power over the methods used to handle its business. It is important that men continuously and intimately involved with court procedures be responsible for court rules. Legislatures cannot deal with the technical problems of court management and procedure effectively. In most States the rulemaking power is lodged in the Supreme Court, a judicial conference, or some other body of judges.

The Commission recommends:

States should reexamine their court structure and organization and create a single, unified system of courts subject to central administrative management within the judiciary. The Commission urges States that have not yet reformed their

court systems to draw upon the experience of those States and organizations that have made advances in this area. Central administration within the judiciary should have the power to make rules and shift manpower to meet changing requirements.

Chapter 6

Corrections

"CORRECTIONS," AMERICA'S prisons, jails, juvenile training schools, and probation and parole machinery, is the part of the criminal justice system that the public sees least of and knows least about. It seldom gets into the news unless there is a jail break, a prison riot, or a sensational scandal involving corruption or brutality in an institution or by an official. The institutions in which about a third of the corrections population lives are situated for the most part in remote rural areas, or in the basements of police stations or courthouses. The other two-thirds of the corrections population are on probation and parole, and so are widely, and on the whole invisibly, dispersed in the community. Corrections is not only hard to see; traditionally, society has been reluctant to look at it. Many of the people, juvenile and adult, with whom corrections deals are the most troublesome and troubling members of society: The misfits and the failures, the unrespectable and the irresponsible. Society has been well content to keep them out of sight.

Its invisibility belies the system's size, complexity, and crucial importance to the control of crime. Corrections consists of scores of different kinds of institutions and programs of the utmost diversity in approach, facilities, and quality. On any given day it is responsible for approximately 1.3 million offenders. In the course of a year it handles nearly 2.5 million admissions, and spends over a billion dollars doing so. If it could restore all or even most of these people to the community as responsible citizens, America's crime rate would drop significantly. For as it is today, a substantial percentage of offenders become recidivists; they go on to commit more, and as chapter 11 shows, often more serious crimes.

For a great many offenders, then, corrections does not correct. Indeed, experts are increasingly coming to feel that the conditions under which many offenders are handled, particularly in institutions, are often positive detriment to rehabilitation.

Life in many institutions is at best barren and futile, at worst unspeakably brutal and degrading. To be sure, the offenders in such institutions are incapacitated from committing further crimes while serving their sentences, but the conditions in which they live are the poorest possible preparation for their successful reentry into society, and often merely reinforce in them a pattern of manipulation or destructiveness.

These conditions are to a great extent the result of a drastic shortage of resources together with widespread ignorance as to how to use the resources available. Moreover, corrections by its very nature must always work at the "end of the line" of the criminal justice system, with those whose problems have overtaxed the resources of other systems.

However, there are hopeful signs that far-reaching changes can be made in present conditions. The Commission found, in the course of its work, a number of imaginative and dedicated people at work in corrections. It found a few systems where their impact, and enlightened judicial and legislative correctional policies, had already made a marked difference; a few experimental programs whose results in terms of reduced recidivism were dramatic. A start has been made in developing methods of classification that will permit more discriminating selection of techniques to treat particular types of offenders. But many of the new ideas, while supported by logic and some experience, are yet to be scientifically evaluated. Nevertheless, the potential for change is great.

As a foundation for its work, the Commission decided that a comprehensive, nationwide survey of correctional operations should be undertaken. Relevant information existed in bits and pieces around the country, but there was no overall picture of American corrections. The structure of probation and parole programs, institutions, theories, and procedures that together make up corrections is extremely complex and diverse. A few jurisdictions have relatively small probation caseloads, an integrated system of institutions, well-trained staffs, and a variety of experimental programs. Others consist of several autonomous and antiquated county jails, a state training school for juveniles, and a huge prison farm where convicts toil under the surveillance of trusties armed with shotguns.

It was necessary for the Commission to survey all of the disparate segments of the system so that its analysis and recommendations would not simply perpetuate the existing state of fragmented and inadequate knowledge. The Commission, therefore, in collaboration with the Office of Law Enforcement Assistance, arranged for the National Council on Crime and Delinquency, an independent, nationwide group with long experience in the corrections field, to undertake the necessary survey. The detailed report of this survey is presented in the corrections task force volume.

BACKGROUND OF CORRECTIONS TODAY

The survey gave the first accurate national picture of the number of offenders under correctional authority on an average day: 1.3 million (table 1). This total is so much larger

Table 1.—Average Daily Population in Corrections

1965:	
Misdemeanant	342,688
Juvenile	348,204
Adult felon	591,494
Total, 1965	1,282,386
1975:	
Misdemeanant	482,000
Juvenile	588,000
Adult felon	771,000
Total estimated, 1975	1,841,000

SOURCES: 1965 figures computed from the National Survey of Corrections and tabulations provided by the Federal Bureau of Prisons and the Administrative Office of the U.S. Courts; 1975 projections computed by the task force on science and technology.

than had ever before been estimated that it has startled even those familiar with the field. It overtaxes the facilities, programs, and personnel of the correctional system badly. Moreover, if present trends in arrests and convictions continue, the system 10 years from now will be facing even more extreme pressures. The juvenile system, because of the rapid increase in the number of young people in the population, will be the most hard pressed. Adult probation and parole treatment will also suffer, because of the trend toward probation or early parole rather than prolonged confinement. In recent years, adult institutional commitments have been leveling off.

Offenders themselves differ strikingly. Some seem irrevocably committed to criminal careers; others subscribe to quite conventional values; still others, probably the majority, are aimless and uncommitted to goals of any kind. Many are disturbed and frustrated youths. Many others are alcoholics, narcotics addicts, victims of senility, and sex deviants. This diversity poses immense problems for correctional officials, for in most places the many special offender groups must be managed within large, general-purpose programs. The superintendent of an institution must meet the challenge of especially hostile and violent inmates, respond appropriately to those who are mentally disordered, guard against the smuggling and use of narcotics, provide instruction and supervision for the mentally retarded, and handle the dangerous and intricate problem of sexual deviance—all within a locked and artificial world.

Beneath the diversities, certain characteristics predominate. A great majority of offenders are male. Most of them are young: in the age range between 16 and 30. The life histories of most of them document the ways in which the social and economic factors discussed in chapters 2 and 3 contribute to crime and delinquency. Education is as good a barometer as any of the likelihood of success in modern urban society; as figure 1 shows, a high proportion of offenders are severely handicapped educationally. Many of them have dropped out of school.

Offenders also tend to have unstable work records and, as shown by figure 2, a lack of vocational skill.

A large proportion come from backgrounds of poverty, and many are members of groups that suffer economic and social disadvantage. Material failure, then, in a culture firmly oriented toward material success, is the most common denominator of offenders. Some have been automatically excluded from economic and social opportunity; some have been disqualified by lack of native abilities; some may simply not have tried hard enough. Many, too, have failed in their relationships with their families and friends. Offenders, adult or juvenile, usually have little self-esteem, and for some it is only when they are undergoing correction that they get a first glimmering of their personal worth.

CORRECTIONAL ADMINISTRATION

The differences among offenders do not account for the

Comparison of Educational Levels —Federal and State Felony Inmates   Figure 1

	Years of School Completed	%	General Population	Inmate Population	%
College	4 years or more	8.4			1.1
	1 to 3 years	9.4			4.2
High School	4 years	27.5			12.4
	1 to 3 years	20.7			27.6
Elementary	5 to 8 years	28			40.3
	4 years to none	6			14.4

Source: U.S. Department of Labor, Manpower Administration, Office of Manpower Policy, Evaluation, and Research, based on data from the U.S. Department of Commerce, Bureau of the Census.

Comparison of Occupational Experience —Federal and State Felony Inmates (Males) Figure 2

	%	General Labor Force	Inmate Prior Work Experience	%
Professional and technical workers	10.4			2.2
Managers and owners, incl. farm	16.3			4.3
Clerical and sales	14.2			7.1
Craftsmen, foremen	20.6			17.6
Operatives	21.2			25.2
Service workers, incl. household	6.4			11.5
Laborers (except mine) incl. farm laborers and foremen	10.8			31.9

[1] All data are for males only; since the correctional institution population is 95 percent male, data for males were used to eliminate the effects of substantial differences between male and female occupational employment patterns.

Source: U.S. Department of Labor, Manpower Administration, Office of Manpower Policy, Evaluation, and Research, based on data from U.S. Department of Commerce, Bureau of the Census.

most salient differences among correctional facilities and procedures. These can be traced, rather, to historical development, administrative fragmentation, and divergent and unreconciled purposes and theories.

Table 2 shows the diversity of American corrections with respect to size and cost.

The Federal Government, all 50 States, the District of Columbia, the Commonwealth of Puerto Rico, most of the country's 3,047 counties, and all except the smallest cities engage in correctional activities—if only maintaining a primitive jail in which to lock up overnight those who are "drunk and disorderly." Each level of government typically acts independently of the others. The Federal Government has no direct control over State corrections. The States usually have responsibility for prisons and parole programs, but probation is frequently tied to court administration as a county or municipal function. Counties do not have jurisdiction over the jails operated by cities and towns.

Responsibility for the administration of corrections is divided not only among levels of government, but also within single jurisdictions. There has been a strong historic tendency for juvenile and adult corrections to follow separate paths. Public support for rehabilitative programs first developed in connection with juveniles. Today, progressive programs for adults resemble progressive programs for juveniles, but more often than not they are administered separately to the detriment of overall planning and of continuity of programing for offenders. The ambiguity and awkwardness resulting from this division is nowhere more apparent than in the handling of older adolescent and young adult offenders, who often defy precise classification and are dealt with maladroitly by both the juvenile and the adult correctional systems.

Much the same is true of the historical barriers that exist between institutional and community programs. Parole and probation services have often held themselves aloof from jails and prisons, and they are frequently run entirely separately. One result often is that the transition between the way an offender is handled in an institution and his supervision in the community is irrationally abrupt. And of course there are also vast differences in many places between programs in such misdemeanant institutions as jails and workhouses, and those in State prisons and training schools.

THE PERSONNEL OF CORRECTIONS

More than 121,000 people were employed in corrections in

Table 2.—Some National Characteristics of Corrections, 1965

	Average daily population of offenders	Total operating costs	Average cost of offender per year	Number of employees in corrections	Number of employees treating offenders
Juvenile corrections:					
Institutions	62,773	$226,809,600	$3,613	31,687	5,621
Community	285,431	93,613,400	328	9,633	7,706
Subtotal	348,204	320,423,000			
Adult felon corrections:					
Institutions	221,597	435,594,500	1,966	51,866	3,220
Community	369,897	73,251,900	198	6,352	5,081
Subtotal	591,494	508,846,400			
Misdemeanant corrections:					
Institutions	141,303	147,794,200	1,046	19,195	501
Community	201,385	28,682,900	142	2,430	1,944
Subtotal	342,688	176,477,100			
Total	1,282,386	1,005,746,500		121,163	24,073

SOURCES: National Survey of Corrections and tabulations provided by the Federal Bureau of Prisons and the Administrative Office of the U.S. Courts.

1965. Only a small proportion of correctional staff had treatment and rehabilitation as their primary function. Twenty-four thousand, or 20 percent of the staff, were probation and parole officers working in the community, and educators, social workers, psychologists, and psychiatrists working in institutions. By contrast, 80 percent of correctional manpower had major responsibility for such functions as custody and maintenance.

Correctional agencies across the country face acute shortages of qualified manpower, especially in positions charged with responsibility for treatment and rehabilitation. Thousands of additional staff are required now to achieve minimum standards for effective treatment and control. Many more thousands will be needed in the next decade.

HISTORY AND THEORY

The oldest part of the correctional apparatus is institutional confinement. Until the middle of the 18th century, execution and such corporal punishments as flogging and pillorying were the principal means by which society dealt with offenders. Their replacement by imprisonment arose from both the growing spirit of humanitarianism that accompanied the "Enlightenment" in Western Europe, and in the effect of the philosophy of utilitarianism developed in the late 18th and early 19th centuries. Criminals were no longer seen as men and women possessed by evil demons that had to be exorcised by corporal punishment or death. They were persons who had deliberately chosen to violate the law because it gave them pleasure or profit.

Imprisonment was seen on the one hand as a punitive sanction to deter lawbreaking by making it painful rather than pleasant. On the other hand, unlike corporal punishment and execution, it gave an offender an opportunity to reflect in solitude over his wrong choices and to mend his ways. Not incidentally, of course, incarceration also prevented an offender from committing further harm against the community, which corporal punishment short of execution did not.

Many legacies of these philosophical developments run through corrections today. They can be seen in much prison architecture for adult felons, grim and fortresslike, with tier upon tier of individual cells arranged chiefly with a view of security. They can be seen in the daily regimen of many such institutions, too, though in most cases this has been mitigated by later correctional movements. The wide gulf between inmates and staff in many prisons, maintained by restrictions on "fraternization," rules of address, and constant rollcalls and inspections, is part of this. Impersonality extends to dress, restrictions on conversation with other prisoners, and the way in which prisoners are marched in groups from cells to dining hall to shop. Cells are usually small and bare, with prisoners locked into them at night and out of them—and into shops, recreation rooms, or simply hallways—during the day. Juvenile training schools, though their architecture and their routine are far less forbidding, too often emphasize in subtle ways that restraint is their primary purpose and treatment a casual afterthought.

A prisoner under this sort of regimen is expected to "do his own time" aloof from staff and other inmates, and his release may often be accelerated or postponed according to his good or bad behavior in this peculiar institutional setting rather than his preparedness to enter the world outside. Many institutions, especially those for juveniles have counselors, teachers, and chaplains whose charge it is to aid in the process of rehabilitation, but their limited role and number typically make significant rehabilitative efforts impossible. Shops and farms or other work activities too often are operated primarily because of their value to the state and conducted in a fashion useless for instruction in skills and habits needed to succeed in the community.

This model of corrections has further inadequacies. With offenders of all kinds confined together and handled indiscriminately without close staff contact, a special inmate culture may develop that is deleterious to everyone, and especially the juvenile, who is exposed for the first time to it. Certain inmates—often the most aggressive—assume control over the others with tacit staff consent; in some adult institutions this situation is formalized through the use of "trusties"—sometimes armed—to carry the burden of close supervision. Rackets, violence, corruption, coerced homosexuality, and other abuses may exist without staff intervention. The physical inadequacy of the older prisons has been compounded in most cases by severe overcrowding. At best, however, their construction is unsuited to most rehabilitative programs. It is difficult to hold group counseling sessions when there are no rooms of a size between cells and the dining hall; difficult to release prisoners during the day to settle themselves into regular jobs in the community when the nearest town is miles away; difficult more generally to promote self-discipline and responsible independence in an institution architecturally dedicated to intimate and constant authoritarian control.

These conditions have given rise to a whole series of

393

changes, beginning as long ago as the latter part of the 19th century. Authorities in most jurisdictions began to realize that mere restraint could not accomplish the purpose of corrections, and that many of the features of prison life actually intensified the problems of offenders. The resulting determination to undertake more positive efforts at reformation was accompanied by the recognition that motivation was more than a matter of rational choice between good and evil, and that psychological treatment might thus be a necessary part of corrections. It was also recognized that the useful occupation of prisoners in shops, farms, classes, and recreation would ease institutional tensions and contribute to an atmosphere less detrimental to rehabilitation.

The reform model reshaped all roles in the correctional system. No longer was the offender regarded as a morally deficient person, to be controlled by a keeper. Instead he became, for some purposes at least, a "patient." The old rule—"Let the punishment fit the crime"—was replaced by a new maxim—"Let the treatment fit the needs of the individual offender."

On the reform model was built a far more complex approach to corrections than had existed before. This new approach began with and has gained most ground with juveniles, who had previously been imprisoned indiscriminately with adults, but now began to be treated separately. A wide range of services was to be provided: Education; vocational training; religious guidance; and eventually psychotherapy in its various forms. Prison schools and counselors would help some; prison industries would accustom others to the beneficial effects of regular employment as against the irregular gains of crime. The main focus was on the individual—on correcting him.

The new ideals led to the development of different kinds of institutions. Medium-security prisons were built that had fences rather than walls and guard towers, rooms rather than cells, locked doors and windows rather than bars. Minimum-security facilities showed even greater departures: Schools where offenders lived in cottages, forestry camps and farms where they lived in barracks without locks and worked without armed surveillance. Facilities were created for women, for youths, for reception and diagnosis, for prerelease and postrelease guidance, for medical and psychiatric treatment, for alcoholics, for addicts, for sexual psychopaths, and for others.

Some of the reforms have been notable. The Federal prison system and several State systems have taken leadership in bringing about many of the changes discussed later in this chapter—from such important atmosphere changes as dining facilities with small tables to modern prison industries and programed learning. The progress that these reforms have made has not been uniform or free from complications, however. The old buildings were built in the stoutest fashion, and it has been difficult to secure their replacement. Today there are 25 prisons in the United States over a hundred years old. Old methods and evils have been perpetuated as well as old architecture. In some States juveniles are still jailed with adults. In a few, the bulk of the corrections population is still employed on vast farms raising cash crops under conditions scarcely distinguishable from slavery. Flogging is still practiced in at least one place as discipline even for such offenses as "overlooking okra"—carelessness in harvesting. But a more pervasive evil is idleness; this is especially destructive where there are no industries, no educational programs, no recreational facilities—only aimless loitering in corridors or yards.

Where it has come, the process of reform has not always been smooth. Those in the field have sometimes lacked the inclination, and have almost always lacked the resources, to evaluate their new programs carefully. There has been a tendency for the correctional field to adopt new or seemingly new programs in an impulsive, sometimes faddish manner, only to replace them later with some more recent innovation. Much supposed progress really has been only circular movement. "New" approaches turn out to be devices tried elsewhere under a different name. The advance guard of corrections in one jurisdiction may be stressing individual and family therapy; in another, vocational training and job placement; and in still another, group treatment relying upon the influence of fellow offenders to accomplish rehabilitation. Frustration in achieving clear results sometimes leads officials to drop one approach and move on to a completely new one, or to add treatment methods one on the other without clearly distinguishing their purposes.

Correction of offenders has also labored under what is coming to be seen as a fundamental deficiency in approach. All of the past phases in the evolution of corrections accounted for criminal and delinquent behavior primarily on the basis of some form of defect within the individual offender. The idea of being possessed by devils was replaced with the idea of psychological disability. Until recently reformers have tended to ignore the evidence that crime and delinquency are symptoms of the disorganization of the community as well as of individual personalities, and that community institutions —through extending or denying their resources—have a critical influence in determining the success or failure of an individual offender.

The responsibility for community treatment and supervision has been entrusted mainly to probation and parole services. As noted, these programs handle far more offenders than do institutions. Probation—supervision in the community in lieu of imprisonment—was first established for juveniles almost a century ago, and is now at least superficially available for both juveniles and adult felons in a majority of States. Very little probation service is available to misdemeanants.

Parole, the postincarceration equivalent of probation, dating from about the same period, is also widely used for juveniles and felons, but seldom for misdemeanants.

Often probation and parole are separately administered, probation as a service to the courts and parole as a part of State correctional agencies. Probation officers typically spend much time preparing sentencing reports for judges in addition to supervising offenders. Parole officers perform like functions for parole boards in providing information relative to decisions to grant or revoke parole.

Supervision consists basically of a combination of surveillance and counseling, drawing partly upon the methods identified with social casework, but distinguished by the need to enforce authoritative limits and standards of behavior. Offenders are put on probation or released on parole subject to certain conditions: That they stay out of trouble; that they maintain regular employment or stay in school; that they not drink or use narcotics; and usually that they obtain permission for such steps as getting married, changing jobs or residence, or leaving the jurisdiction. The probation or parole officer's first duty is to "keep track" of his cases and see that they comply with these conditions. Often he has little time even for this function.

If this were the whole of the job, it still would not be easy to accomplish in most jurisdictions. But in fact probation and parole supervision aims at much more. An officer is expected to offer counseling and guidance and to help in getting a job or in straightening out family difficulties. In practice he is almost always too pressed to do this well. Probation and parole supervision typically consists of a 10- or 15-minute interview once or twice a month, during which the officer questions and admonishes his charge, refers him to an employment agency or a public health clinic, and makes notations for the reports he must file. The great pressures on these officers make it difficult for them to exercise evenly and knowledgeably the tremendous discretion they have in recommending the revocation or continuation of community treatment when offenders under their supervision get into trouble.

There are, of course, many exceptions to this picture, some of them very impressive—experiments with small caseloads of offenders classified on the basis of need and given carefully prescribed treatment, and with agencies that use teams of caseworkers and have specialized services such as psychiatric treatment, legal advice, job placement, and remedial tutoring.

The challenge facing parole and probation officers is increased by the growing sense that the efforts of correctional officials should be directed toward both the offender and the community institutions—school, work, religion, and recreation—with which he must effect a reconciliation if he is to avoid further crimes. It is of little use to improve the reading skills and motivation of a juvenile offender if the community school system will not receive him when he is placed on parole, or if it cannot provide usable instruction for him. It makes little sense for a correctional institution to offer vocational training if an offender cannot find related work when he returns to the community. The process of repairing defects in the individual must be combined with the opening of opportunities for satisfying participation in community life, opportunities that lead toward legitimate success and away from illicit and destructive ways of life. For most offenders, however, the doors to legitimate opportunity are hard to find and harder to open.

There is a growing appreciation within the field of the irrationality that runs through much of correctional practice today: Of having such sharp lines between institutional and community treatment, between juvenile and adult programs, between local jails and State prisons; of spending so much on custody and so little on rehabilitation; of focusing so heavily on security during incarceration and so little on supervision to protect the community once an offender is returned to it.

While recent public opinion polls show increasing public sympathy with rehabilitative goals, conflict and uncertainty about the theories behind and the goals of corrections have impaired broad support for needed experiments and changes. Correctional treatment designed to meet the offender's needs is often (although not always) less burdensome and unpleasant than traditional forms of treatment. Thus, rehabilitation efforts may to some extent conflict with the deterrent goal of the criminal system and, if treatment is in the community instead of in prison, with the goal of incapacitating the offender from committing further crime. But the issue is not simply whether new correctional methods amount to "coddling." A major goal of corrections is to make the community safer by preventing the offender's return to crime upon his release.

COMMUNITY-BASED CORRECTIONS

With two-thirds of the total corrections caseload under probation or parole supervision today, the central question is no longer whether to handle offenders in the community but how to do so safely and successfully. Clearly, there is a need to incarcerate those criminals who are dangerous until they no longer are a threat to the community. However, for the large bulk of offenders, particularly the youthful, the first or the minor offender, institutional commitments can cause more problems than they solve.

Institutions tend to isolate offenders from society, both physically and psychologically, cutting them off from schools, jobs, families, and other supportive influences and increasing the probability that the label of criminal will be indelibly impressed upon them. The goal of reintegration is likely to be furthered much more readily by working with offenders in the community than by incarceration.

Additionally other goals are met. One is economy. In 1965 it cost, on the average, about $3,600 a year to keep a youngster in a training school, while it cost less than one-tenth that amount to keep him on probation. Even allowing for the substantial improvements in salaries and personnel needed to make community programs more effective, they are less costly. This is especially true when construction costs, which now run up to $20,000 for each bed in a children's institution, are included. The differential becomes even greater if the costs of welfare for the families of the incarcerated, as well as the loss of taxable income, are included.

Various studies have sought to measure the success of community treatment. One summary analysis of 15 different studies of probation outcomes indicates that from 60 to 90 percent of the probationers studied completed terms without revocation. In another study, undertaken in California, 11,638 adult probationers who were granted probation during 1956 to 1958 were followed up after 7 years. Of this group almost 72 percent completed their probation terms without revocation.

These findings were not obtained under controlled conditions, nor were they supported by data that distinguished among the types of offenders who succeeded or among the types of services that were rendered. But they are the product of a variety of probation services administered at different times and places and provide some evidence that well planned and administered community programs can be successful in reducing recidivism. These findings, combined with the data from the national survey of corrections showing that probation and parole services are characteristically poorly staffed and often poorly administered, suggest that improvement in the quality of community treatment should be a major goal.

INSURING AVAILABILITY OF PROBATION AND PAROLE SUPERVISION

The Commission's survey of corrections disclosed that there are still a significant number of jurisdictions that lack probation or parole facilities of any sort for misdemeanant offenders. Of the 250 counties studied in the national corrections survey, one-third provided no probation service at all. Institutionalization and outright release on suspended sentence without supervision are the only alternatives in such jurisdictions. Most misdemeanants are released from local institutions and jails without parole; information obtained in the survey from a sample of 212 local jails indicated that 131 of them (62 percent) had no parole procedure. In the other 81, only 8 percent of the inmates were in fact released on parole; thus 92 percent were simply discharged at the expiration of their sentences.

All States appear to have community supervision facilities for juvenile offenders and adult felons, but in some jurisdictions these are no more than nominal. Many small juvenile courts, for example, rely almost entirely on release on suspended sentence in lieu of probation supervision, and their judges attempt to keep a check on those released as best they can, often with the assistance of the local police.

These inadequacies can have serious consequences. Lack of community treatment facilities for misdemeanants and juveniles means the neglect of one of the most important lines of defense against serious crimes, since many persons with juvenile or misdemeanant records graduate to graver offenses. Lack of probation facilities also may mean that many minor and first-time offenders, who would be more suitably and economically dealt with in the community, are instead institutionalized. And lack of supervision, particularly through parole, means that the community is being exposed to unnecessary risks and that offenders are going without assistance in reestablishing themselves in jobs and schools.

The Commission recommends:

Parole and probation services should be available in all jurisdictions for felons, juveniles, and those adult misdemeanants who need or can profit from community treatment.

If a prisoner serves his term without having been paroled, in most places he is released into the community without any guidance or supervision. But in the Federal system, and in several States, when an inmate is released before his maximum term because of good behavior, he is subject to supervision in the community for a period equivalent to his "good time credit." He is released to a parole officer under the same conditions as an inmate who is paroled, and he can be returned to prison to serve out his sentence if he violates those conditions.

The Commission recommends:

Every State should provide that offenders who are not paroled receive adequate supervision after release unless it is determined to be unnecessary in a specific case.

THE NEED FOR INCREASED MANPOWER

The statistics from the national survey of corrections make clear the vastness of the community treatment task and the inadequacy of the resources available to accomplish it. They do not convey the everyday problems and frustrations that result from that disparity. These take many forms. For example:

☐ A probation officer meets with a 16-year-old boy who 2 months previously was placed on probation for having stolen a car. The boy begins to talk. He explains that he began to "slip into the wrong crowd" a year or so after his stepfather died. He says that it would help him to talk about it. But there is no time; the waiting room is full, and the boy is not scheduled to come back for another 15-minute conference until next month.

☐ A parole officer feels that a 29-year-old man, on parole after serving 3 years for burglary, is heading for trouble. He frequently is absent from his job, and there is a report of his hanging around a bar with a bad reputation. The parole officer thinks that now is a critical time to straighten things out—before it is too late. He tries unsuc-cessfully two or three times to reach his man by tele-phone, and considers going out to look for him. He decides against it. He is already far behind in dictating "revocations" on parolees who have failed and are being returned to prison.

☐ A young, enthusiastic probation officer goes to see his su-pervisor and presents a plan for "something different," a group counseling session to operate three evenings a week for juvenile probationers and their parents. The supervi-sor tells him to forget it. "You've got more than you can handle now getting up presentence reports for the judge. Besides, we don't have any extra budget for a psychiatrist to help out."

In these situations the offender is denied the counseling and supervision that are the main objects of probation and parole. Because the probation or parole officer is too over-worked to provide these services, the offender is left on his own. If he does not succeed, he loses and the community loses.

On the basis of information gathered in the corrections survey, it is possible to form a general picture of the magni-tude of need for additional probation and parole officers if they are simply to carry on orthodox supervision at the case-load levels widely accepted as the maximum possible. Figure 3 on the following page shows the average present caseload sizes of probation officers. The findings of the survey are alarming:

☐ In the juvenile field there is an immediate need to in-crease the number of probation and parole officers from the present 7,706 to approximately 13,800. This man-power pool would mean caseloads of 35 offenders per of-ficer, and would permit additional time for the hundreds of thousands of diagnostic investigations needed each year by juvenile courts. It is estimated that a total of 23,000 of-ficers will be required by 1975 to carry out the functions essential to community treatment of juveniles.

☐ For adult felons there is an immediate need for almost three times the number of probation and parole officers currently employed. This estimate again is based on an average caseload size of 35, for while adult probation and parole caseloads have typically been somewhat larger than those of juvenile systems, this difference is more a reflection of historical factors than one justified by a difference in need. On this basis, too, population projections point to a requirement of a total of 23,000 officers in 1975.

☐ The need for officers for misdemeanants is staggering; 15,400 officers are needed as against 1,944 currently employed. The number needed in 1975 is estimated at 22,000. This forecast, unlike those for adult felony and juvenile officers, is based upon needs for officers to supervise only the rather modest proportion of the misdemeanant group that could be aided in the community, plus others to provide minimal screening and classification services for the roughly 5 million persons referred to the lower courts each year. Many of the latter, particularly alcoholics, could be diverted from the criminal justice system if identified in time.

The Commission recommends:

All jurisdictions should examine their need for probation and parole officers on the basis of an average ratio of 35 offenders per officer, and make an immediate start toward recruiting additional officers on the basis of that examination.

Standards for average caseload size serve a useful purpose in estimating the magnitude of present and future needs for probation and parole officers. But in operation there is no single optimum caseload size. Indeed, in the Commission's opinion, it would be a mistake to approach the problem of upgrading community treatment solely in terms of strengthening orthodox supervision to bring caseload sizes down to universal maximum standards. Such an approach would ignore the need for specialized caseloads to deal differently with particular types of offenders, and for changes in the standard procedure that results in an offender being supervised by only one officer.

Furthermore many of the answers to manpower needs must be found outside the mold of the existing system. There is, for example, great promise in employing subprofessionals and volunteers in community corrections. Much work performed today by probation and parole officers could be effectively handled by persons without graduate training in social work or the behavioral science. In fact, organizing teams of workers within which the tasks of investigating, monitoring, helping, and guiding offenders are divided in a logical manner, would permit more specialized and individualized attention.

The use of subprofessionals and volunteers could significantly reduce the need for fully trained officers.

Citizen volunteers have been used with apparent success by some probation departments. Royal Oak, Mich., for example, has utilized volunteers for 6 years and claims a high success rate for the probationers who have received supervision. The General Board of Christian Social Concerns of the Methodist Church, the North American Judges Association, and the National Council on Crime and Delinquency have launched "Project Misdemeanant," a program to encourage other communities to develop programs similar to that in Royal Oak. By 1966, 75 communities in over 30 States had expressed interest, and a number of other such programs were operating or were in the developmental stage.

The State parole agency in Texas uses volunteers as assistants to parole officers. Volunteers contact parolees upon release and help arrange jobs for them or secure their readmission into school. Thereafter volunteers are available to counsel parolees in any problems they may have or simply to serve as the kind of successful friends whom many offenders have never known. The work of the volunteers is closely supervised by professional parole officers, to whom they go for guidance when there are signs of trouble.

The use of paid, subprofessional aides in probation and parole is also promising. Such people, if properly trained and supervised, could, for example, collect and verify information about offenders, work that now takes up much of the time that probation and parole officers could be spending in counseling and arranging community services for offenders.

Subprofessionals could provide positive benefits beyond that of meeting manpower shortages. People who have themselves experienced problems and come from backgrounds like those of offenders often can help them in ways professional caseworkers cannot. Contact with a person who has overcome handicaps and is living successfully in the community could mean a great deal more to an offender than conventional advice and guidance.

To the extent possible, subprofessionals should be prepared for career advancement within the corrections field.

The Commission recommends:

Probation and parole services should make use of volunteers and subprofessional aides in demonstration projects and regular programs.

Caseloads of Probation Officers   Figure 3

Source: National Corrections Survey

Probation Officers with 0-50 cases are responsible for:

11.76 percent of all juvenile cases.

.86 percent of all misdemeanant cases.

3.10 percent of all felony cases.

Probation Officers with 51-70 cases are responsible for:

31.15 percent of all juvenile cases.

8.12 percent of all misdemeanant cases.

9.16 percent of all felony cases.

Probation Officers with 71-100 cases are responsible for:

46.41 percent of all juvenile cases.

14.68 percent of all misdemeanant cases.

20.69 percent of all felony cases.

Probation Officers with over 100 cases are responsible for:

10.68 percent of all juvenile cases.

76.34 percent of all misdemeanant cases.

67.05 percent of all felony cases.

Basic changes also must be made in what probation and parole officers do. They usually are trained in casework techniques and know how to counsel and supervise individuals, but they are seldom skilled in or oriented to the tasks required in mobilizing community institutions to help offenders. Much of the assistance that probationers and parolees need can come only from institutions in the community—help from the schools in gaining the education necessary for employment; help from employment services and vocational training facilities in getting jobs; help in finding housing, solving domestic difficulties, and taking care of medical disabilities.

As chapter 3 has pointed out with respect to juveniles, many offenders are, at the time of their offenses, already rejects and failures in home, school, work, and leisuretime activities. Once they become officially labeled criminal or delinquent, and particularly once they have been institutionalized and their community and family ties have been broken, their estrangement from these primary institutions increases, and their sense of powerlessness to succeed in legitimate ways is accentuated. In many cases, society reacts to their criminality by walling them off from the help they most need if they are to turn away from criminality.

There are many specific barriers to reentry. Perhaps the most damaging are those limiting employment opportunity. The inability of ex-offenders to obtain the bonding needed for certain kinds of employment; licensing restrictions that deny them access to certain kinds of work; and outright ineligibility for many forms of employment. The rituals surrounding the banishment of a lawbreaker are very potent, but there are no rituals to remove from him the label of offender when he seeks to reenter the community.

Even stronger than these formal restrictions are the informal pressures operating throughout the community to "lock out" the person who carries a criminal stigma. Those who profess to believe in rehabilitation often personally shun ex-offenders who seek to return to school, find work, or join recreation groups. Of course, this fear is in some cases legitimate. But when it is not, there is rarely any official assurance to minimize it. There is usually no conference with the parole or probation officer at which a job applicant's background and problems are discussed, or means worked out to enable employers to consult the officer if problems result.

If corrections is to succeed in mobilizing varied community resources to deal more effectively with offenders, it must significantly change its way of operating. Probation and parole officers today direct their energies primarily toward the offender rather than the social environment with which he must come to terms.

Although it is important that present skills in working with individual offenders be retained and improved, much is to be gained by developing new work styles that reach out to community resources and relate them to the needs of the caseload. The officer of the future must be a link between the offender and community institutions; a mediator when there is trouble on the job or in school; an advocate of the offender when bureaucratic policies act irrationally to screen him out; a shaper and developer of new jobs, training, recreation, and other institutional resources.

The Commission recommends:

Probation and parole officials should develop new methods and skills to aid in reintegrating offenders through active intervention on their behalf with community institutions.

A number of changes will be necessary if community corrections is to do this. A basic one is in the internal organization and management of many probation and parole agencies.

Few departments have expanded their concept of programing beyond the basic relationship between an officer and an offender. The resources of staff and of community agencies typically are made available to an offender through the officer to whose caseload he is assigned. There must be more direct relationships between offenders and persons who can help them to find success in legitimate ways.

Instead of giving a single officer total responsibility for an offender, the system needs to draw many persons into the task—teachers, vocational counselors, friends, family members, and employers. The aim must be to change the context of an offender's life as well as his personal orientation to the world around him. Most probation and parole agencies should reexamine their policies and operating procedures: how they assign cases, how they use the time of officers, and how they relate to the surrounding community.

The Youth Services Bureau recommended in chapter 3 as an alternative to adjudicatory treatment of delinquents can both serve and be served by community correctional programs. Such bureaus could constitute a valuable point of referral for probationers and parolees. Corrections, on the other hand, could provide important assistance to the Youth Services Bureaus through diagnosis and investigation, and through provision of special treatment services not involving coercion.

SERVICE PURCHASE

If community institutions can be encouraged to develop policies and operating procedures to help offenders, and to allocate a larger share of resources to them, their chances for success in the community will be greatly increased. Usually, however, a probation or parole officer has no means to encourage community institutions to extend this sort of help.

The Vocational Rehabilitation Administration of the Department of Health, Education, and Welfare has pioneered in the development of a method for helping handicapped persons overcome personal problems that stand in the way of self-sufficient performance in the community. This method, called service purchase, provides counselors with funds that they can use to obtain psychological, vocational, educational, medical, and other services for their clients when the counselors' own agencies cannot provide them. This approach would, in many places, be a valuable tool in reintegration of the offender. The ability to obtain a period of on-the-job training, for example, might well be a critical factor in moving an offender recently released from prison away from his earlier pattern of illegitimate associations and activities.

The Commission recommends:

Substantial service-purchase funds should be made available to probation and parole agencies for use in meeting imperative needs of individual offenders that cannot otherwise be met.

SPECIAL COMMUNITY PROGRAMS

One of the most disappointing experiments in corrections was conducted several years ago in California. The caseloads of some parole officers were greatly reduced to allow more intensive contact. Methods of parole supervision remained static; caseworkers simply had more time to devote to their usual duties of checking on progress in school or work, briefly interviewing parolees, and interceding occasionally in

408

family or personal problems. The performance of parolees in avoiding further trouble with the law did not improve.

Substantial improvement did occur, however, when in a subsequent experiment parolees were divided into subgroups according to their special characteristics, and assigned to different kinds of officers who used different methods. This result has been confirmed and elaborated by an impressive line of research over the past several years. It was the basis for an innovative community program that has attracted national attention. In this experiment, the community treatment project of the California Youth Authority, juvenile court commitments from Sacramento and San Joaquin Counties were first screened to eliminate those offenders—about 25 percent of the boys and 5 to 10 percent of the girls—for whom institutionalization was deemed mandatory. From the remaining cases, assignments were divided randomly between the community project and the regular institutional programs.

The youthful offenders assigned to the community treatment project were placed in caseloads of 10 to 12 per officer. Treatment methods were tailored to meet the individual needs of each youth. They included a wide variety of personal and group counseling, family therapy, tutoring for the marginal or expelled student, occasional short-term confinement to provide essential disciplinary controls, and an increased use of foster homes and group homes.

A principal goal has been to determine the effectiveness of different kinds of treatment for different kinds of delinquents. Current results include striking differences in the responses to differentiated treatment. As the research data accumulate, important clues as to who should and should not be institutionalized are emerging, as well as insights in the specific kinds of treatment and control required for particular offenders.

After approximately 5 years of experimentation, the community treatment project reports that only 28 percent of the experimental group have been subject to parole revocation, as against 52 percent of the comparable control group who were incarcerated. The results have been so encouraging that the California Youth Authority has launched modified versions of the project in high-delinquency areas in Los Angeles (including Watts), Oakland, and San Francisco. By 1966, these community programs were handling a youth population of approximately 600, larger than the capacity of an institution, thus saving some 7 to 8 millions of dollars of construction funds plus the difference in costs between institutional and community treatment.

The Commission recommends:

Caseloads for different types of offenders should vary in size and in type and intensity of treatment. Classification and assignment of offenders should be made according to their needs and problems.

In recent years, too, a number of imaginative programs have been developed that offer a middle ground between the often nominal supervision in the community provided by probation services and confinement in an institution. Some of them involve part-time residential supervision of offenders in small centers situated in their own communities. A significant element of some programs has been a research project to evaluate the effectiveness of the programs. These projects bring together in an extremely useful way practitioners interested in trying new methods and researchers concerned with increasing knowledge.

The prototype for several experimental programs was launched at Highfields, N.J., in 1950. The Highfields program limits its population to 20 boys, aged 16 and 17, who are assigned directly from the juvenile court as a condition of probation. It operates on the premise that corrections has its major impact on an offender during the first 3 or 4 months of contact. The inmates work during the day at a nearby psychiatric institution; in the evening they participate in group counseling sessions.

They are given as much responsibility for their own futures as the staff feels they can manage. Youths who do not respond favorably are transferred elsewhere, but those who do remain must confront their own and each other's problems, and participate actively in solving them.

For example, the boys are not usually released until their peers feel they are ready for freedom in the community. Robert Weber, who studied some 160 programs for juveniles immediately prior to the Commission's work, reported:

If you ask a youth in most conventional institutions, "How do you get out?" you invariably hear some version of "Be good. Do what you are told. Behave yourself." If one asks a youth in a group treatment program, "How do you get out?" one hears, "I have to help myself with my problems," or "when my group thinks I have been helped." This implies a basic difference in the social system of organization, including staff roles and functions. In the large institution the youth perceives getting out in terms of the problem of meeting the institutional need for conformity. In the group treatment program the youth sees getting out in terms of his solutions to his own problems, or how that is perceived by other youths in the group.

The Highfields project has been a model for similar programs elsewhere: The Turrel Residential Center and Essexfields in New Jersey; Pine Hills in Provo, Utah; and other programs in San Francisco and Los Angeles, in Kentucky and New York. The California community treatment project, which was discussed above, is partly based on the Highfields approach. The Provo, Essexfields, and San Francisco versions, unlike Highfields, permit the boys to live at home. Program activity centers on gainful employment in the community, classroom studies, and daily group meetings. The regimen is rigorous.

During the Provo experiment, for example, all boys were employed by the city during the summer. They put in a full day's work on the city streets, the golf courses, the cemetery —wherever they were needed. They were paid 50 cents an hour. After work they all returned to the program headquarters to meet at a group. At 7 in the evening they were free to return home.

The daily group sessions were built around the techniques of "guided group interaction." All group members, not staff alone, were responsible for defining and addressing difficult questions. Such programs seek to discover how much responsibility for their own lives offenders can take and how to reward them for responsible behavior. The basic assumption is that change, if it is to occur, must be shared with others. It is reasoned that if a youth can see others changing and receiving support for doing so, he is most likely to change himself.

Because these programs are located in the community, the problems with which the participants struggle are not the artificial ones of institutional life but the real ones of living with family, friends, school, work, and leisure-time activity. The available evidence indicates that these programs are achieving higher success rates than the institutional alternatives, and at a substantially lower cost.

Another effort to find alternatives to institutions is the program of the New York State Division for Youth. This agency, which is independent of the State training schools and prisons, deals with the offenders served by both. Originally developed to subsidize delinquency prevention programs, it moved into the direct-service field about 5 years

411

ago. For the more delinquent youth, several programs that
are replications of the original Highfields model have been
developed. For the younger or more immature youth, who
needs to be removed from inadequate home or community
situations, the agency provides a series of small forestry camp
operations, which combine work with schooling and group
counseling. And for the youth who needs support in his
efforts to obtain emancipation from a poor home environment, there are residential centers within the cities. The program provides shelter, group guidance, and supportive
counseling by a small staff, but it relies primarily on the educational and employment resources of the community.

The Commission recommends:

**Correctional authorities should develop more extensive com-
munity programs providing special, intensive treatment as an
alternative to institutionalization for both juvenile and adult
offenders.**

CORRECTIONAL INSTITUTIONS

On an average day in 1965, as table 3 shows, there were
some 426,000 persons in correctional institutions. Whatever

Table 3.—Daily Average Number of Inmates in
American Correctional Institutions in 1965

Institutions primarily for adults:	
Federal prisons	20,377
State prisons	201,220
Local jails and workhouses	141,303
Total	362,900
Institutions primarily for juveniles:	
Public training schools	[1] 43,636
Local juvenile institutions	6,024
Detention homes	13,113
Total	62,773
Grand total	425,673

[1] Includes 1,247 Juvenile and Youthful offenders in Federal Bureau of Prisons institutions.

SOURCES: National Survey of Corrections and U.S. Department of Justice, Bureau of
Prisons, "Statistical Tables, Fiscal Year 1965" p. 2.

the differences in type and quality among correctional institutions—from huge maximum-security prisons to open forestry
camps without guards or fences, from short-term detention

homes for juveniles to penitentiaries where men spend most of their lives, from institutions of brutal or stultifying routine to those with a variety of rehabilitative programs—there remains an inherent sameness about places where people are kept against their will.

It arises partly from restraint per se, whether symbolized by walls and guns or by the myriad more subtle inhibitions on personal liberty. It arises from the isolation of the institutional community from the outside world and from the alienation and apartness of the inmate society. It is fed by the strangeness of living apart from families, with no choice about place of residence, selection of intimate associates, or type of occupation—all crucial values that are taken for granted in the world outside.

These restraints have both advantages and disadvantages. On the one hand they serve the function of punishment and deterrence. They also prevent the dangerous offender from committing further crimes in the community during the term of his sentence. And, by keeping him apart from the conditions of community life and subjecting him to a special environment that can be artificially controlled 24 hours a day, they sometimes afford opportunities for rehabilitative treatment that cannot be duplicated in the community.

On the other hand, an artificial environment that works against self-reliance and self-control often complicates and makes more difficult the reintegration of offenders into free society. Sometimes institutions foster conspicuously deleterious conditions—idleness, corruption, brutality, and moral deterioration.

There are many ways in which the advantages of institutionalization can be exploited and the disadvantages minimized. For many offenders, institutionalization can be an extremely valuable prelude to community treatment. For a few, those who must be incapacitated for society's protection if not their own, it is the only possible alternative.

A MODEL FOR INSTITUTIONS

The Commission's national survey of corrections and other studies showed it how far many jurisdictions still were from optimal uses of institutions. It was disturbed to find that much planning for institutional construction, and the attitudes of many officials concerned, indicated that these conditions were not likely to be radically changed in the future.

The Commission believes that there is, therefore, value in setting forth, in the form of a "model," the changes that it sees as necessary for most correctional institutions. There will, of course, continue to be special offender problems that must be dealt with in other kinds of institutions. But in general new institutions should be of the sort represented by the model, and old institutions should as far as possible be modified to incorporate its concepts.

The model institution would be relatively small, and located as close as possible to the areas from which it draws its inmates, probably in or near a city rather than in a remote location. While it might have a few high-security units for short-term detention under unusual circumstances, difficult and dangerous inmates would be sent to other institutions for longer confinement.

Architecturally, the model institution would resemble as much as possible a normal residential setting. Rooms, for example, would have doors rather than bars. Inmates would eat at small tables in an informal atmosphere. There would be classrooms, recreation facilities, dayrooms, and perhaps a shop and library.

In the main, however, education, vocational training, and other such activities would be carried on in the community, or would draw into the institution community-based resources. In this sense the model would operate much like such programs as the Highfields and Essexfields projects. Its staff, like probation and parole officers, would be active in arranging for participation by offenders in community activities and in guiding and counseling them.

Some offenders might be released after an initial period of detention for diagnosis and intensive treatment. The model institution would permit correctional officials to invoke short-term detention—overnight or for a few days—as a sanction or discipline, or to head off an offender from prospective trouble. Even if initial screening and classification indicated that long-term incarceration was called for, and an offender was, therefore, confined in another facility, the community-based institution could serve as a halfway house or prerelease center to ease his transition to community life. It could indeed serve as the base for a network of separate group homes and residential centers to be used for some offenders as a final step before complete release.

The prototype proposed here, if followed widely, would help shift the focus of correctional efforts from temporary banishment of offenders to a carefully devised combination of control and treatment. If supported by sufficiently flexible laws and policies, it would permit institutional restraint to be used only for as long as necessary, and in carefully graduated degree rather than as a relatively blind and inflexible process.

A final advantage of the concept suggested here is that institutions that are small, close to metropolitan areas, and highly diversified in their programs provide excellent settings for research and experimentation and can serve as proving grounds for needed innovations. Not only are they accessible to university and other research centers, but their size and freedom from restrictions foster a climate friendly to inquiry and to the implementation of changes suggested by it.

The Commission recommends:

Federal and State governments should finance the establishment of model, small-unit correctional institutions for flexible, community-oriented treatment.

COLLABORATIVE INSTITUTIONS

Even in institutions committed to longer term custody, many steps can be taken short of this model to improve capacity to contribute to the reintegration of offenders. The most fundamental of these changes may be summed up as the establishment of a collaborative regime in which staff and inmates work together toward rehabilitative goals, and unnecessary conflict between the two groups is avoided.

Institutional communities in which persons are kept against their will tend to generate tension and conflict between the inmates and the staff. The task of preparing the inmate for reintegration into the community becomes lost in elaborate forms of competition, in covert and corrupting reciprocities between guards and inmate leaders, and in forced maintenance of passivity on the part of inmates. This encourages anger toward—and yet complete dependence on—institutional authority.

The collaborative approach seeks to reverse this too common pattern. The custodial staff, for example, is recognized as having great potential for counseling functions, both informally with individual inmates and in organized group discussions. Administrators and business staff likewise have been brought into the role of counselors and assigned rehabilitative functions in some programs. This collaborative style of management is more readily achieved if the institution staff is augmented by persons from the free community with whom inmates can identify. This involves recruiting outsiders who can help the inmate to develop motivation for needed vocational, avocational, and other self-improvement goals. Volunteers and subprofessional aides can be as useful in institutions as in community-based corrections.

Another important dimension of the collaborative concept is the involvement of offenders themselves in treatment functions. Group counseling sessions, for example, provide opportunities for inmates to help each other, through hard and insistent demands for honesty in self-examination, demands that cannot be made with equal force and insight by staff, whose members have not had personal experience in the world of criminal activity. The loosening of inmate-to-staff and of inmate-to-inmate communication tends to reduce the inmate politician's power. Moreover, the "rat" complex, which brings great social stigma and physical danger to an inmate who cooperates with staff in traditional institutions, is greatly diminished.

A delicate balance is involved between giving inmates a meaningful role to play in the life of the institution, and allowing them to usurp authority that should only be carried by staff. The line is still being fashioned in most institutions today, and more experience will be required to decide where it lies in specific areas such as assignment of inmates to job, work, and living units and decisions involving discipline and security.

The Commission recommends:

All institutions should be run to the greatest possible extent with rehabilitation a joint responsibility of staff and inmates. Training of correctional managers and staff should reflect this mode of operation.

EDUCATION AND VOCATIONAL TRAINING

It has been noted that the majority of offenders are severely handicapped by educational deficiencies from succeeding in a labor market that increasingly demands at least a high school education.

The society of delinquents and criminals is especially seductive to those unable to find legitimate pathways to success and self-esteem. Failure is cumulative in the typical case. Poor performance and small reward in the early school years lead to failing and dropping out at the high school level. This, in turn, makes entry into the world of work doubtful. Lack of specific skills is aggravated by inability to cope with time schedules and the standards of diligence and conformity required in most jobs.

Traditional work and vocational training programs within correctional institutions have not effectively solved such problems. A major difficulty in such programs today is the lack of incentives for achievement, which results in low motivation on the part of inmate trainees. Immediate rewards for efficient learning are small. Such long-term rewards as improved employability seem distant and unreal. In fact they often are unreal in the most practical sense that ex-offenders cannot secure the jobs for which they were trained in prisons and juvenile institutions.

Recent experiments in special education for students from culturally deprived neighborhoods have provided both insights and methods that can be transplanted into correctional programs. It is noteworthy that most inmates have had experience in the schools of poor neighborhoods. They have achieved far less academically than their intelligence test scores indicate they can achieve. The way to help them to learn is to make learning a rewarding experience and thus overcome the sense of failure and humiliation they have come to feel as a result of past performances in school.

One of the most promising approaches to this problem is the use of programed learning techniques. Special texts and machines present the material to be learned in small units. The student must master each part before he proceeds to the next. He goes at his own pace. It then becomes possible to use a variety of incentives and rewards for achievement. Programed instruction is discussed further in Chapter 11.

During the past few years there have been several experimental applications of programed instruction to correctional education. The most significant work has taken place in two centers. The Draper Youth Center, a reformatory-type institution in Alabama, has combined programed learning with efforts to change the social climate of the institution. Inmates who progress well in their studies are enlisted in a service corps to help other inmates. College students from nearby Auburn University have been recruited to work in this program. Although no scientific evaluation has been made, informal reports show highly accelerated educational and vocational progress, as well as an apparent reduction in recidivism, on the part of those who participated in the special program.

At the National Training School for Boys, a Federal institution in Washington, D.C., a whole "programed environment" for rehabilitative learning has been created. The inmates have a wide range of choice as to how to occupy themselves, and are rewarded in "points" that are equivalent to money. They have a variety of opportunities to "spend" these points, but they may also be fined for misbehavior and so do not earn many points if they choose to be lazy or indifferent.

This program makes a determined effort to simulate the problems and conditions of life in the outside world. For example, the boys must use earned points to pay rent for especially attractive sleeping quarters or to purchase more desirable meals than those routinely offered. They may also purchase a variety of small items from a commissary or a mail-order catalog. Meals and visits to relatives are paid for with points; special recreational equipment and courses can also be purchased with points. Points may be earned by work, completion of programed courses, or good behavior. Such incentive programs go far toward stimulating inmates to take responsibility for their own lives. They create opportunities for learning how to deal with the very problems they will encounter in the community.

The Commission recommends:

Correctional institutions should upgrade educational and vocational training programs, extending them to all inmates who can profit from them. They should experiment with special techniques such as programed instruction.

The greatest need is at the elementary and secondary level; more than half of adult inmates have not completed elementary school. However, enrichment of programs is much needed at all stages, including college-level courses. Opportunity for bringing the resources of nearby universities into correctional institutions in new and creative ways is great, and is largely unexploited. But it is noteworthy that a "prison college" was recently started in San Quentin by the University of California and the Institute for Policy Studies of the District of Columbia.

There are about 6,000 academic and vocational teachers now employed in the Nation's correctional institutions. It is estimated that an additional 10,700 persons are needed immediately to develop effective academic and vocational programs. In order to close this gap, which is expanding rapidly, substantial subsidies are needed to recruit needed specialists and to provide them with the training required to make them effective in their complex and challenging task.

418

The Commission recommends:

States should, with Federal support, establish immediate programs to recruit and train academic and vocational instructors to work in correctional institutions.

CORRECTIONAL INDUSTRIES

Vocational training can in many cases be best carried out in conjunction with operating prison industries.

Work programs for prisoners were first established for "sturdy beggars" in 16th-century Europe, and were a dominant feature of American reformatories and penitentiaries from the outset. Typically, however, penal work programs have been repetitious drudgery, providing little incentive for diligent or enthusiastic performance. In some instances institutions have been and still are required to be self-supporting or even to show a profit; and work (generally agriculture) is carried on typically without regard for the offender, under conditions that have long since been displaced in the rest of society.

During periods when unemployment was extensive in the outside community and private businesses could not sell their goods, political pressures mounted to prevent prisons from engaging in enterprises seen as competitive. This culminated during the Great Depression in a variety of State and Federal laws designed to restrict the use of prison labor.

Beginning in 1929, with the passage of the Hawes-Cooper Act, the sale of prison-made goods was gradually restricted by Federal and State legislation. Today there are severe constraints upon the development of industrial work programs within correctional institutions. This fact, combined with a frequent attitude of suspicion and resistance on the part of organized labor and business interests, has made idleness a prevailing characteristic of most American prisons and jails.

In the absence of good industrial programs, maintenance and work details are usually so heavily overmanned that offenders do not learn from them the habit of working independently and with dispatch.

Prison-made goods tend to be inferior in design and workmanship to those available from private enterprise. Delivery has been unreliable, and, despite the availability of cheap prison labor, the products frequently cost more than similar items that are privately produced. This is the result of many factors, including the small size of prison shops, the lack of

419

strong administrative support for industrial programs, and the dearth of imaginative and aggressive sales operations.

One of the first requirements for the promotion of more realistic and competitive correctional industries is a clear recognition on the part of the public that gross idleness in penal institutions works a serious detriment to the larger society. As has been noted, work skills are badly needed by many offenders. These skills are best developed under realistic conditions of production. Useful jobs cannot be learned in an environment of indolence and lethargy. Moreover, it is tremendously wasteful to support thousands of persons with no return of goods or services. Of course, increasing the productivity of prison industries would be futile if action also were not taken to increase the market for prison-made goods or, at the very least, increase the current percentage of the State-use market which is now the principal outlet for those goods.

The most extensive and successful use of prison industries is found in the Federal prisons. In 1965 Federal prisoners assigned to industry shops earned an average of $40 per month, according to their skill and productivity, primarily on a piece-rate basis. The industries also paid the cost of vocational training programs in the Federal prisons. The staff includes employment placement officers who help procure post-release jobs for prisoners. In some cases industries and vocational training are supported by private businesses and labor unions and tied to job placement upon release. The Federal system offers a model for the development of prison industries programs in the States, although most States would be unable to duplicate its features without financial assistance from the Federal Government or cooperative arrangements with each other.

The Commission recommends:

States should work together and with the Federal Government to institute modern correctional industries programs aimed at rehabilitation of offenders through instilling good work habits and methods. State and Federal laws restricting the sale of prison-made products should be modified or repealed.

Strong and informed administrative support in State correctional programs will be required to upgrade services and to adopt the practices of private industry. Labor organizations and business firms could be of inestimable help in advising and guiding the development of new programs, and in neutralizing opposition to them.

Even within the limitations of most existing institutions, there are a number of means by which the transition from institution to community can be made less abrupt, and the resources of community institutions drawn upon to help in rehabilitation. Short-term furloughs from institutions have been used most extensively in Mississippi and Michigan, each of which has reported less than 1 percent failure to return. Juvenile institutions have used such procedures successfully, though parsimoniously, at family-gathering times, such as Christmas, Thanksgiving, weddings, and funerals. Furloughs are useful in helping to prevent the deterioration of family ties and in allowing offenders to try newly learned skills, and test the insights they have developed in counseling experiences.

The most striking increase in temporary release from institutions in recent years has been in work-release programs. Introduced in Wisconsin institutions for misdemeanants over 40 years ago, their use spread slowly until large-scale extension to adult felons began in North Carolina in 1959. Favorable experience there led to work-release programs for felons in the early 1960's in South Carolina, Maryland, and other States in rapid succession, and to work-release provisions for Federal prisoners under the Prisoner Rehabilitation Act of 1965.

Despite difficulties inherent in lack of experience in administering them, work-release programs have been highly successful. In North Carolina, where inmates are eligible for work release when they have served a relatively small portion of their sentences, cancellation of work release for serious misbehavior—generally absconding—has occurred in only 15 percent of the cases. Revocation has been lower in the Federal system, where prisoners usually enter work release approximately 6 months before their expected parole date.

With their earnings the work-release prisoners usually pay for their transportation to and from their work, and meet incidental expenses as well. They buy necessary work clothes and tools and pay union fees and income taxes. In some places they have also reimbursed the State for room and board. With the surplus above these expenses they can send money to dependents, pay fines and debts arising from their preprison activities, and save funds to use once they return to the community.

The Federal correctional system has been a leader in the

establishment of special prerelease guidance centers—residential facilities where prisoners stay prior to parole and which help them arrange jobs and other contacts and adjust to reentry into the community. The same principles, on a less formal basis, are reflected in the halfway houses established by a number of State and local jurisdictions, often in cooperation with private agencies.

A number of work releasees and residents of prerelease guidance centers attend school part time or full time in addition to or instead of working. This arrangement sometimes is called study release. Particularly appropriate for juvenile and youthful offenders, it is highly developed at several State establishments resembling the Federal prerelease guidance centers. The New York State Division of Youth, for example, has several centers consisting of selected apartments within large apartment buildings, which serve primarily as alternatives to traditional commitment.

All of the programs described here suggest that crime control can be increased by making the transition from confinement in a correctional institution to freedom in the community a gradual, closely supervised process. This process of graduated release permits offenders to cope with their many postrelease problems in manageable steps, rather than trying to develop satisfactory home relationships, employment, and leisure-time activity all at once upon release. It also permits staff to initiate early and continuing assessment of progress under actual stresses of life.

The Commission recommends:

Graduated release and furlough programs should be expanded. They should be accompanied by guidance and coordinated with community treatment services.

LOCAL JAILS AND MISDEMEANANT INSTITUTIONS

No part of corrections is weaker than the local facilities that handle persons awaiting trial and serving short sentences. Because their inmates do not seem to present a clear danger to society, the response to their needs has usually been one of indifference. Because their crimes are considered petty and the sentences they serve are relatively short, the corrections system gives them low status. Many local jails and misdemeanant institutions are administered by the police or county sheriffs, authorities whose experience and main concern are in other fields. Most facilities lack well-developed recreational and counseling programs, sometimes even medical services. The first offender, the innocent awaiting trial, sometimes juveniles and women are imprisoned with confirmed criminals, drunks, and the mentally disturbed or retarded.

A large majority of the 215 misdemeanant institutions examined in detail in the Commission's survey of corrections have few, if any, rehabilitative programs. Less than 3 percent of the staff perform rehabilitative duties, and some of these work only part time. It would not be uncommon to find a single psychologist—or none at all—for several thousand in-

Table 4.—Distribution of Personnel in Jails and Local Correctional Institutions, 1965

	Number	Ratio of staff to inmates
Social workers or counselors	167	1:846
Psychologists	33	1:4282
Psychiatrists	58	1:2436
Academic teachers	106	1:1333
Vocational teachers	137	1:1031
Custodial officers	14,993	1:9
Administrative and supportive services	3,701	1:38
Total	19,195	1:7

SOURCE: National Survey of Corrections.

mates (table 4). Most teachers and social workers are concentrated in the larger facilities, leaving the great bulk of institutions without any at all.

Since many misdemeanants go on to commit subsequent offenses, and many "graduate" into felons, the general lack of rehabilitative programs is critical.

In a few misdemeanant institutions promising steps have been taken to correct the deficiency. The St. Paul, Minn., workhouse has in the last 8 years substantially improved its work and educational programs. Professional staff is augmented by volunteers. Counseling and testing services for men under 21 years of age are provided through funding by the Office of Economic Opportunity. A work and school release program has been initiated. Since the inception of the release program, a high proportion of the inmates involved appear to have adjusted successfully.

Multnomah County, Oreg. (Portland), is among the jurisdictions that have established special facilities as an adjunct to their county jails. Multnomah's program serves offenders who are sentenced for more than 60 days, apply for transfer and are accepted after case history review and psychological testing. The program includes work, counseling, tutoring by college student volunteers, corrective surgery, and dentistry. Work release has been added recently. Since December 1, 1963, when it received its first inmates, over 500 have been released. The recidivism rate has been estimated at less than 20 percent. The population includes all categories of misdemeanants, including skid row alcoholics and felons who ordinarily would serve prison sentences.

San Diego, Calif., has established five camps to which prisoners sentenced to the county jail are transferred after screening. Men are sent to particular camps according to their needs. One camp accepts only younger prisoners and has a specially trained staff selected for its ability to train and counsel younger offenders.

Such projects illustrate the progress that can be made by implementing reforms directed toward rehabilitation of offenders; they indicate that many of the measures required in institutions for juveniles and adult felons are also applicable to the misdemeanant system. It is not feasible in most States, however, to expect that advances such as these will be made as long as local jails and misdemeanant institutions are administered separately from the rest of corrections.

The Commission recommends:

Local jails and misdemeanant institutions should be integrated into State correctional systems. They should not be operated by law enforcement agencies. Rehabilitative programs and other reforms should be instituted.

The national survey found that in 93 percent of the country's juvenile court jurisdictions, covering 44 percent of the population, there is no place for the pretrial detention of juveniles other than a county jail or police lockup. In 1965, over 100,000 juveniles were confined in adult institutions. Presumably most of them were there because no separate juvenile detention facilities existed. Nonetheless, it is clearly undesirable that juveniles be confined with adults.

Even more undesirable is placing abandoned, neglected, or runaway juveniles in detention, a practice pursued in many communities that do not have shelter facilities under their welfare departments.

The Commission recommends:

Separate detention facilities should be provided for juveniles. All jurisdictions should have shelter facilities outside the correctional system for abandoned, neglected, or runaway children.

A special problem exists in the handling of persons awaiting trial or appeal. The implementation of bail reforms proposed in chapter 5 would go far toward alleviating the present situation in most jurisdictions, where large numbers of persons presenting no particular danger to the community are imprisoned pending trial, often to be released on probation afterwards. There will, of course, continue to be persons who require pretrial custody. However, in large cities they might still feasibly be housed or handled separately from adjudicated offenders.

The Commission recommends:

Wherever possible, persons awaiting trial should be housed and handled separately from offenders.

CORRECTIONAL DECISIONMAKING

The preceding discussion has been about the range of correctional treatment. There is another issue in corrections that has not been touched on—the range of decisions made by correctional personnel and the problems created by the great discretion they exercise. Most of these questions are old ones, but they have become acute with the widening of treatment alternatives and the growing advocacy of greater flexibility in choosing among them.

During the period when restraint was the dominant response to crime, there were only two major statuses to differentiate: In prison being punished and out of prison after having served a sentence. Concern for accurate factfinding and procedural safeguards was therefore focused on adjudication.

Today, however, an offender may be sentenced for an indeterminate length of time, with his release depending on the decision of correctional authorities. He may be referred to any of a wide variety of facilities or treatments on the basis of screening by correctional authorities. And he may be subjected to special discipline or punishment on the basis of determinations from which he has no appeal.

More numerous alternatives also create decision-making problems from the standpoint of effectiveness. Most correctional decisionmaking is to some degree handicapped by the following deficiencies:

First, important data often are not available, data which are essential to the making of sound decisions. In determining whether or not to grant parole for example, decisions usually are based on scanty information collected at the time the offender was committed to the institution. Information on changes that have occurred during confinement is usually either not available or inadequate.

Second, information that is available may be irrelevant to the outcomes which determine whether the decision was sound. It is characteristic of any decision-making process that those involved often are not aware of the particular bits of information they employ in arriving at a judgment. Moreover, the information they do use may, by empirical standards, be unrelated to the judgment being made. The question of relevance cannot be answered by argument but only by careful research.

By withholding certain items of information from the directors of juvenile institutions in England, for example, one study found that prognosis of inmate performance could often be improved. Apparently certain items of information tended to mislead the officials because they attached greater weight to them than was warranted.

A final and related problem is that the volume of information often overloads human capacity for analysis and utilization. The sheer number of offenders under correctional supervision is staggering and is growing rapidly each year. Adequate disposition of these offenders may require tens or hundreds of items of information on each offender at each step in the correctional cycle. The potential of computerized information systems as an aid to meeting this problem is discussed in chapter 11.

DISTINGUISHING DEGREES OF DANGEROUSNESS AND
DETERMINING OPTIMAL DISPOSITION FOR
DIFFERENT OFFENDERS

A core responsibility found in all phases of the correctional process is the requirement of gathering and analyzing that information about the offender that will provide an adequate basis on which to predicate the series of correctional decisions.

Whether the decision be to invoke the judicial process, to choose between probation or imprisonment, to select the appropriate degree of security in a correctional institution, to determine the timing for release from incarceration or the necessity for revocation of parole, the judicial and administrative decisionmakers are concerned with very similar issues.

These issues include:

(1) The extent or degree of threat to the public posed by the individual. Significant clues will be provided by the nature of the present offense, and the length of any prior record;

(2) The extent or degree of an individual's commitment to criminal or delinquent values, and the nature of his response to any earlier correctional programs;

(3) The kind of personal stability and responsibility evidenced in his employment record, residential patterns, and family support history;

(4) The kind of personal deficiencies apparent, including educational and vocational training needs;

(5) The personal, psychological characteristics of the offender that determine how he perceives the world and his relationship to it.

A few correctional research programs are seeking to test the way in which these personal dimensions can be subjected to objective analyses and used as the basis for predicting the probable response to alternative correctional programs. Some progress is evident in both statistical and psychological research experiments.

Central to such evaluation is the necessity for identifying those dangerous or habitual offenders who pose a serious threat to the community's safety. They include those offenders whose personal instability is so gross as to erupt periodically in violent and assaultive behavior, and those individuals whose long-term exposure to criminal influences has produced a thoroughgoing commitment to criminal values that is resistive of superficial efforts to effect change.

For these persons the still primitive state of treatment methodologies can only offer a period of confinement followed by the kind of parole supervision that will provide the requisite control.

Clearly indicated is the need for an improved capability in the information gathering and analysis process and continued experimental development to improve the predictive power of the information gathered. These needs point to increased manpower and the training requisite for the development of sophistication and skill in the investigative-diagnostic process.

Paralleling these general needs is the need for professional clinical personnel to assist in the evaluation of the bizarre acting, seriously disturbed, and mentally deficient offenders, and to provide consultation and advice to the line staff who must deal on a day-to-day basis with this special group.

Improved correctional decisionmaking requires not only better information and personnel but also a wider range of alternative facilities and programs. These are particularly needed when dealing with disturbed or dangerous offenders.

Penal institutions tend to be a kind of catch basin for a myriad of human problems not resolved elsewhere. Correctional staff must deal not only with offenders as such, but with offenders who also are alcoholic, mentally ill or deficient, addicted to narcotics, or driven by psychological pressures to commit sexually deviant acts. The implications of these conditions for needed treatment resources are sobering indeed, if they are faced realistically.

It is true, moreover, that some categories of offenders require special treatment and control, not because they are pathological in a particular way but because they are different from the numerically dominant inmate group. For example, female offenders, especially juveniles, have mainly been provided only with inadequate imitations of the institutional programs used for males, despite factual evidence that their needs and their involvements in criminal activity are strikingly different. Older adolescents and young adults often are not served well by either the adult or juvenile system of corrections.

It would seem obvious that offenders are as different from each other as are people in the general population. Those who are highly skilled and persistent at manipulating and hoodwinking persons in authority must be handled firmly if change is to occur. Others need reassurance about their importance as human beings more than they need firm limits on their behavior. Still others require practical assistance in getting a job or securing needed training, rather than psychological help of any kind. And there are those who need no help at all; they have experienced a legal sanction and will manage ably enough in the community thereafter with only perfunctory contact with authority.

Special offender groups such as alcoholics, derelicts, those with psychological problems, narcotics addicts, gifted people with high IQ's and female offenders may also require very distinct kinds of services that can be provided most effectively and efficiently through specialized treatment. Promising experiments with this kind of classification have occurred in New York and Pennsylvania.

The problems of special offender groups should be approached through efforts to classify and handle them separately wherever this will achieve either improvement in their treatment or alleviation of the conditions under which other inmates are handled. This will require in many cases—particularly for local misdemeanant systems—that jurisdictions join together, as a number are now beginning to do, in operating joint facilities and programs for special offender groups, or alternatively that they contract with neighboring facilities to handle such persons.

The Commission recommends:

Screening and diagnostic resources should be strengthened, with Federal support, at every point of significant decision. Jurisdictions should classify and assign offenders according to their needs and problems, giving separate treatment to all special offender groups when this is desirable. They should join together to operate joint regional facilities or make use of neighboring facilities on a contract basis where necessary to achieve these ends.

Under such a pattern, the Federal Government would be in a particularly advantageous position to undertake the handling of small groups of special offenders who require highly specialized or long-term treatment. Maximum security prisoners and those serving life sentences, are among the groups that could be handled away from local communities.

IMPROVING PAROLE DECISIONS

A particularly critical area of correctional decisionmaking is that which surrounds the granting of parole.

Chapter 5 has suggested a number of improvements in sentencing procedures. Unlike sentencing, which has traditionally been a judicial function, the parole decision is administrative. It is made by correctional authorities or by a special parole board, usually composed of laymen.

While many parole officials are extremely able and knowledgeable, some still are merely political appointees without training and many serve only on a part-time basis. Such a situation is incompatible with the development of the kind of expertise necessary to make a decision which is as complex and important as that made by a sentencing judge.

The Commission recommends:

Parole boards should be appointed solely on the basis of

competence and should receive training and orientation in their task. They should be required to serve full time and should be compensated accordingly.

Parole boards should concentrate on developing and monitoring policy guidelines within which decisions about individual cases could be made fairly and consistently. Where the workload is heavy, boards should review the actions of professional hearing officers rather than attempting to carry on all hearings themselves.

In the main, both juvenile and adult releasing authorities must depend on their staffs for information about persons being considered for release. The quality of staff available to releasing authorities is, therefore, a crucial determinant in effective decisionmaking. Staff must be able to develop and assemble vital information and present it in such a way as to establish its relevance to the decision. Far too typically, the pattern is for an overworked caseworker to attempt to gather information on a prisoner from meager institutional records. Institution officials sometimes form their impressions primarily in terms of whether an individual was docile during confinement, rather than on the basis of his readiness for release into the community.

Another problem arises from the fact that the information on offenders often is fitted into a highly stereotyped format. The repetitious character of parole hearings, coupled with the sameness of reporting style and jargon, make it very difficult for board members to understand the individual aspects of a given case and to assess them wisely.

It seems especially important that research and experimentation should be undertaken to develop improved information for use in making parole decisions and to discover better ways of presenting that information. There should be a flow of information on the performance in the community of offenders previously released, so that parole officials will know who succeeded and who failed to adopt law-abiding ways.

CONCERN FOR THE RIGHTS OF OFFENDERS

As the line between institutional and community treatment becomes increasingly blurred, problems of achieving fairness in decisions relating to release will proliferate. Partial release to the community for work or study, placement in a prerelease residential unit—these are only some of many ways of gradually shifting an offender from life in an institution to

430

life in the community. Given the many shades of gray along that transition route, and the present rapid invention of new variations on the theme, it is increasingly difficult to determine when the shift actually has been made—indeed this is the very point of such correctional strategy.

But many questions arise relative to the decisions that are made as the offender moves away from the institution. These questions become even more acute if it is decided that he should move part or all of the way back. This area of decisions has for a considerable time been the province of parole boards, but such new procedures as work furloughs and educational leaves sometimes place the decisions in the hands of institution officials.

These developments have increased the need to insure that adequate procedures are present to safeguard the rights of offenders. Already such formal decisions as parole revocation are coming to be seen as requiring legal representation of offenders—as the Commission recommends in chapter 5. Less formalized decisions—assignment to particular facilities and treatment programs, return of halfway-house residents to confinement before rather than after trouble—present greater difficulties.

On the one hand, such decisions can vitally affect the lives of offenders, and there is danger that they may be made on the basis of inadequate or incorrect information, or through prejudice. On the other hand, serious problems would be presented by subjecting these and similar actions to all of the traditional legal procedures associated with judicial due process requirements. The law has yet to define limits and standards in this area. But correctional authorities should take immediate steps to insure that there are adequate safeguards by providing for hearing procedures, review of decisions by persons removed from the immediate situation, explicit policy guidelines and standards, and adequate records to support decisions.

Offenders should always have administrative recourse for grievances against officials, and the adequacy of this recourse should be subject to review by some external authority.

The Commission recommends:

Correctional agencies should develop explicit standards and administrative procedures to enable those under correctional control to test the fairness of key decisions affecting them.

Elements of a Modern Correctional System   Figure 4

Police

Screening of Offenders

Committing
Judge

(Probation)

Community Based Programs

Community
Organizations:
Recreational
Religious
Schools
Vocational

Therapy
Programs:
Group
Family
Individual

Residential
Facilities:
Group
Individual

Caseload Supervision

Intensive
Supervision
In Special
Caseloads

Supervision in
Regular
Caseloads

State Agency   (Parole)
Screening
Resources

Institutional
System:
Camps
Open Units
Security Units

These procedures should include gathering and recording facts and providing for independent monitoring and review of the actions of correctional staff.

CREATING CHANGE

The correctional programs of the United States cannot perform their assigned work by mere tinkering with faulty machinery. A substantial upgrading of services and a new orientation of the enterprise toward integration of offenders into community life is needed.

To achieve this end, there must be new divisions of labor, cooperative arrangements between governments, and a better balance between institutional and community programs. There must be a wide variety of techniques for controlling and treating offenders, and arrangements that allow these techniques to be used flexibly and interchangeably. A strategy of search and validation must be substituted for the present random methods of determining how correctional resources should be used. Figure 4 depicts the operational elements of a modern correctional system as recommended by the Commission.

Such pervasive changes will require strong and decisive action. The following points out where responsibility for taking action rests and notes the cost and consequences of inaction.

RESPONSIBILITY FOR ACTION: ROLE OF GOVERNMENT

Certain principles should govern correctional operations:

(1) Correctional operations should be located as close as possible to the homes of the offenders.

(2) Reciprocal arrangements between governments should be developed to permit flexible use of resources. Regional sharing of institutional facilities and community programs should be greatly increased.

(3) Large governmental units should take responsibility for a variety of forms of indirect service to smaller and less financially able units, helping them to develop and strengthen their correctional services.

The Federal Government should assume a large share of responsibility for providing impetus and direction to needed changes. It should take increasing responsibility for helping to upgrade the correctional programs of State and local governments. Ultimately, Federal authorities might provide only those direct services which cannot be operated effectively and economically by State and local governments.

The Federal Government can stimulate action by providing financial and other assistance to State and local governments. Federal financial support can be of crucial importance in developing to capacity to secure, analyze, and disseminate information on the treatment that is most successful with different classifications of offenders; in assisting State and local agencies to recruit and train the many kinds of personnel needed to staff new programs; in providing funds for needed research and demonstration, and curriculum development projects.

State and local activities should reflect the principles outlined above. Some counties and metropolitan areas are sufficiently large to develop comprehensive correctional services of their own. In such cases, the State role might be similar to the Federal role indicated above—providing stimulus for change. Primarily, however, the State governments themselves should develop and administer correctional services, involving local governments as much as possible and decentralizing operations through regional offices. No single pattern of organization will fit the varied conditions that exist; needs in the correctional field are a challenge to imaginative inter-governmental problem solving.

RESPONSIBILITY FOR ACTION: NONGOVERNMENTAL ROLE

A sizable number of nongovernmental organizations operate nationally to improve correctional practices. Among them are the National Council on Crime and Delinquency, the American Correctional Association, the National Association of Training Schools, the Joint Commission on Correctional Manpower and Training, and various affiliated groups. These entities, operating independently of vested interests and of the limitations imposed by public office, have an opportunity to play a most important role in bringing about needed changes in corrections. They can carry out surveys in States and localities, provide consulting services, and help with research and information exchange. Above all, they can inform the public about needs and problems and mobilize the grassroots support required for major change. Public funds should be made available to help private agencies perform these functions, but it is imperative that they maintain a perspective from outside the system in order to be incisive critics and monitors of its operations.

434

At present, university curricula generally ignore the field of corrections. Correctional concerns tend to be invisible to students and faculty at both the undergraduate and graduate level, despite the fact that many disciplines and professions —psychology, sociology, public administration, law, and social work, among others—have legitimate responsibilities in this area. Universities have an indispensable role to play in filling the knowledge gap that exists throughout corrections. However, two hazards should be avoided: Heavily vocational programs which purport to answer questions about how to perform correctional functions without addressing the complexities of what and why and thus further isolate corrections from the university community; and conversely the reluctance of scholars to address the specific problems faced by those charged with the perplexing task of controlling and rehabilitating offenders.

Funds from Federal, State and local governments and private foundations are specifically needed for research; for fellowships and stipends to promising students and to those employed in corrections who want further university training; and for sustained support for internships and field placement programs developed with correctional agencies.

The Commission recommends:

Universities and colleges should, with governmental and private participation and support, develop more courses and launch more research studies and projects on the problems of contemporary corrections.

CONSEQUENCES OF INACTION

It would be satisfying to have available a quantitative statement of the costs and consequences over the decades ahead of continuing the present faltering correctional system, and of the gains that could be achieved through implementation of the recommended changes. How much reduction of crime and delinquency could be achieved over 5, 10, or 20 years? When would the economies implicit in more effective handling of offenders equal or surpass the increased cost of a renovated correctional system? What would be the cost to the Nation, in human lives and suffering as well as in dollars, of inaction in the face of such critical conditions?

It is impossible to answer such questions in quantitative terms. The cost of additional personnel and facilities can be estimated roughly, but there is at present no solid basis in experience for predicting the impact of a changed correctional system.

However, the ineffectiveness of the present system is not really a subject of controversy. The directions of change—toward the community, toward differential handling of offenders, toward a coherent organization of services—are supported by a combination of objective evidence and informed opinion.

The costs of action are substantial. But the costs of inaction are immensely greater. Inaction would mean, in effect, that the Nation would continue to avoid, rather than confront, one of its most critical social problems; that it would accept for the next generation a huge, if now immeasurable, burden of wasted and destructive lives. Decisive action, on the other hand, could make a difference that would really matter within our time.

Chapter 7

Organized Crime

ORGANIZED CRIME is a society that seeks to operate outside the control of the American people and their governments. It involves thousands of criminals, working within structures as complex as those of any large corporation, subject to laws more rigidly enforced than those of legitimate governments. Its actions are not impulsive but rather the result of intricate conspiracies, carried on over many years and aimed at gaining control over whole fields of activity in order to amass huge profits.

The core of organized crime activity is the supplying of illegal goods and services—gambling, loan sharking, narcotics, and other forms of vice—to countless numbers of citizen customers. But organized crime is also extensively and deeply involved in legitimate business and in labor unions. Here it employs illegitimate methods—monopolization, terrorism, extortion, tax evasion—to drive out or control lawful ownership and leadership and to exact illegal profits from the public. And to carry on its many activities secure from governmental interference, organized crime corrupts public officials.

Robert F. Kennedy, when he was Attorney General, illustrated its power simply and vividly. He testified before a Senate subcommittee in 1963 that the physical protection of witnesses who had cooperated with the Federal Government in organized crime cases often required that those witnesses change their appearances, change their names, or even leave the country. When the government of a powerful country is unable to protect its friends from its enemies by means less extreme than obliterating their identities, surely it is being seriously challenged, if not threatened.

What organized crime wants is money and power. What makes it different from law-abiding organizations and individuals with those same objectives is that the ethical and moral standards the criminals adhere to, the laws and regulations they obey, the procedures they use, are private and secret ones that they devise themselves, change when they see fit, and administer summarily and invisibly. Organized crime affects the lives of millions of Americans, but because it desperately preserves its invisibility many, perhaps most, Americans are not aware how they are affected, or even that they are affected at all. The price of a loaf of bread may go up one cent as the result of an organized crime conspiracy, but a housewife has no way of knowing why she is paying more. If organized criminals paid income tax on every cent of their vast earnings everybody's tax bill would go down, but no one knows how much.

But to discuss the impact of organized crime in terms of whatever direct, personal, everyday effect it has on individuals is to miss most of the point. Most individuals are not affected, in this sense, very much. Much of the money organized crime accumulates comes from innumerable petty transactions: 50-cent bets, $3-a-month private garbage collection services, quarters dropped into racketeer-owned jukeboxes, or small price rises resulting from protection rackets. A one-cent-a-loaf rise in bread may annoy housewives, but it certainly does not impoverish them.

Sometimes organized crime's activities do not directly affect individuals at all. Smuggled cigarettes in a vending machine cost consumers no more than tax-paid cigarettes, but they enrich the leaders of organized crime. Sometimes these activities actually reduce prices for a short period of time, as can happen when organized crime, in an attempt to take over an industry, starts a price war against legitimate businessmen. Even when organized crime engages in a large transaction, individuals may not be directly affected. A large sum of money can be diverted from a union pension fund to finance a business venture without immediate and direct effect upon the individual members of the union.

It is organized crime's accumulation of money, not the individual transactions by which the money is accumulated, that has a great and threatening impact on America. A quarter in a jukebox means nothing and results in nothing. But millions of quarters in thousands of jukeboxes can provide both a strong motive for murder and the means to commit murder with impunity. Organized crime exists by virtue of the power it purchases with its money. The millions of dollars it can throw into the legitimate economic system give it power over the lives of thousands of people and over the quality of life in whole neighborhoods. The millions of dollars it can throw into the legitimate economic system give it power to manipulate the price of shares on the stock market, to raise or lower the price of retail merchandise, to determine whether entire industries are union or nonunion, to make it easier or harder for businessmen to continue in business.

The millions of dollars it can spend on corrupting public officials may give it power to maim or murder people inside or outside the organization with impunity, to extort money from businessmen, to conduct businesses in such fields as liquor, meat, or drugs without regard to administrative regulations, to avoid payment of income taxes, or to secure public works contracts without competitive bidding.

The purpose of organized crime is not competition with visible, legal government but nullification of it. When organized crime places an official in public office, it nullifies the political process. When it bribes a police official, it nullifies law enforcement.

There is another, more subtle, way in which organized crime has an impact on American life. Consider the former way of life of Frank Costello, a man who has repeatedly been called a leader of organized crime. He lived in an expensive apartment on the corner of 72d Street and Central Park West in New York. He was often seen dining in well-known restaurants in the company of judges, public officials, and prominent businessmen. Every morning he was shaved in the barbershop of the Waldorf Astoria Hotel. On many weekends he played golf at a country club on the fashionable North Shore of Long Island. In short, though his reputation was common knowledge, he moved around New York conspicuously and unashamedly, perhaps ostracized by some people but more often accepted, greeted by journalists, recognized by children, accorded all the freedoms of a prosperous and successful man. On a society that treats such a man in such a manner, organized crime has had an impact.

And yet the public remains indifferent. Few Americans seem to comprehend how the phenomenon of organized crime affects their lives. They do not see how gambling with bookmakers, or borrowing money from loan sharks, forwards the interest of great criminal cartels. Businessmen looking for labor harmony or nonunion status through irregular channels rationalize away any suspicions that organized crime is thereby spreading its influence. When an ambitious political candidate accepts substantial cash contributions from unknown sources, he suspects but dismisses the fact that organized crime will dictate some of his actions when he assumes office.

President Johnson asked the Commission to determine why organized crime has been expanding despite the Nation's best efforts to prevent it. The Commission drew upon the small group of enforcement personnel and other knowledgeable persons who deal with organized crime. Federal agencies provided extensive material. But because so little study and research have been done in this field, we also secured the assistance of sociologists, systems analysts, political scientists, economists and lawyers. America's limited response to organized crime is illustrated by the fact that, for several of these disciplines, our call for assistance resulted in their first concentrated examination of organized crime.

THE TYPES OF ORGANIZED CRIMINAL ACTIVITIES

CATERING TO PUBLIC DEMANDS

Organized criminal groups participate in any illegal activities that offers maximum profit at minimum risk of law enforcement interference. They offer goods and services that millions of Americans desire even though declared illegal by their legislatures.

Gambling. Law enforcement officials agree almost unanimously that gambling is the greatest source of revenue for organized crime. It ranges from lotteries, such as "numbers" or "bolita," to off-track horse betting, bets on sporting events, large dice games and illegal casinos. In large cities where organized criminal groups exist, very few of the gambling operators are independent of a large organization. Anyone whose independent operation becomes successful is likely to receive a visit from an organization representative who convinces the independent, through fear or promise of greater profit, to share his revenue with the organization.

Most large-city gambling is established or controlled by organized crime members through elaborate hierarchies. Money is filtered from the small operator who takes the customer's bet, through persons who pick up money and slips, to second-echelon figures in charge of particular districts, and then into one of several main offices. The profits that eventually accrue to organization leaders move through channels so complex that even persons who work in the betting operation do not know or cannot prove the identity of the leader. Increasing use of the telephone for lottery and sports betting has facilitated systems in which the bookmaker may not know the identity of the second-echelon person to whom he calls in the day's bets. Organization not only creates greater efficiency and enlarges markets, it also provides a systematized method of corrupting the law enforcement process by centralizing procedures for the payment of graft.

Organization is also necessary to prevent severe losses. More money may be bet on one horse or one number with a small operator than he could pay off if that horse or that number should win. The operator will have to hedge by betting some money himself on that horse or that number. This so-called "layoff" betting is accomplished through a network of local, regional, and national layoff men, who take bets from gambling operations.

There is no accurate way of ascertaining organized crime's gross revenue from gambling in the United States. Estimates of the annual intake have varied from $7 to $50 billion. Legal betting at racetracks reaches a gross annual figure of almost $5 billion, and most enforcement officials believe that illegal wagering on horse races, lotteries, and sporting events totals at least $20 billion each year. Analysis of organized criminal betting operations indicates that the profit is as high as one-third of gross revenue—or $6 to $7 billion each year. While the Commission cannot judge the accuracy of these figures, even the most conservative estimates place substantial capital in the hands of organized crime leaders.

Loan Sharking. In the view of most law enforcement officials loan sharking, the lending of money at higher rates than the legally prescribed limit, is the second largest source of revenue for organized crime. Gambling profits provide the initial capital for loan-shark operations.

No comprehensive analysis has ever been made of what kinds of customers loan sharks have, or of how much or how often each kind borrows. Enforcement officials and other investigators do have some information. Gamblers borrow to pay gambling losses; narcotics users borrow to purchase heroin. Some small businessmen borrow from loan sharks when legitimate credit channels are closed. The same men who take bets from employees in mass employment industries also serve at times as loan sharks, whose money enables the employees to pay off their gambling debts or meet household needs.

Interest rates vary from 1 to 150 percent a week, according to the relationship between the lender and borrower, the intended use of the money, the size of the loan, and the repayment potential. The classic "6-for-5" loan, 20 percent a week, is common with small borrowers. Payments may be due by a certain hour or a certain day and even a few minutes' default may result in a rise in interest rates. The lender is more interested in perpetuating interest payments than collecting principal; and force, or threats of force of the most brutal kind, are used to effect interest collection, eliminate protest when interest rates are raised, and prevent the beleaguered borrower from reporting the activity to enforcement officials. No reliable estimates exist of the gross revenue from organized loan sharking; but profit margins are higher than for gambling operations, and many officials classify the business in the multi-billion-dollar range.

Narcotics. The sale of narcotics is organized like a legitimate importing-wholesaling-retailing business. The distribution of heroin, for example, requires movement of the drug through four or five levels between the importer and the street peddler. Many enforcement officials believe that the severity of mandatory Federal narcotics penalties has caused organized criminals to restrict their activities to importing and wholesale distribution. They stay away from smaller-scale wholesale transactions or dealing at the retail level. Transactions with addicts are handled by independent narcotics pushers using drugs imported by organized crime.

The large amounts of cash and the international connections necessary for large, long-term heroin supplies can be provided only by organized crime. Conservative estimates of the number of addicts in the Nation and the average daily expenditure for heroin indicate that the gross heroin trade is $350 million annually, of which $21 million are probably profits to the importer and distributor. Most of this profit goes to organized crime groups in those few cities in which almost all heroin consumption occurs.

Other Goods and Services. Prostitution and bootlegging play a small and declining role in organized crime's operations. Production of illegal alcohol is a risky business. The destruction of stills and supplies by law enforcement officers during the initial stages means the loss of heavy initial investment capital. Prostitution is difficult to organize and disci-

442

pline is hard to maintain. Several important convictions of organized crime figures in prostitution cases in the 1930's and 1940's made the criminal executives wary of further participation.

Infiltration of Legitimate Business. To have a legitimate business enables the racket executive to acquire respectability in the community and to establish a source of funds that appears legal and upon which just enough taxes can be paid to avoid income tax prosecution. Organized crime invests the profit it has made from illegal service activities in a variety of businesses throughout the country. To succeed in such ventures, it uses accountants, attorneys, and business consultants, who in some instances work exclusively on its affairs. Too often, because of the reciprocal benefits involved in organized crime's dealings with the business world, or because of fear, the legitimate sector of society helps the illegitimate sector. The Illinois Crime Commission, after investigating one service industry in Chicago, stated:

There is a disturbing lack of interest on the part of some legitimate business concerns regarding the identity of the persons with whom they deal. This lackadaisical attitude is conducive to the perpetration of frauds and the infiltration and subversion of legitimate businesses by the organized criminal element.

Because business ownership is so easily concealed, it is difficult to determine all the types of businesses that organized crime has penetrated. Of the 75 or so racket leaders who met at Apalachin, N.Y., in 1957, at least 9 were in the coin-operated machine industry, 16 were in the garment industry, 10 owned grocery stores, 17 owned bars or restaurants, 11 were in the olive oil and cheese business, and 9 were in the construction business. Others were involved in automobile agencies, coal companies, entertainment, funeral homes, ownership of horses and race tracks, linen and laundry enterprises, trucking, waterfront activities, and bakeries.

Today, the kinds of production and service industries and businesses that organized crime controls or has invested in range from accounting firms to yeast manufacturing. One criminal syndicate alone has real estate interests with an estimated value of $300 million. In a few instances, racketeers

443

control nationwide manufacturing and service industries with known and respected brand names.

Control of business concerns has usually been acquired through one of four methods: (1) investing concealed profits acquired from gambling and other illegal activities; (2) accepting business interests in payment of the owner's gambling debts; (3) foreclosing on usurious loans; and (4) using various forms of extortion.

Acquisition of legitimate businesses is also accomplished in more sophisticated ways. One organized crime group offered to lend money to a business on condition that a racketeer be appointed to the company's board of directors and that a nominee for the lenders be given first option to purchase if there were any outside sale of the company's stock. Control of certain brokerage houses was secured through foreclosure of usurious loans, and the businesses then used to promote the sale of fraudulent stock, involving losses of more than $2 million to the public.

Criminal groups also satisfy defaulted loans by taking over businesses, hiring professional arsonists to burn buildings and contents, and collecting on the fire insurance. Another tactic was illustrated in the recent bankruptcy of a meatpacking firm in which control was secured as payment for gambling debts. With the original owners remaining in nominal management positions, extensive product orders were placed through established lines of credit, and the goods were immediately sold at low prices before the suppliers were paid. The organized criminal group made a quick profit of three-quarters of a million dollars by pocketing the receipts from sale of the products ordered and placing the firm in bankruptcy without paying the suppliers.

Too little is known about the effects on the economy of organized crime's entry into the business world, but the examples above indicate the harm done to the public and at least suggest how criminal cartels can undermine free competition. The ordinary businessman is hard pressed to compete with a syndicate enterprise. From its gambling and other illegal revenue—on most of which no taxes are paid—the criminal group always has a ready source of cash with which to enter any business. Through union connections, the business run by organized crime either prevents unionization or secures "sweetheart" contracts from existing unions. These tactics are used effectively in combination. In one city, organized crime gained a monopoly in garbage collection by preserving the business's nonunion status and by using cash reserves to offset temporary losses incurred when the criminal group lowered prices to drive competitors out of business.

Strong-arm tactics are used to enforce unfair business policy and to obtain customers. A restaurant chain controlled by organized crime used the guise of "quality control" to insure that individual restaurant franchise holders bought products only from other syndicate-owned businesses. In one city, every business with a particular kind of waste product useful in another line of industry sold that product to a syndicate-controlled business at one-third the price offered by legitimate business.

The cumulative effect of the infiltration of legitimate business in America cannot be measured. Law enforcement officials agree that entry into legitimate business is continually increasing and that it has not decreased organized crime's control over gambling, usury and other profitable, low-risk criminal enterprises.

Labor Racketeering. Control of labor supply and infiltration of labor unions by organized crime prevent unionization of some industries, provide opportunities for stealing from union funds and extorting money by threats of possible labor strife, and provide funds from the enormous union pension and welfare systems for business ventures controlled by organized criminals. Union control also may enhance other illegal activities. Trucking, construction and waterfront shipping entrepreneurs, in return for assurance that business operations will not be interrupted by labor discord, countenance gambling, loan sharking and pilferage on company property. Organized criminals either direct these activities or grant "concessions" to others in return for a percentage of the profits.

Some of organized crime's effects on labor union affairs, particularly in the abuse of pension and welfare funds, were disclosed in investigations by Senator John McClellan's committee. In one case, almost immediately after receiving a license as an insurance broker, the son of a major organized crime figure in New York City was chosen as the broker for a number of such funds, with significant commissions to be earned and made available for distribution to "silent partners." The youthful broker's only explanation for his success was that he had advertised in the classified telephone directory.

In New York City, early in 1966, the head of one organized crime group was revealed to be a partner in a labor relations consulting firm. One client of the firm, a nationally prominent builder, said he did not oppose unions but that

445

better and cheaper houses could be built without them. The question of why a legitimate businessman would seek the services of an untrained consultant with a criminal record to handle his labor relations was not answered.

LOCATION OF ORGANIZED CRIME ACTIVITIES

Organized criminal groups are known to operate in all sections of the Nation. In response to a Commission survey of 71 cities, the police departments in 80 percent of the cities with over 1 million residents, in 20 percent of the cities with a population between one-half million and a million, in 20 percent of the cities with between 250,000 and 500,000 population, and in over 50 percent of the cities between 100,000 and 250,000, indicated that organized criminal groups exist in their cities. In some instances Federal agency intelligence indicated the presence of organized crime where local reports denied it. Of the nine cities not responding to the Commission survey, six are known to Federal agencies to have extensive organized crime problems. Where the existence of organized crime was acknowledged, all police departments indicated that the criminal group would continue even though a top leader died or was incarcerated.

Organized crime in small cities is more difficult to assess. Law enforcement personnel are aware of many instances in which local racket figures controlled crime in a smaller city and received aid from the paid tribute to organized criminal groups located in a nearby large city. In one Eastern town, for example, the local racket figure combined with outside organized criminal groups to establish horse and numbers gambling grossing $1.3 million annually, an organized dice game drawing customers from four states and having an employee payroll of $350,000 annually, and a still capable of producing $4 million worth of alcohol each year. The town's population was less than 100,000. Organized crime cannot be seen as merely a big-city problem.

CORRUPTION OF THE ENFORCEMENT AND POLITICAL SYSTEMS

Today's corruption is less visible, more subtle and therefore more difficult to detect and assess than the corruption of the prohibition era. All available data indicate that organized crime flourishes only where it has corrupted local officials. As the scope and variety of organized crime's activities have expanded, its need to involve public officials at every level of local government has grown. And as government regulation expands into more and more areas of private and business activity, the power to corrupt likewise affords the corrupter more control over matters affecting the everyday life of each citizen.

Contrast, for example, the way governmental action in contract procurement or zoning functions today with the way it functioned only a few years ago. The potential harm of corruption is greater today if only because the scope of governmental activity is greater. In different places at different times, organized crime has corrupted police officials, prosecutors, legislators, judges, regulatory agency officials, mayors, councilmen, and other public officials, whose legitimate exercise of duties would block organized crime and whose illegal exercise of duties helps it.

Neutralizing local law enforcement is central to organized crime's operations. What can the public do if no one investigates the investigators, and the political figures are neutralized by their alliance with organized crime? Anyone reporting corrupt activities may merely be telling his story to the corrupted; in a recent "investigation" of widespread corruption, the prosecutor announced that any citizen coming forward with evidence of payments to public officials to secure government action would be prosecuted for participating in such unlawful conduct.

In recent years some local governments have been dominated by criminal groups. Today, no large city is completely controlled by organized crime, but in many there is considerable degree of corruption.

Organized crime currently is directing its efforts to corrupt law enforcement at the chief or at least middle-level supervisory officials. The corrupt political executive who ties the hands of police officials who want to act against organized crime is even more effective for organized crime's purposes. To secure political power organized crime tries by bribes or political contributions to corrupt the nonoffice-holding political leaders to whom judges, mayors, prosecuting attorneys, and correctional officials may be responsive.

It is impossible to determine how extensive the corruption of public officials by organized crime has been. We do know that there must be more vigilance against such corruption, and we know that there must be better ways for the public to communicate information about corruption to appropriate governmental personnel.

447

MEMBERSHIP AND ORGANIZATION
OF CRIMINAL CARTELS

Some law enforcement officials define organized crime as those groups engaged in gambling, or narcotics pushing, or loan sharking, or with illegal business or labor interests. This is useful to the extent that it eliminates certain other criminal groups from consideration, such as youth gangs, pickpocket rings, and professional criminal groups who may also commit many types of crimes, but whose groups are ad hoc. But when law enforcement officials focus exclusively on the crime instead of the organization, their target is likely to be the lowest-level criminals who commit the visible crimes. This has little effect on the organization.

The Commission believes that before a strategy to combat organized crime's threat to America can be developed, that threat must be assessed by a close examination of organized crime's distinctive characteristics and methods of operation.

NATIONAL SCOPE OF ORGANIZED CRIME

In 1951 the Kefauver committee declared that a nation-wide crime syndicate known as the Mafia operated in many large cities and that the leaders of the Mafia usually controlled the most lucrative rackets in their cities.

In 1957, 20 of organized crime's top leaders were convicted (later reversed on appeal) of a criminal charge arising from a meeting at Apalachin, N.Y. At the sentencing the judge stated that they had sought to corrupt and infiltrate the political mainstreams of the country, that they had led double lives of crime and respectability, and that their probation reports read "like a tale of horrors."

Today the core of organized crime in the United States consists of 24 groups operating as criminal cartels in large cities across the Nation. Their membership is exclusively Italian, they are in frequent communication with each other, and their smooth functioning is insured by a national body of overseers. To date, only the Federal Bureau of Investigation has been able to document fully the national scope of these groups, and FBI intelligence indicates that the organization as a whole has changed its name from the Mafia to La Cosa Nostra.

In 1966 J. Edgar Hoover told a House of Representatives Appropriations Subcommittee:

La Cosa Nostra is the largest organization of the criminal underworld in this country, very closely organized and strictly disciplined. They have committed almost every crime under the sun . . .

La Cosa Nostra is a criminal fraternity whose membership is Italian either by birth or national origin, and it has been found to control major racket activities in many of our larger metropolitan areas, often working in concert with criminals representing other ethnic backgrounds. It operates on a nationwide

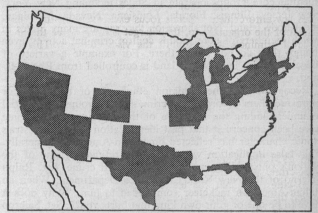

States in which Organized Crime Core Group Members Both Reside and Operate

basis, with international implications, and until recent years it carried on its activities with almost complete secrecy. It functions as a criminal cartel, adhering to its own body of "law" and "justice" and, in so doing, thwarts and usurps the authority of legally constituted judicial bodies . . .

In individual cities, the local core group may also be known as the "outfit," the "syndicate," or the "mob." These 24 groups work with and control other racket groups, whose leaders are of various ethnic derivations. In addition, the thousands of employees who perform the street-level functions of organized crime's gambling, usury, and other illegal activities represent a cross section of the Nation's population groups.

The present confederation of organized crime groups arose after Prohibition, during which Italian, German, Irish, and

Jewish groups had competed with one another in racket operations. The Italian groups were successful in switching their enterprises from prostitution and bootlegging to gambling, extortion, and other illegal activities. They consolidated their power through murder and violence.

Today, members of the 24 core groups reside and are active in the States shown on the map. The scope and effect of their criminal operations and penetration of legitimate businesses vary from area to area. The wealthiest and most influential core groups operate in States including New York, New Jersey, Illinois, Florida, Louisiana, Nevada, Michigan, and Rhode Island. Not shown on the map are many States in which members of core groups control criminal activity even though they do not reside there. For example a variety of illegal activities in New England is controlled from Rhode Island.

Recognition of the common ethnic tie of the 5,000 or more members of organized crime's core groups is essential to understanding the structure of these groups today. Some have been concerned that past identification of Cosa Nostra's ethnic character has reflected on Italian-Americans generally. This false implication was eloquently refuted by one of the Nation's outstanding experts on organized crime, Sgt. Ralph Salerno of the New York City Police Department. When an Italian-American racketeer complained to him, "Why does it have to be one of your own kind that hurts you?", Sgt. Salerno answered:

I'm not your kind and you're not my kind. My manners, morals, and mores are not yours. The only thing we have in common is that we both spring from an Italian heritage and culture—and you are the traitor to that heritage and culture which I am proud to be part of.

Organized crime in its totality thus consists of these 24 groups allied with other racket enterprises to form a loose confederation operating in large and small cities. In the core groups, because of their permanency of form, strength of organization and ability to control other racketeer operations, resides the power that organized crime has in America today.

INTERNAL STRUCTURE

Each of the 24 groups is known as a "family," with membership varying from as many as 700 men to as few as 20. Most cities with organized crime have only one family; New

450

York City has five. Each family can participate in the full range of activities in which organized crime generally is known to engage. Family organization is rationally designed with an integrated set of positions geared to maximize profits. Like any large corporation, the organization functions regardless of personnel changes, and no individual—not even the leader—is indispensable. If he dies or goes to jail, business goes on.

The hierarchical structure of the families resembles that of the Mafia groups that have operated for almost a century on the island of Sicily. Each family is headed by one man, the "boss," whose primary functions are maintaining order and maximizing profits. Subject only to the possibility of being overruled by the national advisory group, which will be discussed below, his authority in all matters relating to his family is absolute.

Beneath each boss is an "underboss," the vice president or deputy director of the family. He collects information for the boss; he relays messages to him and passes his instructions down to his own underlings. In the absence of the boss, the underboss acts for him.

On the same level as the underboss, but operating in a staff capacity, is the *consigliere,* who is a counselor, or adviser. Often an elder member of the family who has partially retired from a career in crime, he gives advice to family members, including the boss and underboss, and thereby enjoys considerable influence and power.

Below the level of the underboss are the *caporegime,* some of whom serve as buffers between the top members of the family and the lower-echelon personnel. To maintain their insulation from the police, the leaders of the hierarchy (particularly the boss) avoid direct communication with the workers. All commands, information, complaints, and money flow back and forth through a trusted go-between. A *caporegima* fulfilling this buffer capacity, however, unlike the underboss, does not make decisions or assume any of the authority of his boss.

Other *caporegime* serve as chiefs of operating units. The number of men supervised in each unit varies with the size and activities of particular families. Often the *caporegima* has one or two associates who work closely with him, carrying orders, information, and money to the men who belong to his unit. From a business standpoint, the *caporegima* is analogous to plant supervisor or sales manager.

The lowest level "members" of a family are the *soldati,* the soldiers or "button" men who report to the *caporegime.* A

451

An Organized Crime Family

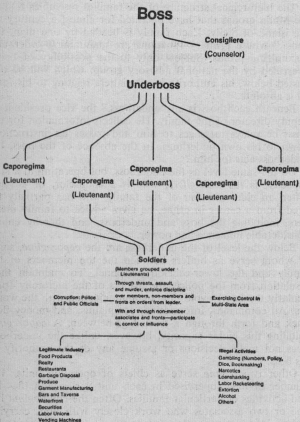

Boss

Consigliere
(Counselor)

Underboss

Caporegima
(Lieutenant)

Caporegima
(Lieutenant)

Caporegima
(Lieutenant)

Caporegima
(Lieutenant)

Caporegima
(Lieutenant)

Soldiers

(Members grouped under
Lieutenants)

Corruption: Police
and Public Officials

Through threats, assault,
and murder, enforce discipline
over members, non-members and
fronts on orders from leader.

Exercising Control in
Multi-State Area

With and through non-member
associates and fronts—participate
in, control or influence

Legitimate Industry
Food Products
Realty
Restaurants
Garbage Disposal
Produce
Garment Manufacturing
Bars and Taverns
Waterfront
Securities
Labor Unions
Vending Machines
Others

Illegal Activities
Gambling (Numbers, Policy,
Dice, Bookmaking)
Narcotics
Loansharking
Labor Racketeering
Extortion
Alcohol
Others

soldier may operate a particular illicit enterprise (e.g., a loan-sharking operation, a dice game, a lottery, a bookmaking operation, a smuggling operation, or a vending machine company) on a commission basis, or he may "own" the enterprise and pay a portion of its profit to the organization, in return for the right to operate. Partnerships are common between two or more soldiers and between soldiers and men higher up in the hierarchy. Some soldiers and most upper-echelon family members have interests in more than one business.

Beneath the soldiers in the hierarchy are larger numbers of employees and commission agents who are not members of the family and not necessarily of Italian descent. These are the people who do most of the actual work in the various enterprises. They have no buffers or other insulation from law enforcement. They take bets, drive trucks, answer telephones, sell narcotics, tend the stills, work in the legitimate businesses. For example, in a major lottery business that operated in Negro neighborhoods in Chicago, the workers were Negroes; the bankers for the lottery were Japanese-Americans; but the game, including the banking operation, was licensed, for a fee, by a family member.

The structure and activities of a typical family are shown in the chart on page 452.

There are at least two aspects of organized crime that characterize it as a unique form of criminal activity. The first is the element of corruption. The second is the element of enforcement, which is necessary for the maintenance of both internal discipline and the regularity of business transactions. In the hierarchy of organized crime there are positions for people fulfilling both of these functions. But neither is essential to the long-term operation of other types of criminal groups. The members of a pickpocket troupe or check-passing ring, for example, are likely to take punitive action against any member who holds out more than his share of the spoils, or betrays the group to the police; but they do not recruit or train for a well-established position of "enforcer."

Organized crime groups, on the other hand, are believed to contain one or more fixed positions for "enforcers," whose duty it is to maintain organizational integrity by arranging for the maiming and killing of recalcitrant members. And there is a position for a "corrupter," whose function is to establish relationships with those public officials and other influential persons whose assistance is necessary to achieve the organization's goals. By including these positions within its

453

organization, each criminal cartel, or "family," becomes a government as well as a business.

The highest ruling body of the 24 families is the "commission." This body serves as a combination legislature, supreme court, board of directors, and arbitration board; its principal functions are judicial. Family members look to the commission as the ultimate authority on organizational and jurisdictional disputes. It is composed of the bosses of the Nation's most powerful families but has authority over all 24. The composition of the commission varies from 9 to 12 men. According to current information, there are presently 9 families represented, 5 from New York City and 1 each from Philadelphia, Buffalo, Detroit, and Chicago.

The commission is not a representative legislative assembly or an elected judicial body. Members of this council do not regard each other as equals. Those with long tenure on the commission and those who head large families, or possess unusual wealth, exercise greater authority and receive utmost respect. The balance of power on this nationwide council rests with the leaders of New York's 5 families. They have always served on the commission and consider New York as at least the unofficial headquarters of the entire organization.

In recent years organized crime has become increasingly diversified and sophisticated. One consequence appears to be significant organizational restructuring. As in any organization, authority in organized crime may derive either from rank based on incumbency in a high position or from expertise based on possession of technical knowledge and skill. Traditionally, organized crime groups, like totalitarian governments, have maintained discipline through the unthinking acceptance of orders by underlings who have respected the rank of their superiors. However, since 1931, organized crime has gained power and respectability by moving out of bootlegging and prostitution and into gambling, usury, and control of legitimate business. Its need for expertise, based on technical knowledge and skill, has increased. Currently both the structure and operation of illicit enterprises reveal some indecision brought about by attempting to follow both patterns at the same time. Organized crime's "experts" are not fungible, or interchangeable, like the "soldiers" and street workers, and as experts are included within an organization, discipline and structure inevitably assume new forms. It may be awareness of these facts that is leading many family members to send their sons to universities to learn business administration skills.

As the bosses realize that they cannot handle the complicated problems of business and finance alone, their authority will be delegated. Decisionmaking will be decentralized, and individual freedom of action will tend to increase. New problems of discipline and authority may occur if greater emphasis on expertise within the ranks denies unskilled members of the families an opportunity to rise to positions of leadership. The unthinking acceptance of rank authority may be difficult to maintain when experts are placed above long-term, loyal soldiers. Primarily because of fear of infiltration by law enforcement, many of the families have not admitted new members for several years. That fact plus the increasing employment of personnel with specialized and expert functions may blur the lines between membership and nonmembership. In organized crime, internal rebellion would not take the form of strikes and picketing. It would bring a new wave of internal violence.

CODE OF CONDUCT

The leaders of the various organized crime families acquire their positions of power and maintain them with the assistance of a code of conduct that, like the hierarchical structure of the families, is very similar to the Sicilian Mafia's code—and just as effective. The code stipulates that underlings should not interfere with the leaders' interests and should not seek protection from the police. They should be "standup guys" who go to prison in order that the bosses may amass fortunes. The code gives the leaders exploitative authoritarian power over everyone in the organization. Loyalty, honor, respect, absolute obedience—these are inculcated in family members through ritualistic initiation and customs within the organization, through material rewards, and through violence. Though underlings are forbidden to "inform" to the outside world, the family boss learns of deviance within the organization through an elaborate system of internal informants. Despite prescribed mechanisms for peaceful settlement of disputes between family members, the boss himself may order the execution of any family member for any reason.

The code not only preserves leadership authority but also makes it extremely difficult for law enforcement to cultivate informants and maintain them within the organization.

Although law enforcement has uncovered the skeletal organization of organized crime families, much greater knowledge is needed about the structure and operations of these organizations. For example, very little is known about the many functions performed by the men occupying the formally established positions in the organizations. In private business identifying a person as a "vice president" is meaningless unless one knows his duties. In addition to his formal obligations, the corporate officer may have important informal roles such as expediter or troubleshooter.

More successful law enforcement measures against the organized crime families will be possible only when the entire range of informal and formal roles for each position is ascertained. Answers to crucial questions must be found: While it is known that "money-movers" are employed to insure maximum use of family capital, how does money move from lower-echelon workers to top leaders? How is that money spread among illicit activities and into legitimate business? What are the specific methods by which public officials are corrupted? What roles do corrupted officials play? What informal roles have been devised for successful continuation of each of the illicit enterprises, such as gambling and usury? Only through the answers to questions such as these will society be able to understand precisely how organized crime maintains a coherent, efficient organization with a permanency of form that survives changes in working and leadership personnel.

THE NATION'S EFFORTS TO CONTROL ORGANIZED CRIME

Investigation and prosecution of organized criminal groups in the 20th century has seldom proceeded on a continuous, institutionalized basis. Public interest and demands for action have reached high levels sporadically, but, until recently, spurts of concentrated law enforcement activity have been followed by decreasing interest and application of resources.

HISTORICAL BACKGROUND

The foothold that organized crime has gained in our society can be partly explained by the belated recognition on the part of the people and their governments of the need for specialized efforts in law enforcement to counter the enterprises and tactics of organized crime. A few law enforcement officials became concerned with the illicit enterprises of Mafia-type groups in the United States near the close of the 19th century. Sustained efforts at investigation were abruptly terminated by the murders of two police officers, one from New Orleans and one from New York City. The multimillion-dollar bootlegging business in the Prohibition era of the 1920's produced intensive investigations by the Treasury Department and the conviction of Chicago racket leader Al Capone.

In the 1930's, the special racket group of Thomas E. Dewey in New York secured the conviction of several prominent racketeers, including the late Lucky Luciano, the syndicate leader whose organizational genius made him the father of today's confederation of organized crime families. In the early 1940's, FBI investigation of a million-dollar extortion plot in the moving picture industry resulted in the conviction of several racket leaders, including the Chicago family boss who was then a member of organized crime's national council.

After World War II there was little national interest in the problem until 1950, when the U.S. Attorney General convened a national conference on organized crime. This conference made several recommendations concerning investigative and prosecutive needs. Several weeks later the well-publicized hearings of the Senate Special Committee under Senator Kefauver began. The Kefauver committee heard over 800 witnesses from nearly every state and temporarily aroused the concern of many communities. There was a brief series of local investigations in cities where the Senate committee had exposed organized crime operations and public corruption, but law enforcement generally failed to develop the investigative and prosecutive units necessary to root out the activities of the criminal cartels.

In 1957 the discovery of the meeting in Apalachin, N.Y., of at least 75 criminal cartel leaders from every section of the Nation aroused national interest again. This interest was further stimulated by disclosures in the hearings of Senator McClellan's Select Senate Committee investigating organized crime's infiltration of labor and business. A concerted Federal enforcement response developed in the 1950's, and special, institutionalized efforts on the local level have been growing slowly since that time.

Following the Kefauver hearings, the Department of Justice commenced a concerted drive against the leading racket figures identified in the hearings. Federal prosecutors throughout the Nation were encouraged to initiate investigations and prosecutions of such persons. As a result, a number of high level organized crime participants were convicted of Federal law violations. Under authority of the immigration statutes, the Department was successful in effecting the deportation of other racketeers. In 1954, the Justice Department formed an Organized Crime and Racketeering (OCR) Section to encourage the continuation of these prosecutive efforts. Efforts to institutionalize an antiracketeering intelligence program were hindered by a lack of coordination and interest by some Federal investigative agencies.

In 1958, after Apalachin, an Attorney General's Special Group on Organized Crime was created in the Department of Justice with regional offices from which intelligence information was gathered and grand jury proceedings conducted, concerning the Apalachin conferees. After trial and reversal of the convictions of 20 of these conferees for conspiring to obstruct justice, the group's functions were assumed by the existing OCR Section.

In September 1960, the Federal Bureau of Investigation began to supply the OCR Section with regular intelligence reports on 400 of the Nation's organized crime figures. But with only 17 attorneys and minimal intelligence information from other Federal agencies, the section could not adequately fulfill its functions, which included coordinating all Federal law enforcement activities against organized crime, accumulating and correlating all necessary data, initiating and supervising investigations, formulating general prosecutive policies, and assisting the Federal prosecuting attorneys throughout the country.

In 1961, the OCR Section expanded its organized crime program to unprecedented proportions. In the next 3 years, regular intelligence reports were secured from 26 separate Federal agencies, the number of attorneys was nearly quadrupled, and convictions increased. Indicative of the cooperation during this enforcement effort was the pooling of information from several Federal agencies for investigative leads in income tax cases. Over 60 percent of the convictions secured between 1961 and July 1965 resulted from tax investigations conducted by the Internal Revenue Service. Several high-level members of organized crime families in New York City were convicted through the efforts of the Federal Bureau of Narcotics.

This is a diagram of an interstate gambling operation that the FBI destroyed. Gamblers based in Brooklyn controlled lottery operations not only in Brooklyn, but in Manhattan and Newark, New Jersey. The Newark "work" (cash and gambling records) went first to a secret location on Varick Street in Manhattan and then, together with the Manhattan "work", to the Brooklyn base where it was processed.

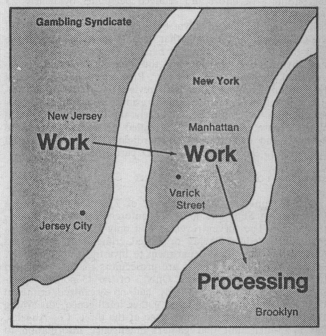

The FBI was responsible for convictions of organized crime figures in New York City, Chicago, and elsewhere. Enactment of statutes giving the FBI jurisdiction in interstate gambling cases resulted in disruption, by investigation and prosecution, of major interstate gambling operations, including "lay-off" betting, which is essential to the success of local gambling businesses.

In 1965, a number of factors slowed the momentum of the organized crime drive. A Senate committee uncovered a few isolated instances of wiretapping and electronic surveillance by Treasury Department agents, and some officials began to question whether special emphasis upon organized crime in tax enforcement was appropriate or fair. The Department of Justice was accused of extensively using illegal electronic surveillance in investigations of racketeer influence in Las Vegas casinos. Federal prosecutors in some large cities demanded independence from OCR Section attorneys and prosecutive policies. Attacks appeared in the press on the intensity and tactics of the Federal investigative and prosecutive efforts. A high rate of turnover among OCR Section attorneys meant discontinuity of effort and reduced personnel by nearly 25 percent.

This combination of adverse circumstances apparently led the OCR Section to believe that it could no longer expect the high degree of cooperation it had received from some Federal investigative agencies, and the intensity of its efforts diminished. In May 1966, however, President Johnson directed Federal enforcement officials to review the status of the national program against organized crime. He restated his determination to continue and accelerate the program. In a White House memorandum he called upon the appropriate agencies and departments to coordinate their activities and cooperate to the utmost with the Department of Justice.

STATE AND LOCAL LAW ENFORCEMENT

The Commission made a survey of 71 cities to determine the extent of State and local law enforcement against organized crime. The survey revealed that only 12 of the 19 cities that acknowledged having organized crime have specialized units within the police department to investigate that activity. In only 6 of those 19 cities are prosecutors specially assigned to work on organized crime. Only 3 of the 43 police departments that answered that they had no organized crime in their area had created units to gather intelligence concerning the possibility of its existence. One of the three, Los Angeles, has a 55-man unit that gathers intelligence information to prevent the expansion of organized crime.

At present, well-developed organized crime investigation units and effective intelligence programs exist within police and prosecutive agencies in only a handful of jurisdictions. There is, however, some evidence that local police and prosecutors are becoming more aware of the threat of organized crime. For example, in Philadelphia, both the police department and the prosecutor have created units to work exclusively in this area. In the Bronx County prosecutor's office responsibility for antiracketeering work has been centralized. The New England State Police Compact is a first step toward

460

regional confrontations of organized crime. In addition to provisions for mutual assistance in a number of areas and for coordination of command training, the compact provides for a centralization of organized crime data to which all members contribute and from which all draw. This system should reduce current duplication and permit a better coordinated attack upon organized crime.

In 1956 the Law Enforcement Intelligence Unit was established in California. This was the first step toward the development of a network for the exchange of data concerning people active in organized crime. The LEIU has since expanded to more than 150 members throughout the Nation. It maintains a central file in California, and information is available to its members on request.

The effectiveness of these State and local efforts is difficult to assess. But only New York and California have developed continuing State programs that have produced a series of convictions against major figures in organized crime. Coordinated police activity has substantially aided this process. On the local level, Chicago and New York City, where the organized crime problem is the most severe, appear to be the only cities in which large, firmly established police intelligence units continue to develop major cases against members of the criminal cartels.

PUBLIC AND PRIVATE CRIME COMMISSIONS

Among the most effective vehicles for providing public information on organized crime are the crime investigating commissions, which exist in a number of States. When established without having to rely on continuing governmental financial support and the resulting potential political pressures, the private crime commission has frequently rendered major service in exposing organized crime and corruption and arousing public interest. The Chicago Crime Commission and the Metropolitan Crime Commission of New Orleans have played major roles in informing the citizens within their jurisdictions of the menace of organized crime and have fulfilled substantial educational, investigative, and legislative functions.

Where a governmentally sponsored nonpartisan crime commission is created, as with the New York State Temporary Commission on Investigation, significant benefits have resulted. Established shortly after the Apalachin meeting, it has through a series of public hearings exposed organized crime and corruption. Recent loan-shark hearings prompted legislative action to make prosecution of such offenders less difficult. The Illinois Crime Commission, through public hearings and the efforts of its own investigators, continually exposes organized criminal activity. A governmental commission in California detailed the operations of criminal cartels in that State in the early 1950's and recommended action that subsequently proved effective.

LIMITATIONS ON CONTROL EFFORTS

Efforts to curb the growth of organized crime in America have not been successful. It is helpful in devising a program for the future to examine the problems encountered in attempting to combat organized crime.

Difficulties in Obtaining Proof. As described above, criminal cartels have organized their groups and operations to insulate their higher echelon personnel from law enforcement and regulatory agencies. Every measure has been taken to insure that governmental investigation, no matter how intensive, will be unable to secure live witnesses, the sine qua non of prosecution. Street workers, who are not members of organized crime families, cannot prove the identities of the upper-level personnel. If workers are arrested for gambling or other illicit activities, the fear instilled in them by the code of nondisclosure prevents their telling even the little they may know. The organization provides money and food for families of incarcerated workers; this helps to keep the workers loyal. Lawyers provided by the cartels for arrested employees preserve the interests of the organization ahead of those of the particular defendant.

Usually, when a crime is committed, the public calls the police, but the police have to ferret out even the existence of organized crime. The many Americans who are compliant "victims" have no incentive to report the illicit operations. The millions of people who gamble illegally are willing customers who do not wish to see their supplier destroyed. Even the true victims of organized crime, such as those succumbing to extortion, are too afraid to inform law enforcement officials. Some misguided citizens think there is social stigma in the role of "informer," and this tends to prevent reporting and cooperating with police.

Law enforcement may be able to develop informants, but organized crime uses torture and murder to destroy the particular prosecution at hand and to deter others from cooperating with police agencies. Informants who do furnish intelligence to the police often wish to remain anonymous and are unwilling to testify publicly. Other informants are valuable on a long-range basis and cannot be used in public trials. Even when a prosecution witness testifies against family members, the criminal organization often tries, sometimes successfully, to bribe or threaten jury members or judges.

Documentary evidence is equally difficult to obtain. Bookmakers at the street level keep no detailed records. Main offices of gambling enterprises can be moved often enough to keep anyone from getting sufficient evidence for a search warrant for a particular location. Mechanical devices are used that prevent even the telephone company from knowing about telephone calls. And even if an enforcement agent has a search warrant, there are easy ways to destroy written material while the agent fulfills the legal requirements of knocking on the door, announcing his identity and purpose, and waiting a reasonable time for a response before breaking into the room.

Lack of Resources. No State or local law enforcement agency is adequately staffed to deal successfully with the problems of breaking down criminal organizations. Just one major organized crime case may take 2 to 3 years to develop and then several more years to complete through prosecution and appeal. Cases may require several man-years of investigative resources. The percentage of investigations that result in arrests is quite low. Requests for increased budgets in government are usually granted only upon a showing of success; i.e., a high number of arrests. An effective organized crime investigative effort may not be able to produce such statistics without years of intelligence gathering, and the drive for statistics may divert investigative energy to meaningless low-level gambling arrests that have little effect on the criminal organizations. Even with these known problems, the organized crime units of all but a few city police departments are staffed by less than 10 men, and only 6 prosecutors' offices have assigned assistants to work exclusively or particularly in organized crime cases.

Effective investigation and prosecution of organized crime require extensive experience. As noted in chapter 5, assistant prosecutors rarely stay in a district attorney's office for more than a few years, if that long. On the investigative level, with the exception of some Federal agencies, assignment to the organized crime intelligence unit may be only a step in an officer's career. The most proficient people are likely to be promoted out of the unit into supervisory positions, and their replacements must then start the difficult job of acquiring the skills for the peculiar demands of organized crime investigation. In addition, few units have any personnel with the necessary accounting and legal knowledge.

Lack of Coordination. Local police are hampered by their limited geographical jurisdiction, and law enforcement has not responded by developing sufficient coordination among the agencies. One gambling operation may range through several police jurisdictions; if only one agency is involved in the investigation, it may be unable to detect key elements of the illegal enterprise. The potential for Federal-local cooperation was illustrated in the past 3 years in Chicago. With search warrant affidavits signed by FBI agents and based on FBI information, Chicago police have arrested almost 1,000 gambling defendants and seized money and wagering paraphernalia valued at approximately $400,000. The monthly gross of gambling sites so raided exceeded $8½ million. Unfortunately, such instances of sustained intensity are extremely rare.

Agencies do not cooperate with each other in preparing cases, and they do not exchange information with each other. Enforcement officers do not trust each other for they are sensitive to organized crime's ability to corrupt law enforcement. Agencies have not developed strategies to overcome these problems and to insure that needed data can be effectively transferred.

Failure to Develop Strategic Intelligence. Intelligence deals with all of the things that should be known before initiating a course of action. In the context of organized crime there are two basic types of intelligence information: tactical and strategic. Tactical intelligence is the information obtained for specific organized crime prosecutions. Strategic intelligence is the information regarding the capabilities, intentions, and vulnerabilities of organized crime groups. For example, the body of knowledge built up by the FBI concerning the structure, membership, activities, and purposes of La Cosa Nostra represents significant strategic intelligence.

At present, most law enforcement agencies gather organized crime intelligence information with prosecution as the immediate objective. This tactical focus has not been accompanied by development of the full potential for strategic intelligence. That failure accounts for the gaps in knowledge, described above, concerning the ways in which criminal cartels organize and operate as a business. Prosecution based merely upon individual violations that come to the attention of law enforcement may result in someone's incarceration, but the criminal organization simply places someone else in the vacated position.

A body of strategic intelligence information would enable agencies to predict what directions organized crime might take, which industries it might try to penetrate, and how it might infiltrate. Law enforcement and regulatory agencies could then develop plans to destroy the organizational framework and coherence of the criminal cartels. Comprehensive strategic planning, however, even with an expanded intelligence effort, will not be possible until relevant disciplines, such as economics, political science, sociology, and operations research, begin to study organized crime intensively.

Failure to Use Available Sanctions. Gambling is the largest source of revenue for the criminal cartels, but the members of organized crime know they can operate free of significant punishment. Street workers have little reason to be deterred from joining the ranks of criminal organizations by fear of long jail sentences or large fines. Judges are reluctant to jail bookmakers and lottery operators. Even when offenders are convicted, the sentences are often very light. Fines are paid by the organization and considered a business expense.

And in other organized crime activity, when management level figures are convicted, too frequently the sentences imposed are not commensurate with the status of the offender.

Lack of Public and Political Commitment. The public demands action only sporadically, as intermittent, sensational disclosures reveal intolerable violence and corruption caused by organized crime. Without sustained public pressure, political office seekers and office holders have little incentive to address themselves to combatting organized crime. A drive against organized crime usually uncovers political corruption; this means that a crusading mayor or district attorney makes many political enemies. The vicious cycle perpetuates itself. Politicians will not act unless the public so demands; but much of the urban public wants the services provided by organized crime and does not wish to disrupt the system that provides those services. And much of the public does not see or understand the effects of organized crime in society.

A NATIONAL STRATEGY AGAINST ORGANIZED CRIME

Law enforcement's way of fighting organized crime has been primitive compared to organized crime's way of operating. Law enforcement must use methods at least as efficient as organized crime's. The public and law enforcement must make a full-scale commitment to destroy the power of organized crime groups. The Commission's program indicates ways to implement that commitment.

PROOF OF CRIMINAL VIOLATION

The previous section has described the difficulties that law enforcement agencies meet in trying to prove the participation of organized crime family members in criminal acts. Although earlier studies indicated a need for new substantive criminal laws, the Commission believes that on the Federal level, and in most State jurisdictions where organized crime exists, the major problem relates to matters of proof rather than inadequacy of substantive criminal laws, as the latter—for the most part—are reasonably adequate to deal with organized crime activity. The laws of conspiracy have provided an effective substantive tool with which to confront the criminal groups. From a legal standpoint, organized crime continues to grow because of defects in the evidence-gathering process. Under present procedures, too few witnesses have been produced to prove the link between criminal group members and the illicit activities that they sponsor.

Grand Juries. A compulsory process is necessary to obtain essential testimony or material. This is most readily accomplished by an investigative grand jury or an alternate mechanism through which the attendance of witnesses and production of books and records can be ordered. Such grand juries must stay in session long enough to allow for the unusually long time required to build an organized crime case. The possibility of arbitrary termination of a grand jury by supervisory judges constitutes a danger to successful completion of an investigation.

The Commission recommends:

At least one investigative grand jury should be impaneled annually in each jurisdiction that has major organized crime activity.

If a grand jury shows the court that its business is unfinished at the end of a normal term, the court should extend that term a reasonable time in order to allow the grand jury to complete pending investigations. Judicial dismissal of grand juries with unfinished business should be appealable by the prosecutor and provision made for suspension of such dismissal orders during the appeal.

The automatic convening of these grand juries would force less than diligent investigators and prosecutors to explain their inaction. The grand jury should also have recourse when not satisfied with such explanations.

The Commission recommends:

The grand jury should have the statutory right of appeal to an appropriate executive official, such as an attorney general or governor, to replace local prosecutors or investigators with special counsel or special investigators appointed only in relation to matters that they or the grand jury deem appropriate for investigation.

When a grand jury terminates, it should be permitted by law to file public reports regarding organized crime conditions in the community.

Immunity. A general immunity statute as proposed in chapter 5 on the courts is essential on organized crime investigations and prosecutions. There is evidence to indicate that the availability of immunity can overcome the wall of silence that so often defeats the efforts of law enforcement to obtain live witnesses in organized crime cases. Since the activities of criminal groups involve such a broad scope of criminal violations, immunity provisions covering this breadth of illicit actions are necessary to secure the testimony of uncooperative or criminally involved witnesses. Once granted immunity from prosecution based upon their testimony, such witnesses must testify before the grand jury and at trial, or face jail for contempt of court.

Federal, State, and local coordination of immunity grants, and approval by the jurisdiction's chief law enforcement officer before immunity is granted, are crucial in organized crime investigations. Otherwise, without such coordination and approval, or through corruption of officials, one jurisdiction might grant immunity to someone about to be arrested or indicted in another jurisdiction.

The Commission recommends:

A general witness immunity statute should be enacted at Federal and State levels, providing immunity sufficiently broad to assure compulsion of testimony. Immunity should be granted only with the prior approval of the jurisdiction's chief prosecuting officer. Efforts to coordinate Federal, State, and local

immunity grants should be made to prevent interference with existing investigations.

Perjury. Many prosecutors believe that the incidence of perjury is higher in organized crime cases than in routine criminal matters. Immunity can be an effective prosecutive weapon only if the immunized witness then testifies truthfully. The present special proof requirements in perjury cases, detailed in chapter 5, inhibit prosecutors from seeking perjury indictments and lead to much lower conviction rates for perjury than for other crimes. Lessening of rigid proof requirements in perjury prosecutions would strengthen the deterrent value of perjury laws and present a greater incentive for truthful testimony.

The Commission recommends:

Congress and the States should abolish the rigid two-witness and direct-evidence rules in perjury prosecutions, but retain the requirement of proving an intentional false statement.

WIRETAPPING AND EAVESDROPPING

In connection with the problems of securing evidence against organized crime, the Commission considered issues relating to electronic surveillance, including wiretapping and "bugging"—the secret installation of mechanical devices at specific locations to receive and transmit conversations.

Significance to Law Enforcement. The great majority of law enforcement officials believe that the evidence necessary to bring criminal sanctions to bear consistently on the higher echelons of organized crime will not be obtained without the aid of electronic surveillance techniques. They maintain these techniques are indispensable to develop adequate strategic intelligence concerning organized crime, to set up specific investigations, to develop witnesses, to corroborate their testimony, and to serve as substitutes for them—each a necessary step in the evidence-gathering process in organized crime investigations and prosecutions.

As previously noted, the organizational structure and operational methods employed by organized crime have created unique problems for law enforcement. High-ranking organized crime figures are protected by layers of insulation from direct participation in criminal acts, and a rigid code of discipline inhibits the development of informants against them. A soldier in a family can complete his entire crime career without ever associating directly with his boss. Thus, he is unable, even if willing, to link the boss directly to any criminal activity in which he may have engaged for their mutual benefit. Agents and employees of an organized crime family, even when granted immunity from prosecution, cannot implicate the highest level figures, since frequently they have neither spoken to, nor even seen them.

Members of the underworld, who have legitimate reason to fear that their meetings might be bugged or their telephones tapped, have continued to meet and to make relatively free use of the telephone—for communication is essential to the operation of any business enterprise. In legitimate business this is accomplished with written and oral exchanges. In organized crime enterprises, however, the possibility of loss or seizure of an incriminating document demands a minimum of written communication. Because of the varied character of organized criminal enterprises, the large numbers of persons employed in them, and frequently the distances separating elements of the organization, the telephone remains an essential vehicle for communication. While discussions of business matters are held on a face-to-face basis whenever possible, they are never conducted in the presence of strangers. Thus, the content of these conversations, including the planning of new illegal activity, and transmission of policy decisions or operating instructions for existing enterprises, cannot be detected. The extreme scrutiny to which potential members are subjected and the necessity for them to engage in criminal activity have precluded law enforcement infiltration of organized crime groups.

District Attorney Frank S. Hogan, whose New York County office has been acknowledged for over 27 years as one of the country's most outstanding, has testified that electronic surveillance is:

the single most valuable weapon in law enforcement's fight against organized crime . . . It has permitted us to undertake major investigations of organized crime. Without it, and I confine myself to top figures in the underworld, my own office could not have convicted Charles "Lucky" Luciano, Jimmy Hines, Louis "Lepke" Buchalter, Jacob "Gurrah" Shapiro, Joseph "Socks" Lanza, George Scalise, Frank Erickson, John "Dio" Dioguardi, and Frank Carbo . . .

Over the years New York has faced one of the Nation's most aggravated organized crime problems. Only in New

York have law enforcement officials achieved some level of continuous success in bringing prosecutions against organized crime. For over 20 years, New York has authorized wiretapping on court order. Since 1957, bugging has been similarly authorized. Wiretapping was the mainstay of the New York attack against organized crime until Federal court decisions intervened. Recently chief reliance in some offices has been placed on bugging, where the information is to be used in court. Law enforcement officials believe that the successes achieved in some parts of the State are attributable primarily to a combination of dedicated and competent personnel and adequate legal tools; and that the failure to do more in New York has resulted primarily from the failure to commit additional resources of time and men. The debilitating effect of corruption, political influence, and incompetence, underscored by the New York State Commission of Investigation, must also be noted.

In New York at one time, Court supervision of law enforcement's use of electronic surveillance was sometimes perfunctory, but the picture has changed substantially under the impact of pretrial adversary hearing on motions to suppress electronically seized evidence. Fifteen years ago there was evidence of abuse by low-rank policemen. Legislative and administrative controls, however, have apparently been successful in curtailing its incidence.

The Threat to Privacy.   In a democratic society privacy of communication is essential if citizens are to think and act creatively and constructively. Fear of suspicion that one's speech is being monitored by a stranger, even without the reality of such activity, can have a seriously inhibiting effect upon the willingness to voice critical and constructive ideas. When dissent from the popular view is discouraged, intellectual controversy is smothered, the process for testing new concepts and ideas is hindered and desirable change is slowed. External restraints, of which electronic surveillance is but one possibility, are thus repugnant to citizens of such a society.

Today, in addition to some law enforcement agents, numerous private persons are utilizing these techniques. They are employed to acquire evidence for domestic relations cases, to carry on industial espionage and counterespionage, to assist in preparing for civil litigation, and for personnel investigations, among others. Technological advances have produced remarkably sophisticated devices, of which the electronic cocktail olive is illustrative, and continuing price reductions have expanded their markets. Nor has man's ingenuity in the development of surveillance equipment been exhausted with the design and manufacture of electronic devices for wiretapping or for eavesdropping within buildings or vehicles. Parabolic microphones that pick up conversations held in the open at distances of hundreds of feet are available commercially, and some progress has been made toward utilizing the laser beam to pick up conversations within a room by focusing upon the glass of a convenient window. Progress in microminiaturizing electronic components has resulted in the production of equipment of extremely small size. Because it can detect what is said anywhere—not just on the telephone—bugging presents especially serious threats to privacy.

Detection of surveillance devices is difficult, particularly where an installation is accomplished by a skilled agent. Isolated instances where equipment is discovered in operation therefore do not adequately reflect the volume of such activity; the effectiveness of electronic surveillance depends in part upon investigators who do not discuss their activities. The current confusion over the legality of electronic surveillance compounds the assessment problem since many agents feel their conduct may be held unlawful and are unwilling to report their activities. It is presently impossible to estimate with any accuracy the volume of electronic surveillance conducted today. The Commission is impressed, however, with the opinions of knowledgeable persons that the incidence of electronic surveillance is already substantial and increasing at a rapid rate.

Present Law and Practice. In 1928 the U.S. Supreme Court decided that evidence obtained by wiretapping a defendant's telephone at a point outside the defendant's premises was admissible in a Federal criminal prosecution. The Court found no unconstitutional search and seizure under the Fourth Amendment. Enactment of Section 605 of the Federal Communications Act in 1934 precluded interception and disclosure of wire communications. The Department of Justice has interpreted this section to permit interception so long as no disclosure of the content outside the Department is made. Thus, wiretapping may presently be conducted by a Federal agent, but the results may not be used in court. When police officers wiretap and disclose the information obtained, in accordance with State procedure, they are in violation of Federal law.

Law enforcement experience with bugging has been much more recent and more limited than the use of the traditional

471

wiretap. The legal situation with respect to bugging is also different. The regulation of the national telephone communication network falls within recognized national powers, while legislation attempting to authorize the placing of electronic equipment even under a warrant system would break new and uncharted ground. At the present time there is no Federal legislation explicitly dealing with bugging. Since the decision of the Supreme Court in *Silverman* v. *United States,* 365 U.S. 505 (1961), use of bugging equipment that involves an unauthorized physical entry into a constitutionally protected private area violates the Fourth Amendment, and evidence thus obtained is inadmissible. If eavesdropping is unaccompanied by such a trespass, or if the communication is recorded with the consent of one of the parties, no such prohibition applies.

The confusion that has arisen inhibits cooperation between State and Federal law enforcement agencies because of the fear that information secured in one investigation will legally pollute another. For example, in New York City prosecutors refuse to divulge the contents of wire communications intercepted pursuant to State court orders because of the Federal proscription but do utilize evidence obtained by bugging pursuant to court order. In other sections of New York State, however, prosecutors continue to introduce both wiretapping and eavesdropping evidence at trial.

Despite the clear Federal prohibition against disclosure of wiretap information no Federal prosecutions of State officers under State laws have occurred.

One of the most serious consequences of the present state of the law is that private parties and some law enforcement officers are invading the privacy of many citizens without control from the courts and reasonable legislative standards. While the Federal prohibition is a partial deterrent against divulgence, it has no effect on interception, and the lack of prosecutive action against violators has substantially reduced respect for the law.

The present status of the law with respect to wiretapping and bugging is intolerable. It serves the interests neither of privacy nor of law enforcement. One way or the other, the present controversy with respect to electronic surveillance must be resolved.

The Commission recommends:

Congress should enact legislation dealing specifically with wiretapping and bugging.

All members of the Commission agree on the difficulty of striking the balance between law enforcement benefits from the use of electronic surveillance and the threat to privacy its use may entail. Further, striking this balance presents important constitutional questions now pending before the U.S. Supreme Court in *People* v. *Berger,* and any congressional action should await the outcome of that case.

All members of the Commission believe that if authority to employ these techniques is granted it must be granted only with stringent limitations. One form of detailed regulatory statute that has been suggested to the Commission is outlined in the appendix to the Commission's organized crime task force volume. All private use of electronic surveillance should be placed under rigid control, or it should be outlawed.

A majority of the members of the Commission believe that legislation should be enacted granting carefully circumscribed authority for electronic surveillance to law enforcement officers to the extent it may be consistent with the decision of the Supreme Court in *People* v. *Berger,* and, further, that the availability of such specific authority would significantly reduce the incentive for, and the incidence of, improper electronic surveillance.

The other members of the Commission have serious doubts about the desirability of such authority and believe that without the kind of searching inquiry that would result from further congressional consideration of electronic surveillance, particularly to the problems of bugging, there is insufficient basis to strike this balance against the interests of privacy.

Matters affecting the national security not involving criminal prosecution are outside the Commission's mandate, and nothing in this discussion is intended to affect the existing powers to protect that interest.

SENTENCING

Criminal statutes do not now authorize greater punishment when the violation was committed as part of an organized crime business. The Model Sentencing Act creates a separate category for such violations. It provides for 30 years' commitment of any felony offender who is so dangerous that the public must be protected from him and whose felony was committed as part of a continuing criminal activity in concert with one or more persons. The Model Penal Code also contains separate provisions for heavier sentences of defendants connected with organized crime.

473

The Commission recommends:

Federal and State legislation should be enacted to provide for extended prison terms where the evidence, presentence report, or sentence hearing shows that a felony was committed as part of a continuing illegal business in which the convicted offender occupied a supervisory or other management position.

This will make it possible to distinguish, for example, between the streetworker in a gambling operation and an office supervisor or higher management person.

There must be some kind of supervision over those trial judges who, because of corruption, political considerations, or lack of knowledge, tend to mete out light sentences in cases involving organized crime management personnel. Consideration should therefore be given to allowing the prosecution the right of appeal regarding sentences of persons in management positions in an organized crime activity or group. Constitutional requirements for such an appellate procedure must first be carefully explored.

APPEALS FROM SUPPRESSION ORDERS

The Commission's recommendation in chapter 5 that prosecutors be permitted to appeal trial court orders suppressing evidence is particularly important in organized crime cases, where so much investigative and prosecutive time has been expended, and where evidence gathering is extremely difficult. Allowing appeals would also help overcome corrupt judicial actions. In gambling cases, particularly, arbitrary rejection of evidence uncovered in a search is one method by which corrupt judges perform their service for organized crime.

PROTECTION OF WITNESSES

No jurisdiction has made adequate provision for protecting witnesses in organized crime cases from reprisal. In the few instances where guards are provided, resources require their withdrawal shortly after the particular trial terminates. On a case-to-case basis, governments have helped witnesses find jobs in other sections of the country or have even helped them to emigrate. The difficulty of obtaining witnesses because of the fear of reprisal could be countered somewhat if governments had established systems for protecting cooperative witnesses.

The Commission recommends:

The Federal Government should establish residential facilities for the protection of witnesses desiring such assistance during the pendency of organized crime litigation.

After trial, the witness should be permitted to remain at the facility so long as he needs to be protected. The Federal Government should establish regular procedures to help Federal and local witnesses who fear organized crime reprisal, to find jobs and places to live in other parts of the country, and to preserve their anonymity from organized crime groups.

INVESTIGATION AND PROSECUTION UNITS

State and Local Manpower. There is, as described above, minimal concentrated law enforcement activity directed at organized crime. Only a few cities have established police intelligence and prosecutorial units specifically for developing organized crime cases. Legal tools such as electronic surveillance and immunity will be of limited use unless an adequate body of trained and expert investigators and prosecutors exists to use those tools properly.

The Commission recommends:

Every attorney general in States where organized crime exists should form in his office a unit of attorneys and investigators to gather information and assist in prosecution regarding this criminal activity.

Investigators should include those with the special skills, such as accounting and undercover operations, crucial to organized crime matters. Members of the State police could be assigned to this unit. In local areas where it appears that the jurisdiction's law enforcement agencies are not adequately combatting organized crime, State police should conduct investigations, make arrests, or conduct searches upon request of any branch of the local government. This should be done without the knowledge of local officials if, because of apparent corruption, it is necessary. The State police should cooperate with, and seek advice from the State attorney general's special unit. For local enforcement,

The Commission recommends:

Police departments in every major city should have a special intelligence unit solely to ferret out organized criminal activity and to collect information regarding the possible entry of criminal cartels into the area's criminal operations.

Staffing needs will depend on local conditions, but the intelligence program should have a priority rating that insures assignment of adequate personnel. Perhaps the enormous amount of manpower devoted to petty vice conditions should be reduced and the investigative personnel for organized crime cases increased. Criteria for evaluating the effectiveness of the units, other than mere numbers of arrests, must be developed.

The background of potential intelligence unit members should be investigated extensively and only the most talented and trustworthy assigned to those units. Salary levels should be such that membership in the unit could be a career in itself.

One of the duties of the police legal advisers recommended in chapter 4 should be consultation with the intelligence unit. Special training programs should be used to teach the necessary skills involved in organized crime investigative work.

Because of the special skills and extensive time involved in organized crime cases, prosecution thereof requires concentrated efforts.

The Commission recommends:

The prosecutor's office in every major city should have sufficient manpower assigned full time to organized crime cases. Such personnel should have the power to initiate organized crime investigations and to conduct the investigative grand juries recommended above.

Special training in these legal tactics should be provided; the prosecutors should work closely with the police units.

Development and dissemination of intelligence. Since the activities of organized crime overlap individual police jurisdictions, the various law enforcement agencies must share information and coordinate their plans.

On the Federal level, enforcement agencies are furnishing a large amount of intelligence to the Organized Crime and

Racketeering (OCR) Section in the Department of Justice. But there is no central place where a strategic intelligence system regarding organized crime groups is being developed to coordinate an integrated Federal plan for enforcement and regulatory agencies.

The Commission recommends:

The Federal Government should create a central computerized office into which each Federal agency would feed all of its organized crime intelligence.

Intelligence information in the OCR Section is now recorded manually in a card catalog. Much information, such as that discovered in grand jury proceedings, has not been incorporated because of limited resources. Many Federal agencies do not submit information on a case until it has been completed. A central office in the Department of Justice should have proper recording facilities and should analyze intelligence information fed to it by all relevant Federal agencies keeping current with events. A pool of information experts from the FBI, Secret Service, Central Intelligence Agency and other departments and private companies should help build the system, which would employ punch cards, tapes, and other modern information storage and retrieval techniques. Each agency, of course, would maintain its own files, but being able to draw upon the capability of the central computer would eliminate duplication of effort and justify the cost of the new operation. A strategic intelligence system necessary to satisfy investigative, prosecutive, and regulatory needs must have specialists in economics, sociology, business administration, operations research, and other disciplines, as well as those trained in law enforcement.

Since organized crime crosses State lines, the Commission recommends the creation of regional organizations, such as that established by the New England State Police Compact. Large States could develop statewide systems, such as exists in New York, as well as participate in regional compacts.

These systems should permit and encourage greater exchange of information among Federal, State, and local agencies. Currently, information sharing proceeds on a personal basis; i.e., information is given officers who, through personal contact with agents of the disseminator, have proved their trustworthiness.

Perhaps a central security system should be developed (like the military system), in which one who has been

Coordinated Effort Against Organized Crime

Commitment of Political Leaders
26 Federal Investigative Agencies
Federal Prosecutors' Units
Federal Regulatory Agencies
Joint Congressional Investigative Committee

Federal Groups

Commitment of Political Leaders
Local Police Special Units
Local Prosecutors' Units
Government Crime Commissions
Grand Jury Reports

Local Groups

Organized Crime

State Groups

Commitment of Political Leaders
State Police Investigations
State Attorney General Intelligence Units
State and Regional Intelligence Groups
State Prosecutors' Units
State Regulatory Agencies
Government Crime Commissions

Private Groups

Commitment of Citizens
Private Crime Commissions
Press and News Media
Social Scientists
Private Trade Associations

cleared to receive information and who demonstrates a need for it can obtain information, whether or not the disseminator and recipient are personally acquainted. Standards for clearance should be established, and any agency with available manpower could conduct the investigation of potential recipients of information.

Sharing information on other than a person-to-person basis of mutual trust will be a delicate, evolutionary process. Preservation of the secrecy of each confidential informant's identity is an absolute requirement for any successful intelligence-gathering agency. Law enforcement agents are loath to make information available when its source could be guessed or inferred. However, great amounts of intelligence can be shared without revealing the possible identity of the informant, and information sharing by means of a mechanical, central security system would still be of great value.

The proposed organized crime intelligence program of the New York State Identification and Intelligence System illustrates one way to solve the problem of keeping the source of information secret. By that system the agency that commits information to central storage would be allowed to choose what other agencies may draw upon those particular data.

The Commission recommends:

The Department of Justice should give financial assistance to encourage the development of efficient systems for regional intelligence gathering, collection and dissemination. By financial assistance and provisions of security clearance, the Department should also sponsor and encourage research by the many relevant disciplines regarding the nature, development, activities, and organization of these special criminal groups.

Federal Law Enforcement. The Attorney General should continue to be the focal point of the Federal enforcement drive against organized crime. The Organized Crime and Racketeering (OCR) Section is the coordinating and policy-making body within the Department of Justice. The Commission believes that greater centralization of the Federal effort is desirable and possible.

Experience in some areas has shown that an effective partnership can be built between OCR Section attorneys and prosecutors in the 94 U.S. Attorneys' offices throughout the Nation. Such cooperation should be the rule for the organized crime program, which should not be the exclusive province of either the OCR Section or the U.S. Attorneys.

Different responsibilities within the Federal agencies have produced investigators with special skills and talents. The expertise of these agents should be used by organizing them into investigative teams that work exclusively on organized crime matters under the direction of the OCR Section.

The Commission recommends:

The staff of the OCR Section should be greatly increased, and the section should have final authority for decision-making in its relationship with U.S. Attorneys on organized crime cases.

The Federal Government could also do much to assist and coordinate the work of State and local organized crime enforcement. There is very little such assistance at present.

The Commission recommends:

A technical assistance program should be launched wherein local jurisdictions can request the help of experienced Federal prosecutors from the OCR Section. The Department of Justice, through the FBI and the OCR Section, should conduct organized crime training sessions for State and local law enforcement officers.

This training could supplement the extensive general enforcement sessions now conducted by the FBI and the narcotics enforcement training offered by the Federal Bureau of Narcotics. The proposed training would concentrate on the development of special investigative and prosecutive techniques necessary in organized crime investigations.

In view of the additional responsibilities cast upon the OCR Section by these recommendations, perhaps its status should be raised to a division-level operation which would be headed by an Assistant Attorney General appointed by the President.

These recommendations for the OCR Section would not remove any of the existing responsibility of Federal investigating agencies.

Legislative Investigations. To give necessary impetus to a continuing drive against organized crime, the public must be constantly informed of its manifestations and influences. The changing nature of organized criminal activities also requires that legislators constantly analyze needs for new substantive and procedural provisions.

The Commission recommends:

A permanent joint congressional committee on organized crime should be created.

A permanent committee would focus the interest of those members of Congress who have in the past displayed concern with the problem, and would involve a greater number of legislators than at present. It could mean that there would be a larger staff to concentrate on the problem and to permit consideration of the implications of any new legislation for organized crime. In addition, the creation of such a committee would place the prestige of the U.S. Congress behind the proposition that organized crime is a national problem of the highest priority.

PUBLIC AND PRIVATE CRIME INVESTIGATING COMMISSIONS

Crime investigating commissions financed by State governments, such as in New York and Illinois, have proved to be effective for informing the public about organized crime conditions. Legislative proposals to combat organized crime also result from the hearings of these committees.

The Commission recommends:

States that have organized crime groups in operation should create and finance organized crime investigation commissions with independent, permanent status, with an adequate staff of investigators, and with subpoena power. Such commissions should hold hearings and furnish periodic reports to the legislature, Governor, and law enforcement officials.

Independent citizen crime commissions in metropolitan areas can provide enlightened resistance to the growth of organized crime and to the formation of alliances between it and politics. A citizen crime commission can give reliable and determined community leadership to assess the local government's effort to control organized crime. It can provide impartial public education, marshal public support for government agencies that have committed resources to special organized crime drives, monitor judicial and law enforcement performance, organize public responses, and enlist business cooperation against infiltration by organized crime.

The Commission recommends:

Citizens and business groups should organize permanent citizen crime commissions to combat organized crime. Financial contributions should be solicited to maintain at least a full-time executive director and a part-time staff.

At this time there are not enough citizen crime commissions functioning effectively in the Nation. A national coordinating headquarters could be established in Washington, D.C., to encourage and guide the creation of new commissions and to provide services to improve existing ones. Private foundation funds should be sought to help establish and administer the headquarters.

It would provide channels for communication among citizen crime commissions, between such commissions and national agencies of government, and between crime commissions and mutual interest associations such as the International Association of Chiefs of Police, the National District Attorneys Association, the National Council on Crime and Delinquency, and others. Such a headquarters could give concerned citizens in any community the technical assistance necessary for initiating a crime commission. In addition to making training personnel available for short-term assignments with local commissions, a headquarters could establish formal procedures for training professionals in crime commission management. A national headquarters could also motivate States and communities to undertake reforms in their criminal justice systems and to deal with other community problems unrelated to organized crime.

PRIVATE AND GOVERNMENT REGULATION

Law enforcement is not the only weapon that governments have to control organized crime. Regulatory activity can have a great effect. One means to diminish organized crime's influence on politics, for example, would be legislation subjecting political contributions and expenditures to greater public visibility and providing incentives for wider citizen contributions to State and local political activity. Tax regulations could be devised to require disclosure of hidden, or beneficial, owners of partnerships and corporations that do not have public ownership.

Government at various levels has not explored the regulatory devices available to thwart the activities of criminal groups, especially in the area of infiltration of legitimate business. These techniques are especially valuable because they require a less rigid standard of proof of violation than the guilt-beyond-a-reasonable-doubt requirement of criminal law. Regulatory agencies also have powers of inspection not afforded to law enforcement. State income tax enforcement could be directed at organized crime's businesses. Food inspectors could uncover regulatory violations in organized crime's restaurant and food processing businesses. Liquor authorities could close premises of organized crime-owned bars in which illicit activities constantly occur. Civil proceedings could stop unfair trade practices and antitrust violations by organized crime businesses. Trade associations could alert companies to organized crime's presence and tactics and stimulate action by private business.

The Commission recommends:

Groups should be created within the Federal and State departments of justice to develop strategies and enlist regulatory action against businesses infiltrated by organized crime.

Private business associations should develop strategies to prevent and uncover organized crime's illegal and unfair business tactics.

NEWS MEDIA

In recent years, the American press has become more concerned about organized crime. Some metropolitan newspapers report organized crime activity on a continuing basis, and a few employ investigative reporters whose exclusive concern is organized crime. The television industry, as well, has accepted a responsibility for informing the American citizen of the magnitude of the problem.

In some parts of the country revelations in local newspapers have stimulated governmental action and political reform. Especially in smaller communities, the independence of the press may be the public's only hope of finding out about organized crime. Public officials concerned about organized crime are encouraged to act when comprehensive newspaper reporting has alerted and enlisted community support.

483

The Commission recommends:

All newspapers in major metropolitan areas where organized crime exists should designate a highly competent reporter for full-time work and writing concerning organized criminal activities, the corruption caused by it, and governmental efforts to control it. Newspapers in smaller communities dominated by organized crime should fulfill their responsibility to inform the public of the nature and consequence of these conditions.

PARTICIPATION BY LOCAL GOVERNMENT LEADERS

Enforcement against organized crime and accompanying public corruption proceeds with required intensity only when the political leaders in Federal, State, and local governments provide aggressive leadership. They are the only persons who can secure the resources that law enforcement needs. They are the only ones who can assure police officials that no illegal activity or participating person is to be protected from proper enforcement action. They are the only ones who can insure that persons cooperating with organized criminal groups are not appointed to public office. They are the only ones who can provide for effective monitoring of regulatory action to expose irregular practices or favors given to businesses dominated by criminal groups. They are the ones who can provide full backing for a police chief who institutes internal inspection, promotion and other practices, as recommended in chapter 4, for controlling police corruption.

Mayors, Governors, and the President of the United States must be given adequate information concerning organized crime conditions. Dissemination of incomplete or unevaluated intelligence about individuals would present grave civil liberties problems. However, government leaders must be made aware of the particular activities of organized crime groups.

The Commission recommends:

Enforcement officials should provide regular briefings to leaders at all levels of government concerning organized crime conditions within the jurisdiction.

The briefings should be supplemented by written reports further describing those conditions as well as current governmental action to combat them. Reports of conditions should also be furnished periodically by the Federal Government to

State and local jurisdictions, and by State governments to local jurisdictions. Reports should be withheld from jurisdictions where corruption is apparent and knowledge by a corrupt official of the information in the report could compromise enforcement efforts.

Public fears of reporting organized crime conditions to apparently corrupt police and governmental personnel must also be met directly. If an independent agency for accepting citizen grievances, such as is suggested in chapter 13, is established, it should be charged with accepting citizen complaints and information about organized crime and corruption.

Information obtained in this way could be forwarded to Federal, State, or local law enforcement officials, or to all of them, at the direction of the agency. Names of sources should be kept confidential if the citizen so requests or if the agency deems it necessary.

The above program is not intended as a series of independent proposals. It represents an integrated package requiring combined action by the American people, its governments and its businesses. Organized crime succeeds only insofar as the Nation permits it to succeed. Because of the magnitude of the problem, the various branches of government cannot act with success individually. Each must help the other. Laws and procedures are of no avail without proper enforcement machinery. Prevention fails unless citizens, individually and through organizations, devise solutions and encourage their elected representatives. Regulation must accomplish what criminal law enforcement cannot. Above all, the endeavor to break the structure and power of organized crime—an endeavor that the Commission firmly believes can succeed—requires a commitment of the public far beyond that which now exists. Action must replace words; knowledge must replace fascination. Only when the American people and their governments develop the will can law enforcement and other agencies find the way.

In many ways organized crime is the most sinister kind of crime in America. The men who control it have become rich and powerful by encouraging the needy to gamble, by luring the troubled to destroy themselves with drugs, by extorting the profits of honest and hardworking businessmen, by collecting usury from those in financial plight, by maiming or murdering those who oppose them, by bribing those who are sworn to destroy them. Organized crime is not merely a few preying upon a few. In a very real sense it is dedicated to subverting not only American institutions, but the very decency and integrity that are the most cherished attributes of a free society. As the leaders of Cosa Nostra and their racketeering allies pursue their conspiracy unmolested, in open and continuous defiance of the law, they preach a sermon that all too many Americans heed: The government is for sale; lawlessness is the road to wealth; honesty is a pitfall and morality a trap for suckers.

The extraordinary thing about organized crime is that America has tolerated it for so long.

Chapter 8

Narcotics and Drug Abuse

IN 1962 a White House Conference on Narcotic and Drug Abuse was convened in recognition of the fact that drug traffic and abuse were growing and critical national concerns. Large quantities of drugs were moving in illicit traffic despite the best efforts of law enforcement agencies. Addiction to the familiar opiates, especially in big-city ghettos, was widespread. New stimulant, depressant, and hallucinogenic drugs, many of them under loose legal controls, were coming into wide misuse, often by students. The informed public was becoming increasingly aware of the social and economic damage of illicit drug taking.

Organized criminals engaged in drug traffic were making high profits. Drug addicts, to support their habits, were stealing millions of dollars worth of property every year and contributing to the public's fear of robbery and burglary. The police, the courts, the jails and prisons, and social-service agencies of all kinds were devoting great amounts of time, money and manpower to attempts to control drug abuse. Worst of all, thousands of human lives were being wasted.

Some methods of medical treatment, at least for opiate-dependent persons, were being tried, but the results were generally impermanent; relapse was more frequent than cure. The established cycle for such persons was arrest, confinement with or without treatment, release, and then arrest again. And the cause of all of this, the drug-prone personality and the drug-taking urge, lay hidden somewhere in the conditions of modern urban life and in the complexities of mental disorder.

Responsibility for the drug abuse problem was not at all

clear. Was it a Federal or a State matter? Was it a police problem or a medical one? If, as seemed evident, it was a combination of all of these, which agencies or people should be doing what? The Conference did not answer these questions, but it did bring to them a sense of national importance and commitment.

The President's Advisory Commission on Narcotic and Drug Abuse was created in 1963 to translate this commitment into a program of action. The Commission's final report, issued in November of that year, set forth a strategy designed to improve the control of drug traffic and the treatment of drug users. The 25 recommendations of that report have been the basis for most of the subsequent Federal activity in this field. Many of them, notably those pertaining to civil commitment for narcotic addicts and the need for Federal controls on the distribution of nonnarcotic drugs, have been or are in the process of being implemented.

This Commission has not and could not have undertaken to duplicate the comprehensive study and report on drug abuse so recently completed by another Presidential Commission. Yet any study of law enforcement and the administration of criminal justice must of necessity include some reference to drug abuse and its associated problems. In the course of the discussion in this chapter, recommendations are made where they seem clearly advisable. In many instances these recommendations parallel ones made by the 1963 Commission.

There have been major innovations in legal procedures and medical techniques during the last few years. There are new Federal and State laws and programs designed to provide treatment both for narcotic addicts charged with or convicted of crime, and for those who come to the attention of public authorities without criminal charge. These laws and programs signify that the Nation's approach to narcotic addiction has changed fundamentally. They are on a creative effort to treat the person who is dependent on drugs.

Careful implementation, evaluation, and coordination of the new programs, some of which are not yet in operation, will be absolutely essential. These are among today's first needs. New ideas are only a first step. Unless the programs they lead to are provided with sufficient money and manpower and are competently administered, no improvement in drug abuse problems can be expected.

THE DRUGS AND THEIR REGULATION

The drugs liable to abuse are usually put into the two classifications of "narcotics" and "dangerous drugs," and the people who abuse them are usually called "addicts" and "users." The terms have been used carelessly and have gathered around them many subjective associations. Some precision is necessary if they are to be used as instruments of analysis.

ADDICTION

There is no settled definition of addiction. Sociologists speak of "assimilation into a special life style of drug taking." Doctors speak of "physical dependence," an alteration in the central nervous system that results in painful sickness when use of the drug is abruptly discontinued; of "psychological or psychic dependence," an emotional desire, craving or compulsion to obtain and experience the drug; and of "tolerance," a physical adjustment to the drug that results in successive doses producing smaller effects and, therefore, in a tendency to increase doses. Statutes speak of habitual use; of loss of the power of self-control respecting the drug; and of effects detrimental to the individual or potentially harmful to the public morals, safety, health or welfare.

Some drugs are addicting, and some persons are addicted, by one definition but not by another. The World Health Organization Expert Committee on Addiction-Producing Drugs has recommended that the term "drug dependence," with a modifying phrase linking it to a particular type of drug, be used in place of the term "addiction." But "addiction" seems too deeply imbedded in the popular vocabulary to be expunged. Most frequently, it connotes physical dependence, resulting from excessive use of certain drugs. However, it should be noted that one can become physically dependent on substances, notably alcohol, that are not considered part of the drug abuse problem. It should be noted also that psychic or emotional dependence can develop to any substances, not only drugs, that affect consciousness and that people use for escape, adjustment or simple pleasure.

NARCOTICS

The dictionary defines a "narcotic" as a substance that induces sleep, dulls the senses, or relieves pain. In law, however, it has been given an artificial meaning. It does not refer, as might be expected, to one class of drugs, each having similar chemical properties or pharmacological effects. It is applied rather to a number of different classes of drugs that have been grouped together for purposes of legal control. Under the Federal laws, narcotics include the opiates and cocaine. Under most State statutes, marihuana is also a narcotic.

The Opiates. These drugs have a highly technical legal definition, but for purposes of this chapter they may be taken to include opium, morphine, their derivatives and compounds and their synthetic equivalents. The opiates have great medical value. They differ widely in their uses, effects, and addiction potential. The most common are morphine and codeine. The former is a principal drug in the relief of pain, the latter in the treatment of cough. Many opiates are prescribed for use in approved medical settings. While the misuse or illicit use (drug "abuse" includes both) of some of these drugs has presented serious problems for State and Federal enforcement agencies, public concern as to the opiates is focused primarily on heroin, a morphine derivative. This is the chief drug of addiction in the United States.

The effect of any drug depends on many variables, not the least of which are the mood and expectation of the taker. Drug effects are therefore best expressed in terms of probable outcomes. The discussion here is selective rather than exhaustive. With these provisos, it may be said that heroin is a depressant. It relieves anxiety and tension and diminishes the sex, hunger, and other primary drives. It may also produce drowsiness and cause inability to concentrate, apathy, and lessened physical activity. It can impair mental and physical performance. Repeated and prolonged administration will certainly lead to tolerance and physical dependence.

This process is set in motion by the first dose. An overdose may lead to respiratory failure, coma and death. With dosages to which a person is tolerant, permanent organic damage does not occur. However, secondary effects, arising from the preoccupation of a person with the drug, may include personal neglect and malnutrition. The ritual of the American addict is to inject the drug intravenously with a needle, and infections and abscesses may be caused by the use of unsterile equipment. Euphoria is an effect often associated with heroin, often reflecting the relief a particular individual gets from chronic anxiety. Among the symptoms of the withdrawal sickness, which reaches peak intensity in 24–48 hours, are muscle aches, cramps, and nausea.

The Bureau of Narcotics maintains a name file of active opiate addicts. As of December 31, 1965, there were 52,793 heroin addicts (out of a total of 57,199 opiate addicts) listed. Most of the names in the file are of persons arrested by State and local police agencies and reported voluntarily to the Bureau on a form the Bureau provides for this purpose. Thus the inclusion of a person's name in the file depends in large measure on his coming to the attention of the police, being recognized and classified as an addict, and being reported. There is some uncertainty at each step. Moreover some police agencies, and many health and medical agencies, do not participate in the voluntary reporting system. There is also no place in the system for persons who use opiates without becoming addicted. For these reasons many people feel that the Bureau's file does not present a complete statistical picture of opiate use in this country. Indeed the Bureau makes no claims of infallibility for the reporting system. It is intended as a device for arriving at a workable estimate of the extent and concentration of opiate addiction. The Commissioner of Narcotics has testified numerous times that the Bureau's figures are only approximations. The State of California is another source for statistics on drug addiction; it maintains a file of addicts-users in the State.

It should also be noted that other estimates of the present addict population, some of which cite figures as high as 200,000, are without a solid statistical foundation.

More than one-half the known heroin addicts are in New York. Most of the others are in California, Illinois, Michigan, New Jersey, Maryland, Pennsylvania, Texas, and the District of Columbia. In the States where heroin addiction exists on a large scale, it is an urban problem. Within the cities it is largely found in areas with low average incomes, poor housing, and high delinquency. The addict himself is likely to be male, between the ages of 21 and 30, poorly educated and unskilled, and a member of a disadvantaged ethnic minority group.

The cost of heroin to the addict fluctuates over time and from place to place. So does the quality of the drug. Five dollars is a commonly reported price for a single "bag" or packet of heroin. The substance purchased ranges in purity from 1 to about 30 percent, the remainder consisting of natural impurities, and adulterants such as lactose and mannitol. Usually the addict does not know the strength of the doses he buys. Today, however, the drug available on the street is generally so far diluted that the typical addict does not develop

491

profound physical dependence, and therefore does not suffer serious withdrawal symptoms.

The basic Federal control law, the Harrison Narcotic Act of 1914, is a tax statute. It is administered by the Bureau of Narcotics, an agency of the Treasury Department. The statute imposes a tax upon the manufacture or importation of all narcotic drugs. Payment of the tax is evidenced by stamps affixed to the drug containers. The statute authorizes transfers of narcotics in the original containers by and to persons who have registered with the Treasury Department and paid certain occupational taxes ranging from $1 to $24 a year. Official order forms must be used in completing these transactions. There is an exception for the physician acting in the course of his professional practice. Unauthorized possession under the statute is a criminal offense, whether or not the drug is intended for personal use. Unauthorized sale or purchase is a criminal offense. Unauthorized importation is made punishable by a separate Federal statute. Unauthorized possession and sale are also criminal acts under the Uniform Narcotic Drug Act, and the control statute in effect in most states.

Heroin occupies a special place in the narcotics laws. It is an illegal drug in the sense that it may not be lawfully imported or manufactured under any circumstances, and it is not available for use in medical practice. All the heroin that reaches the American user is smuggled into the country from abroad, the Middle East being the reputed primary point of origin. All heroin transactions, and any possession of heroin, are therefore criminal. This is not because heroin has evil properties not shared by the other opiates. Indeed, while it is more potent and somewhat more rapid in its action, heroin does not differ in any significant pharmacological effect from morphine. It would appear that heroin is outlawed because of its special attractiveness to addicts and because it serves no known medical purpose not served as well or better by other drugs.

Cocaine. This drug is included as a narcotic under Federal and other laws but, unlike the opiates, it is a powerful stimulant and does not create tolerance or physical dependence. It is derived from the leaves of the coca plant cultivated extensively in parts of South America. At present it is not the major drug of abuse that it once was.

Marihuana. This is a preparation made from the flowering tops of the female hemp plant. This plant often is found growing wild, or it can be cultivated, in any temperate or semitropical climate, including the United States. Most of the marihuana that reaches American users comes from Mexico. There it is cut, dried, and pulverized and then smuggled across the border, either loose or compressed in brick form. It is commonly converted into cigarettes and consumed by smoking. Other derivatives of the hemp plant, such as hashish, which are more potent than marihuana, are rarely found in the United States.

Marihuana has no established and certainly no indispensable medical use. Its effects are rather complicated, combining both stimulation and depression. Much of its effect depends on the personality of the user. The drug may induce exaltation, joyousness and hilarity, and disconnected ideas; or it may induce quietude or reveries. In the inexperienced taker it may induce panic. Or, one state may follow the other. Confused perceptions of space and time and hallucinations in sharp color may occur; the person's complex intellectual and motor functions may be impaired. These effects may follow within minutes of the time the drug is taken. The influence usually wears off within a few hours but may last much longer in the case of a toxic dose. The immediate physiological effects may include nausea and vomiting, but there are no lasting physical effects, and fatalities have not been noted. Tolerance is very slight if it develops at all. Physical dependence does not develop.

There is no reliable estimate of the prevalence of marihuana use. To the limited extent that police activity is an accurate measure, use appears to be increasing. Bulk seizures of marihuana by Federal enforcement authorities totaled 5,641 kilograms in 1965 as against 1,871 kilograms in 1960. Bureau of Narcotics arrests for marihuana offenses about doubled over the same period of time. So did the number of arrests by California authorities.

Marihuana use apparently cuts across a larger segment of the general population than does opiate use, but again adequate studies are lacking. An impressionistic view, based on scattered reports, is that use is both frequent and increasing in depressed urban areas, academic and artistic communities, and among young professional persons. There are many reports of widespread use on campuses, but estimates that 20 percent or more of certain college populations have used the drug cannot be verified or refuted.

Marihuana is much cheaper than heroin. The director of the Vice Control Division, Chicago Police Department, testified in 1966 that the price of marihuana in Chicago was roughly

50 to 75 cents for a single cigarette, roughly $25 for a can the size of a tobacco tin, and from $85 to $125 a pound. Prices tend to be lower nearer the Mexican source.

The Federal law controlling marihuana is a tax statute, enacted in 1937 and enforced by the Bureau of Narcotics. On its face the statute authorizes marihuana transactions between persons, such as importers, wholesalers, physicians, and others, who have paid certain occupational and transfer taxes. But in fact, since there is no accepted medical use of marihuana, only a handful of people are registered under the law, and for all practical purposes the drug is illegal. Unauthorized possession, which in this context means possession under almost any circumstance, is a criminal act under Federal tax law. Sale or purchase of marihuana are also criminal offenses under this statute. Importation is made punishable by a separate statute. Possession and sale are also offenses under the Uniform Narcotic Drug Act, which controls marihuana in most States.

DANGEROUS DRUGS

The term "dangerous drugs" commonly refers to three classes of nonnarcotic drugs that are habit-forming or have a potential for abuse because of their stimulant, depressant or hallucinogenic effect. Central nervous system stimulants and depressants are widely used in medical practice and are not considered dangerous when taken in ordinary therapeutic doses under medical direction. They are available on prescription. Drugs in the hallucinogenic class have not been proven safe for medical purposes and are not legally available in drugstores. Their sole legitimate use at present is by qualified researchers in connection with investigations reported to and authorized by the Food and Drug Administration. There is an exception in the case of peyote, the use of which is authorized in connection with religious ceremonies of the Native American Church.

THE STIMULANTS

The most widely used and abused of the stimulants are the amphetamines, which are known generally as "pep pills." They bear chemical names such as amphetamine sulfate or dextroamphetamine sulfate and particular nicknames such as "bennies" or "dexies" (after trade names of the two drugs). There are dozens of amphetamine preparations in the market. They are prescribed and apparently are medically effective for relief of fatigue, for control of overweight, and in the treatment of mental disorder.

494

The amphetamines cause wakefulness and have the capacity to elevate mood and to induce a state of well-being and elation. This is probably the basis of their medical value. It is also the likely reason for their abuse.

Tolerance develops with the use of amphetamines. This permits gradual and progressive increases in dosage. Too large a dose or too sudden an increase in dose, however, may produce bizarre mental effects such as delusions or hallucinations. These effects are more likely if the drug is injected intravenously in diluted powder form than if it is taken orally in tablet form. Nervousness and insomnia are milder symptoms of abuse. Physical dependence does not develop.

THE DEPRESSANTS

The most widely used and abused of the depressant drugs are the barbiturates. These are known generally as "goofballs." They have chemical names, such as pentobarbital sodium and secobarbital sodium, and particular nicknames, such as "nimbies" and "seccy" (after trade names of the two drugs). There are more than 25 barbiturates marketed for clinical use. They are apparently useful because of their sedative, hypnotic, or anesthetic actions and are most commonly prescribed to produce sleep and to relieve tension and anxiety.

A person can develop tolerance to barbiturates, enabling him to ingest increasing quantities of the drug up to a limit that varies with the individual. Chronic administration of amounts in excess of the ordinary daily dose will lead to physical dependence, resulting, upon withdrawal of the drug, in a sickness marked at peak intensity by convulsions and a delirium, resembling alcoholic delirium tremens or a major psychotic episode. Excessive doses may also result in impairment of judgment, loss of emotional control, staggering, slurred speech, tremor, and occasionally coma and death. Barbiturates are a major suicidal agent. They are also reported, like the amphetamines, to be implicated in assaultive acts and automobile accidents.

Among the other depressants involved in the drug abuse problem are a number of sedative and tranquilizing drugs, introduced since 1950, that are chemically unrelated to the barbiturates, but similar in effect. The best known of these are meprobamate (Miltown, Equanil), glutethimide (Doriden), ethinamate (Valmid), ethchlorvynol (Placidyl), methyprylon (Noludar), and chlordiazepoxide (Librium). There is strong evidence that abuse of these agents may lead to drug intoxication and physical dependence. Suicide by overdose, and deaths during withdrawal from some of the drugs, have also been reported.

THE HALLUCINOGENS

Hallucinogenic, or psychedelic, drugs and the controversy that surrounds them have recently aroused the attention of the mass media and the public. This is certainly due in part to the increasing incidence of their use on college campuses. It may also be due to the emergence of new substances, such as LSD, many times more potent than such older hallucinogens as peyote and mescaline. All these drugs have the capacity to produce altered states of consciousness. Generally they are taken orally.

LSD, the most potent of the hallucinogens, is a synthetic drug made by a chemical process; lysergic acid is the main component in the chemical conversion. Minute amounts of the drug are capable of producing extreme effects. It is usually deposited on sugar cubes in liquid form, although recently it has been found frequently in pill form. Swallowing such a cube or pill is called "taking a trip." A recent publication of the Medical Society of the County of New York described such a trip as follows:

After the cubes, containing 100–600 mcg. [a microgram is one-millionth of a gram] each, are ingested a startling series of events occurs with marked individual variation. All senses appear sharpened and brightened; vivid panoramic visual hallucinations of fantastic brightness and depth are experienced as well as hyperacusis [abnormal acuteness of hearing]. Senses blend and become diffused so that sounds are felt, colors tasted; and fixed objects pulsate and breathe. Depersonalization also occurs frequently so that the individual loses ego identity; he feels he is living with his environment in a feeling of unity with other beings, animals, inanimate objects and the universe in general. The body image is often distorted so that faces, including the user's, assume bizarre proportions and the limbs may appear extraordinarily short or elongated. The user is enveloped by a sense of isolation and often is dominated by feelings of paranoia and fear. If large doses are ingested (over 700 mcg.) confusion and delirium frequently ensue. During LSD use, repressed material may be unmasked which is difficult for the individual to handle. Duration of the experience is usually 4 to 12 hours but it may last for days.

The same publication cited as dangers of LSD: (1) Prolonged psychosis; (2) acting out of character disorders and homosexual impulses; (3) suicidal inclinations; (4) activation of previously latent psychosis; and (5) reappearance of the drug's effects weeks or even months after use. It was reported that between March and December of 1965 a total of 65 persons suffering from acute psychosis induced by LSD were admitted to Bellevue Hospital in New York.

The only legal producer of LSD ceased manufacture in April 1966, and turned over its entire supply of the drug to the Federal Government. A few closely monitored experimental projects involving LSD are still in progress.

Peyote is the hallucinogenic substance obtained from the button-shaped growths of a cactus plant found growing wild in the arid regions of Mexico. Mescaline is a natural alkaloid, which occurs in the same plant. These drugs have appeared in capsule and liquid form and as a powder that can be dissolved in water.

Psilocybin is a substance extracted from a mushroom fungus. It appears in liquid and powder form.

Different degrees of tolerance to the hallucinogens are reported. Physical dependence apparently does not develop.

There is no reliable statistical information on the prevalence of dangerous drug abuse. However, there are indications of widespread and increasing abuse. The former Commissioner of the Food and Drug Administration, for example, has testified that enough raw material was produced in 1962 to make over 9 billion doses of barbiturates and amphetamines combined, and he estimated that one-half of these ended up in the bootleg market. There is no similar estimate of the proportion of the more than 1 million pounds of tranquilizer drugs produced each year that fall into the hands of drug abusers, but the figure certainly is high. A spreading use of the hallucinogens has undoubtedly been caused in part by the activities and advertising of groups formed for the very purpose of promoting experience in these drugs. These groups, or cults, have made broad and appealing claims in regard to the capacity of the hallucinogens to expand the power of the mind to understand self, love, God, and the universe. They are likely to understate the dangers that line the route to such mystical experiences. Whatever the other causes, cases of dangerous drug abuse coming to the attention of school and medical authorities and police officials have been steadily increasing in number.

The prices of illicit dangerous drugs vary sharply in time and place. Some approximate ranges of reported price are from $0.10 to $1 for an amphetamine or barbiturate tablet, from $1 to $10 for a sugar cube saturated with LSD, and from $0.01 to $0.50 for a peyote button. All of these prices represent significant profits to the seller.

A series of Federal enactments that proved inadequate to deal with the traffic in dangerous drugs has given way to the Drug Abuse Control Amendments of 1965. The statute became effective February 1, 1966, and is now the principal Federal law in the field. It limits manufacture, sale, and distribution of any controlled drug to certain designated classes of persons, such as registered wholesale druggists and licensed physicians. It requires that inventories be taken and records of receipts and dispositions be maintained. It places restrictions on the refilling of prescriptions. Criminal penalties are provided for violations, including manufacture, sale, or distribution by unauthorized persons. The first offense is a misdemeanor; the second, a felony. Possession of drugs for personal use is not an offense under this statute.

All of the amphetamines and the barbiturates are controlled by specific language in the statute. In addition, any other drug with potential for abuse because of its depressant, stimulant, or hallucinogenic effect may be placed under control by designation. Some 22 other drugs have been so designated, including all of the hallucinogens and 3 of the tranquilizers discussed above. The statute is enforced by the Bureau of Drug Abuse Control, a newly created agency within the Food and Drug Administration.

Almost all States have some statutory scheme for controlling at least some of the dangerous drugs, but there is complete lack of uniformity in this legislation.

It is obvious that the increasing use of drugs, including particularly those like LSD with great potential for harm, presents a serious challenge to the Nation.

The Commission recommends:

Research should be undertaken devoted to early action on the further development of a sound and effective framework of regulatory and criminal laws with respect to dangerous drugs. In addition, research and educational programs concerning the effects of such drugs should be undertaken.

ENFORCEMENT

Drug enforcement is a question of finding the drugs and the people in the illicit traffic. Both tasks are formidable.

THE DRUGS

Different enforcement considerations are presented by the opiates (meaning heroin for purposes of this section) and marihuana on the one hand, and the dangerous drugs on the other. To get the former into the country requires an illegal act of smuggling, and their possession and sale in virtually every circumstance are criminal offenses over which the State and Federal governments have concurrent jurisdiction. The dangerous drugs for the most part enter the illicit market by way of diversion from domestic supplies. Simple possession of these drugs is not an offense under any Federal statute. Under State law it may or may not be an offense, depending on the State and the drug involved. It should also be noted that not all abuse of dangerous drugs stems from an illicit traffic. Abuse may occur, for example, if a dose of barbiturates greater than that called for in a legal prescription is taken. Not even perfect and total enforcement of the drug laws could prevent abuse of this kind.

By multiplying the number of known addicts by an average daily dose, the Federal enforcement agencies have arrived at the very rough estimate that 1,500 kilograms (1 kilo=2.2 pounds) of heroin a year are smuggled into the United States. On the average, less than one-tenth of this amount is seized by all enforcement agencies combined. The principal foreign sources are thought to be Turkey and to a much lesser extent Mexico and the Far East. In Turkey, the poppy is cultivated legally, and its opium (heroin is a refined product of opium) is an important export commodity; but a substantial part of the annual crop is diverted by the farmer from the government monopoly to the black market, where it brings double the price. In Mexico the cultivation of the opium poppy is itself illicit. It takes place in remote and mountainous terrain.

Raw opium diverted in Turkey is converted to morphine base at points near its source, reducing its bulk by a factor of 10, and then forwarded to clandestine chemical laboratories, mostly in France, for processing into heroin. The finished product is then smuggled into the United States, either directly or indirectly through Canada or Mexico, and proceeds on its course to the consumer. The heroin becomes less pure and more expensive as it moves through the illicit channels of distribution. The same 10 kilos of opium, which are purchased from the Turkish farmer at the black-market price of roughly $350, and which are sufficient to produce roughly one kilo of pure (in this context about 85 percent) heroin, reach the American addict as thousands of doses of substance containing 1 to 30 percent heroin and costing $225,000 or more.

The estimated 1,500 kilograms of heroin illegally entering the country each year represent less than one-half of 1 percent of the licit opium production of the world, and an even smaller fraction of the combined licit and illicit production. The problem is thus how to block a small flow from a vast supply. To do this, the Bureau of Narcotics maintains 12 posts of duty in 3 overseas districts. Nineteen agents were assigned to these posts at the end of fiscal 1966. They work with authorities in the host country in attempting to locate and seize illicit opium and heroin supplies destined for the United States. This effort has had considerable success. In 1965, for example, the agents assisted in 82 investigations which resulted in the seizure of 888 kilograms of raw opium, 128 kilograms of morphine base, and 84 kilograms of heroin. But the effort has obvious limitations. It is somewhat like trying to dam a river at its widest point with much too little material.

The Bureau of Customs maintains a force at ports and along land borders to protect the revenue and to detect and prevent smuggling of contraband, including illicit drugs. This is not solely an enforcement task. Many nonenforcement personnel such as examiners, verifiers, and appraisers of merchandise are involved. Also in the nonenforcement category, although they play a vital role in the suppression of smuggling, are the inspectors, some 2,600 of whom were on the customs rolls at the end of fiscal 1966. These men handle the inspection of persons, their vehicles, and their effects arriving from abroad. In 1965 more than 180 million persons and 53 million vehicles and trains arrived in the United States. Obviously nothing more than a cursory inspection of most of them was possible. Such inspections are not well designed to uncover illicit drugs, which are generally small in bulk and cleverly concealed, but they often do lead to significant seizures and probably deter countless smuggling violations.

The customs enforcement arm is the Customs Agency Service. This is composed of: (1) Customs port investigators and customs enforcement officers. There were 492 such men on duty at the end of fiscal 1966. They conduct vessel and aircraft searches (more than 99,000 vessels and 210,000 aircraft arrived in the United States in 1965), perform uniformed patrol in marked vehicles and carry out plainclothes assignments and surveillances at airports, piers, and border crossing points. (2) Customs agents. These men, 276 of whom were assigned at the end of fiscal 1966, are the top-echelon criminal investigators within the Bureau. They develop intelligence and evidence concerning violations of the criminal statutes within customs enforcement jurisdiction.

Some 65 kilograms of heroin and other illicit narcotics excluding marihuana were seized at ports and borders in fiscal

1966. Approximately one-half of all 1966 customs seizures of illicit drugs resulted from prior information received from informants.

Once heroin enters the country, unless it is seized quickly in the hands of the courier, the job of finding it in significant quantities becomes even more difficult. This is because it is broken up into smaller lots and diluted as it moves through the channels of distribution. Enforcement against the upper echelons of the traffic is the business of the Bureau of Narcotics, which at the end of fiscal 1966 had a force of 278 agents stationed in 13 districts in the country. Lower echelons of the traffic are targets for State and local narcotics enforcement. An accurate total of the personnel engaged in narcotics enforcement in all States and localities is not available, but the number would probably exceed a thousand. Frequently narcotics enforcement is part of the responsibility of local vice control squads. Federal agents seized 156 kilograms of illicit opiates and cocaine in the internal traffic in 1965, 95 kilos of heroin coming in a single seizure. No accurate total is available for illicit narcotic seizures by all States and municipal agencies.

Many of the considerations noted above are applicable to the enforcement of the marihuana laws. More than 5,600 kilograms were seized by Federal authorities in 1965, the majority of it by the Bureau of Customs at points of entry along the Mexican border.

Serious Federal enforcement of the drug abuse control amendments is just beginning. A Bureau of Drug Abuse Control has recently been established within the Food and Drug Administration. It now has 200 agents assigned to 9 field offices. It hopes to have 500 agents assigned by 1970. State and local enforcement is handled by the narcotic units or vice control squads.

The illicit traffic in depressant and stimulant drugs is quite new, and how it operates is only partially understood. It appears to be fed mainly by diversions from the chain of legitimate drug distribution. Diversions are known to have occurred at all points in the chain from the manufacture of the basic chemicals to delivery of the finished dosage forms of the drug to the consumer. Large quantities of the basic depressant and stimulant powders have been ordered from chemical brokers and dealers by persons using fictitious names, indicating firms engaged in research. In some cases, involving diversions of millions of capsules over periods of a few months, drugs have been sold directly to illegal peddlers by manufacturers of the dosage form. In other cases drugs have been diverted by salesmen of manufacturing or wholesale firms, sometimes through the medium of fictitious drugstores. Again millions of tablets have been involved. Unlawful sale by retail pharmacists and by physicians have occurred. So, of course, have larcenies from plants and thefts from interstate shipments. Apparently unregistered drug manufacturers (whose product duplicates the genuine article in substance) and drug counterfeiters (whose product duplicates the genuine article in appearance only) are also major sources of illicit drugs. Fraudulent means of obtaining drugs, such as forging prescriptions, are also practiced.

The hallucinogens are not available for legitimate distribution. In some cases the drugs are smuggled across the Mexican border. In other cases the raw materials are present in large supply in this country, and supplies of peyote have reputedly been obtained by placing an order with a "cactus company" in Texas. LSD, while it may be produced by a relatively simple, chemical process (the raw materials are also under Federal controls), is thought to come frequently from foreign sources, both legal and illegal. The problems of detecting this drug are special ones. It is colorless, tasteless, odorless; one two-hundred and eighty thousandth of an ounce is enough to cause the characteristic effects.

THE PEOPLE

Those involved in illicit drug traffic are either suppliers or consumers. They range from the organized crime boss who organizes 50-kilo heroin shipments, to the college student who smokes a single marihuana cigarette.

The opiate traffic on the east coast is in heroin of European origin and is hierarchical in structure. The importers, top members of the criminal cartels more fully described in chapter 7 of this report dealing with organized crime, do not handle and probably do not ever see a shipment of heroin. Their role is supervisory and financial. Fear of retribution, which can be swift and final, and a code of silence protect them from exposure. Through persons working under their direction the heroin is distributed to high-level wholesalers, who are also members of the cartels. Beyond this point the traffic breaks out of the hands of the organized crime element and becomes increasingly diffuse. Low-level wholesalers are at the next echelon; they are on the neighborhood level. Retailers, street peddlers (who are often themselves addicts) and addicts round out the system.

On the west coast the traffic is in heroin of Mexican origin and is carried on largely by independent operators. The actual

502

smuggling is often done by persons hired for this purpose by the operators.

The marihuana trade resembles the heroin traffic on the west coast. Occasionally the same people are involved, but they are not likely to be major racketeers, or to have dominant positions in the underworld.

Not enough of the people in the dangerous drug traffic have been caught to form valid judgments about the traffic's personnel. It appears the unregistered manufacturers and wholesalers and bulk peddlers are key figures. It has been alleged, but not proved, that trafficking in these drugs has become an activity of organized crime. Certainly the profits are there in the case of the depressant and stimulant drugs. The hallucinogenic drug traffic appears to be less profit oriented than others.

THE TECHNIQUE

The objectives of law enforcement are to reach the highest possible sources of drug supply and to seize the greatest possible quantity of illicit drugs before use. These are difficult goals, given the fact that drug transactions are always consensual. There are no complaining witnesses or victims; there are only sellers and willing buyers. The enforcement officer must therefore initiate cases. He must find and take up positions along the illicit traffic lanes. The standard technique for doing this is undercover investigation during which an officer assumes another identity for the purpose of gathering evidence or making a "buy" of evidence. The use of informants to obtain leads and to arrange introductions is also standard and essential. An informant may or may not be a person facing criminal charges. If he is not, he may supply information out of motives of revenge or monetary reward. More typically the informant is under charges and is induced to give information in return for a "break" in the criminal process such as a reduction of these charges. Frequently he will make it a condition of cooperation that his identity remain confidential.

The payoff in enforcement is the "big case" against the major violator with executive rank in the traffic. This man is hard to identify and harder to implicate with legal evidence. He has a shield of people in front of him, and by not handling drugs himself he removes his liability to prosecution under laws that prohibit possession, sale, or other such acts. The conspiracy laws are the most useful weapon against such a person, and over the years many important convictions have been obtained under these laws on evidence developed by the Bureau of Narcotics and the Bureau of Customs.

Judgments about enforcement results are hard to make. Experience with the opiate laws has been the longest. There are persuasive reasons to believe that enforcement of these laws has caused a significant reduction in the flow of these drugs. The best evidence is the high price, low quality, and limited availability of heroin today as contrasted with the former easy availability of cheap and potent heroin. Arguments based on comparisons on the number of addicts in the general population at different points in time are difficult to assess because of the uncertainties in the estimates being compared. However, there is a widespread conviction that the incidence of addiction in the general population has declined since the enactment and enforcement of the narcotic control laws.

The brunt of enforcement has fallen heavily on the user and the addict. In cases handled by the Bureau of Narcotics, whose activities are directed against international and interstate traffickers, more than 40 percent of the defendants prosecuted are addicts. However, these addicts almost invariably are also peddlers, who are charged with sale rather than mere possession. It is fair to assume that the percentage of addicts among the defendants prosecuted by State and local drug enforcement agencies is even higher. The enforcement emphasis on the addict is due to his constant exposure to surveillance and arrest and his potential value as an informant.

THE NEED TO STRENGTHEN LAW ENFORCEMENT

More customs enforcement is not a simple formula for progress. To begin with, it must be understood that illegal importations of drugs can never be completely blocked. The measures necessary to achieve or even approach this goal, routine body searches being one obvious example, would be so strict and would involve such a burden on the movement of innocent persons and goods that they would never be tolerated. Moreover, the demand and the profits being what they are in the drug traffic, there will always be people willing to take whatever risks are necessary to pass the customs barrier. These conditions make the impact of any enforcement buildup hard to determine in advance. Nevertheless the ports and borders are the neck of the illicit traffic, and it is at these points that the Commission believes a commitment of more men would achieve the most. Illicit drugs regularly arrive at these points in significant quantities and in the hands of people who, while not at the highest, are at least not at the lowest level of the traffic. More frequent interceptions of both the drugs and the people could reasonably be expected if the capacity to enforce customs laws was increased. Other important benefits, in the form of larger revenue collections and the suppression of smuggling generally, would also follow.

Three separate studies of the manpower needs of customs enforcement operations have been made within the last 5 years. Each has arrived independently at the same recommendation: That the enforcement staff be increased by a total of about 600 positions. But only a small fraction of this total has, in fact, been authorized. In the meantime the overall customs workload, from which the enforcement workload is naturally derived, has increased by 5 or 10 percent a year, a rate exceeding every advance estimate. The need for more enforcement staff is thus more urgent now than ever.

The Commission also believes that increases in the nonenforcement personnel of the Bureau of Customs are necessary. In the decade between 1955 and 1965 the number of people entering the United States increased by 50 percent the number of aircraft by almost 100 percent. During the same period the number of inspectors who examine incoming passengers and their baggage increased only 4 percent. Examination today is, therefore, less common and less effective. This is but one example of how much faster than its manpower the customs workload has grown. The inspection force should be augmented. If a sufficient number of new positions were created, not only could regular inspections be improved but greater customs coverage of military shipments might also be possible. In addition, roving inspection teams might be formed and used on a random basis to double or triple the inspection strength at particular ports of entry for short periods of time.

Mail examination is another customs activity that suffers from budgetary and manpower limitations. In 1965 only 5.5 percent of 47.6 million foreign mail packages were examined. The Commissioner of Customs testified in 1966 that the rate of examination should be at least 10 percent to insure against the smuggling of illicit drugs and other contraband and to protect the revenues. He estimated that 60 additional employees, at a cost of about $450,000, could be expected to return between $6 and $8 million annually in duty collections. The Commission believes the addition of these employees would be a sound investment and would offer at least potentially valuable law enforcement benefits.

The Commission recommends:

The enforcement and related staff of the Bureau of Customs should be materially increased.

There are no convenient devices, such as the rate of incoming persons or merchandise, to measure the workload of the Bureau of Narcotics. The need for more funds and more staff is thus hard to document. Yet the simple fact is that the Bureau has numerous complex tasks to perform. It bears the major Federal responsibility for suppression of traffic in illicit narcotics and marihuana. It assists foreign enforcement authorities within their own countries. It assists in training local enforcement personnel in this country. It not only enforces the penal statutes relating to narcotics and marihuana but also administers the laws relating to the legitimate importation, manufacture, and distribution of these drugs. The Commission believes that the Bureau's force of some 300 agents, spread across 10 foreign countries and throughout the United States, is not sufficient. It certainly does not enable the Bureau to divert personnel from the business of making arrests, seizing drugs, and obtaining convictions, to the work of intelligence. Yet given the pyramidal structure of the illicit drug traffic and the limited exposure of those at the top, intelligence activity has a vital place in the enforcement effort.

The Commission recommends:

The enforcement staff of the Bureau of Narcotics should be materially increased. Some part of the added personnel should be used to design and execute a long-range intelligence effort aimed at the upper echelons of the illicit drug traffic.

The Commission also notes that the Federal Government undertook responsibility in respect to dangerous drugs with the enactment of the Drug Abuse Control Amendments of 1965. It is essential that adequate resources be provided to the Bureau of Drug Abuse Control to enable it to carry out these responsibilities.

In enacting the 1965 Drug Abuse Control Amendments, Congress sought to control the traffic in dangerous drugs predominantly by a system of registration, inspection, and recordkeeping. The amendments apply to drugs in intrastate as well as interstate commerce. Thus, once a drug has been placed under control of the amendments, State law cannot exempt from regulation even intrastate commerce in that drug.

Existing State laws dealing with dangerous drugs are strikingly dissimilar. In some States there are none at all. In some States nonmedical distribution and possession are criminal offenses, but there are no recordkeeping or other regulatory provisions. In others a version of the Model State Barbiturate Act, or legislation patterned after the Uniform Narcotic Drug Act, is in effect. In still others dangerous drugs are controlled like any other prescription legend drugs. Some State statutes list particular drugs. Others give an enforcement agency authority to designate drugs having certain characteristics.

The Commission believes that effective control of traffic in dangerous drugs requires a joint Federal-State effort. Such an effort, in turn, requires common State and Federal regulatory provisions. With such provisions there could be a pooling of strength and a division of responsibility. A Model State Drug Abuse Control Act is now being distributed to the States by the Food and Drug Administration. Under this act, which automatically subjects a drug to State control upon its designation under the Federal law, State and Federal authorities could immediately combine to control the drug. With common recordkeeping provisions, State authorities could concentrate their inspectors on retailers, and Federal authorities, on wholesalers.

The Model State Act as drafted is flexible enough to permit States to control drugs not regulated by Federal law and to insert their own provisions respecting possession, penalties, licensing, etc.

The Commission recommends:

Those States which do not already have adequate legislation should adopt a model State drug abuse control act similar to the Federal Drug Abuse Control Amendments of 1965.

The recordkeeping and inspection provisions of the 1965 amendments are at the heart of the Federal dangerous drug regulatory scheme. They are designed to serve several purposes: To furnish information regarding the extent of the dangerous drug problem and the points in the chain of distribution where diversions of drugs occur; to facilitate the detection of violations; and to deter violations. Yet at present the 1965 amendments specifically state:

No separate records, nor set form or forms for any of the foregoing records (of manufacture, receipt, and disposition),

507

shall be required as long as records containing the required information are available.

There are about 6,000 establishments, including 1,000 manufacturers and 2,400 wholesalers, which are required to register and keep records under the amendments. In addition, there are about 73,000 other establishments that are required to maintain records but not required to register. This group includes some 54,000 pharmacies or other retail drug outlets, some 9,000 hospitals and clinics, some 8,000 dispensing practitioners, and some 2,000 research facilities. The Commission simply does not believe that a proper and productive audit of such a mass of records is possible without, at the very least, a provision requiring the records to be segregated or kept in some other manner permitting rapid identification and inspection.

The Commission recommends:

The recordkeeping provisions of the 1965 amendments should be amended to require that records must be segregated or kept in some other manner that enables them to be promptly identified and inspected.

DRUG ABUSE AND CRIME

Drug addicts are crime-prone persons. This fact is not open to serious dispute, but to determine its meaning is another matter. Analysis is best restricted to heroin because of the applicable laws, because of the information available, and because drugs with addiction liability present the clearest issues. In order to obtain an accurate idea of the drug-crime relationship, it is necessary to make a clear distinction between the drug offenses and the nondrug offenses committed by addicts.

DRUG OFFENSES

Addiction itself is not a crime. It never has been under Federal law, and a State law making it one was struck down as unconstitutional by the 1962 decision of the Supreme Court in *Robinson* v. *California*. It does not follow, however, that a state of addiction can be maintained without running afoul of the criminal law. On the contrary, the involvement of an addict with the police is almost inevitable. By definition, an addict has a constant need for drugs, which obviously must be purchased and possessed before they can be consumed. Purchase and possession, with certain exceptions not relevant in the case of an addict, are criminal offenses under both Federal and State law. So is sale, to which many addicts turn to provide financial support for their habits. In many States, the nonmedical use of opiates is punishable, as is the possession of paraphernalia such as needles and syringes designed for such use. In other States, vagrancy statutes make it punishable for a known or convicted addict to consort with other known addicts or to be present in a place where illicit drugs are found.

Thus, the addict lives in almost perpetual violation of one or several criminal laws, and this gives him a special status not shared by other criminal offenders. Together with the fact that he must have continuous contact with other people in order to obtain drugs, it also gives him a special exposure to police action and arrest, and, in areas where the addiction rate is high, a special place in police statistics and crime rate computations.

NONDRUG OFFENSES

The nondrug offenses in which the heroin addict typically becomes involved are of the fund-raising variety. Assaultive or violent acts, contrary to popular belief, are the exception rather than the rule for the heroin addict, whose drug has a calming and depressant effect.

Illicit drugs, as already noted, are expensive. Records compiled by the New York City police are sufficient proof of this. In May 1965, a total of 991 admitted users of heroin were arrested in New York City. The average daily cost of heroin to these users was $14.34. In December of that year, the 1,271 heroin users arrested spent a daily average of $14.04. The price of the drug is not uniform in time or place; it differs in New York and Los Angeles and fluctuates everywhere according to the supply available on the street. But it is never low enough to permit the typical addict to obtain it by lawful means. So he turns to crime, most commonly to the theft of property. Stolen property cannot be converted at full value, especially by an addict who needs to dispose of it quickly. It is said that between $3 and $5 in merchandise must be stolen to realize $1 in cash.

The mathematics of this are alarming. Assuming that each of the heroin addicts in New York City, whose names were on file with the Bureau of Narcotics at the end of 1965, spent $15 a day for his drug, and that in each case the $15 represented the net cash proceeds after conversion of stolen property worth $50, the addicts would be responsible each year for the theft of property valued at many millions of dollars in New York City alone. This amount would, of course, have to be adjusted to take into account the addicts who are in jail or hospitalized; those who obtain the price of heroin either through lawful means or by prostitution, selling of drugs, thefts of cash, or any other method which does not require the conversion of stolen property, and the addicts who are unknown to the authorities. The impact of these adjustments might be enormous but it cannot be accurately measured.

The projected totals are so impressive that they lead one into the easy assumption that addicts must be responsible for most crimes against property where addiction is widespread. But this assumption cannot so easily be verified.

Records compiled by the New York City Police Department indicate that 11.1 percent of those arrested in 1965 for those felonies against property most often committed by addicts were admitted drug (mostly heroin) users. The comparable figure for 1964 was 12.5 percent; for 1963 it was 11.7 percent. The involvement of admitted drug users in arrests for selected felonies against the person was much lower —on the order of 2 percent. The 1965 figure for the involvement of admitted drug users in arrests for petit larceny was 9.8 percent. It is impossible to judge what any of these figures might have been if they had reflected involvement in nondrug offenses of actual instead of admitted drug users.

For the fiscal years 1956–65 inclusive, an average of 8 percent of all persons committed to Federal prisons and other penal institutions had an admitted drug (again mostly heroin) use history. On the other hand, the New York City Department of Corrections reports that surveys taken of its average 1966 population (about 10,000 persons) show that almost 40 percent had an admitted history of drug use.

As of December 31, 1966, there were 4,385 persons identified as users of heroin in the FBI's "Careers in Crime Program"—a computerized record of criminal histories. This data is based on criminal fingerprint cards submitted by local and Federal agencies.

The 4,385 people who were identified as heroin users had an average criminal career (the span of years between the first and last arrest) of 12 years during which they averaged 10 arrests. Six of these arrests on an average were for offenses other than narcotics. Of the total arrests accumulated by heroin users in the property crime and violent crime categories, 26 percent were arrests for violent crimes and 74 percent arrests for property crimes. On the other hand, all criminal offenders in the program (over 150,000) averaged 23 percent arrests for violent crimes and 77 percent for property crimes. Seventy-two percent of all heroin users had an arrest for some other criminal act prior to their first narcotic arrest.

The simple truth is that the extent of the addict's or drug user's responsibility for all nondrug offenses is unknown. Obviously it is great, particularly in New York City, with its heavy concentration of users; but there is no reliable data to assess properly the common assertion that drug users or addicts are responsible for 50 percent of all crime.

More broadly, the Commission's examination of the evidence on the causal connection between drug use and crime has not enabled it to make definitive estimates on this important issue. Since there is much crime in cites where drug use is not thought to be a major problem, to commit resources against abuse solely in the expectation of producing a dramatic reduction in crime may be to invite disappointment. While crime reduction is one result to be hoped for in eliminating drug abuse, its elimination and the treatment of its victims are humane and worthy social objectives in themselves.

PENALTIES

Since early in the century we have built our drug control policies around the twin judgments that drug abuse was an evil to be suppressed and that this could most effectively be done by the application of criminal enforcement and penal sanctions. Since then, one traditional response to an increase in drug abuse has been to increase the penalties for drug offenses. The premise has been that the more certain and severe the punishment, the more it would serve as a deterrent. Typically this response has taken the form of mandatory minimum terms of imprisonment, increasing in severity with repeated offenses, and provisions making the drug offender ineligible for suspension of sentence, probation, and parole.

Federal law was changed twice during the last decade. In 1951, following the post-World War II upsurge in reported addiction, mandatory minimum sentences were introduced for all narcotic and marihuana offenses, 2 years for the first offense, 5 years for the second, and 10 years for third and subsequent offenses. At the same time, suspension of sentence and probation were prohibited for second offenders. In 1956 the mandatory minimum sentences were raised to 5 years for the first and 10 years for the second and subsequent offenses of unlawful sale or importation. They remained at 2, 5, and 10 years for the offense of unlawful possession. Suspension of sentence, probation, and parole were prohibited for all but the first offense of unlawful possession. Many State criminal

511

codes contain comparable, though not identical, penalty provisions.

In support of existing mandatory minimum sentences for narcotics violations, it has been suggested that the high price and low quality of the heroin available on the street and the fact that serious physical dependence on the drug has become a rarity are evidence that there are fewer people willing to face the risk of more severe penalties. On the other hand, with respect to heroin, it has been noted that these trends preceded the pattern of mandatory minimum sentence provisions. And despite the application of such sanctions to marihuana, the use of and traffic in that drug appear to be increasing.

Since the evidence as to the effects of mandatory minimum sentences is inconclusive, the Commission believes that the arguments against such provisions, which appear in chapter 5, are a firmer basis upon which to rest its judgment in the case.

Within any classification of offenses, differences exist in both the circumstances and nature of the illegal conduct and in the offenders. Mandatory provisions deprive judges and correctional authorities of the ability to base their judgments on the seriousness of the violations and the particular characteristics and potential for rehabilitation of the offender.

There is a broad consensus among judges and correctional authorities that discretion should be restored. A 1964 policy statement of the Advisory Council of Judges and repeated testimony by officials of the Bureau of Prisons and Board of Parole are expressions of this consensus.

Application of the mandatory minimums has had some measurable results. The first of these has been a substantial increase in the percentage of the Federal prison population serving sentences for narcotic and marihuana offenses. At the close of fiscal 1965 there were 3,998 drug-law violators confined in all Federal institutions. This number represented 17.9 percent of all persons confined. The average sentence being served by the drug-law violators was 87.6 months, and 75.5 percent of them were ineligible for parole. These figures compare with the 2,017 drug-law violators confined at the close of fiscal 1950, comprising 11.2 percent of all persons confined at that time. The 1950 violators were all eligible for parole, and while average sentence data is not available for that year, it would be safe to estimate that sentences averaged much less than one-half of 87.6 months.

Some differential handling of narcotic addicts after conviction is permitted by the civil commitment laws discussed below, which bypass the penalty provisions. Other devices in the present law also permit some distinctions to be made among drug offenders. First offenders charged with unlawful possession under Federal law are eligible for suspended sentence, probation, and parole. Persons under the age of 22 are eligible for indeterminate sentencing under the Federal Youth Corrections Act. Some State laws distinguish mere possession from possession with intent to sell and provide separate penalties for the two offenses. Informal practices also are common, such as reduction of charge by the prosecutor (whose discretion is not circumscribed by the law) to avoid the mandatory minimum sentence provided for the greater offense.

In its recommendations on mandatory minimums, the President's 1963 Advisory Commission sought to avoid the evils of treating all narcotics and marihuana offenders alike by dividing offenses into four groups:

☐ The smuggling or sale of large quantities of narcotics or the possession of large quantities for sale. This would subject the offender to mandatory minimum sentences. Probation, suspension of sentence, and parole would be denied.

☐ The smuggling or sale of small quantities of narcotics, or the possession of small quantities for sale. This would subject the offender to some measure of imprisonment but not to any mandatory minimum terms. Suspension of sentence would not be available but parole would.

☐ The possession of narcotics without intent to sell. The sentencing judge would have full discretion as to these offenses.

☐ All marihuana offenses. The sentencing judge would have full discretion.

This Commission believes that these graduations as to the seriousness of offense are sound in principle. But, for the reasons set forth above and in the discussion in chapter 5 on sentencing, it does not believe they should be rigidified into legislation. Rather, judges and correctional officials should be relied on to take account of the nature of the offense and the record and status of the offender in making their decisions.

The Commission recommends:

State and Federal drug laws should give a large enough measure of discretion to the courts and correctional authorities to enable them to deal flexibly with violators, taking account of the nature and seriousness of the offense, the prior record of the offender and other relevant circumstances.

It should be noted that parole rights have already been reinstated for Federal marihuana violators by a provision of the Narcotic Addict Rehabilitation Act of 1966.

In submitting the foregoing recommendations, the Commission also wishes to record its concurrence in the view of the Bureau of Narcotics that long terms of imprisonment for major drug violators are essential. The Commission is opposed only to features of existing laws that deny to judges and correctional officials the flexibility to deal with the infinitely varied types of violations and offenders in accordance with facts of each case rather than pursuant to prescribed rigid rules.

MARIHUANA

In addition to suggesting that the penalties provided for narcotics and marihuana offenses be made more flexible, the Commission would like to comment specially on marihuana, because of questions that have been raised concerning the appropriateness of the substantive law applicable to this drug.

The basic Federal control statute, the Marihuana Tax Act, was enacted in 1937 with the stated objectives of making marihuana dealings visible to public scrutiny, raising revenue, and rendering difficult the acquisition of marihuana for nonmedical purposes (the drug has no recognized medical value) and noncommercial use (the plant from which the drug comes has some commercial value in the production of seed and hemp). At the heart of the act are provisions requiring that all persons with a legitimate reason for handling marihuana register and pay an occupational tax, requiring that all marihuana transactions be recorded on official forms provided by the Treasury Department, subjecting transfers to a registered person to a tax of $1 an ounce, and subjecting transfers to an unregistered person to a prohibitive tax of $100 an ounce. Under the Uniform Narcotic Drug Act in force in most States, marihuana is defined and controlled as a narcotic drug.

The act raises an insignificant amount of revenue and exposes an insignificant number of marihuana transactions to public view, since only a handful of people are registered under the act. It has become, in effect, solely a criminal law imposing sanctions upon persons who sell, acquire, or possess marihuana.

Marihuana was placed under a prohibition scheme of control because of its harmful effects and its claimed association with violent behavior and crime. Another reason now advanced in support of the marihuana regulations is that the drug is a steppingstone or forerunner to the use of addicting drugs, particularly heroin.

The law has come under attack on all counts, and the points made against it deserve a hearing.

THE EFFECTS

Marihuana is equated in law with the opiates, but the abuse characteristics of the two have almost nothing in common. The opiates produce physical dependence. Marihuana does not. A withdrawal sickness appears when use of the opiates is discontinued. No such symptoms are associated with marihuana. The desired dose of opiates tends to increase over time, but this is not true of marihuana. Both can lead to psychic dependence, but so can almost any substance that alters the state of consciousness.

The Medical Society of the County of New York has classified marihuana as a mild hallucinogen, and this is probably as good a description as any, although hallucinations are only one of many effects the drug can produce. It can impair judgment and memory; it can cause anxiety, confusion, or disorientation; and it can induce temporary psychotic episodes in predisposed people. Any hallucinogenic drug, and many of the other dangerous drugs, can do the same. Marihuana is probably less likely to produce these effects than such moderately potent hallucinogens as peyote, mescaline, and hashish (another derivative of the plant from which marihuana comes), and much less likely to do so than the potent hallucinogen LSD.

MARIHUANA, CRIME, AND VIOLENCE

Here differences of opinion are absolute and the claims are beyond reconciliation. One view is that marihuana is a major cause of crime and violence. Another is that marihuana has no association with crime and only a marginal relation to violence.

Proponents of the first view rely in part on reports connecting marihuana users with crime. One such report by the district attorney of New Orleans was referred to in the hearings on the 1937 act. It found that 125 of 450 men convicted of major crimes in 1930 were regular marihuana users. Approximately one-half the murderers (an unstated number) and a fifth of those tried for larceny, robbery, and assault (again an unstated number) were regular users. However, the main reliance is on case files of enforcement agencies. Excerpts from these files have been used to demonstrate a marihuana-crime causal relation. The validity of such a demonstration involves three assumptions which are questioned by opponents of the present law: (1) The defendant was a marihuana user. Usually this can be determined only by the defendant's own statement or by his possession of the drug at the time of arrest. (2) He was under the influence of marihuana when he committed the criminal act. Again a statement, perhaps a self-serving one, is most often the source of the information. Chemical tests of blood, urine, and the like will not detect marihuana. (3) The influence of the marihuana caused the crime in the sense that it would not have been committed otherwise.

Those who hold the opposite view cannot prove their case, either. They can only point to the prevailing lack of evidence. Many have done so. The Medical Society of the County of New York has stated flatly that there is no evidence that marihuana use is associated with crimes of violence in this country. There are many similar statements by other responsible authorities. The 1962 report of the President's Ad Hoc Panel on Drug Abuse found the evidence inadequate to substantiate the reputation of marihuana for inciting people to antisocial acts. The famous Mayor's Committee on Marihuana, appointed by Mayor La Guardia to study the marihuana situation in New York City, did not observe any aggression in subjects to whom marihuana was given. In addition there are several studies of persons who were both confessed marihuana users and convicted criminals, and these reach the conclusion that a positive relation between use and crime cannot be established.

One likely hypothesis is that, given the accepted tendency of marihuana to release inhibitions, the effect of the drug will depend on the individual and the circumstances. It might, but certainly will not necessarily or inevitably, lead to aggressive behavior or crime. The response will depend more on the individual than the drug. This hypothesis is consistent with the evidence that marihuana does not alter the basic personality structure.

MARIHUANA AS A PRELUDE TO ADDICTING DRUGS

The charge that marihuana "leads" to the use of addicting drugs needs to be critically examined. There is evidence that a majority of the heroin users who come to the attention of public authorities have, in fact, had some prior experience with marihuana. But this does not mean that one leads to the other in the sense that marihuana has an intrinsic quality that creates a heroin liability. There are too many marihuana users who do not graduate to heroin, and too many heroin addicts with no known prior marihuana use, to support such a theory. Moreover there is no scientific basis for such a theory. The basic text on pharmacology, Goodman and Gilman, *The Pharmacological Basis of Therapeutics* (Macmillan 1960) states quite explicitly that marihuana habituation does not lead to the use of heroin.

The most reasonable hypothesis here is that some people who are predisposed to marihuana are also predisposed to heroin use. It may also be the case that through the use of marihuana a person forms the personal associations that later expose him to heroin.

The amount of literature on marihuana is massive. It runs to several thousand articles in medical journals and other publications. Many of these are in foreign languages and reflect the experience of other countries with the use of the drug and with other substances derived from the hemp plant. The relevance of this material to our own problem has never been determined. Indeed, with the possible exception of the 1944 LaGuardia report, no careful and detailed analysis of the American experience seems to have been attempted. Basic research has been almost nonexistent, probably because the principal active ingredient in marihuana has only recently been isolated and synthesized. Yet the Commission believes that enough information exists to warrant careful study of our present marihuana laws and the propositions on which they are based.

The Commission recommends:

The National Institute of Mental Health should devise and execute a plan of research, to be carried on both on an intramural and extramural basis, covering all aspects of marihuana use.

The research should identify existing gaps in our knowledge of marihuana. A systematic review of the literature will be necessary. The plan should provide for an intensive examination of the important medical and social aspects of marihuana use. It should provide for surveys of the extent of marihuana use and of the nature of such use, i.e., occasional, periodic, or habitual. It should provide for studies of the pharmacology of marihuana and of its immediate and long-term effects. It might also provide for animal studies. The relation of marihuana use to aggressive behavior and crime should certainly be a subject of study. So should the relation between marihuana and the use of other drugs. The Commission of course does not wish to imply that the need for research is confined to marihuana. Much remains to be learned, for example, about the potential uses and dangers of hallucinogenic drugs.

TREATMENT

Until quite recently treatment opportunities for opiate addicts were largely restricted to the two Federal narcotic hospitals at Lexington, Ky., and Fort Worth, Tex. Within the past decade, numerous new programs for the treatment of addiction have been developed. However, there are virtually no programs for the treatment of users of the other dangerous drugs.

LEXINGTON AND FORT WORTH

The Public Health Service hospitals were established, in 1935 and 1938 respectively, for the primary purpose of providing treatment to Federal prisoners who were addicted to narcotic drugs. Voluntary patients, who make up almost one-half the hospital population at any given time, are admitted on a space-available basis after Federal prisoners have been accommodated. Since 1935 there have been more than 80,000 admissions of addict-patients to the two hospitals. The constructed capacity of Lexington is 1,042 beds and of Fort Worth 777 beds.

After withdrawal of the drug and psychiatric evaluation, a wide range of services is available to the patient. These are mainly designed to develop and improve functional skills and to accustom the patient to a stable environment. The recommended length of stay for a voluntary patient is 5 months, but most check out much sooner against medical advice. The hospital authorities are powerless to prevent this.

There is no effective aftercare or supervision in the community, except in the case of a prisoner-patient who is granted parole. The relapse rate is high, but there is growing evidence that it is not as high as the 94 percent rate found in one short-term followup study. Much depends on whether relapse is taken to mean return to drugs once during a period of time or to refer to the drug status of the patient at the end of a period of time. One recent long-term (12-year) followup, using the second method of classification, found that, although 90 of the 100 heroin addicts studied had returned to drug use at some time, 46 of them were drug-free in the community at the time of death or last contact. Among the 30 who were considered to have made the best adjustment, the average length of abstinence was 7 years. Significantly, the best outcomes were found among those who had undergone some form of compulsory supervision after discharge.

THE CALIFORNIA REHABILITATION CENTER

This facility, operated by the California Youth and Adult Corrections Agency, was established in 1961. Most admissions are of addicted misdemeanants and felons convicted in California courts and committed by order of the court.

The program involves a combination of inpatient and outpatient treatment. The addicts are required to remain on inpatient status for at least 6 months, although the average is close to 15 months. During this period they are divided into 60-patient units for purpose of treatment. Work therapy, vocational courses, and a full academic course through high school also are offered.

Upon release to outpatient status, the patients are supervised by caseworkers with special training and small caseloads. Patients are chemically tested for the presence of drugs five times a month, both on a regular and a surprise basis, for at least the first 6 months. Failure of the test or other indications of relapse to drugs results in return to the institution. A halfway house, the Parkway Center, provides guidance for those making a marginal adjustment in the community. The patient becomes eligible for final discharge after 3 drug-free years as an outpatient.

The capacity of the Rehabilitation Center is 2,300 patients. Between September 15, 1961, and December 31, 1965, there were 5,300 admissions. During this period 3,243 persons were transferred to outpatient status. Although many were returned to the center, 1,700 persons remained on such status as of December 31, 1965; 27 persons had been finally discharged.

NEW YORK STATE PROGRAM

Between the effective date of the Metcalf-Volker Act, January 1, 1963, and June 30, 1966, there were 6,799 admissions of addicts to treatment units maintained by the State Department of Mental Hygiene. The majority of these were persons who chose treatment in lieu of prosecution for a crime. The treatment units are located in six State hospitals having a total of 555 beds for addict-patients; they could handle over 2,200 addicts a year. Both inpatient and outpatient phases of treatment were provided.

A new and more comprehensive program for the treatment and prevention of addiction is now planned in New

York under legislation passed in 1966 and administered by a new agency, the State Narcotic Control Commission. Facilities will be greatly expanded, as indicated by a $75 million appropriation for capital construction. The Commission is authorized, among other things, to conduct basic, clinical, and statistical research; to operate rehabilitation and aftercare centers; and to establish a unified program of education, prevention, care, and community referral.

SYNANON

This is a private antiaddiction society founded in 1958. The central location is in Santa Monica, but there are other installations inside and outside California. The organization is made up and managed entirely by ex-addicts, aided by a volunteer medical staff. Membership is voluntary and not always available. The addict who seeks admission must first be screened by a committee. Once admitted, his compulsion to take drugs is countered by "attack" therapy and group pressure. If he does not respond, he can be expelled. If he does, he can move upward to levels of responsibility within the society, perhaps to an executive position. Some members return to the community; others become permanent Synanon residents. As of March 1964, according to its officers, there were 400 drug-free persons affiliated with Synanon.

DAYTOP LODGE

This is a voluntary program serving addicts placed on probation by the local courts in Brooklyn, N.Y. It resembles Synanon in approach, but is supported by a Federal grant and is under court sponsorship. Its capacity, presently 25 addicts, is being expanded.

METHADONE MAINTENANCE

This is an experimental method of treatment for heroin addiction. Its principal sponsors are Drs. Vincent P. Dole and Marie Nyswander. They began their program of research in January 1964, at the Rockefeller University Hospital in New York City. Subsequently treatment units were established at Manhattan General and other New York hospitals. Patients are admitted on a voluntary but selective basis. Motivation and a past record of treatment failures are among the important selection criteria. The patients are free to leave the program at any time. Of the 108 heroin addicts admitted prior to February 1, 1966, 101 were still in the program on that date. The other 7 had been dismissed from the program.

The first phase of the treatment involves hospitalization and withdrawal from heroin. The patient is then started on daily doses of methadone, a synthetic opiate that is itself addicting. The daily doses are gradually increased and finally become stable. The median stable dose is 100 milligrams per day. This phase of the program lasts about 5 weeks. It is followed by release to the outpatient phases of the treatment. These involve supportive contacts with the hospital staff and hopefully lead the patient to a secure and responsible position in society. Many of the outpatients are, in fact, employed or in school. No attempt has yet been made to withdraw any outpatient from methadone.

As used in the maintenance program, the methadone is dissolved in fruit juice and taken orally under supervision. It is always dispensed from a hospital pharmacy, and the outpatients are required to return each day for their doses. No prescriptions have been given to patients for the purchase of methadone at drug stores. The patients must also give daily urine samples for analysis.

According to the sponsors of the maintenance program, methadone given in adequate doses blocks the euphoric effects of heroin and does not itself produce euphoria, sedation, or distortion of behavior. The patients allegedly remain alert and functionally normal.

The question being tested here is whether an opiate drug, regularly administered as part of a medical program, can contribute to the rehabilitation of a heroin addict. The emphasis is on drawing the patient out of the addict community and away from a career of crime and into new social attitudes and relationships. The social rehabilitation of the addict is seen as a more important treatment goal than the medical cure of addiction itself.

The results of the methadone maintenance research are fragmentary. No final judgments about its suitability as treatment or as a public health approach are yet possible.

CYCLAZOCINE TREATMENT

This method involves daily administration of a new drug, cyclazocine, which is a long-acting opiate antagonist and blocks the effects of heroin. The drug is not itself a narcotic. This treatment has been tried, with urinalysis to detect heroin use, on a pilot basis in New York.

Parole is of course not a medical technique, but it may fairly be classified as a form of treatment insofar as it is used to overcome a person's dependence on drugs. Several parole projects, with specially trained staffs carrying small caseloads, are in operation. The theory is that a parole agency, with its authority over the addict, is ideally situated to arrange and coordinate his adjustments in the community. Frequent contact and intensive supervision are necessary. The outpatient phase of the California rehabilitation program mentioned above is a special parole project in method, if not in name. The prototype of such a project, however, was developed in New York.

The 1960 final report of the Special Narcotic Project of the New York State Division of Parole described the results of a study of 344 addict-parolees supervised between 1956 and 1959. Of the total number supervised, 119 offenders had never been declared delinquent, and another 36 had been declared delinquent for reasons not related to drug use. Thus 155, or 45 percent, were found to be abstinent. A followup study of the same project parolees reported that, by the end of 1962, the abstinence rate had fallen to 32 percent. The median length of supervision of the 344 addict-parolees was 15 months in 1962, as against 8 months in 1959. The New York project now operates as the Narcotic Treatment Bureau. As of December 1966, there were 22 parole officers in the Bureau with an average caseload of 30 parolees.

Treatment of narcotic addiction is by no means a certain or perfected medical art. The most remarkable feature of the treatment programs mentioned above, and these represent only a sample, is their diversity of method. Careful and continuing evaluation of these programs, which has often been absent in the past, is imperative. There is great need for better standards for measuring the outcome of treatment. To think only in terms of "cure" is not very meaningful in the case of a chronic illness such as addiction. There is little knowledge about why a good outcome is achieved for one addict but not another, by one method but not another. More trained personnel are desperately needed. Methods of treatment for abusers of nonopiate drugs must be developed, and there is a general need for research effort in the whole area of personality disorder, of which drug abuse is usually a symptom. New facilities will certainly be needed. The $15 million for each of the next 3 years authorized by the Narcotic Addict Rehabilitation Act of 1966 for grants to State and local governments is a bare minimum. States with drug abuse problems but without specialized treatment programs must initiate such programs. Hospitals and medical schools must devote more attention to drug abuse. This is the beginning of what needs to be done.

Two subjects associated with treatment deserve particular mention. One is civil commitment; the other is the use of drugs in medical practice.

CIVIL COMMITMENT

The enactment of laws authorizing or compelling commitment of drug addicts for purposes of treatment has been the most important development in recent years in the drug abuse field. This trend has broad public acceptance; perhaps it has even assumed the proportions of a movement. In candor it must be said that commitment of addicts began as an experiment, born less out of an established body of medical and scientific knowledge than out of a sense of frustration with orthodox procedures and a demand for new approaches. There was growing awareness that drug addiction was a medical illness and that a clearer distinction, which would make some allowance for the quality of compulsion in addiction, should be made between addicts and other offenders.

California was the first State to initiate new procedures, enacting a Civil Addict Commitment Law in 1961. New York followed with the Metcalf-Volker Act in 1962, but this legislation was revised and broadened in 1966. Also in 1966 a Federal commitment law, the Narcotic Addict Rehabilitation Act, was enacted. These statutes represent the most significant legislation in the field.

The results are still too fragmentary, and experience still too limited, to permit anything more than tentative judgments. A process of trial and error still lies ahead. The Commission therefore considers it imperative that the treatment programs be flexible enough to follow each promising idea and technique as it emerges. Most of all, it is essential that the commitment laws be construed and executed to serve the purpose for which they were intended and by which alone they can be justified. This purpose is treatment in fact and not merely confinement with the pretense of treatment.

THE TYPES OF CIVIL COMMITMENT

The expression "civil commitment" is misleading. The fact is that these commitments usually take place at some point during a criminal proceeding. They are denominated "civil"

523

because they suspend that criminal proceeding and because they do not result in penal confinement.

Civil commitment is generally understood to mean court-ordered confinement in a special treatment facility, followed by release to outpatient status under supervision in the community, with provision for final discharge if the patient abstains from drugs and for return to confinement if he relapses. The total commitment is for an indeterminate period not to exceed a prescribed maximum term. The confinement phase usually entails withdrawal of drugs and therapy designed to overcome psychic dependence. The outpatient phase generally includes a variety of supportive services plus some form of periodic testing for the use of drugs.

At least four types of civil commitment can be identified:

1. Commitment on request of noncriminal addicts, i.e., those who are neither charged with crime nor under sentence after conviction of crime. Both State laws and the Federal law offer this with the proviso that the addict must subject himself to a prescribed maximum term.

2. Involuntary commitment of noncriminal addicts. There is provision for this type in the California law (it has produced only a small minority of the admissions since 1961), the recent New York law, and the Federal law. Under each, the addict is entitled to a jury trial on the issue of addiction.

3. Commitment on request or consent of criminal addicts, i.e., those charged with crime but not yet convicted and those who have been both charged and convicted. The New York and Federal laws provide for this type during the preconviction stage of the proceeding only. The California law does not provide for it at all.

4. Involuntary commitment of criminal addicts. All three laws contain provision for involuntary postconviction commitment. None contains provision for involuntary preconviction commitment.

THE ARGUMENTS PRO AND CON

The involuntary commitment of noncriminal addicts and the voluntary commitment of criminal addicts are controversial and raise difficult issues.

The most heated debate centers on the involuntary commitment of the addict who is not accused of crime. Its proponents compare it to the practices of involuntarily committing the mentally ill, or isolating persons with serious contagious diseases; they argue that the addict is both a health risk to himself and a crime risk to others; they point to the evidence that addiction is spread by social contact with addicts rather than by the recruiting efforts of peddlers. These premises, buttressed by the right of a State to protect the general health and welfare of its citizens, lead them to the conclusion that commitment for treatment offers the maximum benefit to the individual and the minimum risk to society. Its opponents dispute both the premises and the conclusions. They contend that at the very least there should be a specific finding that the person to be committed is reasonably likely to commit dangerous acts; that mere proof of addiction is not a sufficient showing that a person is dangerous to himself or others; and that, in any event, the commitment is a subterfuge—it holds out the promise of a known method of treatment, or a reasonable prospect of cure, which does not exist.

These questions are not easily resolved. However, the Commission believes that involuntary civil commitment offers sufficient promise to warrant a fair test. But it must not become the civil equivalent of imprisonment. The programs must offer the best possible treatment, including new techniques as they become available, and the duration of the commitment, either within or outside an institution, must be no longer than is reasonably necessary.

Another group of issues is raised by voluntary commitment to treatment, before conviction, of addicts charged with crimes. The claimed advantages of such a commitment are that the addict can receive immediate treatment and avoid the stigma of criminal conviction. The eligible addict is given the choice of proceeding to trial or being committed. If he elects commitment, the criminal case is suspended pending the completion of treatment.

The objection in principle to this form of commitment is that a defendant, even though mentally competent in a legal sense, can avoid trial simply by asserting the fact of his addiction in a preliminary proceeding. Thus, so contend the critics, the ultimate issue of guilt or innocence is never reached at all.

In practice there are further objections. These relate to:

☐ The period of time within which the addict must exercise his election to undergo treatment. Under the Federal commitment law, the eligible addict must act within 5 days of being advised by the court of his right to elect. Thus the opportunity to consult with counsel is doubtful, and coercion to forego valid defenses is possible.

☐ The inflexible term of commitment. Under both the Federal and the New York laws, the term of commitment is for a period not to exceed 3 years. A person facing a charge carrying an average or expected sentence in excess of 3 years would probably be induced to elect treatment, whereas a person having the same or greater need for treatment, but facing a shorter sentence, would probably elect a trial. Thus the worst offenders would be channeled into the commitment program.

☐ The fact that a mere showing of addiction is sufficient basis for commitment. No existing law makes it a condition of commitment that a relation between the addiction and crime charged be shown. The addict is not even required to establish that his addiction existed at the time of the alleged crime. Thus an addict may be relieved of his obligation to answer a criminal charge, even though his addiction was entirely unrelated to that charge.

☐ The provisions that exclude certain addicts from treatment. The Federal act, for example, makes all of the following classes of addicts ineligible for commitment to treatment before conviction: Those charged with crimes of violence; those charged with unlawfully importing or selling a narcotic drug; those against whom a prior felony charge is pending; those with two or more felony convictions; and those who have been civilly committed because of narcotic addiction on three or more occasions. Some of these exclusions do not appear advisable. Addicts charged with sale of drugs should be eligible for treatment if the primary purpose of sale was to support their addiction. Likewise two prior felony convictions seem an arbitrary basis for exclusion, especially since prior drug felonies are counted. Finally, a history of past treatment failure is not a valid reason to exclude an addict from present treatment. Addiction is a long process and relapse is predictable. Limited treatment goals are the only realistic ones, and the vital question to ask in measuring success is not whether the addict has completely abstained but whether he has improved in the sense of being less dependent on drugs or using them less frequently. The fact of prior relapse says little about present treatment prospects. The Commission believes that, where laws exist permitting voluntary commitment of addicts who have been charged with but not convicted of crime, judges should have broad discretion to admit addicts to treatment. Only those who are dangerous or habitual criminals aside from their addiction should be excluded.

MEDICAL PRACTICE AND ADDICTION

What limits does the law set on the right of a physician to prescribe or administer narcotic drugs to a narcotic addict? This short question raises issues that have been warmly debated for a long time—issues that are not resolved by reference to the general proposition that the statutory and regulatory measures for the control of narcotic drugs are not intended to interfere with the administration of such drugs in legitimate medical practice. The important issues are: How and by whom is the concept of legitimate medical practice defined and given content? Does legitimate medical practice mean the same thing as that practice accepted and followed by a majority of doctors in the community or as that approved by official spokesmen of the medical profession? If so, and if adverse legal consequences attend any departure from legitimate medical practice, how can new medical ideas and techniques safely be developed? What allowance is made for the good faith of a doctor who departs from standard treatment procedures while acting in what he considers to be the best interests of his patient?

Some background is necessary to put these issues into perspective. The Harrison Narcotic Act of 1914 regulates the distribution of narcotics. It requires those whose usual business involves transactions in narcotic drugs (including physicians) to register and pay an occupational tax, and it imposes a commodity tax, evidenced by stamps, on all narcotics manufactured. It further requires that all narcotics be distributed and transferred in original stamped packages, pursuant to order forms provided by the Treasury Department. Failure to comply with these provisions is a criminal offense. Specifically exempted from the operations of the act, however, are prescriptions issued by a physician "for legitimate medical uses" and distribution of drugs to a patient "in the course of his professional practice only." The very obvious but very important point to note here is that the medical practice exemption is part of a criminal statute. A prescription of drugs that falls outside this exemption is much more than a professional mistake on the part of a doctor. It is a prosecutable offense.

The American Medical Association has adopted and issued several statements on the use of narcotics in medical practice. The most recent, which appeared in 1963, and is currently in the process of revision, was prepared in collaboration with the national research Council of the National Academy of Sciences. It may be summarized as follows:

☐ Continued administration of drugs for the maintenance

of addiction is not a bona fide attempt at cure. In other words withdrawal of the drug must be accomplished before the rehabilitation phase of the treatment can begin.

☐ Withdrawal is most easily carried out in a drug-free environment, in specialized wards or installations for narcotic addicts. Under certain circumstances withdrawal may be carried out in other institutional settings, such as psychiatric wards of general hospitals.

☐ Withdrawal on an ambulatory basis (outside an institution) is, as a general matter, medically unsound and not recommended on the basis of present knowledge.

☐ Ambulatory clinic plans (dispensing drugs to outpatient addicts through clinics established for that purpose) or any other form of ambulatory maintenance (giving stable doses to outpatient addicts) are also medically unsound on the basis of present knowledge.

☐ It is proper ethical practice, after consultation and subject to keeping adequate records, to administer narcotics over a prolonged period to patients with chronic incurable and painful conditions when reasonable alternate procedures have failed, or to maintain an aged or infirm addict, when withdrawal would be dangerous to life. Finally it is ethical to administer maintenance doses generally of methadone, a synthetic narcotic, to an addict who is awaiting admission to a narcotic facility, and to administer limited and diminishing doses to an addict during a process of withdrawal.

☐ Research on the problems of narcotics addiction is absolutely necessary and present concepts are open to revision based on the results of such research.

The AMA–NRC statement touches on areas of active controversy—maintenance, clinic plans, and ambulatory treatment. The Bureau of Narcotics accepts it as the authoritative definition of legitimate medical practice against which all medical practice is to be measured. However, there is a small but vocal minority, composed of reputable men within the medical profession, who do not consider it either authoritative or complete. At least some of these men do not regard withdrawal of the addict from drugs as the first, perhaps not even as the ultimate, treatment objective. Some would permit addicts to continue on stable doses of narcotics, either by means of a clinic arrangement or in some other medical setting.

The Commission has no doubt that the AMA–NRC 1963 statement was an accurate expression of the consensus of medical opinion about treatment. It has been given the explicit approval of the Bureau of Narcotics in a widely distributed pamphlet. Whatever the situation might have been before 1963, there is now no reason for any confusion or apprehension on the part of physicians about their legal right to treat addict-patients in most circumstances that are likely to arise.

One dilemma remains. It is equally felt by the medical profession and by agencies charged with enforcement of narcotic statutes. That dilemma is: What action is to be taken in regard to the physician who departs, or is suspected of having departed, from the AMA–NRC standards concerning the dispensing and prescription of narcotic drugs? Such a physician might have acted without the pretense of treatment, or a bona fide physician-patient relationship, in which case he would clearly have violated the law. But he might also have acted in complete good faith following what he considered to be the best course of treatment for his patient. Should he then be subject to a criminal investigation? One visit from an agent of the Bureau of Narcotics might well be enough to cause him to discontinue his method of practice. It might also deter other physicians and discourage new treatment ideas and approaches.

While the AMA–NRC statement leaves room for research looking to the revision of present treatment concepts, the Commission does not believe that this alone provides sufficient guidance. Who is to know where research begins and ends? How many patients may be involved and for how long? Can techniques that have been tried before, and perhaps failed, be tried again? Who is to judge the qualifications of the researcher and the controls built into the program? These plainly do not seem appropriate questions for enforcement agencies, and yet the answers may determine whether there has been a violation of the laws that those agencies enforce.

The Commission believes that the ultimate resolution of these problems depends on closer cooperation and liaison between the medical profession and law enforcement. Some new measures of cooperation are already in effect. In 1965, for example, a national body was formed for the purposes of keeping current the standards of ethical medical practice with relation to narcotics and narcotic addicts and acting in an advisory capacity to the Bureau of Narcotics. This body is composed of the membership of the Committee on Problems of

Drug Dependence, National Academy of Sciences-National Research Council, and of the Committee on Alcoholism and Drug Addiction, American Medical Association Council on Mental Health, meeting jointly. There must be frequent contacts between this body and the Bureau. In accordance with the AMA–NRC 1963 recommendation, responsible medical bodies should also be established in each State to collaborate in the investigation of physicians under question concerning alleged irregularities in prescribing or dispensing narcotics. Questions concerning the proper limits of medical research could also be referred to these bodies. The Commission further believes that, as recommended by the President's Advisory Commission on Narcotic and Drug Abuse in 1963, consideration should be given to clarification of the Bureau of Narcotics regulation which states that a prescription for narcotics "not in the course of professional treatment but for the purpose of providing the user with narcotics sufficient to keep him comfortable by maintaining his customary use" is an unlawful act subject to the penalties of the Federal narcotics laws. This regulation is ambiguous, makes no allowance for research, and has caused much unnecessary misunderstanding.

The inescapable fact is that medical science has not come very far or very fast in this extremely puzzling field. The need for expanded research is fundamental. It is in the interest of both the medical profession and good law enforcement that no obstacles be put in the way of such research.

EDUCATION

In 1963 the President's Advisory Commission on Narcotic and Drug Abuse found that public and professional education in the field was inadequate. It found the problem clouded by misconceptions and distorted by persistent fallacies. Unfortunately these conclusions are as valid today as they were 3 years ago. Misinformation about drugs and their effects is still prevalent, and the measures taken by the Federal Government to correct them are still limited, fragmented, and sporadic. The National Clearinghouse for Mental Health Information within the National Institute of Mental Health (NIMH) collects and disseminates information, but drug abuse is only one of its many concerns, and its audience is largely made up of researchers and other specialists. Similarly, the educational efforts of the Bureau of Narcotics and the Bureau of Drug Abuse Control, while well intended and well executed, are not on the necessary scale. There is a clear present need for a single agency, having a specific mandate for education, to prepare and distribute a broad range of materials, from pamphlets to films, suitable for presentation to target segments of the public, such as college students. The materials must above all be factual.

The Commission recommends:

A core of educational and informational materials should be developed by the National Institute of Mental Health.

This same recommendation was made by the 1963 Commission. Since that time a Center for Studies on Narcotics and Drug Abuse has been established within NIMH. This unit might be the appropriate one to charge with the major Federal responsibility for education. Wherever the responsibility is placed, it should be discharged with the cooperation of other Federal agencies, State and local agencies, universities, and private organizations. Adequate staff and funding should be provided on a priority basis.

The urgent need for a Federal response in education produced at least one hopeful start in 1966. A program to increase understanding of drug problems on college campuses has been undertaken by the National Association of Student Personnel Administrators under a contract with the Bureau of Drug Abuse Control. Regional seminars will be held for the benefit of campus officials. Written materials will be prepared and disseminated, and methods of communicating effectively with students will be explored. This is a useful, but only a very preliminary step. It is aimed at college students only. Moreover the work will end when the contract expires in 1967. The Federal responsibility for education will not expire at the same time.

The Commission believes that the educational function must be given continuing and central direction by a single agency.

Chapter 9

Drunkenness Offenses

TWO MILLION ARRESTS in 1965—one of every three arrests in America—were for the offense of public drunkenness. The great volume of these arrests places an extremely heavy load on the operation of the criminal justice system. It burdens police, clogs lower criminal courts and crowds penal institutions throughout the United States.

Because of the sheer size of the problem and because of doubts that have recently been raised about the efficacy of handling drunkenness within the system of criminal justice, the Commission sought to reexamine present methods of treating drunkenness offenders and to explore promising alternatives. It was not in a position to undertake a comprehensive study of the complex medical, social, and public health problems of drunkenness.

THE EXISTING SYSTEM

DRUNKENNESS LAWS

Drunkenness is punishable under a variety of laws, generally describing the offense as being "drunk in a public place," often without providing a precise definition of drunkenness itself. Some laws include as a condition that the offender is "unable to care for his own safety."

In some jurisdictions there are no laws prohibiting drunkenness, but any drunkenness that causes a breach of the peace is punishable. In Georgia and Alabama, for example, drunkenness that is manifested by boisterous or indecent conduct, or loud and profane discourse, is a crime. Other jurisdictions apply disorderly conduct statutes to those who are drunk in public. In Chicago, for example, the police, having no drunkenness law to enforce, use a disorderly conduct statute to arrest nondisorderly inebriates. Some jurisdictions permit police to make public drunkenness arrests under both State laws and local ordinances.

The laws provide maximum jail sentences ranging from 5 days to 6 months; the most common maximum sentence is 30 days. In some States an offender convicted of "habitual drunkenness" may be punished by a 2-year sentence of imprisonment.

THE OFFENDERS

The two million arrests for drunkenness each year involve both sporadic and regular drinkers. Among the number are a wide variety of offenders—the rowdy college boy; the weekend inebriate; the homeless, often unemployed single man. How many offenders fall into these and other categories is not known. Neither is it known how many of the offenders are alcoholics in the medical sense of being dependent on alcohol. There is strong evidence, however, that a large number of those who are arrested have a lengthy history of prior drunkenness arrests, and that a disproportionate number involve poor persons who live in slums. In 1964 in the city of Los Angeles about one-fifth of all persons arrested for drunkenness accounted for two-thirds of the total number of arrests for that offense. Some of the repeaters were arrested as many as 18 times in that year.

A review of chronic offender cases reveals that a large number of persons have, in short installments, spent many years of their lives in jail. In 1957 the Committee on Prisons, Probation and Parole in the District of Columbia studied six chronic offenders and found that they had been arrested for drunkenness a total of 1,409 times and had served a total of 125 years in penal institutions. A recent article in a Syracuse, N.Y., newspaper illustrates the point even more succinctly:

H_ _ _ _ F_ _ _ _, 69, appeared in Police Court for the 277th time on a public intoxication charge. F_ _ _ _, who has served 16 years in the Jamesville Penitentiary in short terms on the charge, was returned there for a 6-month sentence.

The great majority of repeaters live on "skid row"—a dilapidated area found in most large and medium-size cities in the United States. On skid row substandard hotels and roominghouses are intermingled with numerous taverns, pawn shops, cheap cafeterias, employment agencies that specialize in jobs for the unskilled, and religious missions that provide free meals after a service. Many of the residents—including the chronic drunkenness offenders—are homeless, penniless, and beset with acute personal problems.

THE ARREST OF THE DRUNKENNESS OFFENDER

The police do not arrest everyone who is under the influence of alcohol. Sometimes they will help an inebriate home. It is when he appears to have no home or family ties that he is most likely to be arrested and taken to the local jail.

One policeman assigned to a skid row precinct in a large eastern city recently described how he decided whom to arrest:

I see a guy who's been hanging around; a guy who's been picked up before or been making trouble. I stop him. Sometimes he can convince me he's got a job today or got something to do. He'll show me a slip showing he's supposed to go to the blood bank, or to work. I let him go. But if it seems to me that he's got nothing to do but drink, then I bring him in.

Drunkenness arrest practices vary from place to place. Some police departments strictly enforce drunkenness statutes, while other departments are known to be more tolerant. In fact, the number of arrests in a city may be related less to the amount of public drunkenness than to police policy. Some of the wide variations in police practices can be seen in the table below that compares drunkenness arrests by two police departments known to be guided by policies of strict enforcement (Atlanta, Ga., and Washington, D.C.) to arrests by a department that is considered more tolerant (St. Louis, Mo.).

In some large and medium-size cities, police departments have "bum squads" that cruise skid rows and border areas to apprehend inebriates who appear unable to care for their own safety, or who are likely to annoy others. Such wholesale arrests sometimes include homeless people who are not intoxicated.

Following arrest, the drunk is usually placed in a barren cell called a "tank," where he is detained for at least a few hours. The tanks in some cities can hold as many as 200 people, while others hold only 1 or 2. One report described the conditions found in a tank in this way:

Although he may have been picked up for his own protection, the offender is placed in a cell, which may frequently hold as many as 40–50 men where there is no room to sit or lie down, where sanitary facilities and ventilation are inadequate and a stench of vomit and urine is prevalent.

The drunken behavior of some of the inmates is an added hazard. It is questionable whether greater safety is achieved for the individual who is arrested for his safe keeping.

The chronic alcoholic offender generally suffers from a variety of ailments and is often in danger of serious medical complications, but medical care is rarely provided in the tank; and it is difficult to detect or diagnose serious illness since it often resembles intoxication. Occasionally, chronic offenders become ill during pretrial detention and die without having received adequate medical attention.

If the offender can afford bail, he usually obtains release after he sobers up. In many jurisdictions an offender is permitted to forfeit bail routinely by not appearing in court. Thus, if the arrested person has the few dollars required, he can avoid prosecution; if he has no money, as is usually the case, he must appear in court.

Drunkenness offenders are generally brought before a judge the morning after their arrest, sometimes appearing in groups of 15 or 20. Rarely are the normal procedural or due process safeguards applied to these cases. Usually defendants are processed through the court system with haste and either released or sentenced to several days or weeks in jail. In some cities only those offenders who request it are jailed. In others chronic offenders, who are likely to be alcoholics, are generally sent to jail.

When a defendant serves a short sentence, he is fed, sheltered, and given access to available recreational facilities. In most institutions there is such a lack of facilities and financial

Comparison of Drunkenness Arrests in Three Cities

| | Population (1965 estimates) | Number of arrests (1965) | | | Percentage of all arrests accounted for by: | |
		Drunkenness arrests	Disorderly conduct and vagrancy arrests	All arrests	Drunk arrests	Drunk, disorderly, and vagrancy arrests
Washington, D.C.	802,000	44,792	21,338	86,464	51.8	76.5
St. Louis, Mo.	699,000	2,445	5,994	44,701	5.5	18.9
Atlanta, Ga.	522,000	48,835	22,379	92,965	52.5	76.6

resources that it is not possible to do more. Austin Mac-Cormick, a former New York City Commissioner of Corrections, noted recently:

The appallingly poor quality of most of the county jails in the United States is so well known that it is probably not necessary to discuss this point at any great length. The fact that the majority of all convicted alcoholics go to these institutions, however, makes it imperative that the public, and particularly those thoughtful citizens who are interested in the treatment of alcoholics, never be allowed to forget that our county jails are a disgrace to the country * * * and that they have a destructive rather than a beneficial effect not only on alcoholics who are committed to them but also on those others who are convicted of the most petty offenses.

After serving a brief sentence, the chronic offender is released, more likely than not to return to his former haunts on skid row, with no money, no job and no plans. Often he is rearrested within a matter of days or hours.

In a memorandum of law submitted in a recent case of a homeless alcoholic, defense counsel noted that his client had been arrested 31 times in a period of 4 months and 6 days. Counsel maintained that "it is fair to conclude [in view of three commitments during that period of time] that he must have been arrested once out of every two days that he appeared on the public streets of the District of Columbia."

EVALUATION OF THE EXISTING SYSTEM

EFFECT ON THE OFFENDER

The criminal justice system appears ineffective to deter drunkenness or to meet the problems of the chronic alcoholic offender. What the system usually does accomplish is to remove the drunk from public view, detoxify him, and provide him with food, shelter, emergency medical service, and a brief period of forced sobriety. As presently constituted, the system is not in a position to meet his underlying medical and social problems.

EFFECT ON THE SYSTEM OF CRIMINAL JUSTICE

Including drunkenness within the system of criminal justice seriously burdens and distorts its operations. Because the police often do not arrest the intoxicated person who has a home, there is in arrest practices an inherent discrimination against the homeless and the poor. Due process safeguards are often considered unnecessary or futile. The defendant may not be warned of his rights or permitted to make a telephone call. And although coordination, breath, or blood tests to determine intoxication are common practice in "driving-while-intoxicated" cases, they are virtually nonexistent in common drunk cases. Yet, without the use of such chemical tests, it is often difficult to determine whether the individual is intoxicated or suffering from a serious illness that has symptoms similar to intoxication.

The handling of drunkenness cases in court hardly reflects the standards of fairness that are the basis of our system of criminal justice. One major reason is that counsel is rarely present. Drunkenness cases often involve complex factual and medical issues. Cross-examination could be conducted on "observations" of a police officer such as "bloodshot" and "glassy" eyes, "staggering gait," "odor" of alcohol on defendant's breath. The testimony of an expert medical witness on behalf of the defendant could be elicited.

The extent of police time allotted to handling drunkenness offenders varies from city to city and from precinct to precinct. In most cities a great deal of time is spent. The inebriate must be taken into custody, transported to jail, booked, detained, clothed, fed, sheltered, and transported to court. In some jurisdictions, police officers must wait, often for hours, to testify in court.

There is a commensurate burden on the urban courts. Notwithstanding the fact that an overwhelming caseload often leads judges to dispose of scores of drunkenness cases in minutes, they represent a significant drain on court time which is needed for felony and serious misdemeanor cases. More subtly, drunkenness cases impair the dignity of the criminal process in lower courts, which are forced to handle defendants so casually and to apply criminal sanctions with so little apparent effect.

In correctional systems, too, resources are diverted from serious offenders. After court appearance, some offenders are sent to short-term penal institutions, many of which are already overcrowded. Correctional authorities estimate that one-half the entire misdemeanant population is comprised of drunkenness offenders. In one city it was reported that 95 percent of short-term prisoners were drunkenness offenders.

LINES FOR ACTION

The sheer size of the drunkenness problem in relation to

the very limited knowledge about causes and treatment makes it impossible to speak in terms of "solutions." There are, however, some important and promising lines that the Commission believes should be explored.

TREATING DRUNKENNESS AS NONCRIMINAL

The Commission seriously doubts that drunkenness alone (as distinguished from disorderly conduct) should continue to be treated as a crime. Most of the experts with whom the Commission discussed this matter, including many in law enforcement, thought that it should not be a crime. The application of disorderly conduct statutes would be sufficient to protect the public against criminal behavior stemming from intoxication. This was the view of the President's Commission on Crime in the District of Columbia, which recommended that the District of Columbia drunkenness law "be amended to require specific kinds of offensive conduct in addition to drunkenness."

Perhaps the strongest barrier to making such a change is that there presently are no clear alternatives for taking into custody and treating those who are now arrested as drunks. The Commission believes that current efforts to find such alternatives to treatment within the criminal system should be expanded. For example, if adequate public health facilities for detoxification are developed, civil legislation could be enacted authorizing the police to pick up those drunks who refuse to or are unable to cooperate—if, indeed, such specific authorization is necessary. Such legislation could expressly sanction a period of detention and allow the individual to be released from a public health facility only when he is sober.

The Commission recommends:

Drunkenness should not in itself be a criminal offense. Disorderly and other criminal conduct accompanied by drunkenness should remain punishable as separate crimes. The implementation of this recommendation requires the development of adequate civil detoxification procedures.

Among those seeking alternatives to processing drunkenness cases through the criminal system are the Vera Institute of Justice in New York City and the South End Center for Alcoholics and Unattached Persons in Boston. The Vera Institute has recently undertaken a project to explore the feasibility of using personnel other than the police to pick up drunks. Included in the study is an attempt to determine what percentage of drunks will come to a treatment facility voluntarily. The Vera program would circumvent the criminal process by establishing a system within a public health framework to care for the immediate and long-range needs of the skid row inebriate.

The Boston program, which has received funds from the Office of Economic Opportunity, provides an alternative to the police-correctional handling of the homeless alcoholic. Staff personnel of the Boston South End Center have approached homeless inebriates in skid row and offered them assistance. An official of the program estimates that 80 percent of the people approached in this way responded willingly. The center screens and evaluates the cases and refers homeless alcoholics to appropriate community facilities. In the past year it has handled the cases of over 900 homeless alcoholics.

The importance of developing an alternative to treating drunkenness within the criminal system is underlined by court decisions in two Federal circuits holding that alcoholics cannot be convicted for drunkenness. *Easter* v. *District of Columbia,* 361 F.21 50 (D.C. Cir. 1966); *Driver* v. *Hinnant,* 356 F.2d 761 (4th Cir. 1966). Pursuant to the *Easter* decision, alcoholics are no longer being convicted of public drunkenness in Washington, D.C.

DETOXIFICATION CENTERS

An alternate approach to present methods of handling drunkenness offenders after arrest and a prerequisite to taking drunkenness out of the criminal system is the establishment of civil detoxification centers. The detoxification center would replace the police station as an initial detention unit for inebriates. Under the authority of civil legislation, the inebriate would be brought to this public health facility by the police and detained there until sober. Thereafter, the decision to continue treatment should be left to the individual. Experience in New York and Boston indicates that some alcoholics may be willing to accept treatment beyond the initial "sobering up" period. The center should include such medical services as physical examinations, an emergency-care unit for the treatment of acutely intoxicated persons, and transportation to a hospital, if advanced medical care seems necessary.

The Commission recommends:

Communities should establish detoxification units as part of comprehensive treatment programs.

540

The Department of Justice has recently provided funds to establish detoxification centers as demonstration projects in St. Louis and Washington, D.C. The St. Louis center is already in full operation; plans for the Washington center are under way. Both units have sufficient facilities to house for a period of a few days those who are in need of "drying out." They also have "inpatient programs," in which patients are given high protein meals with vitamin and mineral supplements and appropriate medication to alleviate alcohol withdrawal symptoms. Bath and laundry facilities are available, as are basic clothing and limited recreational facilities. Regularly scheduled Alcoholics Anonymous meetings, film showings, work projects, group therapy, and lectures are part of the program. During their stay patients are counseled by social workers and other staff members.

The police might also bring to such a center intoxicated persons charged with a variety of petty offenses apart from drunkenness, with violations of administrative codes, and with such felony offenses as driving while intoxicated, assault, and larceny. If the police planned to prosecute the case, a summons could be left with the offender to appear in court at a later date. If an intoxicated defendant was charged with committing a felony, the police could make an individual determination as to the most appropriate detention facility. If he seemed likely to appear in court he might be taken to the detoxification facility. Otherwise, he would presumably be taken to the local jail, unless there were adequate detention facilities on the premises of the detoxification center.

AFTERCARE PROGRAMS

There is little reason to believe that the chronic offender will change a life pattern of drinking after a few days of sobriety and care at a public health unit. The detoxification unit should therefore be supplemented by a network of coordinated "aftercare" facilities. Such a program might well begin with the mobilization of existing community resources. Alcoholics Anonymous programs, locally based missions, hospitals, mental health agencies, outpatient centers, employment counseling, and other social service programs should be coordinated and used by the staff of the detoxification center for referral purposes. It is well recognized among authorities that homeless alcoholics cannot be treated without supportive residential housing, which can be used as a base from which to reintegrate them into society. Therefore, the network of aftercare facilities should be expanded to include halfway houses, community shelters, and other forms of public housing.

The Commission recommends:

Communities should coordinate and extend aftercare resources, including supportive residential housing.

The success of aftercare facilities will depend upon the ability of the detoxification unit to diagnose problems adequately and to make appropriate referrals. A diagnostic unit attached to, or used by, the detoxification unit could formulate treatment plans by conducting a thorough medical and social evaluation of every patient. Diagnostic work should include assistance to the patient and his family in obtaining counseling for economic, marital, or employment problems. Subsequent referrals to appropriate agencies will be crucial to the success of the overall treatment plan. The diagnostic unit, through referral to a job and housing service, might also assist the patient in moving out of the deteriorating environment of skid row. Philadelphia has already established a diagnostic and relocation center, which offers diagnostic, recreational, therapeutic vocational counseling, and housing relocation services, including training in social and occupational skills.

RESEARCH

With over five million alcoholics in the country, alcoholism is the Nation's fourth largest health problem. Research aimed at developing new methods and facilities for treating alcoholics should be given the priority called for by the scope of the need.

The Commission recommends:

Research by private and governmental agencies into alcoholism, the problems of alcoholics, and methods of treatment, should be expanded.

The application of funds for research purposes appears to be an appropriate supplement to the proposed detoxification and treatment units. Consideration should be given to providing further legislation on the Federal level for the promotion of the necessary coordinated treatment programs. Only through such a joint commitment will the burdens of the present system, which fall on both the criminal system and the drunkenness offender, be alleviated.

Chapter 10

Control of Firearms

THE ASSASSINATION OF President John F. Kennedy with a mail-order rifle offered a grim and tragic illustration of what can result when firearms are easily available to anyone in the United States. The Commission strongly believes that the increasing violence in every section of the Nation compels an effort to control possession and sale of the many kinds of firearms that contribute to that violence.

During 1963, 4,760 persons were murdered by firearms. During 1965, 5,600 murders, 34,700 aggravated assaults and the vast majority of the 68,400 armed robberies were committed by means of firearms. All but 10 of the 278 law enforcement officers murdered during the period 1960–65 were killed with firearms. And statistics, of course, cannot even indicate the personal tragedy each of these offenses caused.

The issue of firearms control has been debated heatedly throughout the country in the past few years. Many millions of the estimated 50 million privately owned guns in the United States belong to hunters, gun collectors, and other sportsmen. Their representative organizations resist controls over the present easy accessibility of rifles and shotguns. Many other millions of firearms—pistols, revolvers, rifles, and shotguns—are owned by citizens determined to protect their families from criminal attack and their property from loss to burglars. In a nationwide sampling conducted for the Commission by the National Opinion Research Center, 37 percent of the persons interviewed said that they kept firearms in the household to protect themselves. Some citizens who fear assault and robbery in the streets of our cities carry firearms about for self-protection. Many of these firearms owners contend that control over the purchase and possession of firearms conflicts with the need and right to defend themselves, their families, and their property.

Although the Commission believes that controls at all levels of government must be strengthened in order to reduce the probability that potential criminal offenders will acquire firearms, it agrees that the interests of persons desiring such weapons for legitimate purposes must be preserved as much as possible. No system of control, of course, can guarantee that society will be safe from the misuse of firearms, but the Commission is convinced that a strengthened system can make an important contribution to reducing the danger of crime in the United States.

EXISTING FIREARMS CONTROL LAWS

Regulation of firearms in the United States is based upon three Federal laws, various kinds of State legislation, and a large number of local ordinances.

The first of the Federal laws, the National Firearms Act of 1934, applies to machine guns, short-barreled and sawed-off rifles and shotguns, mufflers and silencers, and concealable firearms—not including pistols. The 1934 act requires that possessors register all of these weapons and devices with the Treasury Department, and it imposes annual taxes on firearms manufacturers, importers, and dealers. Taxes ranging from $5 to $200 are also imposed on the transfer of registered weapons and other equipment.

The Federal Firearms Act of 1938 requires the licensing of all manufacturers and dealers who use the facilities of interstate or foreign commerce. It prohibits the knowing transportation of firearms in interstate commerce to, or receipt by, any person who has been convicted of a felony, or who is a fugitive from justice. The law requires that most kinds of firearms imported into or manufactured in the United States bear serial numbers, and it prohibits the interstate transportation of stolen firearms, or those with mutilated serial numbers. The 1938 law also prohibits the licensed manufacturers and dealers from transporting firearms into States in violation of State laws requiring a permit to purchase firearms.

The third Federal law regulating firearms is the Mutual Security Act of 1954, which authorizes the President to regulate the export and import of firearms. Administration of the act has been delegated to the Department of State.

The Department of Defense, which formerly disposed of

its surplus firearms through commercial and other private channels, suspended all such sales several months ago. It is now considering the advisability of destroying surplus or obsolete weapons in the future.

There is a wide diversity in the purpose and scope of State gun control laws:

Twenty-five States require a license to sell handguns at retail, 8 require a permit (or the equivalent) to purchase a handgun, 11 require a waiting period between purchase and delivery of a handgun, 1 requires a license to possess a handgun, 29 require a license to carry a handgun, 19 prohibit the carrying of a concealed handgun, 18 require a license to carry a handgun in a vehicle, 22 prohibit the carrying of a loaded firearm in a vehicle, and 4 States require the registration of firearms.

New York State's Sullivan law is the most stringent firearms control regulation in the United States. The laws of several States require that anyone carrying concealable firearms have a license, but the Sullivan law prohibits anyone from keeping a pistol or revolver in his home or place of business without a license. Further, no one may even purchase a pistol or revolver until he has obtained either a license to possess or a license to carry such a weapon. The New York law does not require a license to possess or carry rifles and shotguns, but does state that they cannot be carried in an automobile or a public place when loaded.

In addition to the State laws, there are many county, city, town, and village ordinances that require licenses for the possession or purchase of firearms.

LIMITED EFFECTIVENESS OF PRESENT LAWS

At first glance, the combined regulatory machinery established by these firearms laws may appear to provide sufficient control. This appearance is misleading. A 1966 Federal Bureau of Investigation survey of the chief administrators of police departments in 10 large cities discloses that all but one believe that the easy accessibility of firearms is a serious law enforcement problem.

On the Federal level, the statutes do little to control the retail and mail-order sale of handguns, rifles, and shotguns. The provision of the Federal Firearms Act of 1938 prohibiting Federal licensees from transporting firearms into States in violation of State laws requiring a permit to purchase firearms has an extremely limited effect. Only eight States have enacted permit laws. If there are local ordinances within a State, but no State law, the Federal provision does not apply. The prohibition against transport of firearms to, or receipt by, felons or fugitives applies only to direct interstate shipment and does not prevent such persons from buying firearms locally after they have been transported from another State. Despite the Federal laws, therefore, practically anyone—the convicted criminal, the mental incompetent, or the habitual drunkard—can purchase firearms simply by ordering them in those States that have few controls.

Strict controls by one State or city are nullified when a potential criminal can secure a firearm merely by going into a neighboring jurisdiction with lax controls, or none at all. While information is sparse, there are strong indications that mail-order houses and other out-of-State sources provide a substantial number of guns to those who commit crimes. One study by the Massachusetts State Police showed that 87 percent of concealable firearms used during the commission of crimes in Massachusetts in a recent year were obtained from sources outside the State.

In order to prevent criminal use of firearms, the police must have some way of following weapons into the hands of the ultimate consumer. But only in four States do police agencies have a method of determining who owns firearms and where they are located. The requirement that each person register firearms—a tool available to law enforcement in almost every industrial nation in the world—has been compared with the State control of automobiles and drivers. At a time when there were very few autombiles, registration was not thought necessary. When automobiles became so numerous that they posed a serious physical threat to society, comprehensive registration was felt to be essential.

A final failing in the present system of control is the ease with which extremely low-priced, and therefore widely available, surplus weapons are brought into the United States from foreign countries. At the present time it is estimated that at least 1 million such weapons are reaching the civilian market each year. During the recent hearings of the Senate Subcommittee on Juvenile Delinquency, law enforcement officials testified that foreign imports accounted for a significant percentage of the total number of firearms coming into their possession as a result of having been used in the commission of crimes. The figures ranged from a low of 18 percent in Washington, D.C., to a high of 80 percent in Atlanta, Ga.

The limited statutory framework within which the State Department must operate prevents any effective control over the importation of firearms. If the import in question does not involve machineguns, sawed-off shotguns, or the other weapons covered by the 1934 National Firearms Act, each transaction is approved routinely, as long as the dealer is a bona fide businessman engaged in a bona fide business transaction.

PUBLIC OPINION ABOUT FIREARMS CONTROL

Public opinion on the subject of firearms control has been sampled several times in the last few years by the Gallup Poll. According to the 1966 poll, a substantial majority of persons interviewed—67 percent—said they favored "a law which would require a person to obtain a police permit before he or she could buy a gun." Even when the same question was put to firearms owners, a majority—56 percent—indicated that they favored police permits to purchase guns.

A second question asked by the Gallup Poll was directed to the problem of guns and juveniles. "Which of these three plans would you prefer for the use of guns by persons under the age of 18—forbid their use completely; put strict regulations on their use; or continue as at present with few regulations?" In response, 27 percent of those questioned and 17 percent of firearms owners said they favored completely forbidding the use of guns by persons under 18; 55 percent of all persons and 59 percent of gun owners said they favored strict regulation; and 15 percent of all persons and 22 percent of the gun owners wanted to continue as at present.

On the question of outlawing all handguns except for police use (a question last asked in 1959) 59 percent of the sample were in favor and 35 percent were opposed.

THE CONTROVERSY ABOUT FIREARMS CONTROL

While the majority of the public favors reasonable firearms control, the National Rifle Association and other citizen groups have provided an effective legislative lobby to represent those hunters, gun collectors, and other persons who oppose additional regulation. Many arguments are offered by this opposition.

The most emotional position—one this Commission must reject outright—is that licensing and registration provisions for handguns, rifles, and shotguns would disarm the public and thus render it easy prey for violent criminals, or an invading or subversive enemy. In fact, all proposals for regulation would permit householders and shopkeepers to continue to possess firearms. Licensing and registration for the legitimate firearms owner would merely add a small measure of inconvenience to the presently largely unregulated mail-order and over-the-counter sales of firearms. It is this inconvenience that appears to be the underlying reason for the opposition to more firearms control. Opponents suggest that laws calling for registration would penalize the law-abiding citizen, who would comply—while not touching criminals who would not comply. They thus conclude that such laws do not address themselves to the real problem of firearms misuse.

Those supporting stricter control of firearms agree that many potential criminal offenders will obtain firearms even with additional laws. But they point to the conclusion of the Senate Subcommittee on Juvenile Delinquency, which found that criminals, for the most part, purchase their firearms through the mails or in retail stores, rather than stealing them. One Police chief from a large western city told an FBI survey that, after permissive State legislation had preempted local controls, there were "several instances of homicide committed within 30 minutes of the time a short firearm was purchased by a person who would not have been granted a permit to purchase one under the former legislation."

During the first year's operation of a Philadelphia ordinance requiring a permit to obtain a firearm, 73 convicted persons were prohibited from purchasing firearms in the city. Federal Bureau of Investigation statistics demonstrate that a higher proportion of homicides are committed with firearms in those areas where firearms regulations are lax, than in those areas where there are more stringent controls. In Dallas, Tex., and Phoenix, Ariz., firearms regulations are fairly weak. In Dallas in 1963, 72 percent of homicides were committed with firearms; in Phoenix 65.9 percent were committed with firearms. In Chicago, where regulations are more strict, 46.4 percent of the homicides were committed with firearms. In New York City, with the most stringent gun controls of any major city in the United States, only about 25 percent of the homicides are committed with firearms.

Opponents of additional controls contend that firearms are dangerous only if misused and that the appropriate legal remedy is to punish illegal use of firearms—not to hamper ownership. Supporters of control argue that it is not enough to rely on the deterrent effect of punishing the wrongdoer after the act to prevent others from misusing guns. They maintain that firearms should be kept out of the hands of those who intend to use them wrongfully.

Opponents of firearms control legislation also rely upon the Second Amendment's guarantee of "the right to bear arms." The Second Amendment, in its entirety, states:

A well regulated Militia, being necessary to the security of a free State, the right of the people to keep and bear Arms, shall not be infringed.

The U.S. Supreme Court and lower Federal courts have consistently interpreted this Amendment only as a prohibition against Federal interference with State militia and not as a guarantee of an individual's right to keep or carry firearms. The argument that the Second Amendment prohibits State or Federal regulation of citizen ownership of firearms has no validity whatsoever.

COMMISSION RECOMMENDATIONS

Since laws, as they now stand, do not accomplish the purposes of firearms control, the Commission believes that all States and the Federal Government should act to strengthen them. Any legislative scheme should maximize the possibility of keeping firearms out of the hands of potential criminal offenders, while at the same time affording citizens ample opportunity to purchase such weapons for legitimate purposes.

It is appropriate to ban absolutely the sale of those weapons no citizen has a justifiable reason for owning.

The Commission recommends:

Federal and State Governments should enact legislation outlawing transportation and private possession of military-type firearms such as bazookas, machine guns, mortars, and anti-tank guns.

In addition, dangerous or potentially dangerous persons should be prohibited from purchasing firearms.

The Commission recommends:

States should enact laws prohibiting certain categories of persons, such as habitual drunkards, drug addicts, mental incompetents, persons with a history of mental disturbance, and persons convicted of certain offenses, from buying, owning, or possessing firearms.

Prevention of crime and apprehension of criminals would be enhanced if each firearm were registered with a governmental jurisdiction. A record of ownership would aid the police in tracing and locating those who have committed or who threaten to commit violent crime. Law enforcement officers should know where each gun is and who owns it.

The Commission recommends:

Each State should require the registration of all hand-guns, rifles, and shotguns. If, after 5 years, some States still have not enacted such laws, Congress should pass a Federal firearms registration act applicable to those States.

Government regulation to prevent those with criminal purposes from purchasing firearms cannot be effective as long as mail-order sales and retail sales to persons living outside the seller's State are not controlled. It is essential, also, to reduce and to regulate the importation into the United States of large numbers of cheap firearms. Since sporting weapons such as rifles and shotguns apparently present less danger of criminal use than do handguns, control over the latter should be more stringent. A truly effective system of regulation requires a meshing of State and Federal action.

The Commission recommends:

Each State should require a person to obtain a permit before he can either possess or carry a handgun. Through licensing provisions, Federal law should prohibit mail-order and other interstate sales of handguns and should regulate such sales of rifles and shotguns.

Federal legislation to implement these goals should prohibit the interstate shipment of handguns except between federally licensed importers, manufacturers, and dealers. A Federal licensee should also be prohibited from selling handguns to an individual not living in the State of the seller. The interstate shipment of shotguns and rifles should be delayed a sufficient time for law enforcement authorities in the buyer's hometown to examine his sworn statement concerning age and other factors affecting his eligibility to purchase such a weapon, and the consent of these authorities should be required before the weapon may be shipped. Antique dealers could continue to operate under reasonable regulations. States may also want to prohibit firearms sales to persons under a certain age, such as 18 or 21, or require parental approval for firearms registration in a minor's name.

Chapter 11

Science and Technology

THE SCIENTIFIC AND TECHNOLOGICAL revolution that has so radically changed most of American society during the past few decades has had surprisingly little impact upon the criminal justice system. In an age when many executives in government and industry, faced with decisionmaking problems, ask the scientific and technical community for independent suggestions on possible alternatives and for objective analyses of possible consequences of their actions, the public officials responsible for establishing and administering the criminal law—the legislators, police, prosecutors, lawyers, judges, and corrections officials—have almost no communication with the scientific and technical community.

More than two hundred thousand scientists and engineers are helping to solve military problems, but only a handful are helping to control the crimes that injure or frighten millions of Americans each year. Even small businesses employ modern technological devices and systems, but the Nation's courts are almost as close to the quill pen era as they are to the age of electronic data processing. The police, with crime laboratories and radio networks, made early use of technology, but most police departments could have been equipped 30 or 40 years ago as well as they are today. Hospitals and clinics draw heavily upon the most recent developments in engineering and medical science, but the overwhelming majority of reformatories, jails and prisons are, technologically speaking, a century or more in the past.

This lack of contact between criminal justice and science and technology is true even in the Federal Government, where, as recently as 1965, the Justice Department was the only Cabinet department with no share of the roughly $15 billion Federal research and development budget.

In order to help bring scientific knowledge and techniques to bear on the problems of criminal justice, the Commission, in collaboration with the Office of Law Enforcement Assistance, established a task force on science and technology in April 1966. The task force was given the job of showing how the resources of science and technology might be used to solve the problems of crime. In the subsequent months, the task force sought:

☐ To identify the problems, immediate and long term, that technology is most likely to help solve, and to suggest the kinds of research and development needed.

☐ To identify and describe crime control problems in a form susceptible to quantitative analysis.

☐ To point out the kinds of important data on crime control and the criminal justice system that are lacking, unreliable or otherwise unusable, and to propose means of correcting such deficiencies.

☐ To analyze problems in crime assessment, police, courts, and corrections as an aid to the Commission and its other task forces.

☐ To suggest organizational formats within which technological devices and systems can be developed, field tested, and rendered useful.

With a scope so broad, and limited time and manpower, only a few problems could be studied in detail. The task force gave major attention to computer technology, information systems, communications engineering, and systems analysis, since these appeared to offer the greatest unrealized potentials for systemwide improvement. Within the criminal justice system, the greatest potential for immediate improvement by technological innovation appeared to be in police operations, and so the task force looked particularly hard at the police and somewhat less hard at courts and corrections. Some of the results are presented here and detailed in the task force report. The results included:

☐ A compilation of field data examining certain relationships between police patrol operations and the apprehension of criminals.

☐ A proposal for improving police responsiveness to calls at minimum cost.

- [ ] A program that could dramatically reduce police radio frequency congestion.
- [ ] A research and development program for developing a semiautomatic fingerprint recognition capability, to replace the present system which cannot regularly trace a criminal with less than a full set of prints.
- [ ] Studies examining possible alternative alarm systems, nonlethal weapons, and other technological innovations for police operations.
- [ ] A procedure for reducing certain unnecessary delays in moving criminal cases through the courts.
- [ ] An examination of how programed learning techniques can be used in the rehabilitation of young offenders.
- [ ] A review of the application of statistical techniques to decisions about treatment of convicted criminals.
- [ ] Methods for making auto theft more difficult, which automobile manufacturers have agreed to incorporate into the design of future models.
- [ ] An exploratory attempt to apply systems analysis to the overall criminal justice system, which produced several highly suggestive but still tentative results.
- [ ] An outline, but not a detailed design, of a national information system for criminal justice agencies.
- [ ] A proposal for a national research and development program.

These results are only illustrations of the potential contributions of science and technology to crime control. They must be developed in detail for each local situation, and they suggest many other opportunities. As illustrations, however, they appear to offer sufficient promise of the potential benefits from science and technology to warrant major further work immediately.

Modern technology can provide many new devices to improve the operations of criminal justice agencies, and particularly to help the police deter crime and apprehend criminals. It is far easier, however, to imagine and develop devices than to choose the ones in which to invest necessarily limited equipment budgets. Technology can indeed fill most reasonable requests and can thereby provide considerable help to law enforcement. We must still decide what devices we want relative to the price we are willing to pay in dollars, invasion of privacy, and other social costs. It is technically feasible, for example, to cut auto theft drastically by putting a radio transmitter in every car in America and tracking all cars continuously. But this might cost a billion dollars and, even more

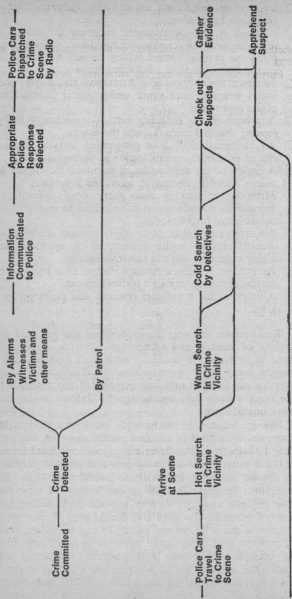

Apprehension Process Figure 1.

Crime Committed ——— Crime Detected
- By Alarms Witnesses Victims and other means ——— Information Communicated to Police ——— Appropriate Police Response Selected ——— Police Cars Dispatched to Crime Scene by Radio

By Patrol

Police Cars Travel to Crime Scene ——— Arrive at Scene ——— Hot Search in Crime Vicinity — Warm Search in Crime Vicinity — Cold Search by Detectives — Check out Suspects

Gather Evidence

Apprehend Suspect

important, create an intolerable environment of unending surveillance. Science can provide the capability, but the public as a whole must participate in the value discussion of whether or not the capability is worth its financial and social costs.

Furthermore, no one can say what most devices or systems will do about crime; little is known of what anything will do about crime. The effect of this or that device upon crime will be speculative until careful field evaluations are conducted. However, not all technological innovations can be postponed until these evaluations are completed. Judgment must identify where technology appears to offer the greatest promise. This may involve some wasted effort, but the urgency of crime control warrants the risk of some waste.

Introduction of appropriate technology is often hindered by budgets, which not very helpfully distinguish between "equipment" and "personnel" rather than between functions such as "general-purpose police patrol" and "investigation of homicide." For example, since a two-man car on continuous patrol costs about $100,000 per year, it would be surprising if patrol operations could not be significantly improved by a capital investment exceeding the current $3,000 per car. But such an investment might severely strain the equipment budget, and might be passed up, even if it could result in a much larger saving in personnel costs. Dollars could be allocated more rationally by making use of the program budgeting techniques now being used by the Federal Government.

Because of the enormous range of technological possibilities, it is essential to begin not with technology but with problems. Technological efforts can then be concentrated where they are most likely to be productive. Systems analysis has been used most successfully in fields like national defense and mass transportation to determine where technological resources can most usefully be directed over a broad field of concern. These techniques and approaches can be usefully applied to the problems of crime control, relating alternative means to desired ends. Because of the importance of this approach, the task force has illustrated how systems analysis might be applied in a small number of cases: To reduce courtroom delay, to speed police response to a call, and to examine the overall criminal justice system in an integrated way.

Because the task force on science and technology brought a new viewpoint and analytical and quantitative techniques to the subject matter, the Commission encouraged it to examine some of the basic problems of crime and crime control not within the traditional boundaries of science and technology. As a result, a number of ideas and conceptions were uncovered that provided significant new insights into the problems with which the Commission dealt. One of several possible examples can serve to illustrate this point. Although it is common knowledge that the number of arrests made each year in the United States for nontraffic offenses is very large (the FBI estimates exceed 6 million), it has never been known what percentage of the population is arrested. This percentage depends strongly on the proportion of arrests that are of persons never before arrested. This proportion is difficult to estimate because of the incompleteness of arrest records. A mathematical analysis performed by the task force used a conservative estimate—one new offender in eight arrests—and indicated tentatively that about 40 percent of the male children living in the United States today will be arrested for a nontraffic offense sometime in their lives. The proportion is even higher for boys living in a city.

If sustained by additional data, these startling results refute the common notion that most people never encounter the criminal justice system, and only a small class of "criminals" do. Although this statistic and many like it are vital to understanding how the system operates, there are no estimates, however tentative, of many such numbers. Reasonable estimates of the numbers connected with crime and the criminal justice system are necessary for a systematic analysis of crime control.

Virtually all the efforts of the Commission have been hampered by the pervasive lack of adequate objective information about crime and the possible effects of various techniques for crime control. Each year, judges in this country pass roughly 2 million sentences. Almost all sentencing decisions are made with little or no information on the likely effect of the sentence on future criminal behavior. About 200,000 policemen spend half of their time on "preventive" patrol. Yet, no police chief can obtain even a rough estimate of how much crime is thereby "prevented." The factfinding, analytical, and experimental methods of science offer one approach to identifying some of the important questions and developing the required information.

POLICE OPERATIONS

Of all criminal justice agencies, the police traditionally have had the closest ties to science and technology, but they have called on scientific resources primarily to help in the solution of specific serious crimes, rather than for assistance in solving general problems of policing. The task force focused its efforts on some illustrative applications of science and technology to the broad problems of police operations.

The police control crime primarily by apprehending criminals and by posing a convincing threat of apprehension. The apprehension process (figure 1) begins either with the detection of a crime by patrol or by a report to the police, followed by the dispatch of police to the scene. Then come search, investigation, interrogation, data gathering, suspect checkouts and arrest, sometimes followed by more investigation and assistance in prosecution. The police field operations centering around apprehension are closely tied to technology. Automobiles, radios, crime laboratories, scientific investigation, and police weaponry are essential technical aids to the operations of a modern police force.

Science and technology can improve the capabilities of the police in the apprehension process. However, many promising developments are inhibited by the lack of data on just what situations confront the police, and by the lack of systematic studies of police patrol and apprehension operations. A number of studies have been undertaken in the past, but much more potential lies in the use of new analysis techniques and the opportunities for computer processing of the data. To try to illustrate some of these potentials, the task force undertook a limited first-hand study of police operations. It then conducted an illustrative cost-effectiveness analysis comparing alternative means of reducing response time. These studies are summarized in this section, followed by an examination of the sequence of stages in the apprehension process—detection, communication to police, police command and control and communications, evidence gathering by fingerprints and analysis by crime laboratories—to identify some of the scientific and technological contributions to each.

ANALYSIS OF FIELD DATA ON APPREHENSIONS

The purpose of this study, conducted with the Los Angeles Police Department, was to identify and assess the influence of various factors in the apprehension process on the solution of crimes. The study was, essentially, an analysis of records: Reports of calls for service, patrol field activity, crimes, detective investigations, arrests, and other case clearances. Data were collected on time delays within the communications-dispatching center and response time in the field.

Of the total of 1,905 crimes examined in the study, 25 percent (482) resulted in arrests or other clearances. Seventy percent of the cleared cases were cleared by arrests, 90 percent of which were made by the patrol force. More than half the arrests were made within 8 hours of the crime, and almost two-thirds of the arrests were made within the first week of the crime.

The most significant factor in clearance is whether or not a suspect is named in the crime report. As shown in figure 2 if a suspect is neither known to the victim nor arrested at the scene of the crime, the chances of ever arresting him are slim. Of the 482 cleared cases, 63 percent involved "named suspects." Of these, about half involved suspects actually known to the victim, about 30 percent were on-the-scene arrests by patrol officers and another 20 percent by store security officers. The majority of the crime cases, a total of 1,556 (82 percent), involved suspects not named in the crime report. Of these, 1,375 (88 percent) were not cleared. Most of the cleared cases with unknown suspects were cleared because of an on-the-scene arrest, initiated either by radio call or by field observation. These results suggested examining the importance of rapid response in catching the suspect at the scene.

Table 1.—Relation Between Response Time and Arrests

Type of call		Average communication center time (minutes)	Average field response time (travel time) (minutes)	Average combined time (minutes)
Emergency	Crime uncleared	1.92	4.38	6.30
	Arrest made	1.11	3.00	4.11
Nonemergency but urgent.	Crime uncleared	3.84	[1] 4.00	7.84
	Arrest made	2.61	2.71	5.32
All other nonemergency	Crime uncleared	7.25	[1] 12.94	[2] 20.19
	Arrest made	5.64	4.56	10.20

[1] Very small sample.
[2] Reflects high proportion of "take report" calls.

From table 1, the overall police response time for emergency calls is seen to average 6.3 minutes for those cases involving crimes subsequently not cleared. The average is only 4.1 minutes for cases in which the police were able to make an arrest. A similar difference exists for the calls classified as nonemergency. Thus, for Los Angeles, on the basis of these data, short response time correlates with ability to make an arrest.

A similar picture results when the probability of arrest is related to response time. When response time was 1 minute, 62 percent of the cases ended in arrest. When all cases with response time under 16 minutes were grouped together, only 44 percent led to arrest. The correlation between arrest and response time may be a cause-and-effect relationship, or it may have developed through some third factor to which both arrest and response time are related. More carefully controlled tests than were possible in the time available are needed to establish a definitive causal relation.

Clearance of Crimes with Named and Unnamed Suspects.

1,905 crimes   Total Clearance Rate = 25%   Figure 2

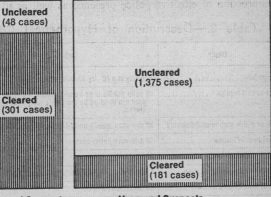

Uncleared (48 cases)	Uncleared (1,375 cases)
Cleared (301 cases)	Cleared (181 cases)

Named Suspects (349 cases) Clearance Rate = 86%

Unnamed Suspects (1,556 cases) Clearance Rate = 12%

The Commission recommends:

Similar studies exploring the detailed characteristics of crimes, arrests, and field investigation practices should be undertaken in large metropolitan police departments.

Among the matters to be considered, as shown by the Los Angeles study, are:

☐ Criteria for priority of dispatching of patrol cars.

- [ ] Design and tests of sets of criteria for emergency response.
- [ ] Assessing in more detail the effects of response time.
- [ ] Sampling incoming calls and following them through activities into the field.
- [ ] Use of equipment, such as portable recording devices, to simplify data collection by the investigating officer.

This kind of factual study could also be extremely valuable in determining the effects on later stages in the criminal process of the questioning of suspects, warning them as to their rights, and introducing counsel into the situation.

SYSTEMS ANALYSIS OF RESPONSE TIME IN
A HYPOTHETICAL CITY

On the basis of the correlation between response time and arrests, and because officials desire rapid response to create an impression of effective police presence as well as to aid in

Table 2.—Description of Hypothetical City

Item	Details
Geography	The city is a 10- by 10-mile square.
Rate of call receipt [1]	40 calls per hour or approximately 350,000 calls per year are handled by the police telephone complaint clerks.
Rate of police mobile unit dispatch	30 one-man mobile units are dispatched per hour.
Total mobile force [2]	40 one-man patrol cars.
Speed of mobile force	25 m.p.h.
Public telephone distribution	1,000 distributed uniformly throughout city.
Patrol time at crime scene	30 minutes average.
Number of call complaint clerks	2 or 3.

[1] This might be typical for a city of about 500,000 population.
[2] Considers only mobile units assigned to patrol functions independent of special detective forces and supervisory vehicles.

apprehension, the task force examined means of reducing response time. In particular, an analysis was conducted to determine how to get the greatest reduction in response time per dollar of cost. This analysis was accomplished by making a mathematical model of the apprehension process in a hypothetical city. Although the numerical values used in this example, being based on averages from several large cities, typify a major city in the United States, any police department would in practice have to use data developed for its specific case.

The hypothetical city is assumed to cover 100 square miles and to have the police force, telephone system, and other variables shown in table 2. A city this size would have a population of about 500,000 and be comparable in population density to Atlanta or Indianapolis.

In the analysis, time delays in the apprehension process were related to system resources (table 3), and costs were as-

Table 3.—Resources Associated With Time Delays in the Apprehension Process

Components of response time	Resources
Time until detection......................	Police patrol unit, sensors, alarms, public's response.
Time from detection until attempt is made to transmit message to police dispatcher.	Police callboxes, police radio network, common carrier telephone, automatic alarm and associated communications.
Incoming message queue waiting time.......	Telephone operators.
Control center response time.............	Police control center Internal operations.
Field force response time.................	Patrol unit, car-location devices.

sociated with each resource. The analysis computes the time reduction and costs associated with various means of reducing response time. The improvements were measured in seconds of delay saved per dollar.

The results of the analysis are summarized in table 4. In the first column the delays caused by each activity are identified. For example, the patrol mobility delay is the time from the termination of the dispatch order to arrival at the scene of the crime. The basic operating unit associated with this activity is a one-man patrol car (col. 2). The number of such units already in use is 40 (col. 3). The amount of this delay is 216 seconds (col. 4). If one additional unit were added, response time would decrease by 4 seconds (col. 5). The patrol unit is expected to be used 264,000 times a year (col. 6). The cost of an additional unit is $50,000 per year (col. 7). Multiplying the delay saved per call per additional unit (col. 5) by the frequency of use (col. 6) and dividing by the cost of the additional unit (col. 7), one obtains the number of seconds saved per dollar, 21.1 seconds (col. 8).

Employing this technique, one can evaluate the changes in other components such as the complaint clerk, public callbox, automatic car locator, and computer and collateral equipment for the communications center. For this case, automating the command center is seen to be the most attractive alternative. If there are only two complaint clerks, adding a third is the next most desirable step. As is shown in table 4, adding a fourth would not be desirable.

Among the conclusions about the hypothetical city that may be drawn from detailed analysis of the sort illustrated are:

☐ Automatic car-locator systems costing $100,000 or less per year to operate would decrease the system delay at least twice as much as a comparable investment in additional patrol units.

☐ Since telephone waiting time is very sensitive to load, an additional complaint clerk would be warranted in places where the clerks are now busy.

☐ Since the hypothetical city already has public callboxes, the incremental value of additional ones would be low. The effectiveness of callboxes is relatively large, so that cities that now keep their callboxes locked should open them to the public.

☐ Random detection of crimes by patrolling cars is an infrequent event, except in the case of stolen cars. A policeman might expect to observe a street robbery once every 14 years.

These results apply directly only to the hypothetical city just described but they suggest what might be learned from similar analyses in real cities.

DETECTION BY ALARMS AND SURVEILLANCE DEVICES

Devices for sounding an alert with no human intervention would have advantages both as a deterrent to criminals and in facilitating the response to an incident. Many devices are available: silver-tape electric alarms, pressure and acoustic sensors, radar, and ultrasonic, infrared, and ultraviolet beams. These devices can protect unattended premises from intrusion by detecting movement in a room or motion across a perimeter.

False alarms are a problem for any alarm system. In Washington, D.C., in 1965, 4,450 alarms were received by the police; 98 percent of them were false. Since answering each false alarm takes an average of about 30 minutes and since patrol cars tend to spend about half their time answer-

Table 4.—Cost-Effectiveness Analysis of Delay Reduction in Hypothetical City

Elements of delay (1)	Basic unit (2)	Number of units currently allocated (3)	Delay time (seconds) (4)	Seconds of delay saved per call per additional unit installed (5)	Frequency of use (calls/year) (6)	Cost per year of additional unit (7)	Seconds of delay saved per dollar allocated (8)
Public access delay	Public callbox	1,000	96	0.0475	10,000	$50	9.5
Telephone queue waiting time	Complaint clerks	2 3	7.2 .042	7.158 .042	350,400 350,400	35,000 35,000	71.7 .42
Delay due to lack of command and control function automation	Computer and related hardware for command and control center.	0	120	90	264,000	200,000	119
Delay due to lack of knowledge of exact position of patrol unit	Automatic car locator system	0	20	18	264,000	100,000	47.5
Patrol mobility delay	1-man patrol car	40	216	4	264,000	50,000	21.1

ing calls, this was approximately equivalent to full-time duty of one patrol car.

New, low-cost private alarm systems are being developed and may become widely installed. These devices can automatically send prerecorded messages directly to the police. As a consequence, the police should expect a significant increase in the number of false alarms. To prevent this increase from seriously disrupting police operations, police departments should establish minimum standards for direct-calling alarm installations. On-site inspection should be required to assure that the alarm itself is mechanically and electrically reliable (usually not a serious problem), that its installation is not subject to simple accidental failure as from blowing wind, and that it is not subject to accidental triggering by the occupants.

Various kinds of street alarm or surveillance networks have been proposed to detect crime in the streets. The proposals range from simple pushbutton alarms to sophisticated pattern-recognizing devices that detect cries of "help." Other sensors include closed-circuit TV cameras (fed to a console at the police station), simple microphones, and magnetic sensors triggered by specially coded devices carried by individuals. To explore these suggestions, the task force has examined several system designs. The automatic systems cost over $1 million per square mile, far too much for most communities. Furthermore, they may pose an insoluble false-alarm problem and so are not recommended. Accessible street emergency communication facilities, discussed below, can serve many of the same functions, and can be developed much more readily.

COMMUNICATIONS TO THE POLICE

The apprehension process can respond only after it gets a call, and a number of things can be done to modify existing street communications equipment to make it easier for a victim or a witness to reach the police.

The victim of a robber careful enough to steal the last dime cannot now use the public telephone. Public telephones can be adapted so that the operator can be reached without using money, as was demonstrated in a recent test in Hartford, Conn. The Bell Telephone System is now planning to extend this capability widely.

Most major cities have a network of police callboxes that are usually inconspicuous and locked. Washington, D.C., has 920 such boxes, or about one every one-fourth mile. During World War II these boxes were painted red, white, and blue, and made available to the public in case of air raids and other emergencies.

The Commission recommends:

Police callboxes should be designated "public emergency callboxes," should be better marked and lighted, and should be left unlocked.

The false-alarm rate for such callboxes would probably be far less than from a mechanical alarm, since a potential prankster would have to reveal his voice. While experience with a police callbox may not turn out to be fully comparable, one metropolitan fire department estimates the false alarm rate for calls received over the telephone to be less than 3 percent, far less than the false-alarm rate for an automatic or a mechanically-actuated alarm.

In trying to call the police from an ordinary telephone, a person may be bewildered by the many police jurisdictions and the various telephone numbers associated with them. In the Los Angeles area alone, there are 50 different telephone numbers that reach police departments within Los Angeles County. It should be possible to have a single telephone number to reach the police directly. England has such a universal emergency number.

The Commission recommends:

Wherever practical, a single police telephone number should be established, at least within a metropolitan area and eventually over the entire United States, comparable to the telephone company's long-distance information number.

This is difficult but feasible with existing telephone switching centers; it appears practical with the new electronic switching systems being installed by the Bell System, and should be incorporated. In the interim, telephone companies should print on each telephone number disc the number of the police department serving that telephone's location.

COMMAND AND CONTROL

Once a call reaches the police, the facts must be sent to the police officers who will respond. This linkage occurs in the police communications center, which performs what the military calls the command-and-control function. Military analysts have given extensive attention to this function.

The communications center's role has increased as the telephone has become the common access to the police, and as more police officers have been equipped with radios. Even though the communications center is the nerve center controlling the minute-by-minute deployment of the police force, it has received surprisingly little attention. It is often squeezed into a spare corner of police headquarters under the command of a sergeant or a patrolman. It operates with obsolete or poorly designed equipment and procedures that have tended to evolve by chance rather than through careful design. A notable exception is Chicago, which invested $2 million in modernizing its center in 1961.

When a person calls the police, a complaint clerk takes the call, decides on the police reaction and its priority, passes the information to the radio dispatcher who then dispatches a car. This gathering, evaluating, and disseminating of information normally takes from 1 to 5 minutes, and occupies 20–50 percent of the total response time. It can take much longer during periods of intense congestion.

Immediate Improvements. Even before considering major new technology, improving such simple aspects of command and control as floor layouts, design of headsets and microphones, and location of control switches and time stamps can improve a center's performance under heavy load. In some centers, the same person serves as the complaint clerk and the dispatcher; in others, the functions are separated. Some centers have a dispatcher handling part of a city; others have several dispatchers all handling calls for the whole city. Such differences, which can affect performance significantly under critical loads, have evidently evolved more from tradition and physical restrictions than as the result of planning. Each of the different possible configurations can be experimentally measured, both in operating centers and under laboratory control in a simulation laboratory. In this manner, standard and emergency plans and procedures can be tested, decision rules can be evaluated, and training and experience can be provided police officers under simulated extreme conditions.

In a riot or other general emergency, the communications center must transform a police department from a loose collection of independent units to a cohesive, coordinated force. Means must be provided to collect and display, rapidly and continuously, all the varieties of tactical intelligence relating to the location of events and the disposition of forces. The communications center staff must be headed by a commander who can assimilate this information and who has the authority to command the available forces. Contingency plans for situations that might arise must be developed and stored in a readily accessible form. These plans can be tested in a simulation laboratory.

The Commission recommends:

A versatile laboratory for continuing simulation of communications center operations, looking primarily toward changes in operating procedures and arrangements, should be established with Federal support.

Computer-Assisted Command and Control. In addition to operating changes, introduction of modern technology can make a significant contribution. The entire police command-and-control function should be subjected to a basic reexamination taking full account of the promising new technological opportunities offered by computers and communications links. The review should not begin with the new technology, however; it should begin by considering questions of when, where, and how to use the police patrol force, and how to respond to various types of routine and emergency situations. It should examine on paper and by experiment the extent to which preventive patrol deters crime, how forces should be allocated by time and by geography, optimum patrol tactics, appropriate conditions for conspicuousness and for covertness, how to respond to riots, and many other questions. The patrol operation will then be able to benefit markedly from computer assistance—much more than from merely automating current procedures.

It is possible to describe the general outlines of a computer-assisted command-and-control system. In such a system, depicted in figure 3, telephone calls to the police are still answered by a complaint clerk, now a "controller." He enters the type of incident, the address, and a priority code into a keyboard connected to a computer. The controller can specify what the situation requires: whether a one- or two-man car should be sent, whether two vehicles should respond, etc. The rest is then automatic.

The computer maintains records of street-address locations and the location and availability of each patrol car, and finds the best car to respond to the call. It prepares a dispatching order that is automatically sent to the selected car as a computer-generated voice message or by some digital data link such as teletype. If the patrol officer does not acknowledge the message within, say, 10 seconds, a second car can be sent on the call.

The dispatch orders, the status of the patrol cars, events in progress, and other basic control information can be displayed by the computer to command officers, who can always countermand the computer-originated orders. They can concentrate on the unusual while the computer automatically handles the routine.

Since response time depends primarily on a car's distance from the call, automatic car-location devices could be tied directly to the computer, so that it could dispatch the closest car. An analysis shows that even a crude system with accuracies of only about ¼ mile radius would ordinarily serve the purpose.

Burglar and other alarms could be linked directly to the computer. If an alarm went off, the computer, knowing the alarm's location, could immediately dispatch the appropriate car without the controller's intervention.

A computer-assisted command-and-control system offers many new possibilities for the deployment of a patrol force. As the crime pattern in a city changes hour by hour, its patrol force could be redeployed to respond to it. As parts of the city are stripped of patrolmen by called-for services, other units could be assigned as backup. Under a riot or other emergency situation, contingency plans could be programed so that appropriate units would be deployed to the emergency, and adequate backup maintained. With all information on calls stored in the computer, complete analysis of the operations of the patrol force could be conducted regularly to aid in assigning forces in response to changing crime patterns.

It is estimated that the total operating cost of such a system for a 100-car city would range from $500 to $2,000 per car for new equipment, $200,000 to $400,000 per year for computer rental, a similar amount for computer personnel, plus $500,000 to $2 million for control-center equipment and design. In measuring the impact of the cost of these items on a police budget, it is relevant to note that a two-man patrol beat costs about $100,000 per year.

The Commission recommends:

An experimental program to develop a computer-assisted command-and-control system should be established with Federal support.

A great deal of analysis and experimentation should precede and accompany the implementation of this proposal. Many possible equipment combinations will have to be weighed, basic organizational and procedural questions will have to be examined. The following programs should be undertaken to implement the system:

☐ Two or three large cities should be funded for a detailed study of their patrol operations in order to determine how they would use a computer-assisted command-and-control system.
☐ As part of the effort, an extensive reexamination of the communications systems should be undertaken to insure that channels are available, and to assess the utility of car locators and mobile teletype.
☐ Based on the results of the studies, one of the cities should be selected for installation of a prototype system.
☐ As the new system is developed, it should first be used in simulated operation in parallel with the manual system, then with a manual backup, and finally, take over control.

The development process will need continual modification and testing and should be guided by an organization experienced in the development of large computer-based systems.

POLICE RADIO COMMUNICATIONS

All dispatch messages must go from the communications center to the mobile patrol force by radio. The most troublesome problem in police radio communications is the critical shortage of radio frequencies available to the police community. A police officer who needs help should not have to wait for a clear frequency. In the Chicago metropolitan area, for example, 38 separate suburban cities with 350 patrol cars must share one frequency. This congestion results in excessive delays and underuse of the police force while patrol officers or dispatchers wait to gain the air. In addition, in emergency situations that require mutual support, neighboring police departments cannot communicate because their radios operate on different frequencies.

The Commission recommends:

Frequencies should be shared through the development of larger and more integrated police mobile radio networks.

A Possible Computer-Assisted Police Command-Control System. Figure 3

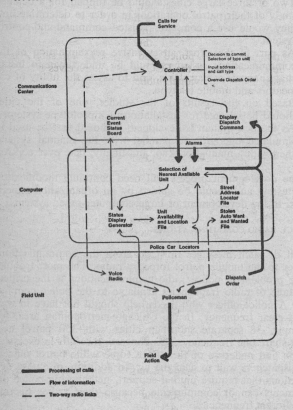

Communications Center

- Calls for Service
- Controller
  - Decision to commit
  - Selection of type unit
  - Input address and call type
  - Override Dispatch Order
- Current Event Status Board
- Display Dispatch Command

Alarms

Computer

- Selection of Nearest Available Unit
- Street Address Locator File
- Stolen Auto Want and Wanted File
- Status Display Generator
- Unit Availability and Location File

Police Car Locators

Field Unit

- Voice Radio
- Dispatch Order
- Policeman

Field Action

▬▬▬ Processing of calls
───── Flow of information
‐ ‐ ‐ Two-way radio links

With sharing of frequencies, each user, when its demand peaks, could use any available capacity, a basic concept employed in telephone and electric-power networks. For instance, if each of two departments uses its private channel 50 percent of the time, then each one finds a busy signal half the time. If they were to share their two channels, a user would find both channels busy only 35 percent of the time. If four such users were to group together, then all channels would be busy less than 20 percent of the time. If their demands peak at different times, then the advantages are even greater.

The relationship between the Federal Communications Commission and the police and other public safety users must be altered so that the FCC no longer receives a separate request from each individual public safety user.

The Commission recommends:

The FCC should require metropolitan areas to submit coordinated requests for additional frequencies, with the manner in which action on a local level is coordinated left to the discretion of local governments.

In suburban communities coordination is likely to come about by police agencies in different jurisdictions sharing frequencies. Core cities may be large enough to be able to develop efficient mobile radio networks for their own use, sharing their own public safety frequencies to balance the peak loads, since schoolbuses, highway maintenance trucks, police cars, etc., have radio demands that peak at different times. With the gradual creation of coordinated networks, the FCC will be in a position to require projection of future needs so that radio frequencies can be allocated more rationally in the future.

The Commission recommends:

Greater use should be made of multichannel radio trunks.

Generally, individual stations (patrol cars, dispatchers) will have to be reached by transmissions coded to trigger a particular receiver on whatever frequency is open at the time, instead of monitoring a single frequency. Selective coding minimizes the present system's inflexible dependence on frequency, but enables the individual user to retain its independence while using the system. It is evident that these techniques will increase the cost of the mobile radio network.

The networks will be less wasteful of radio frequencies, more flexible in use, and more costly to implement than the many small individual networks now existing. Federal Government encouragement in the form of financial support may be necessary.

In addition, frequency space is available in most areas within the VHF TV band between TV stations, and especially within the underloaded UHF TV band. One TV channel can provide over 100 radio channels, but represents only a small loss (2 percent for one UHF channel) to the TV community.

The Commission recommends:

The FCC should develop plans for allocating portions of the TV spectrum to police use.

Communications must be maintained with foot patrolmen and with police officers who have left their cars. Police officials are unanimous in their desire for small portable radios so that patrolmen can call for assistance in any emergency and so that supervisors can maintain closer contact with those they supervise and make more effective use of the entire police force.

Miniaturized transceivers for the officer away from his car and for the foot patrolman would have similar features. Because portable sets will be limited by transmitter power output, both will require base stations—the car for one and probably the precinct house for the other. Large-scale production economies can produce a miniaturized unit at a low cost, perhaps under $150.

The Commission recommends:

The Federal Government should assume the leadership in initiating portable-radio development programs and consider guaranteeing the sale of the first production lots of perhaps 20,000 units.

Such a program would automatically create a standardized portable police radio. A modest standardization program for car radios would add considerable flexibility to a police department's choice of radio suppliers. Gross standardization of size, mounting brackets, receptacles, and control heads can and should be accomplished immediately, and should go far to make it possible to use the products of different manufacturers interchangeably. More detailed standardization of radio

572

equipment is less obviously useful for it could serve to inhibit manufacturers from improving their product. Certain obvious electronic features that involve system compatibility, such as selective codes to trigger receivers, should be standardized as early as practicable.

Teletypes or other digital data links to and from police cars could remove a large part of the normal voice traffic and also provide a paper copy of the message to the car. Because radio signals tend to bounce off buildings and other structures, mobile receivers could produce distortions that result in teletype errors. While digital links could save bandwidth, the need for extra transmissions to eliminate teletype errors could substantially reduce much of that saving. Further investigation of this problem is needed.

FINGERPRINT IDENTIFICATION

Effective police work draws on fingerprint identification capability both to apprehend those who leave what are called latent prints at the scene of a crime and to identify positively persons held in custody.

Positive identification of persons already held is made by searching files structured around a 10-print classification system, since all 10 prints can be obtained from such persons. Manual techniques of 10-print classification and search have been used for more than 50 years, and are limited primarily by the time a search takes. Technical advances here would both speed up police identification and reduce the costs of the present classification and searching procedure.

Unfortunately, the structure of most present files precludes tracing an unknown offender who has left less than a full set of prints. Once a suspect has been taken into custody, his fingerprints can be compared with even a single print recovered from the scene of the crime. By the same token, a single print can be matched against complete prints of a short list of likely suspects. But the process is now entirely manual and so time consuming that it cannot be used to check less than a full set of prints against a national file or even a substantial local file of previous offenders. Most large police departments maintain a specially organized file of single fingerprints of several thousand persistent criminals. Only a small percentage of offenders are in such a file, and only a small percentage of the searches are successful.

Modern computer technology can make feasible the search of a file of even millions of prints with a single latent print. Such a development would also contribute to more efficient positive identification. The FBI, the New York State Identification and Intelligence System, and several industrial organizations have already initiated studies on aspects of the fingerprint recognition problem. Completely automatic recognition capability is desired eventually, but semiautomatic operation—a trained operator working in conjunction with a machine—appears to be the more feasible approach with current technology. Developing the search capability would take several years and be relatively costly.

The Commission recommends:

Two studies leading to the development of a semiautomatic fingerprint recognition system should be undertaken: A basic study of classification techniques and a utility study to assess the value of a latent print-searching capability.

The classification study should develop statistical data on the information contained in fingerprints (e.g., the variations in ridge counts from core to delta for ulnar loops) and ultimately should establish a search procedure based on these data. The utility study should be conducted for the purpose of estimating how many more arrests a few selected law enforcement agencies might have made if they had had a latent fingerprint capability. If an effective procedure is developed and its utility demonstrated, these studies should be followed by an equipment development program.

CRIME LABORATORIES

The crime laboratory has been the oldest and strongest link between science and technology and criminal justice. Because of this tradition, and because the best laboratories, such as the FBI's, are well advanced, the science and technology task force did not devote major attention to criminalistics. There are some excellent laboratories in key locations around the country. However, the great majority of police department laboratories have only minimal equipment and lack highly skilled personnel able to use the modern equipment now being developed and produced by the instrumentation industry. Techniques such as neutron activation analysis and mass spectrometry permit the identification of even smaller pieces of material evidence. Voice prints and photographic developments will expand the ability to detect and apprehend criminals. To bring these advances more directly into police operations, improvements in crime laboratories must proceed in two directions:

☐ Establishment of laboratories to serve the combined needs of police departments in metropolitan areas.
☐ Expansion of research activities in major existing and in new laboratories.

The need for the regional laboratories follows naturally from the increasing expense of facilities and the increasing demand for individuals of superior technical competence. The research is needed to speed the application of new instrumentation possibilities.

NONLETHAL WEAPONS

A patrol officer, in meeting the diverse criminal situations he must face, has a limited range of weaponry—either the short-range nightstick or the potentially lethal handgun. If an officer feels that his life is threatened, he may have to shoot, with the attendant risk that the suspect or innocent bystanders may be killed. If a suitable nonlethal weapon were made available, it could supplement the officer's present arsenal and possibly serve as a replacement for the handgun.

In the past 100 years, 180 New York City policemen have been killed while apprehending suspects. A study of these 180 cases revealed that in every instance the combat range was 21 feet or less and that in most cases it was 10 feet or less. Since 1960, 96 percent of the murders of police officers have been with firearms, and of those 78 percent were with handguns. Thus, in most emergency situations, the officer does not have an opportunity to make a careful weapon selection—nonlethal or lethal—and he should have the services of one weapon or a combined weapon. The weapon should be immediately available and ready for instant use.

For a nonlethal weapon to be an acceptable replacement for a handgun, it must incapacitate its victim at least as fast as a gun. Even then there might be opposition to it. A criminal knowing that he cannot be killed might act more aggressively than he would facing a gun.

The qualities that must be sought in a general purpose nonlethal weapon are almost immediate incapacitation and little risk of permanent injury to the individual who is the target. Survey of a wide range of possibilities leads to the conclusion that these requirements are incompatible with current technology. For example, darts have been used to inject tranquilizing drugs into animals. However, the drugs presently available offer too great a risk, because of the close correspondence between the dose required to incapacitate quickly and a lethal dose. No nonlethal weapon is presently available that could serve as a replacement for the handgun, but a continuing effort to achieve such a weapon should be pursued. In this connection the products of military research should be continually examined for possible applicability.

When a nonlethal weapon is considered as a supplement to the policeman's gun, the requirements for immediate incapacitation can be relaxed. Supplemental nonlethal weapons, such as tear gas or CS gas dispensers in various forms, might be used in circumstances in which an officer's life was not threatened, but it would be necessary for police departments to set careful guidelines specifying the circumstances under which they could be used. Evaluation of public reaction to the use of various nonlethal weapons under various circumstances would be an essential part of research into this subject.

ALLOCATION OF POLICE PATROL RESOURCES

All police departments have the problem of allocating patrol forces—how many men to assign to each shift and to each precinct. Most departments assign men equally to all shifts, which simplifies scheduling but is an inefficient use of manpower. Some departments use a formula that weights the previous year's reported crimes, radio calls, population, etc., for each precinct and then assign the patrol force proportionately to the precinct's weighted score. For example, if there were 1,000 crimes in precinct A and 600 crimes in precinct B, this procedure might suggest transferring officers from precinct B to precinct A. But the conditions in precinct B might be more conducive to deterring crime. If an additional officer in precinct B could suppress 50 crimes whereas one in precinct A could suppress only 10 crimes, then it might be desirable to transfer an officer from A to B.

Estimating this relative effectiveness of a police officer is, of course, extremely difficult, since the number of assigned officers is only one of many factors influencing the crime rate. It is, however, important to develop such an estimate to make efficient use of the police force. Statistical techniques, such as regression analysis, should be used to develop such estimates. Even though the final determination of the effect of an officer on crime must come from controlled experiments in the field, the experiments should be preceded by preliminary analysis so that the experiments can be more productive of both information and crime reduction.

An inherent difficulty of most statistical analysis is its inability to distinguish between cause and effect. For example, in many police precincts, additional officers are assigned as crime increases. Because the additional crime causes additional manpower allocations, the two may appear positively correlated. But this certainly does not permit the blind conclusion that the additional police cause the additional crime. Thus, any results must be used with caution, checking the predictions against actual observations before acting on the results.

The task force undertook a preliminary analysis based on limited data contained in the statistical digests of the Los Angeles Police Department from 1955 to 1965. The standard statistical procedures of regression analysis were used to predict the number of reported serious crimes in each of the department's divisions as a function of the number of patrol officers assigned to the division to get an estimate of the change in the number of serious crimes associated with the reallocation of a patrolman from one division to another.

In the regression analysis for each division, an attempt was made to factor out the effects due to changes in the population, simple time trends resulting from changing characteristics of the population, as well as the number of patrol officers assigned. This model could be improved by adding such variables as median education level of the inhabitants, median income, and by replacing total population with population by age groups, when data become available.

In 4 of the 11 divisions, most of the changes in the numbers of crimes could be accounted for. In these 4, there were differences in the relative effectiveness of assigned patrolmen, suggesting that a shift of officers might have led to a net decrease in crime. To determine the feasibility of this and other related techniques, further theoretical development and trials in actual operations are needed. Several such approaches should be tried to develop methodologies that can be applied by other police departments.

The Commission recommends:

Police departments should undertake data collection and experimentation programs to develop appropriate statistical procedures for manpower allocation.

COURT OPERATIONS

It is a basic precept of our society that justice should not be administered with one eye on the clock and the other on the checkbook. But it is too often the fact that justice in the United States is rationed because of the limited resources at its disposal. At the same time, justice is effectively denied because of inordinate delays between arrest and final disposition. Science and technology can help to achieve the most efficient use of the available resources, provided always that it is recognized that the ends of justice must be served first.

The task force has focused its attention on the processing of defendants through a court, with special emphasis on the reduction of delay. Various solutions to the problem of delay have been suggested by judges, lawyers, and court administrators. Whether or not these solutions would indeed reduce delay can only be determined after they have been put into effect. In order to make preliminary tests of some alternatives without disrupting the operating courts, the task force examined the feasibility of computer simulation techniques for experimenting with various modifications in court procedures.

Because the enormous variety of court systems in the Nation differ in organization and procedure, no single model will serve to represent them all. The approach taken therefore was to test the feasibility of stimulating one of these systems, a court in the District of Columbia. The steps followed were:

(1) describing in detail the organization and structure of the court system for processing felony defendants;
(2) analyzing the available data on felony defendants to determine whether delay occurs and to identify when and where it occurs;
(3) developing a computer simulation of the processing system that could be used to study possible modifications of the system.

TIME DELAY IN A DISTRICT OF COLUMBIA COURT

The time delay problem was approached by analyzing in detail the data on 1,550 felony defendants whose cases commenced by filing of indictment or information in the District Court of the District of Columbia in 1965. The time periods that these defendants were in the court system were compared with the timetable presented in chapter 5. The timeta-

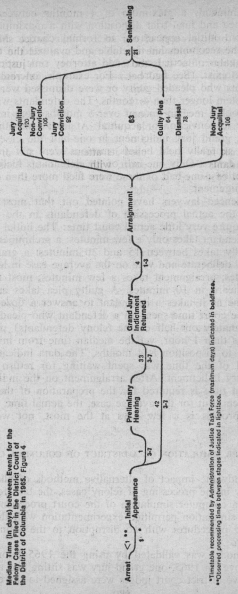

Median Time (in days) between Events for the Felony Cases Filed in the District Court of the District of Columbia in 1965. Figure 4

Arrest △* □** Initial Appearance

1 3-7 Preliminary Hearing

42 3-7 Grand Jury Indictment Returned

4 1-3 Arraignment

33 3-7

Jury Acquittal 120
Non-Jury Conviction 106
Jury Conviction 92

Guilty Pleas 63

Dismissal 78
Non-Jury Acquittal 106

Guilty Pleas 64

Sentencing 38 21

*Timetable recommended by Administration of Justice Task Force (maximum days) indicated in **boldface**.

●●Observed processing times between stages indicated in lightface.

ble recommends a maximum of 4 months between initial appearance and final trial disposition with a maximum of 14 days from initial appearance to formal charge. Measured against the recommended timetable and evaluated in terms of best estimates of actual court and attorney time, appreciable delays do exist. (See figure 4.) For example, one-half of the defendants who pleaded guilty or were dismissed were in the court system longer than 4 months. The defendants who went to trial took a median time of over 5 months from initial appearance to conviction or acquittal. At least a month passed before a grand jury indictment in one-half the cases. Contrary to generally held beliefs, motions were not the main cause of delays. Only one-half of the defendants filed one or more motions; one-half of these were filed more than 40 days after arraignment.

Experienced lawyers have pointed out that most of the steps in the actual processing of defendants in the District Court require very little actual court time: The initial hearing for a defendant takes only a few minutes; a preliminary hearing usually takes between 15 and 30 minutes; a grand jury can hear, deliberate and vote on the average case in less than 30 minutes; arraignment takes a few minutes; most motions can be heard in 10 minutes. A guilty plea takes as much court time as it takes a defendant to answer a dozen questions. The court time spent on a defendant who pleads guilty (approximately one-half of the felony defendants) probably totals less than 1 hour, yet the median time from initial appearance to disposition is 4 months. The data indicated that one-third of the time was spent waiting for return of the grand jury indictment. After arraignment on the indictment, additional time is required for the preparation of the necessary papers. But for the average case, the actual time devoted to this process is a few days at the most, not weeks or months.

COMPUTER SIMULATION OF A DISTRICT OF COLUMBIA COURT

To study the impact of alternative methods of alleviating the delay in the processing of felony cases, the task force developed a computer simulation of the court processing activity. The simulation permitted experimentation with the court operating procedures with no disruption to the actual court operation.

The model was validated by using the 1965 felony data cited above. In 1965, one grand jury was sitting and an average of five district court judges were assigned to the criminal part of the court. Under these conditions, the simulation faithfully reflected the actual court operation: In both there was a median time of approximately 6 weeks between initial presentment and the return of an indictment, and 14 weeks from arraignment to beginning of trial.

Most of the time prior to arraignment was spent waiting at the Grand Jury Division for indictment (5 out of 7 weeks). By simulating the system with a second grand jury sitting part of the time, the wait for indictment was reduced from 35 days to less than 1 day, resulting in a median time of approximately 2 weeks from initial presentment to return of the indictment. Thus, it appears that for a cost of probably less than $50,000 per year for the additional grand jury and associated support resources, the delay from presentment to return of indictment could be reduced by 70 percent. The total delay would be reduced by 25 percent, since the time from arraignment to trial would be unchanged. By requiring motions to be filed and heard within 17 days and increasing the Grand Jury Division resources, without increasing the number of district court judges, the median time from arraignment to trial could be reduced from 15 to 9 weeks. Most felony cases can be properly prepared in 9 weeks. The resulting median total time from initial presentment to trial disposition could then be 3 months compared to over 5 months observed in 1965. The above analyses indicate that the timetable of the Administration of Justice Task Force is practical. More generally, simulation has been found an effective tool for examining reallocation of existing resources or efficient allocation of additional resources.

An additional example of the use of the simulation is in examination of the possible consequences of changes in defendants' behavior resulting from changes in court procedure. It has been argued that one effect of the Bail Reform Act will be to reduce the number of guilty pleas. The impact of various possible reductions of guilty pleas on time in the court system can be tested in the simulation. For example, if the Act had been in effect in 1965, and if it had resulted in reducing the number of defendants who pleaded guilty from 55 percent to 35 percent, then the median times from presentment to trial disposition would have increased approximately 2 weeks, or 10 percent. The additional judge and attorney resources required to maintain their current schedule or the new time table could be determined through the simulation.

An important immeasurable factor not accounted for is the effect of changes in processing on the actions of defendants and court officials. The human in the system adapts to his environment and any changes made to it. The model assumes the various changes made will not affect the feedback process. For this reason, before any changes can be seriously proposed, the results of the simulation must first be thoroughly analyzed and discussed in detail with the court officers.

The Commission recommends:

The simulation techniques developed should be extended to several large urban areas as pilot studies with Federal support to determine their applicability to other court systems and to develop them in further detail.

CORRECTIONS OPERATIONS

The subject matter of corrections comprises three kinds of problems: Techniques for the rehabilitation of offenders, decisions about what treatment to apply to each individual, and means of maintaining custody of prisoners.

Conventional alarms and surveillance devices can increase security and reduce the costs of holding offenders who cannot or should not be released into the community. Information systems and statistical analysis of the information they contain can provide better and more complete information about individual offenders and treatment possibilities in order to find the most suitable treatments. Systems analysis will make it possible to study means for improving the allocation of resources and for examining some of the consequences of modification in operating procedures. Rehabilitation calls primarily for knowledge at the frontiers of the behavioral sciences. The task force has looked into one area of educational technology, programed learning, to assess its potential for improving vocational skills.

PROGRAMED LEARNING TO AID REHABILITATION

Many delinquent careers are associated with failure in school. It is a short route from academic failure to dropping out of school to idleness and unemployment to entry into a spiraling criminal career. Some dropouts fail because they cannot adapt to a classroom social situation. If there were some alternative way of educating them, they might find a rewarding place in the community and refrain from crime.

Programed learning offers one such opportunity. In programed learning, currently being conducted with published booklets in at least two correctional institutions, and experimentally with computers at several research centers, the student works through the educational material on his own, testing his understanding at frequent intervals. Whenever his responses exhibit lack of comprehension, he is diverted back to correct his deficiency. He works at his own pace, he checks his own performance, and he can do most of this alone.

One study at Draper Correctional Center in Alabama found that students completed one academic year of schoolwork in 200 hours of work with programed-learning materials. The average cost per academic year of advancement was under $400. Based on the expected contribution of each year's schooling to future earnings, the discounted future taxes from that year's schooling would be about $800, more than enough to cover the cost of education, without considering the thousands of dollars of criminal-career costs saved and, most important, providing a chance for a fuller life.

About 70 percent of the first class of graduates from the Draper vocational school were two-time losers—men who had previously been jailed, released, and jailed again. Of the 78 youthful offenders who have graduated from this school (which began about 2 years ago) and who have been paroled and placed in jobs, only four have been returned to prison for committing new crimes and six for technical violations of parole conditions. Compared to the usual one-third to two-thirds rate of return to prison, a return rate of between one-seventh and one-eighth is remarkable. These figures are the result of only a preliminary field test of programed aids to instruction at correctional institutions. Much more careful and thorough experimentation is needed before drawing definite conclusions about how much recidivism can be reduced.

Programed learning appears to have significant advantages for educating the identified problem children who find their way into correctional institutions, and also for crime-prone populations in the community. Its use should be encouraged, and further evaluated in controlled circumstances, using conventional teachers or even fellow inmates for supervision. The shortage of adequate programed learning texts, especially in vocational subjects relevant to local job opportunities, is the primary limitation on more effective and wider use of the technique. The development of programed learning materials should be subsidized by the Federal Government.

STATISTICAL TECHNIQUES TO AID DECISIONS

The desirability of developing statistical data to estimate the effects of different sentences and correctional treatment on different types of offenders has been noted in chapters 5 and 6. Information concerning the likelihood that the individual will return to crime is essential. Just as important as the evaluation of the individuals being treated in a correctional system is the evaluation of the treatment itself. Without objective evaluation of methods of treatment, it is difficult, if not impossible, to make rational choices about the kinds of treatment programs that should be developed or about people to whom they should be applied.

Most of the available information about such questions is in one of two forms: "rules of thumb" that have evolved out of experience and are justified or rationalized in large part on the basis of anecdotal histories of operations, and statistical tabulations of operations in which there was neither a control group nor an adequate characterization of the experimental group.

There is a need to correlate both individual characteristics and type of treatment to recidivism as measured by further commission of crimes, arrests, and commitments. Judges and corrections officials need information that will help them decide what treatment to prescribe. They need to know the differential effects of various kinds of treatment on various kinds of individuals. Statistical analyses of large numbers of criminal-career histories will be required to provide these needed correlations.

The Commission recommends:

Statistical aids for helping in sentencing and selection of proper treatment of individuals under correctional supervision should be developed.

In addition to assisting in treatment selection, statistical techniques of experiment design must play an important role in correctional program development, testing, evaluation, and planning. Of all the behavioral areas, offender rehabilitation offers perhaps the best opportunity for reasonably careful experimental control to determine the effects of actions taken. There should be an expanded use of careful, controlled evaluation in the development of correctional programs. Program development should be preceded by careful studies of the specific correctional objectives, and testing should be conducted by personnel qualified in the behavioral sciences and in statistical analysis.

REDUCING CRIMINAL OPPORTUNITIES

Everyone has an obligation to others as well as to himself not to invite crime. Banks, supermarkets, and other businesses take steps to make it more difficult to pass bogus checks; shop and home owners protect against burglary and theft by the use of concealment, alarms, and locks; individuals take precautions such as not carrying large amounts of cash.

There are two important techniques for reducing criminal opportunities: hardening the targets of crime, and inhibiting potential criminals. Automobile design modification to make the car less vulnerable to theft is an example of hardening a target, and street lighting an example of an inhibitor.

INCREASING THE DIFFICULTY OF AUTO THEFT

Auto theft is costly. About 28 percent of the inhabitants of Federal prisons are there following conviction of interstate auto theft under the Dyer Act. In California alone, auto thefts cost the criminal justice system over $60 million yearly. Even more important, auto thefts are primarily juvenile acts. Although only 21 percent of all arrests for nontraffic offences in 1965 were of individuals under 18 years of age, 63 percent of auto theft arrests were of persons under 18. Auto theft represents the start of many criminal careers. In an FBI sample of juvenile auto theft offenders, 41 percent had no prior arrest record. Many of the juveniles who steal automobiles are incompetent drivers and frequently damage the vehicle or injure themselves or others.

Many thefts occur simply because a boy sees an unlocked automobile. The FBI reports that 42 percent of the autos stolen had keys in their ignitions or their ignitions unlocked. Even of those stolen when the ignitions were locked, at least 20 percent were stolen merely by shorting the ignition with tools as simple as paper clips or tinfoil. In one city, the change in the Chevrolet lock (eliminating the unlocked "off" position) in 1965 resulted in about 50 percent fewer 1965 Chevrolets stolen than the previous year's model.

The findings suggest that the easy opportunity to take a car may contribute significantly to auto theft and that thefts by the relatively casual or marginal offender would be reducible by making theft more difficult than merely starting the car. Educational campaigns advising drivers to lock their cars are important, but their effect is difficult to sustain. A more fundamental change in the ignition system and other automobile components is needed. Many possibilities exist. Spring-ejection locks can prevent the driver from leaving the key in the ignition; sturdier housings can enclose the ignition terminals; heavier metal cables can surround the ignition wires; steering wheel locking devices can be used, as is done on several foreign cars. In 1960, the Federal Republic of Germany made the following a part of the highway code: "Passenger cars, stationwagons, and motorcycles should be equipped with an adequate safety device against unauthorized use of vehicles. The locking of the doors and removal of the ignition key are not regarded as safety measures within the meaning of the preceding sentence."

This problem has been discussed by Commission and Department of Justice representatives with the four major automobile manufacturers and they have indicated their desire to develop and install devices to increase the security of their products. These will include making the ignition system connector cable much more difficult to remove from the ignition lock, increasing the ignition key combinations, and locating the ignition system in less accessible places. These basic improvements will be made in some 1968 models. One manufacturer is testing an arrangement that will help reduce the possibility of leaving the key in the ignition lock in an unattended parked car and hopes to install such a device in the 1969 models at the latest.

Although the above steps will contribute to the reduction of auto thefts, the following additional improvements should be carefully considered:

☐ A steering column or transmission lock that immobilizes the car when the gearshift lever is put into the proper position and the key removed. With this type of lock, starting an engine by shorting the ignition does not permit the car to be driven away.

☐ Coupling the above lock with an ignition system that causes the driver to remove the key from the ignition. This can be done by a spring-loaded lock or key that pushes the key out; or by requiring the key to be not only turned, but also pulled out of the ignition in order to stop the engine; or by attaching a buzzer that goes off if the key is left in the ignition when the engine is turned off.

Although the automobile manufacturers are best able to integrate such devices into the design of their vehicles, it is desirable that some Federal agency work with them to establish minimum requirements on the actual implementation. This responsibility could well be assigned to the National Highway Safety Agency as part of its program to establish safety standards for automobiles.

REMOVING THE COVER OF DARKNESS

Improved street lighting is frequently advocated by the police and by highway departments as an important tool for combatting crime. Its proponents assume that adequate street lighting will, first, deter certain types of street crimes by increasing the offender's risk of being detected and, second, enhance the probability of apprehending the offender. These assumptions are fortified by the general sense of security that the individual feels when streets are brightly lit. The police and the public alike frequently remark that they have no proof that improved street lighting reduces crime, but the public does feel safer.

Unfortunately, existing studies do not present definitive conclusions as to the effects of lighting on crime. In 1956, the central business district of Flint, Mich., was relit. Six-thousand-lumen incandescent lights were replaced with 20,000-lumen multiple fluorescent bracket-type lights. A study conducted over a 6-month period indicated that there was a 60 percent reduction in the number of all felonies and misdemeanors, and an 80 percent reduction in larcenies. However, there was, at the same time, an increase in police surveillance in the area. Since the experiment was not adequately controlled, the effects of patrol and relighting are confounded, so that any conclusions on the effects of street lighting alone must be considered only tentative.

In New York City, four police precincts designated as high crime areas were converted from incandescent lighting to mercury vapor lighting. The rate of nighttime crimes dropped by 49 percent after the installation of the lights. After over 80 percent of the city street lighting was modernized over a period of four years at a cost of $58 million, the total number of felonies in the city increased by approximately 43 percent. Due to the extreme difficulty of assessing the effects of the numerous other variables, it is virtually impossible to determine what the felony rate would have been if the lights had not been installed.

The only results it is possible to reach now are:

☐ There is no conclusive evidence that improved lighting
587

would have a lasting or significant impact on crime rates, although there are strong suggestions that it might.

☐ Improved street lighting will reduce some types of crimes in some areas, i.e., given a light and dark street to commit a crime, a criminal will normally choose the dark street.

☐ Improved street lighting accompanied by increased police patrol can reduce crime rates in an area.

☐ When new lighting programs are instituted, police departments should be encouraged to maintain records of crimes in the relighted and adjoining areas. With information on past, present, and projected crime rates and on other relevant variables, it may be possible to assess better the impact of lighting on crime.

SYSTEMS ANALYSIS OF CRIMINAL JUSTICE

THE USEFULNESS AND LIMITATIONS OF SYSTEMS ANALYSIS

The criminal justice system is an enormous complex of operations. Subjecting such a system to scientific investigation normally involves making changes in its operations in order to observe the effects directly. Whenever practical, this kind of controlled experimentation is clearly the best kind. But experimentation inside a system is often impractical and even undesirable, not only because the costs could be prohibitive, but because normal operations are frequently too critical to be disrupted. Instead, the scientist may be able to formulate a mathematical description or "model" of the system in order to illuminate the relationships among its parts. Systems analysis involves construction and manipulation of such mathematical models in order to find out how better to organize and operate the real-life systems they represent. It is desirable to conduct such analyses of the criminal justice system for several reasons:

☐ They develop an explicit description of the criminal justice system and its operating modes so that the system's underlying assumptions are revealed.

☐ They provide a vehicle for simulated experimentation in those instances in which "live" experimentation is unfeasible.

☐ They identify the data that must be obtained if essential calculations are to be made of the consequences of proposed changes.

These advantages must be considered in light of a sober appreciation of what cannot be done by constructing and using models. The cause-and-effect relationships in the real world of criminal justice are so complex and so intricately interwoven that any mathematical description of them is bound to be a gross simplification. At the present time, even the most basic relationships are poorly understood, and the available data contribute little to further understanding. Moreover, in so dynamic a system, the causal relationships themselves are constantly changing and will change further as increased understanding changes people's behavior. Clearly, a system of this magnitude and complexity cannot be studied in detail even descriptively, much less analytically, in a few months by a few people. However, sufficient benefits have accrued from similar analyses conducted on equally complex systems, such as air traffic systems and national economies, to warrant probes in this direction. The State of California has already supported a pioneering study of this sort at the Space General Corp. The task force further developed these approaches in order to lay a foundation on which additional analytical development could be based and also to identify the primary data needs.

Among the capabilities provided by models is the ability to conduct cost-effectiveness analyses. These analyses, applied with particular success in the Department of Defense, provide a means for determining which of several alternative courses of action will provide maximum effectiveness for a given cost, or minimum cost for a given effectiveness. There are many different measures of both cost and effectiveness applicable to crime control programs. Numerical costs include direct dollar costs of operating the criminal justice system, as well as indirect costs such as lost income of offenders who are denied good jobs. Numerical measures of effectiveness include reductions in the rates of the various crimes. Nonquantitative considerations such as justice, individual liberty, rights of privacy, and freedom from fear of victimization are of vital concern, but are beyond the realm of numerical treatment. The techniques of analysis can be brought to bear only on those parts of crime and criminal justice that are amenable to quantification, and these measurable values must always be considered in relation to what are frequently more important, often unquantifiable values in making any decisions about modification of police, court, or corrections operations. The cost-effectiveness approach does not force a quantification of unmeasurable human values. Rather, it sets out those implications that are quantifiable, and thereby permits

589

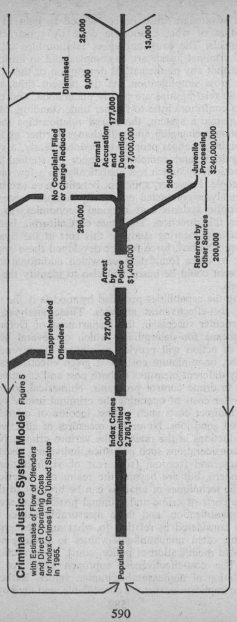

Criminal Justice System Model Figure 5

with Estimates of Flow of Offenders
and Direct Operating Costs
for Index Crimes in the United States
in 1965.

Population

Index Crimes Committed
2,780,140

Unapprehended Offenders

Arrest by Police
$1,400,000

727,000

290,000

No Complaint Filed or Charge Reduced

Formal Accusation and Detention
$7,000,000

177,000

Dismissed

9,000

25,000

13,000

260,000

Juvenile Processing
$240,000,000

Referred by Other Sources
200,000

Number in **boldface** indicates estimated flow of persons arrested for Index crimes.
Numbers in regular type indicate estimated costs incurred at processing stages.

590

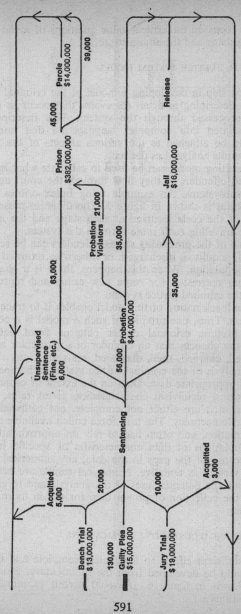

Bench Trial
$13,000,000

Guilty Plea
$15,000,000

Jury Trial
$19,000,000

Acquitted
5,000

20,000

130,000

10,000

Acquitted
3,000

Sentencing

Unsupervised
Sentence
(Fine, etc.)
6,000

Probation
$44,000,000

56,000

Probation
Violators
35,000

35,000

Prison
$382,000,000

63,000

21,000

Jail
$16,000,000

Parole
$14,000,000

45,000

39,000

Release

a sharper focus on the critical value questions of social policy by the legislator and the administrator.

A CRIMINAL JUSTICE SYSTEM MODEL

The first step in developing a model of the criminal justice system is describing in detail the events that occur as offenders are processed through the system. This description is then translated into computer language so that numerical values can be attached to the various aspects of the system and the results analyzed as desired.

The resulting model can be used to calculate what happens to arrested offenders as they flow through the court and corrections subsystems. An example using Index crimes in the United States is shown in figure 5. The diagram presents an estimate of the costs incurred at each stage and the number of people traveling each route through the system.

At some of the processing stages, offenders can be released, dismissed, acquitted, discharged, or otherwise returned to the general population. When this happens, there is a chance of their being rearrested for some new crime and reprocessed through the criminal justice system.

The feedback nature of the model enables it to trace criminal careers. Thus, one product of such a model is a compilation of lifetime criminal career patterns from data that describe the chances that an offender of a particular age will be arrested, charged, tried, dismissed, rearrested, etc.

Any analysis of the criminal justice system is hampered by a lack of appropriate data. Data on the extent of crime, costs of operations, recidivism characteristics, arrest rates, parole violations, etc., are either not complete, not gathered or of questionable accuracy. The task force culled available sources for information, and often had to rely on approximations or on extrapolations of data characteristic of specific jurisdictions. Because of the gaps in the data, any numerical results must be viewed as tentative. Numerical results are presented to illustrate the potential uses of the analysis and to give impetus to the collection of proper data for use in more definitive studies.

SOME SPECIFIC ILLUSTRATIVE APPLICATIONS

With sufficient effort, an adequately complete and detailed model could be developed from the rudimentary, generalized model shown in figure 6. It would permit examination of such questions as:

- [ ] The effects upon court and correctional caseloads and operating costs of a 10 percent increase in police clearance rates.
- [ ] The effects upon court and correctional costs and workloads of providing counsel to all those arrested.
- [ ] The effects upon costs and arrest rates in a particular state of instituting a given community treatment program for certain sentenced offenders.
- [ ] The projected workloads and operating costs of police, courts, and corrections for the next 5 years.
- [ ] The effects upon recidivism and associated costs of statistical techniques that permit sentencing judges to prescribe optimum treatment programs.

However, such analyses require a completeness and detail of description that will take many years of research to develop and will always have elements of uncertainty. As an illustration of the approach, the science and technology task force formulated a preliminary model to examine several issues with existing data, or, where none were available, with hypothetical data.

Criminal Justice Costs of Index Crimes in the United States. Basic to any evaluation of proposed changes in the criminal justice system is knowledge of the current costs of the system. These costs include both the dollar costs and the intangible social costs. The task force was, of necessity, restricted to dollar costs. In fact, not even all of the dollar costs can be considered. This examination omits consideration of the indirect dollar costs, which include items such as lost incomes of witnesses and defendants lawyers' fees, etc. Rather, it is restricted to costs directly incurred by criminal justice agencies.

Fixed and variable costs are allocated to each offense of each type on the basis of estimates, some of them necessarily arbitrary (e.g., allocation of patrol force time to index crimes), of the division of time and effort by police, courts, and corrections. Because of the necessary imperfections in the cost estimates, the percentage distribution of costs among the various Index crimes, and especially the dollar costs, should not be taken as definitive.

Given the time it takes to process an offender at each stage, and the associated costs, it is possible to calculate the direct costs of processing cases in the system by crime type. Figure 6 shows how these costs are attributable to each of the 1965 Index crimes in the United States. It can be seen that the property crimes of burglary, larceny of $50 and over, and

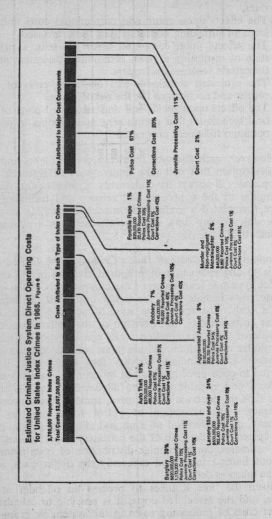

Estimated Criminal Justice System Direct Operating Costs
for United States Index Crimes in 1965. Figure 6

2,780,000 Reported Index Crimes

Total Costs: $2,097,000,000

Costs Attributed to Each Type of Index Crime

Burglary 39%
1,173,000 Reported Crimes
Police Cost 72%
Juvenile Processing Cost 11%
Court Cost 1%
Corrections Cost 10%

Larceny $50 and over 24%
762,400 Reported Crimes
Police Cost 76%
Juvenile Processing Cost 8%
Court Cost 1%
Corrections Cost 15%

Auto Theft 18%
$370,000,000
486,000 Reported Crimes
Police Cost 87%
Juvenile Processing Cost 81%
Court Cost 1%
Corrections Cost 11%

Aggravated Assault 9%
$190,000,000
206,700 Reported Crimes
Police Cost 59%
Court Cost 4%
Juvenile Processing Cost 34%
Corrections Cost 8%

Robbery 7%
$140,000,000
118,100 Reported Crimes
Police Cost 45%
Juvenile Processing Cost 12%
Court Cost 4%
Corrections Cost 42%

Forcible Rape 1%
$25,000,000
22,470 Reported Crimes
Police Cost 39%
Juvenile Processing Cost 14%
Court Cost 5%
Corrections Cost 42%

Murder and
Non-negligent
Manslaughter 2%
$40,000,000
9,850 Reported Crimes
Police Cost 10%
Juvenile Processing Cost 1%
Court Cost 8%
Corrections Cost 81%

Costs Attributed to Major Cost Components

Police Cost 67%

Corrections Cost 20%

Juvenile Processing Cost 11%

Court Cost 2%

594

Table 5.—Total 1965 U.S. Criminal Justice System Costs for Index Crimes [1]

Crime type	Total system costs (millions of dollars)	Number of crimes	System costs per crime (dollars)	Number of arrests	System costs per arrest (dollars)	Career costs [3] (dollars)
Willful homicide	48	9,850	4,900	9,400	5,100	12,600
Forcible rape	29	22,420	1,300	14,300	2,000	9,600
Robbery	140	118,920	1,200	54,300	2,600	13,500
Aggravated assault	190	206,700	920	108,000	1,800	9,400
Burglary	820	1,173,200	700	266,000	3,100	14,000
Larceny of $50 and over	500	762,400	660	144,000	3,500	11,900
Auto theft	370	486,600	760	131,000	2,800	11,000
All Index crimes	2,097	2,780,140	750	727,000	2,900	[2] 12,200

[1] 100 percent of detective force costs and 25 percent of patrol force costs and court and corrections costs were allocated to Index crimes.
[2] Based on Index crimes with the first Index crime arrest occurring at age 16 for the indicated crime.
[3] Based on distribution of first arrests matched to distribution of arrests of individuals under 18 given in the 1965 Uniform Crime Reports.

595

auto theft, which account for 87 percent of the Index crimes, also account for the bulk (81 percent) of the system costs for Index crimes. In figure 6, the system costs for each kind of Index crime are attributed to the major cost components. The results show that corrections accounts for a large portion of the total cost in cases of murder and nonnegligent manslaughter (81 percent), forcible rape (42 percent), and robbery (42 percent), where police clearance rates are high. For property crimes, which have lower clearance rates, police costs are a much larger proportion of the total costs.

Figure 6 shows how these system costs for Index crimes are distributed among the major system components. The processing of juveniles, from courts through corrections, is shown separately in the diagram. The police account for the bulk of the costs, 67 percent. Correctional programs (including probation) are the next largest, accounting for 20 percent.

In table 5 these system costs are presented as the cost per individual crime. The Index crimes other than willful homicide cost the criminal justice system directly about $750 (aside from the social costs of the crime itself and any subsidiary indirect costs). The cost per offender arrested, however, is about $3,000, since there are about one-fourth as many reported arrests as reported Index crimes.

Another costing approach would omit the large amounts of police costs charged to the offenders, and charge them instead as fixed costs of the system. If offenders are charged only with the costs of the detective time spent on the different types of Index crimes, then the cost per offender arrested is cut to about $1,000.

Another important cost is the cost of permitting a person to enter a life of crime. This cost is measured by the total cost to the criminal justice system over the life of the offender for processing him, or the criminal-career cost. The costs accumulate to about $12,000 per individual, despite the relatively low costs per single crime, and demonstrate the value of an investment in preventive programs that would avert criminal careers.

Escalation of Criminal Careers. The model can also be used to examine the differences between the types of crimes for which first offenders are arrested and those for which repeaters are arrested. An example of such an examination is shown in table 6. The results are tabulated according to the order of "seriousness" used by the FBI in its procedure of listing only the most "serious" offense in its statistics in cases of simultaneous multiple offenses. A typical distribution of 1,000 first arrests for index offenses was taken. The criminal careers of these 1,000 individuals were then simulated by cycling through the model, taking the probabilities of rearrest over time, and the distribution among the Index crimes of each group of rearrested persons, broken down according to the crime for which they were rearrested. The simulation

Table 6.—Average Distribution of First Arrests and Lifetime Rearrests for Index Crime Offenders

Offense	First arrests		Lifetime rearrests		Percent change in proportion of total
	Number [1]	Percent of total	Number	Percent of total	
Willful homicide	2	0.2	34	1.1	+450
Forcible rape	6	.6	68	2.3	+280
Robbery	33	3.3	458	15.2	+360
Aggravated assault	32	3.2	194	6.4	+100
Burglary	252	25.2	1,196	39.7	+60
Larceny of $50 and over	518	51.8	739	24.6	−50
Auto theft	157	15.7	321	10.7	−30
Total	1,000	100.0	3,010	100.0	

[1] The distribution of the 1,000 1st arrests is based on the distribution of arrests of individuals under 18 given in the 1965 Uniform Crime Reports.

showed an eventual accumulation of 3,010 subsequent arrests. These include a greater proportion of the more serious offenses than the 1,000 original offenses. For example, homicides, rapes, and robberies were several times more prevalent among the rearrests than among the first arrests. The less serious Index crimes of larceny and auto theft, on the other hand, became less prevalent.

This analysis, though only exemplary, raises questions about why successive arrests apparently are for more serious crimes. It may be due to the aging of the individuals, to the development of antisocial attitudes, or possibly to reactions to treatment by the criminal justice system. This analysis suggests the seriousness, in terms of escalating criminal conduct, of the problem of recidivism. A question to be explored is whether the rearrest probabilities increase or decrease and the serious crimes become more or less prevalent for those who are processed further through the system. Any differences may be the result of differences among individuals who reach the various stages or it may be the result of the treatment itself. Unfortunately, data to examine such basic questions do not now exist, but the questions are sufficiently important to warrant an intensive effort to collect the data, and ultimately, after hypotheses are developed, to conduct appropriate controlled experiments.

As a result of experience with the system model, it has been possible to identify many specific inadequacies in the published data concerning crime and the criminal justice system. These deficiencies fall under two main headings. First, much of the published data are incomplete, inconsistent, and inaccurate. For example, different criminal justice agencies report their operations in inconsistent units: The police report "arrests," the courts report "cases," and corrections agencies report "offenders." Information from different jurisdictions often has different underlying interpretations. In some jurisdictions, stealing from parking meters is burglary, while in others it is larceny. These problems have long troubled criminologists as well as the operating agencies that collect and use the data.

The second class of deficiencies in existing data includes the vast number of instances in which no data at all are available. We know much too little about how various actions of the criminal justice system affect the number and types of crimes committed by different classes of offenders. It is necessary to collect data on recidivism (rearrest probabilities, reconviction probabilities, etc.) by type of crime and by offender treatment. It is important to know how recidivism varies with how far a person travels through the criminal processes (discharged on arrest, prosecution dropped, put on probation, paroled, etc.). This information needs to be correlated with age, crime type, and other relevant variables. While collecting and processing such a large amount of data is clearly a difficult task it is well within the capabilities of today's technology and will be considerably aided by the development of a national criminal justice information system.

CRIMINAL JUSTICE INFORMATION SYSTEMS

THE NEED FOR BETTER INFORMATION CAPABILITIES

The importance of having complete and timely information about crimes and offenders available at the right place and the right time has been demonstrated throughout this chapter and, indeed, throughout this report. With timely information, a police officer could know that he should hold an arrested shoplifter for having committed armed robbery elsewhere. With a more detailed background on how certain kinds of offenders respond to correctional treatment, a judge could more intelligently sentence a second offender. With better projections of next year's workload, a State budget office would know whether and where to budget for additional parole officers.

Modern information technology now permits a massive assault on these problems at a level never before conceivable. Computers have been used to solve related problems in such diverse fields as continental air defense, production scheduling, airline reservations, and corporate management. Modern computer and communications technology permits many users, each sitting in his own office, to have immediate remote access to large computer-based, central data banks. Each user can add information to a central file to be shared by the others. Access can be restricted so that only specified users can get certain information.

Criminal justice could benefit dramatically from computer-based information systems, and development of a network designed specifically for its operations could start immediately. Such systems can aid in the following functions:

☐ *Police patrol*—enabling a police officer to check rapidly the identification of people and property against a central "wanted" file.

☐ *Crime investigation*—providing a police officer or detective with supporting information files such as crime patterns, modus operandi, criminal associates, and perhaps in the future the ability to match latent fingerprints from a crime scene against a central fingerprint file.

☐ *Police deployment*—altering police deployment in response to changing patterns of crime on an hourly, daily, seasonal or emergency basis.

☐ *Sentencing and correctional decisions*—providing more complete history of an offender and his reactions to prior correctional actions; statistical estimates of the effects of different kinds of treatment on different kinds of offenders.

☐ *Development of correctional programs*—analyzing complete case records to evaluate the effectiveness of different programs.

☐ *Protection of individual rights*—assuring that arrest records include court disposition, thereby presenting a fairer picture to the police and to judges; restricting access to certain criminal records after a specified period of good conduct.

☐ *Federal, State, and local budgeting*—collecting uniform statistics on agency operations and workloads, providing a basis for estimating personnel needs and for optimum allocation of men and dollars.

☐ *Research*—providing a collection of anonymous criminal histories to find out how best to interrupt a developing criminal career and to achieve a better understanding of how to control crime.

A PROGRAM FOR AN INTEGRATED NATIONAL
INFORMATION SYSTEM

An integrated national information system is needed to serve the combined needs at the National, State, regional and metropolitan or county levels of the police, courts, and correction agencies, and of the public and the research community. Each of these agencies has information needed by others; an information system provides a means for collecting it, analyzing it, and disseminating it to those who need it. Each can be kept in close communication with the others, and information transferred by voice, by teletype, or computer to computer.

Since law enforcement is primarily a local and State function, the overall program must be geared to the circumstances and requirements of local and State agencies; and, wherever practical, the files should be located at these levels. Even the specifications and procedures of the national system must conform to local needs, and should be developed by people familiar with them.

Table 7, on the following page, depicts a possible structure for a national integrated criminal justice information system. The system contains three kinds of files:

☐ *Inquiry file*—a centralized list of wanted people and stolen property that a police officer can check for immediate response.

☐ *Personal information*—information about individuals with criminal records.

☐ *Statistical information*—data on crimes, on criminal careers, and on the activities of criminal justice agencies.

AN IMMEDIATE-RESPONSE INQUIRY SYSTEM

A police officer frequently needs to know, within a matter

of minutes, whether individuals, or vehicles or other property, are wanted within his jurisdiction or elsewhere. Separate state-wide inquiry systems could provide immediate information on stolen property and persons wanted within the State. An automobile recovered with its own license plates could be checked against the State in which it is registered. For other property and for persons, such an inquiry would theoretically have to be addressed to every State, requiring each State to implement its own system and calling for complex communications to every other State. A second alternative would be to establish a limited number of regional systems centralizing information

Table 7.—Users of Files in an Integrated National Criminal Justice Information System

	Type of file			
	Inquiry	Personal information		Statistics
		Directory [1]	Registry [2]	
Required response time.	Minutes____	Hours_____	Days_____	Weeks.
National_____	Police_____	All criminal justice agencies.	No file kept____	Criminal justice agencies, research projects, Government public information offices.
State_____	___same____	_____same____	Courts and corrections only.	_____same_____
Local_____	_same_	_____same_____	_____same_____	___same_____

[1] Index of record information as to formal contacts with criminal justice agencies.
[2] Collection of related background materials (probation reports, educational records, etc.) kept by some States.

within each region. The regions could be interconnected into a national system or could be kept separate, accepting the penalty of losing track of people or property that cross the regional boundaries. A third alternative is to establish a single national repository to which any State may address inquiries, and into which every State places information.

A national inquiry file (the National Crime Information Center—NCIC) is now being established by the FBI. This file will contain records of all cars reported stolen for more than 24 hours, all persons wanted for extraditable offenses, stolen guns, and all stolen identifiable property valued at over $1,000. This file will be maintained on a computer, with terminals initially connected to 15 police agencies, and with plans to include all States eventually. Any agency with a terminal can enter a record into the file or inquire whether a person or property in custody is listed in the file. It will receive an answer seconds later.

The utility of a fully interconnected national inquiry file depends on the need for interstate and interregional communications and on the need to provide an inquiry capability for those States that do not establish their own files. If such a need should be established, analyses conducted by the science and technology task force indicate that a single central computer is more economical than interconnecting separate regional computers. This result follows from the fact that computer processing and storage costs are much greater than communications costs. It is important that the States, in assessing their own needs and developing their own computer facilities, and the FBI in operating the NCIC, seek to develop information that will provide a basis for a sound decision on the needs for and the form of a national inquiry system.

HANDLING PERSONAL INFORMATION

The most delicate part of any criminal justice information system is the record of previously arrested people and accompanying information about them. Such information is valuable in making prosecution, sentencing, and correctional decisions. But whenever government records contain derogatory personal information, they create serious public policy problems:

☐ The record may contain incomplete or incorrect information.
☐ The information may fall into the wrong hands and be used to intimidate or embarrass.
☐ The information may be retained long after it has lost its usefulness and serves only to harass ex-offenders, or its mere existence may diminish an offender's belief in the possibility of redemption.

Heretofore, the inherent inefficiencies of manual files containing millions of names have provided a built-in protection. Accessibility will be greatly enhanced by putting the files in a computer, so that the protection afforded by inefficiency will diminish, and special attention must be directed at protecting privacy. However, the new technology can create both more useful information and greater individual protection. On the basis of the limited examination it was possible to undertake,

The Commission recommends:

Personal criminal-record information should be organized as follows:

There should be a national law enforcement directory that records an individual's arrests for serious crimes, the disposition of each case, and all subsequent formal contacts with criminal justice agencies related to those arrests. Access should be limited to criminal justice agencies.

There should be State law enforcement directories similar to the national directory, but including less serious offenses.

States should consider criminal justice registries that could record some ancillary factual information (e.g., education and employment records, probation reports) of individuals listed in their State directories. This information must be protected even more carefully than the information in the directories, and would be accessible only to court or corrections officers.

No further background information other than the facts about formal contacts with criminal justice agencies, which are matters of record, should be maintained in the national directory. Any detailed background information would have to come from the individual agencies noted in the directory record. This requirement may pose some added inconvenience in collecting complete histories and in conducting research on criminal careers. However, the potential dangers inherent in a massive central dossier outweigh these disadvantages.

The security of the directory, as with all personal information files, must be carefully protected. Techniques such as auditing users, computer programs and operators, and encoding of files and transmissions should be used to assure that the information is used only for legitimate criminal justice requirements.

The national directory would be similar to a current FBI service. Today, when a police department sends fingerprints to Washington, they are checked against a file of 16 million fingerprints of previously arrested and fingerprinted individuals. The police department then gets positive identification of the individual, and his criminal record or "rap sheet." The process is conducted through the mail and takes about two weeks. About 1,000 fingerprint clerks at the FBI process about 23,000 such fingerprint records each day.

The rap sheet contains a record of all arrests that lead to the submission of fingerprints to the FBI. It is also supposed to contain the court disposition following each arrest, but this information fails to appear in 35 percent of the cases. A police department has no strong incentive for reporting dispositions after the positive identification has been established. Some system of incentives should be developed to assure that court dispositions are recorded. In addition, an individual should be able to learn the contents of his record and have access to a procedure to expunge clearly mistaken arrests, as in cases of mistaken identity or unfounded charge.

The FBI maintains a record until it learns of an individual's death, or until his 75th birthday has passed and he has not been arrested in the previous 10 years. It may be retained even longer because of the difficulty of cleaning out the files. Earlier purging—either destroying the record or putting it in a secure file to which only the most serious crimes would warrant access—would not only increase efficiency but reduce the stigma of a stale arrest. A witness at congressional hearings claimed that "the Christian notion of the possibility of redemption is incomprehensible to the computer." By a policy of early purging of the files, computers permit restoring the notion of redemption to the existing manual files.

The primary entry into the directory would continue to be by means of fingerprints, using the present manual techniques until future automated techniques are developed. In the future, it may be possible to add latent fingerprints and repeating offender "profile" entries capable of being searched by name, personal appearance, or modus operandi.

A majority of States today maintain State identification bureaus similar to the FBI service. These States would presumably continue to maintain their bureaus until there was a more rapidly responding national directory. A number would choose to continue this service in a form modeled after the proposed national directory, particularly in order to maintain criminal records below the threshold of seriousness of the national directory.

Some States might choose to establish State registries that record supplementary information, such as references to school history, employment history, juvenile as well as adult offenses, aptitude-test results, etc., to aid in preparing probation reports and in selecting correctional treatment. Each

State would have to decide for itself what information it wants to retain, recognizing that as more information is included, the potential danger of misuse and the need for limiting access increase.

COMPILING STATISTICAL INFORMATION

During the Commission's investigations, the inadequacy of the available data on crime and on the criminal justice system has become very clear. Statistical information is needed in order to assess the magnitude of the crime problem in the United States and to measure the effectiveness of programs for prevention, enforcement, and correction. The problems of incompleteness, inconsistency, and unreliability of the current data, as well as the outstanding data needs, have been discussed in chapter 2 and in this chapter.

The Commission recommends:

A National Criminal Justice Statistics Center should be established in the Department of Justice. The Center should be responsible for the collection, analysis, and dissemination of two basic kinds of data:

> **Those characterizing criminal careers, derived from carefully drawn samples of anonymous offenders.**

> **Those on crime and the system's response to it, as reported by the criminal justice agencies at all levels.**

In addition, the Center would serve as a central focus for other statistics related to the crime problem, such as costs of crime, census data, and victim surveys. It would have to work in close coordination with the FBI's Uniform Crime Reports Section, the Children's Bureau of the Department of Health, Education, and Welfare, the Federal Bureau of Prisons, and other existing agencies with continuing responsibility for collecting and reporting related statistics. It would combine their information into an integrated picture of crime and criminal justice.

A major task of the Center would be to solicit the cooperation of criminal justice agencies to assure that they compile and submit complete and accurate statistics. The continuing efforts of the FBI to upgrade police statistical reporting have shown how important and difficult this task is. To gain cooperation of local agencies, it would be necessary, first, to establish an understanding of the usefulness of statistics as an operational and management tool, and, second, to create a strong national organization able to collect, process, analyze, interpret, and disseminate the information, and ready to pay the collection costs. The lessons inherent in the collapse in 1945 of the national judicial statistics program—which was manned by one person 10 percent of his time—urge that the effort be well supported when it is undertaken.

SCIENTIFIC AND TECHNOLOGICAL RESEARCH AND DEVELOPMENT PROGRAM

On the basis of the work of the Science and Technology Task Force described in this chapter and in the report of the task force, the Commission believes that science and technology can make a significant contribution to better understanding of the nature of crime and of the operations of the criminal justice system, and to the design and development of valuable technological devices and systems.

The Federal Government should take the initiative in organizing and sustaining a science and technology research and development program. Whether it be equipment development, field experimentation, data collection, or analytical studies, the limited budgets of individual State and local criminal justice agencies cannot provide the necessary investment. Furthermore, the results will be of nationwide benefit. Thus, the Federal Government should support a major science and technology research and development program relating to all areas of criminal justice.

The program should introduce science and technology to criminal justice. The Federal Government should sponsor research, development, test, and evaluation (RDT&E) projects at the local and State levels, especially supporting those widely useful projects that no single agency could support alone. The Government should help criminal justice agencies get the technical support they need to incorporate the results of these projects into their operations. To infuse science and technology directly into day-to-day activities, operations research groups should be established in the larger criminal justice agencies. Finally, to provide the basic fund of knowledge, a major science and technology program should be established in one of the research institutes described in chapters 12 and 13 following. The President's Science Advisory Committee has reviewed and supports these recommendations.

The Commission recommends:

The Federal Government should sponsor a science and technology RDT&E program with three primary components: systems analysis, field experimentation, and equipment-system development.

The systems analysis studies should include development of mathematical models of the criminal justice system and appropriate component parts, and collection of the data needed to apply these models to improving operations. The projects to be undertaken should include:

☐ Model of a State criminal justice system.
☐ Apprehension studies in a police department.
☐ Computer simulation of court processing of cases.

These studies are only extensions of the initial efforts undertaken by the science and technology task force. As the program develops, new problem areas in which systems analysis can be usefully applied will appear, and some of them may turn out to be more productive than the ones already identified.

Field experimentation should be conducted by operating criminal justice agencies in conjunction with individuals or groups competent in experimental research. Many operating innovations are possible, and these should be evaluated in actual use both to test their value and to assess their possible side effects. The experimental projects to be undertaken should include:

☐ Controlled experiments examining various police patrol concepts, such as statistical techniques for allocation of patrol forces, various random patrol patterns, saturation patrolling, etc.
☐ Laboratory simulation of various police command and control systems and procedures.
☐ Statistical analysis relating recidivism to offender characteristics and to correctional treatment possibilities.

These areas again, are only suggestive; many more may be discovered by the criminal justice agencies themselves in their process of self-examination and innovation.

607

A number of basic kinds of equipment should be developed for general use by criminal justice agencies. Some of the promising possibilities include:

☐ Computer-assisted police command and control facility.
☐ Semiautomatic fingerprint system.
☐ Inexpensive portable radio for foot patrolmen and for patrolmen operating away from their car radios.
☐ Automatic patrol car locator.

The RDT&E program would have to be developed in detail by the office administering it. The program would have to be housed in an agency that was sympathetic to research and development, and could attract the high-caliber scientific staff needed to manage the program.

The program would inevitably require technical guidance of a breadth and quality exceeding that which could be expected of any internal technical staff. Advisory committees comprising scientists and criminal justice officials would be needed to review proposals in specific subject areas. In many cases, another government office will be the best choice to manage a specific project; the Army Materiel Command might direct the development of a portable radio, for example. Nonprofit or even profitmaking contractors, as used by the Department of Defense, might furnish broad technical guidance.

TECHNICAL SUPPORT AND ESTABLISHMENT OF
EQUIPMENT STANDARDS

As the Federal Government plays a more important role in aiding criminal justice agencies to share in the products of modern technology, it will become necessary to help them use it effectively. To this end, there will be a need for centralized establishment of technical standards (for radios, computer codes, etc.) and for provision of technical assistance and guidance.

The Commission recommends:

A Federal agency should be assigned to coordinate the establishment of standards for equipment to be used by criminal justice agencies, and to provide those agencies technical assistance.

This organization should be an adjunct to an existing Federal agency already technically strong and familiar with standardization problems. The National Bureau of Standards is one such agency. It could organize committees of users and manufacturers to agree on equipment and communication standards. It would be a center with growing competence in criminal justice equipment problems, and would be staffed by scientists and engineers in the most relevant technologies—electronics, computer sciences, operations research, chemistry, etc. The organization would help criminal justice agencies draw on local technical resources such as consultants, professional societies, and manufacturers, and would help the agencies to assess the products received.

OPERATIONS RESEARCH GROUPS WITHIN CRIMINAL JUSTICE AGENCIES

As an important mechanism for innovation, the large criminal justice agencies, and especially large police departments, should establish small operations research groups with professionally trained scientists, mathematicians, and engineers, including at least one person competent in statistics. The group would analyze the operations, design and evaluate experiments, and provide general technical assistance. Such groups have proved extremely valuable to industry, government, and the military. Certainly each of the 21 police departments, 4 sheriffs' forces, and 12 State police forces with more than 1,000 employees could benefit significantly from such a group.

The Commission recommends:

The Federal Government should encourage and support the establishment of operations research staffs in large criminal justice agencies.

SCIENCE AND TECHNOLOGY PROGRAM IN A RESEARCH INSTITUTE

Probably the most important single mechanism for bringing the resources of science and technology to bear on the problems of crime would be the establishment of a major prestigious science and technology research program within one of the research institutes discussed in chapters 12 and 13. The program would create interdisciplinary teams of mathematicians, computer scientists, electronics engineers, physicists, biologists, and other natural scientists, and would

609

require psychologists, sociologists, economists, and lawyers on these teams. The institute and the program must be significant enough to attract the best scientists available, and to this end, the director of this institute must himself have a background in science and technology or have the respect of scientists. Because it would be difficult to attract such a staff into the Federal Government, the institute should be established by a university, a group of universities, or an independent nonprofit organization, and should be within a major metropolitan area. The institute would have to establish close ties with neighboring criminal justice agencies that would receive the benefit of serving as experimental laboratories for such an institute. The research program might require, in order to bring together the necessary "critical mass" of competent staff, an annual budget which might reach $5 million, funded with at least a 3-year lead time to assure continuity.

The Commission recommends:

A major scientific and technological research program within a research institute should be created and supported by the Federal Government.

Chapter 12

Research—Instrument for Reform

The Commission has found and discussed throughout this report many needs of law enforcement and the administration of criminal justice. But what it has found to be the greatest need is the need to know.

America has learned the uses of exploration and discovery and knowledge in shaping and controlling its physical environment, in protecting its health, in furthering its national security, and in countless other areas. The startling advances in the physical and biological sciences are products of an intellectual revolution that substituted the painful and plodding quest for knowledge for the comforting acceptance of received notions. The Nation has invested billions of dollars and the best minds at its disposal in this quest for scientific discovery. The returns from this investment are dramatically apparent in the reduction of disease, the development of new weapons, the availability of goods, the rise in living standards, and the conquest of space.

But this revolution of scientific discovery has largely bypassed the problems of crime and crime control. Writing for the Boston Crime Survey in 1927 Felix Frankfurter observed that the subject was "overlaid with shibboleths and cliches" and that it was essential to "separate the known from the unknown, to divorce fact from assumption, to strip biases of every sort of their authority." The statement is no less true today.

Few domestic social problems more seriously threaten our welfare or exact a greater toll on our resources. But society has relied primarily on traditional answers and has looked almost exclusively to common sense and hunch for needed changes. The Nation spends more than $4 billion annually on the criminal justice system alone. Yet the expenditure for the kinds of descriptive, operational, and evaluative research that are the obvious prerequisites for a rational program of crime control is negligible. Almost every industry makes a significant investment in research each year. Approximately 15 percent of the Defense Department's annual budget is allocated to research. While different fields call for different levels of research, it is worth noting that research commands only a small fraction of 1 percent of the total expenditure for crime control. There is probably no subject of comparable concern to which the Nation is devoting so many resources and so much effort with so little knowledge of what it is doing.

It is true, of course, that many kinds of knowledge about crime must await better understanding of social behavior. It is also true that research will never provide the final answers to many of the vexing questions about crime. Decisions as to the activities that should be made criminal, as to the limits there should be on search and seizure, or as to the proper scope of the right to counsel, cannot be made solely on the basis of research data. Those decisions involve weighing the importance of fairness and privacy and freedom—values that cannot be scientifically analyzed. But when research cannot, in itself, provide final answers, it can provide data crucial to making informed policy judgments.

There is virtually no subject connected with crime or criminal justice into which further research is unnecessary. The Commission was able to explore many of these subjects in connection with its work, and to develop the data that underlie the recommendations made in this report. Many of its projects sought to open up new areas of knowledge; many drew on the prior work of scholars, governmental agencies, and private organizations. Crime is a continuing and urgent reality with which we must deal as effectively as we can. We cannot await final answers. The alternatives are not whether to act or not, but whether to act wisely or unwisely.

Some Commission research has served to mark out paths along which further exploration should proceed. The pilot survey of criminal victims shows a great potential for discovering the extent and the nature of unreported crime. Such surveys should be conducted on a continuing basis, so their usefulness can be tested further. The Commission's studies of police-community relations were as extensive as any previously undertaken, but, of course, this extremely complicated and crucial subject deserves and requires continuing study. The science and technology task force's study of the relationship between police response time and the apprehension of suspects has suggested the value of changing various procedures so as to reduce response time, but it remains for the police to apply this analysis to their specific situations, to experiment with the suggested changes and to discover what happens in practice.

Naturally, in the course of its studies the Commission discovered many areas it had neither the time nor the resources to explore, although it was clear that there was a vital need that they be explored. For example, the effects on law enforcement and crime of legal restrictions on such police practices as interrogation and search and seizure are not known; ways of testing those effects accurately must be developed. There is no present technique for measuring the deterrent effects on criminal activity of the imposition, removal or change of sanctions; such a technique is badly needed.

It would obviously be futile to attempt to catalog all the kinds of research that are needed. We do not even know all the questions that need to be asked. But we do know many of them and we also know that planning and organizing the search for knowledge is a matter of highest importance.

PLANNING AND ORGANIZING RESEARCH

Research is many kinds of activity. It is gathering and analyzing facts. It is conducting and evaluating operational experiments. It is devising methods for testing the effects of change. It is searching for the motivations of human behavior. Obviously there is a need here for a wide variety of talents. Sociologists, lawyers, economists, psychiatrists, psychologists, physical scientists, engineers, statisticians, mathematicians—all these and more are needed. There is likewise opportunity for a wide variety of organizations and institutions. Too little is known about the various uses and limitations of different methods of organizing for research to permit the prescription of any one mold for future research efforts. Indeed it is essential that such efforts take many different forms.

RESEARCH BY OPERATING AGENCIES

There is no activity, technique, program, or administrative structure in the criminal justice system that is so perfect it

613

does not need to be systematically scrutinized, evaluated, and experimented with. Police patrol and police investigation, personnel structures, communication systems and information systems, community relations programs and internal investigation programs; court business methods and court organization, plea bargaining and ways of providing defense counsel, the selection of prosecutors and the training of judges; prison industry programs and prison design, halfway houses and juvenile training schools, parole decisions and parole techniques are a few of the hundreds of subjects that should be studied.

Operating agencies should obviously concern themselves with this kind of research. But it is clear that the criminal justice system does not have the means to conduct research entirely on its own. Few people working in any part of the system at the present time have the scholarly training to use the sophisticated methods of gathering and analyzing facts, inventing experiments, and using controls that research requires. The system's administrators must call upon the universities, foundations, social service agencies, and industrial corporations for help—must open their doors and reveal their secrets.

Chapter 1 mentioned the inertia of the criminal justice system, its slowness to make even those changes that everyone agrees are necessary. Perhaps the most damaging expression of that inertia has been the failure of most police, court, and correctional officials to recognize how little they know and how important to America it is for them to know more. Doubtless many of them have been so busy merely keeping abreast of their day-to-day work that they have had no time for contemplation and study. Doubtless some, who are aware of the need, have looked at the system's limited resources and have concluded that trying to fill that need was hopeless. But beyond these real and formidable obstacles there is in the criminal justice system a reluctance to face hard facts, a resistance to innovation, a suspicion of "outsiders," a fear of the kind of criticism that objective appraisal may lead to that, until they are overcome, will make significant programs of research difficult, if not impossible, to plan and organize.

The Commission is well aware that no recommendation it can make will overcome reluctance, resistance, suspicion, and fear; it is well aware of how little mere adjuration and exhortation are likely to accomplish; it is well aware that many mayors, Governors and legislators, to whom the system is responsible and to whom it must look for leadership and funds, have been no more eager to face this problem than police, courts, or correctional officials have been; it is well aware that the scholarly community has been slow to interest itself in the problems of crime and criminal justice, and to offer its skills and services. It can only note that some of the operating agencies that have recognized their responsibility for research have found ways of improving their effectiveness. All too few have accepted this responsibility.

The Commission recommends:

Criminal justice agencies such as State court and correctional systems and large police departments should develop their own research units, staffed by specialists and drawing on the advice and assistance of leading scholars and experts in relevant fields.

INDEPENDENT RESEARCH

Of course, there is no sharp line between the kind of research that operating agencies can do, and the kind that is more appropriately the responsibility of independent researchers. Often the line is blurred, as when a researcher uses a police department or a court or a prison as a subject for research study, and what is learned is a direct benefit to the agency. The Vera Institute's bail study in the New York City courts is an excellent example. On the other hand, many of the problems of crime and crime control require research not directly related to day-to-day operations of the criminal justice system. This is obviously true of such subjects as the relationship between crime and poverty, the impact of organized crime on the economy, the scope of unreported crimes, or the nature and extent of gambling, to offer but four of a multitude of possible examples. Whatever the nature of the inquiry, those outside the system generally have a greater freedom to question long accepted assumptions, to explore radically new modes of action, and to conduct long-range research which might lead to basic alterations in the structure and functioning of operating institutions.

The independent research which has been done in the past has been centered in law schools and sociology departments of universities. Much of it has been the work of professors working alone or with one or a few graduate students. This form of research has produced significant contributions to our learning and will continue to be a major source of new data and new ideas, but there are large areas where it is inadequate. Since the complexities of crime cut across many disci-

615

plines, and many projects require a group of people working together, it is important that there be some collaborative, organized research projects and centers. Individual scholars can add to our knowledge of the causes of various kinds of criminal behavior. But to develop a comprehensive plan for combating organized crime, for example, it would be helpful to bring together economists, sociologists, and lawyers.

In recent years a few departments or centers specifically for the study of crime and criminal justice have developed at universities. Such centers bring together persons from a number of relevant fields for collaborative research. One promising example is the Center for Studies in Criminal Justice at the University of Chicago, recently funded by the Ford Foundation. Its projects draw on the work of scholars from law, sociology, psychiatry, and other fields. Its advisory committee includes police officials, judges, and correctional officials. Its projects include studies of deterrence, alternative methods of treatment of offenders, legal aid for jail inmates and slum dwellers, and compensation for victims of crimes of violence. Other criminal research centers include those at the University of California, Georgetown University, and the University of Pennsylvania.

Some criminal research activity has developed outside of the university framework. The Vera Institute has launched a broadly conceived research program in New York City, which includes studies of police questioning, night courts, and drunkenness. The American Bar Foundation has completed several programs of research into the administration of criminal justice, and has begun others. The California Institute for the Study of Crime and Delinquency works closely with correctional agencies in the State but was designed to be "free from both the constraints of political government and institutions of higher learning," and to "bridge the gap between the interests of crime control administrators and those of academic researchers." The National Council on Crime and Delinquency has sponsored significant amounts of research, in addition to disseminating work of others.

The Commission believes that institutions for organized research in this field are of great significance and that more private and governmental financial support should be provided for this purpose, though not to the exclusion of other efforts.

The Commission recommends:

Substantial public and private funds should be provided for a

number of criminal research institutes in various parts of the country.

Some of the institutes might be expansions of existing research centers. They should be sufficiently well-financed so they can attract highly qualified persons from the social and natural sciences, the law, business administration and psychiatry, to work together and with criminal justice agencies. Some of their work should be directed at practical problems facing operating agencies and major policy issues facing legislators. In addition, there should be opportunity for broader inquiry, including challenges to the basic assumptions of any part of the present system of justice. They could study such especially puzzling forms of criminal activity as white collar crime, professional crime and organized crime. They could study the need for and the effects of controversial police procedures. While these institutes should not be controlled or dominated by the Federal Government, they could play an important role in providing ideas and data to the Department of Justice in connection with State and local aid programs described in chapter 13, and in evaluating innovative proposals suggested for Federal support.

Most of these institutes should be at universities since it seems likely, at least in the foreseeable future, that the leading scholars in this field would prefer to work in a university setting. The ability to draw on faculty and students of law, architecture, medical, and business schools, and social and physical science departments would provide a broad base for the institute's work. A university-based institute would be in a favorable position to train the research personnel that criminal justice agencies need so badly. And it could, through special seminars or degree courses, provide administrators and specialists from the agencies with a broader understanding of the whole problem of crime and its control and the advantages to be gained from research. Through its ties to the university, the institute would promote the infusion of the results and attitudes of research into the professional training of lawyers, policemen, and correctional workers.

The Commission finds persuasive the suggestion that has been made to it that one of these institutes should be independent of any single university and should not rely on Federal financial support except as "seed money." When the establishment of an institute of criminology in New York City was under study, the bar association committee that considered the matter concluded:

The very idea of such a criminology center or institute, if it is to justify its reason for being, is that it be not subordinated to the professional, vocational, or even educational, objectives of institutions or organizations seeking or serving other and narrower or broader goals in the community. It is for that reason that the Committee found itself in complete agreement with its reporter that the kind of criminological center or institute contemplated should, as a matter of strong preference, not be associated with any particular university, professional school, governmental or private organization devoted to other purposes, or committed to any narrow professional purpose or particular evil or amelioration in the administration of the criminal law. Breitel, Foreword to Radzinowicz, *The Need for Criminology, p. vii (1965).*

Such an institute could be set up jointly by a number of universities, as was the Brookhaven National Laboratory. Its continuing financing could be drawn from a number of foundations and, particularly, from business corporations.

Other forms of independent institutes are possible. For example, an institute that had the application of science and technology to criminal administration as one of its primary concerns might be established in affiliation with one of the present, nonprofit scientific corporations that undertake military research for the Government.

The Commission recognizes that in view of the dearth of skilled and interested researchers in this field, such institutes cannot be set up overnight. However, it urges that immediate steps be taken to set up one or two without delay and that as soon as possible no less than four be established in different parts of the country.

A substantial part of the funding of these institutes should come from private sources. But whatever form these institutes take, and ideally they should take a variety of different forms, major support by the Federal Government would be essential, at least in the beginning. Chapter 13 proposes such support as part of the overall Federal program. For the institutes to attract the best people and to be effective in their work it is essential that Federal funds be provided on a basis that does not impair the independent administration of the research program.

Of course, even if several institutes were set up, their work should constitute only part of the research activity in this field. Work by individual scholars, by existing and new privately financed centers, will still be necessary, and adequate financing for these efforts is no less essential than for the institutes.

The Commission recommends:

Universities, foundations, and other private groups should expand their efforts in the field of criminal research. Federal, State, and local governments should make increased funds available for the benefit of individuals or groups with promising research programs and the ability to execute them.

NATIONAL FOUNDATION FOR CRIMINAL RESEARCH

The Commission believes it essential that some national body act as a focus for research efforts in the field of crime and its control, stimulating vitally needed projects, providing more effective communication between those doing research, and disseminating what is learned. Thus, where a police department experiments with important new techniques, someone should be concerned that the effects of these techniques are scientifically evaluated, and that other police departments find out what is learned. If a city court judge is considering methods for reducing delay, there should be some place he can check to see what has been tried elsewhere and with what success. If whole areas of crucial importance such as drug abuse, police misconduct, or white-collar crime continue to be shrouded in darkness, someone should have responsibility for seeing that money and talent are mustered to seek data and make proposals.

The need for stimulation, coordination, and dissemination is now met only in a limited, fragmentary, and often haphazard way. In view of the enormous increase in research activity and the variety of research organizations envisaged in this report, it seems desirable that there be a Federal agency with overall responsibility for research. This agency should not displace private and governmental agencies seeking to perform this function, but by collaborating with them, should seek to insure as broad and effective a program of research and dissemination as possible. It should serve as a clearinghouse of research and information for the benefit of Federal, State, and local agencies and private institutions.

While there are some obvious advantages to having this agency in the Department of Justice, the Commission believes that the long-range goal should be to establish an independent agency—a National Foundation for Criminal Research. Like the National Science Foundation, it should be financed by an annual appropriation from Congress. Its independent status would insure its freedom from the pressures and immediate needs of any Federal agency responsible for criminal administration. Such independence would also make it more attractive to leading scholars in the field, on whom its success would depend.

The Commission recommends:

A National Foundation for Criminal Research should be established as an independent agency.

The Commission recognizes that to establish a National Foundation for Criminal Research at the same time that the new aid program proposed in chapter 13 is being developed, would present a serious risk of confusion and competition for already scarce research personnel. It is essential that the new Justice Department program embody a major research component, if it is not simply to perpetuate present failures in many areas. This is particularly important at the outset when difficult decisions must be made about what meets the standards justifying Federal aid. There is too little research now being done in this field and very few skilled researchers to do it. Furthermore, the establishment of a National Foundation for Criminal Research presents organization and funding problems which the Commission has not fully explored. Therefore, it may be desirable to defer the establishment of such a foundation until the proposed new Justice Department agency is established. In that event, one of the early responsibilities of this agency should be to develop detailed plans for an independent foundation and to work toward its establishment.

Chapter 13

A National Strategy

AMERICA CAN CONTROL CRIME. This report has tried to say how. It has shown that crime flourishes where the conditions of life are the worst, and that therefore the foundation of a national strategy against crime is an unremitting national effort for social justice. Reducing poverty, discrimination, ignorance, disease and urban blight, and the anger, cynicism or despair those conditions can inspire, is one great step toward reducing crime. It is not the task, indeed it is not within the competence, of a Commission on Law Enforcement and Administration of Justice to make detailed proposals about housing or education or civil rights, unemployment or welfare or health. However, it is the Commission's clear and urgent duty to stress that forceful action in these fields is essential to crime prevention, and to adjure the officials of every agency of criminal justice—policemen, prosecutors, judges, correctional authorities—to associate themselves with and labor for the success of programs that will improve the quality of American life.

This report has shown that most criminal careers begin in youth, and that therefore programs that will reduce juvenile delinquency and keep delinquents and youthful offenders from settling into lives of crime are indispensable parts of a national strategy. It has shown that the formal criminal process, arrest to trial to punishment, seldom protects the community from offenders of certain kinds and that therefore, the criminal justice system and the community must jointly seek alternative ways of treating them. It has shown that treatment in the community might also return to constructive life many offenders who quite appropriately have been subjected to formal process.

This report has pointed out that legislatures and, by extension, the public, despite their well-founded alarm about crime, have not provided the wherewithal for the criminal justice system to do what it could and should do. It has identified the system's major needs as better qualified, better trained manpower; more modern equipment and management; closer cooperation among its functional parts and among its many and varied jurisdictions; and, of course, the money without which far-reaching and enduring improvements are impossible.

Finally, this report has emphasized again and again that improved law enforcement and criminal administration is more than a matter of giving additional resources to police departments, courts, and correctional systems. Resources are not ends. They are means, the means through which the agencies of criminal justice can seek solutions to the problems of preventing and controlling crime. Many of those solutions have not yet been found. We need to know much more about crime. A national strategy against crime must be in large part a strategy of search.

WHAT STATE AND LOCAL GOVERNMENTS CAN DO

Almost every recommendation in this report is a recommendation to State or local governments, the governments that by and large administer criminal justice in America. A special difficulty of writing the report has been finding terms general enough to describe criminal administration in 50 States and thousands of local communities, and at the same time specific enough to be helpful. The Commission is acutely aware that the report does not discuss many distinctive local conditions and problems, that its descriptions often are quite broad, that no one of its recommendations applies with equal force to every locality, that, indeed some of its recommendations do not apply at all to some localities.

On the whole the report concentrates on cities, for that is where crime is most prevalent, most feared, and most difficult to control. On the whole the report dwells on the criminal justice system's deficiencies and failures, since prescribing remedies was what the Commission was organized to do. Some States and cities are doing much to improve criminal administration; their work is the basis for many of the report's recommendations. Finally, because the report is a national report, it is not and cannot be a detailed manual of instructions that police departments, courts and correctional systems need only to follow step by step in order to solve their problems. It is of necessity a general guide that suggests lines along which local agencies can act.

PLANNING—THE FIRST STEP

A State or local government that undertakes to improve its criminal administration should begin by constructing, if it has not already done so, formal machinery for planning. Significant reform is not to be achieved overnight by a stroke of a pen; it is the product of thought and preparation. No experienced and responsible State or city official needs to be told that. The Commission's point is not the elementary one that each individual action against crime should be planned, but that all of a State's or a city's actions against crime should be planned together, by a single body. The police, the courts, the correctional system and the noncriminal agencies of the community must plan their actions against crime jointly if they are to make real headway.

The relationships among the parts of the criminal justice system and between the system and the community's other institutions, governmental and nongovernmental, are so intimate and intricate that a change anywhere may be felt everywhere. Putting into effect the Commission's recommendation for three entry "tracks" in police departments could involve the rewriting of civil service regulations, the revision of standard police field procedures, the adjustment of city budgets, possibly the passage of enabling legislation. A reform like organizing a Youth Service Bureau to which the police and the juvenile courts, and parents and school officials as well, could refer young people will require an enormous amount of planning. Such a bureau will have to work closely with the community's other youth-serving agencies. It will affect the caseloads of juvenile courts, probation services and detention facilities. It will raise legal issues of protecting the rights of the young people referred to it. It could be attached to a local or State government in a variety of ways. It could offer many different kinds of service. It could be staffed by many different kinds of people. It could be financed in many different ways.

Most of the recommendations in this report raise similar problems. Later in this chapter a large-scale program of Federal support for State and local agencies is sponsored. If this program is adopted, States and cities will need plans in order to secure their share of Federal funds.

Furthermore, concerted and systematic planning is not only a necessary prelude to action. It is a spur to action. The best way to interest the community in the problems of crime is to engage members of it in planning. The best way to mobilize the community against crime is to lay before it a set of practical and coherent plans. This report often has had occasion to use the word "isolation" to describe certain aspects of the relationship between the criminal justice system and the community. State and city planning agencies could do much to end that isolation.

The Commission recommends:

In every State and every city, an agency, or one or more officials, should be specifically responsible for planning improvements in crime prevention and control and encouraging their implementation.

It is impossible, of course, to prescribe in a national report the precise forms that State or city planning agencies should take. No two States have identical constitutions or penal codes or crime problems. State-city relationships vary from State to State, and often within States according to the size of cities. County governments have more or less power, depending on the State. Municipal government takes many forms. However, there are certain principles that are universally applicable.

First, much of the planning for action against crime will have to be done at the State level. Every State operates a court system and a corrections system, and has responsibility for certain aspects of law enforcement. State legislatures, as a rule, control local finances. The States are in the best position to encourage or require the coordination or pooling of activities that is so vitally necessary in metropolitan areas and among rural counties. Many States have units, some independent and some a part of the Governor's office, that are actively engaged in planning in the field of juvenile delinquency.

In addition, a number of Governors have responded to the President's suggestion in March 1966, that they establish State planning committees to maintain contact with this Commission during its life and with other interested Federal agencies, to appraise the needs of their State criminal systems, and to put into effect those proposals of the Commission that they find to be worthwhile. The Commission urges all Governors to establish similar committees.

Second, much of the planning will have to be done at the municipal level. The problems of the police and, to a certain extent, of the jails and the lower courts are typically city problems. Welfare, education, housing, fire prevention, recreation, sanitation, urban renewal, and a multitude of other functions that are closely connected with crime and criminal justice are also the responsibility of cities. In some cities members of the mayor's or the city manager's staff, or advisory or interdepartmental committees, coordinate the city's anticrime activities; in most cities there is as yet little planning coordination.

Third, close collaboration between State and city planning units is obviously essential. Representatives of a State's major cities should serve on the State body, and staff members of the State body should be available to the city bodies for information and advice. Money, manpower, and expertise are in too short supply to be squandered in activities that duplicate or overlap each other and, conversely, when there is no collaboration there is always a risk that some important field of action will be overlooked.

Fourth, however much the structure and composition of planning units vary from place to place, all units should include both officials of the criminal justice system and citizens from other professions. Plans to improve criminal administration will be impossible to put into effect if those responsible for criminal administration do not help to make them. On the other hand, as this report has repeatedly stressed, crime prevention is the task of the community as a whole and, as it has also stressed, all parts of the criminal justice system can benefit from the special knowledge and points of view of those outside it. Business and civic leaders, lawyers, school and welfare officials, persons familiar with the problems of slum dwellers, and members of the academic community are among those who might be members of planning boards, or who might work with such boards as advisers or consultants.

Fifth and finally, planning boards must have sufficient authority and prestige, and staffs large enough and able enough, to permit them to furnish strong and imaginative leadership in making plans and seeing them through.

The first thing any planning unit will have to do is to gather and analyze facts: Statistics about crime and the costs and caseloads of the criminal justice system; knowledge about the programs and procedures being used in its own jurisdiction, and about those that have proved successful elsewhere; data about the social conditions that appear to be linked with crime; information about potentially helpful individuals and organizations in the community.

In few States or cities has information of these kinds been compiled systematically. Gathering facts will be an invaluable process for any planning body, not only because of the importance of the facts themselves, but also because they will have to be gathered from people and organizations experienced in crime prevention and criminal administration: Judges, correctional officials, police officials, prosecutors, defense counsel, youth workers, universities, foundations, civic organizations, service clubs, neighborhood groups.

Those people and organizations can be combined into a network of support for the changes the planning body will propose. Such a network will be able to do much to overcome resistance to change, or fear of it, inside and outside the criminal justice system, by showing how changes can be made carefully and practically.

On the basis of the facts it gathers, the planning body will be able to appraise objectively and frankly the needs of its State or city and the resources that are available for meeting those needs. It would ask, for example, whether in its jurisdiction police training is adequate; whether the lower and juvenile courts are failing in any of the ways cited by the Commission; whether the correctional system is beginning to make fundamental improvements of the sort the Commission has found are widely needed.

It will discover needs that can be met rapidly by putting into effect programs that have succeeded in other places; for example, bail reform projects, systems for the assignment of defense counsel to indigents, police standards commissions, rehabilitation programs in jails, sentencing institutes for judges. An excellent model of how much a planning body can do is the work of the President's Commission on Crime in the District of Columbia, which undertook a comprehensive study of the criminal justice system and other agencies concerned with crime and delinquency in the District, and made detailed recommendations for change.

The one caution about planning bodies the Commission feels it must make is that they not serve as an excuse for postponing changes that can be made immediately. For example, most police departments could immediately add legal advisers to their staffs, or launch police-community relations programs. In many cities there is no question about whether more prosecutors and probation officers are needed in the lower courts; they clearly are and they should be provided at once. Sentencing councils could be organized with no more effort than it would take for a number of judges to arrange to meet regularly. Other recommendations that one jurisdiction or another could put into effect at once, without elaborate planning, will be found in the pages of this report. Simple changes that can be made immediately should be, not only because justice demands it, but because making them will contribute to create a climate in which complicated, long-range reform will be feasible.

MAJOR LINES FOR STATE AND LOCAL ACTION

MONEY

The most urgent need of the agencies of criminal justice in the States and cities is money with which to finance the multitude of improvements they must make. As is set forth in the next section of this chapter, the Commission believes that Federal financial support of improved criminal administration in the States and cities is necessary and appropriate. But even more essential is an increase in State support. Plans for change must include realistic estimates of financial requirements and persuasive showings of the gains that can be achieved by spending more on criminal administration.

A central task of planning bodies and the network of agencies and individuals working with them will be to mobilize support, within legislatures and by the public, for spending money on innovation and reform. The collaboration of police, prosecutors, correctional officials, and others involved in the agencies of justice is crucial in this, for they know best how vital the need for greater resources is, and how little is accomplished by identifying scapegoats or resorting to simplistic answers as solutions to the complicated problems of crime and criminal justice.

PERSONNEL

The Commission has found that many of the agencies of justice are understaffed. Giving them the added manpower they need is a matter of high priority for protection of public safety and of the rights of individuals accused of crime. But even more essential is a dramatic improvement in the quality of personnel throughout the system. Establishment of standard-setting bodies, such as police standards commissions that exist in several States, is one approach to this problem. Better and more numerous training programs are another. State and city planning groups must consider to what extent each operating agency can and should provide its own training and to what extent metropolitan, statewide, or regional programs should be developed instead.

If the agencies of justice are to recruit and retain the able, well-educated people they badly need, they will have to offer them higher pay and challenging and satisfying work. For example, it is clear to the Commission that until the single recruitment and promotion "track" that now prevails in all police forces is abandoned, upgrading of the police will be extremely difficult. Thus, one of the first and most difficult tasks of planning bodies will be to consider major changes in the personnel structures of the agencies of justice.

PROGRAMS TO MEET NEW NEEDS

This report has described how modern urban life has burdened the criminal justice system with a range of almost entirely new problems. It has attempted to suggest promising ways of dealing with them. For example, it outlines a model for future development in corrections that predicates treatment on a new kind of facility: A small institution, located in the community it serves, that can be used flexibly for short-term incarceration and as a base for intensive community treatment. It has proposed police communications centers that take advantage of modern technology. It has described how necessary it is, in the interest of preventing delinquency, for the community to reassess the current practices of schools, welfare departments, and housing officials, particularly in poor neighborhoods. It has proposed, as a new alternative to criminal disposition for less serious juvenile offenders, Youth Services Bureaus that would provide them with a variety of treatment services and keep them from being grouped with serious criminals. It has proposed greatly strengthened community relations programs to improve respect for law and increase police effectiveness in the highest crime neighborhoods of America's cities. In addition, broader methods of meeting problems presented by the increasing complexity and anonymity of life in large urban areas are obviously important. Thus, some cities may wish to consider developing procedures or agencies—of which the ombudsman, which has proved useful in a number of other countries, is only one possible model—to assist citizens in understanding and dealing with the many official agencies that affect their lives. These are only a few important examples of the many new services the Commission recommends that State and local planning bodies develop.

In many instances establishing new programs will be costly. The Commission is therefore recommending that the emphasis of proposed Federal financial aid be placed on innovation. The Commission further recommends that State and local governments carefully consider the feasibility and desirability of devoting to new programs increasing proportions of the funds allocated to crime control.

ORGANIZATION AND PROCEDURES OF AGENCIES OF JUSTICE

An important matter for planning units and operating agencies to consider is how the police, the courts, and corrections can improve their organization and their operations. Since there are throughout the Nation many examples to draw on, and since legislative action often will not be required, early and substantial improvements can be made. Such of the Commission's proposals as those for regularizing the procedures in pretrial disposition of cases and in sentencing; for providing clearer guidance by police chiefs to field officers on such matters as the making of arrests in domestic disputes, drunkenness and civil disturbance situations; and for developing a "collaborative" regime within prisons, can be considered almost at once, and acted upon without legislative action and, in many instances, without significant increases in spending.

The success of such changes in the States or cities where they have been made should greatly help the agencies in States and cities where they have not been made to act promptly. Planning bodies and other State and local groups may find themselves chiefly providing support, encouragement and continuing pressure for change. In some cases it may be desirable for State or local agencies to obtain suggestions from recognized professional or governmental groups such as the International Association of Chiefs of Police or the Bureau of Prisons as one means of identifying specific needs and possible ways of meeting them.

LAW REFORM

While many improvements in the system of criminal justice do not require legislative action other than the appropriation of funds, others do require new laws or changes in existing laws. Proposals for court reorganization may even require constitutional change. Therefore, at an early stage in their work, planning bodies should appraise the needs for legislative change. Legislative changes could include such diverse actions as enacting new gun control laws; amending existing laws to aid in organized crime prosecutions; changing legal disabilities of former prisoners; and enacting controls over dangerous drugs that are uniform with Federal law.

More general and fundamental reevaluation is also called for. A number of State legislatures, including those in Illinois, California, and New York, have recently completed or are now engaged in major revisions of their criminal codes. For States that have not yet addressed this problem, the carefully formulated provisions of the American Law Institute's Model Penal Code serve as a valuable starting point. In many places there are bar associations and other groups with continuing interest in law revision; clearly such groups should be involved in the planning process. Governors and State legislatures should also give strong consideration to appointing law revision commissions comparable to that established by the Congress for review of all Federal criminal statutes.

WHAT THE FEDERAL GOVERNMENT CAN DO

Although day-by-day criminal administration is primarily a State and local responsibility, the Federal Government's contribution to the national effort against crime is crucial. The Federal Government carries much of the load of financing and administering the great social programs that are America's best hope of preventing crime and delinquency, and various of its branches concern themselves actively with such specific criminal problems as preventing juvenile delinquency, and treating drug addiction and alcoholism.

The Federal Government has the direct responsibility for enforcing major criminal statutes against, among other things, kidnapping, bank robbery, racketeering, smuggling, counterfeiting, drug abuse and tax evasion. It has a number of law enforcement agencies, a system of criminal courts and a large correctional establishment. Some of the Commission's recommendations, notably those concerning organized crime, drug abuse, firearms control and the pooling of correctional facilities and of police radio frequencies, are addressed in part to the Federal Government.

The Federal Government has for many years provided information, advice and training to State and local law enforcement agencies. These services have been extremely important. In many towns and counties, for example, the Federal Bureau of Investigation's on-site training programs for police officers and sheriffs are the only systematic training programs available. The Department of Justice, under the Law Enforcement Assistance Act of 1965, has begun to give State and city agencies financial grants for research, for planning, and for demonstration projects.

The Commission wants not only to endorse warmly Federal participation in the effort to reduce delinquency and crime, but to urge that it be intensified and accelerated. It believes further that the Federal Government can make a dramatic new contribution to the national effort against crime by greatly expanding its support of the agencies of justice in the States and in the cities.

FEDERAL PREVENTION PROGRAMS

The Federal Government is already doing much in the field of delinquency prevention. An Office of Juvenile Delinquency and Youth Development, which funds research and demonstration projects by both governmental and nongovernmental State and local agencies, is an important part of the Department of Health, Education, and Welfare. The office is supporting projects, to give only a few examples, aimed at providing job training and opportunities to delinquents; enabling school dropouts to continue their education; controlling the behavior of youthful gangs; involving young people in community action; devising alternatives to juvenile court referral and finding ways to give delinquents the support and counseling they do not get from their families. The same Department's Children's Bureau has for years given technical aid to police and juvenile court personnel. The Vocational Rehabilitation Administration in the Department has recently developed job training programs specifically designed for delinquent young people. The Commission is convinced that efforts like these are of great immediate, and even greater potential, value, and urges that they be strengthened.

Other Federal programs of greater scope work against delinquency and crime by improving education and employment prospects for the poor and attacking slum conditions, associated with crime. Such work and job training programs as the Neighborhood Youth Corps, the Job Corps, the Youth Opportunity Centers, and Manpower Development and Training Act programs provide training, counseling, and work opportunities essential to break the pattern of unemployability that underlies so much of crime today. The Elementary and Secondary Education Act programs and the Head Start work with preschool children are aimed at readying disadvantaged children for school, improving the quality of slum education and preventing dropping out. Community action programs and the new Model Cities Program are concerned with strengthening the social and physical structure of inner cities, and thus ultimately with delinquency and crime prevention. As chapter 1 of this report has pointed out, a community's most enduring protection against crime is to right the wrongs and cure the illnesses that tempt men to harm their neighbors.

AN EXPANDED FEDERAL EFFORT

In the field of law enforcement and administration of justice the Federal contribution is still quite small, particularly in respect to the support it gives the States and cities, which bear most of the load of criminal administration. The present level of Federal support provides only a tiny portion of the resources the States and cities need to put into effect the changes this report recommends. The Commission has considered carefully whether or not the Federal Government should provide more support for such programs. It has concluded that the Federal Government should. In reaching this conclusion it has been persuaded, first, by the fact that crime is a national as well as a State and local, phenomenon; it often does not respect geographical boundaries. The FBI has demonstrated the high mobility of many criminals. Failure of the criminal justice institutions in one State may endanger the citizens of others. The Federal Government has already taken much responsibility in such fields as education and welfare, employment and job training, housing and mental health, which bear directly on crime and its prevention. As President Johnson stated in his 1966 Crime Message to Congress:

Crime does not observe neat, jurisdictional lines between city, State, and Federal Governments. . . . To improve in one field we must improve in all. To improve in one part of the country we must improve in all parts.

Second, simply in terms of economy of effort and of feasibility, there are important needs that individual jurisdictions cannot or should not meet alone. Research is a most important instance. Careful experimentation with and evaluation of police patrol methods, for example, or delinquency prevention programs, means assembling and organizing teams of specialists. They can best be marshaled with the help of the Federal Government. It is also important to make available the sorts of information that every jurisdiction in the Nation needs access to every day: wanted person and stolen property lists, and fingerprint files, for example. Furthermore, the Federal Government can do much to stimulate pooling of resources and services among local jurisdictions.

Third, most local communities today are hard-pressed just to improve their agencies of justice and other facilities at a rate that will meet increases in population and in crime. They cannot spare funds for experimental or innovative programs or plan beyond the emergencies of the day. Federal collaboration can give State and local agencies an opportunity to gain on crime rather than barely stay abreast of it, by making funds, research, and technical assistance available and thereby encouraging changes that in time may make criminal administration more effective and more fair.

The Federal program the Commission visualizes is a large one. During the past fiscal year the Federal Government spent a total of about $20 million on research into crime and delinquency, and another $7 million, under the Law Enforcement Assistance Act, on research and demonstration projects by local agencies of justice. The Commission is not in a position to weigh against each other all the demands for funds that are made upon the Federal Government. And so it cannot recommend the expenditure of a specific number of dollars a year on the program it proposes. However, it does see the program as one on which several hundred million dollars annually could be profitably spent over the next decade. If this report has not conveyed the message that sweeping and costly changes in criminal administration must be made throughout the country in order to effect a significant reduction in crime, then it has not expressed what the Commission strongly believes.

The Commission's final conclusion about a Federal anti-crime program is that the major responsibility for administering it should lie with the Department of Justice, and that the official who administers it for the Attorney General should be a Presidential appointee, with all the status and prestige that inheres in such an office. In the Department of Justice alone among Federal agencies there is a large existing pool of practical knowledge about the police, the courts and the correctional system. The Federal Bureau of Prisons and the Federal Bureau of Investigation, each of which is already expanding its own support of State and local agencies, are parts of the Department of Justice. The Department of Justice has a Criminal Division, one of whose most important sections is concerned with organized crime and racketeering. It has the recently established Office of Criminal Justice, which has concentrated on criminal reform. Many of the research and demonstration portions of the Commission's program are already authorized under the Law Enforcement Assistance Act, which is administered by the Department of Justice. If it is given the money and the men it will need, the Department of Justice can take the lead in the Nation's efforts against crime.

In proposing a major Federal program against crime, the Commission is mindful of the special importance of avoiding any invasion of State and local responsibility for law enforcement and criminal justice, and its recommendation is based on its judgment that Federal support and collaboration of the sort outlined below are consistent with scrupulous respect for —and indeed strengthening of—that responsibility.

THE COMMISSION'S PROGRAM

The program of Federal support that the Commission recommends would meet eight major needs:
(1) State and local planning.
(2) Education and training of criminal justice personnel.
(3) Surveys and advisory services concerning organization and operation of criminal justice agencies.
(4) Development of coordinated national information systems.
(5) Development of a limited number of demonstration programs in agencies of justice.
(6) Scientific and technological research and development.
(7) Institutes for research and training personnel.
(8) Grants-in-aid for operational innovations.

STATE AND LOCAL PLANNING

The Commission believes that the process of State and local planning outlined in the preceding section of this chapter should be a prerequisite for the receipt of Federal support for action programs. It believes further that such planning should itself receive Federal support, and it recommends that planning grants be made available for this purpose. The Department of Justice has already made grants of up to $25,000 to a number of State planning committees formed during the past year. It is clear that planning support in considerably larger amounts will be necessary if States and cities are to conduct a careful assessment of their needs and of ways to meet them.

This report has emphasized many times the critical importance of improved education and training in making the agencies of criminal justice fairer and more effective. The Federal Government is already involved to a limited degree in providing or supporting education and training for some criminal justice personnel. The FBI provides direct training of police officers at its academy in Washington and in the field. The Department of Justice's new Law Enforcement Assistance program has supported police curriculum development and training demonstration projects; the Department of Health, Education, and Welfare has done some research on education and training in the fields of juvenile corrections, mental health and delinquency prevention; and the Department of Labor has recently initiated in a few large cities programs under the Manpower Development and Training Act to help prepare young men from slum areas for police work.

The Commission believes that Federal financial support to provide training and education for State and local criminal justice personnel should be substantially increased. Such support might take several forms. In the field of medicine forgivable loans have been used to help defray the costs of college education and to provide an incentive for further work in the field. Another plan would be to subsidize salary payments to personnel on leave for training or longer study programs, or to their interim replacements. Curriculum development programs like those conducted by the National Science Foundation are also much needed if those from different parts of the criminal justice system are to be jointly instructed in such subjects as, for example, the treatment of juveniles or the problems of parolees.

A seminar for police chiefs, sponsored by the Office of Law Enforcement Assistance and held at the Harvard Business School in the summer of 1966, exposed the chiefs to the methods and insights of modern business administration in a way that they felt was invaluable, and created new interest in the managerial problems of the police among professors at the school. Such advanced programs hold great promise for breaking down the isolation in which many criminal justice agencies now operate.

Some examples of badly needed and promising programs for education and training are:

Police

☐ State police standards commission programs to establish minimum recruitment and training standards, and to provide training, particularly through the establishment of regional academies or programs for medium-and small-size communities.
☐ Graduate training in law and business administration for police executives through degree courses or special institutes.
☐ Curriculum development and training for instructors in police academies and police training programs.
☐ Special training programs in such critical problems as organized crime, riot control, police-community relations, correctional supervision of offenders being treated in the community, the use by police and juvenile court intake personnel of social agencies in the community.
☐ Programs to encourage college education for police in liberal arts and sciences, including scholarship and loan support, and curriculum development to guide college police-science programs away from narrow vocational concentration.

Administration of Justice

☐ Special programs to educate and train judges, prosecutors, and defense counsel for indigents.
☐ Orientation in correctional and noncriminal dispositions for prosecutors and judges.
☐ Training for court administrators.

Corrections

☐ Education and training of rehabilitative personnel, including teachers, counsellors, and mental health personnel.
☐ Training custodial personnel for rehabilitative roles.
☐ Education and orientation of personnel for research and evaluation in experimental treatment methods.

As these examples indicate, it is proposed that Federal aid in this area would be directed toward meeting special needs: Training new types of personnel, developing programs if none now exist, and encouraging the acquisition of advanced skills.

Many criminal justice agencies willing to consider making changes are not sure what their needs are or how their practices compare to the best practice of the field. They need experienced advice about how to put changes into effect. State and local officials whom the Commission has consulted have pointed out that ineffectual administration can negate otherwise promising attempts to increase effectiveness against crime, and have urged that the Federal program help with this problem.

Management studies already have a long history in law enforcement. Organizations like the IACP and the Public Administration Service have conducted them since the 1920's. The Children's Bureau has provided specialized assistance to many of the Nation's juvenile courts. In corrections, the Bureau of Prisons provides increasingly extensive consulting services to local authorities, having recently set up a special office to do so. The Justice Department's new Office of Criminal Justice has been able, with a relatively small amount of explanation and advice, to help stimulate local bail reform efforts. These valuable services have touched but a few of the thousands of agencies that could benefit by surveys and expert advice.

The Commission does not believe that the Federal Government itself should provide the staff to conduct studies or advise the very large number of local agencies that might wish such services. Federal assistance should be aimed instead at developing State or regional bodies with the skills to perform these services. In addition, the Federal Government could contract with private groups to conduct surveys and studies. Advice and studies by expert groups could become a valuable adjunct to the continuing work of State and local planning bodies. For example, they could assist police agencies that desire to reorganize their community relations programs, or correctional agencies seeking to establish halfway houses. In such cases, the studies might be a forerunner to more substantial grant-in-aid support.

INFORMATION SYSTEMS

Another way in which the Federal Government can collaborate with State and local criminal justice systems is by helping to improve the collection and transmission of information needed by the police, courts, and corrections agencies in their day-to-day work. The FBI already makes much important data available to local police agencies from its fingerprint files. The National Crime Information Center, now being developed by the FBI, will provide instantaneous response to computer inquiry by local agencies for information on stolen automobiles, wanted persons, certain identifiable types of stolen property, and the like.

In addition to this "hot" information, data on offenders needed by prosecutors, courts and correctional authorities should be collected and made centrally available. As is further discussed in chapter 11 on science and technology, the goal should be to develop an index drawn from the records of the criminal justice agencies across the country. With such an index a sentencing judge, for example, could learn where information might be found bearing on an offender's response to treatment in other jurisdictions. Disclosure of the information itself would remain, as at present, entirely within the discretion and control of the individual agency that held it. This would help avoid the dangers of developing national "dossiers," but would greatly speed collection of data for making decisions on disposition of cases—a major source of present delays and injustice.

At the State and local levels, enforcement activities against organized crime groups are for the most part nonexistent or primitive, as chapter 7 of this report has shown. A principal need in this field is an effective system for receiving, analyzing, storing, and disseminating intelligence information. Many of organized crime's activities are national in scope, and even its small operations usually spill across city, county, and State lines. If investigators and prosecutors in separate jurisdictions are to make any headway at all against organized crime, they must work together; especially they must share information. There should be within the Department of Justice a computerized, central organized crime intelligence system that handles information from all over the country. This system should be the center of a federally supported network of State and regional intelligence systems, such as those now being developed in New York and in the New England States.

In addition to information needed for operations, there should be available on a centralized basis statistical information on the criminal justice system itself. This is needed for assessing requirements and effectiveness. The FBI's Uniform Crime Reports service should be closely coordinated with this program, which also would include court, probation, prison, and parole statistics on such information as numbers and dispositions of cases, time intervals, and costs. Complementing such data would be special intensive surveys—of crime victims or insurance claims, for example—designed to ascertain more accurately the patterns of crime.

There are at present no centralized crime statistics apart from the UCR, although for many years it has been generally agreed in the field that the absence of information on all aspects of the criminal system has seriously impeded important research. Correlation of comprehensive statistics with surveys and other new methods for analyzing facts about crime is important not only to develop a national picture of crime's seriousness, but to provide a gauge by which police and other agencies can accurately determine the effect of their efforts on the amount of crime. The victimization survey undertaken by the Commission has shown the feasibility and usefulness of such surveys, in combination with UCR data, as the basis for statistical indices as comprehensive as those prepared by the Federal Government in the labor and agricultural fields.

SPECIAL DEMONSTRATION PROJECTS

The Federal administering agency should be authorized to finance in a few places major demonstration projects designed to show all cities and States how much major changes can improve the system of criminal justice. For example, support could be provided to a police force that was prepared, on the basis of an organization study, to make fundamental personnel, management, and operational changes; or to a State or city wishing to plan for entirely new combinations of service between community-based correctional institutions and noncriminal agencies. The demonstration project authorization should also be broad enough to support cooperative programs under which various jurisdictions share needed services, such as police dispatching or short-term detention facilities, or even totally pooled police services.

In the earlier stages of the Federal program, these few major projects could serve as the primary laboratories for research and training, and the experience gained through them would provide a reference point for much of the work done by States and local communities under operational grants-in-aid. Thus, there should be special authorization for the systematic dissemination of the results of demonstration projects and for bringing State and local officials from other areas together to see model programs in operation.

Chapter 11 of this report has shown that the skills and techniques of science and technology, which have so radically altered much of modern life, have been largely untapped by the criminal justice system. One extremely useful approach to innovation is the questioning, analytical, experimental approach of science. Systems analysis, which has contributed significantly to such large-scale government programs as national defense and mass transportation, can be used to study criminal justice operations and to help agency officials choose promising courses of action.

Modern technology can make many specific contributions to criminal administration. The most significant will come from the use of computers to collect and analyze the masses of data the system needs to understand the crime control process. Other important contributions may come, for example, from:

☐ Flexible radio networks and portable two-way radios for patrol officers;
☐ Computer assisted command-and-control systems for rapid and efficient dispatching of patrol forces;
☐ Advanced fingerprint recognition systems;
☐ Innovations for the police patrol car such as mobile teletypewriters, tape recorders for recording questioning, and automatic car position locators;
☐ Alarms and surveillance systems for homes, businesses and prisons;
☐ Criminalistics techniques such as voice prints, neutron activation analysis and other modern laboratory instrumentation.

The Federal Government must take the lead in the effort to focus the capabilities of science and technology on the criminal justice system.

It can sponsor and support a continuing research and development program on a scale greater than any individual agency could undertake alone. Such a program will benefit all agencies.

It should stimulate the industrial development, at reasonable prices, of the kinds of equipment all agencies need. A useful technique might be to guarantee the sale of first production runs.

It should provide funds that will enable criminal justice

agencies to hire technically trained people and to establish internal operations research units.

It should support scientific research into criminal administration that uses the agencies as real-life laboratories.

RESEARCH

The need for research of all kinds has been discussed in chapter 12. There should be Federal support for specific research projects by individual scholars, and by universities or research organizations. In many instances such projects should be carried out in conjunction with large police departments, correctional institutions, or other operating agencies. In addition to such project grants, the Commission believes the Federal Government should provide support for a number of institutes specifically dedicated to research into crime and criminal justice. Such institutes would bring together top scholars from the social and natural sciences, law, social work, business administration and psychiatry, and would be able to deal with the criminal justice system, from prevention to corrections, as a whole. Presumably most of these research institutes would be located at universities, although, as noted in chapter 12, one or more might be independent.

These institutes would serve as the foundation for the other parts of the Federal program described here, both in the substance of the research they undertook and in the availability of their staff members as top-level consultants. They could provide training, through special seminars or degree courses, for senior administrators and specialist personnel. They could undertake studies of the effectiveness of various education and training programs. They could provide much of the data needed to conduct organization and operations studies, and seek and test new techniques for implementation. They could take major responsibility for analyzing data developed by the national information systems and they would propose and evaluate important new demonstration programs and provide consulting services.

GRANT-IN-AID SUPPORT FOR NEW PROGRAMS

In addition to the forms of support described above, a major part of the Federal program should be grants-in-aid for a broad range of innovative State and local programs. The standards of this part of the program should preclude continuing support for such normal operational expenses as those for basic personnel compensation, routine equipment like police cars, or replacement of physical facilities like jails and courthouses. Support would instead be given to major innovations in operations, including especially the coordination of services among the parts of the system of criminal administration and among agencies in different jurisdictions.

The possibilities for such programs are as wide as the range of innovations State and local authorities propose to undertake. They might include:

☐ New police operations such as the storefront Community Service Officer program; sophisticated communications equipment; and regional laboratory facilities.
☐ Construction and operation of new corrections facilities to serve as a nucleus for community-based programs.
☐ Temporary salary support for new specialized personnel, such as computer experts, court management specialists, and classification or treatment experts for correctional facilities.

The Commission is confident that this eight-point program, if fully implemented, will do much to bring crime under control.

WHAT CITIZENS AND THEIR ORGANIZATIONS CAN DO

Given enough time and money, specialists can do dramatic things. They can prolong human life. They can make deserts bloom. They can split the atom. They can put men on the moon. However, specialists alone cannot control crime. Crime is a social problem that is interwoven with almost every aspect of American life; controlling it involves changing the way schools are run and classes are taught, the way cities are planned and houses are built, the way businesses are managed and workers are hired. Crime is a kind of human behavior; controlling it means changing the minds and hearts of men. Controlling crime is the business of every American institution. Controlling crime is the business of every American.

HOW INDIVIDUALS CAN HELP TO REDUCE CRIME

That every American should cooperate fully with officers of justice is obvious. The police cannot solve crimes that are not reported to them; the courts cannot administer justice fairly and surely if citizens will not serve as witnesses and jurors. In an earlier society the peace was kept, for the most part, not by officials but by the whole community. Constables were citizens who served their community in turn and magistrates were local squires. That society no longer exists except, perhaps, in a few remote rural areas. But the complexity and anonymity of modern urban life, the existence of professional police forces and other institutions whose official duty it is to deal with crime, must not disguise the need—far greater today than in the village societies of the past—for citizens to report all crimes or suspicious incidents immediately; to cooperate with police investigations of crime; in short, to "get involved."

The Chicago Police Department has had much success with "Operation Crime-Stop," a formal campaign to involve citizens. A special police emergency number that connects callers directly to a dispatcher has been established and widely publicized. Citizens are urged to report suspicious occurrences and are given official commendation when they do report or help the police in other ways. Washington, D.C., and several other cities have similar programs. In some cities taxi drivers and other citizens with radios in their vehicles are organized to assist the police by transmitting information useful in apprehending offenders. Under some State statutes active concealment of a felony is itself an offense as it was at common law. Even if there are no special programs or penalties, every citizen should recognize that he is duty bound to assist the police.

People can do much to insure their own safety and that of their families and belongings by reducing the opportunities for crime. Many crimes would not occur if individuals had proper locks on their doors and windows and enough lighting to discourage prowlers, and if they took such simple preventive action as not letting newspapers or milk bottles accumulate as a sign that a house is unoccupied. Keys left in the ignition or an unlocked ignition account for more than 42 percent of the cars that are stolen.

The citizen's responsibility runs far deeper than cooperating with officials and guarding against crime, of course. Much more important is a proper respect for the law and for its official representatives. People who sneer at policemen; people who "cut corners" in their tax returns; landlords who violate housing codes; parents who set bad examples by their own disrespect for the law, or who wink at their children's minor offenses, contribute to crime. Delinquents—and adult criminals as well—often try to justify their actions by saying

643

that the only difference between them and "respectable citizens" is that they were unlucky enough to be caught.

PARTICIPATION BY INDUSTRY, RELIGIOUS INSTITUTIONS, AND OTHER PRIVATE GROUPS

As members of groups and organizations outside the official agencies of justice, citizens can play even a greater part than they can as individuals in helping to reduce crime. Private businesses, welfare agencies and foundations, civic organizations, and universities can contribute much toward impelling official agencies to reform themselves and toward helping them do it. There are some impressive examples of what such groups can do when they turn their attention to crime.

In Chicago and New York the YMCA and other agencies supported by contributions pioneered the concept of "detached workers" for juvenile gangs. Research projects conducted by the Vera Institute of Justice in New York sparked the bail reform movement, and the Institute is now exploring new ways of handling drunks. Law schools and bar associations have led the development of legal aid and defender programs. Church groups in St. Louis and Chicago opened the first halfway houses for released prisoners. The student service organization at Harvard University was one of the first groups to run regular programs to teach prison inmates. Such projects indicate that private groups have a growing interest and involvement in crime problems, but they still do far less about crime than about such matters as health, education or recreation.

BUSINESS, INDUSTRY, AND LABOR UNIONS

Business and industry are in a particularly favorable position to help the criminal justice system. They have the financial and technical resources that are essential both for developing new equipment to modernize law enforcement and justice, and for devising means to protect against crime. The jobs they can provide can do much to prevent delinquency and reintegrate offenders into society.

The Commission's task force on science and technology explored a number of the important ways in which industry might apply technological innovations to protecting lives and property from crime. It discussed with the automobile industry, for example, such new ways to combat auto theft as ignitions that buzz when a key is left in a turned-off lock, or expel the key; special shielding around ignition cables to prevent "jumping"; and steering column or transmission locks. Automobile manufacturers have already assured the Commission that they will incorporate such devices in future models.

The same sort of effort is needed on such problems as making alarm systems less expensive and less susceptible to false alarms. Alteration of telephone equipment to permit free dialing to the police from public telephones, adoption of a uniform police number, and development of equipment that would automatically record the location from which the call is made are other examples of how private business could contribute to reducing crime.

There are several noteworthy recent examples of successful programs in which business, industry and organized labor have collaborated with correctional authorities. For example, at the Federal penitentiary at Danbury, Conn., the Dictograph Corp. trains in the penitentiary and then employs, on work release or parole, microsoldering technicians for hearing aid manufacture; IBM trains key punch operators, programers and systems analysts, hiring some itself while others are employed elsewhere; and the International Ladies' Garment Workers' Union has established a program to train sewing machine repairmen on machines furnished by several local companies, and provides a card to graduates enabling them to find employment upon release.

The experience of the Bureau of Prisons with these programs indicates that there is a vast, largely untapped willingness on the part of business and labor to cooperate in employment programs in corrections. This bodes well for the success of the growing number of work-release programs in various States, and represents an encouraging change from industry's and labor's traditional hostility toward prison industries, expressed in restrictive State and Federal laws on prison industry activities. If employers overcome their reluctance to hire and unions to admit persons with arrest or conviction records, and if irrational prohibitions on licensing such persons for occupations and trades are removed, correctional agencies will have much more chance to succeed in their task.

The cooperation of business and labor is also essential to make jobs available to young people from slum areas and to help give them the skills and attitudes necessary for successful integration into working life. Several companies have run programs for the Job Corps; many more have provided jobs through the Neighborhood Youth Corps and the Youth Opportunity Centers, programs of the Department of Labor. But here, as with employment of offenders, much more can be done through less formal, entirely private initiative. Chambers of commerce, labor union locals, and service clubs are logical bases for community programs to advise young people about employment and place them in jobs.

Individual employers, too, can contribute substantially to crime prevention through special programs to train and hire young people who have had some trouble with the law. There are obvious risks, though many can be offset through bonding —arranged perhaps with Government guarantees. However much recruitment, training, and employment programs for delinquents and ex-convicts may cost, the price cannot possibly be as great as that paid for the almost total failure, up to now, to bring criminals and potential criminals back into the working world.

PRIVATE AGENCIES AND FOUNDATIONS

Private social service agencies and foundations, concerned with counseling, health and welfare aid, have long carried major responsibility for delinquency prevention. Professional associations such as the International Association of Chiefs of Police, the National Council on Crime and Delinquency, the ABA and local bar associations, the American Law Institute, and others have led for many years the attempt to raise standards and rationalize the criminal justice system. In recent years a number of private organizations like the Ford Foundation have supported research and demonstration projects in various parts of the criminal area, bridging the gap between agencies active in the field and those that concentrate on planning and standard setting. Work of all these sorts is vitally necessary for comprehensive progress in reducing crime. Private groups can identify needs and problems that have not been officially recognized and undertake programs that would be too experimental or controversial for public agencies.

There are, of course, distinct discouragements to work by private social agencies in the criminal area. Usually progress is very difficult to achieve. Those who need to be helped are often hostile, sometimes dangerous, and seldom promise to be truly outstanding citizens even if rehabilitated.

It is not surprising, then, that most private agencies, with very limited resources, have concentrated on serving persons whose problems are less intractable than those of the delinquent or criminal. But the extent to which official agencies, even some antipoverty programs, continue to shun people with criminal records emphasizes the importance of attention to the criminal area by private agencies that can better afford than official ones to risk the failures that are a necessary consequence of experimental work.

RELIGIOUS INSTITUTIONS

The important contribution churches, synagogues, and other religious institutions can make to crime prevention is evident. They are leading exponents and guardians of the community's moral and ethical standards. They have the ability to understand and teach in their largest context the great principles of honesty and honor, of compassion and charity, of respect and reverence that underlie not only the Nation's laws but its entire being. They have the power to move men's spirits and sway their minds.

They have the power, too, to do many practical things. Many religious institutions have. Inner-city churches have done valuable work with youth gangs and released offenders. A particularly noteworthy contribution has been made by the Faith Opportunities Project of the Chicago Conference on Religion and Race. This project, partially financed by the Office of Economic Opportunity, makes a point of finding deserting fathers, particularly those who have deserted because they are unemployed, finding them jobs, and returning them to their families. During one 6-month period 2,500 families were reunited, and 89 percent of them remained that way for at least 90 days.

COMMUNITY AND PROFESSIONAL ORGANIZATIONS

The most dramatic example in the country of a 'citizens' group that has addressed itself forcefully and successfully to the problems of crime and criminal justice is the Anti-Crime Crusade in Indianapolis. In 1962, the day after a 90-year-old woman had been hit on the head and robbed on the street, 30 Indianapolis women, representing a cross section of the community, met to devise ways of making the streets safer. The organization, which has no dues, no membership cards, no minutes and no bylaws, now involves some 50,000 women, in 14 divisions. It has stimulated the city to improve street lighting. It has secured jobs for young people, helped school dropouts return to school, involved thousands of adolescents in volunteer work for social service agencies and clinics. It has organized campaigns for cleaning up the slums. It has sponsored police recruits. It has observed the operation of the courts and publicized their shortcomings. It has helped parole officers with their work. It has campaigned for pay raises for policemen and formed block clubs to improve slum neighborhoods. This list is only a random selection of the crusade's activities, and only an indication of what concerned citizens can do.

Every group in a community can do something about crime or criminal justice. PTA's and other school groups, for example, could concentrate on the school's role in delinquency prevention and reintegration of offenders; volunteer parents could promote closer contact with slum parents, lead field trips and other activities to compensate for culturally deprived backgrounds, tutor in remedial work, and serve as teacher aides. Suburban groups might pair with those in the inner city for such projects. Hospitals could join together to institute narcotics programs and treatment centers for drunkenness offenders. Businessmen's groups would be well suited to conducting employment programs. Neighborhood clubs and settlement houses have set up recreation programs and a wide range of other services. All of these efforts must be greatly strengthened, an endeavor that will require increased financial support by government and private foundations.

Bar associations and other professional groups have an important role in encouraging legislatures and official agencies to implement changes such as those recommended by this report. A special bar association group in Illinois, for example, drew up that State's pioneering new criminal code. The IACP has been active in promoting police standards and training councils. The National Council of Juvenile Court Judges has promoted reforms in juvenile justice. The American Bar Foundation is now publishing a series of volumes reflecting an intensive 10-year study of law enforcement and criminal justice in three States, most of it completely new and of great importance.

COLLEGES AND UNIVERSITIES

Higher education has played an uneven part in criminal justice. A few law schools have engaged for years in research, and in representation of indigent defenders; their professors have been responsible for a major share of modern criminal legislation and much of the informed criticism of the criminal process. On the other hand, until recently little emphasis was given to preparing students to practice criminal law. Universities like the University of California at Berkeley and Michigan State University have had police science departments for several decades, but they have existed too much in isolation from the rest of the academic community. The same thing is to a large extent true of teaching and research in the corrections field.

All operating agencies of justice urgently need the close contact with academic thought that could be achieved through use of faculty consultants; seminars and institutes to analyze current problems and innovations; advanced training programs for judges, police administrators, and correctional officers; and more operational research projects and surveys conducted in conjunction with agencies of justice.

CONCLUSION

At its end, as at its beginning, this report on crime and criminal justice in America must insist that there are no easy answers. The complexity and the magnitude of the task of controlling crime and improving criminal justice is indicated by the more than 200 specific recommendations for action, and the many hundreds of suggestions for action, that this report contains. These recommendations and suggestions are addressed to cities, to States, to the Federal Government; to individual citizens, and their organizations; to policemen, to prosecutors, to judges, to correctional authorities, and to the agencies for which these officials work. Taken together these recommendations and suggestions express the Commission's deep conviction that if America is to meet the challenge of crime it must do more, far more, than it is doing now. It must welcome new ideas and risk new actions. It must spend time and money. It must resist those who point to scapegoats, who use facile slogans about crime by habit or for selfish ends. It must recognize that the government of a free society is obliged to act not only effectively but fairly. It must seek knowledge and admit mistakes.

Controlling crime in America is an endeavor that will be slow and hard and costly. But America can control crime if it will.

Table of Recommendations

CRIME IN AMERICA—CHAPTER 2

The Commission's study of the nature, volume, and trends of crime in America reveals at many points the need to develop additional and improved information and understanding about crime. To assist each city administration and agency of justice in insuring that its citizens are being informed of the full rate of crime in their community, the Commission recommends that cities and police departments that have not already done so adopt centralized procedures for handling reports of crime from citizens and establish the staff controls necessary to make such procedures effective. To promote a clearer public understanding of the differences between crimes of violence and property crimes, the Commission recommends that the trend in the FBI's Uniform Crime Reports toward separate treatment of these crime categories be carried further and that the present Index of reported crime be broken into wholly two separate parts.

JUVENILE DELINQUENCY AND YOUTH CRIME—CHAPTER 3

The most effective way to prevent crime is to assure all citizens full opportunity to participate in the benefits and responsibilities of society. Especially in inner cities, achievement of this goal will require extensive overhauling and strengthening of the social institutions influential in making young people strong members of the community—schools, employment, the family, religious institutions, housing, welfare, and others. Careful planning and evaluation and enormous increases in money and personnel are needed to expand existing programs of promise and to develop additional approaches.

Such efforts are especially crucial for those youths, now too often overlooked, who have already demonstrated delinquent tendencies. The community must not wait until such tendencies manifest themselves in serious criminal acts. Measures short of formal adjudication can help such youths find their way to appropriate assistance programs, and minimize the reinforcing and stigmatizing effects of full criminal treatment. For this purpose Youth Services Bureaus should be established to coordinate and provide needed programs. The bureaus should accept both delinquents and nondelinquents but devote special resources to intensive treatment of delinquents.

The formal juvenile justice system should concentrate on those cases in which a need for coercive court authority has been demonstrated. Proceedings in these more serious cases must be characterized by safeguards commonly accepted as necessary to protect persons subject to coercive state authority, including counsel, confrontation of complainants, and exclusion of improper evidence. At all stages in the juvenile justice system, there is need for greater clarification and regularization in the exercise of discretion. Detention pending court determination, for example, must be based on clearly articulated standards and reduced to a minimum. The police in their dealings with juveniles should attempt to divert cases from the criminal process wherever appropriate and without coercive stationhouse adjustment procedures. In exercising discretion the police should also observe the most scrupulous standards of procedural fairness and personal impartiality.

Housing and Recreation

Families

Involving Youths in Community Life

Schools

Employment

The Juvenile Justice System

POLICE—CHAPTER 4

Widespread improvement in the strength and caliber of police manpower, supported by a radical revision of personnel practices, are the basic essentials for achieving more effective and fairer law enforcement. Educational requirements should be raised to college levels and training programs improved. Recruitment and promotion should be modernized to reflect education, personality, and assessment of performance. The traditional, monolithic personnel structure must be broken up into three entry levels of varying responsibility and with different personnel requirements, and lateral entry into advanced positions encouraged.

The need is urgent for the police to improve relations with the poor, minority groups, and juveniles. The establishment of strong community relations programs, review of all procedures in light of their effect on community relations, recruitment of more minority group members, and strengthening of community confidence in supervision and discipline, all aim at making the police more effective in high-crime areas. Increased effectiveness also requires that law enforcement improve its facilities and techniques of management—particularly that it utilize manpower more efficiently, modernize communications and records, and formulate more explicit policy guidelines governing areas of police discretion. The pooling of services and functions by police forces in each metropolitan area can improve efficiency and effectiveness.

Community Relations

Personnel

Organization and Operations

COURTS—CHAPTER 5

A number of important reforms are necessary to enable courts to operate with the dignity and effectiveness many now lack. Substantial changes in the processing of criminal cases and increases in the number and caliber of judges, lawyers and administrators are essential to fairer and more effective justice. To rationalize procedures in the crucial and often neglected pretrial stage, bail practices must be reformed; guilty plea negotiation regularized; and discovery expanded. Early diversion of appropriate cases to noncriminal treatment should be encouraged. Sentencing reforms—such as revision of criminal codes, improved fact-gathering, sentencing councils and institutes for judges—are needed to promote consistent and informed decisions.

The right of defendants to counsel must be extended and defense counsel's role broadened. Improvements must be made in the methods used to select, compensate, and educate counsel. Better procedures are needed to remove judges from political influence and supervise their performance. Several Commission recommendations are aimed at strengthening prosecutors' offices, and encouraging better formation of policy guidelines and procedures for the exercise of discretion. State governments should take a more vigorous role in coordinating local prosecution through stronger State attorneys general and the creation of State councils of prosecutors.

Court structures should be reformed to unify felony and

misdemeanor courts, overhaul or abolish the justice of the peace system, and provide firm, central administrative responsibility within the courts. The procedures used by the courts to monitor and schedule their work should be modernized and professional talent brought to the administration of courts.

The Lower Courts

Initial Stages of a Criminal Case

Court Proceedings

Sentencing Policies and Procedures

CORRECTIONS—CHAPTER 6

The wholesale strengthening of community treatment of
offenders and much greater commitment of resources to their
rehabilitation are the main lines where action is needed to
make correctional treatment more effective in reducing recidivism. Correctional programs of the future should be built
around small centers, located in the communities they serve.
These would be better suited than present facilities for flexible treatment, combining the short-term commitment sufficient for most offenders with a variety of partial release or
community corrections programs in which job training, educational, and counseling services would be provided or coordinated by the center's staff. Careful screening and classification of offenders is essential so that handling can be individualized to suit the needs in each case. So, too, is greater emphasis on evaluation of the effect of various programs on different offenders.

Much can be done to advance corrections toward such

goals with existing facilities, but large increases in skilled diagnostic, rehabilitation, and research personnel are needed immediately. A new regime should be inaugurated in institutions to involve all staff, and encourage inmates to collaborate as much as possible, in rehabilitation. Prison industries must give more meaningful work experience. Counseling, education, and vocational training programs for inmates must be strengthened. Greater use should be made of release for work and education, of halfway houses, and of similar programs to ease the offender's reintegration in society.

Community-Based Corrections

Correctional Institutions

Correctional Decisionmaking

Research and Training

ORGANIZED CRIME—CHAPTER 7

Success in combating organized crime will require a greater
commitment of resources and imagination at all levels of government, directed toward investigation and prosecution and
also toward attacking criminal syndicates through regulatory
laws. A coordinated network of investigative and prosecutive
units is needed, provided with legal tools necessary for gathering evidence—including investigating grand juries and the
power to grant witnesses immunity. Investigation must be
carried out with a broader focus than merely the prosecution
of individual cases; research for building longer range plans
should draw on sociologists, economists, and experts from
other disciplines.

Proof of Criminal Violations

Investigation and Prosecution Units

Noncriminal Controls

NARCOTICS AND DRUG ABUSE—CHAPTER 8

The growing problem of narcotics and drug abuse in this country must be attacked by strengthening all approaches: Law enforcement, rehabilitation and treatment of drug users, and public education on the dangers involved. This is partly a matter of increased resources, such as for customs control; for the Bureau of Narcotics (especially to strengthen its long-range intelligence); and for expansion of treatment. There is also need for intensified research, and for careful implementation, evaluation, and coordination of the many new and promising programs for control.

Enforcement

Research and Education

DRUNKENNESS—CHAPTER 9

Present efforts to find alternatives to treatment of drunkenness within the criminal system should be pursued vigorously. One of the most promising possibilities is the construction of detoxification centers with medical services and therapy for short-term detention. A network of aftercare facilities and services should also be established to which referrals could be made after diagnosis at a detoxification center.

CONTROL OF FIREARMS—CHAPTER 10

The increasing violence in the Nation demands that governments at all levels strengthen control of possession and sale of the firearms that contribute to that violence. Additional laws requiring registration of firearms and permits for those who possess or carry them, prohibiting their sale to and possession by certain potentially dangerous persons, and preventing transportation and sale of military-type weapons are needed. Such restrictions would not need to interfere with legitimate sporting or antique collecting interests.

SCIENCE AND TECHNOLOGY—CHAPTER 11

The potential contributions of science and technology in the field of law enforcement and criminal justice have scarcely been tapped; a strong research program to develop them is necessary. This program should be initiated through Federal support. It should cover both basic research studies and systems analysis, and development of specific technological innovations. The Commission's task force on science and technology explored a number of specific areas where science might make a contribution, particularly in increasing law enforcement effectiveness. It found a number of lines for improving police response-time for apprehension of criminals. Coordinated information systems covering immediate-response inquiries, law enforcement criminal records information, and statistics on criminal justice agency operations should be established.

Police Operations

Court Operations

Correctional Operations

RESEARCH—CHAPTER 12

Expanded research is essential for preventing crime and improving the effectiveness of criminal justice. It must be conducted by operating agencies; universities, foundations, and research corporations; private industry; and government institutes. It must attempt a more complete assessment of the volume, nature, and causes of crime. It must look more carefully at the way the criminal justice system operates. Change need not wait upon the gaining of such knowledge; only through innovation and evaluation of operations can most of it be obtained.

A NATIONAL STRATEGY—CHAPTER 13

The Commission's recommendations must be implemented through a strategy for change involving all levels of government, private groups, and every American citizen. Control of crime requires three very basic emphases: Preventing delinquency before it ever becomes a matter for the criminal justice system to deal with; providing the agencies of justice with adequate resources; and pushing forward the search for better knowledge about crime and how best to handle it.

Control of crime and improvement of criminal justice are basically State and local concerns. Governments at this level must begin by planning the changes needed: gathering facts, setting priorities, and mobilizing resources needed for action. But legislatures—and the public—must also be willing to spend a great deal more to secure safety and justice. And officials and citizens must be willing to undertake often difficult reforms. The role of the Federal Government must be to lead and coordinate change through providing financial and technical assistance and support of research. Private groups and individuals can join in—indeed lead—the process of change, through activities ranging from doing volunteer work to employing released offenders. And the support of every citizen is crucial to all other progress in controlling crime.

Additional Views of Individual Commission Members

ADDITIONAL VIEWS OF MISS BLATT

*". . . Godlessness as a basic cause of
crime and religion as a basic cure . . ."*

Thorough as the Commission's studies have been and comprehensive as its valuable recommendations are, its report seems deficient to me in that it neglects to recognize godlessness as a basic cause of crime and religion as a basic cure.

The report acknowledges the necessity for activating religious institutions in the war on crime, and it mentions some of the excellent work religious groups have done in youth work and along similar lines.

But nowhere does the report mention the Ten Commandments which underlie our Judaeo-Christian culture. Nor does it mention the God who created all of us, who gave us the Ten Commandments, who enforces a law higher than ours and who administers the ultimate justice.

Admittedly, it would not be within the province of the Commission to recommend how to combat the godlessness so prevalent today and so basically at the root of so much of our crime problem. Nor could the Commission properly outline how religion, as a moral force distinct from an institutional group, could help control crime.

But just as the report recognizes the obvious relationship of poverty and ignorance and discrimination to an increasing crime rate, it should recognize that man's alienation from his God has also been a crime-inducing factor.

It is true that the all too frequent unwillingness of many religious groups and of many presumably religious individuals to live by and not just to profess the moral precepts common to all religions has all too frequently blunted the effectiveness of religion in preventing crime. Nevertheless, properly used, religion is a real weapon. In my personal opinion, it is the best weapon. And it should be used.

My feeling is that we unquestionably should, as the Commission suggests, improve family life and the school system and every other human institution. In so doing we will undoubtedly help prevent crime.

To do these things, however, without renewing and revitalizing religious life, won't be enough.

Somehow or other we must restore to every citizen's everyday living that same belief in God's love and justice which was characteristic of our countrymen in an earlier and less crime-ridden period of our history.

We were a God-fearing people at one time, and proud of it. We must be that again if we expect to see the crime rate substantially reduced.

ADDITIONAL VIEWS OF DR. BREWSTER, JUDGE BREITEL, MRS. STUART, AND MR. YOUNG

Despite our strong feelings that the Commission and its staff have done an outstanding job in a very limited period of time with some of the most difficult problems that our Nation faces, we feel compelled to note that the Commission has not confronted many major unanswered questions about narcotics and dangerous drugs. This is one field in which an open-minded, questioning inquiry is necessary. This is one field in which reliance upon assumptions, emotional biases, and the acceptance of traditional viewpoints is most dangerous. Many persons concerned with the problem have for years been questioning whether the criminalization of narcotics and marihuana distribution has not served to defeat the objective of controlling and perhaps eliminating drug abuse and the crime associated with it. The gnawing question to which there has never been a satisfactory answer is whether this policy of criminalization, which raises the cost and increases the difficulty of obtaining drugs, does in fact make the drug user a proselytizer of others in order that he may obtain the funds to acquire his own drugs. There is also the unusually difficult question of whether the compulsion of the addict to obtain drugs and the moneys to purchase them causes him to commit collateral crime that otherwise he might not commit.

In this important area the Commission has been unable to face the fundamental questions. Instead, for reasons that are quite understandable but in our view not justifiable, it assumes that the laws and the traditional methods of enforcement which have obtained for over 50 years, are the only proper ways in which to meet the problem. It makes this assumption at a time when the use of narcotics and other drugs may have become intensified, and all of the moral, economic, and criminal law problems associated with these vices may be greater than ever.

That the Commission and its staff were capable of open-minded imaginative analysis in other difficult areas is demonstrated by the way the report deals with such matters as the assessment of crime and the application of scientific thinking and methods to solving problems of criminal justice. These successes, and the objective analysis of the operations of criminal justice agencies generally, make all the more contrasting the Commission's failure to have the staff explore an equally new approach to narcotics and drugs. There is no field in which the problems and failures frighten Americans more.

We recognize that there were practical limitations, apart from the short time the Commission was given to do its work. It is not easy to question the views of the many National and State law enforcement agencies of high quality and experience, which have been struggling heroically with the problem along traditional lines for over a half century. It is also difficult to attempt to raise anew questions that were, or should have been, explored by another Presidential commission limited to this problem, which concluded its work only 3 years ago. It is particularly difficult to remove from one's own mind and from the minds of others the idea that, because there is correlation of events, one must be the cause of the other. But the fact—the obvious fact—that so many criminals are also users of narcotics or marihuana, and that there has been an escalation in the use and the amount and kind of drugs, does not necessarily mean that drug abuse is a cause of crime. It is difficult to persuade people that they should at least consider whether both are simply the effects of common causes—that delinquents resort both to drugs and to crime for more deep-seated reasons than that the one causes the other.

We feel impelled to make these remarks because, while we do not know the answers or have the data to disprove what

667

we believe to be the unproven presuppositions of the traditional approach, we are convinced that the time must come when this Nation will have to consider from entirely new and unbiased viewpoints the associated but distinguishable problems involving narcotics, marihauna, hallucinogens, and other dangerous drugs. The time will come when we will have to determine causal relations and consider the possibility that traditional methods of law enforcement produce more rather than less crime, particularly of a collateral character. We have done as much in providing new approaches in the field of corrections and, more recently, in the field of bail reform. We first questioned and then proved that traditional approaches were producing exactly the reverse of what had been the design. The present report is so hospitable to the broadest kind of research that we can hope that there will be opportunity to reevaluate the present bases of our drug laws.

ADDITIONAL VIEWS OF MESSRS. JAWORSKI, MALONE, POWELL, AND STOREY

We have joined our fellow members of the Commission in this report and in commending it to the American people. This supplemental statement is submitted in support of the report for the purpose of opening up for discussion—and perhaps for further study and action—areas which were not considered explicitly in the report itself. These relate to the difficult and perplexing problems arising from certain of the constitutional limitations upon our system of criminal justice.

CONSTITUTIONAL LIMITATIONS

The limitations with which we are primarily concerned arise from the Fifth and Sixth Amendments to the Constitution of the United States as they have been interpreted by the Supreme Court in recent years. The rights guaranteed by these amendments, and other provisions of the Bill of Rights, are dear to all Americans and long have been recognized as cornerstones of a system deliberately designed to protect the individual from oppressive government action. As they apply to persons accused of crime, they extend equally to the accused whether he is innocent or guilty. It is fundamental in our concept of the Constitution that these basic rights shall be protected whether or not this sometimes results in the acquittal of the guilty.

We do not suggest a departure from these underlying principles. But there is a serious question, now being increasingly posed by jurists and scholars,[1] whether some of these rights have been interpreted and enlarged by Court decision to the point where they now seriously affect the delicate balance between the rights of the individual and those of society. Or, putting the question differently, whether the scales have tilted in favor of the accused and against law enforcement and the public further than the best interest of the country permits.

It is concern with this question which prompts us to express these additional views. As the people of our country must ultimately decide where this balance is to be struck, it is important to encourage a wider understanding of the problem and its implications.

In 1963 Chief Judge Lumbard of the Court of Appeals of the Second Circuit warned:

*[W]e are in danger of a grievous imbalance in the administration of criminal justice * * *.*

In the past forty years there have been two distinct trends in the administration of criminal justice. The first has been to strengthen the rights of the individual; and the second, which is perhaps a corollary of the first, is to limit the powers of law enforcement agencies. Most of us would agree that the development of individual rights was long overdue; most of us would agree that there should be further clarification of individual rights, particularly for indigent defendants. At the same time we must face the facts about indifferent and faltering law enforcement in this country. We must adopt measures which will give enforcement agencies proper means for doing their jobs. In my opinion, these two efforts must go forward simultaneously.[2]

The trends referred to by Judge Lumbard have had their major impact upon law enforcement since 1961 as a result of far-reaching decisions of the Supreme Court which have indeed effected a "revolution in state criminal procedure."[3]

[1] See Friendly, *The Bill of Rights as a Code of Criminal Procedure*, 53 Calif. L. Rev. 929 (1965); Schaefer, *Police Interrogation and the Privilege Against Self-Incrimination*, 61 Nw. U.L. Rev. 506 (1966); Traynor, *The Devils of Due Process in Criminal Detection, Detention and Trial*, 33 U. Chi. L. Rev. 657 (1966).

[2] Lumbard, *The Administration of Criminal Justice: Some Problems and Their Resolution*, 49 A.B.A.J. 840 (1963). Judge Lumbard is chairman of the American Bar Association's Criminal Justice Project.

[3] George, *Constitutional Limitations on Evidence in Criminal Cases* 3 (1966).

The strong emotions engendered by these decisions, for and against both them and the Court, have inhibited rational discourse as to their actual effect upon law enforcement. There has been unfair—and even destructive—criticism of the Court itself. Many have failed to draw the line, fundamental in a democratic society, between the right to discuss and analyze the effect of particular decisions, and the duty to support and defend the judiciary, and particularly the Supreme Court, as an institution essential to freedom. Moreover, during the early period of the Court's restraint with respect to State action, there were many examples of gross injustice in the State courts and of indefensible inaction on the part of State legislatures. In short, there was often a pressing need for action due to neglect elsewhere, and many of the great decisions undoubtedly brought on by such neglect have been warmly welcomed.

Whatever the reason, the trend of decisions strikingly has been towards strengthening the rights of accused persons and limiting the powers of law enforcement. It is a trend which has accelerated rapidly at a time when the nation is deeply concerned with its apparent inability to deal successfully with the problem of crime. We think the results must be taken into account in any mobilization of society's resources to confront this problem.

THE ACCUSATORY SYSTEM

In any attempt to assess the effect of this trend upon law enforcement it is necessary to keep in mind the essential characteristics of our criminal system. Unlike systems in many civilized countries, ours is "accusatory" in the sense that innocence is presumed and the burden lies on the State to prove in a public trial the guilt of the accused beyond reasonable doubt. The accused has the right to a jury trial, and —in most if not all States—the added protection that a guilty verdict must be unanimous.

Other characteristics which have marked our system include the requirements of probable cause for arrest, prompt arraignment before a judicial officer, indictment or presentment to a grand jury, confrontation with accusors and witnesses, reasonable bail, the limitation on unreasonable searches and seizures, and habeas corpus.

Argument and controversy have swirled around the interpretation and application of many of these rights. The drawing of a line between the obvious need for police to have reasonable time to investigate and the right of an accused to a prompt arraignment occasioned one of the most intense controversies.[4]

There also has been serious dissatisfaction with the abuse of habeas corpus and especially the flood of petitions resulting from decisions broadening the power of Federal courts to review alleged denials of constitutional rights in State courts.[5] No other country affords convicted persons such elaborate and multiple opportunities for reconsideration of adjudication of guilt.[6]

Another constitutional limitation, affecting criminal trials and now being increasingly questioned,[7] requires that a conviction be set aside automatically whenever material evidence obtained in violation of the Bill of Rights was received at the trial. The purpose of the rule is not related to relevance, truth or reliability, for the evidence in question may in fact be the most relevant and reliable that possibly could be obtained. Rather, the reason assigned for the peremptory exclusion is that there is no other effective method of deterring improper action by law enforcement personnel.

ESCOBEDO AND MIRANDA

But the broadened rights and resulting restraints upon law enforcement which have had the greatest impact are those derived from the Fifth Amendment privilege against self-incrimination and the Sixth Amendment assurance of counsel.

The two cases which have caused the greatest concern are *Escobedo* v. *Illinois* [8] and *Miranda* v. *Arizona.* [9] In *Miranda*

[4] See *Mallory* v. *United States,* 354 U.S. 449 (1957).

[5] *Fay* v. *Noia,* 372 U.S. 391 (1963); *Townsend* v. *Sain,* 372 U.S. 293 (1963). In 1941 fiscal year there were only 127 petitions; by 1961 there were 984. The number escalated to 3,531 in 1964; during the first 6 months of fiscal 1965 there were 2,460 applications (an increase of 32.7 percent over the previous 6 months' period). See 90 A.B.A. Rep. 463 (1965). The *Townsend* case, to take one dreary example, was in the courts for more than 10 years after conviction of the defendant, with 6½ years being consumed in various habeas corpus proceedings. The great majority of these petitions are not meritrious. See Ibid.

[6] The Commission's report, ch. 5, contains helpful recommendations as to what the States can do to minimize frivolous habeas corpus petitions.

[7] See Friendly, *supra* at 951–53.

[8] 378 U.S. 478 (1964).

[9] 384 U.S. 436 (1966).

the requirements were imposed that a suspect detained by the police be warned not only of his right to remain silent and that any statement may be used against him at trial, but also that he has the right to the presence of counsel and that counsel will be furnished if he cannot provide it, before he can be asked any questions at the scene of the crime or elsewhere. The suspect may waive these rights only if he does so "voluntarily, knowingly and intelligently" and all questioning must stop immediately if at any stage the person indicates that he wishes to consult counsel or to remain silent.

Although the full meaning of the code of conduct prescribed by *Miranda* remains for future case-by-case delineation, there can be little doubt that its effect upon police interrogation and the use of confessions will drastically change procedures long considered by law enforcement officials to be indispensable to the effective functioning of our system. Indeed, one of the great State chief justices has described the situation as a "mounting crisis" in the constitutional rules that "reach out to govern police interrogation." [10]

THE FATE OF POLICE INTERROGATIONS

If the majority opinion in *Miranda* is implemented in its full sweep, it could mean the virtual elimination of pretrial interrogation of suspects—on the street, at the scene of a crime, and in the station house—because there would then be no such interrogation without the presence of counsel unless the person detained, howsoever briefly, waives this right. Indeed, there are many who now agree with Justice Walter V. Schaefer who recently wrote:

The privilege against self-incrimination as presently interpreted precludes the effective questioning of persons suspected of crime.[11]

In *Crooker* v. *California,* the Court recognized that an absolute right to counsel during interrogation would "preclude police questioning—*fair as well as unfair * * *.*"[12] Mr. Justice Jackson, familiar with the duty and practice of the trial bar, perceptively said:

[10] Traynor, *supra* at 664. Chief Justice Traynor discussed this "mounting crisis" in the Benjamin N. Cardozo Lecture at the Association of the Bar of the City of New York on Apr. 19, 1966, prior to the Court's decision in *Miranda.*

[11] Schaefer, *supra* at 520. See also Justice Schaefer's first lecture in the 1966 Julius Rosenthal Lectures, Northwestern University Law School 8 (unpublished manuscript).

[12] 357 U.S. 433, 441 (1958), the holding of which was overruled in *Miranda, supra* at 479 n. 48. [Emphasis in original.]

[A]ny lawyer worth his salt will tell the suspect in no uncertain terms to make no statement to police under any circumstances.[13]

There will, it is true, be a certain number of cases in which the suspect will not insist upon his right to counsel. If he makes admissions or a formal confession, the question whether his waiver of counsel was "voluntarily, knowingly and intelligently" made will then permeate all subsequent contested phases of the criminal process—trial, appeal and even post conviction remedies. And the prosecution will bear the "heavy" burden of proving such waiver; mere silence of the accused will not suffice; and "any evidence" of threat, cajolery or pressure by the government will preclude admission.

The employment of electronic recorders[14] and television possibly may enable police to defend such an interrogation if conducted in the station house. But in the suddenness of a street encounter, or the confusion at the scene of a crime, there will be little or no opportunity to protect police interrogation against the inevitable charge of failing to meet *Miranda* standards. The litigation that follows more often than not will be a "trial" of the police rather than the accused.

There are some who argue that further experience is needed to determine whether police interrogation of suspects is necessary for effective law enforcement. Such experience would be helpful in defining the dimensions of the problem. But few can doubt the adverse impact of *Miranda* upon the law enforcement process.

Interrogation is the single most essential police procedure. It benefits the innocent suspect as much as it aids in obtaining evidence to convict the guilty. Mr. Justice Frankfurter noted:

Questioning suspects is indispensable in law enforcement.[15]

The rationale of police interrogation was well stated by the Second Circuit Court of Appeals in *United States* v. *Cone:*

The fact is that in many serious crimes—cases of murder, kidnapping, rape, burglary and robbery—the police often have no or few objective clues with which to start an investi-

---

[13] *Watts* v. *Indiana*, 338 U.S. 49, 59 (1949) (dissenting opinion).

[14] As recommended in *Model Code of Pre-Arraignment Procedure* § 4.09 (Tent. Draft No. 1, 1966).

[15] *Culombe* v. *Connecticut*, 367 U.S. 568, 578 (1961), quoting *People* v. *Hall*, 413 Ill. 615, 624, 110 N.E. 2d 249, 254 (1953).

gation; a considerable percentage of those which are solved are solved in whole or in part through statements voluntarily made to the police by those who are suspects. Moreover, immediate questioning is often instrumental in recovering kidnapped persons or stolen goods as well as in solving the crime. Under these circumstances, the police should not be forced unnecessarily to bear obstructions that irretrievably forfeit the opportunity of securing information under circumstances of spontaneity most favorable to truth-telling and at a time when further information may be necessary to pursue the investigation, to apprehend others, and to prevent other crimes.[16]

THE FUTURE OF CONFESSIONS

The impact of *Miranda* on the use of confessions is an equally serious problem. Indeed, this is the other side of the coin. If interrogations are muted there will be no confessions; if they are tainted, resulting confessions—as well as other related evidence—will be excluded or the convictions subsequently set aside. There is real reason for the concern, expressed by dissenting justices, that *Miranda* in effect proscribes the use of all confessions.[17] This would be the most far-reaching departure from precedent and established practice in the history of our criminal law.

Until *Escobedo* and *Miranda* the basic test of the admissibility of a confession was whether it was genuinely voluntary.[18] Nor had there been any serious question as to the desirable role of confessions, lawfully obtained, in the

---

[16] 354 F. 2d 119, 126, *cert. denied*, 384 U.S. 1023 (1966). Perhaps the best published statement of the considerations favoring in-custody interrogation is that found in the *Model Code of Pre-Arraignment Procedure*, Commentary § 5.01, at 168–74 (Tent. Draft No. 1, 1966). See also Bator & Vorenberg, *Arrest, Detention, Interrogation and the Right to Counsel: Basic Problems and Possible Legislative Solutions*, 66 Colum. L. Rev. 62 (1966); Friendly, *supra*, at 941, 948.

[17] Mr. Justice White, joined by Mr. Justice Harlan and Mr. Justice Stewart, said "[T]he result [of the majority holding] adds up to a judicial judgment that evidence from the accused should not be used against him in any way, whether compelled or not." *Miranda* v. *Arizona, supra* at 538 (dissenting opinion).

[18] Indeed, until very recently and back through English constitutional history, a distinction had been made between the privilege against self-incrimination and the rules excluding compelled confessions. See Morgan, *The Privilege Against Self-Incrimination*, 34 Minn. L. Rev. 1 (1949); 3 Wigmore, *Evidence* 819 (3d ed. 1940). But see *Bram* v. *United States*, 168 U.S. 532, 542 (1897). In the United States, the common law and the due process clauses of the Constitution were

criminal process. The generally accepted view had been that stated in an early Supreme Court case:

[T]*he admissions or confessions of a prisoner, when voluntary and freely made, have always ranked high in the scale of incriminating evidence.* [19]

It is, of course, true that the danger of abuse and the difficulty of determining "voluntariness" have long and properly concerned the courts. Yet, one wonders whether these acknowledged difficulties justify the loss at this point in our history of a type of evidence considered both so reliable and so vital to law enforcement.

THE "PRIVILEGE" AND CRIMINAL TRIAL

The impact upon law enforcement of the privilege against self-incrimination as now construed by the Court is not confined to the *Miranda* issues of interrogation and confession. The privilege has always protected an accused from being compelled to testify; it now prevents any comment by judge or prosecutor on his failure to testify; and it limits discovery by the prosecution of evidence in the accused's possession or control.[20] It was not until 1964 that the privilege was held applicable to the States by virtue of the 14th amendment,[21] and

---

construed to provide a voluntariness standard for the admissibility of confessions. See *Developments in the Law—Confessions*, 79 Harv. L. Rev. 935 (1966). The Fifth Amendment was adopted in 1791. Before that time, in England and in this country, the privilege was construed to apply only at judicial proceedings in which the person asserting the privilege was being tried on criminal charges; at preliminary hearing the magistrate freely questioned the accused without warning of his rights and any failure to respond was part of the evidence at trial, such evidence being given by testimony of the magistrate himself. See Morgan, *supra* at 18. Dean Wigmore and Professor Corwin suggest that the intent of the framers of the Fifth Amendment was to retain these limitations upon the privilege. See Corwin. *The Supreme Court's Construction of the Self-Incrimination Clause*, 29 Mich. L. Rev. 1, 2 (1930); 8 Wigmore, *Evidence* § 2252, at 324 (McNaughton rev. 1961).

[19] *Brown* v. *Walker*, 161 U.S. 591, 596 (1896). Moreover, as Judge Friendly has pointed out: "[T]here is no social value in preventing uncoerced admission of the facts." Friendly, *supra* at 948.

[20] See 8 Wigmore, *Evidence* § 2264 (McNaughton rev. 1961). Beyond the trial itself, the privilege protects grand jury witnesses (*Counselman* v. *Hitchcock*, 142 U.S. 547 (1892)); witnesses in civil trial (*McCarthy* v. *Arndstein*, 266 U.S. 34 (1924)); and witnesses before legislative committees (*Emspak* v. *United States*, 349 U.S. 190 (1955); *Quinn* v. *United States*, 349 U.S. 155 (1955)).

[21] *Malloy* v. *Hogan*, 378 U.S. 1 (1964).

the final extension came in 1965 when the Court held invalid a State constitutional provision permitting the trial judge and prosecutor to comment upon the accused's failure to testify at trial.[22]

The question is now being increasingly asked whether the full scope of the privilege, as recently construed and enlarged, is justified either by its long and tangled history or by any genuine need in a criminal trial.[23] There is agreement, of course, that the privilege must always be preserved in fullest measure against inquisitions into political or religious beliefs or conduct. Indeed, the historic origin and purpose of the privilege was primarily to protect against the evil of governmental suppression of ideas. But it is doubtful that when the Fifth Amendment was adopted it was conceived that its major beneficiaries would be those accused of crimes against person and property.

Plainly this is an area requiring the most thoughtful attention. There is little sentiment—and in our view no justification—for outright repeal of the privilege clause or for an amendment which would require a defendant to give evidence against himself at his trial. But a strong case can be made for restoration of the right to comment on the failure of an accused to take the stand.[24] As Justice Schaefer has said:

[I]t is entirely unsound to exclude from consideration at the trial the silence of a suspect involved in circumstances reasonably calling for explanation, or of a defendant who does not take the stand. It therefore seems to me imperative that the privilege against self-incrimination be modified to permit comment upon such silence.[25]

Any consideration of modification of the Fifth Amendment also should include appropriate provision to make possible reciprocal pretrial discovery in criminal cases. One spe-

---

[22] *Griffin* v. *California*, 380 U.S. 609 (1965).

[23] See, e.g., McCormick, *The Scope of Privilege in the Law of Evidence*, 16 Texas L. Rev. 447 (1938); Schaefer, *supra;* Traynor, *supra;* Warden, *Miranda—Some History, Some Observations and Some Questions,* 20 Vand. L. Rev. 39 (1966).

[24] See Traynor, *supra* at 677: "I find no inconsistency in remaining of the opinion that a judge or prosecutor might fairly comment upon the silence of a defendant at the trial itself to the extent of noting that a jury could draw unfavorable inferences from the defendant's failure to explain or refute evidence when he could reasonably be expected to do so. Such comment would not be evidence and would do no more than make clear to the jury the extent of its freedom in drawing inferences."

[25] Schaefer, *supra* at 520.

cific proposal, meriting serious consideration, is to accomplish this by pretrial discovery interrogation before a magistrate or judicial officer.[26] The availability of broad discovery would strengthen law enforcement as well as the rights of persons accused of crime,[27] and would go far to establish determination of the truth as to guilt or innocence as the primary object of our criminal procedure.

OTHER COUNTRIES LESS RESTRICTIVE

We know of no other system of criminal justice which subjects law enforcement to limitations as severe and rigid as those we have discussed. The nearest analogy is found in England which shares through our common law heritage the basic characteristics of the accusatory system. Yet, there are significant differences—especially in the greater discretion of English judges and in the flexibility which inheres in an unwritten constitution. There is nevertheless a developing feeling in England, parallel to that in this country, that criminals are unduly protected by the present rules. The Home Secretary of the Labor Government, speaking of proposed measures to aid law enforcement, recently said:

The scales of justice in Britain are at present tilted a little more in the favor of the accused than is necessary to protect the innocent.[28]

One of the measures recommended by the Labor Government is to permit a majority verdict of 10, rather than the historic unanimous vote of all 12 jurors.[29] Leading members of the English bar are pressing for further reforms. After pointing out that "the criminal is living in a golden age," Lord Shawcross has commented:

The barriers protecting suspected and accused persons are

[26] Schaefer, *supra* at 518–20.

[27] The Commission's report emphasizes the need for broader pretrial discovery by both the prosecution and the defense.

[28] Address of the Rt. Hon. Roy Jenkins, M.P., Secretary of State for the Home Department, National Press Club, Washington, D.C., Sept. 19, 1966. Mr. Jenkins, in emphasizing the deterrent effort of swiftness and certainty in justice, also said: "Detection and conviction are therefore necessarily prior deterrents to that of punishment, and I attach the greatest possible importance to trying to increase the chances that they will follow a criminal act."

[29] The rule in Scotland long has been that a simple majority vote suffices to convict.

being steadily reinforced. I believe our law has become hope-lessly unrealistic in its attitude toward the prevention and de-tection of crime. We put illusory fears about the impairment of liberty before the promotion of justice.[30]

Among the reforms being urged in England are major modifications of the privilege against self-incrimination, broadened discovery rights by the state, and the adoption of a requirement that accused persons must advise the prosecution in advance of trial of all special defenses, such as alibi, self-defense, or mistaken identity. Another change suggested would allow the admission in evidence of previous convic-tions of similar offenses, although convictions of dissimilar crimes still would not be admissible.[31]

THE FIRST DUTY OF GOVERNMENT

In the first chapter of the Commission's report the serious-ness of the crime situation is described as follows:

Every American is, in a sense, a victim of crime. Violence and theft have not only injured, often irreparably, hundreds of thousands of citizens, but have directly affected everyone. Some people have been impelled to uproot themselves and find new homes. Some have been made afraid to use public streets and parks. Some have come to doubt the worth of a society in which so many people behave so badly.[32]

The underlying causes of these conditions are far more funda-mental than the limitations discussed in this statement. Yet, prevention and control of crime—until it is "uprooted" by long-range reforms—depends in major part upon effective law enforcement. To be effective, and particularly to deter crimi-nal conduct, the courts must convict the guilty with prompt-ness and certainty just as they must acquit the innocent. Soci-ety is not well served by limitations which frustrate reason-able attainment of this goal.

[30]Address by Lord Shawcross, Q.C., Attorney General of Great Brit-ain, 1945–51, before the Crime Commission of Chicago, Oct. 11, 1965, reprinted in U.S. News & World Report, Nov. 1, 1965, pp. 80–82. See also Shawcross, *Police and Public in Great Britain,* 51 A.B.A.J. 225 (1965).

[31] See statements of Viscount Dilhorne (Q.C. and Lord Chancellor, 1962–64 and Attorney General, 1954–62), and Lord Shawcross, as re-ported in The Listner, Aug. 11, 1966, pp. 190, et seq.

[32] Commission's General Report, ch. 1.

We are passing through a phase in our history of understandable, yet unprecedented, concern with the rights of accused persons. This has been welcomed as long overdue in many areas. But the time has come for a like concern for the rights of citizens to be free from criminal molestation of their persons and property. In many respects, the victims of crime have been the forgotten men of our society—inadequately protected, generally uncompensated, and the object of relatively little attention by the public at large.

Mr. Justice White has said: "The most basic function of any government is to provide for the security of the individual and of his property." [33] Unless this function is adequately discharged, society itself may well become so disordered that all rights and liberties will be endangered.

RIGHTING THE IMBALANCE

This statement has reviewed, necessarily without attempting completeness or detailed analysis, some of the respects in which law enforcement and the courts have been handicapped by the law itself in seeking to apprehend and convict persons guilty of crime.

The question which we raise is whether, even with the support of a deeply concerned President [34] and the implementation of the Commission's national strategy against crime, law enforcement can effectively discharge its vital role in "controlling crime and violence" without changes in existing constitutional limitations.

There is no more sacred part of our history or our constitutional structure than the Bill of Rights. One approaches the thought of the most limited amendment with reticence and a full awareness both of the political obstacles and the inherent delicacy of drafting changes which preserve all relevant values. But it must be remembered that the Constitution contemplates amendment, and no part of it should be so sacred that it remains beyond review.

Whatever can be done to right the present imbalance through legislation or rule of court should have high priority. The promising criminal justice programs of the American

[33] *Miranda* v. *Arizona, supra* at 539 (dissenting opinion).

[34] In his recent State of the Union Address, President Johnson said: "Our country's laws must be respected, order must be maintained. I will support—with all the constitutional powers I possess—our Nation's law enforcement officials in their attempt to control the crime and violence that tear the fabric of our communities." State of the Union Address, Jan. 10, 1967.

Bar Association and the American Law Institute should be helpful in this respect. But reform and clarification will fall short unless they achieve these ends:

☐ An adequate opportunity must be provided the police for interrogation at the scene of the crime, during investigations and at the station house, with appropriate safeguards to prevent abuse.

☐ The legitimate place of voluntary confessions in law enforcement must be reestablished and their use made dependent upon meeting due process standards of voluntariness.

☐ Provision must be made for comment on the failure of an accused to take the stand, and also for reciprocal discovery in criminal cases.

If, as now appears likely, a constitutional amendment is required to strengthen law enforcement in these respects, the American people should face up to the need and undertake necessary action without delay.

CONCLUSION

We emphasize in concluding that while we differ in varying degrees from some of the decisions discussed, we unanimously recognize them as expressions of legally tenable points of view. We support all decisions of the Court as the law of the land, to be respected and enforced unless and until changed by the processes available under our form of government.

In considering any change, the people of the United States must have an adequate understanding of the adverse effect upon law enforcement agencies of the constitutional limitations discussed in this statement. They must also ever be mindful that concern with crime and apprehension for the safety of their persons and property, as understandable as these are today, must be weighed carefully against the necessity—as demonstrated by history—of retaining appropriate and effective safeguards against oppressive governmental action against the individual, whether guilty or innocent of crime.

The determination of how to strike this balance, with wisdom and restraint, is a decision which in final analysis the people of this country must make. It has been the purpose of this statement to alert the public generally to the dimensions of the problem, to record our conviction that an imbalance exists, and to express a viewpoint as to possible lines of remedial action. In going somewhat beyond the scope of the Commission's report, we reiterate our support and our judgment that implementation of its recommendations will have far reaching and salutary effects.

MR. BYRNE, CHIEF CAHILL, AND MR. LYNCH CONCUR IN THIS STATEMENT.

The Commission and Its Operations

I. THE COMMISSIONERS

NICHOLAS DEB. KATZENBACH, CHAIRMAN

Washington, D.C.; Under Secretary of State; U.S. Army Air Force, 1st Lieutenant, prisoner of war, awarded Air Medal With Three Clusters, 1941–45; Rhodes scholar, 1947–49; attorney, Department of the Air Force, 1950–52; Professor of Law, Yale Law School, 1952–56; Professor of International Law, University of Chicago, 1956–61; Assistant Attorney General, Office of Legal Counsel, 1961; Deputy Attorney General, 1962–65; Attorney General of the United States, 1965–66.

GENEVIEVE BLATT

Harrisburg, Pa., attorney; Phi Beta Kappa; Secretary of Internal Affairs, Member, State Board of Pardons, State of Pennsylvania, 1955–67.

CHARLES D. BREITEL

New York, N.Y.; Associate Judge, Court of Appeals of the State of New York; Deputy Assistant District Attorney, New York County, staff of Thomas E. Dewey, special rackets investigations, 1935–37; Assistant District Attorney, New York County, 1938–41; Chief of Indictment Bureau, 1941; Counsel to Governor, State of New York, 1943–50; Justice, Supreme Court of New York, 1950–52; Associate Justice, Appellate Division (First Department), Supreme Court of New York, 1952–66; Advisory

Committee, Model Penal Code, American Law Institute; Chairman, Special Committee on the Administration of Criminal Justice, Association of the Bar of the City of New York; Council, American Law Institute.

KINGMAN BREWSTER, JR.

New Haven, Conn.; President, Yale University; U.S. Navy, Lieutenant, 1942–46; Assistant Professor of Law, Harvard Law School, 1950–53; Professor of Law, Harvard Law School, 1953–60; Provost, Yale University, 1960–63; author, "Anti-Trust and American Business Abroad" (1959); "Law of International Transactions and Relations" (with M. Katz, 1960).

GARRETT H. BYRNE

Boston, Mass.; attorney; District Attorney, Suffolk County, Mass.; Member, Massachusetts House of Representatives, 1924–28; President, National District Attorneys Association, 1963–64; President, Massachusetts District Attorneys Association, 1963–64; President, National District Attorneys Foundation.

THOMAS J. CAHILL

San Francisco, Calif.; Chief of Police, San Francisco; entered San Francisco Police Department as patrolman, 1942; Big Brother of the Year Award, 1964; Liberty Bell Award, San Francisco Bar Association, 1965; Vice President, International Association of Chiefs of Police, 1963– ; Chairman, Advisory Committee to the Governor on the Law Enforcement Section of the Disaster Office of the State of California; Chairman, Advisory Committee to the School of Criminology, City College, San Francisco; Member, National Advisory Committee, National Center on Police-Community Relations, Michigan State University.

OTIS CHANDLER

San Marino, Calif.; Publisher, Los Angeles Times; U.S. Air Force, 1st Lieutenant, 1951–53; Senior Vice President, the Times-Mirror Co.; Member, Board of Directors, Associated Press, Western Airlines, Union Bank.

LEON JAWORSKI

Houston, Tex.; attorney, senior partner, Fulbright, Crooker, Freeman, Bates & Jaworsik; U.S. Army, Colonel, Chief, War Crimes Trial Section, European Theater, Legion of Merit, 1942–46; President, Houston Bar Association, 1949; President, Texas Civil Judicial Council, 1951–52; President, American College of Trial Lawyers, 1961–62; President, Texas Bar Association, 1962–63; Special Assistant U.S. Attorney General, 1962–65; Special Counsel, Attorney General of Texas, 1963–65; Executive Committee, Southwestern Legal Foundation; trustee, Houston Legal Foundation; Fellow, American Bar Foundation; U.S. Member, Permanent (International) Court of Arbitration; Member, National Science Commission; Chairman, Governor's Committee on Public School Education, State of Texas.

THOMAS C. LYNCH

San Francisco, Calif.; Attorney General, State of California; Assistant U.S. Attorney, 1933–42; Chief Assistant U.S. Attorney, 1943–51; District Attorney, San Francisco, Calif., 1951–64; Fellow, American College of Trial Lawyers; Advisory Committee on Prearraignment Code, American Law Institute.

ROSS L. MALONE

Roswell, N. Mex.; attorney, partner, Atwood & Malone; U.S. Navy, Lieutenant Commander, 1942–46; Deputy Attorney General of the United States, 1952–53; President, American Bar Association, 1958–59; President, American Bar Foundation; Trustee, Southwestern Legal Foundation; Council, American Law Institute; Board of Regents, American College of Trial Lawyers; Board of Trustees, Southern Methodist University.

JAMES BENTON PARSONS

Chicago, Ill.; Judge, U.S. District Court, Northern District of Illinois; U.S. Navy, 1942–46; teacher, Lincoln University of Missouri, 1934–40, city schools of Greensboro, N.C., 1940–42, John Marshall Law School, 1949–52; Assistant Corporation Counsel, city of Chicago, 1949–51; Assistant U.S. Attorney, 1951–60; Judge, Superior Court of Cook County, Ill., 1960–61; Member, Committee on Administration of Probation System, Judicial Council of the United States; Chicago Commission on Police-Community Relations; Illinois Academy of Criminology.

LEWIS FRANKLIN POWELL, JR.

Richmond, Va.; attorney, partner, Hunton, Williams, Gay, Powell & Gibson; U.S. Army Air Force, Colonel awarded Legion of Merit, Bronze Star, Croix de Guerre With Palms, 1942–46; Member, Virginia State Board of Education, 1961– ; President, American Bar Association, 1964–65; Trustee, Washington and Lee University and Hollis College; Board of Regents, American College of Trial Lawyers; Vice President, American Bar Foundation; Trustee and General Counsel, Colonial Williamsburg, Inc.

WILLIAM PIERCE ROGERS

Bethesda, Md.; attorney, partner, Royall, Koegel, Rogers & Wells (New York and Washington); Assistant U.S. Attorney, New York

County, 1938–42, 1946–47; U.S. Navy, Lieutenant Commander, 1942–46; Chief Counsel, U.S. Senate War Investigating Committee, 1948; Chief Counsel, Senate Investigations Subcommittee of Executive Expenditures Committee, 1948–50; Deputy Attorney General, 1953–57, Attorney General of the United States, 1957–61; Member, U.S. Delegation, 20th General Assembly, United Nations, 1965; U.S. Representative, United Nations Ad Hoc Committee on Southwest Africa, 1967; Member, President's Commission on Crime in the District of Columbia, 1965–67; Fellow, American Bar Foundation.

ROBERT GERALD STOREY

Dallas, Tex.; attorney, partner, Storey, Armstrong & Steger; Phi Beta Kappa, Order of Coif; U.S. Army, 1st Lieutenant, 1918–19, Colonel, Bronze Star, Legion of Merit, 1941–45; Assistant Attorney General, State of Texas, 1921–23; Executive Trial Counsel for the United States, trial of major Axis war criminals, Nuremberg, Legion of Honor (France), 1945–46; Dean, Southern Methodist University Law School, 1947–59; President Texas Bar Association, 1948–49; President, American Bar Association, 1952–53; Member, Hoover Commission, 1953–55; President, Inter-American Bar Association, 1954–56; American Bar Association Gold Medal, 1956; Vice Chairman, U.S. Civil Rights Commission, 1957–63; President, Southwestern Legal Foundation.

JULIA DAVIS STUART

Spokane, Wash.; President, League of Women Voters of the United States; Governor's Tax Advisory Council, State of Washington, 1958; Chairman, Citizens Subcommittee on School Finance, State of Washington Legislature, 1960; National Municipal League Distinguished Citizen Award, 1964; Member, National Citizens Commission on International Cooperation, 1965.

ROBERT F. WAGNER

New York, N.Y.; attorney; New York State Assembly, 1938–41; U.S. Army Air Force, Lieutenant Colonel, 1942–45; New York City Tax Commission, 1946; Commissioner of Housing and Buildings, New York City, 1947; New York City Planning Commission, 1948; President, Borough of Manhattan, N.Y., 1949–53; Mayor, New York City, 1954–66.

HERBERT WECHSLER

New York, N.Y.; Harlan Fisk Stone Professor of Constitutional Law, Columbia Law School; Assistant Attorney General, State of New York, 1938–40; Special Assistant U.S. Attorney General, 1940–44, Assistant Attorney General of the United States, 1944–46; Member, U.S. Supreme Court Advisory Committee on Rules of Criminal Procedure, 1941–45; Oliver Wendell Holmes

Lecturer, Harvard Law School, 1958–59; Director, American Law Institute; Reporter, Model Penal Code, American Law Institute; Member, New York State Temporary Commission on Revision of the Penal Law and Criminal Code; Member, Executive Committee, Association of the Bar, City of New York; author, "Criminal Law and Its Administration" (with J. Michael, 1940); "The Federal Courts and the Federal System" (with H. Hart, Jr., 1953); "Principles, Politics and Fundamental Law" (1961).

WHITNEY MOORE YOUNG, JR.

New Rochelle, N.Y.; Executive Director, National Urban League; Dean, Atlanta University School of Social Work, 1954–60; Member, President's Committee on Youth Employment, 1962; Member, President's Committee on Equal Opportunity in the Armed Forces, 1963; Member, President's Commission on Technology, Automation, and Economic Progress, 1965–66; Member, Special Presidential Task Force on Metropolitan and Urban Problems, 1965–66; Member, Advisory Committee on Housing and Urban Development, Department of Housing and Urban Development; President, National Conference on Social Welfare; Member, Advisory Board, A. Philip Randolph Institute; Member, National Board, Citizens Crusade Against Poverty; Trustee, Eleanor Roosevelt Memorial Foundation; author, "To Be Equal" (1964).

LUTHER W. YOUNGDAHL

Washington, D.C.; Senior Judge, U.S. District Court, District of Columbia; U.S. Army, artillery officer, World War I: Judge, Municipal Court, Minneapolis, Minn., 1930–36; Judge, District Court, Hennepin County, Minn., 1936–42; Associate Justice, Supreme Court of Minnesota, 1942–46; Governor of Minnesota, 1947–51; Judge, U.S. District Court, District of Columbia, 1951–66.

II. HOW THE COMMISSION DID ITS WORK

The President's Commission on Law Enforcement and Administration of Justice was established on July 23, 1965, by President Lyndon B. Johnson, who instructed it to inquire into the causes of crime and delinquency and report to him, early in 1967, with recommendations for preventing crime and delinquency and improving law enforcement and the administration of criminal justice.

At the first Commission meeting, in September 1965, the Commission with the advice of its staff designated specific subjects in which intensive work was to be undertaken. The staff, on the basis of further consultation with the Commission members and experts in various fields, prepared preliminary work plans relating to these subjects. It also began the task—which extended through the full term of the Commission—of gathering and analyzing data and the views of consultants and advisers and preparing, for Commission review and analysis, drafts of material looking to the development of the final report.

The work of the Commission was initially divided into four major areas: Police, courts, corrections, and assessment of the crime problem. Concentrating on each was a task force consisting of a panel of Commission members, a number of full-time staff members, and consultants and advisers. As the Commission's work proceeded, special task forces or working groups were formed to give special attention to organized crime, juvenile delinquency, narcotics and drug abuse, and drunkenness. Early in 1966, the task force on science and technology was organized as a collaborative undertaking by the Commission, the Office of Law Enforcement Assistance of the Department of Justice, and, with direct responsibility for the work, the Institute for Defense Analyses.

The full-time staff began as only a few and grew to number more than 40. It included lawyers, police officials, correctional personnel, prosecutors, sociologists, psychologists, systems analysts, juvenile delinquency prevention planners, and professional writers and editors. Many were professors on leave from universities; criminal justice officials on leave from Federal, State, and local agencies; or experts on loan from various Federal departments, including Justice, HEW, Treasury, Labor, Army, and Navy.

To direct the staff work, the President appointed, as Executive Director, James Vorenberg, on leave as Professor at Harvard Law School, who had been serving as the first Director of the Office of Criminal Justice in the Department of Justice. The Deputy Director, Henry S. Ruth, Jr., had been a prosecutor in the Department of Justice's Oganized Crime and Racketeering Section, and later a member of the Office of Criminal Justice.

The four Associate Directors of the Commission and their areas of primary responsibility were: Police—Gene S. Muehleisen, on leave as the Executive Officer of the Commission on Peace Officer Standards and Training in the California Department of Justice; corrections—Elmer K. Nelson, on leave as Professor of Public Administration at the University of Southern California; assessment of the nature and scope of crime—Lloyd E. Ohlin, on leave as Professor on Sociology at Columbia University and director of Research of Columbia's School of Social Work; courts—Arthur I. Rosett, a former Federal prosecutor who was an attorney in private practice. In addition, Alfred Blumstein of the Institute for Defense Analyses was director of the science and technology task force.

The Commission's research and inquiries took many forms, a few of which are suggested below. Surveys were conducted in connection with work on police-community relations, professional criminals, unreported crime, and correctional personnel and facilities. The corrections survey, sponsored jointly by the Commission and the Office of Law Enforcement Assistance, is only one example of the numerous projects in which the Office of Law Enforcement Assistance and the Commission collaborated. This survey and the survey of unreported crime were the first nationwide studies ever made of those areas. Over 2,200 police departments were asked by questionnaire what field procedures they had found especially effective against crime. Field observers acquainted themselves with police patrol practices and procedures in lower criminal courts. Commission staff and representatives visited correctional institutions, met with groups of residents in slum areas, and interviewed professional criminals and prison inmates.

The Commission also had the benefit of data and suggestions from Federal agencies including the Federal Bureau of Investigation; the Bureau of Prisons; the Criminal Division of the Department of Justice; various divisions of the Department of Health, Education, and Welfare; the Department of the Treasury; the Department of Labor; and the Bureau of the Budget, to name a few. Members of the Office of Criminal Justice and staff and citizen advisers of the President's Committee on Juvenile Delinquency and Youth Crime assisted in a number of areas. Similar assistance was received from numerous State and local agencies and from officials in some foreign countries.

The Commission sponsored many conferences, large and small, concerning mentally disordered offenders, riots and their control, correctional standards, plea bargaining, and the Federal role in crime control, to mention only a few. Commission members or staff met with rural southern law enforcement officials, government officials, practitioners, scholars, and others. One conference brought scientists and businessmen together to consider ways of working together against crime. Another inquired into the legal manpower problems of the criminal system. A third was attended by representatives of the State committees appointed by many Governors in response to the President's request that groups be formed in each State to plan and implement reform of criminal systems and laws. In this connection, the Commission staff also worked with State and local criminal justice personnel to obtain information on the operation of the law enforcement and criminal justice systems in their States and the likely effect of Commission proposals on those systems, and to assist State officials in planning research and programs in their States.

Advice was sought at every step from experts in law enforcement, criminal justice, and crime prevention. Many of them, acting as consultants to the Commission, prepared useful background papers. A few of these papers served as the basis for chapters of the separate task force reports and many are published as appendices to the task force reports. A few leading scholars from corrections, police work, and law came to Washington and worked with the staff on a full-time basis during the summer of 1966. The principal role of most of the consultants, however, like that of the many other persons of knowledge and experience who served the Commission as advisers, was as a sounding board for new ideas, proposed recommendations, and materials being developed for Commission consideration. In addition, the Commission invited the views of professional organizations in many areas related to crime.

The full Commission met seven times, for 2 or 3 full days each time. The meetings often led to new proposals or new lines the staff was instructed to explore. Discussion at the meetings centered on drafts sent Commission members in advance and focused chiefly on major issues and findings, although a number of specific stylistic and other drafting changes emerged as well.

In addition to the meetings of the Commission as a whole, members participated on a continuing basis in preparing materials and developing the final report, both informally—by letter, telephone, and visits with staff—and as formally constituted panels (sometimes with the inclusion of outside experts). In the early months, these panels played an important role in proposing directions the Commission's work would take. And before consideration by the full Commission, staff papers were reviewed by the several Commission members assigned by the Chairman to the given area and then usually reworked by the staff in light of the comments received.

While the members of the Commission have considered carefully the entire report, this does not necessarily mean that there is complete agreement with every detail of each recommendation or statement. Except where otherwise noted, however, there is agreement with the substance of every important conclusion and recommendation. The nature of the general agreement and the extent of incidental disagreement are those to be expected when members of a Commission individually have given serious thought to a major and complex problem, and have sought to achieve a joint resolution in furtherance of the Commission's task as a deliberative body.

As will be noted in the preface to each task force volume, those underlying volumes were prepared by the staff on the basis of its studies and those of consultants. The materials in the task force volumes were distributed to the entire Commission and discussed generally at Commission meetings, although more detailed discussion and intensive review were the responsibility of a panel of several Commission members attached to each task force. While, to the extent noted in the preface of the task force volumes, individual members of the panel may have reservations on some points covered in the task force volumes but not reflected in the Commission's general report, the task force volumes have the general endorsement of the panels.

The final product of the Commission's work will consist of this report; the reports of the several task forces; and appendices containing consultants' papers, documentation, and other explanatory and supporting material.

Consultants and Advisers

I. CONSULTANTS

GENERAL

Anthony G. Amsterdam, Professor, University of Pennsylvania Law School, Philadelphia, Pa.

Jan Deutsch, Associate Professor, Yale University Law School, New Haven, Conn.

Arnold Enker, Professor, University of Minnesota Law School, Minneapolis, Minn.

Daniel Freed, Acting Director, Office of Criminal Justice, Department of Justice

Howard Heffron, Professor, University of Washington Law School, Seattle, Wash.

Sanford H. Kadish, Professor, University of California Law School, Berkeley, Calif.

Michael March, Assistant to Chief, Education, Manpower and Science Division, Bureau of the Budget

Frank Remington, Professor, University of Wisconsin Law School, Madison, Wis.

Arnold Sagalyn, Director of Law Enforcement Coordination, Department of the Treasury

Donald A. Schon, President, Organization for Social and Technical Innovation, Cambridge, Mass.

Harry Subin, Associate Director, Vera Institute of Justice, New York, N.Y.

ADMINISTRATION OF JUSTICE

Norman Abrams, Professor of Law, University of California, Los Angeles, Calif., Special Assistant, Criminal Division, Department of Justice

Sheldon Elsen, attorney, New York, N.Y.

Gilbert Geis, Professor, California State College at Los Angeles, Los Angeles, Calif.

Abraham S. Goldstein, Professor of Law, Yale University, New Haven, Conn.

Zona F. Hostetler, Consultant, Office of Economic Opportunity

Louis L. Jaffe, Professor of Law, Harvard University, Cambridge, Mass.

Arthur B. Kramer, attorney, New York, N.Y.

John S. Martin, Jr., attorney, Nyack, N.Y.

Monroe E. Price, Associate Professor of Law, University of California, Los Angeles, Calif.

Lee Silverstein, Research Attorney, American Bar Foundation, Chicago, Ill.

Patricia M. Wald, Commissioner, President's Commission on Crime in the District of Columbia

Lloyd L. Weinreb, Assistant Professor of Law, Harvard University, Cambridge, Mass.

ASSESSMENT OF CRIME

Albert D. Biderman, Senior Research Associate, Bureau of Social Science Research, Inc., Washington, D.C.

Egon Bittner, Associate Professor of Sociology and Resident, Langley Porter Neuro-Psychiatric Institute, University of California Medical Center, San Francisco, Calif.

Sol Chaneles, Director of Child Sex Victimization, American Humane Association, New York, N.Y.

Karl O. Christiansen, Professor, Det Kriminalistiriske Institute, Copenhagen, Denmark

Jerome Daunt, Chief, Uniform Crime Reporting Section, FBI, Department of Justice

Samuel Dunaif, M.D., Supervising Psychiatrist, Jewish Family Service, New York, N.Y.

Otis Dudley Duncan, Professor, Department of Sociology, University of Michigan, Ann Arbor, Mich.

Phillip Ennis, Senior Study Director, National Opinion Research Center, University of Chicago, Chicago, Ill.

Robert Fogelson, Associate Director, Department of History, Columbia University, New York, N.Y.

Howard Freeman, Professor, School of Social Work, Brandeis University, Waltham, Mass.

Jack Gibbs, Professor, Department of Sociology, Washington State University, Pullman, Wash.

Gilbert Geis, Professor, California State College at Los Angeles, Los Angeles, Calif.

Donald Goldstein, Research Assistant, Bureau of Social Science Research, Inc., Washington, D.C.

Leroy C. Gould, Assistant Professor, Department of Sociology, Yale University, New Haven, Conn.

Reginald Lourie, M.D., Director of Psychiatry, Children's Hospital, Washington, D.C.

Jennie McIntyre, Assistant Professor, Department of Sociology and Anthropology, University of Maryland, College Park, Md.

Sheldon Messinger, Vice Chairman, Center for the Study of Law and Society, University of California, Berkeley, Calif.

Samuel Meyers, Research Associate, Bureau of Social Science Research, Inc., Washington, D.C.

Kriss Novak, Assistant Professor, Department of Sociology, Wisconsin State University, Whitewater, Wis.

Fred Powledge, Brooklyn, N.Y.

Albert J. Reiss, Jr., Professor, Department of Sociology, University of Michigan, Ann Arbor, Mich.

Peter Rossi, Director, National Opinion Research Center, University of Chicago, Chicago, Ill.

Philip C. Sagi, Professor of Sociology, University of Pennsylvania, Philadelphia, Pa.

Leonard D. Savitz, Associate Professor, Department of Sociology, Temple University, Philadelphia, Pa.

Stephen Schafer, Professor, Department of Sociology-Anthropology, Northeastern University, Boston, Mass.

Karl Schuessler, Professor, Department of Sociology, Indiana University, Bloomington, Ind.

Milton Shore, National Institute of Mental Health, Public Health Service, Department of Health, Education, and Welfare

James F. Short, Dean, Graduate School, Washington State University, Pullman, Wash.

Jerome H. Skolnick, Center for Study of Law and Society, University of California, Berkeley, Calif.

Irving Spergel, Professor, School of Social Service Administration, University of Chicago, Chicago, Ill.

Don D. Stewart, Washington, D.C.

Denis Szabo, Director, Institute of Criminology, University of Montreal, Canada

Adrianne W. Weir, Research Analyst, Bureau of Social Science Research, Inc., Washington, D.C.

Marvin Wolfgang, Director, Center of Criminological Research, University of Pennsylvania, Philadelphia, Pa.

James Woolsey, Yale University, New Haven, Conn.

CORRECTIONS

William T. Adams, Assistant Director, Joint Commission on Correctional Manpower and Training, Washington, D.C.

Myrl E. Alexander, Director, U.S. Bureau of Prisons, Department of Justice

Gordon Barker, Professor, Department of Sociology, University of Colorado, Boulder, Colo.

Sanford Bates, Pennington, N.J.

Bertram Beck, Executive Director, Mobilization for Youth, New York, N.Y.

Alan Breed, Superintendent, Northern California Youth Center, Stockton, Calif.

Bertram S. Brown, M.D., Deputy Director, National Institute of Mental Health, Public Health Service, Department of Health, Education, and Welfare

Milton Burdman, Director, Division of Parole and Community Service, Department of Corrections, Sacramento, Calif.

Richard Clendenen, Professor, Criminal Law Administration, University of Minnesota Law School, Minneapolis, Minn.

Fred Cohen, Professor of Law, University of Texas Law School, Austin, Tex.

John P. Conrad, Chief, Division of Research, Department of Corrections, Sacramento, Calif.

Thomas F. Courtless, Director of Criminological Studies, George Washington University Institute of Law, Psychiatry, and Criminology, Washington, D.C.

Roger Craig, attorney, Washington, D.C.

LaMar Empey, Director, Youth Studies Center, University of Southern California, Los Angeles, Calif.

T. Conway Esselstyn, Professor of Sociology, San Jose State College, San Jose, Calif.

Joseph P. Fitzpatrick, S.J., Associate Professor and Chairman, Department of Sociology, Fordham University, New York, N.Y.

Robert H. Fosen, Research Director, Joint Commission on Correctional Manpower and Training, Washington, D.C.

Ben Frank, Task Force Director, Joint Commission on Correctional Manpower and Training, Washington, D.C.

Marcia Freedman, Research Associate, Office of Conservation of Human Resources, Columbia University, New York, N.Y.

Thomas E. Gaddis, Consultant, Research and Development, Division of Continuing Education, Oregon System of Higher Education, Portland Continuation Center, Portland, Oreg.

Gilbert Geis, Professor, California State College at Los Angeles, Los Angeles, Calif.

Daniel Glaser, Chairman, Department of Sociology, University of Illinois, Urbana, Ill.

Douglas Grant, Program Director, New Careers Development Project, Sacramento, Calif.

Keith S. Griffiths, Chief of Research, Department of Youth Authority, Youth and Adult Corrections Agency, Sacramento, Calif.

David H. Gronewold, Professor, School of Social Work, University of Washington, Seattle, Wash.

Edward J. Hendrick, Superintendent of Prisons, Department of Public Welfare, Philadelphia, Pa.

Harland L. Hill, Director, Research and Development, Institute for the Study of Crime and Delinquency, Sacramento, Calif.

Garrett Heyns, Executive Director, Joint Commission on Correctional Manpower and Training, Washington, D.C.

Barbara Kay, Task Force Director, Joint Commission on Correctional Manpower and Training, Washington, D.C.

John T. Kilkeary, Center Director, Bureau of Prisons, Prerelease Guidance Center, Chicago, Ill.

Charles King, Executive Director, Wiltwyck School for Boys, New York, N.Y.

Barbara Knudson, Department of Sociology, University of Minnesota, Minneapolis, Minn.

Howard Leach, Consultant, New Mexico Council on Crime and Delinquency, Albuquerque, N. Mex.

Robert B. Levinson, Chief, Psychology Services, Federal Bureau of Prisons, Department of Justice

Milton Luger, Director, New York State Division of Youth, Albany N.Y.

Austin MacCormick, Executive Director, The Osborne Association, Inc., New York, N.Y.

Matthew Matlin, Editor, National Council on Crime and Delinquency, New York, N.Y.

John M. Martin, Professor, Department of Sociology and Anthropology, Fordham University, New York, N.Y.

Malcolm Matheson, Visiting Assistant Professor, School of Public Administration, University of Southern California; Deputy Director of Corrections,

Province of British Columbia, Canada

Boyd C. McDivitt, Deputy Director, Office of Probation, New York, N.Y.

Richard F. McGee, Administrator, Youth and Adult Corrections Agency, Sacramento, Calif.

Roma K. McNickle, Editor, Joint Commission on Correctional Manpower and Training, Washington, D.C.

William G. Nagel, Executive Secretary, Governor's Council for Human Services, State of Pennsylvania, Harrisburg, Pa.

Sherwood Norman, Director of Detention Services, National Council on Crime and Delinquency, New York, N.Y.

Lawrence Pierce, Chairman, New York State Narcotic Addiction Control Commission, Albany, N.Y.

Barbara Pittard, Assistant Professor, Department of Sociology, Georgia State College, Atlanta, Ga.

Kenneth Polk, Director, Research and Evaluation, Lane County Youth Project, Eugene, Oreg.

Walter Reckless, Professor of Sociology, Department of Sociology and Anthropology, Ohio State University, Columbus, Ohio

Milton G. Rector, Director, National Council on Crime and Delinquency, New York, N.Y.

Ernest Reimer, Chief, Correctional Program Services Divisions, California Department of

694

Corrections, Sacramento, Calif.

Henry Reining, Jr., Dean, School of Public Administration, University of Southern California, Los Angeles, Calif.

Mark S. Richmond, Deputy Assistant Director, Community Services, Federal Bureau of Prisons, Department of Justice

Ted Rubin, Judge, Juvenile Court, Denver, Colo.

Charles Shireman, School of Social Work, University of Chicago, Chicago, Ill.

Gerald M. Shattuck, Professor, Department of Sociology and Anthropology, Fordham University, New York, N.Y.

Clarence Schrag, Professor of Sociology, University of Southern California, Los Angeles, Calif.

Saleem A. Shah, National Institute of Mental Health, Public Health Service, Department of Health, Education, and Welfare

Louis Tomaino, Director, Southwest Center on Law and the Behavioral Sciences, University of Texas, Austin, Tex.

Robert Trimble, Executive Assistant to the Director, National Council on Crime and Delinquency, New York, N.Y.

Fred Ward, Southern Regional Director, National Council on Crime and Delinquency, Austin, Tex.

Marguerite Q. Warren, Principal Investigator, Community Treatment Project, California State Youth Authority, Sacramento, Calif.

Robert Weber, Institutional Consultant, National Council on Crime and Delinquency, New York, N.Y.

Leslie T. Wilkins, Professor, School of Criminology, University of California, Berkeley, Calif.

DRUNKENNESS

David Pittman, Director, Social Science Institute, Washington University, St. Louis, Mo.

Peter Hutt, attorney, Washington, D.C.

JUVENILE DELINQUENCY

Ivar Berg, Associate Professor, Department of Business Administration, Columbia University, New York, N.Y.

Virginia M. Burns, Chief, Training Administration, Office of Juvenile Delinquency and Youth Development, Welfare Administration, Department of Health, Education, and Welfare

Aaron Cicourel, Professor, Center for Study of Law and Society, University of California, Berkeley, Calif.

Sanford J. Fox, Professor, Boston College Law School, Brighton, Mass.

Don M. Gottfredson, National Council on Crime and Delinquency, Davis, Calif.

Paul Grams, Research Assistant, Merrill-Palmer Institute, Detroit, Mich.

Robert F. Johnson, Executive Director, Wieboldt Foundation, Chicago, Ill.

Edwin M. Lemert, Professor, Department of Sociology, University of California, Davis, Calif.

Henry D. McKay, Division Chief, Division of Community Studies, Institute for Juvenile Research, Department of Mental Health, Chicago, Ill.

Kenneth Polk, Associate Professor, Department of Sociology, University of Oregon, Eugene, Oreg.

Hyman Rodman, Senior Research Associate, Merrill-Palmer Institute, Detroit, Mich.

Margaret K. Rosenheim, Professor, School of Social Service Administration, University of Chicago, Chicago, Ill.

Seymour Rubenfeld, National Institute of Mental Health, Public Health Service, Department of Health, Education, and Welfare

Walter E. Schafer, Assistant Professor, Department of Sociology, University of Oregon, Eugene, Oreg.

William H. Sheridan, Assistant Director, Division of Juvenile Delinquency Service, Children's Bureau, Welfare Administration, Department of Health, Education, and Welfare

Leonard W. Stern, Chief, Demonstration Programs, Office of Juvenile Delinquency and Youth Development, Department of Health, Education, and Welfare

Jackson Toby, Professor, Department of Sociology, Rutgers University, New Brunswick, N.J.

Robert D. Vinter, Associate Dean, School of Social Work,

University of Michigan, Ann Arbor, Mich.

Carl Werthman, Research Assistant, Center for Study of Law and Society, University of California, Berkeley, Calif.

Marvin E. Wolfgang, Drector, Center of Criminological Research, University of Pennsylvania, Philadelphia, Pa.

NARCOTICS

Dennis S. Aronowitz, Assistant Professor of Law, Washington University, St. Louis, Mo.

Richard H. Blum, Professor, Project Director, Psychopharmocology Project, Institute for the Study of Human Problems, Stanford University, Stanford, Calif.

Jonathan O. Cole, M.D., Chief, Psychopharmocology Research Branch, National Institute of Mental Health, Public Health Service, Department of Health, Education and Welfare

Arthur D. Little, Inc., Cambridge, Mass.

Michael P. Rosenthal, Assistant Professor of Law, Rutgers University, Camden, N.J.

ORGANIZED CRIME

G. Robert Blakey, Associate Professor, Notre Dame Law School, Notre Dame, Ind.

Donald R. Cressey, Dean, College of Letters and Science, University of California, Santa Barbara, Calif.

John Gardiner, Professor, Department of Political Science, University of Wisconsin, Madison, Wis.

Rufus King, attorney, Washington, D.C.

Ralph Salerno, Central Intelligence Bureau, New York City Police Department, New York, N.Y.

Gus Tyler, Director, Department of Politics, Education, and Training, International Ladies' Garment Workers' Union, New York, N.Y.

POLICE

Richard H. Blum, Professor, Stanford University, Stanford, Calif.

Allen P. Bristow, Associate Professor, Department of Police Science and Administration, California State College at Los Angeles, Los Angeles, Calif.

William P. Brown, Professor, State University of New York, Albany, N.Y.

James E. Carnahan, Associate Professor, Department of Police Science and Administration, California State College at Los Angeles, Los Angeles, Calif.

Edward V. Comber, Project Director, Criminal Justice Information Systems Design Study, California Department of Justice, Sacramento, Calif.

J. Shane Creamer, First Assistant U.S. Attorney, Philadelphia, Pa.

William F. Danielson, Director of Personnel, City of Berkeley, Calif.

Harry Diamond, Associate Professor, Department of Police Science and Administration, California State College at Los Angeles, Los Angeles, Calif.

George D. Eastman, Headquarters Representative, Public Administration Service, Chicago, Ill.

John Fabbri, Chief of Police, South San Francisco, Calif.

Edward A. Farris, Professor of Police Science, New Mexico State University, University Park, N. Mex.

James L. Fyke, Field Representative, Public Administration Service, Chicago, Ill.

Raymond Galvin, Assistant Professor, School of Police Administration and Public Safety, Michigan State University, East Lansing, Mich.

A. C. Germann, Professor, Department of Criminology, California State College at Long Beach, Long Beach, Calif.

Herman Goldstein, Professor, University of Wisconsin Law School, Madison, Wis.

G. Douglas Gourley, Professor and Chairman, Department of Police Science and Administration, California State College at Los Angeles, Los Angeles, Calif.

John Guidici, Captain, Oakland Police Department, Oakland, Calif.

Richard O. Hankey, Professor, Department of Police Science and Administration, California State College at Los Angeles, Los Angeles, Calif.

William H. Hewitt, Assistant Professor and Chairman, Department of Police Science, State University of New York, Farmingdale, N.Y.

Roy E. Hollady, Chief of Police, Fort Collins, Colo.

Norman C. Kassoff, Supervisor, Police Training Unit, International Association of Chiefs of Police, Washington, D.C.

Joseph Kimble, Chief of Police, San Carlos, Calif.

Richard Laskin, Associate Professor, Department of Political and Social Science, Illinois Institute of Technology, Chicago, Ill.

G. Stephen Lloyd, Field Representative, Public Administration Service, Chicago, Ill.

Joseph D. Lohman, Dean, School of Criminology, University of California, Berkeley, Calif.

Lawrence S. Margolis, Special Assistant U.S. Attorney for the District of Columbia, Department of Justice

Gordon E. Misner, Visiting Associate Professor, School of Criminology, University of California, Berkeley, Calif.

Richard A. Myren, Dean, School of Criminal Justice, State University of New York, Albany, N.Y.

David L. Norrgard, Field Representative, Public Administration Service, Chicago, Ill.

George W. O'Connor, Director, Professional Standards Division, International Association of Chiefs of Police, Washington, D.C.

Bruce T. Olson, Police Administration Specialist, Institute for Community Development and Services, Michigan State University, East Lansing, Mich.

J. Kinney O'Rourke, Executive Director, Massachusetts League of Cities and Towns, Boston, Mass.

Margaret G. Oslund, Department of Political and Social Science, Illinois Institute of Technology, Chicago, Ill.

Wesley A. Pomeroy, Undersheriff, San Mateo County Sheriff's Police Department, San Mateo, Calif.

Norman E. Pomrenke, Assistant Director, Institute of Government, University of North Carolina, Chapel Hill, N.C.

Louis Radelet, Professor, School of Police Administration and Public Safety, Michigan State University, East Lansing, Mich.

Leonard E. Reisman, President, John Jay College of Criminal Justice, The City University of New York, New York, N.Y.

Gerald Robin, Office of National Analysts, Philadelphia, Pa.

Jewell L. Ross, Captain (retired), Berkeley Police Department, Berkeley, Calif.

James D. Stinchcomb, Supervisor, Police Education Unit, International Association of Chiefs of Police, Washington, D.C.

Patricia M. Wald, Commissioner, President's Commission on Crime in the District of Columbia

John B. Williams, Associate Professor, Department of Police Science and Administration, California State College at Los

Angeles, Los Angeles, Calif.

SCIENCE AND TECHNOLOGY

Mary Ellen Angell, Institute for Defense Analyses, Arlington, Va.

James E. Barr, Chief, Safety and Special Radio Services Bureau, Federal Communications Commission

Thomas Bartee, Professor, Harvard University, Cambridge, Mass.

Mandell Bellmore, Associate Professor, The Johns Hopkins University, Baltimore, Md.

Robert Brooking, Communications Engineer, City of Burbank, Calif.

Albert Bush-Brown, President, Rhode Island School of Design, Providence, R.I.

Ronald Christensen, University of California, Berkeley, Calif.

Joseph Coates, Institute for Defense Analyses, Arlington, Va.

Robert Cohen, Institute for Defense Analyses, Arlington, Va.

Jerome Daunt, Chief, Uniform Crime Reporting Section, FBI, Department of Justice

P. A. DonVito, Washington, D.C.

Ronald Finkler, Institute for Defense Analyses, Arlington, Va.

Saul I. Gass, International Business Machines, Inc., Rockville, Md.

Leonard Goodman, Bureau of Social Science Research, Washington D.C.

Norbert Halloran, International Business Machines, Inc. Yorktown Heights, N.Y.

Janice Heineken, Institute for Defense Analyses, Arlington, Va.

William Herrmann, Police Consultant, Rand Corp., University of Southern California, Los Angeles, Calif.

Thomas Humphrey, International Business Machines, Inc., Houston, Tex.

Herbert Isaacs, Los Angeles, Calif.

Sue Johnson, Glen Head, N.Y.

Robert Jones, CEIR, Inc., Bethesda, Md.

Vincent Keenan, Paoli, Pa.

Peter Kelly, Kelly Scientific Corp., Washington, D.C.

Jerry Kidd, National Science Foundation

Ray Knickel, Kelly Scientific Corp., Washington, D.C.

Richard Larson, Massachusetts Institute of Technology, Cambridge, Mass.

Peter Lejins, Professor, University of Maryland, College Park, Md.

Charles McBride, Massachusetts Institute of Technology, Cambridge, Mass.

Lois Martin, Institute for Defense Analyses, Arlington, Va.

Robert Muzzy, Research Associate, Ohio State University, Columbus, Ohio

Franz Nauta, CEIR, Inc., Bethesda, Md.

Joseph Navarro, Institute of Defense Analyses, Arlington, Va.

William Offutt, International Business Machines, Inc., Rockville, Md.

Lloyd Perper, Tucson, Ariz.

S. Rothman, TRW Systems, Redondo Beach, Calif.

Thomas Schelling, Professor, Harvard University, Cambridge, Mass.

Marsha Smith, Institute for Defense Analyses, Arlington, Va.

Peter Szanton, Bureau of the Budget

Jean Taylor, Institute for Defense Analyses, Arlington, Va.

Claude Walston, International Business Machines, Inc., Gaithersburg, Md.

Herbert Weiss, Litton Systems, Inc., Van Nuys, Calif.

Leslie T. Wilkins, Professor, University of California, Berkeley, Calif.

Marvin Wolfgang, Director, Center of Criminological Research, University of Pennsylvania, Philadelphia, Pa.

II. ADVISERS

ADMINISTRATION OF JUSTICE

Francis A. Allen, Dean, University of Michigan Law School, Ann Arbor, Mich.

Richard Arens, Professor of Law, McGill University, Montreal, Canada

Sylvia A. Bacon, Assistant Director, President's Commission on Crime in the District of Columbia

Gary Bellow, Deputy Director, California Rural Legal Assistance, Los Angeles, Calif.

Charles L. Decker, Major General, U.S. Army (retired), Director, National Defender Project of the National Legal Aid and Defender Association, Washington, D.C.

Richard A. Green, Project Director, A.B.A. Special Project for Minimum Standards for the

Administration of Criminal Justice, New York, N.Y.

Lois R. Goodman, Washington, D.C.

Geoffrey Hazard, Jr., Administrator, American Bar Foundation, Chicago, Ill.

Richard A. Lavin, attorney, Newark, N.J.

Peter Lowe, Professor of Law, University of Virginia, Charlottesville, Va.

Frank Miller, Professor of Law, Washington University, St. Louis, Mo.

Tim Murphy, Judge, Court of General Sessions, Washington, D.C.

Herbert Packer, Professor of Law, Stanford University, Stanford, Calif.

A. Kenneth Pye, Associate Dean, Georgetown University Law

Center, Washington, D.C.

Harold Rothwax, Director, Legal Services, Mobilization for Youth, New York, N.Y.

Barbara Roffwarg, New York, N.Y.

Murray L. Schwartz, Professor of Law, University of California, Los Angeles, Calif.

Ted Small, staff attorney, Office of Criminal Justice, Department of Justice

James Thompson, Professor of Law, Northwestern University, Chicago, Ill.

Jack Weinstein, Professor of Law, Columbia University, New York, N.Y.

ASSESSMENT OF CRIME

Dana Barbour, Office of Statistical Standards, Bureau of the Budget

Belton Fleischer, Professor, Department of Economics, Ohio State University, Columbus, Ohio

Donald P. Kenefick, Director, National Association of Mental Health, New York, N.Y.

Gerald Levinson, Bureau of Prisons, Department of Justice

James McCafferty, Research and Evaluation Branch, Administrative Office of the U.S. Courts

Thorsten Sellin, Professor of Sociology, University of Pennsylvania, Philadelphia, Pa.

Philip Selznick, Director, Center for the Study of Law and Society, Berkeley, Calif.

Henry Sheldon, Bureau of the Census

Stanton Wheeler, Sociologist, Russell Sage Foundation, New York, N.Y.

CORRECTIONS

Stuart Adams, Project Director, Prison College Project, University of California, Berkeley, Calif.

Dean Babst, Research Associate, Joint Commission on Correctional Manpower and Training, Washington, D.C.

James V. Bennett, Consultant, Bureau of Prisons, Washington, D.C.

George Beto, Director, Texas Department of Corrections, Huntsville, Tex.

Harold Boslow, M.D., Superintendent, Patuxent Institute, Jessups, Md.

Donald E. Clark, Sheriff, Multnomah County, Portland, Oreg.

Arthur Cohen, National Institute of Mental Health, Public Health Service, Department of Health, Education, and Welfare

John Coons, Professor of Law, Northwestern University, Chicago, Ill.

Joseph B. Dellinger, Correctional Service Federation, Baltimore, Md.

Fred Fant, New York State Division of Probation, New York, N.Y.

Paul H. Gebhard, Institute for Sex Research, Indiana University, Bloomington, Ind.

Paul Gernert, Chairman, Penn-

701

sylvania Board of Parole, Harrisburg, Pa.

Howard Gill, Director, Institute of Correctional Administration, American University, Washington, D.C.

Abraham Goldstein, Professor of Law, Yale University, New Haven, Conn.

Don M. Gottfredson, Director of Research, National Parole Institute, Davis, Calif.

John Grace, Commissioner, Salvation Army, New York, N.Y.

Alfred Hantman, Chief, Criminal Section, U.S. Attorney's Office, Washington, D.C.

Solomon Kobrin, Institute of Juvenile Research, Chicago, Ill.

Belle Lead, Lieutenant Colonel, Volunteers of America, New York, N.Y.

Peter Lejins, Professor, Department of Sociology, University of Maryland, College Park, Md.

Arthur R. Mathews, Jr. Director, Project on Mental Illness and Criminal Law, American Bar Foundation, Chicago, Ill.

A. Louis McGarry, M.D., Law and Medicine Center, University School of Medicine, Boston, Mass.

C. F. McNeil, Director, Social Welfare Assembly, New York, N.Y.

Herman G. Moeller, Assistant Director, Bureau of Prisons, Department of Justice

James Murphy, Assistant Director, Office of Law Enforcement Assistance, Department of Justice, Washington, D.C.

Abraham G. Novick, Executive Director, Berkshire Farm for Boys, Canaan, N.Y.

Joshua Okun, Professor of Law, Georgetown University Law Center, Washington, D.C.

Emery Olsen, Emeritus Dean, School of Public Administration, University of Southern California, Los Angeles, Calif.

Russell Oswald, Chairman, New York State Parole Board, Albany, N.Y.

Asher R. Pacht, Chief, Clinical Services, Division of Corrections, Department of Public Welfare, Madison, Wis.

Mauris Platkin, M.D., Chief of Service, John Howard Pavilion, St. Elizabeth's Hospital, Washington, D.C.

Samuel Polsky, Professor of Law and Legal Medicine, Temple University, Philadelphia, Pa.

Sanger Powers, Director, Division of Corrections, Wisconsin Department of Public Welfare, Madison, Wis.

Ross Randolph, Director, Department of Public Safety, Springfield, Ill.

Ames Robey, M.D., Medical Director, Massachusetts Correctional Institute, Bridgewater, Mass.

Donald H. Russell, M.D., Director, Court Clinics Program, Division of Legal Medicine, Brookline, Mass.

Russell O. Settle, M.D., Director of Law and Psychiatry,

Menninger Foundation, Topeka, Kans.

Saleem A. Shah, Center for Studies of Crime and Delinquency, National Institute of Mental Health, Public Health Service, Department of Health, Education, and Welfare

E. Preston Sharp, Executive Secretary, American Correctional Association, Washington, D.C.

Charles Smith, M.D., Chief Medical Officer, Federal Bureau of Prisons, Department of Justice

Heman Stark, Director, California State Youth Authority, Sacramento, Calif.

John A. Wallace, Director, New York City Office of Probation, New York, N.Y.

Russell L. Wilson, Board of Control, Des Moines, Ia.

Frederick Wiseman, Department of Sociology, Brandeis University, Waltham, Mass.

DRUNKENNESS

H. David Archibald, Executive Director, Addiction Research Foundation, Toronto, Canada

Leonard Blumberg, Philadelphia Diagnostic and Relocation Center, Philadelphia, Pa.

Sidney Cahn, Institute for the Study of Human Problems, Stanford University, Stanford, Calif.

Michael Laski, Project Codirector, St. Louis Detoxification Center, St. Louis Police Department, St. Louis, Mo.

Rosemary Masters, Attorney,

Vera Institute of Justice, New York, N.Y.

Frank Mateker, Captain, Director, Planning and Research Division, St. Louis Police Department, St. Louis, Mo.

Richard Merrill, Attorney, Washington, D.C.

John M. Murtagh, Justice, New York Supreme Court, New York, N.Y.

Thomas Plaut, Assistant Chief, National Center for Prevention and Control of Alcoholism, National Institute of Mental Health, Public Health Service, Department of Health, Education, and Welfare

Earl Rubington, School of Alcohol Studies, Rutgers University, New Brunswick, N.J.

Irving Shandler, Director, Philadelphia Diagnostic and Relocation Center, Philadelphia, Pa.

Thomas Shipley, Philadelphia Diagnostic and Relocation Center, Philadelphia, Pa.

Walter Stanger, Philadelphia Diagnostic and Relocation Center, Philadelphia, Pa.

Herbert J. Sturz, Director, Vera Institute of Justice, New York, N.Y.

Ralph F. Turner, Professor, School of Police Administration and Public Safety, Michigan State University, East Lansing, Mich.

JUVENILE DELINQUENCY

Lisle C. Carter, Jr., Assistant Secretary for Individual and Family Services, Department of

Health, Education, and Welfare

Forrest E. Conner, Executive Secretary, American Association of School Administrators, Washington, D.C.

J. Dudley Diggs, Judge, La-Plata, Md.

Orman W. Ketcham, Judge, Juvenile Court of the District of Columbia

James H. Lincoln, Judge, Juvenile Division, Detroit, Mich.

I. Richard Perlman, Chief, Juvenile Delinquency Studies Branch, Division of Research, Children's Bureau, Welfare Administration, Department of Health, Education, and Welfare

George B. Raison, Jr., Judge, Chestertown, Md.

Aubrey E. Robinson, Jr. Judge, Juvenile Court, Washington, D.C.

Bernard Russell, former Director, Office of Juvenile Delinquency and Youth Development, Department of Health, Education, and Welfare

Rosemary C. Sarri, Professor, School of Social Work, University of Michigan, Ann Arbor, Mich.

James W. Symington, former Executive Director, President's Committee on Juvenile Delinquency and Youth Crime

Philip B. Thurston, Judge, Family Court of New York, New York, N.Y.

Walter G. Whitlatch, Judge, Juvenile Court, Cleveland, Ohio

NARCOTICS

David Acheson, Special Assistant to the Secretary (for Enforcement), Department of the Treasury

Carl L. Anderson, Chief Program Consultant, Center for Studies of Narcotic and Drug Abuse, National Institute of Mental Health, Public Health Service, Department of Health, Education, and Welfare

Dale C. Cameron, M.D., Superintendent, St. Elizabeth's Hospital, Washington, D.C.

David Deitch, Executive Director, Daytop Village, Inc., New York, N.Y.

Vincent P. Dole, M.D., Senior Physician and Professor, Rockefeller University, New York, N.Y.

John Enright, Assistant to the Commissioner, Bureau of Narcotics, Department of the Treasury

John Finlator, Director, Bureau of Drug Abuse Control, Food and Drug Administration, Department of Health, Education, and Welfare

James H. Fox, Acting Chief, Center for Studies of Narcotic and Drug Abuse, National Institute of Mental Health, Public Health Service, Department of Health, Education, and Welfare

George Gaffney, Deputy Commissioner, Bureau of Narcotics, Department of the Treasury

F. M. Garfield, Special Assistant to the Commissioner for Drug Abuse Control, Food and Drug Administration, Department of Health, Education, and Welfare

Francis Gearing, M.D., Research Unit, School of Public Health, Columbia University, New York, N.Y.

Henry L. Giordano, Commissioner, Bureau of Narcotics, Department of the Treasury

Kenneth R. Lennington, assistant to the Director for Regulatory Operations, Food and Drug Administration, Department of Health, Education, and Welfare

Dean Markham,[1] Special Assistant to the President, Great Lakes Carbon Corp., Washington, D.C.

Aloysius J. Melia, Deputy Commissioner, Trials, New York City Police Department, New York, N.Y.

Donald S. Miller, Chief Counsel, Bureau of Narcotics, Department of the Treasury

Herbert S. Miller, Senior Research Attorney, Institute of Criminal Law and Procedure, Georgetown University Law Center, Washington, D.C.

Henry E. Peterson, Chief, Organized Crime and Racketeering Section, Criminal Division, Department of Justice

Robert Rasor, M.D., Medical Officer in Charge, U.S. Public Health Service Hospital, Lexington, Ky.

Richard J. Tatham, Chief of the Alcoholic and Drug Addiction Program, Development Office, D.C. Department of Health, Washington, D.C.

ORGANIZED CRIME

Julia Benson, Amherst, Mass.

Louis C. Cottell, Deputy Inspector, Central Intelligence Bureau, New York City Police Department, New York, N.Y.

William Duffy, Captain, Intelligence Division, Chicago Police Department, Chicago, Ill.

Robert Herman, University of California, Santa Barbara, Calif.

George Gaffney, Deputy Commissioner, Bureau of Narcotics, Department of the Treasury

William G. Hundley, Attorney, Falls Church, Va.

Aaron Kohn, Executive Director, Metropolitan Crime Commission, New Orleans, La.

Eliot Lumbard, Special Assistant to the Governor of New York for Law Enforcement, Albany, N.Y.

Henry E. Peterson, Chief, Organized Crime and Racketeering Section, Criminal Division, Department of Justice

Virgil Peterson, Director, Chicago Crime Commission, Chicago, Ill.

Alfred Scotti, Chief Assistant District Attorney, New York County, New York, N.Y.

Harold E. Yarnell, Captain, Intelligence Division, Los Angeles Police Department, Los Angeles, Calif.

[1] Deceased

POLICE

Claude Abercrombie, Jr., Sheriff, Douglas County, Douglasville, Ga.

Charles R. Adrian, Professor and Chairman, Department of Political Science, University of California, Riverside, Calif.

Douglas W. Ayres, City Manager, Salem, Oreg.

David A. Booth, Associate Professor, Department of Political Science, University of Kentucky, Lexington, Ky.

C. Beverly Brily, Mayor, Nashville, Tenn.

Thomas Brownfield, Special Agent Supervisor, FBI, Department of Justice

Robert L. Carter, General Counsel, National Association for the Advancement of Colored People, New York, N.Y.

Joseph Casper, Assistant Director, FBI, Department of Justice

George E. Causey, Deputy Chief, Metropolitan Police Department, Washington, D.C.

Ben Clark, Sheriff, Riverside County, Calif.

Donald E. Clark, Sheriff, Multnomah County, Portland, Oreg.

James Cotter, Inspector in Charge, FBI National Academy, FBI, Department of Justice

John Creer, County Commissioner, Salt Lake City, Utah

Thompson S. Crockett, Professor of Police Science, St. Petersburg Junior College, St. Petersburg, Fla.

Jerome Daunt, Chief, Uniform Crime Reporting Section, FBI, Department of Justice

C. D. deLoach, Assistant to the Director, FBI, Department of Justice

Leonard J. Duhl, Special Assistant to the Secretary of the Department of Housing and Urban Development, Washington, D.C.

Woodrow W. Dumas, Mayor, East Baton Rouge, La.

Edward L. Epting, Sergeant, San Francisco Police Department, San Francisco, Calif.

Paul E. Estaver, Dissemination Officer, Office of Law Enforcement Assistance, Department of Justice

Rev. Walter E. Fauntroy, Director, Washington Bureau Office, Southern Christian Leadership Conference, Washington, D.C.

Thomas F. Fitzpatrick, Director, Bureau of Special Services and Intelligence, San Francisco Police Department, San Francisco, Calif.

Arthur Q. Funn, General Counsel, National Urban League, Inc., New York, N.Y.

Charles R. Gain, Deputy Chief, Oakland Police Department, Oakland, Calif.

Robert R. J. Gallati, Director, New York State Intelligence and Identification System, Albany, N.Y.

Bernard Garmire, Chief of Police, Tucson, Ariz.

Peter F. Hagen, Inspector, Los

Angeles Police Department, Los Angeles, Calif.

William Harpole, Sheriff, Oktibbeha County, Starkville, Miss.

Patrick Healy, Executive Director, National League of Cities, Washington, D.C.

William W. Hermann, Police Consultant, Rand Corp., University of Southern California, Los Angeles, Calif.

James C. Herron, Captain, Philadelphia Police Department, Philadelphia, Pa.

Roderic C. Hill, Lieutenant General, Adjutant General, California National Guard, Sacramento, Calif.

William Hollowell, Sheriff, Sunflower County, Indianola, Miss.

John E. Ingersoll, Chief of Police, Charlotte, N.C.

Adolph C. Jacobsmeyer, Major, St. Louis Police Department, St. Louis, Mo.

John J. Jemilo, Deputy Assistant Director, Office of Law Enforcement Assistance, Department of Justice

Herbert T. Jenkins, Chief of Police, Atlanta, Ga.

Mark E. Keane, City Manager, Tucson, Ariz.

John T. Kelly, Deputy Chief of Police, Chicago, Ill.

Hubert O. Kemp, Chief of Police, Nashville-Davidson County, Tenn.

Floyd Mann, former Superintendent, Alabama Highway Patrol; Chambers County Sheriff's Office, Langdale, Ala.

Daniel H. Margolis, Attorney, Washington, D.C.

Robert E. McCann, Director of Training, Chicago Police Department, Chicago, Ill.

William P. McCarthy, Inspector, New York Police Department, New York, N.Y.

Roy McLaren, Director, Field Operations Division, International Association of Chiefs of Police, Washington, D.C.

Karl A. Menninger, M.D., Chief of Staff, The Menninger Foundation, Topeka, Kans.

Raymond M. Momboisse, Deputy Attorney General, California Department of Justice, Sacramento, Calif.

William Mooney, Special Agent Supervisor, FBI, Department of Justice

Patrick V. Murphy, Assistant Director, Office of Law Enforcement Assistance, Department of Justice

Joseph D. Nicol, Superintendent, Illinois Bureau of Criminal Identification and Investigation, Joliet, Ill.

John F. Nichols, District Inspector, Detroit Police Department, Detroit, Mich.

Harvard Norred, Chief of Police, Gwinnept County, Lawrenceville, Ga.

Peter J. Pitchess, Sheriff, Los Angeles County, Los Angeles, Calif.

George H. Puddy, Executive Officer, California Police Officers' Standards and Training Commission, Sacramento, Calif.

Thomas Reddin, Chief, Los Angeles Police Department, Los Angeles, Calif.

Rudy Sanfillippo, Task Force Director, Joint Commission on Correctional Manpower and Training, Washington, D.C.

Lloyd G. Sealy, Assistant Chief Inspector, New York Police Department, New York, N.Y.

Carleton F. Sharpe, City Manager, Kansas City, Mo.

Daniel J. Sharpe, Inspector, Rochester Police Department, Rochester, N.Y.

Robert Sheehan, Professor, Department of Law Enforcement Administration, Northeastern University, Boston, Mass.

R. Dean Smith, Director, Research and Development Division, International Association of Chiefs of Police, Washington, D.C.

Charles L. Southward, Brigadier General, Assistant Chief for Army National Guard, U.S. National Guard Bureau, Washington, D.C.

Daniel Stringer, Sheriff, Cherokee County, Canton, Ga.

Quinn Tamm, Executive Director, International Association of Chiefs of Police, Washington, D.C.

Carl C. Turner, Major General, Provost Marshal General, Department of the Army, Washington, D.C.

William Veeder, City Manager, Charlotte, N.C.

Nelson A. Watson, Project Director, Research and Development Division, International Association of Chiefs of Police, Washington, D.C.

Leon H. Weaver, Professor, School of Police Administration and Public Safety, Michigan State University, East Lansing, Mich.

James Q. Wilson, Associate Professor of Government, Director, Joint Center for Urban Studies of Massachusetts Institute of Technology and Harvard University, Cambridge, Mass.

Minor Keith Wilson, Assistant Chief of Police, Chicago Police Department, Chicago, Ill.

O. W. Wilson, Superintendent, Chicago Police Department, Chicago, Ill.

Orrell A. York, Executive Director, Municipal Police Training Council, Albany, N.Y.

SCIENCE AND TECHNOLOGY

A. B. Cambel, Director, Research and Engineering Support Division, Institute for Defense Analyses, Arlington, Va.

M. U. Clauser, Lincoln Laboratories, Massachusetts Institute of Technology, Cambridge, Mass.

James Fletcher, President, University of Utah, Salt Lake City, Utah

Eugene Fubini, Vice President, International Business Machines, Inc., Armonk, N.Y.

Jesse Orlansky, Research and Engineering Support Division,

Institute for Defense Analyses, Arlington, Va.

Thomas Reddin, Chief, Los Angeles Police Department, Los Angeles, Calif.

David Robinson, Office of Science and Technology, Executive Office of the President

Robert Sproull, Vice President for Academic Affairs, Cornell University, Ithaca, N.Y.

A. Tachmindji, Assistant Director, Research and Engineering Support Division, Institute for Defense Analyses, Arlington, Va.

James Q. Wilson, Associate Professor of Government, Director, Joint Center for Urban Studies of Massachusetts Institute of Technology and Harvard University, Cambridge, Mass.

Adam Yarmolinsky, Professor of Law, Harvard University, Cambridge, Mass.

IMPLEMENTATION

Seymour S. Berlin, Director, Bureau of Inspections, Civil Service Commission

Don L. Bowen, Executive Director, American Society for Public Administration, Washington, D.C.

Henry Cohen, First Deputy Human Resources Administrator, New York, N.Y.

Morris W. H. Collins, Jr., Professor of Law, University of Georgia, Athens, Ga.

Bernard L. Gladieux, Attorney, New York, N.Y.

Ferrel Heady, Director of Institute of Public Administration, University of Michigan, Ann Arbor, Mich.

T. Norman Hurd, Budget Director, State of New York, Albany, N.Y.

Dwight Ink, Assistant Secretary for Administration, Department of Housing and Urban Development

Roger W. Jones, Special Assistant to the Director, Bureau of the Budget

Herbert Kaufman, Professor, Department of Political Science, Yale University, New Haven, Conn.

Evelyn Murphy, Organization for Social and Technical Innovation, Cambridge, Mass.

William Pincus, Public Affairs Program, Ford Foundation, New York, N.Y.

Randall B. Ripley, Research Associates, Brookings Institutions, Washington, D.C.

Herbert Shepard, Organization for Social and Technical Innovation, Cambridge, Mass.

Elmer B. Staats, Comptroller General of the United States, General Accounting Office

David T. Stanley, Member Senior Staff, Brookings Institution, Washington, D.C.

Robert Steadman, Director, Committee for Improvement in

709

Government, Committee for
Economic Development

Frederick Wiseman, Organization for Social and Technical Innovation, Cambridge, Mass.

Adam Yarmolinsky, Professor of Law, Harvard University, Cambridge, Mass.

Afterword

The President's Commission was diligently served by a host of consultants and advisers; they helped compile the nine supplementary Task Force Reports corresponding to the substantive areas of the Report: The Police, The Courts, Corrections, Juvenile Delinquency and Youth Crime, Organized Crime, Assessment of Crime, Narcotics and Drug Abuse, Drunkenness, and Science and Technology. Other consultants' findings were published from time to time by the Commission, or, as in the case of a study of police misconduct, by a *New York Times* scoop.[1]

The Task Force Reports were a mixed lot. Some of them were just that: faceless reports which did little more than amplify and "flesh out" the basic chapter of the main report. Others, such as the Organized Crime Report, replicated the main report chapter but appended interesting material by named consultants. The Juvenile Delinquency Report was by far the longest and contained the most speculative information, especially in the numerous attached studies. Of particular interest was the Narcotics Report which vividly highlighted the differences between the Commission and some of its consultants, especially in the controversial area of criminal penalties for possession of heroin and marihuana.

The following section is devoted to excerpts from and comments on the Task Force Reports and supplementary consultants' papers. Since many of the most intriguing findings in the whole collection of documents are contained in the latter

[1] See *Misconduct Laid to 27% of Police in 3 Cities' Slums, The New York Times,* July 7, 1968, p. 1, Col. 3.

papers more attention will be devoted to them, proportionally, than to the more bland (and often watered-down) staff reports themselves.

The reader should perceive my bias, so that he may go beyond my choices to sample other materials, if he so wishes. Because I think that the Commission failed to face numerous problems of American criminal law and its enforcement, my first prejudice dictates that I excerpt those documents which do so. For instance, the Commission recommendation that mandatory minimum sentences for possession of narcotics be abolished does not, I think, adequately deal with the problems. In fact the strong recommendations for reduction in criminal penalties made by Professors Blum and Aronowitz (and other consultants) are, to me, more important than the tepid recommendation of the main and staff reports. Consequently I have stressed these because, to the average reader, the arguments are not generally available. I even wonder whether the proposed narcotics bill making possession of LSD a federal crime would have gotten as far as it did (passage by the House of Representatives as of this writing), had the Commission not ignored the advice of its consultants.

I also think that the Organized Crime Report is deficient in its failure to analyze or even devote much comment to the relationship between the substantive criminal law and the Mafia. Professor Thomas C. Schelling's paper, *An Economic Analysis of Organized Crime*, raises the issue whether our national preoccupation with so-called "crimes without victims" —gambling, narcotics, sex laws, abortion—has, in fact, created a criminal monopoly in the provision of services greatly desired by many people. I have also included portions of Chapter Eight of the Report on the Courts which deals with the same problem, albeit quite inadequately.

I have also chosen certain exerpts because they amplify certain otherwise sketchy information contained in the main report. The material is of sufficient importance, I think, to warrant the fuller treatment afforded by the Task Force materials. Also, such amplification tends to focus on some of the critical issues. One shortcoming of the main report is its format, which tends to make all analysis equal and all recommendations apparently of the same magnitude. The recommendations were not scaled in the order of their importance, the areas of concern were not highlighted, and the resulting amorphousness may tend to inhibit rather than foster, adequate appreciation of the virtues of the Report. I have used the Task Force findings to give some coherence to the welter of proposals put forth by the Commission. Finally, I have not included any discussion of the Report on Drunkenness and Science and Technology because the first topic is adequately covered in the main report and the second is uncontroversial.

Juvenile Delinquency and Youth Crime

This is, perhaps, the most speculative Task Force Report as well as one of the most difficult to read because of the prevalence of sociological jargon. Initially, it should be noted that this report contains numerous papers written by sociologists; these documents featured a certain particularized orientation toward social rather than individual explanations for the causes of crime. The Report makes this clear:

Study and research tend increasingly to support the view that delinquency is not so much an act of individual deviancy as a partner of behavior produced by a multitude of social influences. . . .

Thus delinquency is defined—and this may be difficult for many Americans to accept—as a condition of social maladjustment by various people to American norms and of the existence of numerous cultures within American with disparate norms.

The Report, perhaps pessimistically, notes that mere economic and social cures may not have the magical effect of changing habits and integrating deviants into middle-class society. Thus,

Sociological research has discovered little durable evidence to support the contention that poverty, broken homes, and . . . parental unfitness—alcoholism, sexual immorality, or cruelty —are in themselves causes of delinquency.

Indeed the Report haltingly recognizes that sociological analysis cannot quite explain all social deviancy because it is obvious that not all who come from broken homes and suffer other deprivations become delinquents or criminals. Theoretically, if certain "causes" of delinquency exist in the environment then all those subject to the environment should be affected in the same way. If they are not, then other factors are at work, and, perhaps, these factors can never be known. There appears to be an interplay of physical environment, parental attitudes, and, perhaps, some inheritance factors; and, of course, pure chance. We just don't know what the

713

"mix" is or exactly what elements need to be changed in order to effect broader personal changes.

The complexity of the "mix" is demonstrated by the abundance of specific sociological and psychosociological theories which purport to account for delinquency. The following excerpts provide a (very) superficial insight into the theories and their contradictions:

Two major theories of delinquency causation argue that delinquent commitments result from blockages in the attainment of highly valued success goals.

*   *   *

When internal controls are sufficiently weak, or when illegitimate patterns of behavior are readily accessible, some of these youth reject or rebel against legitimate patterns of conduct and at the same time collectively adopt new illegitimate commitments and standards as an alternative avenue to status and status symbols or as means of striking back at the middle class world that produced goal-frustration in the first place.

*   *   *

Some youth become delinquent because of a basic lack of commitment to conventional, middle-class adult roles and to community standards of behavior. [One analyst] takes the position that many lower-class youth become delinquent not because of deprivation or goal frustration but because their behavior is a simple reflection of "lower-class culture" which they have learned. In other words, they have been acculturated into a way of life that in the natural course of things calls for behavior that is consistent with the 'focal concerns' of 'trouble, toughness, smartness, excitement, fate, and autonomy,' but that is inconsistent with the conventional standards of the larger community. Implicit in this theory is that lower-class youth have become committed but to a set of standards and values that are antithetical to dominant norms and values. Lower-class norms call neither for achievement and conformity in school nor for conformity with community laws.

*   *   *

Another theory suggests that lower-class individuals stretch their values, and approve both lower and middle-class values. They have a wider range of values, but also a lower degree of commitment to any of the values in the range. As a consequence, they are more open to the possibility of acts that are defined as delinquent by the official representatives of society.

The foregoing theories share the assumption that a certain "breaking away" from conventional patterns occurs; they tend to deemphasize the role of family and social controls in preventing this process. Other theories are based on the ineffectiveness of such controls:

An analyst hypothesized that delinquency is likely to result when personal and social controls break down.

* * *

Another suggested that four attitude and behavior patterns are influential in controlling juvenile delinquency: "(1) Direct control imposed from without by means of restriction and punishment, (2) internalized control exercised from within through conscience, (3) indirect control related to affectional identification with parents and other noncriminal persons, and (4) availability of alternative means to goals and values."

* * *

Yet another pointed to social disorganization—living in a slum or high-delinquency area or being an immigrant or migrant—as the breakdown of social controls and a cause of delinquency. The absence of effective discipline was an indicator of family disorganization and another form of social control failure. But most of [this] emphasis is concerned with the factor of inner control, the development of a child's self-concept and superego. Intensive longitudinal studies of boys in a high delinquency slum area who do not become delinquent revealed that these boys, chosen by their teachers, compared over a period of years with a group of delinquents, were marked especially by an excellent self-concept—they evaluated their families favorably; they evaluated their school experiences favorably; and they were confident of their ability to stay out of trouble.

Another theory is premised on the assumption that disruptive family conditions of lower class life create "premature autonomy" for many children. The child is forced to make decisions for himself and tends to be resentful when others, such as school officials, attempt to exercise authority and control. This may occur quite early in life.

The discipline associated with the loose organization and female focus that characterize many inner-city families has

715

also been related by social scientists to the development of what has been termed "premature autonomy" and to consequent resentment of authority figures such as policemen and teachers. Often child-rearing practices are either very permissive or very stern—the latter reinforced physically. In the first instance, the child is on his own, in charge of his own affairs, from an early age. He becomes accustomed to making decisions for himself and reacts to the direction or demands of a teacher or other adults as to a challenge of his established independence. Strictness is not objectionable in itself, when it is seen as fairminded and well meant. But where strictness amounts simply to control by force, the child harbors resentment until the day when he can successfully assert physical mastery himself.

* * *

The posture of premature autonomy is carried directly into the schools and the result is the 'predelinquent.' As early as the first and second grade, his teachers find him wild, distracted, and utterly oblivious to their presumed authority. He gets out of chairs when he feels like it; begins fighting when he feels like it; and all of this is done as if the teacher were not present. Even the best teachers find him virtually unmanageable in groups, even though the best teachers also seem to like these boys.

Once the boys begin proving they are 'tough,' there seems to be little the school can do to stop them. If they are suspended, they come to school anyway; and if they are transferred from one class to another they return to the first class or to whatever teacher they happen to like. The social system of the third grader is an arena of social life that very much needs to be explored. It is certainly the beginning of the 'delinquent career,' and in some respects it seems to be its wildest phase. The boys seem immune to sanctions, and thus bullying, theft, and truancy are often blatantly displayed. It is not really until the fifth or sixth grade that organized gangs begin to form, and, in a certain sense, it is not until this age that the boys can be brought under systematic group control.

Other theories incorporating features of the aforementioned ones have been posited,[2] and the interested reader is referred

---

[2] *The Gluecks' classic delinquency research study compared 500 delinquent boys with 500 controls, equated for age, IQ, ethnic deprivation and residence in underprivileged neighborhoods. Some of the significant differences they reported were: (1) the family backgrounds of the delinquents' parents revealed more mental retardation, more emotional*

to the consultant's papers to the Task Force Report. Despite the profusion, several of the consultants clearly favored the view that delinquent groups essentially shared middle class values "but were deprived of the opportunity to participate in their realization."

There is reason to believe that, while young people frequently act out, it is because they want in. While some behavior is antisocial or even self-destructive, it is, to some extent, a way of letting society know the concerns of youth. While youth voices are often heard condemning and rejecting the larger society, youth continues to see itself as part of that larger society; it seeks the challenge of involvement, desires, rather than rejects, commitment, and searches for valid opportunities around which to build such commitment.

*   *   *

. . . perceived prospects for future occupational status was found to be a far more important determinant of 'rebellion' than social or economic origin.

*   *   *

. . . rebellion . . . occurs when future status is not closely related to present performance. When a student realizes that he has not achieved status increment from improved current performance, current performance loses meaning. The stu-

---

disturbances, more drunkenness, more criminality; (2) more fathers were poor workers and poor wage earners, and more families were on public welfare relief; (3) there was more incompatibility and conflict in the parental marriages; (4) more mothers failed to provide adequate supervision for the children, and parents knew less about the activities of their delinquent sons; (5) fathers were more lacking in warmth, sympathy, and affection toward their sons; and the boys did not perceive their fathers as suitable objects for emulation; (6) the picture of the mothers' relationship to their delinquent sons was less clear and consistent than that of the fathers, in that some mothers were overprotective, while others were indifferent and rejecting; (7) the total impression was of compelling evidence that the family backgrounds and atmosphere of the delinquent boys was less positive than those of the control boys.

*   *   *

These and many other studies support the presence of familial factors in various forms of juvenile delinquency. It must be kept in mind, however, that delinquency is caused by a variety of complex factors and that the family is not the sole determination of behavior. Further, as was indicated earlier, the way in which the family functions is highly dependent on its relationships with community institutions. The present lack of fit between many families and institutions calls for basic and radical changes in institutional policies and programs.

dent becomes hedonistic because he does not visualize achievement of long run goals through current self-constraint. He reacts negatively to a conformity that offers nothing concrete. He claims autonomy from adults because their authority does not promise a satisfactory future.

* * *

More indirect evidence is contained in a number of studies which show that the greater the extent to which youth perceive future opportunities as closed, the greater the delinquency.

Most of the foregoing theories closely relate delinquency to adverse educational experiences. Thus teachers in slum schools with their middle-class values teaching a middle-class curriculum, judging and labeling students as "delinquents" and "troublemakers" (or just plain incompetents) also play a crucial role in causing disappointment, cynicism, and, for many, ultimate delinquency. This is the current staple of much popular literature.[3]

First, we contend that the traditional emphasis on individualism in this country, while responsible for much of our growth and vitality, has at the same time been responsible for a pervasive middle class emphasis on exclusion of certain groups from full participation and opportunity: Negroes; the poverty stricken; people in trouble, including adult criminals and ex-criminals, delinquents, and deviants in school; and adolescents in general. We further contend that the middle class school is the primary agent for perpetuating this 'exclusion orientation.' Therefore, we believe a major reorientation of the values taught in those schools is essential.

* * *

While certain handicaps are frequently present, the school itself contributes to failure by not designing its program, curriculum, and techniques of instruction so that such deficiencies are taken account of and effectively offset, and so that the life experiences and cultural assets of such children are used and built on in a positive way.

* * *

Advocates of this position point to research indicating that (1) most lower income children do recognize the importance of education and place a high personal value on educational

<hr/>

[3] Jonathan Kozol's *Death at an Early Age* won the National Book Award for 1967.

*success and attainments; (2) most of them do have the poten-
tial to learn and to develop into capable, responsible, and
productive adults; and (3) many of them have shown remarkable development under educational conditions different
from those prevailing in most schools, especially in the urban
slums.*

* * *

*The way in which the school responds to early signs of
misbehavior may have a profound influence in either diverting the youngster from or propelling him along the path to a
delinquent career. Not all teachers have trouble with 'difficult' youngsters. Some, especially sensitive to what lies behind
insolence and disobedience, adopt a firm but positive attitude
that allows the task of learning to be carried on, if not always
under placid conditions.*

* * *

*Other teachers simply submit, ignoring as best they can
commotions and disruptions of classroom routine—an alternative that avoids head-on conflict with autonomy-seeking
youth but at the same time deprives them of instruction even
when they choose to accept it.*

* * *

*Many teachers, on the other hand, assume a right to
unquestioning obedience. There results a sometimes ceaseless
conflict between teacher and child. The child's assertions of
autonomy are dealt with by the teacher, and eventually the
school administration, as misbehavior, and sanctioned in a
variety of ways. By labeling the youth a troublemaker and
excluding him from legitimate activities and sources of
achievement, the sanctions may reinforce his tendency to
rebel and resist the school's authority. Nor is it easy for him
to reform; grades lowered for misconduct, the stigma of assignment to a special class, and records of misbehavior passed
on both formally and informally from teacher to teacher
make his past difficult to live down. The conception he forms
of himself as an outsider, a nonconformer, is of particular
importance. With no other source of public recognition, such
negative self-images become attractive to some young people,
and they begin to adapt their behavior to fit the labels applied
to them. A process of defining and communicating a public
character occurs, and some young people in a sense cooperate in actually becoming the delinquents they are said to be.*

Yet, even this theory is challenged:

Regardless of whether the delinquent is ambitious and capable, ambitious and incapable, or unambitious and incapable, the school is sketched as a monolith of middle class personnel against which he fares badly.

Yet data collected by observation and interview over a 2-year period on the educational performances and classroom experiences of lower class gang members suggests that pitting middle class schools against variations in the motivation and capacity of some lower class boys is at best too simple and at worst incorrect as a model of the problems faced by the delinquents.

First, some of the 'trouble' that gang boys get into takes place on school grounds but outside the classroom.

* * *

Second, during middle adolescence when the law requires gang members to attend school, there seems to be no relationship between academic performance and 'trouble.' Gangs contain bright boys who do well, bright boys who do less well, dull boys who pass, dull boys who fail, and illiterates.

Finally, the school difficulties of these boys occur only in some classes and not others.

The Report agrees that the most significant environmental factor is not poverty but rather the pace of social change within a community. Although rapid social change may create as many problems in suburbia as in the inner city, the Report's orientation is toward the latter:

Societies where there is little or no change are rigid . . . and there is little opportunity for delinquency or rebellion . . . Where change is rapid . . . the traditional institutional ways of dealing with problems are not effective answers. . . .

* * *

The particular form of delinquency in any society is related in fundamental ways to other characteristics of that society. A society that places a high premium on freedom over order, that prizes material success, and that encourages mobility aspirations is not likely to be able to contain all its members within a conventional mold. Delinquency is one way to break that mold. Short of a major change in values, such as a return to a more traditional, pre-industrial way of life, members of our society may have to tolerate a fairly high amount of nonconformity among youth.

These considerations should serve to caution against an assumption that delinquency can be wiped out by one or an-

other crash program, while leaving all else in society un-changed.

Since America is nothing, if not rapid change, and, often, such change occurs in poverty areas, a certain amount of criminal conduct will become inevitable. Perhaps we should not deplore that "hard core" conduct, for we may be loath to relinquish the benefits accompanying change. In addition, we shall simply be hard pressed to give up our traditional "ways of doing things." As the Report notes:

[M]any aspects of the American ethic, our freedom, our be-nevolent attitude toward rapid social change . . . our encour-agement of mass migrations . . . in or near large urban cen-ters . . . may produce the delinquency we deplore. . . .

Another vital characteristic of middle-class society is its drive to conform and its (relative) intolerance of conduct, not necessarily dangerous, which is "different." We tend to treat even occasional acts of deviance as somehow sympto-matic of dangerous tendencies and invoke the clanking armor of the criminal (or nearly criminal) law to deal with them. In short, we overreact. In overreacting, we apply labels; in la-beling we somehow segregate "bad" children from their com-patriots:

Since many antisocial activities are unplanned outbursts of childhood and adolescent frustration, many offenders will ma-ture to productive adulthood if they are not labeled as de-linquent and stigmatized by correctional processes.

*   *   *

The conclusion that the court processing rather than the behaviors in some way helps to fix and perpetuate delin-quency in many cases is hard to escape.

There are other data which suggest that formal efforts by the juvenile court to shape the course of childhood and ado-lescent development away from hypothetically dire directions in the large may be gratuitous or self-defeating. The refer-ence is to facts or common knowledge that most youth pass through epochs in their lives when they engage in activities definable in other than their contexts as delinquency. Chil-dren normally play hookey, help themselves to lumber from houses under construction, snitch lipstick or other items from 10-cent stores, swipe some beer, get a little drunk, borrow a car, hell around, learn about sex from an available female or prostitute, or give the old man a taste of his own medicine. Transitional deviance not only is ubiquitous in our society but universal to all societies.

*　　*　　*

Delinquency is a vague and slippery concept indeed. Acts that may serve to get a juvenile labeled delinquent are enormously varied. Many of our difficulties at all stages of prevention, adjudication, and correction are rooted in the tremendous variety of acts that may at different times and places be defined as delinquent. The following, for example, were all causes for official police contacts with juveniles in a major east coast city in recent months: selling flowers without a permit, possession of an air rifle, loitering, neglect of minor children, breaking and entering, assault and battery, and armed robbery. Moreover, activity regarded in one area as 'normal' will be regarded as delinquent in another area even in the same jurisdiction. It follows that discussions of delinquency are likely to be plagued by definitional problems.

Indeed, in the words of one sociologist, "deviance is not a quality of the act a person commits, but rather a consequence of the application by others of rules and sanctions to an 'offender.'"

Several papers are concerned with this problem and its consequences:

Social groups create deviance by making the rules whose infraction constitutes deviance, and by applying those rules to particular people and labeling them as outsiders. The deviant is one to whom that label has successfully been applied; deviant behavior is behavior that people so label.

*　　*　　*

At the very least it is possible to assert with considerable confidence that while crime and delinquency are likely to occur in all income groups, the particular types that preoccupy us as a society are concentrated among males in lower income groups living in urban centers. Once again, values are operative, and have the effect of coloring the priorities in our indignations. Homicides on city streets (or, more likely, as the result of payday arguments in the kitchens of low-income homes) thus concern us a good deal more in most discussions of crime than hazards of fatal shock from faulty domestic appliances sold to the public by manufacturers, demonstrably harmful drugs that deform babies, pesticides that poison con-

sumers, or steering mechanisms that cripple or kill motorists. And this is not simply a cynical assertion. Our tolerance for "big deviance" is reflected in the ruling by the Internal Revenue Service permitting damages paid to victims of the electrical conspiracy, in the 1960's, to be deducted from corporate income for tax purposes, as '. . . ordinary and necessary business expenses.'

Of course in rebuttal we might say that every dominant social group in every society makes rules and punishes violators. Would not the "relativistic" approach taken by social scientists undermine the very basis of organized society—a recognized authority which makes rules for the continued viability of that society? If America is a white middle-class society, why shouldn't it enforce its norms?

The answer to these perfectly reasonable questions is both "yes" and "no." "Yes" in the sense that, obviously, dominant social groups will continue to create and enforce their norms —that must be regarded as a "given" in the social equation. "No" in the sense that the ability of these groups to formulate rules is subject to legal bounds—the Constitution and laws enacted under it. Clearly, majority rule cannot preclude minority dissent, at least in the form of speech because we, as a Nation, have Constitutionally dedicated ourselves to this proposition. We also have agreed to observe certain procedural rights for everyone, deviant or not, in Federal and State Bills of Rights.

America also is not a homogenous society, as are most other nations. We pride ourselves on our commitment to "diversity," to "pluralism," to the ability of competing social groups to find meaningful if not necessarily complete outlets for their life styles within the broader social framework. We must recognize that America is not simply a PTA America, a white middle-class America, an American Legion America, but rather it is a multipurpose social organism. We cannot even define juvenile delinquency or crime without a recognition of social diversity:

A question basic to th[is] exploration . . . is the capacity of American society as a whole to tolerate diversity. . . .

*   *   *

In attempting to deal with the problems . . . are we proceeding with the end in mind of eventually producing behavior which is acceptable to that which is traditionally 'white middle-class'? [I]f our goal is to encourage and provide for a di-

*versity of cultural and economic styles of life . . . then . . .
our strategy for changing 'deviant' behavior will be governed
by very different assumptions about behavior itself.*

Another germane question is whether conformity can best
be achieved by the criminal law or by other social processes.
Even if we tend to overlabel conduct as "deviant," and over-
look diversity as a desirable social goal, the real problem is
whether we seek conformity through punitive or other
means. We have largely chosen to *coerce* rather than encourage conformity through the use of criminal sanctions.

This might be true for several reasons: other socializing institutions are weak. We have no national church or Council
of Elders to exercise moral wisdom. Although many Americans are churchgoers, they go to different churches. Also, we
cannot be sure of just what kind of influence religious institutions exercise over them. Most people are not very religious,
and their conduct is affected by other factors in the environment—materialism, the notion of progress—which frequently
vary significantly from church teaching.

We still regard government with suspicion, or at least when
its purposes conflict with personal economic goals. Government is still thought of as "big," and even liberals have become disenchanted with federal spending programs. The Constitution is essentially a scheme for limiting the powers (and,
inevitably, the functions) of government because of our peculiar historical heritage. If "government derives its power
from the consent of the governed," we give that consent only
grudgingly. Certainly there are few who would claim that
government has much legitimate authority over fundamental
social decisions.

If Americans think in terms of "natural law"—the existence of an ideal social and political State guaranteeing each
man his freedom—we utilize that concept to limit governmental encroachment upon that freedom. Our political arguments tend to be couched in the rhetoric of "constitu-
tionalism," and that rhetoric automatically involves an assumption that government is not to have moral authority.
Well-meaning politicians—and most of us would agree, on
particular issues—argue that on the one hand "X" condition
is deplorable, and on the other that "good will," "private enterprise," or some other such agency is better equipped than
government to alleviate that condition.

Perhaps, paradoxically, because our social institutions are
weak we come to rely on the law. We make a fetish of "Law
and Order" and are often hypocritical in the process, for

those who advocate the maxim in one area often deplore it in another (where their interpretation of the Constitution tells them that the exercise of governmental authority is illegal.) Law can either encourage good, or discourage evil, and, in controlling social deviancy, we often opt for the latter. We do not reward people for being good, but punish them for being bad. The Law operates petulantly and sulks; it should, perhaps, raise men's aspirations and, hopefully, their conduct. Probably most Americans, were they polled on the question, would equate "Law" and "Criminal Law." We use the law because we feel that no other sanction could possibly be effective. If we are to ask of social deviants that they conform, perhaps we should ask it in different ways; yet we do not know how.

Perhaps different people should be asking the questions; for there is a clear tendency to allow "experts" to take over the function of labeling rather than merely dealing with deviancy.

The current trends toward professionalization in the field of delinquency prevention and control services may lead toward a broader category of persons being defined as 'in need of service' than in the past. For there is at least a modicum of evidence that the more sophisticated personnel become, the greater is their tendency to see symptoms of problem behavior, and therefore the greater the tendency to engage in some form of intervention. It is the very feeling of confidence in the sophisticated techniques of modern intervention methods that may serve as justification for placing children in special therapeutic settings, in residential treatment centers, and in institutions thought to be beneficial for them. Thus a study of police relations with juveniles suggests that the more professional a police system is, the larger is the percentage of the juvenile population formally charged with delinquency. A study of judges suggests that those with more therapeutically oriented attitudes were somewhat more willing to commit children to institutions, and an authority on youth correctional systems who has surveyed them around the country is left with the strong feeling that it is the states with the most professional services that implicate the largest number of children in the official agencies and institutions.

Even those scientists who see deviant conduct as a search for identity probably fall into this category, for the existence of identity is socially determined. In fact the Task Force discussion would be clarified by an admission that the search for identity also involves a desire to destroy present identity.

Of course we should be upset by dangerous deviance, by the violent manifestations of social disorientation. We should eagerly seek "cures."

This study lends support to the view that the criminal career is frequently the result of a gradual process of habituation to forms of illegal behavior. It does not, of course, indicate what proportion of adult criminals developed by this process, but since more than 60 percent of all juvenile delinquents have adult criminal records, and since a large proportion of these are known to have engaged in serious offenses, this group, in the aggregate, must constitute a large part of the criminal population.

After all, dangerous deviance may be a tip-off to later criminal conduct. The Task Force papers are pessimistic about solutions. One study of male delinquents in Illinois training institutions concluded that:

But do we know enough about delinquency to specify the ways in which even a moderate reduction could be brought about? In terms of verified knowledge, the answer must be an unqualified no. There is, of course, a vast body of literature reporting numerous research findings, and suggesting a variety of plausible theories of delinquency causation and control. But when experiments have been conducted, the results have not been encouraging. Indeed, as of now, there are no demonstrable and proven methods for reducing the incidence of serious delinquent acts through preventive or rehabilitative procedures.

* * *

The principal findings indicate that little success attends present efforts to rehabilitate these children.

* * *

Thus, it can be concluded that the behavior of significant numbers of boys who become involved in illegal activities is not redirected toward conventional activity by the institutions created for that purpose.

As with adult correctional endeavors (to be discussed later), new goals may be necessary:

One form of reaction is to have no formal disposition at

726

all. The court procedures, may be enough to deter the offender from further unlawful activity. He may be less likely to repeat an offense if there is no correctional program put into effect in his behalf. It is precisely this possibility that led the framers of the New York Family Court Act to allow for 'no-disposition,' following the determination of fact. Relatively little use has been made of this alternative so far, but there is a feeling that its use could be systematically increased. Thus one very real and possibly very meaningful alternative is simply to invoke no disposition whatsoever.

*   *   *

It may well be that whatever impact is obtained by staying in an institution is accomplished during the first two weeks or months of that stay and conceivably within the first few days. Extremely short terms, of course, do not allow for intensive treatment over a long period of time in a controlled environment. But the obvious advantages of very short terms would seem to require that the burden of proof should be on those who argue that a long term is really necessary. In a short-term stay, the offender may not lose his standing in his school, nor will he necessarily suffer the presumed stigma of commitment to a traditional penal institution.

*   *   *

The evidence seems to suggest, however, that a self-healing process tends to operate in most areas except in those close to the heart of the city where rapid change is a permanent characteristic. Given time, order tends to replace disorder. The adults learn to play satisfactorily the different roles in our industrial and commercial life, some new institutional forms are created and some old institutional forms are modified to meet new problems. All of these developments tend to create the web of institutional bliss which constitutes the basis for a stable social order.

*   *   *

There is some evidence to suggest that most gang boys have a conception of how and when their careers as "delinquents" will end. Most look forward to becoming stable and dependable husbands in well-run households, despite their reluctance to voice these expectations around one another and despite the fact that some become fathers out of wedlock along the way. Their images of family life make it clear that the great majority expect to be holding down some kind of conventional occupation when they become 'adults.' During most of the years spent in gangs, however, these occupational

*concerns are neither salient nor relevant. The boys under-
stand that as long as they are defined and define themselves
as 'youth,' they are not the people they will someday become;
and for this reason they have little difficulty identifying with
two apparently conflicting sets of attitudes, values, and behavior patterns.*

* * *

*Rates of delinquency should be decreasing in those areas
which are moving toward institutional stability. This appears
to be the case in several areas of Negro population in Chicago where the population has had several decades to make
an adjustment to urban life.*

Although the causes of delinquency may be complex, and
the cures unknown, one solution must involve the elimination
of poverty. Of course poverty is a social evil, and its elimination is worthwhile for many reasons. The main Report and
the Task Force conclusions may be viewed as ingenuous attempts to endorse and bolster the President's Poverty Program, a crucial issue at the time the Report was issued; but
whatever the uses of the argument, its internal validity is apparent:

*Juvenile delinquency is disproportionately found among Ne-
groes, as is lower-class status, slum residence, unemployment,
and various indices of family breakdown. The question is:
How do we unravel this tangle of problems? Do we place
first priority upon enhancing family stability or employment
stability, for example? Our opinion is that [emphasis should
be] upon the latter for two reasons. One is the research evidence which suggests that the main direction of the causal relationship is from instability of employment to family
instability. The second is that it seems easier to have a direct
impact upon employment stability than upon family stability.*

Although the first seven words of that statement might be
open to question,[4] its perhaps undramatic conclusion is not.
If we do not really understand juvenile delinquency, and if
our attempts to cope with it have failed, what can be said for
the procedures by which we judge a child to be "delinquent"?

[4] Professor Ivan Berg, in a consultant's paper notes:

*The serious bias is not that published data overstate the criminality
occurring in low-income population groups, but that the categories . . .
have the effect of understating the delinquency of other social groups.*

The first problem is, of course, to define "delinquency"; for no procedure can be meaningful unless it can operate on something substantive. Legal definitions of the term are incredibly loose, so that all sorts of conduct are encompassed within its broad rubric. Truants, "stubborn" children, runaway children, as well as those who have committed specific antisocial acts are lumped together in the definition. Perhaps, as Constitutional principles of due Process of Law become increasingly applied to juvenile proceedings, at least some of the open-ended definitions will be tightened.

The disposition of serious juvenile cases occurs in juvenile courts throughout the land. One great vista of the 19th century American dream of justice resulted in the creation of this supposedly unique institution to rehabilitate wayward youth. Presumably no degrading criminal record would be attached to someone found delinquent, and informal procedures would insure sympathetic disposition of the case.

. . . the postulates of specialized treatment and resulting reclamation basic to the juvenile court have significantly failed of proof, both in implementation and in consequences. The dispositions available for most youths adjudicated delinquent are indistinguishable from those for adult criminals: probation with a minimum of contact—much less supervision worthy of the name—with a probation officer who commonly does not have time to uncover underlying problems but can only spot-check the probationer's conformance with such arbitrary rules as early curfew, total abstinence from alcohol and tobacco, isolation from companions deemed undesirable (who may be his best friends); or institutionalization in what is often, as a result of overcrowding and understaffing, a maximum security warehouse for youths. The vaunted intermediate and auxiliary measures—community residential centers, diversified institutions and institutional programs, intensive supervision—with which youth was to be reclaimed have come to pass only sporadically, hampered by lack of money, lack of staff, lack of support, lack of evaluation.

*   *   *

In addition to behavior that would be criminal on the part of an adult, delinquency includes behavior illegal only for a child: Conduct uniquely children's—truancy, incorrigibility —and conduct tolerated for adults but objectionable for children—smoking, drinking, using vulgar language, violating curfew laws, hanging around in bars or with felons or gamblers.

The provisions on which intervention in this category of cases is based are typically vague and all-encompassing: Growing up in idleness and crime, engaging in immoral conduct, in danger of leading an immoral life. Especially when administered with the informality characteristic of the court's procedures, they establish the judge as arbiter not only of the behavior but also of the morals of every child (and to a certain extent the parents of every child) appearing before him. The situation is ripe for over-reaching, for imposition of the judge's own code of youthful conduct. One frequent consequence has been the use of general protective statutes about leading an immoral life and engaging in endangering conduct as a means of enforcing conformity—eliminating long hair, levis, and other transitory adolescent foibles so unsettling to adults. One need not expound the traditional American virtues of individuality and free expression to point out the wrongheadedness of so using the juvenile court; it is enough to reflect that the speed with which such fads come and go is equaled only by the strength of their resistance to outside attack.

The Dream of the 19th century became the Nightmare of the 20th. Rather than discuss the shortcomings of the juvenile court system in the abstract, or by quoting from the Task Force critique (which is devastating), some language from Justice Fortas' landmark opinion in *In Re Gault* should be sufficient:

But it is important, we think, that the claimed benefits of the juvenile process should be candidly appraised. Neither sentiment nor folklore should cause us to shut our eyes, for example, to such startling findings as that reported in an exceptionally reliable study of repeaters or recidivism conducted by the Stanford Research Institute for the President's Commission on Crime in the District of Columbia. This Commission's Report states:

'In fiscal 1966 approximately 66 percent of the 16- and 17-year-old juveniles referred to the court by the Youth Aid Division had been before the court previously. In 1965, 56 percent of those in the Receiving Home were repeaters. The SRI study revealed that 61 percent of the sample Juvenile Court referrals in 1965 had been previously referred at least once and that 42 percent had been referred at least twice before.'

Certainly, these figures and the high crime rates among juveniles to which we have referred could not lead us to conclude that the absence of constitutional protections reduces crime, or that the juvenile system, functioning free of constitutional inhibitions as it has largely done, is effective to reduce crime or rehabilitate offenders.

* * *

The early conception of the juvenile court proceeding was one in which a fatherly judge touched the heart and conscience of the erring youth by talking over his problems, by paternal advice and admonition, and in which, in extreme situations, benevolent and wise institutions of the State provided guidance and help 'to save him from a downward career.' Then, as now, goodwill and compassion were admirably prevalent. But recent studies have, with surprising unanimity, entered sharp dissent as to the validity of this gentle conception. They suggest that the appearance as well as the actuality of fairness, impartiality and orderliness—in short, the essentials of due process may be a more impressive and more therapeutic attitude so far as the juvenile is concerned.

* * *

Under traditional notions, one would assume that in a case like that of Gerald Gault, where the juvenile appears to have a home, a working mother and father, and an older brother, the Juvenile Judge would have made a careful inquiry and judgment as to the possibility that the boy could be disciplined and dealt with at home, despite his previous transgressions. Indeed, so far as appears in the record before us, except for some conversation with Gerald about his school work and his 'wanting to go to . . . Grand Canyon with his father,' the points to which the judge directed his attention were little different from those that would be involved in determining any charge of violation of a penal statute. The essential difference between Gerald's case and a normal criminal case is that safeguards available to adults were discarded in Gerald's case. The summary procedure as well as the long commitment were possible because Gerald was 15 years of age instead of over 18.

* * *

If Gerald had been over 18, he would not have been subject to Juvenile Court proceedings. For the particular offense immediately involved, the maximum punishment would have been a fine of $5 to $50, or imprisonment in jail for not more than two months. Instead, he was committed to custody

731

for a maximum of six years. If he had been over 18 and had committed an offense to which such a sentence might apply, he would have been entitled to substantial rights under the Constitution of the United States as well as under Arizona's laws and constitution. The United States Constitution would guarantee him rights and protections with respect to arrest, search and seizure, and pretrial interrogation. It would assure him of specific notice of the charges and adequate time to decide his course of action and to prepare his defense. He would be entitled to clear advice that he could be represented by counsel, and, at least if a felony were involved, the State would be required to provide counsel if his parents were unable to afford it. If the court acted on the basis of his confession, careful procedures would be required to assure its voluntariness. If the case went to trial, confrontation and opportunity for cross-examination would be guaranteed. So wide a gulf between the State's treatment of the adult and of the child requires a bridge sturdier than mere verbiage, and reasons more persuasive than cliché can provide.

Justice Fortas' comments on the necessity to preserve civil liberties in juvenile court proceedings are, as we shall see, equally applicable to voluntary commitment of narcotics addict programs and other "rehabilitative" proceedings.[5]

A boy is charged with misconduct. The boy is committed to an institution where he may be restrained of liberty for years. It is of no constitutional consequence—and of limited practical meaning—that the institution to which he is committed is called an Industrial School. The fact of the matter is that, however euphemistic the title, a 'receiving home' or an "industrial school" for juveniles is an institution of confinement in which the child is incarcerated for a greater or lesser time. His world becomes 'a building with white-washed walls, regimented routine and institutional laws. . . .' Instead of mother and father and sisters and brothers and friends and classmates, his world is peopled by guards, custodians, state employees, and 'delinquents' confined with him for anything from waywardness to rape and homicide.

In view of this, it would be extraordinary if our Constitution did not require the procedural regularity and the exercise of care implied in the phrase 'due process.' Under our Consti-

5 See pp. 739-42 herein.

tution, the condition of being a boy does not justify a kanga-roo court.

Narcotics and Drug Abuse

The staff section of the Task Force Report on Narcotics and Drug Abuse is as bland as the corresponding data in the main Report. We are told that the problem of narcotics law enforcement is thorny, although—without specification of examples—the enforcement process works.

> *There are no complaining witnesses or victims; there are only sellers and willing buyers. The enforcement officer must therefore initiate cases. He must find and take up positions along the illicit traffic lanes. The standard technique for doing this is undercover investigation during which an officer assumes another identity for the purpose of gathering evidence or making a 'buy' of evidence. The use of informants to obtain leads and to arrange introductions is also standard and essential. An informant may or may not be a person facing criminal charges. If he is not, he may supply information out of motives of revenge or monetary reward. More typically the informant is under charges and is induced to give information in return for a 'break' in the criminal process such as a reduction of those charges. Frequently he will make it a condition of cooperation that his identity remain confidential.*
>
> *The payoff in enforcement is the 'big case' against the major violator with executive rank in the traffic. This man is hard to identify and harder to implicate with legal evidence. He has a shield of people in front of him, and by not handling drugs himself he removes his liability to prosecution under laws that prohibit possession, sale, or other such acts. The conspiracy laws are the most useful weapon against such a person, and over the years many important convictions have been obtained under these laws on evidence developed by the Bureau of Narcotics and the Bureau of Customs.*

This section also restates the main Report's conclusion that there is a distinction between marihuana and the more severe opiates such as heroin:

> *Marihuana is equated in law with the opiates, but the abuse characteristics of the two have almost nothing in common. The opiates produce physical dependence. Marihuana does not. A withdrawal sickness appears when use of the opi-*

733

ates is discontinued. No such symptoms are associated with marihuana. The desired dose of opiates tends to increase over time, but this is not true of marihuana. Both can lead to psychic dependence, but so can almost any substance that alters the state of consciousness.

The main Report's recommendation that mandatory minimum sentences for narcotics offenses be eliminated is dutifully echoed with, of course, the slightest disclaimer:

State and Federal drug laws should give a large enough measure of discretion to the courts and correctional authorities to enable them to deal flexibly with violators, taking account of the nature and seriousness of the offense, the prior record of the offender and other relevant circumstances.

It should be noted that parole rights have already been reinstated for Federal marihuana violators by a provision of Public Law 89–793.

In submitting the foregoing recommendations, the Commission also wishes to record its concurrence in the view of the Bureau of Narcotics that long terms of imprisonment for major drug violators are essential.

The dynamite is to be found in the consultant's papers appended to this rather vacuous report. Professor Richard H. Blum in *Mind-Altering Drugs and Dangerous Behavior: Dangerous Drugs*, begins the assault with an opening foray against popular conceptions of the nature of drug use:

It is best to begin with a few general statements designed to put drug use and drug effects in perspective. In the first place, it is clear that our interest should be not in what drugs as such do, but rather in what people do after they take drugs. Drugs may modify behavior but they do not create it. Our focus must remain on the persons taking drugs rather than on the pharmaceuticals alone. The second fact to bear in mind is that no mind-altering drug, taken with the range of dosage that allows the person taking the drug any choice of actions (when the dosage becomes so great that choice behavior is eliminated, the outcome is then usually stupor, coma, shock, psychosis or death), ever has a single uniformly predictable behavior outcome. The general classifications used for these drugs, for example 'sedatives' or 'stimulants' are misleading; these only describe probable outcomes for certain persons under certain conditions. Within normal dosage ranges there will be among a group of persons or even for the same person on different occasions a variety of behavior outcomes. These outcomes will be partly and sometimes largely determined by factors other than the pharmaceutical substance itself, for example by the person's expectations of what the drug should do, his current moods and motives, the social setting in which the drug is used, the tasks he is performing and so forth. Consequently one must be careful not to assume that the popular terminology employed for classes of drugs is an accurate description of their effect. For example, LSD is called a 'hallucinogen' but the research to date shows that hallucinations are one of the infrequent experiences reported by persons taking LSD. Marihuana is classified as a 'narcotic' under some laws: nevertheless, it seems more likely to produce intoxicating effects similar to alcohol.

*   *   *

Crime associated with hallucinogen use appears to have been minimal. Police reports before a California legislative committee emphasized disturbances of the peace rather than felonies. Occasional accounts of homicide, violence, resisting arrest, etc., have not been subject to followup case studies. It would appear that insofar as decent citizens take hallucinogens their behavior will remain lawful. We may expect that with the expansion of hallucinogen use to delinquent groups —and perhaps because it is now unlawful in some States, so that its use becomes criminal—a greater frequency of crime will be reported. A tangential remark is offered here. It is the person, not the drug, which is 'responsible' for criminal acts. When an already delinquent youth takes LSD and commits yet another delinquent act, it may well be that the timing or expression of the delinquency is shaped by the drug-induced state of mind, but—as an example—aggression will not be a drug phenomenon.

One of the great public fears about marihuana involves the belief that this essentially harmless substance will somehow increase craving for more dangerous drugs as well as general criminality, presumably because of a loosening of inhibitions. After reviewing the scanty evidence, Blum concludes:

Case history material suggests that many identified heroin users have had earlier experiences with marihuana, but their 'natural history' is also likely to include even earlier illicit use of cigarettes and alcohol. The evidence from our college students and utopiate and news articles is clear that many persons not in heroin-risk neighborhoods who experiment with

735

marihuana do not 'progress' to 'hard' narcotics. [In addition] there is no reliable evidence that marihuana 'causes' crime.

He also raises the question of the appropriateness of the criminal law, especially where no conduct harmful to others has occurred:

Many sociologists and criminologists contend that arrest and subsequent experiences when one is treated as a criminal produce many injurious consequences and increase the likelihood of expanded rather than reduced criminal and socially maladaptive behavior. Especially in the field of drugs where use is a crime regardless of whether or not any other damaging behavior occurs has there been discussion of the undesirable features of 'turning the person into a criminal' through treating him like one and exposing him to contact with 'genuine' offenders. As an alternative it is often recommended that criminal prosecution be limited to criminal behavior as such (i.e., crimes against person and property) and that drug use be handled (a) as a normal phenomenon, since this is a drug-using society except (b) when dependency occurs or other behavioral toxicity (aberrant actions, suicidal impulses, psychosis, etc.) emerges at which time the person may be subject to medical-psychological-social rehabilitation efforts. The evidence for arrest and prosecution as methods more likely to create a criminal out of a drug abuser than to correct him remains very contradictory. The situation is complex and no simple predictions seem tenable. It is made more complicated by the lack of assurance that ordinarily psychiatric-social rehabilitation efforts will work either. Even so, it can be argued that on grounds of economics and humanity it may be better to handle any person abusing drugs (that is anyone dependent and acting in damaging ways) by other than criminal procedures.

He argues, as a good clinician, that we should be more concerned with what the person is and what he does rather than with what he takes. He asks the society to put the entire drug problem into a presently unfamiliar perspective:

. . . the extreme feelings apparent, and the catering to bias in popular and purportedly authoritative publications, reflect more, we believe, than a reasonable worry about drugs.

* * *

. . . people are worried about people, not about drugs except as these are a mirror reflecting distress. What people are

said to do because of drugs—to rob and steal and rape, to injure and kill one another on the highways, and to become dependent and psychotic—these are the things that people do and we—all of us—have good reason to be upset about them. But people do not need drugs to act in these frightening and damaging ways; and the general evidence is that drugs in fact play a very small part in the production of our overall rates of trouble.

Professor Blum also wrote a paper entitled *Mind-Altering Drugs and Dangerous Behavior: Narcotics,* wherein he pleads for greater understanding of drug addiction as a symptom of sickness:

Viewed from almost any standpoint, opiate dependency is agreed to be but a symptom of psychological disorder (even if its origins are social or even genetic). To work so hard at symptom suppression through means which cannot be shown to correct the offender is dubious. To attend so fixedly to behavior which is, in some ways, only an incidental criminological concern raises serious doubts about the economy of our efforts. Our recommendation here is limited; we ask that serious attention be given to changing the focus of police control to exclude from criminal penalty the acquisition or possession of opiates without intent to sell.

This paper ties in the problem of addiction with that of questionable law enforcement and takes issue with the staff (and Commission) assertion that, somehow, despite the obvious injustices, the system works against the large drug pushers:

The endeavors of law enforcement in particular are an increasing subject for public debate and of court decisions. Given the nature of opiates use as a vice in which only consenting parties are involved, the demand upon the police to identify and provide sufficient evidence for and conviction of drug users has lead to a number of functional or adaptive police responses of a controversial nature, these including the use of informants, promise of immunity, near-entrapment, drug purchases by undercover agents, invasions of privacy (wire tapping, etc.) and constitutional violations involved in search and seizure. One cannot blame the police for evolving techniques to combat offenses that the law and public sentiment require they combat. One does wonder if the cost of this effort—not only in terms of dollars and police time but in terms of the bad police-judiciary relations resulting from cases brought to the higher courts and in terms of the rate of recidivism among apprehended addicts—may not exceed the community value received. The solution sometimes proposed is that the police disregard the user and concentrate on the pusher. At the street level these appear to be one and the same person. At the higher level of importation and whole-sale distribution, police efforts have not met with noticeable success in spite of the most dedicated endeavors.

His conclusion that:

Unless one is willing to make dramatic and controversial changes in policy and law, ones admittedly leading to un-known changes in drug behavior, one cannot reasonably ex-pect much change either in present police practices or in ad-dict careers. Superficial changes in agency jurisdiction, num-bers of enforcement or treatment personnel, or availability of funds for present operations would signify a less than genuine wish for basic changes.

is an implied and well-deserved criticism of the Commission's emphasis on more, rather than less, enforcement of the nar-cotics laws. In another paper Blum takes issue with the ap-parent feeling of the Commission that public attitudes do not permit any fundamental change in our harsh and punitive measures of dealing with the complexities of drug use, so that bold and enlightened measures would be rejected by the American people.

He notes that:

Harris poll results show most Americans to be environmental determinists; they say the causes of crime are in early envi-ronment, broken homes, poor upbringing and the like. Some also attribute crime to mental illness. Only 8 percent spoke in motivational terms, saying people were criminals for 'kicks.' A few spoke in terms of their being 'born bad.' These highly deterministic explanations are followed by consistent empha-sis on preventive and helpful efforts in crime reduction, as opposed to suppression and punishment. Seventy-six percent favored working with young people as the means to crime re-duction, only 16 percent proposed to strengthen the police. Another indication of the willingness of the public to accept less punitive approaches is found in the fact that only 38 per-cent favor capital punishment: 47 percent are opposed and

738

15 percent unsure. Finally the pollster asked people what prisons should be like. Only 11 percent said that punishment should be the main purpose of imprisonment; 77 percent favored rehabilitation.

Professor Michael Rosenthal is concerned with the relationship of traditional principles of American criminal law to narcotics addiction. If someone is to be punished, he can (in general) only be found guilty of a crime if he "intends" to commit the act which is deemed criminal. The lack of ability to form such intent is at least one reason for not invoking criminal sanctions against chronic alcoholics, although the Supreme Court, in a five to four decision, recently disagreed. Our concept of insanity is closely related to the fundamental belief that a person "so far gone" as to be unable to control his conduct should not be punished because of the absence of intent. Although the question of intent (called *mens rea* by lawyers) is a complex one and totally inapplicable to certain forms of crime, generally economic ones, we instinctively look for it.

Also, if a person cannot control his conduct he cannot exercise the ability to choose to do so; therefore any punishment seeking to deter him will be inoperative. This is the crux of Rosenthal's analysis:

It would seem inappropriate to invoke the criminal process against persons who have lost control over the use of dangerous drugs solely because these persons are drug users. Once a person has lost control over his use the existence of a user offense such as use or simple possession will not deter his use. Having lost control, he cannot choose to conform his conduct to the requirements of the law by refraining from use. He is nondeterrable.

The argument is crucial where narcotics addition is concerned. The Supreme Court has already decided that to punish a person for the "crime" of being a narcotics addict violates the Eighth Amendment's prohibition against "Cruel and Unusual Punishments." If we can only punish a person for what he does rather than for what he is (for instance, New York has held the Eighth Amendment applicable to its vagrancy law) then can we punish him for conduct directly and inevitably related to what he is? If a narcotics addict possesses narcotics because he cannot will himself not to, isn't it mere hyperbole to punish him for possession rather than for addiction? Numerous attacks are being mounted by concerned and compassionate lawyers and scholars on "possession" laws on this theory. Had the Commission opted for Professor Rosenthal's analysis, perhaps some of the bruising and expensive battles (in the Courts) would not have to be fought.

Many have found a deceptively simple solution to the problem of the criminal sanction in the magical refrain "civil commitment of narcotics addicts." "Civil Commitment" is often a euphemism for criminal commitment, since the clear desire of society is to get rid of the troublesome addict whether he has been shown to be dangerous or not, or whether he has committed a crime or not, by avoidance of the stigmatizing criminal process. Here, the growing "scientism" of our Society plays an invidious role. The Rhetoric goes: Sick people should be treated; they should be restored to some sort of social usefulness. Scientists can discern just who is sick, and, therefore, socially unproductive. If we somehow call the process "noncriminal," our fears of civil liberties violations will dissolve. This theory, operative in the juvenile courts until the *Gault* decision (discussed elsewhere), is as dangerous here as there. Professor Rosenthal notes:

It must be emphasized that even were the evidence which might support long periods of isolation for use or possession by addicts and habitual users of such drugs clearer, a determination that a person could be isolated merely because he has lost control over the use of a drug would depart from principles which at the very least require a determination that the particular individual to be isolated poses a danger to himself or to society.

Professor Dennis Aronowitz in another paper concurs for both this reason and because of the simple fact that meaningful treatment of addiction is unknown:

The facade of benevolence generally associated with civil commitment programs does not avoid the danger that such programs can be used as a means of circumventing ordinary criminal safeguards in order to remove "undesirables" from society and to keep them in custody for long or indefinite periods during which there is little expectation of providing efficacious treatment. There is some evidence which indicates that achieving these ends was intended when the New York Legislature recently adopted a compulsory commitment program for noncriminal addicts.

Both professors are not particularly impressed with the secondary argument that civil commitment is necessary to keep addicts from committing other crimes. Although Rosenthal "boot-straps" his argument by quoting from Aronowitz, the point is well taken.

Isolation would be based on the view that addicts and habitual users commit crimes and sell drugs to support their habits, or for other reasons, and introduce nonaddicts to drugs. This view has been advanced to support long periods of isolation for narcotics and addicts irrespective of whether a particular addict has committed a crime other than possession or use. In his report to the Commission, Professor Aronowitz shows that the known facts do not warrant such treatment with respect to narcotics addicts. The known facts certainly do not warrant it in the case of addicts and habitual users of 'medically depressant and stimulant drugs.'

Of course, the crucial question is whether and to what extent Society may forecast (and take preventative though not necessarily criminal measures against) potential crime, and both Professors Aronowitz and Rosenthal deal with the matter only indirectly. To answer this we should first note that any compulsory incarceration is quasi-criminal in nature and should conform to at least minimal standards of fairness, if not the entire gamut of the Bill of Rights. Also, Society should demonstrate, by an overwhelming abundance of proof, that a certain "condition" is so clearly and imminently dangerous to the community that involuntary detention is necessary. Rosenthal's last quoted statement clearly demonstrates that Society has failed to meet that burden of proof (indeed, the way in which most compulsory commitment laws are written preclude consideration of this very element). Procedural safeguards, such as those involved in the way in which the fact of addiction is determined, also must be adhered to.

Professor Rosenthal's statement that:

. . . the possibility that repeal of existing prohibitions on simple possession and use [of marihuana] might increase use is not deemed sufficient reason for retaining them, especially when it is far from clear that lifting these restrictions would lead to a large increase in habitual use or in use by persons likely to become dependent on heroin or other drugs.

raises the issue of the social effect of the repeal of criminal sanction. The counterargument to his proposition is that repeal involves a form of social sanction, of encouragement to participate in conduct because it is now "legal." I shall offer some tentative analysis in the section concerned with the substantive criminal law, because the question relates equally well to repeal of antihomosexual and antigambling (as well as other vice) laws.

The necessary and understandable question of just what treatment works for the narcotics addict cannot be readily answered. If addiction is undesirable and personally harmful, Society should have some interest in rehabilitating the lost souls who are afflicted. What can we do, beyond the felt inadequacies of education and exhortation? Professor Jonathan O. Cole's paper on *The Treatment of Drug Addicts* offers some tentative and, perhaps, hopeful conclusions. This discussion should not end in a frustrating morass, and here Cole's analysis is relevant:

There is overwhelming consensus, based on a good deal of evidence, on a few statements about the outcome of treatments of heroin addicts.

1. Methadone treatment during the acute withdrawal phase is safe, sound, and reasonable and is superior to the use of nonopiate tranquilizers and sedatives.

2. The relapse rate following simple institutionalization (medical or penal) and release without aftercare or rehabilitation is very high.

3. Three classes of opiate addicts may show a somewhat better prognosis for abstinence independent of treatment:

(a) Medical addicts—patients becoming addicted in the course of treatment by physicians for real or functional physical complaints.

(b) Physicians or other professional addicts.

(c) Older heroin addicts.

4. Enforced parole or aftercare leads to less readdiction or reimprisonment than minimal or no aftercare treatment.

5. Most heroin addicts do not cooperate well in formal interview-type dynamic psychotherapy or casework of the sort ordinarily provided to middle-class psychoneurotics.

6. Most heroin addicts have a large array of needs and inadequacies over and above their use of narcotics—no money, no place to live, no readily marketable job skills, low frustration tolerance, low interest in or experience with the usual activities and pressures of the 'square' world, plus, usually, difficult family situations, plus low motivation to solve any of these problems and little trust in professional therapists.

Given the above as a reasonably probable set of facts, it is interesting to note that programs claiming substantial (if often undefined) success may be superficially very different (e.g., Synanon, Daytop Lodge, the California Rehabilitation Center, New York City's intensive parole methadone, cyclazocine, frequent urine testing) but all have several elements in common:

1. Considerable outside pressure to stay off drugs—provided in Synanon by group pressure and in more penal programs by a real threat of return to an institution.

2. Reasonably frequent supportive contact with the treatment agency.

3. Some assistance or encouragement to get a job and find a suitable place to live.

The Police

The Police Task Force shares the main Report's concern with the problem of the policeman's informal role; it chides the police for an unwillingness to scrutinize their own procedures and basic policies. Although all aspects of law enforcement, especially the discretionary ones, cannot be legislated, more administrative flexibility and guidelines can be utilized. The Report notes that police flexibility is necessary because of the conditions under which policemen operate, legislative default in laying down guidelines, and judicial inability to establish and enforce specific rules of conduct. The Report notes that there is a judicial rule-setting trend "inspired in large part by a prevalent assumption that police are unwilling or unable to develop proper policies and to conform their practices to these policies."

The Report cannot find any governmental agency apart from the police which can institute guidelines for police conduct. Legislative controls are inadequate because legislatures are simply not in the business of laying down detailed rules; the judiciary which handles police conduct only on a case-by-case basis is not an appropriate agency except in limited instances. What about the prosecutor's office? In some respects, it would seem to be the logical agency: often assistant district attorneys work closely with detectives investigating a particular case. They know police problems. They are respected by the police. Since at least one police function is to initiate prosecution, prosecutorial supervision might be appropriate.

The Report is intriguingly vague about this:

The prosecutor has an important responsibility in the devel-

743

opment of appropriate law enforcement policies. But there are practical reasons why his involvement cannot [be adequate]. Usually, the prosecutor, particularly in large urban areas, confines his principal attention to cases in which there is a desire to prosecute or to issues which are important to the political life of the community. He seldom, for example, becomes involved in the development of a policy for settling domestic disturbances or dealing with the down-and-out drunk or streetwalking prostitute.

In general, instructions or guidelines issued by the prosecutor relating to procedures for the prosecution of criminal cases will be accepted and followed by the police, particularly if the prosecutor is viewed by the police as seriously interested in the effective prosecution of the case in court. But neither the police nor the prosecutor assume that the prosecutor has the responsibility either to stimulate or participate in the development of administrative policies to control the wide range of police practices.

If better police practices are necessary, if intradepartmental attitudes are insufficient to achieve desirable change, and if trained prosecutors are in the favorable position of understanding both police needs and the public expectations of police performance, the solution could lie in a merger of the police and prosecutorial function. Certainly nothing in the foregoing quoted sections of the Report demonstrates that there is any *necessary* reason to believe that this scheme would not work.

Judicial sanctions will not work. If the famous decision in *Miranda* vs. *Arizona* exemplifies an attempt to apply sanctions in the area of confessions, then the recent *Terry, Peters* and *Sibron* cases demonstrate judicial inability to extend rules to on-the-street conduct of policemen. Since the police function to suppress crime, their daily activities do not necessarily result in arrests and court procedures. In *Terry,* the Supreme Court recognized that "punishing" the police by excluding evidence (the normal penalty inflicted for violation of an accused's Constitutional rights) is inappropriate and ineffective here. Given police unwillingness, judicial frustration, and legislative inability, shouldn't we look to the prosecutor's office for possible relief?

Such relief is needed, in part, because of the "stop" and "frisk" problem. The Report did not distinguish between two types of "stop," as did the Supreme Court in *Terry.* Often policemen in high-crime areas (i.e. ghettos) "roust" people almost at will, partly to keep everyone "shook up" and partly to find incriminating evidence. Sometimes stops are for more esoteric reasons. In San Francisco, "juveniles are frequently stopped when they travel outside their own neighborhood." Also, "police are suspicious and make field interrogations of certain individuals because of clothing, hair and walking mannerisms." The Court, in *Terry*, unequivocally condemned that type of stop; and the Commission and its Task Force also should have done so. The Court did sanction stops in particular situations where the police officer has "specific and articulable facts which, taken together with rational inferences from those facts," would lead a "man of reasonable caution" to believe that a crime was being, had been, or was about to be committed.

How many of the (alleged) 400,000 stops occurring in San Diego each year can be justified, even under this broad rationale? Unfortunately we have little information on the subject. But since more than 90 percent of stops involve no further action whatever, perhaps it would be safe to say that three-quarters of those are totally unjustified. The Task Force also noted that in New York, 81.6 percent of the stops involved frisks, although New York Law states—and the *Terry* case demands—that frisks may be undertaken only if there is a reasonable suspicion of physical danger.

The Task Force went beyond the generalized comments of the main Report to establish some "stop" and "frisk" rules. These rules may or may not be Constitutional, but at least they constitute a serious attempt to draw the boundary lines:

Field interrogations should be conducted only when an officer has reason to believe that a person is about to commit or has committed a crime, or that a crime has been committed and he has knowledge of material value to the investigation. . . . Field interrogations should not be used at all for minor crimes like vagrancy and loitering.

Adequate reason should be based on the actions of the person, his presence near the scene of a crime, and similar factors raising substantial suspicion, and not on race, poverty, or youth. . . .

The stop should be limited in time. The sole purpose should be: (a) to obtain the citizen's identification; (b) to verify it by readily available information; (c) to request cooperation in the investigation of a crime; and (d) to verify by readily available information any account of his presence or any other information given by the person.

*The citizen should be addressed politely; and should receive a
suitable explanation of the reasons for the stop.*
[A search may be made only when safety is involved.]
*Officers should be required to file a report each time a stop is
made. . . .*

The main Report does not mention two onerous (and totally illegal) arrest practices; arrests for investigation and for
harassment. "Although there is no legal basis for arresting
persons simply as a means of detaining them while an investigation of their possible involvement in crime is conducted,
this has been a common practice in a number of departments," notes the Task Force. The few available statistics indicate that such arrests are totally ineffective as even a bad
law enforcement tool.

The comments on harassment arrests are equally negative:

*Arrests for minor crimes, such as vagrancy, disorderly con-
duct, use of obscene language, loitering, failure to move on,
blocking the street or sidewalk, drunkenness, drinking in
public, and curfew violation constitute almost one-half of all
arrests made each year in the United States. There is evidence that such arrests create great antagonism against police
officers in slum communities.*

* * *

*Minor crime statutes are frequently misused. They are em-
ployed as a means of clearing undesirables or unsightly persons from the street or driving them out of town, aiding the
police in detaining a suspected person during an investigation
of a more serious crime, and regulating street activity in slum
neighborhoods.*

These laws are also used against gamblers and higher echelon members of the Mafia, with as little success as against
bowery drunks. Their only function is to create a "siege mentality" in slum areas (also where "hippies"—the latest victims
—congregate), and to temporarily inconvenience the mob-
sters.

The Task Force is concerned with the problem of community strain between the poor and the police. The police believe that impoverished areas of the city present greater
threats to their safety. Because police recruits often belong to
a class or ethnic group "on the way up," a certain bias
against those left behind seems to develop. Perhaps the most
influential factor contributing to the hostility, however, is not
the policeman's initial attitude but his work-role. In a large

bureaucracy where advancement is subject to informal as well as formal criteria, the young recruit looks for the "signals" which will tell him whether certain conduct pleases his superiors. Since the police department seems to be particularly susceptible to this, desirable changes must start at the top and not with the rookie:

The precise extent to which prejudice affects the conduct of the officer on the street is not known. Social scientists, however, believe that discriminatory action is influenced not only by individual attitudes, by the social structure, and by the views of the rest of the group, but also by the policies of the organization.

Although this baffling statement may not seem to say much it does emphasize the difficulty of effecting change in a bureaucratic system.

The Task Force Report was cautious about the allied question of misconduct. It noted that "the use of racial epithets . . . appears to be widespread," but found it difficult to generalize about conduct as distinct from attitudes. Thus one survey of police attitudes allegedly showed that 37 percent of the policemen questioned believed that they could use force when someone acted disrespectfully toward them. This was the most frequently cited single primary reason for its use. Also, "the officers believed that the only way to treat certain groups of people, including Negroes and the poor, is to treat them roughly." Unfortunately the same survey showed that the police really do not engage in the kind of conduct they ostensibly endorse, thus raising the question of the influence of attitude on conduct.

We all would like our police officers to be unprejudiced and dispassionate. This would truly make them professionals, for the essence of professionalism is its disregard for the personal qualities of the clientele. Because there is little likelihood that sweeping changes in the nation's collective police psyche will occur in the foreseeable future, we should investigate the phenomenon of attitude-conduct more closely. Americans do tend to believe that people will act according to their beliefs; accordingly, we have laws preventing Communists from holding certain positions. Police departments themselves are combed to find Birch Society or Klan adherents.

Yet the issue is not that simple. The necessary questions are whether (a) the belief or (b) the strength with which it is held is more important; whether the believer's role in the bureaucracy tends to modify the belief, or, conversely, whether the job role is shaped and defined by the belief; and whether strong leadership by superiors can overcome undesirable beliefs. Presumably we are committed to the sanctity of belief (and only penalize illegal conduct). Yet we do perceive that under certain circumstances even the possibility that belief will influence conduct justifies various restrictions. The police are a particularly sensitive agency, and we cannot disregard the vital public interest in insuring an unprejudiced force. Perhaps the best answer is that belief can be taken into account to determine motive, but only when conduct is illegal or violates departmental rules.

Police brutality is, of course, deplorable and unjustifiable. The Report is equivocal about its existence—"The Commission was not able to determine the extent of physical abuse . . . since recent studies have generally not been systematic." A Commission study only later revealed noted that physical abuse is rather frequent,[6] although presumably considerably less so than in the freewheeling days of the 1920's. The Task Force Report noted that civil rights leaders believed that brutality has lessened; but for some unknown reason the footnote reference for this statement unfortunately is missing.

Another form of misconduct that is of serious social significance, though completely overlooked by the main Report, is the often indiscriminate use of police firearms. The Task Force was rather shocked by a finding that "in a medium sized city . . . officers fired guns more than 300 times in a two-year period, and over one-third were during automobile chases involving juveniles." The Task Force offers a useful and humane guide to the use of such weapons:

Deadly force should be restricted to the apprehension of perpetrators who, in the course of their crime, threatened the use of deadly force, or if the officer believes there is a substantial risk that the person whose arrest is sought will cause death or serious bodily harm if his apprehension is delayed. The use of firearms should be flatly prohibited in the apprehension of misdemeanants, since the value of human life far outweighs the gravity of misdemeanor.

* * *

Deadly force should never be used [where the officer suspects that a crime has been committed or that a particular person committed it]. An officer should have witnessed the crime or should have sufficient information to know as a virtual cer-

[6] See Footnote No. 1 herein.

tainty, that the suspect committed an offense for which the use of deadly force is permissible.

*   *   *

An officer should not be permitted to fire at felony suspects when [he] believes that the suspect can be apprehended reasonably soon thereafter without the use of deadly force. . . .

*   *   *

Officers should never fire from a moving vehicle.

*   *   *

. . . Department regulations should require a detailed written report on all discharges of firearms. . . .

Community reactions to the police are the subject of a separate chapter in the Task Force Report. The main Report barely alludes to the problem of community belief in the extent of police brutality. The Task Force notes that in Watts,

Nearly 47 percent of all respondents and 60 percent of all those from 15 to 29 years of age believed that there was at least some police brutality. Of those who had answered 'a lot' and 'a little', approximately half claimed that they had witnessed it.

Whether or not the surveys indicated substantive or little minority group satisfaction may be irrelevant; superficial surveys may not truly reflect the degree of hostility, partly because "playing the white man's game" may mitigate the severity of the responses. Thus:

Surveys may not accurately reflect the full extent of minority group dissa'isfaction with the police. In-depth interviews with members of minority groups frequently lead to strong statements of hostility, replacing the neutral or even favorable statements which began the interview.

Minority groups often feel that authority is exercised quite arbitrarily against them. The Task Force appears to agree: *[A] study of disorderly conduct arrests of both adults and juveniles in the District of Columbia found that in almost a quarter of them the arrest had been made only for loud and boisterous talking or obscene remarks to the police.*

*   *   *

Demeanor appears to affect police disposition after arrest as well as arrest in the first instance. Juvenile offenders and po-

licemen interviewed in . . . San Francisco . . . estimate that demeanor is the major factor in 50 to 60 percent of juvenile dispositions.[7]

Although the Task Force concurs in the Commission's negative attitude toward civilian review boards, it provides impressive evidence on both (a) the shortcomings of present internal review procedures, and (b) the fact that civilian review boards work without impairing police efficiency. Thus:

Several methods of discouraging complaints have been practiced in the past. In one large eastern city, for example, the police department used to charge many of those who filed complaints of police misconduct with filing false reports with the police. In 1962, 16 of 41 persons [almost 40 percent] who filed complaints were arrested for filing false charges. . . . Officers sometimes told prospective complainants that all statements must be made under oath, and that they could be charged with false reporting. . . . the practice, as of 1966 [in the District of Columbia] was to drop criminal charges against a person if he would agree to withdraw his complaint or agree not to file one. Similar procedures have discouraged complaints in New York and other localities.

* * *

In Philadelphia, the police review board found in 1959 'that it seemed to be standard police procedure to charge a person with resisting arrest or disorderly conduct whenever the person charges the police with brutality.' It also found some evidence that two complainants had been intimidated—one by arrest at the completion of the hearing, and one by harassment before it. Following the board's recommendations, the Commissioner ordered that such practices be 'immediately discontinued.' However, [a] University of California study found that there is still 'fear of police retaliation if a complaint is lodged against a police officer.'

Also:

[T]he boards have had some success. The Philadelphia Police Commissioner has shown a willingness to voluntarily follow the civilian review board's recommendations in most cases. In 1959, Police Commissioner Gibbons testified in court, in answer to a question whether the board had harmed morale,

7 See pp. 721-24 herein.

that 'the board has not only aided me, but has aided the police department.' . . . and while the rank-and-file officers generally oppose the board, [a] University of California study concluded that morale had not been perceptibly impaired. The Rochester director of public safety has also said that the board had not impaired the efficiency or morale of the police in that city. The President's Commission on Crime in the District of Columbia concluded that the Washington board 'has impressed the Commission with its desire to be fair and thorough." The members of the boards generally have been distinguished citizens and the procedures adopted appear to be fair.

*   *   *

[S]ome minority leaders believe that the board is ineffective, and a few even believe that it has no value. However, most find that the board does alleviate tensions at least to some extent, and show confidence in it by referring applicants. But perhaps most important, the University of California study found that the complainants themselves were favorably impressed with the treatment they received. The study concluded that the board 'has worked as an avenue of redress for civilian grievances against members of the police force.'

The Courts

This report is primarily concerned with the problem of the enormous discretion vested in the prosecutor to bring defendants to trial, or to drop the charges. Pretrial disposition of accused persons is secret and virtually without standards. Probably, in large cities, informal policies do exist; but the report gives us no information about this. It notes that prosecutors may try some cases when in justice there should be no criminal proceedings, and may drop serious ones because of a lack of information about the suspect:

The system for making the charge decision remains generally inadequate. Prosecutors act without the benefit of direction or guidelines from either the legislature or higher levels of administration: their decisions are almost entirely free from judicial supervision. Decisions are to a great extent fortuitous because they are made on inadequate information about the offense, the offender, and the alternatives available. At this stage in the process the prosecutor generally knows only a few bare facts about the offense. He generally knows little about the accused, except perhaps what is revealed by a prior criminal record. In many places little consideration is given to cases where guilt is apparent but criminal sanctions seem inappropriate. Often cases are prosecuted that should not be. Often offenders in need of treatment, supervision, or discipline are set free without being referred to appropriate community agencies or followed up in any way.

Court trials should be reserved for serious habitual offenders, not for the occasional and sporadic law violator. Although police may be forced to arrest participants in street brawls, for instance, the prosecutor would be perfectly justified in not pressing the charges. This report notes that the criminal code defines crimes, not criminals. The latter task is the duty of the prosecutor.

A wise district attorney should establish standards by which to judge whether prosecution is desirable in a particular case. The Report suggests six guidelines: (1) the seriousness of the crime; (2) general policy on prosecution of certain crimes; (3) the defendant's mental stability and (4) the existence of other community agencies which might be of greater benefit to him; (5) the chance of success of alternative treatment) and (6) the impact of the crime on community standards.

The Report recognizes the existence and persuasiveness of "plea bargaining" but wants it to be formalized. Most defendants (generally 80 to 90 percent) plead guilty to a charge which is either (a) a reduced version of the original charge, or (b) one retained while others are dropped. The process by which someone is induced to plead guilty—very often, at the first instance, by his own attorney—is the result of a "bargaining" compromise. Our system of criminal procedure would break down overnight if "plea bargains" were abolished.

The present system has several defects: The prosecutor may "overcharge"—charge a high degree of the crime, even in the absence of evidence—to obtain bargaining leverage. He may charge several crimes, often because the criminal code divides certain acts into separate and distinct crimes. Often the "overcharged" crime carries a severe possible penalty; severe enough to scare a defendant into pleading guilty to a crime with a lesser punishment. For most defendants, the prime consideration is the sentence (or, often, whether the charge is reduced to a misdemeanor). The prosecutor may offer "deals" to one particular defendant and deny them to others without apparent reason. He may make rash promises (or even hints) of sentencing recommendations, and may be unable to keep them. Since the process is secret, a defendant who feels that the bargain was not kept (because the judge imposed a higher sentence than expected) has little chance of withdrawing his plea.

The system has given rise to numerous attacks on their guilty pleas by defendants who claimed that the pleas were either coerced by improper pressures, or were given in exchange for promises never kept. Generally these suits arise out of the judge's failure to play the "game." Thus the Task Force Report recognizes that the bargain must be a true one binding everyone, including the judge:

> . . . it is essential to the successful working of the system that the judge accept the arrangements worked out between defense counsel and the prosecutor. Because of doubts over the legality of the negotiated plea, prosecutors and defense counsel typically avoid all reference in court to the sentence to be imposed until after the plea has been tendered and accepted, and engage in the pious fraud of making a record that the plea was not induced by any promises. Since the judge's sentence remains to be pronounced, the defendant does not achieve the control he sought in negotiating unless he has confidence that the judge will accept the arrangement. The defendant is interested in controlling the exercise of sentencing discretion, not in a lawsuit over a motion to withdraw his guilty plea because of disappointment over the sentence later imposed. The typical unreviewability of the exercise of sentencing discretion only sharpens the point. The credibility of the system requires, then, that the judge hold his power to reject the agreement in careful reserve. If there is to be any effective judicial participation in the process, rather than mere judicial acquiescence in an agreement worked out between the parties, such participation must come at an earlier stage of the proceedings.

The proper administration of Justice from the prosecutor's perspective is often adversely affected by this informal system. Since "plea bargaining" is tied into a court system called upon to dispose of a voluminous number of cases, defendants who properly should be tried for serious crimes slip through the net of the harassed prosecutor who is compelled to make instantaneous decisions without knowledge of the facts or of the defendant's prior criminal record. Thus both the prosecutor and defense counsel may be frustrated by the process:

> There are many serious problems with the way that the plea bargaining system is administered. In the first place bar-

gaining takes place at a stage when the parties' knowledge of their own and each other's cases is likely to be fragmentary. Presentence reports and other investigations into the background of the offender usually are made after conviction and are unavailable at the plea bargain stage. Thus the prosecutor's decision is usually made without the benefit of information regarding the circumstances of the offense, the background and character of the defendant, and other factors necessary for sound dispositional decisions. In too many places the acceptance of pleas to lesser offenses, which began as a device to individualize treatment, becomes routine, with a standard reduction for certain charges.

* * *

Too often the result may be excessive leniency for professional and habitual criminals who generally have expert legal advice and are best able to take full advantage of the bargaining opportunity. Marginal offenders, on the other hand, may be dealt with harshly, and left with a deep sense of injustice, having learned too late of the possibilities of manipulation offered by the system.

* * *

As a result there is no judicial review of the propriety of the bargain—no check on the amount of pressure put on the defendant to plead guilty.

The Report wisely proposes that plea bargaining be formalized so that all defendants have the opportunity to participate in it, and that standards for such bargaining be formulated by district attorneys. The facts of the case should be agreed upon; and written reasons, justifying the propriety of the bargain, be presented in open court. Judges should participate and be bound by the decision as to sentencing—the crucial decision for all parties concerned.

The Report is silent about the relationship between sentencing, plea bargaining, and the overpunitive quality of American law. Instead of meeting the problem directly, the Report finds the solution in improved plea bargaining techniques rather than overall reform:

Plea negotiations concerning charges provide an opportunity to mitigate the harshness of a criminal code or to rationalize its inconsistencies and to lead to a disposition based on an assessment of the individual factors of each crime. The field over which these negotiations may range is broad; the defendant's conduct on a single occasion may justify separate

754

charges of robbery, larceny, assault with a deadly weapon, assault, or disorderly conduct. Some of these offenses are felonies, while others are misdemeanors, and the maximum sentences may range from 30 years to less than 1 year. Conviction of a felony may involve serious collateral disabilities, including disqualification from engaging in certain licensed occupations or businesses, while conviction of a misdemeanor may not. The prosecutor often has a wide range of penal provisions from which to choose. His choice has enormous correctional implications, and it is through charge bargaining that in many courts he seeks to turn this discretion to his own advantage.

Charge reduction may be used to avoid a mandatory minimum sentence or a restriction on the power to grant probation. In these instances the agreed plea becomes a way of restoring sentencing discretion when it has in part been eliminated from the code. Charge reduction is also used to avoid the community opprobrium that attaches to conviction of certain offenses. Thus to avoid being labeled a child molester or homosexual, the defendant may offer to plead guilty to a charge such as disorderly conduct or assault.

Society cannot really tolerate the kind of *ad hoc* accommodation between formal and informal norms implied by this process. Public agitation grows, essentially law-abiding people are swept into the net, and a legal credibility gap ensues. At times, Courts actively attempt to mitigate the harshness of the mandatory sentences. The Report recognizes this, but also in misplaced context:

Where prosecutors have sought the imposition of long mandatory sentences, the courts often have refused to enforce the statutes or have narrowed their application. In Detroit, for example, the judges' opposition to the mandatory 20-year minimum sentence for sale of narcotics is so great that they have almost always refused to accept guilty pleas to that offense and have instructed defense counsel and prosecutors to negotiate for a reduction of the charge of possession or use. During the first four years after the mandatory penalty was enacted in 1952, there were only 12 sale-of-narcotics convictions out of 476 defendants originally charged with sale. Under the former New York Penal Law the courts construed the term 'convicted' in the statute requiring increased sentences for habitual offenders as not including instances where an offender had previously been found guilty of a felony but had received a suspended sentence.

By denying adequate sentencing discretion to the courts, the legislatures have unintentionally increased the bargaining power of the prosecutor in plea negotiations.

* * *

The severity of most mandatory sentences and the prosecutor's ability to avoid them can give the prosecutor an undue advantage in plea negotiations. As Prof. Donald Newman has noted:

Defendants with a number of prior felony convictions are potentially susceptible to long sentences or separate convictions as habitual criminals. It is not an uncommon practice for prosecutors to mention this to recidivistic defendants, and there is little doubt that this exerts a strong pressure on them to 'cooperate' with the state by pleading guilty.

The nullification of mandatory sentencing provisions suggests the need for a more flexible means of effectuating legislative sentencing policy. This need might be satisfied by repealing mandatory sentences which have proved unworkable and by enacting statutory standards to guide the courts and correctional authorities in the exercise of their discretion.

Although the statement is true, the problems will continue to exist even in the absence of mandatory minimum sentences where substantive, almost unbridled sentencing discretion exists, and the defendant knows that judges are prone to imposing high minimums.

The Report recognizes that sentencing practices within different jurisdictions, and often within even the same state, are not uniform. American penological thought has never quite determined just why people should go to prison, although in the 19th century we led the world in emphasizing the goal of rehabilitation. The Report discerns at least four goals—isolation from society, deterrence of others, rehabilitation, and revenge—which often are in conflict. The present system is expensive, and at least in terms of rehabilitation it is wasteful and a failure:

A review of a number of such studies in the various States and in the Federal prison system leads to the conclusion that despite considerable variation among jurisdictions, roughly a third of the offenders released from prison will be reimprisoned, usually for committing new offenses, within a 5-year period. The most frequent recidivists are those who commit

*such property crimes as burglary, auto theft, forgery, or lar-
cency, but robbers and narcotics offenders also repeat frequently. Those who are least likely to commit new crimes
after release are persons convicted of serious crimes of violence—murder, rape, and aggravated assault.*

The degree of public concern often determines the penalty.
When airline highjacking occurred in 1965, Attorney General
Clark argued for the imposition of capital punishment. This
proved to be somewhat embarrassing in 1968, when he
sought to abolish the death penalty for all federal crimes.
Some particular subjects of continuous public outrage, such
as the sale of marihuana, are severely punished by long minimum sentences. In Michigan, for instance, there is a 20-year
mandatory sentence for this crime. In Massachusetts, a second offender must receive a minimum 5-year sentence.

Sentence severity deforms the administration of criminal
justice. In early 19th century England, the prevalence of capital punishment for more than 200 crimes resulted in a reduction of convictions rather than of crimes. Juries flagrantly
flouted the law and either acquitted defendants, or found that
thefts were for lesser amounts (despite the lack of evidence)
than those for which the ultimate penalty was exacted. When
the system became intolerable enough, it was changed.

Today, we are faced with the same problem:

*The statutory lengths of sentences are reflected in the sen-
tencing practices of the courts. More than one-half of the
adult felony offenders sentenced to State prisons in 1960 were
committed for maximum terms of 5 years or more; almost
one-third were sentenced to terms of at least 10 years. And
more than one-half of the prisoners confined in State institutions in 1960 had been sentenced to maximum terms of at
least 10 years. There is a substantial question whether sentences of this length are desirable or necessary for the majority of felony offenders. The experience of a number of other
countries throughout the world that rely on relatively short
prison sentences for most offenders supports the view that
long sentences properly may be reserved for the special case.
In addition there are indications that despite the long sentences initially imposed, the administrators of penal systems
in this country in practice have relied on shorter periods of
confinement. Of the approximately 80,000 felony prisoners
released in 1960 from State institutions, the median time actually served before first release was about 21 months; only*

8.7 percent of the prisoners released actually served five years or more.

The American penal reform movement in the 19th and early 20th centuries stressed the virtue of granting substantial discretion to trial judges to determine sentences so that they might comport with information about the criminal himself. In short, the law punished the crime and not the criminal.

The Report is caught in the dilemma of simultaneously arguing against fixed and lengthy terms of imprisonment and against too great judicial discretion. It notes that there was an "unjustified disparity" in sentencing, which leads to "judge shopping" for a favorable determination.[8] The dilemma can be narrowed only by an abolition of mandatory minimum sentences and a confinement of flexibility within both generous boundaries and known standards. Appellate review of sentences is also a necessity because appellate courts serve the invaluable function of regulating the trial courts under their jurisdiction to insure fairly uniform treatment. Of course the most radical answer could be to legislatively reduce lengthy maximum sentence statutes. Ironically we impose very long sentences for many crimes, and the longest of these are for acts generally committed by law-abiding citizens who have lost their heads once in their lives and might never do so again.

For most offenders, the crucial question is not guilt but the length of sentence. The Report, as we have seen, heavily emphasizes the relationship between plea bargaining and the defendant's expectations of sentence. The most vital single factor in the sentencing process is the presentence report prepared by probation departments; they constitute the sole basis for sentencing by most judges. In line with the main Report's recommendation that elementary fairness mandates review of the report by defense counsel to determine factual correctness, in certain cases the Task Force attempts to reconcile this fundamental right with Society's claim to secrecy:

. . . three arguments have been made against disclosure of the presentence report to the defendant or his counsel. The first is that disclosure would tend to dry up sources of information.

*   *   *

. . . it is argued that disclosure would cause unreasonable

---

[8] The Report pointed out some grisly instances of disparity. In one embezzlement case, involving $24,000, where defendant used the money to gamble, the sentence was 117 days; in another, in the same state, a defendant of good background received 20 years.

delay. Defendants could be expected to challenge everything in the report, and the resulting complexity of litigation might cause courts to dispense with presentence reports altogether. Finally, it is argued that disclosure of certain parts of the report would be harmful to rehabilitative efforts, especially psychiatric evaluations and unfavorable comments by the probation officer who might be assigned to supervise the defendant.

While these considerations indicate some limitations on the extent to which the report should be disclosed, a sound general rule would give the defendant or his attorney the right to examine the report, but it would also permit the court to withhold particular information when good cause is shown. Under the Model Penal Code, for example, the court must advise the defendant of the 'factual contents and conclusions' of the presentence report but is not required to disclose the sources of confidential information. Another accommodation of the competing interests might be to permit the court to withhold factual statements when there are reasons for non-disclosure that outweigh the defendant's interest in ensuring the accuracy of important information in the report. Such occasion may arise when disclosure of a statement would be harmful to rehabilitation or when disclosure of a factual statement is tantamount to disclosure of its source, and the identity of the source should be withheld.

Experience in several jurisdictions indicates that a general rule favoring disclosure can operate fairly and without undesirable consequences. In the U.S. District Court for the District of Maryland, for example, presentence reports are prepared in two parts: The bulk of the information is set forth in a document which is made available by the judge to defense counsel in chambers; at the same time a cover sheet containing the probation officer's recommendation, any confidential information, and any data which might injure the defendant's relationships with others is submitted separately. The latter document is not shown to defense counsel, although the judge discusses it with him. This disclosure policy has not resulted in any loss of sources of confidential information or in any instances of unfavorable reactions by defendants against sources of information or probation officers.

The Report's one and a half pages about capital punishment are as equivocal as the parallel passage in the main Report. Does capital punishment deter crime? The statistical answer (not only in England cited by the Report, but also in some 69 other countries which have abolished the death penalty) clearly indicates that there is no relationship between the homicide rate and the death penalty. The Report notes that the death penalty has an "undesirable impact on the administration of justice," results in "unwarranted acquittals," and "is most frequently imposed and carried out on the poor, the Negro, and the members of unpopular groups." It is no longer even a popular form of punishment, since polls indicate that approximately one-half of the American people favor its abolition while about 42 percent support its retention. The Attorney General of the United States recently went on record in favor of complete abolition for federal crimes, and the Supreme Court has been nibbling away at it for thirty years. After giving all the arguments for abolition, the Task Force shrugs its collective shoulders.

Although the Report devoted only 7 pages to the massive ineffectiveness of the lower criminal courts (more was needed), the indictment is damning enough. The Report draws a vivid picture of an urban arraignment court:

Following arrest, the defendant is initially presented in court, often after many hours and sometimes several days of detention. In theory the judge's duty is to advise the defendant of the charges against him and of his rights to remain silent, to be admitted to bail, to retain council or to have counsel appointed, and to have a preliminary hearing. But in some cities the defendant may not be advised of his right to remain silent or to have counsel assigned. In others he may be one of a large group herded before the bench as a judge or clerk rushes through a ritualistic recitation of phrases, making little or no effort to ascertain whether the defendants understand their rights or the nature of the proceedings. In many jurisdictions counsel are not assigned in misdemeanor cases; even where lawyers are appointed, it may not be made clear to the defendant that if he is without funds he may have free representation. One Commission staff report notes:

In cases observed no defendant was told that he had a right to remain silent or that the court would appoint a lawyer to represent him if he were indigent, notwithstanding the court rule that counsel will be assigned whenever a defendant may be sentenced to more than six months or fined more than $500. We were told that at least one judge takes great care to advise defendants fully, but the three judges we observed did not.

The judges have little time to give detailed consideration to the question of bail. Little is known about the defendant other than the charge and his prior criminal record. The result is that bail is based on the charge instead of on the cir-

cumstances of each case; high money bonds are almost in-
variably set by established patterns, and large numbers of de-
fendants are detained.

* * *

The initial appearance is also the final appearance for most
defendants charged with misdemeanors or petty offenses.
While those who can afford to retain counsel are released on
bond to prepare for trial at a later date or to negotiate a dis-
position, a majority of defendants pleads guilty immediately,
many without advice of counsel. Pleas are entered so rapidly
that they cannot be well considered. The defendant is often
made aware that if he seeks more time, his case will be ad-
journed for a week or two and he will be returned to jail.
[*the staff report notes:*]

Most of the defendants . . . pleaded guilty and were sen-
tenced immediately, without any opportunity for allocution
[*the right to make a statement to the judge*]. *When they tried*
to say something in their own behalf, they were silenced by
the judge and led off by the bailiff. . . .

The lower courts process most offenders; they are often the
only point of contact between the average citizen (usually in
traffic cases) and the criminal law system. The Report's finding that a "massive overhaul" is needed is accurate.

In 1962, lower courts processed some 4 million misdemeanor cases. Judges and other court officials encourage
quick pleas of guilty, or trials which are little more than 15-
second farces. Since, in misdemeanor cases, there are no presentence reports, sentences tend to be either too short (for
hardened criminals) or too long (for occasional offenders).
A new approach is required by the "disturbing rate of recidivism among offenders processed through the lower courts."
Of course public attitudes toward the court system, the quality of the judiciary, and the necessity for rehabilitation must
be taken into account when analyzing any particular reform
proposal. The evidence is not encouraging.

The Report also condemns present bail practices. The bail
system automatically operates against the poor, as do many
of our penal practices. Bail is imposed under the same pressures that debilitate all lower court activities so that few facts
are ascertained by the overworked judge. Detention facilities
are too costly; family dislocation and the resultant social
costs (such as relief) are often profound. Bail detainees may

lose their jobs. In addition, "pretrial detention increases the likelihood of conviction."

The Report recommends devices such as statutory limitation on the period of pretrial detention, increased use of summons rather than arrest to bring an accused into the court's jurisdiction, and station-house release after fingerprinting and booking have occurred.

The Report particularly condemns the almost fatal equation between poverty and likelihood of conviction. The poor person has no money to obtain investigative resources or expert witnesses (and the courts have not held that the State is required to furnish them), cannot obtain bail, and is subject to imprisonment for failure to pay a fine. An appendix to the Report depicts the syndrome of frustration that bedevils the impoverished defendant:

When B [an accused shoplifter] is before the judge, the clerk reads her a summary statement of the charges against her and recites to trial and counsel phrased in the words of the pertinent statute or court ruling. Spoken at high speed, in a dull monotone, phrased in legal jargon, the charges and the rights are frequently unintelligible.

B can plead guilty at her first appearance or ask for a trial. She can also request an adjournment to consult or obtain counsel. The various jurisdictions differ on whether a misdemeanant who cannot afford counsel is entitled to appointed counsel. Until recently in Washington, D.C., the court appointed counsel from a 'mourners' bench' and left it to the lawyer and his new client to negotiate a fee. In New York City, a Legal Aid lawyer is appointed minutes before the arraignment of an indigent defendant. In Miami, there is no representation provided for indigent misdemeanants; in Los Angeles, less than 10 percent of all misdemeanants have counsel at arraignment. In all events, more misdemeanants than felons lack representation. It may be harder for the defendant to qualify as an indigent misdemeanant than as an indigent felon, either because he has scraped up a small, automatically disqualifying bail bond or because the counsel fees involved are so small. Without counsel, defendant B is almost certain to plead guilty.

Even with counsel, however, pressures are strong in a high volume misdemeanor court to plead guilty and hope for, or bargain for, leniency. Assigned counsel often get no pay for representation at this level; retained counsel put into the case only the time equivalent of the $50 or $75 they can get out of it, and public defenders have only a few minutes' frantic conference with their clients outside the courtroom to decide on a plea or request for adjournment.

Trial is not an attractive prospect for an indigent misdemeanant or his lawyer. It can mean a new round of bail bonds or weeks in jail awaiting trial. Complexities of proof may be just as great as in felony trials; thorny legal issues can arise: problems of illegal search and seizure, unlawful arrests, or coerced confessions. But public funds are almost never available for investigators or expert witnesses in these courts. Preliminary hearings are usually waived because lawyers cannot take the time.

*   *   *

A defendant in jail cannot help counsel locate witnesses, persuade them to testify, nor restage his story on the actual scene. He is unavailable for spot calls to check details or last-minute conferences to plan strategy; jail may be on the edge of town and the visiting hours inconvenient for busy counsel.

*   *   *

In the absence of a cadre of independent investigators, the defendant has to rely for this information on pretrial criminal discovery. But neither the names of government witnesses nor their prior statements to the police or to the grand jury, even those of a codefendant, are generally available in advance through discovery; their stories cannot be checked out for error—purposeful or inadvertent. They cannot even be contacted personally to see if they have any information helpful to the defense. Their FBI records cannot be secured.

The indigent defendant, on the other hand, must often disclose what he expects his witnesses to testify in order to obtain a free subpoena. The government has its corps of fingerprint, ballistics, and handwriting specialists; it has laboratories in which to test and analyze the evidence. The government also possesses the real evidence itself: the prints, the bullet, the blood, the signature. The results of these tests may be available through discovery, but to counter these tests effectively the defense needs its own experts to view the original evidence. This means double trips and double expert fees, once to analyze and again to testify. Funds from public sources for expert defense witnesses are always limited; often they are nonexistent.

*   *   *

Defendant B, after conviction, is ultimately granted probation. She will be required to report to a probation officer *downtown at the court at his convenience. She must stay in the area. She cannot change jobs, move, alter her marital status without permission, frequent places where liquor is sold, or stay out late. She cannot associate with other law offenders. She must obey all laws. If she does not have a job, she must try 'diligently' to get one. Restitution may have to be made. In some counties, the costs of providing her with a legal defense must be repaid as a condition of probation.*

The Report, happily, assumes that subtle discrimination against the poor has no place in a system of criminal justice. The question of whether the system should be bent to accommodate the poor is a vexatious one. All systems can be "beaten" by the right combination of circumstances, even fortuitous ones; as President Kennedy said (and lived to prove), "Life is unfair." Of course the issue is not whether life in the abstract is unfair, but whether human institutions contribute to its inadequacies and whether and to what extent elimination of institutional unfairness is a desirable social goal. Perhaps the question has been misstated. It is often argued in terms of "giving" the poor man the same resources enjoyed by the affluent to "beat" the law. Because some fish escape the net of law enforcement, should we allow many more to do so? If, as the Supreme Court has indicated, poverty should not be a factor in the provision of State services for persons accused of violating the law, does this imply a positive obligation to supply services normally provided for by private funds? If we are to place the poor on exactly the same footing as the rich, then an enormous increase in overall investigative resources must be supplied at state expense. If we are to ignore this obligation, then our only duty is to insure that the State grants the poor the same rights which the State presently can withhold—such as trial transcripts, etc.

The issue should be resolved by a recognition that the integrity of the system suffers when *any* impediment to the fact-finding process exists. Recent Supreme Court decisions in the area of criminal procedure have emphasized a concern about maintaining this integrity. If state withholding of a service goes to the fact-finding process, such as the refusal to trace down an alibi witness, then such conduct violates elementary norms of decency and therefore the right to "Due Process of Law."

Such discrimination should not become imbedded in the system. Of course the foregoing formulation implies that the State will have to virtually do at its own expense exactly what wealthy private parties can do at theirs, but certain responsibilities will remain with the individual. For instance, instead of the right to choose his own attorney, an individual will have to accept a judicially selected one, and this involves many risks. Theoretically, choice of counsel does not affect the fact-finding process. But the risks are precisely the same, for individuals retaining counsel often make gross errors.[9]

One exception to this standard would be to allow the appointment of an attorney desired by a poor person where such an attorney is willing to serve; the present system foists an attorney on a hapless and occasionally unwilling client. Although the Task Force does not recommend this, there is no reason why even an appointed attorney should not be "chosen" by his client wherever possible. The only objection to this would be where attorneys (and there are some) "solicit" impoverished clients, especially where counsel fees are paid by the State. Canons of Ethics could be enforced to minimize this danger. Presumably other safeguards, such as a required degree of criminal trial experience, could be built into the system.

Although both the main Report and the Task Force eschew analysis of the trial process itself, since the overwhelming majority of cases never reach that stage, both evince some concern for one particular problem that makes a criminal trial a nightmare for defense counsel: his inability to obtain the substance of the prosecution's case. Often defense counsel "flies blind" during a criminal case. He may have little idea of the nature of the prosecution's case, of the identities of witnesses to be presented by his adversary, and of the tangible incriminating evidence. There are few Perry Masons in the criminal courts, and it is only the lucky attorney who manages to upset the credibility (or, especially in the case of eyewitnesses, the ability) of a witness on cross-examination. The training manuals for defense counsel all note that he should never ask a question to which he does not already know the answer, because the result is likely to be a damaging rather than a helpful answer. Unfortunately the manuals are of little help in the din of courtroom battle.

The element of ignorance, generously called by some "the sporting element," is most inappropriate where human life and liberty are concerned; yet precisely here, where it is most

---

[9] In fact it could be argued that the middle class suffers more than the poor class from problems of incompetence of counsel; for people with some money can choose but have little practical choice, since the attorneys they are likely to get will probably not have much criminal court experience. The poor have virtually no choice, but are often represented by able and, most importantly, trained attorneys from legal aid societies.

needed, it is almost totally absent. In the average civil lawsuit for money such a situation is impossible, for the procedure called "discovery" has long existed. Thus an opponent's case is laid on the (otherwise bare) table by the simple ability to question him and his key witnesses about their version of the facts of the case. The main Report laconically states that: "In most cases expanded mutual discovery by [both parties] within constitutional limits is desirable." To this, the Task Force adds:

When discovery is not available, the parties negotiate in ignorance.

One major factor inhibiting fuller discovery in criminal cases is that the criminal defendant, unlike the civil defendant, cannot constitutionally be compelled to testify or produce proof. Thus criminal discovery is sometimes seen as a unilateral benefit to the defendant at the expense of the prosecution. In part this difficulty may be met by expanded discovery by the prosecution within constitutional bounds, along the lines suggested by recent amendments to the Federal Rules of Criminal Procedure and by court decisions in some States. Undoubtedly the problem of mutuality and other unique features of the criminal process make it unlikely that the broad mandatory discovery found in civil cases will soon be common in criminal cases. But there is a clear need to expand the exchange of information between the parties before trial within the special limitations of criminal prosecutions.

The extent to which a defendant has a right of discovery of the prosecution's evidence varies throughout the country, both with respect to the information which is discoverable and the procedures which are available. In California, where discovery rules have developed as a result of appellate decisions, the broadest discovery for defendants is recognized. There a defendant has a right to copies of his own statements, to copies of witnesses' statements, to the results of any scientific tests, to the names of witnesses, and to a transcript of any grand jury proceeding if the trial judge believes that they are necessary for a fair trial.

* * *

The timing of discovery also merits attention. When statements of witnesses have been withheld from the defense before trial, there remains little reason to continue to withhold such statements once the witness has testified. At this stage the danger of evidence being manufactured to meet the line of testimony and the danger of witness intimidation are not increased by discovery, while the defendant's need for such statements to facilitate cross-examination is great. In the Federal courts there is a statute which provides that prior statements of a witness be made available to the defendant as a matter of right after the witness has testified. Many States, however, continue to require that defense counsel make a special showing of need or that the judge review the statements to determine whether they can be of use to the defense before granting discovery. The former practice places upon counsel the almost impossible burden of establishing the usefulness of a document he has never seen; the latter requires the judge, whose knowledge of the case is limited to what he has heard in the courtroom, to make a judgement as to the significance of the statements to the defendant's case, a judgement which defense counsel alone is competent to make. Therefore, to the extent that a witness' statements relating to his testimony have not been made available to the defense prior to the witness' appearance in court, they should be made available as of right prior to cross-examination.

The great contemporary issue of representation for the impoverished is intimately tied to the question of whether our entire legal system needs revamping to create classes of attorneys and, more importantly, judges. Although the Task Force is gingerly about the subject, the plain truth is that many lower-court judges are incompetent. We have proceeded on the theory of "enlightened amateurism" for centuries.

Law is one of the few professions where postlegal training for a technical specialty does not exist. As the Report notes:

The American trial judge receives no formal training or apprenticeship in the judicial function. He generally assumes the bench with no knowledge of the art of judging other than perhaps some experience as a trial lawyer, an experience which rarely includes extensive criminal practice.

*　　*　　*

The length of judicial careers in this country justifies a substantial investment in preservice and inservice training. There are indications that judges of courts of general jurisdiction serve on the average more than 25 years. In several Western European countries, where the choice between the practice of law and a career on the bench is usually made immediately after graduation from law school, one who aspires to be a judge undergoes a specialized course of instruction, often consisting of a number of years of post-law school training.

In many countries there are requirements for lengthy periods of inservice training, first as court clerks, then as apprentice judges with gradually increasing responsibilities in actual cases. Finally, those who survive the training and apprenticeship programs are rated by the judicial hierarchy, and only those who best meet defined criteria are chosen to become judges.

"Training" suggestions are not enough. As the criminal law becomes more complex, "professionalization" is as necessary here as it appears to be with the police. This issue deserved more substantial analysis than it received.

Ten pages of the Report on the Courts are concerned with the substantive criminal law. In addition to the inadequacy of treatment clearly evident within such a necessarily scanty analysis this problem logically belongs to the area of *Crime and its Assessment,* to be discussed later herein. Accordingly, commentary on those 10 pages is reserved for later discussion.

Corrections

The number of people subject to various correctional processes, including release on parole or probation, will grow to an estimated 1,841,000 in 1975. The fate of these and of the institutions which govern them is the subject of the Report on Corrections. Here again the picture is dismal.

Offenders should be classified. The Report chooses four basic categories. The prosocial offender is one who is fundamentally law-abiding but for some reason (often economic) is pressured into crime. He should be subject to as little correction as possible. If he is neurotic, then psychiatric treatment is the best hope for his recovery. Of course many of the "worst" offenders, especially those who commit homicides, fall into this category. Is the Report suggesting that those we most often fear, and therefore, more harshly punish, be released? If it is, then we have reached the *desideratum* in penal treatment.

The Report then identifies the antisocial offender. He is a product of a criminal subculture, and, for him, the best treatment would involve a change of environment. Presumably this is the most frequent offender, and in some ways the most troublesome. Assuming that an individual of this type has committed a crime that calls for a short jail sentence. Should we impose the maximum sentence possible because of his propensity to return to an antisocial environment? Should we require that he change environments—stop associating with his friends—as a condition of early release? Should we have the right to keep him incarcerated indefinitely until he willingly chooses to abandon his antisocial environment? The civil liberties problems in this realm are substantial, and the Task Force should have paid more attention to them.

The pseudosocial individual is the "typical" deranged personality; he has certain psychological needs (such as power desires) which require psychological treatment. Unfortunately for him the prospects are "discouraging," and he presents almost insoluble problems for any criminal justice system. He may also be convicted of a relatively innocuous crime, but his need for lengthy confinement may be great.

The asocial individual has no identification with others, makes minimum demands, and resembles the last enumerated type insofar as psychological aid is necessary. The Report proposes group therapy to aid in establishing relational ties to others.

If psychiatrists may not be in complete agreement with these categories they are nevertheless useful ones; for they demonstrate that people commit criminal acts for different reasons, and the disposition of their cases must of necessity differ.

These categories are a bit too sophisticated for the average judge, and one wonders whether sentencing—or, to get away from that pejorative term, rehabilitation commitment—should not be left to those who are more expert. This would present other problems. The distressing inclination of experts is to incarcerate for lengthy periods for "humane" purposes, and any such process should insure at least judicial supervision over absolute length of incarceration. We can abdicate too many decisions to experts, especially where "hospitalization" becomes the rubric for indefinite imprisonment. Clearly, greater coordination is necessary; but we can never forget that a reasonable term of imprisonment is a fundamental civil liberty even of one convicted of a crime. The Eighth Amendment proscribes cruel and unusual punishments, and, hopefully, its strictures do not apply only to institutions formally designated as prisons.

In this connection, George Bernard Shaw once observed that to oppose capital punishment is to oppose punishment in general. Perhaps all convicted persons should be released on probation immediately; if they were, the recidivism rate might not be higher. As the Report notes:

Probation services have been characteristically poorly staffed

769

and often poorly administered. Despite that, the success of those placed on probation, as measured by not having probation revoked, has been surprisingly high. One summary analysis of outcomes observed in 11 probation studies indicates a success rate of from 60 to 90 percent. A survey of probation effectiveness in such states as Massachusetts and New York, and a variety of foreign countries, provides similar results with a success rate at about 75 percent. An exhaustive study was undertaken in California when 11,638 adult probationers granted probation during the period 1956–58 were followed up after 7 years. Of this group, almost 72 percent were successful in terms of not having their probation revoked.

Of course, this would have to be combined with a law requiring employers not to discriminate in their hiring practices against ex-convicts; a step the Task Force avoids recommending, despite its evident necessity:

A survey conducted in 1966 by the Minnesota Division of Adult Corrections gives an idea of employer policies on hiring offenders. Among 983 firms, it found that almost 40 percent indicated at least a general reluctance to hire offenders for any position. Another 28 percent would hire them for specific jobs only. Perhaps these attitudes toward offenders are similar to those expressed by the average citizen. In any case, they represent a substantial barrier to employment and a challenge to correctional agencies.

The Report recognizes that Family and Community are indispensable institutions for the correctional process:

Few would challenge the all-important role of the family as the universal social institution that nurtures, protects, and shapes the individual from infancy to independence.

The Report recognizes that correction is best achieved within the community, not in an alien institutional setting:

In the supervised community group treatment program the youth sees getting out in terms of his solution to his own problems, or how that is perceived by other youths in the group.

The Report finds various forms of resistance to community treatment centers. "An exaggerated concern for security and the belief in autonomous institutional reponsibility for handling offenders combine to limit innovation and the develop-nent of community ties." Here, again, public attitudes must undergo radical change.

Although the Report opts for halfway houses, work-release programs, and even study-release in small unit institutions, it fails to stress adequately the need for continuing concern with the total environment of the released or about to be released inmate. Just as prisons were heralded as a great 19th century American reform (praise now seen as quite premature), so work-release and the other innovations stressed by the Report will prove illusory and ineffective without close follow-up supervision. The experiences of foreign countries (especially the Scandinavian ones and Australia) are invaluable on this point; unfortunately the peculiarly American orientation of the Report precludes analysis of those quite relevant findings.

The Report also does not quite face the issue of changing the environment where the family, or the environment, or the offender's peer group have contributed to the crime. After all, what community are we talking about when we enthuse over community treatment centers?

The Report also stresses the need for correctional institutions and devices for misdemeanants. Since only the vagaries of legal definition rather than substantive distinctions differentiate felonies from misdemeanors, there is no logical reason for denying correctional facilities at this level. And yet, local jails are inadequate:

In the vast majority of city and county jails and local short-term institutions, no significant progress has been made in the past 50 years.

* * *

In the second decade of this century, Louis Robinson wrote:
'From many points of view, the jail is the most important of all our institutions of imprisonment. The enormous number of jails is alone sufficient . . . to make [one] realize that the jail is, after all, the typical prison in the United States. . . . From two-thirds to three-fourths of all convicted criminals serve out their sentence in jails. But this is not all. The jail is, with small exception, the almost universal detention house for untried prisoners. The great majority, therefore, of penitentiary and reformatory prisoners have been kept for a period varying from a few days to many months within the confines of a county or municipal jail. Then, too, there is the class, not at all unimportant in number, of individuals, who,*

having finally established their innocence, have been set free after spending some time in the jail awaiting trial. Important witnesses also are detained in jail, and it is used at times for still other purposes, even serving occasionally as a temporary asylum for the insane. The part, therefore, which the jail plays in our scheme of punishment cannot be overestimated. Whether for good or for evil, nearly every criminal that has been apprehended is subjected to its influence.'

Now, in the seventh decade, this statement by Robinson and his comments on filth, neglect, and maladministration still accurately describe the role and status of jails and short-term institutions in the United States.

Probation is often meaningless because supervising officers are overworked. Where imprisonment has occurred (and in many states a misdemeanor sentence can run to three years or more) parole should be considered, although it is not.

The Task Force notes, but passes over the implications of the fact that many public services in America are highly political. Clearly, then, one of the great problems with the judiciary is its political character. The same is lamentably true of our correctional institutions:

In many jurisdictions the administrative framework of institutional corrections is a basic barrier to establishment of collaborative regimes focused on reintegration of offenders into the community. The position of warden in State prisons too often has been a political reward. It has carried numerous fringe benefits, such as a lavish residence, unlimited inmate servants, food and supplies from institutional farms and warehouses, furnishings, and a large automobile. Furthermore, for anyone who enjoyed power, the warden's position was most attractive, for his control over both inmates and staff tended to be quite autocratic. Conditions in institutions for juveniles have often resembled those in prisons in this respect, although juvenile institutions usually have been more closely linked administratively with parole and other community correctional services than have adult prisons.

The problems of American Society cannot be solved until the removal of political considerations from our correctional institutions occurs; given our attitudes, such occurrence is highly unlikely.

Many special offenders present problems which society does not know much about solving, quite apart from their criminal manifestations. This is true to a large extent with mental ill-ness and also with alcoholism and narcotic addiction. Igno-rance about treatment methods has indeed been one of the reasons why offenders such as drunks and sexual psychopaths have been brought into the criminal system in the first place. Without means of cure, society has been interested chiefly in securing custody of these people who are—or at least are thought to be—a threat to the peace. This has been provided by corrections, but unfortunately simple incapacitation has come in many cases into direct conflict with newer knowledge and theories about treatment.

Much of mental illness and retardation, for example, is now viewed outside corrections as best treated in a normal commu-nity setting as far as possible. In the late 19th and early 20th centuries, intense correctional interest in retardation as a probable major cause of crime, resulted in the building of a number of special institutions for "defective delinquents" and permanent incarceration of large numbers of retarded per-sons. But these facilities, and the theories they represent, are very much at odds with modern belief that most retarded per-sons can be trained to do useful menial tasks and care for themselves in sheltered surroundings in the community.

Similar evolution in medical thought has occurred with re-spect to many sexual psychopaths. Yet public fear of the acts which such persons may indeed commit has hindered correc-tions in resorting to such new treatment methods. And with respect to the large number of offenders with mental problems who are legally responsible for criminal acts they have com-mitted, penal purposes have restricted community treatment as they have in the case of other offenders.

The cultural climate of the Nation also has influenced the very way we think about offenders. We believe in Progress, in Free Will, and we vigorously oppose all theories of Determin-ism, including Economic Determinism to the extent that we simply cannot understand the environmental factors that make "crime." The tenacity of that belief was recognized by the Report. How do we cope with it? As yet the answers are unknown.

Organized Crime

The Task Force Report on Organized Crime merely re-peats the equivalent Commission chapter. Thus we are told that the syndicate offers "goods and services that millions of Americans desire even though declared illegal by their legislatures." The dreary statistics about gambling and other criminal activities are repeated. The involvement of organized crime in legitimate business is again noted: "One criminal syndicate alone has real estate interests, with an estimated value of $300 million." Again, we are told that "the cumulative effect of the infiltration of legitimate business in America cannot be measured."

There is the occasional surprise. "Protection is easier to arrange through one agency than through many." We learn that the syndicate was not displeased when a large number of Suffolk County police departments united into one agency.

Even vigorous law enforcement may have negative consequences:

[A gambling drive] solved the recruitment problem of the syndicate, as [the] drive successfully stampeded the independents into the arms of the syndicate for protection, and the syndicate can now pick and choose those operators whom they wish to admit.

Increased coordination of antiorganized crime efforts must be undertaken, although there are numerous impediments. Even on the federal level itself coordination is less than complete, partially because of the fact that criminal conviction against syndicate members are hard to obtain. The Report notes that:

Efforts to institutionalize an antiracketeering intelligence program were hindered by a lack of coordination and interest by some federal investigative agencies.

Coyly, the names of those agencies are not mentioned; the common belief is that the FBI is the gravest offender simply because of its own parochial pride and high conviction rate, both of which would be endangered by serious involvement with organized crime. Perhaps the situation has changed since the early 1960's when the Organized Crime and Rackets Section of the Justice Department was hindered by lack of cooperation, but the evidence is inconclusive.

Some police chiefs even deny the existence of organized crime in their bailiwicks, and the Report is properly skeptical of these less than realistic appraisals.

The Report is clearly unhappy with the present "intolerable" status of the laws relating to wiretapping and bugging. It views these electronic devices as absolutely necessary to combat organized crime because much of criminal activity is, of necessity, carried on by telephone. Its recommendation that Congress pass a carefully circumscribed law permitting electronic eavesdropping was probably instrumental in the passage of the Crime Control Act of 1968. Some provisions of that controversial law will be discussed briefly at the end of this analysis.

Several consultants' papers analyzed the relationship between law and mores, and posed the question of just which will have to change. One in particular, a study of a community called "Wincanton", emphasized that most Americans have very little knowledge of the specific connections between gambling and political graft. Americans tolerate gambling, but quickly (if sporadically) root out corruption. Where hard evidence of the latter is accumulated, quick "reform" action follows. The study concluded that:

When the voters have called for clean government, they have gotten it, in spite of loose bidding laws, limited civil service, etc.

This study of corruption posited the (to many, peculiar) theory that social stability is fostered by corruption:

Because of . . . conflicts between legal norms and actual popular attitudes, several political scientists have concluded that corruption can perform the valuable function of permitting the continued existence of society. Instead of a direct confrontation between the norm and the facts, corrupt enforcement of the laws can permit quiet fulfillment of both sets of values. . . . Until legal norms coincide with popular values, these corruptly induced adjustments allow the society to run more smoothly.

Professor Thomas C. Schelling of Harvard picked up that theme and wrote what may be the most significant paper in the entire series of reports. His *Economic Analysis and Organized Crime* was an attempt to study crime as an economic phenomenon subject to the same "laws" that operate in what he calls the "upperworld."

He believes that such a study is necessary because it "could help in identifying the incentives and limitations that apply to organized crime; in evaluating the different kinds of costs and losses due to crime; in restructuring laws and programs to minimize the costs, wastes and injustices that crime entails; and in restructuring the business environment in which organized crime occurs with a view to reducing crime, or, at least, its worst consequences." He wonders why gambling (a social service desired by many), is apparently amenable to a high degree of monopoly organization; and abortion (also a service to many), apparently is not. He tends to regard all social activity for which a demand exists as part of the "system," and notes that: "It may be that modern society 'contracts out' some of its regulatory functions to the criminals themselves."

The role of the law in this analysis is crucial. "If the law is not enforced, there is a scarcity out of which to make profits." Because criminal laws act to raise the costs of doing business, a certain number of competitors, or potential competitors, never enter or leave the particular endeavor. Because the costs of obtaining criminal services are raised, a certain scarcity sets in. Of course the classic American example of this is the "great experiment" with prohibition. Prohibition created a scarce supply of desired goods and led to the growth of organized criminal elements in controlling that supply; abolition of prohibition opened the field to legitimate competitors, cut profits, and sent the Mafia scurrying elsewhere for business.

The more enterprises are made illegal, the greater the danger of creation of organized criminal activities. This has economic implications. "Essentially the question is whether the goal of somewhat reducing [the occurrence of certain acts] is or is not outweighed by the costs to society of creating a criminal industry."

Professor Schelling outlines five possible costs to society of making particular activities criminal: (1) criminality is a form of protective tariff for those in the industry, and thereby diminishes competition; (2) it is an incentive to police corruption; (3) it induces contempt for criminal laws by ordinary people; (4) it may increase other and related criminal activities, such as stealing by narcotics addicts; and (5) it increases the power of criminal organizations.

He envisions two possible social solutions to the problem of organized crime. The first would be to provide alternative services: For instance, loansharking flourishes because legal financial channels are closed; perhaps they could be opened under certain government guarantees for the lenders.

The second solution would doubtless gall most Americans: The underworld itself could be assigned certain services; prostitutes could receive physical checkups; medical advice could be dispensed to junkies; clinics to examine women for pregnancy could be established so that a nonpregnant woman need not undergo an abortion to determine her status, and a pregnant one could have an abortion under medically acceptable supervision.

Before our collective gorge rises, we should realize that a certain amount of informal assignment of functions already exists. Peace in the underworld is kept by the syndicate which acts to control trigger-happy individuals who might upset the public peace. Layoffs on illegal gambling are handled by the syndicate which insures an adequate supply of money for the "hard-hit" bookie, thus minimizing brutal collection attempts by wronged bettors. As we shall see, another alternative would be legalization; hopefully, the prohibition experience might be repeated.

Crime and Its Impact

The greatest incidence of crime is not one man's brutality against another; it is the self-brutality of men living in undesirable social and economic conditions. The Task Force Report on *Crime and Its Impact—An Assessment,* makes the point vividly:

> *What the crimes of that week in [a section of Chicago] strongly suggest is that, although there is always some danger in the city of being robbed and perhaps injured on the street and a considerable danger of being burglarized, what people have to fear most from crime is in themselves; their own carelessness or bravado; their attitudes toward their families and friends, toward the people they work for or who work for them; their appetites for drugs and liquor and sex; their own eccentricities; their own perversities; their own passions. Crime in Town Hall that week, like crime anywhere any week, consisted of the brutal, frightening, surreptitious, selfish, thoughtless, compulsive, sad and funny ways people behave toward each other.*

America has always been—or Americans have always felt themselves to be—crime-ridden:

> *There has always been too much crime. Virtually every generation since the founding of the Nation and before has felt itself threatened by the spectre of rising crime and violence.*
> *A hundred years ago contemporary accounts of San Francisco told of extensive areas where 'no decent man was in*

*safety to walk the street after dark: while at all hours, both night and day, his property was jeopardized by incendiarism and burglary.' Teenage gangs gave rise to the word 'hoodlum'; while in one central New York City area, near Broadway, the police entered 'only in pairs, and never unarmed.' A noted chronicler of the period declared that 'municipal law is a failure * * * we must soon fall back on the law of self preservation.' 'Alarming' increases in robbery and violent crimes were reported throughout the country prior to the Revolution. And in 1910 one author declared that 'crime, especially its more violent forms, and among the young is increasing steadily and is threatening to bankrupt the Nation.'*

Crime and violence in the past took many forms. During the great railway strike of 1877 hundreds were killed across the country and almost 2 miles of railroad cars and buildings were burned in Pittsburgh in clashes between strikers and company police and the militia. It was nearly a half century later, after pitched battles in the steel industry in the late thirties, that the Nation's long history of labor violence subsided. The looting and takeover of New York for 3 days by mobs in the 1863 draft riots rivaled the violence of Watts, while racial disturbances in Atlanta in 1907, in Chicago, Washington, and East St. Louis in 1919, Detroit in 1943 and New York in 1900, 1935, and 1943 marred big city life in the first half of the 20th century. Lynchings took the lives of more than 4,500 persons throughout the country between 1882 and 1930. And the violence of Al Capone and Jesse James was so striking that they have left their marks permanently on our understanding of the eras in which they lived.

*　　　*　　　*

Although it is not possible to identify all the factors that affect the rise and fall in public alarm about crime, it is a constantly recurring public theme. A legal scholar recently took a look over the literature of the past 50 years and noted that each and every decade produced prominent articles about the need for strong measures to meet the then-current crisis in crime. Periodically throughout the century, there have been investigating committees of the Congress, of the State legislatures, and special commissions of cities to deal with the particular crime problem of the time. It may be that there has always been a crime crisis, insofar as public perception is concerned.

778

The Report admonishes the public not to be surprised if a high crime rate continues. The evidence indicates that, if anything, it will rise. The Juvenile Delinquency Report makes this clear:

One sign of greater difficulties ahead is the rising ratio of nonwhite workers joining the labor force—the workers who suffer most from lack of adequate education and training, shortage of unskilled jobs, and discriminatory barriers to employment. Between 1965 and 1970, the number of nonwhite youth reaching 18 will increase by 20 percent over the 1965 level. During the same period, the white population in the same age group will actually decrease, and will not regain the 1965 figure of 3.3 million until 1970. During the 5-year period after that, the number of nonwhite 18-year-olds will again increase by 20 percent while the number of white 18-year-olds will increase by only 10 percent.

And young people compose the category of workers with the highest unemployment rate. In 1965 the average unemployment rates for youth between 16 and 24 decreased somewhat from the peak reached in 1963. But the unemployment rate of youth aged 16 to 21 was over 12.5 percent, two and one-half times that for all workers. The 1.1 million young people unemployed represented, therefore, one-third of the jobless workers in the country, and for them the familiar syndrome—minority group member, school dropout, unemployed—holds stubbornly true. Of the 26 million young people who will enter the labor force during the 1960's, an estimated 25 percent will not have completed high school. Only 45 percent will be high school graduates. Only 26 percent will have graduated from or even attended college.

The true meaning of the rate becomes clearer when we compare our criminal statistics with those of other countries. Comparative homicide rates, as reflected in the recent gun control controversy, has enlightened and, perhaps, shocked us; the same is true for other crimes.[10] The Report, unfortu-

---

[10] *High Southern homicide rates were at least in part due to a tradition of resort to violence as a means of settling family arguments and personal disputes that had been carried over from frontier days and maintained, especially in the lower classes, because of the particular social and economic history of the region. Such traditions have been found among the poor and the depressed in many countries, often in particular regions that are isolated. They are found not only in the South but also in the slums of the larger cities. Such traditions of high violence have often been accompanied by very low rates of suicide.*

nately, barely touches on the fascinating subject of comparative criminology in only four paragraphs and leaves us unsatisfied by its conclusion that:

It is clear . . . that there are great differences in the rates of crime among the various countries.

The Report soberly informs us that there are 1.1 million full-time criminals in the United States. They could earn 5 billion dollars in illegitimate enterprises (the question is, of course, whether they would be employable in the society), and their activities cost the society a great deal of money. Unfortunately, in assessing those costs, the Report does not meaningfully distinguish between differing social costs involved in transfers of wealth (as in robbery) as distinct from its destruction (as in murder and arson). It does not deal with the question raised by Professor Schelling: "What [is] it worth to reduce crime, and to whom is it worth it?"

Cost allocation is also interesting. Crimes such as arson, robbery, burglary, and larceny, often perpetrated by the poor, cost Society approximately 574 million dollars per year. Employee theft and shoplifting weigh in at 1.3 billion dollars, and embezzlement, another white-collar crime, adds 200 million dollars to the total. Embezzlement itself is only exceeded in cost by burglary. Thus we can surmise not that there is necessarily more white collar crime, but that the "take" from that form of activity is greater than that involved in street crime for the simple reason that the victims are richer. When a poor person steals, he generally does so from another poor person. Probably this generalization is a safe one to draw; any other would be hazardous.

The Report is stumped for solutions: "It is not possible, on the basis of current studies, to determine which of these explanations [for occurrence of crimes in certain inner-city areas] will provide the most fruitful guide to action." Since the Report has no clear idea of what will "solve" the kind of crime attributable to social disorganization, it cannot provide clear alternative choices to those Americans who believe that crime is caused by a breakdown of moral standards. A Gallup Poll finding that only 12 percent of the American people believe that unemployment and poverty are the "causes" of crime is dispiritedly cited.

One consultant's paper notes that we should not necessarily jump to the obvious conclusion:

The redistribution of goods through theft and resale might constitute a significant subsidy to certain groups in our society; its curtailment might have significant side effects which should be explored.

But it goes no further. Another even raises the fundamental problem of whether Science and Technology might not do what men seem unable to accomplish. "Increased use of locks may be far more effective in reducing burglary and auto theft than an increase in police patrol."

It is ironic that the question of the substantive criminal law and its limitations was of such minor importance to the Commission. For some reason, the ten pages devoted to the subject appear in the Courts rather than in the Impact study. None of the problems discussed by the Task Force can be dealt with until we decide just what we want the criminal law to do. Narcotics and Drug Abuse, Organized Crime, Crime and Its Impact, Juvenile Delinquency, the Police, all these subjects are tied to the present law.[11] The Drunkenness Task Force was forthright in recommending abolition of criminal sanctions for that peculiar medical problem. That candor is not duplicated in the recommendations concerning other substantive criminal laws, although the analyses are straightforward enough:

Available information indicates that laws against fornication, adultery, and heterosexual deviancy are generally unenforced. In New York, where adultery was the only ground for divorce until recently, there were countless divorces based on documented instances of adultery but no adultery prosecutions. Certainly there is no greater enforcement of prohibitions against premarital sexual relations. In many if not most jurisdictions adultery and fornication laws have been repealed in practice, although in form they persist on the books. There is surely some truth in Thurman Arnold's comment that these laws 'survive in order to satisfy moral objections to established modes of conduct. They are unenforced because we want to continue our conduct, and unrepealed because we want to preserve our morals.'

*   *   *

Homosexual practices are condemned as criminal in virtually all States, usually as a felony with substantial punish-

---

11 Of course, as we have seen, some of the consultants' papers did emphasize decrease of criminal sanctions. Professor Rosenthal's paper on Narcotics and Drug Abuse states: Neither use nor simple possession of marihuana should be the subject of criminal prohibition by either the Federal Government or the States.

ment. There are some attempts at enforcement, particularly in cases involving public conduct, solicitation, or corruption of the young. When the activity is private and consensual, however, the deterrent efficacy of law enforcement is limited; only the indiscreet have reasons for fear.

Homosexuality entails deviation from social mores and the flouting of community attitudes having greater apparent capacity to deter and shape conduct than that possessed by the criminal law. It is questionable whether there is significant additional deterrent force provided by the criminal sanction above that coming from other forms of social pressure not to engage in such acts. Moreover, the present penal system is no better suited than other social institutions to deal with the homosexual or to rehabilitate or reintegrate him. In addition, the presence of these laws creates opportunities for extortion, and opens the door for discriminatory enforcement.

* * *

Abortion laws are another instance in which the criminal law, by its failure to define prohibited conduct carefully, has created high costs for society and has placed obstacles in the path of effective enforcement. The demand for abortions, both by married and unmarried women, is widespread. It is often produced by motives and inclinations that manifest no serious dangerousness or deviation from the normal on the part of the people who seek it. These factors produce the spectacle of pervasive violations but few prosecutions.

It has been estimated that as many as a million abortions are performed each year in this country, while the arrest rate is not more than one per thousand abortions performed. Two-thirds of all abortions are reportedly performed on married women. Available indications are that only 8,000 to 10,000 of these are legal abortions conducted in a hospital setting.

* * *

The present state of the law presents particularly acute problems for conscientious parents and physicians faced with weighty reasons for terminating pregnancy in a jurisdiction where the law is restrictive or its standards are vague and uncertain. Since some highly reputable physicians regard the law as an injustice and want to protect their patients against incompetent abortions available on the black market, large numbers of reputable citizens find themselves in the position of law violators. This tends to contribute to antagonism and resentment toward those who enforce the law.

* * *

To use the criminal law against a substantial body of de-cent opinion, even if it be minority opinion, is contrary to our basic tradition. . . .

. . . Criminal liabilities which experience shows to be unen-forceable because of nullification by prosecutors or juries should be eliminated from the law. Such nullification usually points to a situation of divided community opinion. Also, 'dead letter' laws, far from promoting a sense of security in the community, which is the main function of penal law, actually, (impair) that security by holding the threat of prosecution over the heads of people whom we have no in-tention to punish.

The Reports could conceivably have been influential. They could have influenced legislatures to change some of their outmoded definitions of crime. Instead, we find strewn through these pages homilies such as:

Despite this nonenforcement [of many sex laws] and the costs the presence of these laws on the books can impose, there is understandable and deeply felt reluctance to repeal them. This stems from a fear that the affirmative act of re-peal might be mistaken as an abandonment of social disap-proval for the prohibited acts and an invitation to license. Opponents of repeal emphasize the symbolic effect of unen-forced laws and the difficulty of removing what may be an inappropriate sanction without appearing to condone the for-bidden act. The appropriateness and the scope of criminal sanctions with respect to these sexual activities deserves dis-cussion and analysis by those concerned with the improve-ment of criminal administration.

*   *   *

In the final analysis each legislature must decide whether preserving a given criminal penalty is justified by the costs.

When the Report says,

[I]t may be useful to call attention to the undesirable conse-quences of indiscriminately dealing with undesirable conduct by making it criminal . . .

it is essentially begging the question. When one Task Force observes that legal prohibition creates risk, and risk encour-ages the Mafia so that "hence in some measure crime is en-couraged . . . by the criminal law itself," it has clumsily struck to the heart of many of our vital problems.

If the analysis is disappointing, it nevertheless pinpoints the areas of potential change. Small gambling is almost a "natural" human activity which should not be criminally punished. The drug abuse laws could be profitably reexamined from this perspective. Bad-check and nonsupport criminal statutes are used as weapons to compel monetary restitution. Although they appear to work well in this guise, perhaps other processes—such as easier forms of traditional civil law suits—could be substituted for them.

Disorderly conduct and vagrancy laws, under which 10 percent of all arrests occur, are vague. The latter "crime" encompasses loitering, being about with no visible means of support, and other undesirable conduct; status and condition rather than actual acts are punished under these nebulous definitions. These laws are used to effect other (unstated) goals of law enforcement, such as keeping streets free of undesirables during tourist season in large cities. These hidden goals are improper ones. Recommendations for tightening of definitions rather than their abolition do not solve the problem.

Laws affecting sexual conduct are characterized by several vices. These laws are rarely enforced, and such lack of enforcement creates disrespect for law in general. When these laws are enforced (often against sexual deviants, such as homosexuals), they do not alleviate the conduct. "It is questionable . . . whether private homosexual laws are deterrents." Once the laws are enforced, punishment of deviates leads to no desirable rehabilitation. "[T]he present penal system is no better suited than other social institutions to deal with the homosexual or to rehabilitate or reintegrate him." These failures are known and are admitted. Patchwork will not suffice when the tire has corroded.

The Report is equivocal about abortion laws, but notes that: "The time is overdue for realistic examination of the abortion laws." (Why did it not undertake such "realistic examination?") It advocates legalizing abortion where there is a danger of ill health for the child or mother, or physical or mental defect, and where conception has been caused by rape or incest. On the crucial and controversial issue of permitting abortions for nonmedical reasons the Report notes:

The evils of uninhibited abortions are sufficiently serious to warrant discriminating use of the criminal penalty.

Abolition of criminal sanctions for socially undesirable conduct, it is often argued, means that Society, in some measure, by lifting restrictions, is endorsing or encouraging such conduct. In other words, the criminal law serves not only the function of defining and punishing socially dangerous acts but also of enunciating contemporary community standards of generally accepted conduct. To remove this would be to remove one source of community pressure to conform.

The relationship between Law and Conduct, in this analysis, is simplistic. People will be deterred by Law from doing evil; they will be encouraged to exhibit their true bestial natures in the absence of Law. And yet, the Task Force Reports emphasize—expecially the Report on Juvenile Delinquency —that Law, per se, is not a vital factor [either as deterrent or encouragement] in many people's lives. People do what they do, especially in the area of morals and sex, because they want to; or because local community standards encourage such conduct. Also, many people violate the Law *because* of its existence. Some of the Task Force papers, particularly those of Professors Blum and Aronowitz, emphasize the potential attraction of criminality to many who might not otherwise experiment with narcotics. Professor Goffman's paper in the Juvenile Delinquency Report also makes this clear in the context of juvenile identity-seeking.

In addition, disrespect for Law in general apparently grows (although there is no proof of this) when certain unpopular extant laws are not enforced, or worse, only rarely enforced. Cynicism and contempt can greet vice-squad activities, especially when those activities affect lower-class conduct only. Bribery and other forms of corruption always seem to accompany strict law enforcement. Prohibition is the most startling example of this. The Law is viewed as something that can be "beaten." Where organized crime is involved, the Law becomes a cost of doing business.

Also, there is no hard evidence to support the theory. Were more Americans encouraged to drink after rather than during prohibition? Are more homosexuals surfacing since 1963 in Illinois, where that state abolished criminal penalties for acts committed by adult consenting homosexuals? If the burden of proof falls on the opponents of abolition, as I think it should, it clearly has not been met.

The final argument in favor of abolition is simply that of integrity. If the State has no business meddling in personal affairs, then it should keep out of those affairs *even if* abstinence encourages more undesirable conduct. We have decided that the State should not meddle in certain "privileged" relationships, such as between husband and wife, priest and penitent, lawyer and client, doctor and patient, even though some criminal conduct is undoubtedly encouraged by the very existence of these relationships. Surely the price we would pay by abolishing these privileges would be far in excess of what we might gain. The price we *do* pay for sporadic enforcement of our impossibly puritanical criminal laws is also far outweighed by the loss of freedom and of human dignity which inevitably accompanies those laws. The loss of freedom and dignity is as great, if not greater, among law enforcers as it is among law violators; this breeds cynicism not only in the minds of victims, but also in the minds of the police.

Police alienation from the Society has in a large measure been caused by the necessity to dig into the trash heap of human conduct. Cynicism among law enforcers can jeopardize democracy, especially when we consider the vast powers enjoyed by the police and their potential for abuse. Increasing such cynicism is in itself simply a price we cannot afford to pay if we are to remain a viable Democracy.

CONCLUSION

It seems that several millennia rather than merely a year and a half have elapsed since the Crime Commission reported. Riots threaten to engulf our cities, the crime rate apparently is rising precipitously, and almost daily politicians declare war against crime in the streets. The Riot Commission has reported its doleful findings; we await the heady generalities of the Violence Commission.

Instead of "realistic reexaminations" of our criminal laws, we have had a strengthening of many of their repressive features. As we engage in "The Crime War," to a great extent it is a "Manufactured Crusade" (both terms constitute the title of a new book on the subject). Presumably we shall continue to lose the War but, nevertheless, wage the Crusade.

The characteristic piece of legislation of recent years is, of course, the Crime Control Act of 1968. Title II purports to overrule Supreme Court decisions in several significant cases; it is patently unconstitutional. Title III is the new bugging and tapping law; it was largely written by Professor Blakey of Notre Dame Law School, and embodies his recommendations to the Crime Commission (to be found in the Task Force Report on Organized Crime). Although the traditional argument justifying electronic surveillance (covering all of one and a half pages) is couched in terms of national security and antiorganized crime needs, Title III expands the list (albeit within limits) for federal officers and virtually without limit for State prosecutors (any "crime dangerous to life, limb, or property"); surveillance order may be issued on applicant's "belief" that a crime was being or was about to be committed.

Here there is no requirement for "probable cause," or even "reasonable suspicion" to justify such a belief, although the judge must have such "probable cause" before he issues the interception order. There is a requirement that the prosecutor particularly describe "the type of communications sought to be intercepted"—a neat trick, because it is hard to pinpoint a "type" of conversation which has not as yet occurred. In emergencies related to national security, or to "conspiratorial activities characteristic of organized crime" (the latter term is undefined in the statute), any law enforcement officer specially designated—and doubtless many will be—by a prosecutor can intercept without a judge's order. He must then apply for an order within the comparatively leisurely time of 48 hours. Undoubtedly there will be many emergencies.

The Act also contains a vague and, perhaps, unconstitutional provision penalizing the crossing of state lines to instigate riots.

President Johnson regretfully signed the Law in apparent recognition of political reality. That reality has also decimated his poverty program, although the Administration's current attitude toward its own proposals here was noticeably lukewarm to start with. Thus the national legislature has chosen to follow certain recommendations of the Crime Commission and to ignore others. The complexities have been overlooked, and the simplicities have become part of the "Law of the Land."

Would things have been any different if there had been a different sort of Commission, or if many of its most valuable recommendations had not been tucked away in obscure places in the Task Force Reports? We do not know, and, perhaps, can never tell. From one vantage point (mine) a better attempt to enlighten the American people about "crime" should have been made, for its own sake if for no other reason.

In this era of concern for crime, often hysterical concern, certain truths established by both the main and the Task Forces Reports should be reiterated. Americans will have to accept the inevitability of a certain amount of crime despite even a maximal effort to suppress it. Crime is endemic to a rapidly changing Society, and America has always been precisely that. As part of a Task Force Report notes:

This high a rate of crime in the State [California] that has so often been in the forefront of development of effective, progressive systems of law enforcement and criminal justice is, in many ways, disturbing. California is today the recognized leader in the field of police professionalization. It has a corrections system that is one of the three or four best in the country. Its youth authority has been a pioneer in the effective treatment of juveniles. It is the only State with a really effective bureau of criminal statistics. It has a high standing among the States in terms of general economic and educational levels and the provision of health and other social services.

On the other hand, California has been, throughout the last 30 years, the recipient of one of the great migrations in history. And whether migration is itself as important a cause of crime as is sometimes asserted or not, in large quantities it is clearly unsettling and disruptive of the social order. Population within the State has tripled within the last 30 years and has been increasing at a rate of more than 4 percent a year, creating tremendous economic and social problems.

*   *   *

Finally, with respect to delinquency, it might be said that a certain amount of this form of deviancy has always existed, will continue to exist, and perhaps should exist. In the sense discussed by Emile Durkheim, crime is normal, and perhaps even, in some quantity, desirable. Not only does the existence of delinquency provide the collective conscience an opportunity to reinforce its norms by applying sanctions, but the presence of deviancy reflects the existence of something less than a total system of control over individuals. Moreover, there appear to be personality traits among many delinquents that could be viewed as virtues if behavior were rechanneled. For instance, Sheldon and Eleanor Glueck noted, in 'Unraveling Juvenile Delinquency,' that among 500 delinquents compared to 500 nondelinquents, the delinquent boys were characterized as hedonistic, distrustful, aggressive, hostile and, as boys who felt they could manage their own lives, were socially assertive, and defied authority. The nondelinquents were more banal, conformistic, neurotic, felt unloved, insecure, and anxiety-ridden. The attributes associated with the delinquents sound similar to descriptions of the Renaissance Man who defied the authority and static orthodoxy of the middle ages, who was also aggressive, richly assertive, this-world rather than other-world centered, and was less banal, more innovative, than his medieval predecessors. The Glueck delinquents also sound much like our 19th century captains of industry, our 20th century political leaders and corporation executives. The freedom to be assertive, to defy authority and orthodoxy may sometimes have such consequences as crime and delinquency. But it is well to remember that many aspects of American ethos, our freedom, our benevolent attitude toward rapid social change, our heritage of revolution, our encouragement of massive migrations, our desire to be in or near large urban centers, and many other values that we cherish, may produce the delinquency we deplore as well as the many things we desire.

Despite this rather telling description, the same Report can only offer frustratingly little in solution, for, in truth, we know little about the specific relationship between cultural factors and crime. Those cultural factors may persist even when the last slum has been razed:

The Commission believes that age, urbanization, and other shifts in the population already under way will likely operate over the next 5 to 10 years to increase the volume of offenses faster than population growth. Further dipping into the reservoirs of unreported crime will likely combine with this real increase in crime to produce even greater increases in reported crime rates. Many of the basic social forces that tend to increase the amount of real crime are already taking effect and are for the most part irreversible. If society is to be successful in its desire to reduce the amount of real crime, it must find new ways to create the kinds of conditions and inducements—social, environmental, and psychological—that will bring about a greater commitment to law-abiding conduct and respect for the law on the part of all Americans and a better understanding of the great stake that all men have in being able to trust in the honesty and integrity of their fellow citizens.

* * *

Attempts are being made to improve the educational and occupational status of those living in delinquency areas; and efforts have also been directed toward inducing stronger community organization within depressed areas thereby reducing the alienation of residents of these areas from the larger society. In addition, physical regeneration of these areas has been advocated. In other words, attempts are directed toward the solution of the 'American dilemma.' The American dilemma is a resultant of the belief that all men are created equal (or perhaps more accurately, that all men have not only an opportunity but an obligation to be successful) in conjunction with the reality that some individuals in our society are disadvantaged, they do not have equal opportunities to succeed. Thus, most current attempts at delinquency and crime prevention are directed toward opening the opportunity structure.

There is no doubt that some, even many, individuals will be 'saved' by such procedures. Many individuals will probably have better 'life chances' as a result of such programs, particularly if educational and vocational programs are directed toward the mutual problems of increasing skill dilution, increasing skill obsolescence, and increasing occupational specialization.

But it still remains to be determined whether or not there will be a decrease in the rates of crime and delinquency as a result of such programs. It must be recognized that a new differential patterning of crime and delinquency rates over geographical areas may develop as a result of these programs. One finding which suggests that significant inroads into crime and delinquency rates may not occur as a result of programs directed primarily at changing traditionally hard-core delinquency areas is that crime rates have increased rapidly in rural areas and areas peripheral to urban centers (suburbs) over the past two decades. This has especially been the case as suburbs have become employment centered rather than residentially centered and have taken on the characteristics of central areas of urban units.

[From Judith A. Wilks, Ecological Correlates of Crime and Delinquency in Task Force Report, Crime and Its Impact—An Assessment.]

Of course some of the myths must be shattered. We are all criminally inclined, although most of us resist crimes of violence (probably because violence is unnecessary):

There is a common belief that the general population consists of a large group of law-abiding people and a small body of criminals. However, studies have shown that most people, when they are asked, remember having committed offenses for which they might have been sentenced if they had been apprehended. These studies of "self-reported" crimes have generally been of juveniles or young adults, mostly college and high school students. They uniformly show that delin-

quent or criminal acts are committed by people at all levels of society. Most people admit to relatively petty delinquent acts, but many report larcenies, auto thefts, burglaries, and assaults of a more serious nature.

One of the few studies of this type dealing with criminal behavior by adults was of a sample of almost 1,700 persons, most of them from the State of New York.

*　　*　　*

Ninety-nine percent of the respondents admitted they had committed one or more offenses for which they might have received jail or prison sentences.

No particular racial or national group has a monopoly on criminal activity, and traditional American suspicion of the unintegrated foreigner and the stranger and his propensity toward crime is unwarranted:

The differences between the Negro and white arrest rates for certain crimes of violence have been growing smaller between 1960 and 1965. During that period, considering together the crimes of murder, rape, and aggravated assault, the rate for Negroes increased 5 percent while the rate for whites increased 27 percent. In the case of robbery, however, the white rate increased 3 percent while the Negro rate increased 24 percent. For the crimes of burglary, larceny, and auto theft the Negro rate increased 33 percent while the white rate increased 24 percent.

*　　*　　*

The problem of public stereotyping of certain nationality groups [during the 1930's] as inherently criminal is not unlike the criminal stereotyping of the Negro and other minority groups today. These early studies did not attempt to refute the clearly demonstrable fact that the crime rates of certain nationality groups were disproportionately high. Instead, they amassed evidence to show that while this fact was attributable, in some measure, to the social and cultural traditions of these groups, mainly it was a consequence of the socially disorganized nature of the conditions under which they were forced to live. The overwhelming thrust of the evidence was that the high rates of crime were not a consequence of being German, Irish, Scandinavian, Polish, Italian, or Slavic, but a consequence of their life situation.

Without recognition of these fundamentals, we will not win any "war" against crime. Indeed, we can only wage the conflict with obsolete weapons—and we shall lose both the war and much of our democratic heritage.

Index

[This index has been keyed to the index in the official U. S. Government Printing Office edition of THE CHALLENGE OF CRIME IN A FREE SOCIETY. It does not include entries in the Introduction or Afterword.]

797

803

brutality 244

807

Service purchase
defined, 408
recommendation of Commission, 408
Shaw, Clifford, 132, 174
Sheppard decision, 340
Silverman v. *United States*, 472
Simulation techniques, 580–582
Slums
as ghettos, 132
attitudes, 180, 195
crime as a reaction to conditions, 67, 130–135
crime rates, 133–135
cycle of poverty, 209
example of successful professional criminal, 191
failure of social institutions, 177–178
families, 185
see also family factors contributing to delinquency
homes, 181–182
neighborhood as perceived by juveniles, 182
overcrowding, 184
recreation facilities, 183
religious institutions, 647
schools, 209
see also school, slum
violence, 183
Soldier, in organized crime, 453–454
South End Center for Alcoholics and Unattached Persons in Boston, Mass., 539
Space General Corporation, 593
Special narcotic project of the New York State Division of Parole, 522
Special project for minimum standards for the administration of criminal justice of the American Bar Association, 338, 339, 343
St. Louis Police Department, 261, 289
Standard metropolitan statistical areas 301
Stanford Research Institute, 150
State committees on criminal administration, 624, 634
State National Guard, 299–300
State planning committees, 634
States in which organized crime members reside and operate, 449
Stationhouse summons project, 132
Stimulants
illicit traffic, 500–504
medical use, 494, 495
see also amphetamines
Street workers, 192
Subcommittee on Improvements in Judicial Machinery of Senate Judiciary Committee, 362
Suffolk County, Long Island, N.Y., 308
Sullivan law of New York, 545
Summons, 329
Supreme Court decisions
addiction: *Robinson* v. *California*, 508

defense counsel
Gideon v. *Wainwright*, 366
Miranda v. *Arizona*, 367
Powell v. *Alabama*, 366
electronic surveillance
People v. *Berger*, 473
Silverman v. *United States*, 472
firearms, 549
immunity of witness, 346
juvenile court procedures
Gault v. *United States*, 230
Kent v. *United States*, 85
police investigation, 248
police procedures: *Miranda* v. *Arizona*, 94, 367
publicity
Estes, 340
Sheppard, 340
search warrants: *Gouled* v. *United States*, 313
segregation: *Brown* v. *Board of Education of Topeka*, 197
Survey research center, 96
Sutherland, Justice Edwin H., 157, 366
Synanon, 520
Systems analysis
applications
correctional system, 582–583
crime control, 562
criminal justice system, 386, 589, 592–596
cost-effectiveness analysis by, 593
in R.D.T. & E. programs, 606
limitations, 589–592

Task force on science and technology
insights, 557
results of research, 553–555, 607
study of police apprehension process, 611–612
task, 552
Technological devices
budgetary limitations on introduction, 552-553
limited use in criminal justice system, 552, 641
police use
in apprehension process, 564, 640
in communications center, 569
in crime laboratories, 574–575
Theft
automobile
arrest of juveniles for, 64, 585
as a misdemeanor, 94
as a professional crime, 64
causes, 587–588
cost, 64, 585
ignition unlocked, 261
inquiry systems, 602
losses, 64
minimum requirements for devices to prevent, 587–588
number of cases, 64
prevention, 587–588, 644–645
solution, 20, 65

Norbert Wiener

THE HUMAN USE OF
HUMAN BEINGS:
Cybernetics and Society   Q57   **$1.45**

*The single most important and influential
work on man's role in an automated world;
with an afterword by Walter A. Rosenblith*

Alan Harrington

LIFE IN THE CRYSTAL
PALACE   NS20   **95¢**

*The eminent novelist's classic report on the
subtle and deadly charm of corporation life*

Erich Fromm

ESCAPE FROM FREEDOM DS35   **$1.65**

*The famous psychologist's most important
work—an investigation into the causes of
man's submission to tyranny*

Michael Curtis, Editor

THE NATURE OF POLITICS:
A Sourcebook in the Dynamics
of Modern Political Science   M104   **$1.95**

THE GREAT POLITICAL
THEORIES, Volume I   W236   **$1.25**
From Plato and Aristotle to
Locke and Montesquieu

THE GREAT POLITICAL
THEORIES, Volume II   W237   **$1.25**
From Burke, Rousseau and Kant
to Modern Times

Russell Kirk

THE CONSERVATIVE MIND D6   **$1.65**

*The definitive history of conservative
thought, placing modern conservatism in
its historical perspective*